D. H. LAWRENCE:
THE MAN AND HIS WORK

The Formative Years: 1885-1919

ALSO BY

EMILE DELAVENAY

D. H. Lawrence and Edward Carpenter

D. H. LAWRENCE
THE MAN AND HIS WORK

The Formative Years: 1885-1919

Emile Delavenay

---

*Translated from the
French by Katharine
M. Delavenay*

Southern Illinois University Press
Carbondale and Edwardsville

D. H. Lawrence: The Man and His Work,
The Formative Years, 1885-1919
is translated from a longer version
in French entitled *L'Homme et
la Genèse de son Oeuvre: Les Années
de Formation: 1885-1919*, published by
Librairie C. Klincksieck, Paris, in 1969

International Standard Book Number 0-8093-0603-4
Library of Congress Catalog Card Number 70-190586

Published in Great Britain by
William Heinemann Ltd. and in the United States by
Southern Illinois University Press

Printed in Great Britain

CONTENTS

PART TWO:
THE EXILE: 1912–19

ACKNOWLEDGMENTS

The author is grateful to Laurence Pollinger Ltd, the Trustees of the Estate of the late Mrs Frieda Lawrence, William Heinemann Ltd and the Viking Press Inc. for permission to use copyright material by D. H. Lawrence and Frieda Lawrence, and to Jonathan Cape Ltd and J. R. Wood Esq. for permission to quote from Jessie Chambers's writings, letters and memoirs: © 1969, 1972 by J. R. Wood.

Acknowledgments are also made to the following copyright holders of works from which he either quotes briefly or to which he refers: The Society of Authors and Jonathan Cape Ltd (John M. Murry: *Son of Woman*; *Reminiscences of D. H. Lawrence*; *Between Two Worlds*); The Society of Authors and Constable & Co (Katherine Mansfield: *Letters*; *Letters to J. M. Murry*; *Journal*); George Allen & Unwin Ltd (Edward Carpenter: *Love's Coming of Age*; *The Art of Creation*; *The Drama of Love and Death*. Ford Madox Ford: *Mightier than the Sword*. Bertrand Russell: *Portraits from Memory*. Sir Stanley Unwin: *The Truth about Publishing*); Curtis Brown Ltd and Faber and Faber Ltd (Ottoline Morrell: *Ottoline, The Early Memoirs of Lady Ottoline Morrell*); Chatto & Windus Ltd (Catherine Carswell: *The Savage Pilgrimage*. David Garnett: *the Flowers of The Forest*; *Golden Echo*. Sir Compton Mackenzie: *My Life and Times, Octave Five*); Constable & Co Ltd (Lady Glenavy: *Today we will only gossip*); Miss Helen Corke (*Neutral Ground: D. H. Lawrence, The Croydon Years*, and a private letter); David Higham Associates and Barrie and Rockliff Ltd (Lady Cynthia Asquith: *Haply I Remember*; *Remember and be Glad*); Hutchinson & Co Ltd (Sir Compton Mackenzie: *The South Wind of Love*. Lady Cynthia Asquith: *Diaries 1915–1918*); Faber and Faber Ltd (H. M. Daleski: *The Forked Flame*); Victor Gollancz Ltd (Ford Madox Ford: *Return to Yesterday*); Grove Press Inc. (Hilda Doolittle: *Bid me to Live, a Madrigal*, Copyright © 1960 by Norman Holmes Pearson. Reprinted by permission of Grove Press Inc.); William Heinemann Ltd (Richard Aldington: *Portrait of a Genius, But . . . .* Harry T. Moore: *The Intelligent Heart*); The Hogarth Press Ltd and Harcourt Brace Jovanovich Inc. (Leonard Woolf: *Beginning Again*; *Downhill all the Way*); Macdonald & Co (Publishers) Ltd (Douglas Goldring: *Life Interests*); Methuen & Co Ltd (F. A. Lea: *The Life of John Middleton Murry*); Rupert Hart-Davis Ltd (Mark Gertler: *Selected Letters*. John Maynard Keynes: Lord Keynes *Two Memoirs*); The Estate of Cecil Gray and A. P. Watt & Son (Cecil Gray: *Peter Warlock*; *Musical Chairs*); Harcourt Brace Jovanovich Inc. (David Garnett: *The Golden Echo*); Weidenfeld and Nicolson Ltd, the International Council for Philosophy and Humanistic Sciences and UNESCO (Jean Réal: "The Religious Conception of Race: Houston Chamberlain and Germanic Christianity" in *The Third Reich*); *The Daily Telegraph* (15 November 1915: Report on *The Rainbow* Police Court Case).

ILLUSTRATIONS

(between pages 160 and 161)

---

1. D. H. Lawrence's birthplace, 8a Victoria Street, Eastwood, Nottinghamshire.
2. The Lawrence family in about 1893.
3. King's Scholar, 1905.
4. Lawrence in 1908.
5. Haggs Farm, Underwood, Nottinghamshire.
6. Jessie Chambers in about 1913.
7. Louie Burrows.
8. Alice Dax and her daughter in about 1916.
9. Helen Corke.
10. Frieda von Richthofen, aged eighteen.
11. D. H. Lawrence in about 1913.
12. David Garnett.
13. Portrait of Lady Ottoline Morrell by Augustus John.
14. Lawrence at Garsington Manor in 1916.
15. The Ashmole phoenix rising from its flames.
16. Home Office minutes concerning *The Rainbow* (1)
17. Home Office minutes concerning *The Rainbow* (2)
18. Home Office minutes concerning *The Rainbow* (3)
19. Home Office minutes concerning *The Rainbow* (4)
20. Lady Cynthia Asquith.
21. Bertrand Russell in 1916.
22. With Frieda, Katherine Mansfield and Middleton Murry.
23. "Mystic Nativity" by Botticelli.
24. "Madonna degli Ansidei" by Raphael.
25. Ducks swimming among lotus flowers, from a pavement in Medinet-Habu.
26. The Meidum Geese, Cairo Museum.
27. Wrestlers at Beni-Hassan.
28. The chakras.
29. "The Merry-Go-Round" by Mark Gertler.

FOREWORD

The French version of this book was begun in 1932 as a Sorbonne doctoral thesis, at a time when Lawrence was the subject of impassioned debate and when it seemed desirable to relate any assessment of his works to a full and factual study of his experience and personality. Various reasons, among them the effects of the Second World War on private lives and careers, led to this study being put aside entirely, when already in a fairly advanced stage. By the time the opportunity occurred to devote the necessary time to it once more, the world in which it had been undertaken had sunk into the past, Lawrence's reputation had fluctuated and risen again to new heights, and my own experience in fields other than the study and teaching of English literature had been widened in a manner not irrelevant to the evaluation of the message Lawrence felt he must convey. On rereading what I had written many years before, I gained the conviction that much of it had stood the test of time and of research by others, some of whom had started working on Lawrence at about the same time as I. It seemed worth while to pursue a task on which much labour had been expended at a time when I was, so to speak, among the pioneers.

Not only did it seem useful to publish the results of my early research, some of which were entirely new; there was also the problem, to quote Professor Daiches, of "coming to terms" with Lawrence in the light of my new experience: for instance, to look at a legend which had developed in my own lifetime in the perspective of my own intimate knowledge of life in Britain at war: to relate Lawrence's ideas and their artistic transposition into novels to my own concern, in the United Nations Secretariat and UNESCO, with the problems of race relations, education and the whole question of the raising of human life above or up to a bare subsistence level. Lawrence is a writer who does not leave one alone, and the way he saw the problems of civilization is a challenge to much of the humanitarian work of recent decades, and forces choices on his reader.

The French book, which was completed in 1968 and published in 1969, naturally bears the marks of this change of emphasis from mainly literary to broader human values. The present English version, undertaken in 1970, is in the greater part direct translation, but a few chapters have been remodelled, newly available material has been incorporated and certain factual or interpretative sections have been as far as possible brought up to date. I owe my wife an immense debt not only for translating a very long book,

with constant reference to the original Lawrence passages quoted, para-
phrased or analysed, but for detailed criticism and suggestions such as only a
translator deeply immersed in the subject can offer.

This book in no way claims to be the last word on Lawrence: as long
as there are new readers the last word on Lawrence will never be said. It
rests on one basic assumption and has been written with three main preoccupations in mind. The assumption is that the utterer of a literary message
can be described and circumscribed with reference to his experience, his
environment, his psychological characteristics and to the specific features of
the time and place of his psychological and intellectual formation. Of course
the author of the message cannot be "explained", but he can be observed and
approached historically so as to increase a reader's chances of perceiving the
message with a minimum of distortion.

My first preoccupation when this work was begun was therefore to ascertain as many relevant facts as possible about Lawrence's early years, in order
to grasp the vital problems of his developing personality at Eastwood and
Croydon. Thanks to Janko Lavrin, I made the acquaintance of Jessie Chambers
Wood, and our correspondence over several years, as well as our conversations and the substance of two intimate memoirs, which she wrote specially
for me and unfortunately destroyed before she died, are part of the original
material for this book. Her letters to me, and what I had saved in my notes
from the two memoirs, have appeared in full (in English) in an Appendix to
the original French version of this book, published by Messrs Klincksieck of
Paris. Much of the same material was arranged by Jessie Chambers for publication in her *D. H. Lawrence, a Personal Record*, but in this book the reader
will find, for the first time to my knowledge, an unequivocal statement of
the nature and extent of what Lawrence saw as his sexual failure with his
first love.

With the help of Jessie Chambers's memories, it became possible to
see in perspective Lawrence's other affairs between 1908 and 1912. On
reading the French version, Miss Helen Corke kindly thanked me "for the
light it throws upon much that has always puzzled me when trying to
account for the issues of the David-Muriel-Helen relationship".* The light is,
of course, thrown by Jessie Chambers's confessions in her manuscript
memoirs. Thanks to these, it also became possible to interpret correctly the
allusions to other women in the letters to Louie Burrows, and to try and
sort out the tangle of the love affair with Alice Dax, whose open avowal
that she had been Lawrence's mistress† is too often overlooked.

In my endeavour to get as close to the facts as possible, I also devoted considerable time to the study of such problems as that of the possible motiva-

---

*Letter of 4 May 1969.
†Frieda Lawrence: *The Memoirs and Correspondence*, p. 246.

tions behind the *Rainbow* prosecution in 1915, trying to get beyond vague statements and opinions. I have tried to see Lawrence's attitude to the First World War not in the romanticized, pacifist atmosphere of the thirties, but in the way it struck his contemporaries in 1915—not all of whom saw in him the persecuted genius, the victim of official busybodies. That Lawrence suffered is evident, but much of the suffering was of his own tragic making, as his *Collected Letters* show the attentive reader.

For Lawrence's life with Frieda the sources are many: contemporary accounts by their friends, Frieda's own books, Lawrence's letters, and also his poems, and short stories as written or rewritten in 1913–14, so highly revealing of the shock as well as the early delight of life with a woman so different from any he had so far known. Here the points of convergence of letters and literary works are many, and I have felt free to exploit them, as far as seemed reasonable, as biographical evidence.

My second preoccupation was to relate Lawrence's writings, as far as possible, to the ideas which he had absorbed from reading and conversations, on the assumption that, for a man such as he, ideas are part of one's life experience. The most immediate task was to establish a check-list of his known reading, and in this the information provided by Jessie Chambers, as later published in her book, was invaluable. After 1912 the *Collected Letters* provide a good deal of information, although they by no means reveal the full extent of Lawrence's vast reading. He would borrow books from most of his acquaintance and read what he found in the many houses lent to him: to give but one instance, we do not know what he may have read on his honeymoon with Frieda in 1912, when they were lent Alfred Weber's chalet in Bavaria, and the changes in his "philosophy" about that time may conceivably be connected with such reading. I hope to have carried a little further the excellent work of W. Y. Tindall on Lawrence's theoretical sources; there remains much to be done in this field, if only to relate him more precisely to the change of climate from the nineteenth to the twentieth centuries which, with him, not only coincides with his new life with a German wife, but corresponds to something wider and more general at the end of the Edwardian age.

My third concern was to observe a strictly chronological approach to Lawrence's works as being the only scientific one: if the aim is to understand what the writer meant in any given work, comparison with the work of his contemporaries can be illuminating, whereas comparison with later works may be especially misleading in the case of a man who did not hesitate to change his mind over the years. We find in the theoretical writings which he called his "philosophy", such as "Study of Thomas Hardy", as well as in his letters, the key to scenes in the novels written at about the same time. Thus, rather than separate arbitrarily the works of imagination from the critical and theoretical, I have chosen to study them together phase by phase, endeavouring for each period to see as far as possible the whole man at work in the creative process.

In so doing I have tried to relate Lawrence to his time: this will become increasingly necessary as well as more feasible as memoirs and archives on the years 1910 to 1930 become available. In seeking to "come to terms" with Lawrence, I have naturally been influenced by the experience of the years after 1935. It is impossible for my generation to forget that some of the ideas which attracted Lawrence as early as 1915 were subsequently mobilized in the service of the worst crimes against mankind. To recall that fact after Bertrand Russell is not to charge Lawrence with the crimes, but to issue a warning and a call for vigilance. It is idle to speculate as to what Lawrence's attitude might have been to events after his death. The problem is not there, but in the conception of the future of man which Lawrence's works, in the period considered, offer us. It will be clear to the reader that I find no comfort in and have no sympathy with that conception, while trying to understand how Lawrence may have been brought to form it. It strikes me as regressive and reactionary, in *Women in Love* as in *The Plumed Serpent*. It also seems to me essential to try to understand it for purposes of education.

Lawrence claimed that "the essential function of art is moral"; a morality, he added, "which changes the blood, not the mind":* in other words he saw in literature an instrument at the service of some ambitious but vague programme for changing mankind. While the prophet in him wanted to use his art for a purpose, the poet was content with that he called "poetry of the present". That contradiction is found in all his works, to a greater degree perhaps than with any among his contemporaries who also allowed the tradition of hero-worship inherited from romanticism to shade off into artist-worship. In many of his writings Lawrence treads delicately between the two, and the Lawrence legend as it exists today is also on that borderline. What I have tried to do is to see him as a specimen of the species *man*, with human weaknesses and human greatness, an infinite capacity for suffering and enjoyment, and the gifts of a great writer.

While it is impossible to thank all those who have helped me in this work over the years, special thanks are due not only to my translator, but to Mme Raymonde Jackson for typing the manuscript with infinite vigilance, and to Mrs Patricia Newnham for her valuable critical assistance in preparing it for publication.

* *Studies in Classic American Literature,* p. 170.

PART ONE:

CHILD OF THE MIDLANDS

I

CHILDHOOD: 1885–1901

Eastwood

David Herbert Richards Lawrence, third son of John Arthur Lawrence and of Lydia Beardsall, was born on 11 September 1885 in the Nottinghamshire mining village of Eastwood.

Eastwood straddles a piece of rising ground twelve miles north-west of Nottingham overlooking the valley of the Erewash, whose narrow waters mark the boundary between the counties of Nottinghamshire and Derbyshire. To the north-east the mining country is bounded by wooded heights, last relic of the ancient Forest of Sherwood. The once purely agricultural land of the valley is now dotted with mine-shafts and blast furnaces. Among endless rows of grimy brick cottages, in every village stand enthroned the three local potentates: the mine, the Methodist chapel and the brewery. From the steep, narrow lanes leading out into the countryside from the main street of Eastwood (the road from Nottingham to Derby by way of Ripley) the mine-shafts and the smoking slag heaps can be glimpsed below.

In the meanest of these lanes—despite its royal appellation of Victoria Street—stands Lawrence's birthplace. Short and steep, the narrow roadway is flanked on both sides by single-storey cottages, or rather by two buildings divided into vertical sections by gutter pipes and by the front doors of the different dwellings. The house itself stands next to a yard or stable entry, its narrow façade pierced by three openings. A broad, high window surmounted by a kind of cornice doubtless served as shop window for the little haberdashery once run by Mrs Lawrence. Across it is drawn one of those heavy lace curtains dear to the working-class housewife. In comparison, the door beside it appears mean and narrow, and above it a pane of glass has been let in, presumably to relieve the darkness of the entrance. The upper storey boasts a single window. With its whitewashed sills and lintels, it is the humblest of workmen's homes in this bleak village, depressing in its poverty and ugliness.

The Lawrence family

John Arthur Lawrence, son of a Nottingham tailor who had come to Eastwood to work in the service of the mining company of Barber, Walker & Co,[1] was married in 1875. After working for a time in Sutton-in-Ashfield and Old Radford, he had returned to his native village to work as a butty. The term "mining contractor", used by Mrs Clarke,[2] though not inexact is liable to give a somewhat exaggerated idea of his social status. A butty was a miner paid not by the day but by the ton of coal extracted. There would be three or four men working under him and sometimes he would have a partner. The Company paid the butty for the coal extracted by the whole team, and the wages they earned were divided between him and his fellow-workmen. The weekly wage naturally varied with the yield of the stall allotted to the butty. A good miner such as Mr Lawrence was at the time of his marriage could sometimes earn as much as £5 a week. But since he did not get on with his superiors, he was allotted increasingly unprofitable stalls, so that his average weekly wage was reduced to little more than £2 10s. In the summer partial laying-off period, he might even bring home a mere 16s.[3] Since extra earnings went in drink and not in savings, the Lawrences must often have seen difficult times when the pit was temporarily shut down in the summer season.

The Walter Morel of *Sons and Lovers* is a complete and up to a point impartial portrait of John Arthur Lawrence.[4] Tall and well set-up, his face framed by a thick and curly black beard, his upper lip covered by a luxuriant moustache, he had a fine crop of wavy black hair, a ruddy complexion and eyes that flashed with fire.[5] A period as chorister in Brinsley Church had helped to cultivate his naturally melodious voice. As a man, the collier was certainly not lacking in charm—the sheer physical appeal of the strong swimmer and accomplished dancer. Seeing him in retrospect as he must have been in the days of his youth, his children were able to understand how it was that their mother had come to marry him.

Life in the mine had worn him down; the slack habits of the miner, his drunkenness, the puritanical intolerance of his wife, had soon made him an abject figure in the eyes of his children; his inarticulate nature added to his difficulty in communicating with them.[6] Totally unlettered (he had begun to earn his own living at the age of seven), he was clearly incapable of sharing his wife's literary tastes, so that, while his whole family strained with one endeavour towards the middle classes, the father remained absolutely of the people, without the least desire to rise, either morally or socially.[7]

On those evenings when he came straight home from the mine, after a meal and a wash he would spend his time cobbling shoes, mending holes in saucepans and kettles, cleaning the works of the clock, or making fuses for the mine: finding true happiness in those moments when a man can express an idea not in words but in creative gesture, mind shaping matter as though they were one. His children admired his skill at these small tasks, and loved to lend a helping hand on such good-humoured evenings.[8]

But more often than not, instead of coming home as soon as he reached the open air, he would call in at the pub and spend a good part of his pay, generously standing his friends a drink when the week had been a good one. When, as sometimes happened, he came home drunk, there would follow scenes of brutality probably much like those described in *Sons and Lovers*.[9] The quarrels and the ill-treatment suffered by their mother filled the children with fear and hatred and they, too, began to despise their father and to shut him out almost entirely from their lives.[10]

Lydia Lawrence certainly had many reasons for feeling different from her husband. As the daughter of an engineer in the Sheerness dockyard, she belonged to the lower middle class, and, as a former schoolmistress, was not uncultured; she was also an avid reader and had tried her hand at poetry.[11] Above all her character was firmly anchored in the strong and harsh puritan tradition of striving for moral betterment and domination over both self and environment. Lawrence speaks of his maternal grandfather as "proud of his fair skin and blue eyes but more proud still of his integrity", a man who "preferred theology in reading and who drew near in sympathy to one man, the Apostle Paul". Hard and ironical, he "ignored all sensual pleasure". From this cold and authoritarian puritan the daughter inherited both her "proud and unyielding" character and her abomination of poverty.[12]

The favourite distraction of this frail little woman, with her high, broad brow, brown silken curls and honest, searching gaze, was to talk with educated men on such topics as religion, philosophy or politics. She seemed, however, doomed to encounter only infirmity of purpose in the men she was to love. At twenty she fell in love with the son of a well-to-do tradesman who dreamt of entering the ministry, but, owing to financial losses, was obliged to fall back on teaching. She subsequently heard that he had married his landlady, a rich widow of forty.[13]

At a Christmas party in Nottingham, at the age of twenty-three, Lydia Beardsall made the acquaintance of John Arthur Lawrence.[14] She was fascinated by those very traits which made him so different from her family and herself: his warm, spontaneous laughter, his cheerful character, his natural good-heartedness. To the austerely puritan girl, the naïve sensual delight, the sheer relish of the passing moment radiated by this man came as a revelation. Her "ladylike" manners, the purity of her speech, free of all traces of local accent, attracted the young man. They were married a year from this first meeting.

After only six months of happiness, Lydia Lawrence was to discover her husband's failings and to understand how greatly the environment she had entered differed from her own. She thought she had made him a teetotaller, but it was not long before he took to drinking again. Little by little she came to realize the deep divergence between their two natures: living in the present, given entirely to fleeting impressions, the collier was a truly primitive soul, whereas she sought always to improve herself by a constant effort of the will. In time she came to feel nothing but contempt for his weak character, and seems even to have reproached herself for ever having loved him. Aware of a certain social degradation from daily contact with working-class life, she transferred to her children the full strength of her desire to return to the middle classes, as well as her need for spiritual communion with minds as well-developed as her own. This alienation from her husband and the passionate need for spiritual contact with her growing children became the subject of the first part of Sons and Lovers.

As far as time allowed, Mrs Lawrence continued to read and cultivate her mind. She borrowed books from the village library; she liked to receive visits from the Congregational minister, with whom she would discuss religion and philosophy.[15] She also took an active interest in the local "Co-op", and as secretary of the Women's Guild was even called upon to read an occasional paper, to the boundless admiration of her children.[16]

These tastes, however, in no way detracted from her housework, which both the writer and his sister have described with pride: the highly polished furniture, the walls deliberately bare of the cheap and tawdry ornaments that she despised. It is not difficult to conceive the constant struggle of this workman's wife determined to maintain a well-ordered household and never allow her children to go dirty or ill-dressed. Though it was not more richly furnished, there was always something special about the Lawrence home which made it different from those of all their neighbours.[17]

The children could have had no very clear perception of the opposition between their parents' characters; perhaps no more than a dim awareness of their mother's greater dignity, of a love from her at once more active and more tender; thus the father, rarely present, came in time to be regarded as a stranger in the home. So radical an opposition, even if fully understood only at a later date, was bound to leave traces on the writer's mind and may well have fostered in him a dualist conception of personality: in later life his father and mother became for him, as it were, two poles of attraction towards which he was alternately drawn—one representing all the brutality of instinctive life, as well as its simplicity and soundness; the other a symbol of the struggle of mind and will to triumph over instinct, towards a view of life imposed from above.

David Herbert, known to the family as "Bert", was the last child but one. The eldest, George Arthur, appears to have left no deep impression on his brother. Seven or eight years older than Bert, he was apprenticed at an early age to an uncle in the picture-framing trade in Nottingham with whom he went to live. It may not be irrelevant to point out that in Sons and Lovers, a fictionalized autobiography of D. H. Lawrence, the name of Arthur is given to a younger brother of the hero, Paul Morel.

The real role of elder brother—of admired, beloved model—is given by Lawrence, as indeed it seems to have been given by his mother, to the next son, William Ernest, whom the novelist calls William Morel. The two sisters, Emily, three-and-a-half years older than Bert, and Ada, two years younger, he combines in the character of Annie, elder sister of Paul Morel. Emily's influence on her brother seems to have been slight, whereas Ada will be found at her brother's side on a number of occasions in the course of his life and works, sometimes in surprising guises. In *Sons and Lovers*, for example, Jessie Chambers claimed to recognize many of Ada's traits in the hero's younger brother Arthur.

The younger Lawrence children thus grew up with the shining example of William Ernest ever before their eyes. Intelligent and hard-working, as soon as he left primary school he proceeded to earn his living while continuing his education; the first part of *Sons and Lovers* contains a detailed description of his youth. At twenty-one he obtained a promising situation in a London shipping office. Two years later he was dead of pneumonia, complicated by erysipelas, his strength overtaxed by his work, his studies and the life of pleasure he led under the influence of the flighty girl he was engaged to marry. His rapid rise, his exuberant character, left an indelible mark on the minds of his younger brother and sisters. The shock caused by his death no doubt had deep repercussions on the character of his mother, and, hence, on the destiny of Bert himself. Mrs Lawrence had devoted all her strength to helping William Ernest in his social advancement; she had protected him against his father's outbreaks of violence and opposed his wish to send him down the mine.[18] In return, the young man had defended his mother against his father's drunken brutality and brought her home his wages.[19] With a single stroke his death destroyed the best part of such hope as his mother was still prepared to place in life.

The children shared in all their mother's joys and cares. The father was shut off from the spiritual life of the family by his uncouth habits, his drunkenness and his own bad conscience. So much so that when a mining accident exiled him for a time to hospital in Nottingham, his family, lacking for nothing thanks to various Benefit Societies, settled down almost joyfully to life without him. Without admitting it to one another, they found themselves regretting that his approaching recovery would soon bring him home.[20]

When Bert was about two years old the Lawrence family went to live in the Breach,[21] which consisted of six blocks of colliery houses, two rows of three, twelve houses in a block, ranged at the bottom of the slope leading down northwards from Eastwood towards Brinsley. The Lawrences' house, which stood at the end of a row, was a little larger than the others, giving them a slight superiority over their immediate neighbours. Certainly it was an improvement on the mean little cottage in Victoria Street. Mrs Lawrence now enjoyed the use of a garden surrounded by a low privet hedge; the house was relatively spacious, and from the front it did not look too bad. But the kitchen, where the family lived, opened out on to a "scrubby" back garden and the ashpits in the sordid alley which ran between the blocks.

Five years later, the Lawrences moved up to a better house in Walker Street. Its bay windows looked out over Underwood Hill and High Park Woods, over the whole countryside familiar to readers of *The White Peacock* and *Sons and Lovers*.[22] To the children this was the beloved home, never to be remembered without a pang of heartache, half delight in memory and half anguish at the thought of years now gone for ever. In front of the house stood an old ash tree, and when the north wind swept the Derbyshire hills its groaning branches terrified the children in their beds. The "demoniacal" shrieking of the tree mingled with the noise of the returned drunkard quarrelling with his wife. Awakened and trembling, Bert would listen terrified to this strange symphony:

> Then he heard the booming shouts of his father, come home nearly drunk, then the sharp replies of his mother, then the bang, bang of his father's fist on the table, and the nasty snarling shout as the man's voice got higher. And then the whole was drowned in a piercing medley of shrieks and cries from the great, windswept ash-tree. The children lay silent in suspense, waiting for a lull in the wind to hear what their father was doing. He might hit their mother again. There was a feeling of horror, a kind of bristling in the darkness, and a sense of blood. They lay with their hearts in the grip of an intense anguish. The wind came through the tree fiercer and fiercer. All the cords of the great harp hummed, whistled, and shrieked. And then came the horror of the sudden silence, silence everywhere, outside and downstairs. What was it? Was it a silence of blood? What had he done?[23]

It is difficult to exaggerate the potential effect of such scenes on the development of an over-sensitive child. The whole tenor of his education, both at school and at chapel, reinforced by his mother's influence, could not but drive Lawrence to condemn his father, and to respect and love with all his heart his deserving and devoted mother. In the formative years of Lawrence's personality, his father's influence was either non-existent or completely negative.

The child

If we are to believe certain passages of his novel (perhaps not entirely exempt from traces of his contemporary reading of such poems as Baudelaire's "Bénédiction"), D. H. Lawrence came into this world under the sign of hatred. His mother had "dreaded this baby like a catastrophe, because of her feeling for her husband". Since she no longer loved her husband "she had not wanted this child to come".[24] When only two weeks old the baby developed bronchitis.[25] His mother feared he was "unhealthy or malformed":[26]

> ... she noticed the peculiar knitting of the baby's brows, and the peculiar heaviness of its eyes, as if it were trying to understand something that was pain. She felt, when she looked at the child's dark, brooding pupils, as if a burden were on her heart ... With all her force, with all her soul she would make up to it for having brought it into the world unloved. She would love it all the more now it was here; carry it in her love.[27]

Did the infant's surprised and brooding eyes suggest to her some sort of predestination?[28] Without knowing why, the mother in *Sons and Lovers*, gazing at the setting sun and wondering what will become of her son, cries out on a sudden impulse, "I will call him Paul."[29] Mrs Morel named her son after the Apostle, just as Mrs Lawrence had named hers after David, the predestined shepherd boy, with whom the writer was to identify himself on more than one occasion.

The first photographs of Bert show an alert, attentive, almost laughing schoolboy. In one well-known family group his face and that of his mother are remarkable for their intelligence and delicacy of feature, while William Ernest attracts attention by the intensity of his gaze, concentrated on some inner vision. An unmanageable crop of hair, which looks blond in the photograph, hides part of Bert's high forehead. His drooping lower lip, however, bears no resemblance to the tight-lipped, determined dignity and constraint of his mother's mouth. This photograph does not at all give the impression of a melancholy child excessively aware of the unhappiness of his home. It suggests rather a sensitive disposition, perhaps a mobility of character greater than that of his brothers and sisters.

In *Sons and Lovers*, possibly with the legitimate aim of artistic simplification, Lawrence insists on the sad and sensitive character of Paul Morel. But the novelist simplifies and probably magnifies childhood memories, and both distance and literary influences help to colour a more complex reality. The pallid child of *Sons and Lovers*, resembling his mother with his slight build, his hair darkening from blond to red and finally deep brown, is not altogether the Bert Lawrence revealed in his sister's book; though on the whole exact, the portrait is incomplete. His intense affection for his mother, his sadness during his father's bouts of drunkenness, his anxiety in the face of the ever-present threat of an accident in the mine, his delicate health and weak chest, such are the traits of Paul Morel the child which would seem also to be true of young Bert Lawrence:

> As a rule he seemed old for his years. He was so conscious of what other people felt, particularly his mother. When she fretted he understood, and could have no peace. His soul seemed always attentive to her.[30]

But when all was going well at home the child was happy and would spend many carefree hours playing with companions of his own age. Boys' games, such as football and cricket, did not attract him. With his sisters he would read such adventure stories as *Coral Island, The Swiss Family Robinson* or *The Gorilla Hunters*. Later he enjoyed the works of Marryat and Fenimore Cooper.[31] But in the main his evenings would be spent in the roadway with his sisters and their friends, inventing new games for them to play, and, on nights when his mother was not at home, embarking with them on curious culinary experiments. His favourite games were games "of make believe"— for he seems to have developed very early his marked gift for invention. And he was always happy when he could roam over the fields, gathering the earliest wild flowers, culling plants for Mrs Lawrence's herb beer or picking blackberries for jam.[32]

It is hardly surprising that he should have been painfully shy. Nervous by temperament, brought up for the most part close to his mother, used to the society of girls rather than that of boys, his shrinking attitude may have expressed a subconscious link between the brutality of his father and the indifference of the external world. His terror when obliged to confront strangers is described in *Sons and Lovers*: on Friday afternoons Paul Morel would be sent to collect his father's wages at the payroom of the mine. With beating heart he waited for the little bald pay-clerk to call the name Morel: he did not even dare to shout "Present" loud enough to be heard and suffered "convulsions of self-consciousness" when it was his turn to step forward to claim his father's due. He carried off the money with trembling fingers, suffering "the tortures of the damned".[33] Similar torments beset him when he had to go into the public house to meet his father coming from the mine. The vulgarity of the place revolted him; he dared not even ask for a lemonade in front of all the heavy drinkers: he felt the eyes of the landlady upon him, half pitying, half resentful of his abstinence.[34] Shyness and the stiff pride of a well-brought-up child combined to make him appear gauche and stupid.

Religious education

Mrs Lawrence was a Congregationalist, her husband preferred the public house; the children followed their mother to the chapel and were brought up in her faith. The population of the Erewash mining district, in common with almost all the industrial North, attended the chapels of one or another of the nonconformist sects. For these colliers and their wives, religion was restricted almost entirely to a code of moral behaviour based on Hebrew asceticism. Provided the absolute truth of the Bible was admitted, there was a reasonable measure of tolerance regarding dogma. But the very language of worship and current moral code would ceaselessly recall evangelical rules of conduct and Christian austerity: common norms of behaviour for the working population were indeed the sole link between the various sects, the only effective expression of a constraining group mentality. The religious ideal of the nonconformist went no further than prescribing good behaviour according to a purely negative conception postulating the weakness and wickedness of human nature.

In this religion the Bible and the hymns alone still offered the imagination some of the wonder and magic of life. But poetry and mysticism were alien to men of such rigid character as the tyrannical father in the Lawrence story called "The Christening".[35] The opening chapter of *The Lost Girl* conveys vividly the small-mindedness and austerity of his childhood, and in *Twilight in Italy* Lawrence recalls with a shiver "the stiff null propriety which used to overcome us, like a sort of deliberate, self-inflicted cramp, on Sundays".[36]

Bitter experience had only reinforced in Mrs Lawrence the puritan attitudes inherited from her father. Her hatred of vice and her self-righteousness were increased by life with her husband, in her eyes the living image of moral weakness. Regular attendance at religious service was expected from all and formed part of the system by which the children were to raise themselves to a superior level, thus bettering their social rank. So three times every Sunday they would go to chapel, attending morning and evening service, and in the afternoon a Sunday School conducted by an excellent but ferocious-looking blacksmith with a taste for martial hymns.[37] They also belonged to the Band of Hope, and had all signed a pledge never to drink alcohol.

"There's a serpent in the glass, dash it down!"
they would sing with fervour,
"Dare to be a Daniel, dare to stand alone."[38]

In later life Lawrence was to look back upon this education with characteristically puritan pride and unreserved appreciation:

> I think it was good to be brought up a Protestant: and among Protestants, a Nonconformist, and among Nonconformists a Congregationalist. Which sounds Pharisaic. But I should have missed bitterly a direct knowledge of the Bible, and a direct relation to Galilee and Canaan, Moab and Kedron, those places that never existed on earth ... So, altogether, I am grateful to my "Congregational" upbringing. The Congregationalists are the oldest Nonconformists, descendants of the Oliver Cromwell Independents. But they avoided the personal emotionalism which one found among the Methodists when I was a boy.[39]

The influence of religion on Lawrence's development can scarcely be overestimated. Like Cromwell's Independents, he would always need to feel that he was one of the Righteous, so that, shy as the boy was, he too displayed the "cheek, that was the outstanding quality of chapel men". A special kind of cheek, as Lawrence explains in *Apocalypse*, "authorized from above, as it were",[40] which might equally well be called a form of democratic pride characteristic of men accustomed to run the affairs of their religious community for themselves, convinced that if they respect the moral law in the next world they will be among the first. We can hear the Puritan speaking in "Pomegranate":

> You tell me I am wrong.
> Who are you, who is anybody to tell me I am wrong:
> I am not wrong.[41]

Ada Clarke has rightly pointed out that the hymn sung by the young teetotallers, "Dare to be a Daniel, dare to stand alone", assumed an almost prophetic value in her brother's mouth. How often in the future was he not to show the moral fanaticism, the savage energy of the convinced puritan preaching his cause with indefatigable zeal against all-comers.

In an article already quoted, "Hymns in a man's life" and again in *Apocalypse*, Lawrence tried to define what he retained of permanent value from his religious upbringing. While he may not have been aware to what extent he was following the traditions of the sect even in his rebellion against the morality of his environment, at all events he found alive in his heart, and with all the old magic, the memory of the hymns sung in childhood. Neither dogma, which never was of primary importance in the eyes of his sect, nor the Bible, so often interpreted in accordance with a fixed and arbitrary system that it was "temporarily killed" for him,[42] have the same importance as the hymns his mother used to sing to them at home, and which he learnt and sang again and again in school, in chapel and at Sunday School. As he says himself, "Here is the clue to the ordinary Englishman—in the Non-conformist hymns",[43] which "live and glisten in the depths of man's consciousness in undimmed wonder, because they have not been subjected to any criticism or analysis".

The Hebrew names conveyed for him no geographical reality,[44] but an inner and ideal universe:

> Each gentle dove and sighing bough
> That makes the eve so fair to me
> Has something far diviner now
> To draw me back to Galilee.
> O Galilee, sweet Galilee,
> Where Jesus loved so much to be,
> O Galilee, sweet Galilee,
> Come sing thy songs again to me!

To me the word Galilee has a wonderful sound. The Lake of Galilee! I don't want to know where it is. I never want to go to Palestine. Galilee is one of those lovely, glamorous worlds, not places that exist in the golden haze of a child's half-formed imagination. And in my man's imagination it is just the same.[45]

Steeped in the Bible before reaching an age at which he could hope to understand its language, he was to respond above all to its poetry. His imagination was able to develop all the more freely because the meaning of the hymns and Bible stories was so vague: his vision was of some promised land wrapped in a distant haze, a land where all his dreams would come true. In the twilight glow he glimpsed the vague but radiant image of the Redeemer:

> Sun of my soul, Thou Saviour dear,
> It is not night if Thou be near . . .

The harvest of the farms bordering on his smoke-smirched village was one in his mind with the marvel of "Canaan's pleasant land" where "waved the golden corn".[46] The poetic urge to an imaginary better world would thus assert itself powerfully on the child's fancy, strengthening his tendency to escape from ugly reality into worlds of his own making, better calculated to satisfy the secret longings of his soul.

The schoolboy

Because of his delicate health Bert Lawrence was not sent to school until he was six. Although living in the town of Eastwood, he was domiciled in the parish of Greasley and therefore attended the primary school of this village, a Nottinghamshire County Council non-denominational school.[47]

At the age of thirteen he won a scholarship to Nottingham High School, where he spent three school years, from September 1898 to July 1901, the secondary studies of scholarship holders at that time lasting three years only. He seems to have been an intelligent and hard-working pupil. His first term report, published by Mrs Clarke, shows him to have been gifted in languages.[48]

After starting in the Shell Form, a class for pupils under observation, he was soon put into the Lower Modern IVth, and in July 1899 gained fifth place in this class. At Easter 1900 he moved up from the Upper Modern IVth into the Modern Vth, where he was sixteenth in July. By the time he left school, he had reached the Modern VIth.[49]

We have little information on Lawrence's schooldays. His only descriptions were written after he was twenty-five, and the accuracy of certain of his memories may well be questioned.

The most significant reminiscence—but hindsight all the same—is found in an article entitled "Slaves of Civilization":

I shall never forget the anguish with which I wept, the first day. I was captured. I was roped in. The other boys felt the same. They hated school because they felt captives there. They hated the masters because they felt them as jailers. They hated even learning to read and write. The endless refrain was: "When I go down pit you'll see what —— sums I'll do."[50]

In *Sons and Lovers* Lawrence seems deliberately to have avoided all reference to Paul Morel's schooldays, in order to place greater insistence on his life at home. All he says is that "when he was seven, the starting school had been a nightmare and a torture to him. But afterwards he liked it."[51] No doubt this first allusion to his education can be accepted as the nearest approach to the child's real feelings. It is only later that the novelist takes up the theme of the schoolchild "enslaved by civilization". Moreover, in the biography of Ursula Brangwen, he insists on the secondary school as her opportunity to escape from an over-noisy home and the drab reality of her village.[52]

Once he had overcome his initial shyness, Lawrence was thus reasonably happy in his first places of study. Mrs Clarke asserts that he "learnt things easily and did not dislike school".[53] He does not, however, appear to have attracted any measure of attention at the High School: when interrogated, several of his contemporaries failed to remember him at all.[54] As he did not practise any sport, his personality would doubtless not make any great impression in such a highly traditional institution. Shy and proud, easily hurt if his ability was not immediately recognized,[55] he must have been one of those pupils who may pass unnoticed for years until the day when, favourable circumstances permitting, they suddenly reveal exceptional talent.

The influence of Lawrence's secondary education is thus difficult to define: apart from the purely practical value of all the knowledge acquired during these three years, and a few scattered indications of a more subtle order which can be gleaned from his works, there is little enough to go on. The home background, the positive action of his mother and the negative influence of his father, as well as the pressure of social and religious environment, are of greater significance. Towards the end of his fifteenth year everything seems to have conspired to make of him a timid boy, confiding only in his own family, affectionate with his mother and sisters, knowing that the outside world awaited him but fearful of launching out to conquer it. Proud, but unsure, he does not appear to have had any very particular ambition, or any plan for the future.[56] For the next few years he will be drifting with events: indeed, the course taken by his life appears almost to have been determined by chance.

2

ADOLESCENCE: 1901–06

The period of Lawrence's adolescence is marked not so much by the external circumstances of his life—important though their consequences were—as by an intellectual and emotional growth inseparable from his feelings for Jessie Chambers, known as Miriam to readers of *Sons and Lovers*. A chronological account of those five years would tend to disperse the essential elements of his inner development, and thus to distract attention from the problems basic to the formation of his personality. The events of his adolescence will therefore be considered here in the light of these important problems.

Haywood's

Lawrence left Nottingham High School in July 1901, towards the end of his sixteenth year.[1] Almost at once he addressed to the local surgical goods firm of Haywood an application for a job, composed by his brother Ernest in his best business style, stressing the boy's education and excellent references.[2] Tremulously Bert went with his mother to the interview fixed by Mr Haywood. The sight of the wooden leg and elastic stockings on the firm's notepaper had filled him with alarm. He was, however, taken on, and began his working life as a clerk at 8s. a week.[3] Mrs Clarke confirms that the picture in *Sons and Lovers* of life at Jordan's, and Paul Morel's first impressions in this new world, are applicable to Lawrence's experience at Haywood's.[4] The boy spent twelve hours a day in the factory, with a brief interval for dinner at one o'clock and a few minutes' break for tea. He rose at six, left the house three-quarters of an hour later to catch the seven-fifteen train from Kimberley station. At eight o'clock he sorted the mail, copied the letters and passed on to the workshop instructions for carrying out the orders received. The rest of the morning was spent preparing the parcels for the midday post, after which things were generally quiet till tea-time. Then came the rush for the evening post: letters and invoices to write, parcels to tie up and weigh, addresses to inscribe, stamps to stick on, all in time for the postman to carry off in his bag when he called in on his evening round.

Bert then ran to catch the eight-thirty train which enabled him to reach home at twenty-past nine, after a walk of nearly two miles from the station. No wonder that after a few months of this existence, wilting in the dark and airless atmosphere and exhausted by the long hours, he should have fallen ill.

Not that his commercial experience was hateful to him. Everyone at Jordan's is shown in a favourable light; from the owner, somewhat on the rough side but fundamentally a good sort, to Fanny, the sentimental hunchback; from the head of Paul's department, an inoffensive type with a "saloon bar" flavour, to Polly, the brisk little overseer of the elastic-stocking workshop, who took the lad under her wing. Bert seems to have got on excellently with both clerks and work girls; above all he enjoyed the busy times, when the whole factory seemed to hum with a single rhythm, men and women working in a united effort, though Paul (or perhaps rather his creator, the Lawrence of 1912) claimed to note a marked difference in the way the two sexes applied themselves to their work.

No doubt Lawrence was then the type of boy to be interested in his work, to absorb himself in the daily round and eventually adapt himself to the situation. But such resignation was not achieved without certain inner struggles, without protests, which, in *Sons and Lovers*, are retrospectively expressed more strongly than they could have been in 1901.

As soon as he felt the obligation to look for work, Paul Morel had become aware of being "a prisoner of industrialism": he dreaded "the business world, with its fixed system of values, its impersonality"; he hated to have to appear before strangers to be accepted or rejected.[5] Such, in the novel, are the first brief indications of a future Lawrentian theme. During these months of apprenticeship he makes out that he learnt to detest the mechanization of the individual and of the intellect by industrial life, the reduction of a man to a mechanical function. In a brief scene, he indicates with picturesque naïveté how commercial life puts blinkers on the mind. When Paul Morel appears before him, Mr Jordan asks him to translate an order written in French for *deux paires de bas de fil gris sans doigts*.[6] The lad hesitates for a moment on the word *doigts*, then mutters "fingers". For Mr Jordan, who does not manufacture gloves, the word could only mean "toes".

Pneumonia

Not long after the death of Ernest an attack of penumonia brought to an end, after only three months, a type of existence for which Lawrence was clearly little suited. There is no reason to question either the date or the authenticity of the scene described in *Sons and Lovers*. The accuracy of the smallest details carries complete conviction:

> At last, on December 23, with his five shillings Christmas box in his pocket, Paul wandered blindly home. His mother looked at him, and her heart stood still.
> "What's the matter?" she asked.
> "I'm badly, mother," he replied. "Mr Jordan gave me five shillings for a Christmas box!"
> He handed it to her with trembling hands. She put it on the table.
> "You aren't glad!" he reproached her; but he trembled violently.
> "Where hurts you?" she said, unbuttoning his overcoat. It was the old question.
> "I feel badly, mother."
> She undressed him and put him to bed. He had pneumonia dangerously, the doctor said.[7]

He was saved by his mother's care and by the deep tenderness which bound them to each other:

> Paul was very ill. His mother lay in bed at nights with him; they could not afford a nurse. He grew worse, and the crisis approached. One night he tossed into consciousness in the ghastly, sickly feeling of dissolution, when all the cells in the body seem in intense irritability to be breaking down, and consciousness makes a last flare of struggle, like madness.
> "I s'll die, mother!" he cried, heaving for breath on the pillow.
> She lifted him up, crying in a small voice:
> "Oh, my son,—my son!"
> That brought him to. He realized her. His whole will rose up and arrested him. He put his head on her breast, and took ease of her for love.[8]

This pathetic scene illustrates dramatically the strength of the boy's love for his mother, at the same time throwing light upon the deep reasons he would always have to respect his mother's wishes and avoid causing her distress.

Eastwood British School

After a few weeks' convalescence with an aunt living in Skegness[9] and several months' rest, Lawrence obtained a post as a primary school pupil-teacher in the British School in Eastwood. In *The Rainbow*, he has described under the name of St Philip's[10] the drab mock-Gothic stone building, squatting low within its railed asphalt yard, with "horrible dry plants shadowily looking through the windows".

Since the Education Act of 1902 had increased the number of secondary schools and prolonged the duration of the studies of scholarship holders from three to four years, the old system of pupil-teachers was in the process of disappearing. It consisted of turning young people into teachers before they had received any real education. Some of them left primary school only to return immediately as pupil-teachers. The headmaster checked their teaching methods while supervising their further studies. No doubt this explains why the big classroom of the British School was divided into two sections by a glass partition, enabling the headmaster to keep a permanent eye on his subordinates and their pupils.

It is difficult to make out Lawrence's attitude towards his new profession. His own later allusion to "three years' savage teaching of collier lads"[11] is the only first-hand evidence of this period of his life. Ursula Brangwen's career at St Philip's was recounted in *The Rainbow* at a time when the novelist had fresh in his memory his experience at Davidson Road School in Croydon. The dismal picture of Ursula's life as a pupil-teacher, of her timidity when confronted with a furtive or rebellious class, of her painful struggle to impose discipline and apply rigid and mechanical teaching methods, should serve as a reminder that this new life was just as likely to revolt Lawrence as his factory apprenticeship. Even more, perhaps, if it is remembered that teaching must at first have seemed to offer at least some prospect of liberation and promotion to an easier life.[12]

Yet *Sons and Lovers* does provide indirect proof that he found the teaching routine less severe than that of the factory. Paul Morel returns to Jordan's after ten months' rest. And it is interesting to note that, even while transposing, Lawrence sticks closely enough to reality to invent some alleviation of Paul's work. In point of fact, Lawrence had a half-day's holiday every Wednesday and from 1903 onwards he attended evening classes at Ilkeston, where a district Training Centre for pupil-teachers had been established.

In *Sons and Lovers* this actual improvement is faithfully recorded in fiction as follows:

> When he returned to the factory the conditions of work were better. He had Wednesday afternoon off to go to the Art School—Miss Jordan's provision —returning in the evening. Then the factory closed at six instead of at eight on Thursday and Friday evenings.[13]

In reality Bert had even more free time than Paul, and found new opportunities to cultivate his mind. He worked well at the Ilkeston centre and in December 1904 did extremely well in the King's Scholarship examination, his name appearing among the first eleven candidates for the whole of England.[14] The fact that he had forgotten to register for the examination suggests, however, some indifference towards scholastic success. At all events he showed typical shyness and self-consciousness when he declared that the examiners had been too lenient and had probably corrected his papers "after a good dinner",[15] an attitude entirely belied by the more self-satisfied tone of the letter written to *The Teacher* shortly afterwards, and reproduced, accompanied by a snapshot of him, in that journal on 25 March 1905:

> My schoolmaster showed me the first issue of your paper, and I at once recognized its merits and ordered one for myself. Needless to say, I have continued to take it ever since. I consider it of the greatest help to any student in our profession. I have always found that the courses of study contained in *The Teacher* have an originality which is very pleasing and instructive ... I consider *The Teacher* a first-class magazine for teachers; it is eminently practical and yet has an intellectual chatty tone which is very charming.
>
> I have been teaching for two years and a half, and until March of last year received my instruction from Mr G. Holderness, headmaster of the Eastwood British School. In that month, however, I obtained permission to attend the Ilkeston Centre, and there I received the greatest assistance from the Principal, Mr T. A. Beacroft.[16]

In June 1905, as advised by Mr Beacroft, he sat for the London Matriculation Examination. Placed in the Second Division, he became eligible to continue his studies at Nottingham University College as a non-fee-paying student. Since, however, he still had to meet his own expenses, he decided to wait until he had saved the necessary money. This explains why another year elapsed before he registered at the college. From 1901 to 1902 he remained at the British School as an Uncertificated Teacher earning £65 a year.[17]

At the age of twenty-one, freed from the burden of exams, he turned his hand to writing and began work on the novel which, after several years, was to become *The White Peacock*. It is at this point that Lawrence's literary and emotional life moved into the foreground, while the outside world and formal education receded gradually.

In the course of three years' teaching at the British School the shy and studious schoolboy, the "new lad" at Haywood's factory, the pupil-teacher terrorized by his class, were transformed into a bowler-hatted young man of twenty-one,[18] whose high stiff collars forced his chin up and increased his habitual expression of transparent self-esteem, putting at least one child of his acquaintance in mind of the Mad Hatter![19] Bert Lawrence, the miner's son, now looks every inch the gentleman and is drinking at the founts of wisdom. Although his means were still very slender, he was not really poor by Edwardian standards; in 1906, for instance, he was able to treat his family to a seaside holiday. Like so many other young people to whom the university stands as the great symbol of hope, he was setting out to conquer the world, tormented by a secret desire to play a role in literature and inscribe his name among the annals of the great.

*

By the time he set off for Nottingham University College, Lawrence had already acquired a solid and varied literary culture: one might almost say that he had already unwittingly founded the university of his dreams in the little valley which forms the setting for *The White Peacock*. His friendship with Jessie Chambers and their common love of literature had acted as powerful stimulants to the cultivation of his natural gifts. Her country background provided a striking contrast to his own daily life, complementing it and profoundly influencing the development of his personality and talent from the age of fifteen onwards.

Haggs Farm

When Bert was fifteen, his mother had taken him to visit a new friend, Mrs Chambers, whose acquaintance she had made one Sunday evening coming out of chapel and who had not long since come with her family to live at Haggs Farm.[20] For the adolescent Lawrence, this was the beginning of a long and precious intimacy with the farm and its inhabitants. Beginning in his last term at High School, he would spend almost every Wednesday half-holiday at the farm. During his convalescence, he would go as often as he could, soon behaving and being accepted as one of the family. Until his departure for Croydon, seven years later, "the Haggs" was for Lawrence in every sense a home from home.

The farm lies about a mile and a half from Eastwood on the edge of a little wood standing on either side of Willey Water brook. The path leading to the farm leads off the main road near the top of Underwood hill. Once there, the boy could forget the industrial scene and see only the green meadows, High Park Woods beyond the shallow valley of the Dumbles, and Annesley Park to the north-east. The plain and homely farmhouse, two-storeyed and red-tiled, stood at right-angles to the barns and stables—a typically rustic, old-fashioned English dwelling, with ivy-framed casements, gabled porch and attic windows. To the boy from Eastwood it was an island of rest, with its surrounding woods, fields and expanse of sky, out of earshot of the panting machinery of the mine and the clank of shunting trucks, a haven from the ubiquitous coal dust blackening all it touched in the valley below. It is easy to see the pull of such a paradise on a lad as acutely alive as the young Lawrence to the beauty of the countryside.

To know the Chambers is as important as to know the novelist's own parents. The father, then at the height of his powers, was kept busy with the farm and milk round. The fund of culture and intelligence behind the cheerful farmer's simplicity is revealed in several vivid scenes of the early novels. Lawrence rarely brings him into the foreground, yet his personality is familiar to readers of *The White Peacock* (Mr Saxton) and of *Sons and Lovers* (Mr Leivers), as that of a man of happy and steady disposition. Bert once told Jessie he would have liked him for a father.[21]

Mrs Chambers, "a small frail woman, rosy, with great dark brown eyes", was a little weary of the solitude of the farm.[22] For Lawrence, she represented a new type of woman, gentle and emotional. His own mother was practical, realistic and active; Jessie's mother less so. Inclined to be mystical, she "exalted everything—even a bit of housework—to the plane of a religious trust". The spiritual atmosphere surrounding her attracted Bert; with her it was easier for him to penetrate beyond the external values of ordinary things.[23]

A Christian, not of the same austere type as Mrs Lawrence, she insisted on faith rather than on works, and sought in all humility to "turn the other cheek"; she failed, however, to instil this doctrine into her sons, whose reaction was to behave roughly and treat their mother with a shade of irony.[24] Between her and the older boys—Alan, two years senior to Lawrence, Hubert and Bernard, thirteen and eleven—there reigned a "feeling of jangle and discord" which seems to have disturbed Lawrence considerably, for in the two novels which describe the Chambers family he repeatedly harks back to it.

The other children, though playing less important parts in the writer's life, all appear in his work: the eldest girl May, a schoolteacher in a neighbouring village, remained friendly with Lawrence all through the long-drawn-out episodes of his love for Jessie, always judging him clearsightedly; Emily and Mollie were fused into a single minor character in *The White Peacock*; David, the youngest son, showed a lively affection for Bert, which seems to have been reciprocated.

At the Haggs, Lawrence found an atmosphere completely different from that of his own home. The father was easy to get on with; the mother infused into family life the same almost religious quality she would give to the discovery of a wild flower or a nesting bird, helping Bert to "sift the vital fact from the experience"[25]—a characteristic description of his future literary talent. In the evenings everyone would gather round the lamp for parlour games, usually inspired by Lawrence. There might be chess, or whist, or else, on many a happy night, a sing-song round the old piano, or charades, at which he was an excellent performer. Sometimes he would organize a Shakespeare reading at which each would take a different part, and often the whole family would join in ardent debates on the week's reading or articles from the *Daily News*. It was Lawrence who provided the entertainment, news from the outside world; at the same time he found in his new friends a reinforcement of his personality, an acceptance and encouragement his own family does not seem to have given him. When he had been painting,[26] he would bring his sketches to show the Chambers, whose admiration was tempered with constructive criticism. He also wrote the family long letters in which he exercised his budding talent.

The life of the farm itself also brought new joys, and once he had penetrated beneath the rough exterior of the boys he became their friend. Underneath

their superficial rudeness he felt "a strange gentleness and lovableness".[27]
They showed their friendship by inviting him to share their work, and as
they worked together so the bond grew stronger:

> "Will you come out with me on the fallow?" asked Edgar, rather hesi-
> tatingly.
> Paul went joyfully, and spent the afternoon helping to hoe or to single
> turnips with his friend. He used to lie with the three brothers in the hay piled
> up in the barn and tell them about Nottingham and about Jordan's. In return,
> they taught him to milk, and let him do little jobs—chopping hay or pulping
> turnips—just as much as he liked. At Midsummer he worked all through the
> hay-harvest with them, and then he loved them.[28]

A keen friendship sprang up between Bert and Alan, "a rationalist who was
curious, and had a sort of scientific interest in life". In the fields, in the loft
where they would do carpentry on rainy days, Lawrence would pass on his
knowledge to Alan, and teach him the songs they loved to sing in chorus as
they worked.[29]
The whole family was thus enveloped in the warm glow of Bert's youthful
friendship:

> He loved the family so much, he loved the farm so much; it was the dearest
> place on earth to him. His home was not so lovable. It was his mother. But
> then he would have been just as happy with his mother anywhere. Whereas
> Willey Farm he loved passionately. He loved the little pokey kitchen, where
> men's boots tramped, and the dog slept with one eye open for fear of being
> trodden on; where the lamp hung over the table at night, and everything was
> so silent. He loved Miriam's long, low parlour, with its atmosphere of
> romance, its flowers, its books, its high rosewood piano. He loved the gardens
> and the low buildings that stood with their scarlet roofs on the naked edges of
> the fields, crept towards the wood as if for cosiness, the wild country scooping
> down a valley and up the uncultured hills on the other side. Only to be there
> was an exhilaration and a joy to him. He loved Mrs Leivers, with her unworld-
> liness and her quaint cynicism; he loved Mr Leivers, so warm and young and
> lovable; he loved Edgar, who lit up when he came, and the boys and the
> children and Bill—even the sow Circe and the Indian game-cock called
> Tippoo.[30]

The depth of the impression left on Lawrence by these years of intimacy
with the Chambers and the life of the farm may be judged by a letter written
many years later, in 1928, to the youngest Chambers brother, David:

> Whatever I forget, I shall never forget the Haggs—I loved it so. I loved to
> come to you all, it really was a new life began in me there ... Oh, I'd love to
> be nineteen again, and coming through the Warren and catching the first

glimpse of the buildings. Then I'd sit on the sofa under the window, and we'd crowd round the little table to tea, in that tiny little kitchen I was so at home in. *Son' tempi passati, cari miei! quanto cari, non saprete mai!*—I could never tell you in English how much it all meant to me, how I still feel about it.[31]

Lawrence's personality was enriched by contact with beings so different from his own family and by the life of the farm and its ever-present link with nature. In his mind Haggs Farm came to stand for all that was the opposite of Eastwood, of Nottingham, of all that was meant by the mine, the factory and the mechanical daily round. In Lawrence's mind the upper valley of the Dumbles always stood for escape from industrialism and its constraints, the gate to a paradise where man might rediscover the secret of lost instincts.

Jessie

During his many visits to the Haggs during his convalescence, Lawrence seems scarcely to have noticed Jessie, a shy girl a year younger than himself. According to him, she made the first advance by inviting him to come to see the swing.[32] Gradually there grew up between them a vital friendship which turned imperceptibly into love. The conflict between this love and Lawrence's devotion to his mother became the main theme of the second part of *Sons and Lovers*. The novelist made a genuine effort to retrace his memories to their source, aided in this by notes provided by Jessie, who nevertheless was deeply hurt by the picture given of their relationship.[33] As biographical material, the version of events and the interpretations of character given in *Sons and Lovers* fall far short of the required objectivity. As far as Jessie's character is concerned, the novel can serve only when Lawrence is recounting actual events without working in any explanation, or when his interpretation coincides with that of his model. Shortly after his death, Jessie wrote a record of their common experience, remarkably free from bitterness.[34] The only time she read *Sons and Lovers* was in manuscript in 1912 and its influence on her own account can therefore be discounted. With the help of her manuscript, of which she authorized the use for this study, and of the subsequently published book for which it formed the basis,[35] it is possible to attempt an impartial reconstruction of the painful story.

The first problem is to discover today what Jessie was like between 1901 and 1906. Not that the works of Lawrence, from *The White Peacock* to the poems and short stories of what may be called the "Miriam cycle", do not abound in portraits; but most of these show her somewhere between the ages of nineteen and twenty-five. All written after 1906, they are more than probably tinged with hindsight. Only in *Sons and Lovers* does Lawrence attempt to sketch the girl's development. On first acquaintance she seemed to him a shy and awkward child:

She was about fourteen years old, had a rosy dark face, a bunch of short black curls, very fine and free, and dark eyes; shy, questioning, a little resentful of the strangers, she disappeared.[36]

Soon afterwards, as he came upon her wearing a "discoloured old blue frock and broken boots", moving dreamily about the farm kitchen, he was reminded of King Cophetua's beggar maid:

She was nearly sixteen, very beautiful, with her warm colouring, her gravity, her eyes dilating suddenly like an ecstasy.

Lawrence was to associate these brown eyes—her mother's eyes—with certain moral traits, and he frequently describes them: dark, liquid, gentle, vulnerable, changeable and expressive:[37]

Suddenly, her dark eyes alight like water that shakes with a stream of gold in the dark . . . All the life of Miriam's body was in her eyes, which were usually dark as a dark church, but could flame with light like a conflagration.[38]

Her habitual gestures, too, are often noted: sitting at the window, biting her finger; pensively putting her little finger in her mouth and removing it with a little pop.[39]

Her body was not flexible and living. She walked with a swing, rather heavily, her head bowed forward, pondering. She was not clumsy, and yet none of her movements seemed quite *the* movement. Often, when wiping the dishes, she would stand in bewilderment and chagrin because she had pulled in two halves a cup or a tumbler. It was as if, in her fear and mistrust, she put too much strength into the effort. There was no looseness or abandon about her.[40]

Awkward and lacking in self-assurance, she does not even know the names of the flowers in her own garden; she is unmercifully teased by her brothers; she dare not even let a hen peck from her hand, and only pride and fear of seeming inferior to them induces her to try; on the swing she cannot let herself go, her terror almost makes her lose consciousness as Paul thrusts her higher and higher, whereas he is transformed into "a piece of swinging stuff" and soars through the air "every bit of him swinging like a bird that swoops for joy of movement".[41] As physically described in *Sons and Lovers* Jessie Chambers does not differ greatly from Jessie Wood in later years.

Up to this point we can safely follow Lawrence; but can he be believed when he goes on to paint the complete portrait of romantic girlhood? It is as though he wanted to endow the individual with all the characteristics of the type, even at the cost of truth. Ashamed of her ignorance, irritated by her brothers' mockery, his Miriam escapes into a dream world where she could "think herself somebody".[42] Detesting the drudgery of housework, she takes refuge in a universe peopled by Walter Scott heroes, or else in religious reverie. For her "Christ and God made one great figure which she loved tremblingly and passionately when a tremendous sunset burned out the western sky".[43] In this dream world she was a princess, momentarily transformed into a swine-girl. For her nothing counted but this fantasy life in which she enjoyed all the consideration she so much desired. Shuddering at the "vulgarity of her fellow choir-girls and the common-sounding voice of the vicar",

> ... she held not her father in too high esteem because he did not carry any mystical ideals cherished in his heart, but only wanted to have as easy a time as he could, and his meals, when he was ready for them.[44]

As to Ursula in *The Rainbow*, and indeed Lawrence himself, the real world offered her only one avenue of escape towards more congenial activities: education.

> She could not be princess by wealth or standing. So she was mad to have learning whereon to pride herself. For she was different from other folk, and must not be scooped up among the common fry. Learning was the only distinction to which she thought to aspire.[45]

It is all very well for Paul Morel, clerk in a surgical goods factory, to look down upon Miriam's burning wish to educate herself; but Lawrence was certainly not exempt from a similar desire to better himself through education, and from a certain diffidence concerning his own social position.

Escape through literature

At first Jessie was shy with the newcomer, "fearing to be set at nought, as by her own brothers". She was, however, attracted by the somewhat romantic charm of

> ... this boy who ... looked something like a Walter Scott hero, who could paint and speak French, and knew what algebra meant, and who went by train to Nottingham every day ... Here was a new specimen, quick, light, graceful, who could be gentle and who could be sad, and who was clever, and who knew a lot, and who had a death in the family.[46]

He was gentler than her brothers, and aroused her interest despite her scorn and hatred for the whole of the male sex. He, on the other hand, seemed "scarcely to observe her".

> Then he was so ill, and she felt he would be weak. Then she would be stronger than he. Then she could love him. If she could be mistress of him in

his weakness, take care of him, if he could depend on her, if she could, as it were, have him in her arms, how she would love him![47]

What child of fifteen, moved by a "will to power", would thus deliberately decide to take a young man under her protection? Surely this is one of those tempting but dangerous interpolations inspired by hindsight, of which the biographer should beware.

Soon the girl's portrait is being distorted in a way characteristic of Lawrence's intuitive method of 1912. He attributes to Miriam some of his own tendencies which her influence may indeed have helped to develop in him. Paul would go into the fields with Mrs Leivers and her daughter and, finding flowers or a bird's nest, would interpret them poetically, often attributing spiritual intent to natural phenomena. To Miriam, this "gave new life to everything" and her eager response was to Paul a "strange stimulant", encouraging his gift for quickening nature with spiritual life. It is, however, always Paul who speaks, who explains and describes:

> Anthropomorphic as she was, she stimulated him into appreciating things thus, and then they lived for her. She seemed to need things kindling in her imagination or in her soul before she felt she had them. And she was cut off from ordinary life by her religious intensity which made the world for her either a nunnery garden or a paradise, where sin and knowledge were not, or else an ugly, cruel thing. So it was in this atmosphere of subtle intimacy, this meeting in their common feeling for something in nature, that their love started.[48]

Yet before he ever met Miriam, Paul was evoking the mine to his mother in a living image: "Look how it heaps together, like something alive—a big creature that you don't know."[49] The anthropomorphism Lawrence attributes to Miriam is that of Paul Morel, and, indeed, his own.

But Jessie certainly did prompt him to express himself in spoken and written words. He asked her why she was always sad, and compared her expansive nature somewhat unfavourably with his mother's austere reserve. Gradually his letters to "the Haggites" were addressed to Jessie only, and the day came when he reproached her for having shown one to her parents.[50] As their personalities developed, so their friendship deepened; together they discovered new sources of aesthetic pleasure in the world around them:

> We had explored every one of the grassy ridings in the wood, and knew the different character of each part. I loved the wood passionately; the shade, the murmur of the trees, the sense of adventure, the strong scent of the undergrowth, the sudden startled call of a pheasant, the whir of a partridge's wing were things of importance to us.[51]

Shortly after Bert's illness, Jessie became a pupil-teacher at Underwood. When he went to the British School, he continued to visit the farm every

Saturday, not only for the pleasure given and received, but also to work, since he and Jessie were now both studying for the same examination. He undertook to teach her algebra, but she had difficulty in following his swift explanations, so he would be impatient and rough with her and occasionally lose his temper altogether. Afterwards he would accuse himself of torturing her. Such scenes would leave him strangely disturbed:

> She never reproached him or was angry with him. He was often cruelly ashamed. But still again his anger burst like a bubble surcharged; and still, when he saw her eager, silent, as it were, blind face, he felt he wanted to throw the pencil in it; and still, when he saw her hand trembling and her mouth parted with suffering, his heart was scalded with pain for her. And because of the intensity to which she roused him, he sought her.[52]

This phase of their friendship, which lasted from about seventeen to twenty, was dominated by their passion for education and a common enjoyment of the beauties of their world, whether natural or literary. Jessie "was possessed by two great thirsts, for knowledge and for beauty, and without some prospect of satisfying both, life had no value" for her.[53] On Friday nights, on her way home from Ilkeston, she would call at Bert's home, when he was usually alone, while his mother was out shopping, and they would read poetry together. He also began to teach her French. In the course of long discussions they would compare their characters; Bert found her "very high and very deep", whereas he himself was "comparatively shallow but very broad".[54]

Together they embarked upon a veritable orgy of literature. Lawrence had already made the acquaintance of more exalted works than the adventure stories of his childhood, thanks to a green-bound collection of *The World's Famous Literature* which his family treated with all the veneration due to a relic of his brother Ernest.[55] After his pneumonia, Lawrence began to bring to the farm young people's books such as *Little Women*, *Alice in Wonderland*, the works of Anthony Hope and Rider Haggard. Watts Dunton's *Aylwin* he lent to Jessie when he was about seventeen, only to be seized with qualms at the idea that certain melodramatic scenes might terrify her, and hence upset her mother.[56] The works of Scott played an important part in their friendship, but while, according to *Sons and Lovers*, it is Miriam who eagerly devours the romantic tales of the Border novelist, it seems probable that Lawrence was equally enthusiastic. On Thursday evenings they used to go together to replenish their stock of books at the Mechanics' Institute Library in Eastwood. Bert would walk part of the way home with Jessie, discussing their reading as they went, or lingering to wonder at a wild rose bush in bloom or some other miracle of nature:[57]

> Lawrence and I would go together to choose the books for our respective families and then set off for my home literally burdened with books. During

the walk we discussed what we had read last, but our discussion was not exactly criticism, indeed, not criticism at all, but a vivid re-creation of the substance of our reading . . . Scott's novels in particular we talked over in this way and the scenes and events of his stories were far more real to us than our actual surroundings.[58]

Lawrence felt a certain affinity with David Copperfield, and the whole Chambers family followed enthusiastically the "thrilling adventures" of Gerard in *The Cloister and the Hearth*. The two young people imagined themselves in the principal roles of *Lorna Doone*, re-enacting it in fantasy on the wooded slopes of their own Annesley. Jessie also remembers Bert's "glow of tender delight at Cranford". And all this meant to them so much more than mere reading: "It was the entering into possession of a whole new world, a widening and enlargement of life."[59]

The seeds of love

This friendship between two young people sharing an intense spiritual life naturally led to a love as deep as its approach was insidious, its true nature being long obscured by their many pretexts for being in each other's company. To his mother's complaints of his lateness on evenings when he walked part of the way home with Jessie, Lawrence replied, "I do like to talk to her"; indeed, until he was about nineteen he seems to have remained unaware of the gradual change in their mutual feelings.

So slow and unconscious was this change that it is impossible to date it exactly either from *Sons and Lovers* or from Jessie's memoirs. Two scenes, both difficult to place with any certainty, do, however, seem to mark "the beginning of a conscious sympathy" between the two of them. During the Easter holiday (1904?), Bert had organized several expeditions on foot with a party of young people, the self-styled Eastwood "Pagans":[60]

> On one of these walks I had a sudden flash of insight which made me see Lawrence in a totally new light. We were returning from one of our tramps, walking along anyhow, singly, or in twos and threes. I happened to find myself walking alone beside the hedge, admiring the bronze tips of the maple. Suddenly I turned and looked back and saw Lawrence bending over an umbrella. Something in his attitude held me transfixed; there was a look of intense suffering, and the image of Christ on the cross flashed into my mind. For a second I was overwhelmed, as if by a vision, and seemed to see him as a man destined to suffer. I walked up to him, and asked him what was the matter.
>
> "It was Ernest's umbrella, and mother will be so wild if I take it home broken," he said.

We walked along together, but I did not tell him what I had seen. I think this was the beginning of a conscious sympathy between us. Probably I was seventeen at this time.[61]

Lawrence gives a different, less lucid version of this scene: he seems to suggest that while Jessie already felt love for him, he for his part was not at all sure of his feelings. But the next scene shows clearly that he himself was slipping into a new attitude towards Jessie.

Another Easter ramble took the group to a country church decorated for the festival:

In the fonts hundreds of white narcissi seemed to be growing. The air was dim and coloured from the windows, and thrilled with a subtle scent of lilies and narcissi. In that atmosphere Miriam's soul came into a glow. Paul was afraid of the things he mustn't do; and he was sensitive to the feel of the place. Miriam turned to him. He answered. They were together. He would not go beyond the Communion-rail. She loved him for that. Her soul expanded into prayer beside him. He felt the strange fascination of shadowy religious places. All his latent mysticism quivered into life. She was drawn to him. He was a prayer along with her.[62]

Shy as she was with the other boys, Jessie sympathized with the profound isolation she perceived in him. On the way home, aware of his weariness, she "kept close" to him and he "left himself in her hands".[63]

The bond of poetry

The key to their relationship remained the shared spiritual exaltation inspired by the discovery of great literature. From the age of eighteen Lawrence began to reflect, to try to deduce from a book a lesson, a critical impression. He regretted that George Eliot should have "gone and spoilt" *The Mill on the Floss* by the "marriage" (sic) of Maggie to the cripple Philip. *Jane Eyre* fascinated him, although he "seemed to brood" over the cold passion binding Jane to Rochester. Thackeray was a favourite, particularly *Vanity Fair*. His interest was aroused by *Esmond*, and by the essay on Swift in *English Humourists of the Eighteenth Century* and the "strange" story of Swift's love for Stella. Round about this time he and Jessie even embarked on—but rapidly abandoned—the ambitious project of reading the Bible together from beginning to end.

After this, the chronology of Jessie's record of their reading becomes less clear, no doubt on account of the very profusion of her memories and the difficulty of sifting them when certain works were read again and again over a period of several years. This is particularly true of the poets.

For Christmas and on his birthday, Lawrence generally received the collected works of one of the great poets. Longfellow he loved and Tennyson played an important role in his spiritual life. Lyrical passages from "Maud", "Ulysses", "Morte d'Arthur", "The Lotos Eaters", "The Lady of Shalott" and "Locksley Hall" were among his favourites.

These he would read to Jessie time and time again. His reading of certain verses of "Locksley Hall"—perhaps the poet's curse against "the social wants that sin against the strength of youth"—gave her the impression he was trying to tell her something about himself.[64]

In 1904, when Jessie was eighteen, he arrived one day with Palgrave's *Golden Treasury of English Songs and Lyrics*, and for a time poetry became the realm of their passionate discoveries:

> Lawrence carried the little red volume in his pocket and read to me on every opportunity, usually out in the fields. He must have read almost every poem to me at one time or another.[65]

In Jessie's memory the poems of the Romantics from Book IV—"getting nearer our own day", as Lawrence used to say "significantly"—stand out most clearly: Shelley, Wordsworth, Keats, whose "La Belle Dame sans Merci" seemed to them to have the tang of their own wet meadows. Other favourites were Cowper's poems to Mary Unwin, Robert Burns, the mystic Herbert's "Gifts of God", while the "perfection and intimacy" of Shakespeare's sonnets were a source of frequent wonder.[66]

In other words, the lyrical heritage of most literate Englishmen, centred on the two great themes of love and nature, with an occasional suggestion of a preoccupation with the after-life. Naturally it would be vain to seek in the *Golden Treasury* all that Palgrave voluntarily excluded from it: the great philosophical, epic and narrative gems of English poetry. His little anthology did, however, educate the taste of Lawrence and his friend in the minor genres, above all attuning their ear to simplicity and truth in the expression of feeling by ordinary human beings. Indeed, they seem to have been almost instinctively attracted to the best the book contained. What is significant is the deep communion of feeling such poetry offered these two ardent souls. The close bond of their common love of poetry and of nature made it possible for them to misinterpret their mutual feelings, poetry providing fuel not only to feed the secret flame of their passion but also, unknowingly, to sublimate and lift it to the spiritual plane.

Living in a world of their own, full of presentiments of future glory, they remained unconscious of their growing love:

> Towards one another we were utterly unselfconscious, too content with the present to look into the future, and too deeply interested in the great question of literature to think of personal relations. Even then I had the feeling that our

walks and talks through the damp autumn night were important, and would be memorable. I felt that I was in the presence of greatness, and the facts of poverty and obscurity were irrelevant.[67]

First signs of a vocation

Bert had now reached his twentieth year, and had passed his matriculation examination. Free of examinations for some time, he began to think of writing. Naturally this venture too he shared with Jessie, his chief confidante, who knows as no one else the story of this period of his spiritual life. One day he asked her whether she had ever thought of writing. "All my life," she replied and was almost surprised to learn that he too had the same intention. Lawrence was all for an immediate start: "Lots of the things we say, things you say, would go ever so well in a book."[68] Not long afterwards, he told her "weightily" that he thought he "had something to say" and that his future work would be "didactic". At this time he was reading Emerson, Thoreau and Carlyle, completely engrossed by *The French Revolution* and reading with Jessie *Sartor Resartus* and *Heroes and Hero-Worship*.[55] May there be some connexion between the awakening of his didactic vocation and the reading of three authors whose ideas were certainly not without influence on his own?

One day Lawrence announced to Jessie that his work would be poetic: she "caught fire at the thought". But he feared people might think him mad: "a miner's son, a poet?"—remaining unconvinced by Jessie's sincere attempt to make him see the irrelevance of his fear.[70]

The problem of the predestination of the great man preoccupied him: speaking of Shakespeare as a writer in perfect harmony with his time, he added pensively:

Every great man—every man who achieves anything, I mean—is founded in some woman. Why shouldn't *you* be the woman I am founded in?[71]

He could not conceive that, once great and famous, he could be separated from the girl with whom he had developed step by step. But love itself remained outside their immediate consciousness:

We did not speak of love, but we knew it lay ahead, something that would have to be resolved. But the time was not ripe, and the world that created itself around us when we were together was of such a nature that we wished to prolong it while we could. In this, of course, we acted unconsciously, only there was a feeling of something between us that was precious and fragile.[72]

It may be objected that Jessie speaks only for herself: did Lawrence in fact love her as much as she suggests? There can be little doubt of this, despite the tendency of *Sons and Lovers* to show Miriam more in love than Paul: witness the title "Lad and girl love" and such comments as "he was a fool who did not know what was happening to himself",[73] when Paul affirms that they are only friends. Or again, various minor incidents in Jessie's account and Lawrence's more or less conscious dream of a marriage like that of Blake and his wife, whose "marvellous" story he described to her.[74]

Mother intervenes

The chapel morality of Eastwood disapproved of their long walks and frequent visiting, and Lawrence was teased about it. Almost believing it, he replied that they were only friends and, indeed, his awareness of an undercurrent of hostility to Jessie's influence made him all the more inclined to continue to misinterpret the nature of his feelings. No doubt he vaguely associated this hostility with the general disapproval for any signs of love often shown in nonconformist circles until the day when, safely married, a couple joins the ranks of the respectable. To quote a typical example, Alice Hall, a friend later to serve Lawrence as a model for several pen-portraits, was a firm ally of Mrs Lawrence in her determination to discourage Bert from falling in love with Jessie. Her favourite pastime,

> if she happened to see a courting couple walking together, if they were perfect strangers it made no difference, was to walk close behind them to dog their footsteps, and make them so self-conscious and uncomfortable, that that walk at least was a failure.[75]

Mrs Lawrence soon began to reproach her son for coming home late, and for tiring himself out unnecessarily, adding that it was "disgusting—bits of lads and girls courting". Fearful of hurting his mother, but incapable of giving up Jessie, Bert confessed to the latter that he would have to be home earlier.[76] Incidents such as that of the broken umbrella had already shown Jessie how he dreaded wounding his mother; in the face of his family's hostility, and to Mrs Lawrence's evident satisfaction, she even stopped calling at Bert's house on Friday evenings.[77]

On Easter Monday 1906 there took place an incident which provoked a deep change in their relationship.

In *Sons and Lovers* this scene does not seem to be in its right chronological place, Lawrence having probably shrunk from exposing the exact nature of his mother's role in the destruction of his love. By restoring it to its rightful order we may enable the reader to perceive how, from this moment onwards, Lawrence attributes to Miriam his own inhibitions, his own shrinking from the thought of love. This curious transference of his own feelings to Miriam subsequently becomes so frequent that in the novel their reciprocal attitudes are difficult to disentangle. Perhaps it would be simplest to quote the scene as Jessie remembered it after nearly thirty years.

Visiting the Lawrences after chapel on Easter Sunday, she had observed the marked hostility of his mother and elder sister. Bert promised to come and see her early the next afternoon, and she went home "with a singing in [her] heart". Next day, Lawrence did not come until late in the afternoon; he looked strange, ignored Jessie's reproaches, and behaved ill-humouredly. Finally he began to "speak in a strained voice":

> "This—this friendship between us—is it keeping even? Is it getting out of balance?"
>
> "I don't know what you mean? I think it's even—I think it's balanced."
>
> "The trouble is—I'm afraid—you may be getting too fond of me."
>
> "I don't know. I haven't thought about it," I replied, with truth. "But why are you saying this?" I asked in deep dismay.
>
> "Well—they were talking last night—mother and Emily. They want to know if we are courting. They say we must either be engaged or not go about together. It's the penalty of being nineteen and twenty instead of fifteen or sixteen."
>
> I began to understand.
>
> "Ah—I always thought your mother didn't like me," I said.
>
> "It isn't that. You mustn't think that," he urged. "It's for your sake. She says it's not fair to you—I might keep you from liking someone else. She says I ought to know how I feel." He spoke with difficulty. "I've looked into myself and I cannot find that I love you as a husband should love his wife. Perhaps I shall—some day. If I do, I'll tell you. What about you? If you think that you love me, we'll be engaged. Do you?"
>
> . . . I told him I didn't know whether I loved him or not; I hadn't thought about it, and anyhow I couldn't be engaged under such circumstances. I am not sure whether he was glad or sorry. Things became blank, and I had to make a great effort to attend to what he was saying in a dull voice.[78]

Jessie wanted to break off altogether: he begged her to do nothing, not to sacrifice their friendship; his mother had said they need not give up everything, only make sure exactly where they stood. They could go on with her French lessons and their walks back from Chapel on Sundays, but in future Alan or one of the children should go with them.[79] Nevertheless they felt their life collapsing around them, their love nipped in the bud. Jessie, who did not know until the age of twenty-one the meaning of the words "love—as a husband should a wife", nevertheless felt confusedly that Lawrence, in denying that he loved her in this way, was holding back from her an important part of his love.[80] A barrier had arisen between them, and from then on their relations were painful and tormented, Lawrence's attitude becoming tense and strange.

That he was, in fact, rent by an internal conflict will appear from an analysis of several scenes in *Sons and Lovers*, of which the writers' highly debatable interpretation of the two characters provides no valid explanation.[81]

But first it is important to settle the question of the role played by Mrs Lawrence in her son's feelings and conduct towards Jessie. The relations of mother and son can be viewed without any preconception, taking into account in the first place only the simplest reasons susceptible of arousing in Mrs Lawrence the undoubted hostility she showed towards Jessie. It would be dangerous to introduce into this debate all that Lawrence, either under the influence of psychoanalysis or in reaction against Freud, was in later years to say about maternal love and the Oedipus complex. *Sons and Lovers* was written before he knew anything about psychoanalysis other than what he might have picked up from Frieda's conversation and an occasional discussion in the columns of *The New Age*; it was based on a factual outline provided by Jessie. Understanding the responsibility of his mother in the destruction of their love, the girl was determined to make Bert admit this to himself.[82] She did not, however, allow any theory to slip into her account, and if the novel distorts events by interpretation, it is for personal rather than theoretical reasons. We can thus start from the facts as related in the novel, without fear of deviating too far from reality.

We already know that Mrs Lawrence, disappointed in her marriage, had transferred to her sons all her own frustrated hopes and ambitions.[83] She frankly wanted to see them enter situations which would enable them "to climb into the middle classes", to which her own family had belonged.[84] She wanted not only to follow and encourage their intellectual development, but also to live with and through them the spiritual life she herself had been unable to share with any man.

Ernest had seemed destined to fulfil these desires. But almost as soon as he arrived in London, he fell in love with a shallow, flighty girl.[85] Mrs Lawrence suffered to see him wasting his love and his money on the giddy creature and had tried to get him to break off his engagement.

After Ernest's death, all that remained to her was her youngest son, who also nearly died shortly after. It was her love that saved him, and she determined to see her life fulfilled in his worldly successes:

> Paul was going to distinguish himself. She had a great belief in him, the more because he was unaware of his own powers. There was so much to come out of him. Life for her was rich with promise. She was to see herself fulfilled. Not for nothing had been her struggle.[86]

With Bert she shared her joys and miseries,[87] turning to him as to the man of the house, relying on him for action and support.[88]

She suffered to see him giving his evenings to Jessie, leaving her alone at home,[89] and as a boy of sixteen starting to come home late, risking his delicate health by losing precious hours of sleep. Was he also to become emotionally involved too young, compromising his future and his health? Already he was giving to another the best of his time and of his mind. Hence her jealousy, her reproaches and her coldness towards Jessie whenever she ventured to call on Bert at home.[90]

No doubt Mrs Lawrence also feared that her son might enter into a premature marriage or, worse still, a secret liaison, unacceptable to her puritan morality and presenting even greater dangers. Might she not also have nourished the hope that a brilliant match might crown his social advancement, whereas his love for a village schoolmistress would compromise it for ever?[91] The theme of the "mixed marriage" between a man of the people and a woman of the aristocracy or upper middle class is an early preoccupation and one that recurs often in Lawrence's work. No doubt pursuing this maternal line of advice, Ada later told him that Frieda Weekley, *née* von Richthofen, with whom he was subsequently to link his fate, was "the sort of woman he should marry".[92]

The dangers of a liaison were brought home very vividly to the young man soon after the scene in which he had announced to Jessie that he could not love her "as a husband should". He was most upset to learn that one of his friends, George H. Neville, had "got a girl into trouble".[93] His mother had taken the opportunity to lecture him on "the terrible consequences of five minutes of self-forgetfulness". "Thank God," he burst out to a startled Jessie, "I have been saved from that . . . so far."[94]

Bert's family, and to a certain extent a number of his friends, seem to have shared his mother's animosity towards Jessie.[95] Yet nothing in *Sons and Lovers* suggests that the girl's character was in any way obnoxious. And had it been so, why should Lawrence have gone on seeing her in spite of the constant and ill-concealed hostility of his family? It may, of course, have been one of those family rivalries, not uncommon in working-class milieux, the Lawrences feeling that one of them was breaking away and exploring with a "foreigner" mental regions inaccessible to them. Or was it that they feared something different from themselves, something incomprehensible to them, perhaps that very active spiritual life Lawrence tries to define as Miriam's "romanticism", her desire to elevate and sublimate the emotions?[96] Jessie suggests this explanation:

> I have come to the conclusion of late years that his mother must have been afraid of me; there was something in me she did not understand and she feared me because of it.[97]

With this conflict ends the first phase of Lawrence's prolonged adolescence. He was soon to enter a new world, to encounter ideas until then outside his moral universe. But his personality was to bear the imprint of a deep disorder, the seeds of which could be perceived in the dualism by which he was already tortured and divided. Was this the result of the conflict between his filial affection and his growing love? Or can it be traced back to deeper, and probably earlier, formative experiences? It may well be, indeed, that other causes, such as the contrast between the characters of his parents, may have encouraged a natural predisposition to project his own duality on those around him and to consolidate it by endorsement sought not in facts, but in his interpretation of them. All that can be said with certainty is that at this stage of his development Lawrence's psychological nature shows a characteristic and fundamental dualism. The next two years brought no solution to the internal rift.

3

NOTTINGHAM UNIVERSITY COLLEGE: 1906–08

University

Under intense emotional strain, strongly drawn to literature and driven by an urge to find expression for a still ill-defined ego, Lawrence entered Nottingham University College in September 1906 at the age of twenty-one. In such circumstances it is easy to see why he failed to find either in his studies or in his teachers a solution to the pressing and indeed obsessive emotional problems then foremost in his mind. Lawrence himself later declared that these two years brought "mere disillusion, instead of the living contact of men".[1] Yet he certainly derived from his brief university career material and intellectual advantages which must not be overlooked.

Having successfully passed his matriculation examination, he had the choice of enrolling for a three-year course leading to a London B.A. (Nottingham not then having the Royal Charter requisite for the granting of degrees), or of studying for two years for a Teacher's Certificate. The longer course then provided an opportunity for the better Normal Department students to specialize to a certain extent, and add a recognized degree to their diploma in education. In the ordinary course of events Lawrence should have become a three-year student, but this meant learning Latin (which he had not taken at school), in order to pass the Intermediate examination, first step to a B.A. The head of the Normal Department promised him special tuition in Latin and Lawrence also arranged to have private lessons with the Eastwood Congregational minister. After one term's Latin, however, he informed Jessie "with obvious satisfaction" that the professor could no longer spare the time to tutor him, so that, "glad to be rid of the bother of working for a degree, he settled down to his writing and the ordinary two-year course".[2] The prospect of earning his living a year earlier may have been another factor in this decision.

His programme of studies is easy to retrace. The Board of Education regulations provided that two-year students should "pursue their general knowledge while receiving a special preparation for the profession of their choice".[3]

As regards the Principles of Teaching, Lawrence seems to have opted for the second of two alternative courses, which included: elementary psychology; the elements of logic; the influence of school education on character; school organization; methods of teaching elementary school subjets; hygiene; and leading ideas and movements in elementary education in England since 1839. He must thus have made a close study of the theory of the acquisition of knowledge, of practical teaching methods, and of current pedagogical ideas. We also know from Jessie that he read two works from her own syllabus: *Home and School Life* by T. C. Rooper, and *The Herbartian Psychology applied to Education* by J. Adams.[4]

In English Literature he chose the first of four alternative "schemes". Prescribed general reading included: *Macbeth*, Book I of *The Faerie Queene*, Macaulay's "Essay on Bacon", Kingsley's *Westward Ho!* and the *Memoirs of Colonel Hutchinson*. Detailed study was devoted to: *A Midsummer Night's Dream*, "Comus", "Lycidas", *Arcades*, *Areopagitica* and selected essays by Bacon, which, Jessie noted, Lawrence "detested".

An outline course on the structure and history of the English language was also obligatory. There can have been very little in this syllabus that was new to Lawrence, who was by then remarkably well versed in English prose and poetry. Since the regulations stipulated that the period of history studied should correspond to the literary course selected, he made a quite thorough study of the English Renaissance, acquiring a fair knowledge of the period and often reverting in his works to certain aspects of sixteenth-century English history and literature.[5]

According to the Board of Education list of results for 1909, Lawrence did not, however, obtain "distinctions" in either Education or English. Jessie recalls some disappointment that his literary efforts were not better rewarded. He did, however, distinguish himself in Mathematics, History and Geography, and in the optional subjects of French and Botany. He attributed his success in history to his possession and study of Motley's *Rise of the Dutch Republic*, which means that he chose the first option covering the period from Henry VII to Oliver Cromwell. His reading at this time also seems to have included Prescott's *Conquest of Peru*.[6]

Lawrence clearly enjoyed the prescribed musical course, which seems to have been mainly vocal: the college song book became a favourite both at home and at the Haggs.[7] *The White Peacock* frequently illustrates his continued fondness for music.[8] Heroes of both *The Trespasser* and *Aaron's Rod* are professional musicians. His youthful drawings, reproduced in Mrs Clarke's biography, are straightforward sketches from nature or copies of existing works. They show some talent and serve to demonstrate Lawrence's early interest in an art he was to practise all his life.[9]

His choice of optional subjects is also revealing of his personal tastes and tendencies. The alacrity with which Latin was abandoned makes it difficult to believe his claim to Jessie that he had been translating the *Georgics* aloud to Alan while thatching haystacks in the Greasley fields![10] From Croydon, his letters to Jessie would sometimes end with the salutation "*Jamque vale*": a Greek phrase, so he explained, possibly in jest, meaning "Farewell, already and so soon" (sic).[11] While some scattered Latin quotations in *The White Peacock* suggest that he thought it desirable to display his learning, the translations from the Latin scribbled in the margin of Jessie's Schopenhauer suggest that his knowledge could scarcely have been more than elementary.

Botany seems to have held a fascination for him, possibly increased by the fact that a relatively new friend, Louie Burrows, was also reading it; though the converse, of course, may equally well be true. Lawrence had always loved plants, their sudden growth in spring, the mystery of their flowering. On his walks he was always on the look-out to discover and show his friends "the first primrose, or the fascinating male and female flowers of the larch".[12] For Ursula Brangwen, disillusioned with her college studies, botany alone came to have any meaning:

> Suddenly she threw over French. She would take honours in botany. This was the one study that lived for her. She had entered into the lives of the plants. She was fascinated by the strange laws of the vegetable world. She had there a glimpse of something working entirely apart from the purpose of the human world.[13]

The syllabus dealt with the structure and life-history of flowering plants, with special reference to reproduction, nutrition and adaptation to surroundings. Was Lawrence already seeking in such studies an escape from certain human problems, in particular personal difficulties imputed by him to that mental consciousness which he already felt to be encroaching on vegetative and animal life? Was the attraction of plant-life that of another world, in which his fantasy could have full play? Was he already longing for mindlessness in sex activity? The seeds of certain of these ideas are to be found in works written during his college years, but it is not clear to what extent they had in fact developed by that time.

French, like botany, was a youthful passion. Lawrence had learnt French at school, had continued to study it during his years as pupil-teacher, and had taught it to Jessie. Their reading had begun with simple works such as *Picciola, Jettatura, Un Philosophe sous les Toits*. Later came *Pêcheur d'Islande, Lettres de mon Moulin*, followed by the great masters: Balzac, Flaubert, Maupassant. To this list must be added George Sand, de Musset and Anatole France, read later in Croydon, and no doubt many others of which Jessie never heard.[14] In *The White Peacock* Lawrence mentions *Le Roman d'un Jeune Homme Pauvre*, Maeterlinck, whose *Trésor des Humbles* he read at Croydon, and Maupassant; in *Sons and Lovers*, *Tartarin*, Renan's *Life of Jesus*, Verlaine and Baudelaire.

This reading, beginning before and continuing well after Lawrence's years at University College, went far beyond the Teacher's Certificate syllabus, which in fact prescribed neither specific works nor authors, nor indeed the study of any particular period of French literature. The examination aimed, in fact, only at testing the candidates' knowledge of the language by means of not very difficult translations from and into French. While his written French, as appears from his letters to Louie Burrows, did not rise above school standards, his extensive reading placed him well above the level of most of his fellow-students.

Just as botany was for him a means of escape, so the French character and language appealed to him by all that differentiated them from his own environment, from which he was anxious to set himself apart. As he once told Jessie, "If English people don't like what I write, and I think it's probable they won't, I shall settle in France and write for the French."[15] He liked to imagine that one of his ancestors had been a French *émigré*. With Jessie, as indeed with Louie, he used French as a private code, giving her a book of poems inscribed *Pour la Curieuse* and watching with scorn her family's attempts to decipher the enigmatic dedication.[16] In the margin of Jessie's Schopenhauer, he wrote "*Qu'en pensez-vous?*" and insisted on her keeping in French a diary of her private thoughts.[17] That he should thus see in a foreign language primarily a medium of expression enabling him to become momentarily free of his environment, may well be another sign of his deep need for evasion and for make-believe. In *The White Peacock*, Lettie seizes every opportunity to speak French, even making impassioned speeches to herself in "a mad clatter of French" which leaves poor George totally befogged.[18] Lawrence soon took to ending, and even introducing, his letters with a foreign greeting,[19] a harmless mannerism none the less suggestive of an escapist tendency, a reluctance to accept consistency in expression. Moreover, writing in 1928 to David Chambers, whose knowledge of Italian he had no reason to presume, he resorts to that language to convey deep feeling, as though he dared not make such an avowal in all the nakedness of plain English.[20] In his letters to Louie, however, he will sometimes use French as a means of conveying to her criticism of her family—a sort of private language.

Meanwhile, having entered University College at an age when most students left it and chosen to read for a Teacher's Certificate instead of a B.A., Lawrence found himself among classmates certainly less talented and probably less mature and serious-minded than himself. The level of study must have seemed to him very low, considering all the culture he had absorbed on his own between the ages of sixteen and twenty-one. He certainly found himself something of a misfit, and failed to discover any professor willing to take special pains with an exceptional and original student. Instead of entering wholeheartedly into the life of the college, and making a personal effort to derive from it the maximum advantage it might have offered him, he seems to have held himself somewhat timidly aloof. Later he was to express strong criticism of University College, without a thought for the difficulties encountered by the teaching staff.

Lawrence was never the man to surmount an initial disappointment, and Jessie remembered clearly the mortification he suffered at the treatment received by his first English essay, on the subject of "Autumn", in which he had "tried to strike an arresting note". The essay was returned to him "heavily scored in red ink with corrections, emendations and exhortations in the best manner of an elderly schoolmistress putting a forward youth in his place", and he was told to write it again, giving "a proper essay this time".[21] No wonder he sometimes felt that the normal students were treated "like school-kids" and hated to see his talent belittled by teachers he considered had no right to judge him.

Treated merely as one of the herd when he would have liked to be the beloved disciple of some revered master, he may already have sensed in the university the same death principle he later described in school and factory: everything was mechanical, devoid of life. The institution had killed the spirit to which it owed its creation. The mystic enamoured of the absolute is always disillusioned by the Church, which must militate in the relative. This is the great disenchantment Lawrence has described in the college life of Ursula Brangwen, beginning with her first contact with her fellow-students:

> She wanted all the students to have a high pure spirit, she wanted them to say only the real, genuine things, she wanted their faces to be still and luminous as the nuns' and the monks' faces.
> Alas, the girls chattered and giggled and were nervous, they were dressed up and frizzed, the men looked mean and clownish.[22]

Yet to Ursula the sanctity of knowledge redeemed the mock-mediaeval college building, raising it above its commonplace surroundings; once inside its "shell", the outside world seemed to her to grow remote while "the echo of knowledge filled the timeless silence":

> She would not consider the professors as men, ordinary men who ate bacon, and pulled on their boots before coming to college. They were the black-gowned priests of knowledge, serving for ever in a remote, hushed temple. They were the initiated, and the beginning and the end of the mystery was in their keeping.[23]

The higher the hope, the greater the disillusionment: Ursula falls from absolute hope to total negation. By the start of her second year the life had gone out of her studies:

The professors were not priests initiated into the deep mysteries of life and knowledge. After all, they were only middlemen handling wares they had become so accustomed to that they were oblivious of them. The life went out of her studies, why, she did not know. But the whole thing seemed sham, spurious; spurious Gothic arches, spurious peace, spurious Latinity, spurious dignity of France, spurious naïveté of Chaucer. It was a second-hand dealer's shop, and one bought an equipment for an examination. This was only a side-show to the factories of the town . . . It was a little apprentice-shop where one was further equipped for making money. The college itself was a little slovenly laboratory for the factory.[24]

Was Lawrence really so acutely disillusioned by his college years? Or was he not rather touching up the colours, once he came to write *The Rainbow*, between 1912 and 1915, some time after his final break with teaching and all that Nottingham had represented? This may well be so, though Ursula's experience does seem, as far as can be verified, broadly to represent that of her creator: their ages and the main lines of their experience are identical. Lawrence's disenchantment certainly crystallized round his unsatisfied desire to find among his teachers some kind of guide and master or even, as Jessie thought, a father-figure "to give him a spiritual and intellectual lead into life itself". Only his French teacher, Professor Ernest Weekley, seems to have aroused in him a degree of admiration as a gentleman and scholar: "He's my favourite Pro," he told Jessie. "He's the only gentleman among the lot."[25]

Yet at least one of Lawrence's teachers seems to have judged him with a lucidity which does credit to the system he so violently and unjustly criticized. The Report of his Director of Studies shows an almost prophetic insight into the potential value of this "well read, scholarly and refined student" as a teacher, provided "he gets into the right place". This place, the Director felt, would not be with "a large class of boys in a rough district: he would not have sufficient persistence and enthusiasm but would be disgusted". Noting his bias towards "humanistic studies", and his capacity to stimulate the interest of his pupils, he regrets "a want of that persistent driving home and recapitulation which are necessary" and remarks that "though very fluent he sometimes has an obvious difficulty in finding words suitably simple", concluding that "with an upper class in a good school, or in a higher school he could do work quite unusually good, especially if allowed a very free hand".[26]

Lawrence's disillusionment with university life at the time of his studies might easily, however, be overestimated. Jessie, for one, believes that "his capacity for enjoyment was much too strong for college to make him un-happy".[27] Lawrence passed his final examination with four distinctions, and his two years in college at least resulted in the appreciable material advantage of his being able to obtain a relatively well-paid teaching post. It is true that to him this appeared less important than it would have done to many others. His pride in his culture, in particular in his knowledge of French, comes out clearly in *The White Peacock*, where Cyril, the narrator, shows an almost insolent delight in comparing the superiority of his own culture with that of George, his farmer friend, with whom he "talked endlessly" while they worked:

> I would give him the gist of what I knew of chemistry and botany, and psychology. Day after day I told him what the professors had told me: of life, of sex and its origins, of Schopenhauer and William James . . .[28]

Lettie's cultural attainments inspire in her a self-conceited coquetry, not unlike that later displayed by Ursula before another farmer, Anthony Schofield.[29] In his first novel Lawrence flaunts his culture at the slightest opportunity. He himself described a photograph of himself taken at this time as "the portrait of an intellectual prig".[30] Is it not probable that the Lawrence of 1913, looking back at his former self, may have played up his disillusionment to exonerate himself from the charge of a certain naïve self-complacency? "Nothing is so hateful as the self one has left," he wrote in 1911:[31] such revulsion may very well have prompted him to reconstruct his image in *The Rainbow* in such a way as to fit in better with his current conceptions.

Lawrence was still living in Eastwood, making the daily journey to Nottingham and back, and continuing to see Jessie frequently. In their common exploration of literature, they were now gradually approaching the great contemporaries. *Rosmersholm*, *The Lady from the Sea*, *Hedda Gabler* were all read with her family round the table at the Haggs. Bert's admiration for the inextricable mixture of autobiography and of fiction in *Lavengro* made Jessie wonder if he were not perhaps thinking of one day following in Borrow's footsteps. The poems and prose of Meredith, Gissing and Hardy constituted "the constant background" to their life. The poets retained their place of honour, Browning becoming a great favourite. Lawrence read *Paracelsus* and *The Ring and the Book*, and best of all he liked the shorter poems: "Andrea del Sarto", "One Word More", "Porphyria's Lover", "Never the Time and the Place" and "Rabbi Ben Ezra", which he would read to Jessie over and over again "usually on a Saturday evening after supper".[32]

One whole aspect of Lawrence's culture was thus bound up with his relations with Jessie; his emotional problems, rather than his studies, were the constant focus round which were to develop certain decisive features of his character and intelligence. Nottingham University College may have provided him with the raw materials of knowledge, but only his own strife-ridden heart could mould them into shape. To the problems of a late and apparently prolonged period of puberty, was added the conflict between his upbringing and his nascent sensuality.

Puritanism and sensuality

After the scene of Easter Monday 1906, Lawrence's attitude towards Jessie becomes difficult to understand, at least as it is portrayed in *Sons and Lovers*, where events are hardly ever presented without an interpretative twist. Chapters VII and VIII in particular abound in obscure or ambiguous passages.

Having explained to Jessie that between them there could be no more than friendship, Bert thought he could continue his visits as before. Significantly, he offered to become engaged to her if she "thought she loved him": had she been capable of snatching him away there and then from the influence of his family, would he have acquiesced? Was he really not aware that he loved her, or was he trying to transfer to her the burden of decision? What he did accept was in fact a situation so equivocal as to torture the girl far more than a clean break could ever have done. Divided between filial love and his feelings for the constant companion of his adolescence, he was to take the easy path, that of doing nothing in the hope that things would work out by themselves. For the first time we see him pulled in opposite directions by two attachments, unable to make a decision and to act in accordance with his own desires.

At a crucial moment in his psychic development, when another might have acted as a man conscious of what he wanted and making his own decisions, he obeyed his mother's orders in circumstances where no amount of filial respect can substitute for personal choice. That is the precise meaning of the term "mother-fixation" as applied to Lawrence. At a moment demanding an adult choice, he retreated into an infantile attitude.

By accusing Jessie of romanticism, he hid from himself the fact that the romantic is he who refuses to choose, who wants to eat his cake and have it. The romantic was himself. In comparison with the sentimental Paul Morel, the real Jessie appears essentially sound and rational.

Up to 1909 and even 1910 Lawrence hovers on the brink of passionate love like a starving dog which dares not seize a proffered bone. The maladjustment between his aspirations and his acts grew into a habit which he could not break. At a moment when life demanded an adaptation to new conditions of existence, tortured by a shrinking shame he was to take many years to overcome, Lawrence constantly deferred the necessary readjustment. Apparently more or less uninformed of the normal development of sex, it was impossible for him to face clearly and openly the phenomena he experienced within himself.

If we are to believe Lawrence, Jessie was overcome with shame at the thought that she could feel physical love for him, and tried to salve her conscience by praying to God to make her love him in a purely sacrificial spirit:

> But, Lord, if it is Thy will that I should love him, make me love him—as Christ would, who died for the souls of men. Make me Love him splendidly, because he is Thy son.[33]

But, after all is said and done, Jessie remains sole judge of the authenticity of this prayer, which nothing in the rest of the story seems to corroborate. Moreover, by proposing nothing more than friendship, what possibility other than sacrifice did Lawrence offer her? Naturally she had to sublimate her passion, an operation offering no great problem for most young girls of her day and age. For her, the rare physical contacts between them had only the vaguest and most innocent significance.

Lawrence, on the contrary, was continually on his guard with her as a result of his mother's warning, and seems to have been unable even to endure the slightest touch. The fierce puritan in him made him conceal both his mounting desire and the shame with which it filled him; he tried his utmost to sublimate it in an effort not to admit to himself the conflict between his passion and his filial love. But, unable to repress his desire completely, he suffered equally whichever way the battle went:

> Sometimes, as they were walking together, she slipped her arm timidly into his. But he always resented it, and she knew it. It caused a violent conflict in him. With Miriam he was always on the high plane of abstraction, when his natural fire of love was transmuted* into the fine stream of thought. She would have it so. If he were jolly and, as she put it, flippant, she waited till he came back to her, till the change had taken place in him again, and he was wrestling with his own soul, frowning, passionate in his desire for understanding. And in this passion for understanding her soul lay close to his; she had him all to herself. But he must be made abstract first.
>
> Then, if she put her arm in his, it caused him almost torture. His consciousness seemed to split. The place where she was touching him ran hot with friction. He was one internecine battle, and he became cruel to her because of it.[34]

Was it really the girl who "would have it so"? Jessie, on the contrary, maintains:

> If I had so much as laid a finger on his sleeve, I should have been spurned as the incarnation of temptation; although I did not know to what. Once a word of endearment escaped him, but he drew himself up and repudiated it with vehemence.[35]

* "Transmitted" is the word used in the Secker and Penguin editions. It is probably a misprint for "transmuted".

In August 1906 she spent two weeks' holiday with the Lawrences at Mablethorpe in Lincolnshire. A strange scene, twice repeated in the course of subsequent seaside holidays, left an indelible trace in her memory. As the moon rose "orange and enormous" over the rim of the sandhills a sudden wave of physical desire seems to have swept over Lawrence whose "blood seemed to burst into flame", as though he could "scarcely breathe". Surprised by his agitation, Jessie asked what was the matter:

> He turned and looked at her. She stood beside him, for ever in shadow. Her face, covered with the darkness of her hat, was watching him unseen. But she was brooding. She was slightly afraid—deeply moved and religious. That was her best state. He was impotent against it. His blood was concentrated like a flame in his chest. But he could not get across to her. There were flashes in his blood. But somehow she ignored them. She was expecting some religious state in him. Still yearning, she was half aware of his passion, and gazed at him, troubled.
>
> "What is it?" she murmured again.
>
> "It's the moon," he answered, frowning.
>
> "Yes," she assented. "Isn't it wonderful?" She was curious about him. The crisis was past.
>
> He did not know himself what was the matter. He was naturally so young, and their intimacy was so abstract, he did not know he wanted to crush her on to his breast to ease the ache there. He was afraid of her. The fact that he might want her as a man wants a woman had in him been suppressed into a shame. When she shrank in her convulsed, coiled torture from the thought of such a thing, he had winced to the depths of his soul. And now this "purity" prevented even their first love-kiss. It was as if she could scarcely stand the shock of physical love, even a passionate kiss, and then he was too shrinking and sensitive to give it.
>
> As they walked along the dark fen-meadow he watched the moon and did not speak. She plodded beside him. He hated her, for she seemed in some way to make him despise himself.[36]

Jessie's account of this and similar scenes at Robin Hood's Bay and Flamborough Head discreetly reveals their real nature: the conflict between desire and repression:

> When the final beauty of the moonlight broke upon us it seemed as if this power exploded within him. I cannot remember now what he said, but his words were wild, and he seemed to be in some great distress of mind, and possibly also of body. In some way I seemed to blame; he upbraided me bitterly. I was very miserable and distressed, because I did not know what I had done wrong. Then he blamed himself and spent himself upon me in a torrent of passionate words.[37]

As an adolescent Lawrence was clearly tortured by desires he could not satisfy. He refused to admit his love for Jessie: casual affairs with other women, even had they been easy to come by, would have been repugnant to him. Used from infancy to the company of his mother and sisters rather than to masculine companionship, brought up by his mother to "respect" women, he found it impossible to adapt to his new needs, and his non-conformist background reinforced his natural predisposition to be shy with women. But if Lawrence found no means of satisfying either Jessie or his mother, to say nothing of himself, he did at least join battle with the religious and moral principles in which he had been reared. In the end, and relatively late, he was to find some sort of solution to his inner conflicts in an attempt to reject chapel morality and in the belief that complete surrender to the senses could lead to the promised land. Jessie Chambers remains the chief witness for this evolution, on which Lawrence's letters to Louie throw little light. To what extent the circle of W. E. Hopkin and his wife, and of Alice Dax (who plays an increasing role in his life from 1908 on) influenced his religious emancipation does not appear from the evidence available on the college years.

Exactly when did he lose his Christian faith and settle for what he himself aptly described as "religious Agnosticism"?[38] In his article "Hymns in a Man's Life", he affirms that he lost his faith at sixteen,[39] but it seems more likely that his religious crisis dates from student years, at some time between the ages of twenty and twenty-two. Paul Morel was twenty-one when he "began to question the orthodox creed" and a year later he too had arrived at a form of agnosticism which Lawrence calls "the *Renan Vie de Jésus* stage",[40] at the same time remaining so profoundly respectful of questions of faith that he was "deeply shocked" when one of the Chambers boys let fall an "irreverent remark" concerning the Communion service.[41]

His intellectual emancipation, so gradual that it was not to affect his conduct until late 1909, thus began with his college years. Schopenhauer, read at about this time, seems to have done more than anyone else to incite him to doubt. The edition Lawrence read was a mediocre translation of *Selected Essays*,[42] including the whole or parts of "The Vanity of Existence", "On Women", "On Religion", "The Metaphysics of Love" and "On Suicide".

That most closely studied was the "Metaphysik der Geschlechtsliebe" (Metaphysics of Sexual Love), somewhat expurgated by the translator who had not seen fit to translate "*Geschlecht*" (sex); on it he scribbled translations of all the Latin and German quotations, sometimes underlining a passage or scoring it in the margin. We shall have occasion to revert to the traces of Schopenhauer's influence in *The White Peacock*.[43] Meanwhile the dialogue "On Religion" could not possibly have failed to strengthen his student doubts.

At about the same time, possibly under the influence of his work in psychology and botany, Lawrence began to take an interest in the materialist thought of the second half of the nineteenth century: the reading of Huxley's *Man's Place in Nature*, Darwin's *Origin of Species*, Haeckel's *Riddle of the Universe*, was closely followed by the study of Locke, Berkeley, Stuart Mill, Herbert Spencer and William James. Jessie, who dates his reading of James from this period, whereas "A Modern Lover" would seem to place it in the Croydon years,[44] pertinently records her feeling that "he tried to fill a spiritual vacuum by swallowing materialism at a gulp".[45]

Almost simultaneously French literature must have revealed to him a conception of life completely different from the local brand of puritanism, bringing all its weight to bear in favour of his newly-developing ideas. The open-mindedness and sexual tolerance of Balzac and Flaubert, the obsessions of Maupassant, the subtleties and violence of Baudelaire and Verlaine were a revelation to him. None of the English writers he had so far read, not even the most searching and courageous, not even George Eliot or Thackeray, had dared to portray human nature with the audacity of the nineteenth-century French novelists and poets. Technique apart, this was certainly what Lawrence was seeking in their works. Paul Morel used Baudelaire and Verlaine to convert Miriam to the cult of the flesh:

> He made her copy Baudelaire's "*Le Balcon*". Then he read it for her. His voice was soft and caressing, but growing almost brutal. He had a way of lifting his lips and showing his teeth, passionately and bitterly, when he was much moved. This he did now ... she could not understand why he got into such a tumult and fury. It made her wretched. She did not like Baudelaire, on the whole—nor Verlaine.
> "Behold her singing [sic] in the field
> Yon solitary highland lass."[46]
> That nourished her heart. So did "Fair Ines". And
> "It was [sic] a beauteous evening, calm and pure,
> And breathing holy quiet like a nun." [sic]
> These were like herself. And there was he, saying in his throat bitterly,
> "Tu te rappeleras [sic] la beaûté [sic] des caresses."[47]

He also brought her Maupassant, as though to initiate her into the world of the senses which, so he imagined, was for her a dim and distant region.[48] Such efforts to win her over to a materialistic conception of existence suggest that he was trying to exteriorize his own internal conflict, as though by converting her to his newly-acquired views he would obtain proof positive of their value.

The liberating influence of French literature was reinforced at this time by that of painting. Nottinghamshire, it may be noted in passing, is a county which for several centuries has proved particularly rich in artists.[49] An important religious art centre before the Reformation, the subsequent concentration of lace-making and other artisan industries no doubt attracted good designers and stimulated local talent. Nottingham had a good museum, with a reasonably good art gallery and frequent exhibitions.

Lawrence had at one time taken art lessons from a local pottery designer[50] and had followed drawing classes in college. He made the hero of *Sons and Lovers* a painter, and in *The White Peacock* he alludes to many English artists. The reproductions which Lettie shows to the young farmer are a revelation to him. Especially that of Maurice Greiffenhagen's "Idyll",[51] given to Lawrence by his new friend Blanche Jennings. Against a background of flowers and greenery a muscular and swarthy youth clad in the hide of an animal is bestowing a kiss on the mouth of a pallid maiden who, tense and rigid under her flowing draperies, stands with averted head as though petrified by this voracious kiss. Excited by this picture, George is emboldened almost to the point of declaring his desire to Lettie.[52] Lawrence must have found in it something deeply satisfying; for he copied it not once but several times.[53] The plastic arts certainly helped him to rid himself of his nonconformist embarrassment at the sight of nudity.

His reaction to Aubrey Beardsley is characteristic: Cyril in *The White Peacock* surely speaks for Lawrence:

> I came upon reproductions of Aubrey Beardsley's "Atalanta", and of the tail-piece to "Salome", and others. I sat and looked and my soul leaped out upon the new thing. I was bewildered, wondering, grudging, fascinated. I looked a long time, but my mind, or my soul, would come to no state of coherence. I was fascinated and overcome, but yet full of stubbornness and resistance.[54]

He immediately takes the book down to the Mill to try out its effect on Emily (i.e. Jessie). Thereupon the irresolute George, having seen the Beardsleys once more, almost plucks up the courage to ask for Lettie's hand:

> And the more I look at these naked lines, the more I want her. It's a sort of fine sharp feeling, like these curved lines . . . Has she seen these pictures? . . . If she did, perhaps she'd want me—I mean she'd feel it clear and sharp coming through her.[55]

It is no mere coincidence that Lawrence's doubts began with his increasing sexual awareness. In this lies part of the explanation of his religious crisis which, in addition to its intellectual aspects, clearly has deep-seated emotional origins. Jessie noted that when reading the philosophers Lawrence sought not an objective understanding of their intentions but the solution to problems then preoccupying him. Somewhat naïvely he saw in Berkeley's immaterialism, for example, a temporary solution to his own perplexity: "If God does not exist in my consciousness, then for me God does not exist."[56] He then proceeded to apply the same reasoning to Jessie, in an even more naïve attempt to rid himself of all responsibility towards her,[57] an application of doctrine which would certainly have startled the good Bishop of Cloyne!

> In all his reading he seemed to be groping for something that he could lay hold of as a guiding principle in his own life. There was never the least touch of the academic or the scholastic in his approach. What he read was to be applied here and now; he seemed to consider all his philosophical reading from the angle of his own personal need.[58]

This procedure is clearly noticeable in *Sons and Lovers*: for a time the Leivers shared the Morels' pew in chapel, and Paul delighted to feel his two loves "uniting under the spell of the place of worship". Afterwards he would walk home with Miriam and her brother:

> At this time he was beginning to question the orthodox creed. He was twenty-one, and she was twenty. She was beginning to dread the spring; he became so wild, and hurt her so much. All the way he went cruelly smashing her beliefs. Edgar enjoyed it. He was by nature critical and rather dispassionate. But Miriam suffered exquisite pain, as, with an intellect like a knife, the man she loved examined her religion in which she lived and moved and had her being. But he did not spare her. He was cruel. And when they went alone he was even more fierce, as if he would kill her soul. He bled her beliefs till she almost lost consciousness.[59]

This struggle, renewed *every spring*, is in fact an attempt by Lawrence to free himself from the effects of his religious upbringing, from the nonconformist morals imbibed from his early environment. The sadistic way Paul attacks Miriam's beliefs at the same time as his own is primarily directed against his own principles, against his own ingrained habit of chapel-trained good behaviour. Did he perhaps hope that, by this harsh criticism of the beliefs he shared with Jessie, he could persuade her of the legitimacy of desires he dared not openly admit even to himself? For it is clear that he still needed to convince himself that they were not immoral, and to readjust his whole concept of women and his attitude towards them.

Before the end of his two college years, however, this strange conflict took on a new aspect: Paul's hesitations between Miriam and Clara, in *Sons and Lovers*, correspond in fact to increasingly complex feminine relationships. In contrast to the pure spirituality attributed to Miriam, the composite character of Clara symbolizes the mainly physical attraction of a woman less tenderly loved, but who for some time satisfies the young man's sensual desires. At first, however, Lawrence's dualism of the flesh and of the mind took a simpler form, at least in what he thought fit to reveal to Jessie.

Dualism

At Whitsun of the year 1906, he brought to Jessie the first pages of what was to become *The White Peacock*. He wanted to know whether she thought the dialogue natural and the characters convincingly developed. At about the same time he insisted she should keep a diary in French in which she was to write nothing but her thoughts. When correcting these notes, which, Jessie says, were "mostly a love letter",[60] he would adopt a cold, pedagogical air, only sometimes letting drop a personal remark. One day he noted in the margin, "*Pour faire croître quelque chose, il faut le supprimer*", and a little later: "*Quant à moi, je suis grand animal*" (sic). She understood at once what he meant by the first phrase; the second she refused to believe, but he nodded emphatically insisting, "Yes, I am, I am."[61]

Towards the beginning of his Nottingham studies, his attitude to Jessie began to change. One day he found himself wishing she were a man, adding immediately that "it wouldn't have been any good because then you wouldn't have cared about me".[62] It was at this point that, tormented by his failure to define their relationship satisfactorily, he brought her the short stories of Maupassant, in an attempt to win her over to a materialist view of life. In Schopenhauer's "Metaphysics of Love" he discovered a justification of platonic love between two young persons of different sexes. And one evening at about this time, reading to Jessie the sixteenth chapter of St John, he left out verse 21 in great embarrassment:

A woman, when she is in travail, hath sorrow because her hour is come.[63]

Undoubtedly he felt an invisible barrier rising between them, and for this, in *Sons and Lovers*, he blames sometimes the one sometimes the other.[64]

Finally he began to try to define the dualism which, he maintained, characterized his nature: there were in him two men, one which loved Jessie and the other incapable of loving her. He explained to her in all seriousness that while there were some things for which he needed her, in the very depth of his being, for others he would need another woman. He had begun to dissect her personality, comparing her to Emily Brontë, intense, introspective, and without a strong intellect, whereas he at this time "trusted entirely in the intellect".[65] Later she was "a Burne-Jones damsel",[66] and finally in a letter written on her twenty-first birthday she became "a holy nun":

What I see is the deep spirit of you, and that I love and can go on loving all my life. You are a nun—look, I give you what I would give a holy nun. So you must let me marry a woman whom I can love and embrace and make the mother of my children.[67]

Jessie was convinced he was wrong, that love could not be thus divided into the physical and the spiritual. Lawrence, however, was insistent: he had found in one of his fellow-students at Nottingham University College a fitting object for the desires of his "other half", and he began to speak of the possibility of marrying Louie Burrows.[68] Jessie would remain his inspiration while his wife would satisfy his every physical need. Jessie protested that if he married another she could have no more to do with him; that such a situation would be intolerable both for Louie and herself. Though dropped for a time, the subject was one to which they would return from time to time, and often a forced note would creep into the young man's voice, as though it was himself he was seeking to convince. One day he said to Louie in Jessie's presence: "When one can't attain to genuine love one has to make shift with the spurious."[69]

George Saxton, in *The White Peacock*, hesitates in the same way between Lettie and Meg: one representing a deep love, the other mere physical attraction. He loses Lettie because he is timid and gauche, and with Meg he degenerates into a debased and brutish life. To a character conceived during these years of hesitation Lawrence was obviously attributing some of his own problems.

Lawrence was to go on fluctuating between these two girls, as if his mother's attitude towards his first love had so accustomed him to this type of internal conflict as to render him incapable of firm decision. The denial of his first love once accepted, he seems almost to take pleasure in heaping dualism upon dualism: opposing Louie to Jessie, physical desire to spiritual communion. During the Croydon years which were to follow, his growing impatience with his own indecisions made him seek a hopeless solution in a string of contradictory affairs.

But even as early as 1908 his inner conflict was complicated by a new element, unknown to Jessie. Although the order of events, undoubtedly of some psychological importance, has not been definitely established, it was certainly in the spring of this year that Alice Dax, wife of an Eastwood chemist, began to play a role in Lawrence's life. His relations with her were to last until immediately after his meeting with Frieda Weekley. Alice Dax was the main model for Clara Dawes in *Sons and Lovers*: Clara has not only her physical appearance but also many of her traits of character. The name Dawes, borrowed from a real-life Eastwood family, though close to that of Dax, was sufficiently different to put readers off the scent if, as seems probable, Lawrence wished to keep his relations with Mrs Dax secret from all but a few close mutual friends.

In order to understand fully the evolution of Lawrence's love life, it is necessary to anticipate by referring at this point to an undated event confided by Willie Hopkin to Harry T. Moore, which probably took place in 1909, if not a little earlier. George Neville had already told Moore that "a woman in

Eastwood initiated Lawrence to sexual life", and Hopkin confirmed that he once inadvertently heard "a married woman" tell his first wife:

> Sallie, I gave Bert sex. I had to. He was over at our house struggling with a poem he couldn't finish, so I took him upstairs and gave him sex. He came downstairs and finished the poem.[70]

Alice Dax, a close friend of Sallie Hopkin, was this married woman. A letter from her to Frieda Lawrence can leave no doubt that she was still Lawrence's mistress at the time he met his future wife. In 1912, it was to her and to Jessie that he revealed his liaison with Frieda before he left for Germany. Willie Hopkin's daughter, Enid Hilton, has described Alice Dax as an emancipated woman "years ahead of her time", advanced in dress, thought and house decoration, almost completely uninhibited and, like Sallie Hopkin, devoted to the feminist cause: visitors to their homes included leading suffragettes, socialists and trades-union leaders, amongst them Mrs Pankhurst, Keir Hardie, Ramsay MacDonald, Philip Snowden, Edward Carpenter, Margaret Bondfield and Annie Besant.[71]

Early in 1908, through Alice Dax, Lawrence had made the acquaintance of a Liverpool post office employee, Blanche Jennings, to whom he wrote regularly between April 1908 and January 1910, long, bantering, somewhat coy letters in which amorous and literary confessions are interspersed with innuendoes concerning the writer's "softening" influence on the character and "aesthetic appreciation" of Alice Dax. She, at the time this correspondence begins, was about to give birth to her first child, Eric. Lawrence found in Blanche Jennings a less severe critic of the first version of *The White Peacock* than Alice Dax, who found it "too full of moods",[72] concerned only "with whether such people exist"—about which the author "did not care a damn".[73] This correspondence also shows that during 1908, as in Croydon in 1909, Jessie Chambers was no longer Lawrence's only confidante: the young Lawrence takes full advantage of the chance to "scatter the secrets of his soul" in his letters to a "safe wise elder", enjoying feminine companionship without any of the physical risks of an actual female presence.[74]

Alice Dax appears in this correspondence as someone whose judgments intimidate him (according to Enid Hilton she was "almost brutally frank")[75] but who is subject to his influence on the aesthetic plane and tends to regard him somewhat maternally. "Mrs Dax", he wrote to Blanche Jennings in 1908, "has become somewhat fond of me, so that I am elder brother of my sweet little Phyllis ... or Eric ... who is so long in coming."[76] Jessie Chambers certainly knew of this relationship and even took some part in the activities of the socialistically-minded group to which the Hopkins and the Daxes belonged: she was also aware that Mrs Dax "gave Lawrence plenty of provocation"; but all her life she believed that he had never "taken advantage" of such advances and that the story of Clara was either invented or was based on Helen Corke or Frieda.[77] The story of Lawrence's prolonged liaison with Alice Dax certainly remained a well-guarded secret, known mainly to the Hopkin family and Lawrence's sister Ada.

4

CROYDON: 1908–12

When Lawrence left Nottingham University College in July 1908 there were in Nottinghamshire more elementary schoolteachers than the county could employ. Moreover, he was not prepared to accept a salary of less than £90 a year. He was interviewed unsuccessfully in September for a Manchester post, then for one in Croydon, which he took up on 12 October 1908. He was to stay there until his resignation on 9 March 1912, following his serious illness of November 1911.

The Midland boy at first faced the new world of London and its suburbs with timidity and trepidation. His life, his occupations, his feelings during those crucial three years, have for some time been known, though still superficially, through some forty letters in the Huxley volume and the letters to Blanche Jennings and Rachel Annand Taylor in *The Collected Letters*. The recently published volume of letters to Louie Burrows adds a few new insights, mainly into his feelings during 1911: but for a consistent picture of these years we still depend on the narratives of Jessie Chambers, especially on the two memoranda written for the present author. Yet neither these narratives nor the letters can provide as good material for an intimate biography as Lawrence's own poems. While enlightening us on his reactions to incidents of his inner life, they do not offer however any key to the actual facts. Lawrence has himself issued an invitation to interpret them with the help of his biography:

> ... no poetry ... should be judged as if it existed in the vacuum of the absolute. Even the best poetry, when it is at all personal, needs the penumbra of its own time and place and circumstance to make it full and whole.[1]

In spite of this shortcoming, the Croydon poems contain vital evidence of their author's states of mind and we find in them many details which, once the main biographical facts are sorted out for this highly complex period of his emotional life, throw light on the mental evolution of the man who, during this period, was to undertake the writing of *Sons and Lovers* partly in an attempt to recover from the prolonged crisis of his adolescence.

Croydon

When the time came to leave Eastwood for life in an unknown London suburb, Lawrence was far from cheerful. The emotion of those last days is sensitively conveyed in *The White Peacock*, where the narrator Cyril, "eyes dark with pain", suffers deeply at breaking the tie which binds him to his little group of friends.[2] Bert paid a farewell visit to Haggs farm. When he left, Jessie walked with him as far as the last gate. Taking a lingering look at farm and woods, he leaned towards her, murmuring sadly *"la dernière fois"*. She burst into tears and he put his arm around her, kissing her, tenderly stroking her cheek and saying that he was "sorry, sorry, sorry". Invited to a goodbye tea-party at the Lawrences' next day, Jessie found him looking like a condemned man, white and wretched.[3]

On his second day in Croydon, he sent her a letter "like a howl of terror": how could he live away from them all, how teach a class from which he shrank "with the anguish of a sick girl"? Cut off from his roots, he feared he would "grow into something black and ugly, like some loathsome bird". But he had written to his mother that everything was all right, and begged Jessie not to reveal the truth.[4]

Soon, however, he settled down well enough in his new surroundings. He found lodgings in the home of J. W. Jones, a northerner like himself, and the friendly family atmosphere soon put him at his ease. His fondness for the Jones's baby delighted Mrs Lawrence, who opined that it would help to "keep him pure".[5]

Little by little London too became touched with magic: the great arc lamps pouring their light in golden patches "on the restless darkness", the traffic "floating in and out of the cavern" of the great railway terminals, "the soft fascinating flow of the limbs of men and women" intoxicated the young poet with strange nectar "sipped out of the eyes" of the passers-by. Soon he began to love the town for the ever-changing spectacle it offered him, its swift succession of sights, sounds and colours, unknown in his home country.[6]

Lawrence the teacher

Davidson Road School was "a fine red place—new and splendid",[7] which seems at first to have attracted all the rowdiest boys in the neighbourhood; small wonder the inexperienced teacher dreaded facing his classes of tough South London lads.[8] At first he had some trouble keeping order,[9] but soon adapted himself to work and discipline, apparently to the complete satisfaction of his headmaster. He seems to have taught in most sections, but was more particularly entrusted with "art training" in the upper classes and science teaching throughout the school. The success of Davidson School owed much to his intelligent and progressive teaching and he was soon on friendly terms with the headmaster, a cultured and kindly man who, in recommending Lawrence for a headship in 1912, insisted on the originality and efficacy of his teaching methods.[10]

Yet Lawrence certainly suffered deeply from his exile and the demands of teaching and maintaining discipline on his nervous energy. To Blanche Jennings he compares himself to "a quivering greyhound set to mind a herd of pigs".[11] No doubt his fatigue and depression were exacerbated by quite different factors, without which he might have found it easier to put up with the more thankless tasks of his profession. That he did genuinely suffer is borne out by *The Rainbow*, in which Ursula's horror and disgust with corporal punishment are vividly conveyed. Several of the poems he wrote in Croydon bear out the autobiographical nature of Ursula's experience at St Philip's.

"Last Lesson in the Afternoon" describes the lassitude of the master waiting for the final bell, the pack of unruly children, the weariness in the face of a pile of blotted copy-books and "the scrawl of slovenly work"; the discouragement of knowing the utter vanity of the endless effort:

> So, shall I take
> My last dear fuel of life to heap on my soul
> And kindle my will to a flame that shall consume
> Their dross of indifference: and take the toll
> Of their insults in punishment?—I will not!—
> I will not waste my soul and my strength for this.[12]

On a snowy afternoon, the imagination of the school-bound poet "pattering the lessons ceaselessly" escapes outside to where "the snow descends as if the sky shook in flakes of shadow down" and "all things are in silence".[13]

The continual effort of maintaining discipline, the inevitable need to punish, undoubtedly upset and exhausted his sensitive nature. After administering punishment, the poet feels abandoned by God:

> Desolate I am as a church whose lights are put out
>   And doubt enters in drearness . . .
> Like a flower that the frost has hugged and let go, my head
> Is heavy, and my heart beats slowly, laboriously,
>   My spirit is dead.[14]

Each poem distils a feeling of the unreality of school-teaching, the artificiality of the forced contact with unruly children. Occasionally, it is true, the master feels a glow of pleasure to see his pupils' questioning eyes upon him, "as tendrils reach out yearningly, slowly rotate until they touch the tree". In his loneliness, he finds occasional solace in the eager young lives "intertwining" with his own.[15] Even so the opposition is clear between his personal life, as opposed to his social self, and a profession offering few unconventional rewards. This dualism is particularly striking in the poem "Discipline".[16] Lawrence had tried to inspire his boys, "to win their souls", but they turned on him and tried to violate his soul, so that all that remained was for him to "let them live, the boys", not "to trespass on them with love" but to withdraw into himself until such time as he could give love "where it is wanted", reserving for Jessie alone the sanctuary of his inmost being.

Thus the Lawrentian conflict between the social and the deeper self becomes clear: faced with human labour, of which he is quite capable of doing his full share, he turns more and more towards that intense personal life which to him was alone worth living: literature and love, two facets of the same reality.

Reading: literary début

Lawrence continued to read avidly during these three years, acquainting himself thoroughly with contemporary European literature. Croydon Public Library was a fund of new treasures. Jessie and Blanche Jennings, and to some extent Louie, were kept abreast of his reading, and on occasion fervently adjured to read without delay those works which had particularly impressed him: Doughty's strange *Adam Cast Forth*, for example, Francis Thompson's "Essay on Shelley", or Swinburne's *Atalanta in Calydon*, which he recommended to Jessie. George Moore apparently became an admired model, Lawrence sending Jessie both *Evelyn Innes* and *Esther Waters*. Whitman's *Leaves of Grass* was "one of his great books", Jessie receiving at this time a number of self-styled "Whitmanesque" poems of his own composition.[17] Whitman's disciple Edward Carpenter, whose works he had known through the Dax-Hopkin circle at Eastwood, continued to interest him, and he was in 1910 to take a copy of his poems to Helen Corke.[18]

The discovery of Nietzsche in Croydon Public Library he kept to himself, only references to the "Will to Power" convincing Jessie that "he had come upon something new and engrossing". Besides the Russians—Pushkin, Turgenev, Tolstoy, Dostoevsky, Gorki—he read his great English elders: Wells, Bennett, Galsworthy, Conrad, Samuel Butler and many more, including Synge, W. H. Hudson, Gilbert Murray's translations from the Greek, Sterne, Burns, Anatole France, George Sand, de Musset. The "two great poetic lights in his firmament" at this time were Baudelaire and Verlaine,[19] although by 1911 after meeting Edward Garnett he was to find Verlaine "toshy".[20] Allusions contained in *The White Peacock* and in the *Letters*, as well as information supplied by his Davidson Road colleague A. W. McLeod, add relatively little to this list: Maeterlinck,[21] d'Annunzio, Chekhov, the Dutch naturalist Querido, whose *Toil of Men* made a considerable impression,[22] Richard Jefferies, a man after his own heart, whose *The Open Air* he read in 1909;[23] Jens Peter Jacobsen's *Nils Lyhne, Le Rouge et le Noir*,[24] William Morris, Rachel Annand Taylor and a translation of Verhaeren.[25]

Much as he appears to have read at this time, he was writing even more: many poems date from this period, during which he not only redrafted and published *The White Peacock*, but wrote a number of short stories as well as two new novels: *The Trespasser* and the first draft of *Sons and Lovers*. He was eager to make a living from his writing, in order to give up a profession he regarded as a treadmill. By 1911, as his correspondence shows, he was in touch with several editors and personalities in the literary world, and while his headmaster has testified to the conscientiousness with which he continued to perform his "school work", his leisure time was clearly given up entirely to reading, writing and frequenting a growing circle of literary and other friends.[26]

So far he had made almost no effort to break into literary circles. As early as 1908 he had suffered a rebuff. An admirer of the weekly articles by G. K. Chesterton appearing in the *Daily News*, which he regularly read at the Chambers', Lawrence had plucked up courage to ask for the critic's opinion on one of his own essays or short stories. After several weeks his manuscript arrived back with a note from Mrs Chesterton to the effect that her husband regretted his inability to give an opinion, owing to pressure of work. Deeply chagrined, the collier's son swore never to submit another line to anyone,[27] though in 1909 he did, in vain, offer short stories—some of them written in collaboration with Louie—to "Mags" and to a literary agency.[28]

In December 1909, Lawrence introduced the Chambers to the first number of *The English Review*; the family decided to subscribe and Jessie soon suggested to Lawrence that he should send some of his own works to this enterprising periodical. "Send whatever you like," he answered, after a first ungracious refusal, thus confirming his previous assurance to Jessie that "all his poetry belonged to her".[29] In June she sent off "Discipline", "Dreams Old and Nascent", and "Baby Movements", and in August received from the editor, Ford Madox Hueffer, a letter asking the author to call on him at his office. As soon as Lawrence came back from holiday in Shanklin Jessie gave him the letter, incurring Mrs Lawrence's subsequent displeasure for interfering in things which did not concern her.[30]

On his return to London, he went to see Hueffer, and through him was at once launched into London literary circles, an experience which both "excited and tired him very much".[31] Hueffer introduced him to William Heinemann, who in January 1911 published *The White Peacock*, and in the summer of 1911 he made the acquaintance of Edward Garnett, who was to prove a very precious friend and counsellor.

Emotional life: Jessie, Agnes, Alice

At this moment in his life, when to the demands of a literary début were added those of regular teaching, Lawrence's emotional life by no means provided the calm, comfort and balance of which he stood in need. Haunted by his mother's long agony and by thoughts of death, from 1909 onwards, he enmeshed himself in a veritable net of hesitant and conflicting emotional moves, culminating in an acute despair which finds reflection in everything he then wrote. In one sense, all three novels of that period, *The White Peacock*, *The Trespasser* and *Sons and Lovers*, treat of the failure of love, the horror and fascination of death, leading to thoughts of suicide; indeed, all the elements making for such pessimism are to be found in the writer's own life at this time.

During 1908 and in early 1909, Lawrence was retailing to Blanche Jennings the story of his amorous preferences and the progress of his various loves. In May 1908 he speaks of Jessie, though without naming her, as "one girl who is in love with me and whom I do not love", who cares deeply for his writing but whose criticism is valueless because she "approves too much". Alice Dax, on the contrary,[32] is too "sane" a critic, "like a mother who reads her son's school essay". He longs to fall in love, because love is "the fundamental vibration of the life force". While perfect friendship with a man seems to him preferable to love, it is as difficult to achieve as "magnificent love" between a woman and himself. In the long run it is probably better if marriage is based on "sexual sympathy" rather than on an understanding of souls. Kissing a girl on the mouth is an act so charged with "a positive electricity, a current of creative life", that he could never do it. Yet at Christmas 1908 he has kissed "a certain girl", with whom he is half in love, although "too conscious, vaguely troubled". Does Blanche Jennings agree, he asks, that

> ... in love, or at least in love-making ... the woman is always passive, like the girl in the "Idyll"—enjoying the man's demonstration, a wee bit frit—not active? I prefer a little devil—a Carmen—I like nothing passive. The girls I have known are mostly so; men always declare them so, and like them so; I do not.[33]

In the same letter he asks her to convey to Mrs Dax, then in Liverpool, "my—my—regards", the shade of hesitation being perhaps indicative of some recent significant change in their relationship.[34]

Through all this, his long and complicated romance with Jessie pursued its course. During his first year in Croydon he was still hesitating between her and Louie Burrows. To Jessie he wrote regularly every week, sending her poems, mostly dealing with his new life. He invited her to come and spend a weekend with him, which she did in May 1909.[35] A little later, in July, it is Louie's turn, and he plans to take her to hear Tetrazzini at Covent Garden.[36]

In the autumn of 1909 a new friend, Agnes Holt,[37] a Croydon school-mistress, comes into his life, but his ardour quickly cools when he finds his advances repelled. The episode is, however, highly indicative of his state of mind. To Jessie he continues to speak obsessively of his desire to marry. Once, after a violent scene in which he reproached her vehemently for being Psyche to his Amor, he declared, threateningly, that if things did not change, he would "go from woman to woman" until he was satisfied. Not long afterwards he told her of his latest girl, "a teacher here", whom he had "almost" made up his mind to marry. He urges Jessie to come and see him; he is anxious to show her his poems, a play that he has written, and his "possible fiancée". In November she goes up to Croydon: despite her long and tiring day, Lawrence insists on talking until after two o'clock in the morning, asking her what she wants of life, what her future plans are, telling her of Agnes Holt and of his vague desire to have a mistress, since marriage remains materially impossible. Does she think Agnes will agree to accept him as a lover? "It depends on how much she is in love with you," Jessie replies, thankful of a chance to close the conversation and to go to bed. When in her room she was surprised to hear what seemed like a knock on the door. She did not respond, listened, but heard nothing further.[38]

If he wanted to make her his mistress, why so much beating about the bush? And if that was not what he was after, if the whole conversation was not merely a ruse to discover to what extent she was still bound by the old provincial moral code, why such an astounding lack of tact?

No understanding of Lawrence's state of mind in late 1909 is possible without detailed reference to the poems and novels dealing with this period. The first twenty or so *Collected Poems* probably date from his college years, the most important being "The Wild Common" and "Virgin Youth". The first, quite close in style to some of Edward Carpenter's poems, exalts the beauty of the naked lad, the joy of the swimmer, voluptuously enfolded, swayed and lifted by the deep pond waters. Sensual ecstasy in the presence of nature is a recurrent theme in the poems of the period and seems to imply only a faint association, if any, between sensuality and the female body. "Virgin Youth", however, at least as it first appeared in *Amores*, in its less bold but more significant original version, expresses less the ecstasy of life than the disquietude of the shy young puritan faced with the sudden upsurge of sensual feeling. Intelligence and will both suspended, the adolescent "quivers awake" under the "wild strange tyranny" of his body until

> ... the bursten flood of life ebbs back to my eyes,
> Back from my beautiful, lonely body
> Tired and unsatisfied.[39]

London life was not calculated to calm or dim such ill-directed desires. No doubt the lovers Lawrence watched walking two by two in the freedom of the great anonymous city[40] were less furtive than those of Eastwood, to say nothing of the temptations readily offered by the "hard-faced creatures" of Piccadilly Circus and Hyde Park. Probably he had little difficulty in resisting their advances, but they could not fail to increase the urgency of his desire for initiation into what were for him quasi-religious mysteries. Though the poet was still paralysed by shyness, his preoccupations reveal themselves clearly in his writings.[41]

One poem in particular, which seems to date from his London period, expresses the timorous and helpless desire of the adolescent, and the weary burden of his unwilling chastity. This poem is entitled "Restlessness".[42] It was not included in the 1928 *Collected Poems*, either because Lawrence no longer liked it, or because he thought that "Virgin Youth", entirely rewritten, expressed clearly all that he had previously tried to stammer out more clumsily, perhaps, but also with greater sincerity.

At the open door of his room, the poet stands looking out at the night, holding out his hand to catch the raindrops. He will go out into the fecund night seeking in the bewildering darkness a mate for his "hungry" soul. On the waves of the night he casts the net of his eyes, ears, hands and feet to catch the faces of the women as they pass, to "cherish the wet cheeks and hair a moment", looking earnestly for one who will answer

> With a laugh and a merry wildness that it was she
> Who was seeking me, and had found me at last to free
> Me now from the stunting bonds of my chastity.

Alone among the indifferent crowd, he curses himself for an aimless, desirous fool, who forgets that he can always "linger over the huddled books on the stalls", always lose himself in literature, his one faithful mistress. Then suddenly the futility of this solution bursts upon him:

> But oh, it is not enough, it is all no good.
> There is something I want to feel in my running blood,
> Something I want to touch; I must hold my face to the rain,
> I must hold my face to the wind and let it explain
> Me its life as it hurries in secret.

But this again solves nothing, and indeed until his twenty-fifth year Lawrence seems to have found no acceptable way out. In the end he was to ask Jessie to become his mistress pending marriage. Why then did he wait so long?

For many years his mother's hostility seems to have prevented him from acknowledging to himself the nature of the attraction he felt towards Jessie. During his time in college, it seemed to him inconceivable to ask a girl whom he loved and respected to satisfy his sexual needs. But the very ambiguity of his attitude was a source of torment to him, even driving him on one occasion to wish Jessie were a man.[43] Nor did his friendships with young men of his own age exclude some element of desire and shy attempts at sensual contact,[44] hardly to be wondered at in view of the repression of his natural instincts before they could find an outlet. Thus for several years already, Lawrence had been convinced that he did not love Jessie "as a husband should a wife": it seems to have been beyond his powers to face the truth openly.

Nor had he the least idea that Jessie might have sensual feelings: brought up in the Victorian convention of "respect" for the weaker sex, he found it impossible to persuade himself that a woman could "give herself" without degradation. With Jessie he only twice ventured to talk about sex. Chesterton having written that the man who spoke of sex to a woman was a brute, Lawrence and Jessie agreed that, on the contrary, the brute was "the man who could not speak properly to a woman about sex". After which he confessed to having overheard some commercial travellers in a train talking obscenely about sex in a way which seemed to have "bruised his consciousness".[45] The second time he claimed for himself the right to "know all about" the realities of love, while insisting that Jessie should remain in comparative ignorance, from which she concluded that "the whole question of sex had for him the fascination of horror and that in his repudiation of any possibility of a sex relation between us he felt that he paid me a deep and subtle compliment".[46]

Imagining himself incapable of desiring nice girls of his acquaintance, he would be seized by a sort of paralysis in their presence:

> ... He believed in simple friendship. And he considered that he was perfectly honourable with regard to her. It was only a friendship between man and woman, such as any civilized persons might have.
>
> He was like so many young men of his own age. Sex had become so complicated in him that he would have denied that he ever could want Clara or Miriam or any woman whom he *knew*. Sex desire was a sort of detached thing, that did not belong to a woman.[47]

In the same way Tom Brangwen, a sensitive youth, "fresh as a plant", for whom love was "the most serious and terrifying business", is caught and rent between his horror of loose women and his impotence in face of any others.[48]

Yet a woman was clearly needed to polarize Lawrence's unsatisfied and still hesitant and undirected sex instincts. Such seems to have been the conclusion to which he reluctantly came when he began to speak of marrying Louie. It is as if the dualism between spiritual love and physical attraction, created and encouraged by his puritanical upbringing, his mother's hostility towards Jessie and his own timidity, had indefinitely prolonged the uncertainties and hesitations of early adolescence.

Lawrence had so often assured Jessie that his love for her was entirely intellectual and spiritual, that one easily imagines the shock, "disturbing but at the same time inevitable", she felt when at Christmas 1909 he arrived at the Haggs to announce to Jessie that he had broken with Agnes Holt, that "he had really loved her all along and that all their long association had only been a preparation for *une intimité d'amour*". Marriage, he continued, was for the moment "inexpedient": he was not earning enough money, and was still contributing to the upkeep of his family. An official engagement was equally impossible, no doubt because it would have meant a break with his family. But why should they not ignore the rules of common morality, which for them had no more value? Since marriage is essential only when there are children, all they had to do was to be careful. Jessie agreed in principle, though with the reservation, coldly received by Lawrence, that it would not be "honourable" to take advantage of the hospitality of his landlady, Mrs Jones.[49]

The priggish short story "A Modern Lover"[50] recalls this scene and provides an interesting self-portrait of Lawrence at this time. The hero, Cyril Mersham (who has many points in common with the Cyril/Lawrence of *The White Peacock*), has left his provincial home and has been living for two years in "a large city in the south" where he has learned "nice" manners. He returns to the farmhouse home of his friend Muriel, and savours the cultural difference now dividing him from her collier and farmer brothers. In the little parlour still hang the watercolours he now detests because he had painted them during his adolescence and "nothing is so hateful as the self one has left".[51] He relives the hours of his youth, spent with Muriel in a passionate quest for culture; he looks complacently at a photograph of "a sensitive, alert, exquisite boy", himself at twenty-one.[52] He admits that he no longer shrinks from the idea of kissing her. Up to now they have only speculated and poetized together, but "life's no good but to live":

> "Not," he continued, with slow, brutal candour—"Not that I know any more than I did then—what love is—as you know it—but—I think you're beautiful—and we know each other so well—as we know nobody else, don't we? And so we . . ."[53]

They are interrupted by a rival, Vickers, over whom Cyril easily demonstrates his intellectual superiority; once Vickers has gone, Muriel accompanies Cyril a little way and they take up their previous conversation. He admits his self-conscious reason for wanting to try with her the experiment of sex: "because, well, with you I can be just as I feel, conceited or idiotic, without being afraid to be myself".[54] Is she willing to come to him just naturally as she used to come to church with him, not reluctantly, and having to be coaxed? But they part on a note of estrangement, for he cannot tolerate Muriel's eminently feminine fears of the risks of a liaison, nor the revulsion she feels at the necessity for "creeping in the dark".[55]

Thus Lawrence turns for sexual satisfaction to a woman with whom he feels no shyness and, to do him justice, to one with whom he was bound by spiritual ties. But he was afraid that Jessie (clearly recognizable as Muriel, a name by which he sometimes called her)[56] would be too submissive, too hesitant. He would have preferred a bolder woman, who would take the initiative in love:

> Perhaps it was her very submission which trammelled him, throwing the responsibility of her wholly on him, making him shrink from the burden of her.[57]

He would have liked her more fearless than himself. Cyril asks Muriel, is she not happy? What does she want? "Yes, what do I?" she replies with a "rash challenge which pricks him": but to which he fails to respond. If only she would come right out and say that she loved and desired him.[58]

Lawrence expected much of love: it was to be a revelation, a religious ecstasy: Jessie was to come to him as she went to church. Possession, he told her, was a "great moment in life", "a concentration of all strong emotions". There was "something divine in it".[59] Tom Brangwen too had "an innate desire to find in a woman the embodiment of all his inarticulate, powerful religious impulses".[60]

A decisive event in Lawrence's life may have taken place between the Christmas holidays of 1908 and those of 1909, when Lawrence finally made his proposal of free love to Jessie: the rebuff of a similar and almost simultaneous proposal to Agnes Holt, announced to Blanche Jennings in the letter telling her of his new intentions towards Jessie, cannot explain everything. Was it at this point that Mrs Dax initiated him into sexual love? This might perhaps account for the otherwise inexplicable sudden cry of triumph contained in a letter he wrote to Blanche Jennings from Rottingdean in May 1909, in which he tells her how Mrs Dax is changing, how much more womanly she is becoming, and then, right out of the blue, bursts out with the remarkable announcement that he is now grown up—"tremendously grown up, well I don't care if you won't believe it, it's truth".[61] Had Alice Dax, after his initiation, perhaps made him understand the nature of his love for Jessie and persuaded him to put it to the ultimate test? Clara Dawes, in *Sons and Lovers*, sends Paul to Miriam in this way, but *before* she becomes his mistress.

Some doubt is thrown on Lawrence's sincerity towards Jessie, and indeed on the autobiographical truthfulness of his novel, by the very letter in which he tells Blanche Jennings of his break with Agnes Holt because she has refused to recognize the "animal" in him;[62] he is at his old trick of revealing to one girl what he is hiding from the other:

> I have been sick of her some little time. At Christmas an old fire burned up afresh . . . It is the old girl, who has been attached to me for so long . . . She is

coming to me for a week-end soon; we shall not stay here in Croydon, but in London. The world is for us, and we are for each other—even if only for one spring—so what does it matter![63]

This, as it happens, is the last of the published letters from Lawrence to Blanche Jennings; the sudden interruption of the correspondence remains unexplained. It is noticeable that between January and December 1910 Lawrence almost ceases to write to Louie, sending her in all three postcards and seven letters in eleven months.[64]

As at the university, the higher the hopes, the greater the disillusionment. After Lawrence's brief illness (in February 1910) which seems to have been due to overwork and nervous tension, Jessie came to Croydon in March to spend a weekend with him. While Jessie Chambers does not state that this was their first attempt at love-making, it is highly probable that it was. The following week he wrote to tell her "the great good" she had done him, how he needed to have her "to be near, to touch and to hold", and how he wished they "could have a little house" together.[65]

At Easter, Lawrence devoted much time to his mother; he and Jessie had no more than a few long talks and walks together. Already, possibly under the influence of his family and probably disillusioned by their first experiment in sex, he was beginning to criticize Jessie. He was soon profoundly distressed —at least this is what he told Jessie—by the "discovery" that a woman other than herself could rouse his senses. Alice Dax, he said, had been to see him in London, and they had gone to Covent Garden to hear Richard Strauss's *Elektra*. The music had so affected him, that taking Mrs Dax back to her hotel he had "very nearly" been unfaithful to Jessie. This at any rate was what he wrote, and Alice Dax gave Jessie a concordant, and presumably concerted, version of the incident. He could not promise never to succumb to similar temptations.[66] From then onwards he was constantly begging Jessie not to try to hold him. "I must always return to you," he told her, recounting the story of Hercules and the tunic of Nessus, "but you must never try to keep me."

During the Whitsuntide holiday, the lovers snatched a few days of physical intimacy. According to Jessie the times of their coming together, presumably including the weekend in March, "would not exhaust the fingers of one hand".[66a] Jessie's evidence is definite on the point that two poems, "Lilies in the Fire" and "Scent of Irises", refer to that Whitsun holiday; both express the failure and shame of the "great experiment of sex"; so does Lawrence's later and posthumously published account in the Prologue to *Women in Love*, as will be seen below. It is hardly surprising that Lawrence failed to arouse in Jessie the ardour for which he hoped: his approach could scarcely have been more clumsy. His frank and "earnest injunction" not to count on his fidelity was not calculated to encourage uninhibited and passionate response on the part of a sensitive girl, simultaneously at grips with the "difficult and irksome" conditions of open-air love-making, her natural fears of the consequences and the qualms of her own conscience. Despite the generous carpet of spring flowers—lady-smocks and may-blobs, cowslips and buttercups, their pollen glazing Jessie "with a sheen of gold", her lover's passion could not bridge "the gulf that came between" them, and Jessie could only let herself be "once more . . . taken like a sacrifice, in the night invisible".[67]

The memory of these moments of ill-shared passion was clouded by

The open darkness which then drew us in,
The dark which then drank up our brimming cup.[68]

Love brought not ecstasy but shame, mutual embarrassment and, for the man, the "deep humiliation" of seeing himself accepted rather than desired:

I am ashamed, you wanted me not to-night.
And it is always so, you sigh against me.
Your brightness dims when I draw too near, and my free
Fire enters you like frost, like a cruel blight.[69]

Without reflecting that he was remarkably lacking in elements of comparison, that the fault was not necessarily all Jessie's, that he had no right to judge and condemn her on the strength of such a limited experience, Lawrence was ready to break off the relationship there and then. "After a week of love" (the Whitsun holiday?), Paul Morel announces to his mother that he will no longer see Miriam.[70] And just as Paul leaves Miriam abruptly for Clara, so Lawrence at once throws himself into a new adventure, with Helen, while keeping secret from both Jessie and Helen his, it would seem, simultaneous affair with Mrs Dax.

The Prologue to *Women in Love*, written in 1916, gives Lawrence's definitive version of the failure of his sexual attempt with Jessie, in the guise of Hermione. Jessie could not know of its existence when she recognized herself in the Hermione of the novel.[70a] Not only does it corroborate that recognition, but it contains Lawrence's most frank and outspoken confession and his acknowledgment of moral responsibility.

The Prologue dwells at some length on the protracted spiritual relationship between Birkin and Hermione: a Birkin who, like Lawrence, wrote "harsh, jarring poetry" under which, like Jessie, Hermione "suffered".[70b] In an early phase, which is reminiscent of Lawrence's early manhood at Eastwood, they had "nights of superfine ecstasy of beauty" after which "his body was grey and consumed, and his soul ill". At such times "they penetrated further and further into the regions of death".[70c] Then they were separated, when, like Lawrence to Croydon, Birkin "went away to his duties and work". Birkin "ran about from death to death", the death of work, and that of "a love based entirely on ecstasy and on pain, and ultimate death".[70d]

In view of the poems which refer to Lawrence's love-making with Jessie, and of her own statement that she detected "a forced note in L's attitude, as if he was pushed forwards in his sensual desires—and a lack of spontaneity",[70e] it is difficult not to treat the following as autobiographical:

> He did not even desire her: he had no passion for her, there was no hot impulse of growth between them, only this terrible reducing activity of phosphorescent consciousness . . .
>
> He did not call this love. Yet he was bound to her, and it was agony to leave her. And he did not love any one else. He did not love any woman. He *wanted* to love . . .
>
> He did not love Hermione, he did not desire her. But he wanted to force himself to love her and to desire her. He was consumed by sexual desire, and he wanted to be fulfilled. Yet he did not desire Hermione. She repelled him rather. Yet he *would* have this physical fulfilment, he would have the physical activity. So he forced himself towards her.

The description of Hermione's hopeless resignation to the physical aspects of love is reminiscent of the tone and very wording of the poems:

> She did not want him either. But with all her soul, she *wanted* to want him. She would do anything to give him what he wanted, that which he was raging for, this physical fulfilment he insisted on. She was wise, she thought for the best. She prepared herself like a perfect sacrifice to him. She offered herself gladly to him, gave herself to his will.
>
> And oh, it was all such a cruel failure, just a failure. This last act of love which he had demanded of her was the keenest grief of all, it was so insignificant, so null. He had no pleasure of her, only some mortification. And her heart almost broke with grief.
>
> . . . She wanted him to take her, to break her with his passion, to destroy her with his desire, so long as he got satisfaction . . .
>
> But he was not capable of it, he failed. He could not take her and destroy her. He could not forget her. They had too rare a spiritual intimacy, he could not now tear himself away from all this, and come like a brute to take his satisfaction. He was too much aware of her, and of her fear, and of her writhing torment, as she lay in sacrifice. He had too much deference for her feeling. He could not, as he madly wanted, destroy her, trample her, and crush a satisfaction from her. He was not experienced enough, not hardened enough. He was always aware of her feelings, so that he had none of his own. Which made this last love-making between them an ignominious failure, very, very cruel to bear.[70f]

So Hermione "despised him that he could not destroy her"; and he "hated her, for her incapacity in love, for her lack of desire of him, her complete and almost perfect lack of any physical desire towards him". Birkin—and in this we find once more Lawrence after the 1910 Whitsun holiday—"went to other women, to women of purely sensual, sensational attraction, he prostituted his spirit with them. And he got *some* satisfaction".[70g]

Helen: the death of Mrs Lawrence

Early in 1909 he had made the acquaintance of Helen Corke, a Croydon colleague. That same year Helen had spent a few days' holiday in the Isle of Wight with her music master, Herbert Baldwin Macartney, who on returning to his wife and family had committed suicide. Informed of this by a mutual friend, Lawrence soon asked Helen to let him read the "retrospective" diary[71] in which she had recorded this tragic story. Towards the beginning of 1909, he began, with her consent, to expand the "theme" into a novel, called at first "The Saga of Siegmund", later to become *The Trespasser*.

In May 1910 he insisted on Jessie meeting his new friend, later telling her that in order to write his new novel "he must have Hélène". It was understood that this was to be a purely temporary affair, dictated by the overriding interest of literature and "only for the writing of the book".[72] Lawrence, as usual, seems to have consulted Jessie before the party most directly interested, who was not at this point particularly inclined to throw herself into a new adventure.[73]

Her wings singed in the flame of a tragic passion, by her own account Helen was not prepared to take more than a friendly interest in the eager and awkward young man determined to lure back to the living this new Persephone whose recent ordeal had changed the sun "into a mere ball of gas" and the sound of the violin into "the scraping of hairs upon catgut".[74] Together they went for long walks in London and over the Surrey Downs, talking of art and literature, Meredith and Corot, "pondering and probing at the major mysteries of existence", evoking ancient gods and sensing peace and fulfilment in the sweet "rank evening mist".[75]

By July 1910 the first draft of *The Trespasser* was completed,[76] and Jessie decided the time had come to put an end to an untenable situation. Taking Lawrence at his word, she wrote to suggest "a break with Helen" and using some such phrase as "all or nothing" to define her position. Annoyed, Lawrence then told her he wanted to end their relationship: even their letters were to cease. Shortly afterwards Jessie wrote to Helen to let her know that Lawrence was now free. The two women met again and soon became close friends. All that summer Lawrence continued to press his "demands" on Helen, to whom he showed his writing, and with whom he enjoyed long and intimate literary discussions.[77]

In the autumn Mrs Lawrence's fatal illness began. Her lingering death from cancer plunged her son into the depths of despair, intensifying his already marked tendency to pessimism. In unforgettable passages of *Sons and Lovers*,[78] Lawrence has conveyed the full horror of that autumn, the grief of the children powerless to relieve their mother's suffering. Two very short poems, "Suspense" and "Endless Anxiety",[79] describe the nervous exhaustion, the alternating waves of fear and relief of the interminable wait for news of her release from agony.

Every other weekend Lawrence went to Nottingham to be with his mother. One day he brought her an advance copy of *The White Peacock*, specially bound for her.[80] He was writing a new novel, then called "Paul Morel", telling the story of his mother's youth and marriage, her sorrows and her disillusionments. By 18 October he completed the first chapters,[81] working in his mother's room, just as Paul Morel painted his finest pictures by his mother's sick-bed,[82] talking with her as he painted.

Helen had so far responded coldly to "David's" attentions, still refusing to drink in the poet's "bowl of kisses".[83] She repulsed him and he hated her for it, "as a man hates the dreaming woman he loves but who will not reply".[84] He resented the physical coldness of "this woman who likes to love me" but who wanted only to gather "the flowers of all my mud".[85] Once more he was up against the spirituality of a woman preferring to be his intellectual companion rather than the instrument of his pleasure.

One day in October, Helen accompanied Jessie to Nottingham on a cheap day-ticket in order just to be able to travel back with Lawrence, who had gone to see his mother. This is the journey described in the poem "Excursion Train".[86] The poet is filled with renewed hope of regeneration through love. Cannot the train—"shot arrow of travel"—fly sheer into the sky of a tomorrow free of pain and sorrow? But Helen turns her head obstinately towards the night. Her "stiff reluctancy" puts an end to his dream of sinking with her into an "utter sleep", until they become as one. The poem ends in a fervent prayer to Helen to

> Strip me naked, touch me light,
> Light, light all over
> For I ache most earnestly for your touch,
> Yet I cannot move, however much
> I would be your lover.[87]

Is not this the same lover who was petrified at the thought of taking responsibility for Jessie, substituting words for deeds, spinning out in discussion a painful situation as though it were the woman's role to put an end to it?

Did Helen let herself be persuaded? The poems more than suggest it. In the poem "Release" ("Reproach" in the original version of *Amores*) Lawrence has expressed the complex feelings that her acceptance inspired in him.[88] The lover is a black cloud charged with electricity, the woman is the earth drinking the lightning from the agonized sky, discharging the ache of the wound, washing from her lover's eyes the thought of death.

> . . . Earth of my atmosphere, stone
> Of my steel, lovely white flint of desire,
>   You have no name.[89]

Helen, however, did not appreciate being nameless, even if she thereby became the earth struck by this dark Jupiter. Lawrence soon began to reproach her for her love of abstraction, her lack of sensuality; and the incipient resentment, already discernible in the early poems to Helen, reached full spate in the violent invective of "A Spiritual Woman".[90] Why must she see "only a mean arithmetic on the face of things"? Why shake her lover like a kaleidoscope, which she joggles incessantly without finding the pattern she desires? Why not let him kiss her into blind unconsciousness?

Lawrence was at this point looking to love to obliterate his grief. Haunted by the sight of his beloved mother's suffering, a woman was to him a means of taking his mind away from her, of obtaining momentary relief from the knowledge of reality. Such is the only possible interpretation of the poem "Release", particularly in the light of the following passage in *Sons and Lovers*, and irrespective of whether Clara here stands for Helen, for Alice Dax (who admitted her secret meetings with him by the Trent), or for both:

> And she pressed him to her breast, rocked him, soothed him like a child.
> So he put the trouble aside for her sake, to take it up again immediately he was
> alone. All the time, as he went about, he cried mechanically. His mind and
> hands were busy. He cried, he did not know why. It was his blood weeping.
> He was just as much alone whether he was with Clara or with the men in the
> White Horse. Just himself and this pressure inside him, that was all that existed.
> He read sometimes. He had to keep his mind occupied. And Clara was a way of
> occupying his mind.[91]

But Helen did not give Lawrence the ecstasy he longed for (to which, moreover, his own state of mind can hardly have been conducive). He was still seeing Jessie; and another poem, also of the "awful autumn" of November 1910, alludes obscurely to a meeting described in *Sons and Lovers*.[92]

Jessie has refused the poet "the dour communion", but as she caresses his hair and brows, he wonders whether they might not at this moment seize together the keys of the kingdom so rarely vouchsafed by God. Perhaps he could have baptized himself in the well of her love to achieve "the right rare passion"? This poem refers to an attempt at reconciliation, even if still tinged with fear of failure; but the scene in *Sons and Lovers* conveys only Paul's conflict between the love, now physical, he feels for Miriam, and his anguish at his mother's approaching death.

A few weeks later, early in December, came Mrs Lawrence's final agony and death and for her son the beginning of a period of yet more heart-rending despair, a year so arid that at times the writer seems almost to lose his reason. A new complication in his emotional life certainly contributed to his bitterness, to his feeling of impotence in the face of life now that he was deprived of the woman who had always made his decisions for him. "Out of the blue", he suddenly proposed to Louie Burrows.

Louie

As usual he immediately confides in someone he scarcely knows, in the poetess Rachel Annand Taylor. He recounts to her the same day how "in the train, quite unpremeditated, between Rothley and Quorn", he has proposed to Louie; and he also reveals his feeling of guilt towards Jessie, who loves him "to madness", but "demands his soul", which belongs for ever to his mother and that nobody can ever have again. Louie he describes as "say Rhoda Fleming or a commoner Anna Karenina", who loves him with a "fine, warm, healthy love" and who will "never plunge her hands through my blood and feel for my soul". His relief is evident from his conclusion: "Ugh —I have done well—and cruelly—tonight."93

To Jessie he wrote, about a week before his mother's death, announcing his engagement to Louie, saying he had met her in the train and "suddenly asked her to marry" him, although he "never meant to". After his mother's funeral Jessie told him he ought not to involve the innocent Louie in the complexities of his relationship with Helen and herself. "With should and ought I have nothing to do," replied Lawrence coldly.94

After that he and Jessie met rarely, while Helen Corke broke with Lawrence, or at least reduced their liaison to the friendly if ironical terms illustrated in the short story "The Witch à la Mode",95 in which the heroine Winifred is clearly the Helen of *The Trespasser* and of the poems. The circumstances are those of Lawrence at this time: the distant new fiancée, the return to Croydon: "after months of separation they dove-tailed into the same love and hate". But the new fiancée, too, proved incapable of giving Lawrence the ecstatic and serene love he almost religiously desired. Lawrence's letters to Louie Burrows (who had by September 1911 become headmistress of the Church of England School at Quorn), while they scarcely ever express any depth of feeling, testify to a growing irritation with the shortcomings he found in a fiancée whose whole life shows her to have been a woman of character and ability. He did not like being cross-examined about his other women, especially about Jessie:

I told J. she could marry me if she'd ask me. Unawares I had let our affair
run on: what could I do! But she wouldn't have me so—thank God. I don't
want to marry her—though she is my very dear friend. She has not any very
intrinsic part of me, now—no, not at all.

As for the other three—you were one & J. another: well, I lied. They only
liked & flattered me. I am a fool. One is a jolly nice girl who is engaged now &
whom I hope you will know. She's a schoolmistress in Yorkshire. One is a little
bitch, & I hate her: and she plucked me, like Potiphar's wife: and one is nothing.
I'll tell you verbatim when you ask me.[96]

Having thus admitted part of the truth about Jessie, Agnes Holt, Helen
and Alice Dax and thrown a smoke-screen around his affairs, he goes on to
try to make himself "common", wishing he "were just like ordinary men. I
am a bit different— & God knows, I regret it."

Disagreements with Louie over his strained finances and his expenditure,
signs of her jealousy because Jessie still writes to him, his irritation because of
her parents' "bigoted" views and puritanical codes of behaviour gradually
lead to outbursts such as this:

Will you, I wonder get through life without ever seeing through it? I will
never, if I can help it, try to disturb any of your faith. You will secure yourself
by praying for my conversion, eh?—There the balance. Am I ironical again?[97]

Sexual frustration when the too-proper fiancée rejects his many advances
soon enters into the picture: "I say only that is wicked which is a violation
of one's feeling and instinct";[98] and Louie's prudery is a constant violation.
Lawrence refuses to show her his poetry—about which she shows signs of
mild jealousy. Here again, the poems contain the best clue to the state of his
mind, and show the clarity of his retrospective diagnosis of the troubles into
which this engagement had plunged him.

The cycle of poems relating to Louie, whom Lawrence calls "the other
woman, the woman of 'Kisses in the Train' and 'Hands of the Betrothed'",[99]
reveal the depth of his new disillusion. "Hands of the Betrothed" is a cruel
evocation of a beautiful and attractive woman with unresponsive eyes,
sensual, but too poor in spirit to free herself of her girlish prudishness:

Her tawny eyes are onyx of thoughtlessness,
Hardened they are like gems in time-long prudery;
Yea, and her mouth's prudent and crude caress
Means even less than her many words to me . . .[100]

Her hands move like heavy birds, or stir "like a subtle stoat", but her
thoughts seem elsewhere:

Dreaming—God knows of what, for to me she's the same
Betrothed young lady who loves me, and takes good care
Of her maidenly virtue and of my good name.[101]

True, these verses are more incisive in *The Collected Poems* than in their original version in *Amores*: by slight redrafting, Lawrence has clarified an already harsh assessment.

Too good, and not subtle enough to understand him, such is his final judgment of his fiancée. At a moment when his life appears to him in its most tragic light, when his soul is spent in the grief of bereavement, he finds in her no real chord of sympathy; nor is she a girl to help him reach oblivion by offering herself freely to her lover. Their mutual misunderstanding was to last for over a year; in December 1911 Lawrence wrote from his sick-bed to Edward Garnett:

> My girl is here. She's big, and swarthy, and passionate as a gipsy—but good, awfully good, churchy. She rubs her cheek against me, just like a cat, and says: "Are you happy?" It makes me laugh. But I am not particularly happy, being only half here, yet awhile. She never understands that—so I have to pitch all my wits against her. It's very weird.[102]

And to his sister a few months earlier:

> I never want Lou to understand how relentlessly tragic life is—not that. But I want her not to jar on me by gawkishness, and that she must learn . . . I am glad you like Louie. When she is a bit older she'll be more understanding.[103]

One cruel and violent poem, "Under the Oak", expresses the same irritation and perhaps also something of the same nostalgia for the girl who had been so closely interwoven with his spiritual life, and who shares with him his "ancient curse".

A man is gazing at the stars, a woman of little spirit at his side: clearly the Lawrence whose thoughts, haunted by the memory of his mother, have for long dwelt on death. While to him the stars "flash signals, each one dreadful", his companion, "twittering to and fro", remarks tritely on the beauty of the night. And the poet bursts forth cruelly:

> What thing better are you, what worse?
> What have you to do with the mysteries
> Of this ancient place, of my ancient curse?
> What place have you in my histories?[104]

Socially uprooted

Two failures in love, the loss of his mother, a burdensome engagement: the year 1910 indeed took heavy toll of Lawrence, especially when it is remembered that to all these setbacks was added a growing sense of social uprooting from his native soil. Despite the evidence of his sister,[105] and a recrudescence of literary activity after meeting Edward Garnett,[106] the year 1911 brought little to alleviate his despair, though the illness with which it ended does seem to have helped to resolve the crisis, at least on the practical plane.

Neither his day-to-day existence, his teaching nor his writing was able to resuscitate him, or renew his love of life. From his correspondence with Edward Garnett and Louie it is clear that his greatest desire was to publish as much as possible, in order to begin to earn his living by writing and give up a profession of which he was growing increasingly impatient.[107] His health was failing, he had difficulty in writing what was to become *Sons and Lovers*, and his acute nervousness worried both family and friends. On a holiday in Wales with his sister and Louie, which had begun after much discussion with his fiancée about her family's insistence on some sort of chaperone,[108] he "was never still a minute", running "up and down the crags like a man possessed";[109] he went almost at once from Wales to Shirebrook to relax in the Dax household. In October, Jessie found him pale and thin. His brother George reported that he would call out in his sleep, thinking he was being murdered.[110] Work became impossible; the dry centrally-heated air of the classrooms made him feel "really rotten": he caught cold, and thought often of leaving school.[111]

His first novel had had some success, several critics foreseeing a brilliant future for its youthful author. But in Eastwood offence was taken, particularly by the family of Alice Hall (portrayed in the novel under the too closely similar name of Alice Gall),[112] at the freedom with which he had described local things and people, as well as at certain innocent enough expressions Eastwood considered "daring", despite the fact that his publisher had already made him remove or modify one or two offending phrases.[113] "The publishing of the book has brought me very little but bitterness," Lawrence wrote to an admirer; "a good many folk have been hostile—practically all America" (sic).[114] Nor did he, ill-dressed and often penniless as he was, yet feel at home in the literary world of Garnett and of Hueffer, while publishers were a constant source of irritation.[115]

Where then did his real roots lie? In the old world of Eastwood, among the simple folk with whom he had now little enough in common? Two short stories written early in 1911 insist clumsily on how far he had travelled from his origins. In "A Modern Lover" Cyril Mersham visits his friend Muriel at the family farm after two years in a southern city. The uncouth manners of her brothers, their rough eating habits and their stumbling words, are torture to the Londoner, who, exaggerating his own elegance, begins to speak in an English "exquisitely accurate", pronounced with the southern accent, very different from the heavily-sounded speech of the home folk.[116] His affectation increases their awkwardness and Cyril chats away "with added brightness and subtlety", conscious that by so doing he is irrevocably "removing himself from them, though he had loved them".[117]

Muriel has a suitor, Tom Vickers, "a healthy male", intelligent but simple, "who can add two and two but never xy and yx". Cyril has no difficulty in disposing of him and recapturing Muriel, despite the "beautiful lustihood", the "handsome, healthy animalism" of his rival. His self-satisfaction knows no bounds, and he proceeds to pose, drawling languidly, using quaint turns of speech, and bewildering poor Tom, in short behaving like a very raw recruit to the rank of gentleman, his airs and graces no more than a thin veneer.[118]

"The Soiled Rose",[119] later to become "The Shades of Spring", is yet more enlightening. Here Lawrence is called Syson, Jessie becomes Hilda and the imaginary rival is the "manly" gamekeeper, Pilbeam. Syson speaks French, and quotes Verlaine before this country bumpkin who cannot even speak good English. The polite, refined manners of Syson are contrasted with the roughness of the keeper. But the climax comes when Syson, secretly annoyed at seeing himself replaced in the affections of the girl he loved, suddenly strikes his thigh with his gloves and rises to his feet, leaving his rival with a distant politeness which is the height of ridicule. In the original version of this story, the opening conversation of the two men reveals even more clearly Syson's affectation, snobbishness and secret jealousy.[120]

A certain snobbery was thus beginning to intervene between Lawrence and his former friends. He took offence when Jessie's mother addressed a letter to him as "Mr Lawrence" instead of the "D. H. Lawrence, Esq." requisite for gentlemen.[121] Park Lane houses inspired in him bitter reflections not far removed from envy.[122] Some of his letters to Louie reveal an intolerably patronizing attitude towards the Leicestershire schoolmistress. On his way to Hueffer's flat in Holland Park "the spectacle of London's opulence" caused him to burst out to Jessie with the arrogance of a Rastignac that he would make £2,000 a year! On the same occasion he astonished her by the importance he attached to the fact that Hueffer was leaving them to visit a *Lady* something or other.[123] Yet in this new, cold literary world he was dogged by homesickness for the old simplicity, the affectionate warmth of the common people from whom he sprang,[124] and he willingly sought refuge in a society like that he created in *The White Peacock*, where class distinctions are blurred to the point of almost total disappearance; the distance separating George Saxton, the farmer, from Leslie Tempest, son of the great mine-owner, for instance, being practically ignored.

No doubt Lawrence was sincere when he wrote to Jessie:

Last night I dined with celebrities, and to-night I am dining with two R.A.s, but I'd give it all up for one of our old evenings in the Haggs parlour.[125]

Although conscious of his rise in the social world and somewhat dazzled by the prestige he acquired in his own eyes from his sudden entry into the

world of letters, he appears unsure as to whether this is really the path he
wants to follow.

Ever since childhood he had in fact suffered from a sense of class which was
all the keener and more insidious for its not being intellectually apprehended.
No doubt it sprang originally from the wound to his mother's pride of
having "come down" in the world. Witness the child's shrinking dread
before the pay clerk at the colliery, the shame of being sent to claim his
father's wages—reaction typical of the poor, to whom money and those who
handle it are both hated and religiously respected. Similarly in *Sons and Lovers*,
on their one visit to a restaurant, Mrs Morel and Paul behave with the shame-
faced humility of the poor,[126] and in *The White Peacock* George Saxton at
the hotel "could never get over the feeling he was trespassing".[127] Frieda
has recorded Lawrence's memory of suffering bitterly at being dropped by a
High School friend who learned he was a miner's son.[128] As an adolescent
Lawrence doubted not his genius, but the contradiction between his vocation
and his position as "a collier's son". At Nottingham University College he
resented being looked down on as a future teacher. "It's different with the
engineers," he used to say, "you should see the way they go about the
place."[129]

A young man as sensitive as Lawrence had the choice of bracing himself
to face suffering and setting out to conquer a world which, even if as yet
unaware of his genius, would one day be forced to recognize it; or of with-
drawing into himself to avoid all painful contacts. Lawrence almost invariably wavered between these two solutions. Family pressure was certainly
towards social advancement, and by putting him in touch with Hueffer
Jessie definitely contributed to this, though perhaps without realizing the
inevitable link between literary success and entry into the worldly life of
London and a different moral environment. But Lawrence was no vulgar
opportunist. He was too hesitant, too unstable and too sensitive to pursue
wholeheartedly the path to success: simply to go on living seemed to him
to require a miracle of energy.[130] Too proud, too, with an almost morbid
pride wounded at the least rebuff, the slightest suspicion of indifference on the
part of publisher or critic.[131] His shyness condemned him in advance to
suffer from the changes of background necessitated by his education and the
career of his choice. In his isolation from his former friends it was nostalgia
for his roots, rather than false shame, which beset him as he was suddenly
thrust into a new world, where, in 1910, men of his own class were still
something of a rarity.

Despair

Apart from Garnett, his sister Ada and Louie are his main correspondents
during 1911. The death of his mother revived his family feeling, and his

sister seems to have been the only person to whom he could communicate some of his most intimate thoughts at this time. He was no longer seeing Jessie, and only rarely writing to her. Since his engagement he was seeing less of Helen. He insists strongly on the bonds which bind him to his sister:

> Don't be jealous of her [Louie]. She hasn't any space in *your* part of me. You and I—there are some things which we shall share we alone, all our lives . . . you are my own *real* relative in the world—only you. I am yours: is it not so?[132]

To Ada he confides his sadness, his disgust:

> Sometimes I have a fit of horror which is very hard to put up with . . . we pay heavily for this boon of living . . . At present I find the only antidote is work . . . It gets the days over, at any rate . . . I am tired of life being so ugly and cruel. How I long for it to turn pleasant. It makes my soul heave with distaste to see it so harsh and brutal . . .[133]

Life is "relentlessly tragic": and in that spring of 1911 tragedy is Lawrence's preferred literary genre. To his friend Sallie Hopkin he sends *Riders to the Sea*, *The Trojans*, *Oedipus* and the *Bacchantes*.

> They are tragedies, but all great works are. Tragedy is beautiful also. This is my creed. But sometimes also it leaves me full of misery.[134]

Solitude is scarcely the answer to despair; nevertheless Lawrence deliberately isolates himself. He feels cut off from other men, all company is abhorrent to him. He refuses to spend the Easter holidays at Eastwood. Towards his father his feelings are astonishingly hard and bitter.[135] His first novel has just appeared and Eastwood people will regard him a curiosity; he will go on holiday elsewhere with Ada. He detests, he abominates Eastwood, and would like to see it swept from the face of the earth. Nor does anything bind him to his everyday companions in London. He neither has nor wants close friends:

> Folks aren't company for me: I am as much alone with the friends here as if I were solitary. But how used one gets to a lonely life. I'm sure I've now no intimate friends here, and don't want any. I am sufficient unto myself and prefer to be left alone . . . In the things that matter one has to be alone in this life or nearly alone. I never say anything to anybody but sometimes I can hardly swallow the meals. And there is no refuge from one's own thoughts day after day . . . Bear a thing as if it weren't there—that's the only way. Folk hate you to be miserable and to make them a bit miserable . . . The tragic is the most vital thing in life . . . the lesson is to learn to live alone.[136]

From this period date most of the poems on the death of his mother, which form an important part of *Rhyming Poems*. "Monologue of a Mother" (1912–13) and "End of Another Home Holiday"[137] had shown his mother as a tragic figure, the great hopes of her youth disappointed first by her husband, and then by sons growing up into strangers, bent on their own pursuits. So she begs the love of her youngest son, who is irked by this "inexorable love". Haunted by her "yearning-eyed" figure with "grey bowed head", he seeks to understand why his mother's love should thus pursue him with

> A hoarse, insistent request that falls
> Unweariedly, unweariedly,
> Asking something more of me,
> Yet more of me.[138]

With the death of his mother this struggle against maternal love is over. But something in himself has died with her, and he can think only of the happiness he might have given her "to make requite" for all her life "of asking and despair".[139]

In death his mother "sleeps like a bride, dreaming her dream of perfect things"[140] and the son sings to her the love song of "The Virgin Mother": a tender farewell in which he swears always to be true to the woman who gave him life, to live on "to plough the difficult glebe of the future". Yet tempted by escape into death, the poet envies the "sweet still" calm of his dead mother and is reluctant to turn away to face the fierce ordeal of life.[141]

Soon after this first reaction began "the long haunting of death in life".[142] Often no more than an acute longing for his dead mother, the memory of her last weeks suddenly revived by a wisp of cigarette smoke evoking the thin grey strands of her hair.[143] A yellow leaf hopping in the wind would arouse him sharply from a dream in which he was reliving hour by hour his mother's agony.[144] In death, his mother carried with her his "missal book of fine flamboyant/Hours", leaving her son only a cold and withered sky, a grey and shadowy world.[145] He relives his childhood, hears the frail notes of the old piano accompanying a Sunday evening hymn. His manhood is "cast down in the flood of remembrance" and he weeps "like a child for the past".[146]

The dead woman calls to him, inviting him to leave this world of sorrow; he feels the vanity of all man's "patterings" and "the silence waiting in its last completeness to drown the noise of men". Neither the song of the lark nor all man's strivings can ever

> . . . change the darkness,
> Nor blench it with noise;
> Alone on the perfect silence
> The stars are buoys.[147]

One half of the moon shines in the sky, the other half is buried with his mother in the tomb, symbol of the "troth with the dead that we are pledged to keep", and between the two halves strange beams still carry fearful messages.[148] Lawrence makes some effort to invert the image and draw from it some encouragement for living,[149] but there are moments when the "Call into Death" prevails:

> As a pigeon lets itself off from a cathedral dome,
> To be lost in the haze of the sky; I would like to come
> And be lost out of sight with you, like a melting foam.
> For I am tired, my dear, and if I could lift my feet
> My tenacious feet, from off the dome of the earth
> To fall like a breath within the breathing wind
> Where you are lost, what rest, my love, what rest![150]

He would willingly leave his mortal body, with its shame and pain, and "would laugh with joy" to see it lie like so much "lumber".[151] Sometimes he seems to draw a certain pride and strength from the knowledge of the exceptional depth of his suffering; "wonder-ridden", he has the gift of tongues, so that shadows "tell him things" and he can see beneath the real world a universe "of subtle ghosts".[152]

What does it matter if he burns up "the fuel of life"? Beneath the flame lies a shadow, inviolate core of his whole being.[153]

Such strength is not only illusory but dangerous, and the mystic shadow haunting the poet's soul fills him with mad dreams more often than it fortifies him to continue the struggle. Certain poems show Lawrence on the road to hallucination and madness, and their sincerity is proved beyond a doubt by a comparison with those scenes of *Sons and Lovers* in which Paul's reason seems to hover in the balance:

> So the weeks went on. Always alone, his soul oscillated, first on the side of death, then on the side of life, doggedly. The real agony was that he had nowhere to go, nothing to do, nothing to say, and *was* nothing himself. Sometimes he ran down the streets as if he were mad; sometimes he was mad; things weren't there, things were there. It made him pant. Sometimes he stood before the bar of the public-house where he had called for a drink. Everything suddenly stood back away from him. He saw the face of the barmaid, the gabbling drinkers, his own glass on the slopped, mahogany board, in the distance. There was something between him and them. He could not get into touch. He did not want them; he did not want his drink. Turning abruptly, he went out. On the threshold he stood and looked at the lighted street. But he was not of it or in it. Something separated him . . .[154]

Paul would then go home and drink, or, finding work impossible, would hurry off to a club where he could play cards or billiards, or find a barmaid with whom he would flirt meaninglessly. His own image in a mirror filled him with disgust:

He dared not meet his own eyes in the mirror; he never looked at himself. He wanted to get away from himself, but there was nothing to get hold of. In despair he thought of Miriam. Perhaps—perhaps—?[155]

Lawrence too was haunted by strange visions; his nerves were raw, the slightest sensation summoned up in him a world of dreams:

> The acrid scents of autumn,
> Reminiscent of slinking beasts, make me fear
> Everything, tear-trembling stars of autumn
> And the snore of the night in my ear . . .[156]

Drunk, he wanders about streets become a "phantom show" in which dream and reality are indissolubly mingled. Arc-lamps are roses, lighting up a thousand ghost flowers: hawthorn and white lilacs, laburnum and its "golden lees". The red flowers of the hawthorn are flags plunged in pale blood:

> Blood shed in the silent fight
> Of life with love and love with life,
> The battling for a little food
> Of kisses, long seeking for a wife
> Long ago, long ago wooed . . .[157]

Was it his mother or Jessie that the poet thus "wooed long ago"? Both are now too far away to save him from this haunted road. The white flowers of the chestnut trees are "erect young girls" tempting his disordered imagination; a white lilac is a woman in a lace mantilla, the scent of a purple lilac the insistent call of another; the laburnum, "shimmering her draperies down", is seen as a naked body glimmering in the night. "Two and two are the folk that walk", but "alone and wavering home" along the haunted road goes the poet. "And never a girl like a chestnut flower/Will tiptoe into my room."[158]

And even in his "own room's shelter" the shadows of the trees thrown by the outside street-lamp become a group of strange women. The wind "breaks and sobs in the blind" and the tall women weep, swooping by the bed, beckoning, rushing away, and beckoning again. Has he profaned some female mystery?[159]

This female mystery is his real obsession: the inexplicable failure of his love life, the strange pact binding the living son to the dead mother. Haunted by erotic images, nervous and apprehensive, he can see no reason for living other than the obligation to carry on his mother's effort.[160] More than once tempted to give up, and follow her into annihilation and darkness, he nevertheless turns with tight lips and clenched fists towards light and life.[161]

This crisis seems to have reached its climax in the late spring or early summer of 1911. He found it increasingly difficult to concentrate on his novel "Paul Morel", and the tone of his letters to Louie became more abrupt. It was perhaps only to be expected that the prolonged crisis should be followed by a physical collapse and in mid-November he fell ill with pneumonia. For some time he was nursed in Croydon by his sister Ada, with a visit from Louie over Christmas.[162] As soon as he was well enough to travel he went to convalesce in Bournemouth, returning to Eastwood via The Cearne, Edward Garnett's house in Sussex, at the beginning of February. The doctor advised him to give up teaching: he was threatened with tuberculosis of the lungs.[163]

His illness had given him time to reflect on his various love affairs although it had not resolved all his contradictions. He had written to Louie from The Cearne asking to be released from their engagement. The doctor had advised him not to marry, and he did not "have the proper love to marry on".[164] While staying with Garnett, he had also written to Helen, "a letter that didn't please" her, suggesting a meeting at The Cearne. His host was "beautifully unconventional", he pleaded. "Everyone knew what that meant," is Helen Corke's final comment.[165]

He arrived at Eastwood a few days later determined to put an end to his engagement. In the course of his long crisis he seems moreover to have passed from his former excessive shyness to a sort of swaggering Don Juanism: witness an obscure allusion in a letter to a mysterious "Jane", kissed with a heavy heart at Marylebone, an affair at a Midlands dance, and the poems "Don Juan" and "Hymn to Priapus" which reflect that mood.[166]

On 12 February 1912, with a detachment indicative of his feelings, he gave Garnett a cruel, almost flippant account of his final break with Louie,[167] a scene he later transposed in *The Rainbow*, where it is Ursula who breaks with Anton, and Anton who weeps.[168]

At that same time he went to stay at Shirebrook with the Daxes and seems to have attempted once more to make it up with Jessie. As though he could not do without her whenever he needed to steep himself in the deep sources of literary creation, he had seen her again in the autumn of 1911, and had consulted her about his latest novel. During his convalescence he had entirely rewritten *The Trespasser*,[169] and between the two drafts of this novel had started work on "Paul Morel".[170] The sickness and death of his mother, and possibly the frustration of his engagement, had slowed down this work, though he did, in fact, complete several short stories during this period, one of them—"Two Marriages", later to become "Daughters of the Vicar"—of considerable length.[171]

In October 1911 he had sent to Jessie, in manuscript, the first two-thirds of "Paul Morel", asking her what she thought of it. It was, broadly speaking, the life of Mrs Lawrence, told rather sentimentally; neither the farm nor Miriam's family figured in it, and the girl herself was placed in an entirely different setting from that of Haggs Farm. Jessie suggested to Lawrence that he should relate the story of his mother's life as it had actually happened, and include the death of Ernest. He took her at her word, entirely recasting the novel and even including a picture of the Chambers' household, which she had *not* suggested. He asked her to write what she could remember of their early days together as a help to him, because, he said, he did not remember those days as well as she did. These notes, drafted by Jessie during Lawrence's illness, she gave him on his first visit after his return.[172] The writing of the second version of *Sons and Lovers* then went on apace and Lawrence passed on the manuscript to Jessie as he wrote it, a dozen or so pages at a time.

Jessie had already tried to make Lawrence understand the role played by his mother in the destruction of their love: she had sent him a short story relating the incidents of 1906 and he had replied: "It was the slaughter of the foetus in the womb . . . They tore me from you, the love of my life."[173] She now advised him to treat his mother's story and her own with realism, thinking that if he could work out artistically and within himself the problems of their lives, he would rid himself of his obsession with regard to his mother and become a free and whole man.[174]

Was Lawrence turning towards Jessie in the hope of a reconciliation? The two short stories[175] he finished writing or rewriting during his convalescence show that he had been giving much thought to the failure of his first love: his imagination seems to have lingered long on Jessie, on the farm, on their common experience; and while this nostalgia is tinged with disillusion, this is perhaps due rather to the fear of seeing himself supplanted by some robust and simple rival than to any doubt as to the depth of his own feeling. The poem "After Many Days" deals with the first meeting with Jessie after a long break.

Lawrence had for some time refused to admit to himself the bitterness of their separation.[176] Could they not draw closer to each other again, unite the two violent and flaming hearts which beat under the easy flow of "slipping words"? This meeting is also described in the last pages of *Sons and Lovers*,[177] where Paul, still incapable of "taking what was his", longs desperately for Miriam to make the gesture which would finally unite them: "If she could rise, take him, put her arms round him and say 'You are mine', then he would leave himself to her." But, as so often in the past, the wall of inhibitions which had been raised between them kept them apart: Jessie had an impulse to move to his side when, as clearly as though he actually uttered the words, she seemed to hear him say "Don't imagine, because Mother's dead, that you can claim me . . ." They tried to talk things out, Lawrence maintaining that he did not want to marry yet, that he must move about, perhaps go to Germany to visit his mother's relatives by marriage. If after a year neither of them had found anyone else, they might get married. Jessie's heart "went cold, because the idea of marriage *'faute de mieux'* with Lawrence above all was a terrible prospect". She saw again his intense loneliness, his separation, and, as always, she was "overcome with pity".[178]

They met again several times. One day Lawrence told Jessie he had refused an invitation to lunch from his former professor of French, whom he had consulted about a possible lectureship at a German university.[179] A few days later, meeting Jessie in Nottingham, he told her he would have to go after all, Mrs Weekley having written—"I can't refuse the lady." He lunched with the Weekleys somewhere between 14 and 21 March. Meeting him as arranged after the lunch, Jessie found him intrigued by his hostess, whom he described, looking slightly puzzled, as "modern German".[180] On 17 April, in a letter to Garnett, Lawrence was singing the praises of "the woman of a lifetime" with whom he was to elope to Germany in May.[181]

This brings to a close the long and troubled chapter of Lawrence's youthful loves. Delighted by the early pages of the new version of Sons and Lovers, Jessie was soon "bewildered and dismayed" by his treatment of their own relationship: she realized that this was a death-blow to the long friendship which had meant so much to her. She had naïvely credited him with super-human powers of detachment, whereas in fact the bond with his mother remained so strong that to Lawrence any approach to Jessie involved a sense of disloyalty to his mother. He continued to send her the manuscript, the final instalment of which she read some time in March. After several unhappy meetings with a "defensive" Lawrence, who "knew what he had done" but was "powerless to help himself", Jessie, "unable to speak about it", handed him her written observations on the book. They met for the last time by chance at her sister's cottage, a few days before he left for Germany. He had lost the desperate look of the past months, but, for once, was tongue-tied. They parted "like casual acquaintances" and in June he wrote from Germany to tell Jessie, in the strictest confidence, of his new attachment.[182]

The following winter, at the suggestion of Edward Garnett, Jessie related in simple novel form the long and painful story of her youth, hoping by so doing to free herself for ever of the past. This novel, Eunice Temple, she sent to Garnett, who thought Lawrence ought to see it; from certain "bits" she noticed later in The Rainbow, it seemed to Jessie he had indeed read it. In 1913 she received a remarkably obtuse letter in which he spoke of "the ups and downs" of his life with Frieda, adding that they "discussed her endlessly" and would like her to come out to them some time if she would care to. Used as she was to "shocks and blows" from Lawrence, Jessie felt the time had come to break off completely. At the suggestion of her sister May, she sent Lawrence's letter back to him. Determined to sever every remaining link between them, she then destroyed her own novel and, as far as she possibly could, "every line of his writing" she possessed.[183]

To Louie he addressed several amiable notes from Germany and Austria before, "feeling like a beast", he confided from Gargnano that he was "living here with a lady whom I love". To the confession he added a partial lie: "I never deceived you, whatever—or did I deceive you? I may have done even that. I have nothing to be proud of."[184]

Helen Corke was kept in ignorance of Lawrence's new adventure, of which she learnt from Jessie, when, in the course of a journey they made together in Germany in 1913, Helen suggested they might visit him in Bavaria.[185]

His liaison with Alice Dax seems to have continued until the last moment. In February, Lawrence sent successively to Helen Corke and Mrs Dax a number of *The Hibbert Journal* on Bergson, in which he was particularly interested. In February and again in March he was at Shirebrook, staying with Mr and Mrs Dax, a visit of which there may be echoes in the scene of *Sons and Lovers* where Paul reconciles Clara with her husband.

The secret of this long liaison was well kept by those directly concerned, as well as by the few Eastwood intimates who knew of it. Some time after the publication of the novel Alice Dax wrote to Jessie Chambers: "I have read *Sons and Lovers* and I *swear* it is not true."[186] Jessie believed her. Yet Alice told a friend that Lawrence had at one time, possibly as late as 1912, wanted her to go away with him. She had refused to leave husband and son. A letter she wrote to Frieda Lawrence in 1935 from Enid Hilton's house after reading *Not I, but the Wind* . . . confirms the extent to which the love scenes between Paul and Clara were based on reality, and suggests that only Lawrence's meeting with Frieda brought this liaison to an end:

> I have always been glad that he met you, even from the day after the event, when he told me about you, and I knew that he would leave me. I was never *meet* for him and what he liked was not the *me* I was, but the *me* I might-have-been—the potential me which would never have struggled to life but for his help and influence . . . I fear that he never even enjoyed morphia with me—always it carried an irritant—we were never, except for one short memorable hour, whole: it was from that hour that I began to see the light of life.[187]

5

EARLY WORKS

W e have until now considered Lawrence's work only in so far as it contributes to our knowledge of his psychological development. The moment has now come when his early works can be studied not so much as finished products, but rather from the angle of what may be called the creative dynamics of their content. This implies an attempt to discover subtle links between the artist's creative self and the artefact, and to trace the processes by which the latter, emerging from the writer's living experience, comes to embody certain ideas which in turn will not only shape the man's destiny and character, but also start on an independent life of their own.

The writer's early work comprises three novels, a considerable number of short stories, two plays and many poems. Lawrence begins a story, leaves it aside for a period of months or years, returning to it if he sees a chance of publication.[1] Dissatisfied with a first version, he would rewrite it from beginning to end, often under the influence of entirely new ideas, completely transforming its meaning. This is also true of the novels: *The White Peacock* was rewritten three times between 1906 and 1910;[2] *The Trespasser* at least twice, between March 1910 and January 1912;[3] *Sons and Lovers*, begun in 1910, was recast in 1911, and revised in Germany and Italy in the course of 1912.[4] Like the short stories collected and published in the volume entitled *The Prussian Officer and Other Stories*, this novel bears the mark of the new phase in Lawrence's life and of the corresponding important changes in his thinking and behaviour. The greatest caution is therefore necessary in trying to draw from these works any exact conclusions as to the writer's state of mind at any given moment. Wherever possible, reference should be made to the earliest version known and available.

I. EARLY SKETCHES

At least three stories date from the time of his very earliest attempts at writing. In December 1907 a Nottingham newspaper offered a prize of three guineas for the best Christmas story: Lawrence at once wrote three but, since only one could be entered in his name, he asked Jessie and Louie to submit the other two stories, each under her own name. The story submitted by Jessie, "A Prelude to a Happy Christmas",[5] won the prize, which was immediately handed over to its real author. A simple scene of life at Haggs Farm at Christmas time, the principal charm of this rough sketch lies in its exact yet whimsical description of persons and things. Some preoccupation is already visible with the social difference between the rich, cultured and elegant heroine and the young farmer she consents to marry. There is something indefinably feminine about the whole atmosphere, presaging that of his first novel, and it is to *The White Peacock* "cycle" that "A Prelude" undoubtedly belongs.

Lawrence himself submitted "A Fragment of Stained Glass", which subsequently appeared, in what Jessie Chambers is sure was an entirely rewritten version, in *The English Review* of September 1911 and, once more considerably retouched, in the 1914 collection.[6] The final revision certainly eliminated much of the repetitiousness as well as the many naïvetés and clichés of the earlier version, but a fair amount of redundancy and clumsiness remains. The story, inspired by an old local chronicle, is read to the author by a clergyman friend. A serf, who has avenged himself on his master by arson, is fleeing through snow and cold to the forest haunts of Robin Hood, accompanied by the miller's daughter who is in love with him. They are stopped by the gleams of the illuminated stained-glass window of a chapel; the girl urges him to try to catch a piece of the faery red fire. The man climbs up the face of the window and, breaking it, falls back blood-smeared to the earth, clutching only a poor fragment of rough black stone, but which shines in the sunlight like a drop of blood.

Though complicated, the symbolism is quite clear: man must strive to conquer the imagination of the woman he loves: while she, exacting and insatiable, drives the lover to the gates of death to satisfy her selfish and fanciful demands. Was Lawrence already trying to say this in 1907? It seems doubtful. His original intention was more likely to write a local and historical piece; the clumsy archaic style (perhaps owing something to Scott and even Chaucer) and the opening artifice, probably inspired by Flaubert's "Légende de Saint Julien l'Hospitalier", both point to a simple literary exercise, to which a symbolic interpretation was added at a later date.

"The White Stocking", Lawrence's third competiton entry, was an idealized picture of his mother as a young girl going to a ball at Nottingham Castle and drawing out a long white stocking in mistake for a pocket handkerchief.[7]

The earliest version of "Goose Fair", although Jessie Chambers did not remember Lawrence speaking of it until the publication of *The English Review* version of February 1910, seems to date from the same period as these

first three stories.[8] The 1914 version also varies considerably from that in
The English Review. Again primarily a literary exercise, reminiscent in some
respects of Maupassant and Flaubert, it is also a period piece: Nottingham's
famous Goose Fair in the autumn of 1871, during the crisis in the lace and
knitted-goods trade caused by the Franco-Prussian war. Unemployment had
led to violence; factories were burned down and it was even whispered that
certain manufacturers, tempted by high insurance benefits, might not have
been entirely innocent.

But these events are only the background against which the main story is
played out. Lois Buxton, daughter of a rich industrialist, is engaged to
William Selby, whose father, a lace manufacturer, is a self-made man, with
limited financial reserves, whose business suffers from the slump. Lois tries
in vain to persuade William to stay for dinner, but he makes off on the
pretext that duty calls him to the factory as, in these troubled times, anything
may happen. In the night the factory burns to the ground. William fails to
reappear and while Lois imagines him dying heroically in defence of his
property, she reads in her father's heavy silence a tacit accusation against the
Selbys. The next morning she learns that William has spent the night in gaol
for molesting a goose-girl and her flock in the company of the merry gang
of comrades he had been so eager to rejoin! The girl's anguish turns to cold
condemnation and near triumph: she now has the upper hand.

The text as revised in *The Prussian Officer* eliminates those traits which
made Lois a romantic figure "stilling her sighs" and half in love with tragedy.
Instead the emphasis is on the struggle between the sexes, and the "bitter
contempt" of the young man forced to submit to her on account of his ruin
and the discovery of his lie.

The construction of the story remains poor: it opens *à la* Maupassant with
a long portrait of the goose-girl, who then completely disappears for a dozen
pages. Nor has all trace of naïveté been eliminated from the final version,
from which it is clear, for instance, that Lawrence's idea of "a superior culture"
is still very limited.

The White Peacock

Nevertheless both "Goose Fair" and "A Fragment of Stained Glass" show an
attempt at objectivity, an exercise on historical and local data as far removed
as possible from the writer's own experience. Nothing suggests that the
literary device which consists in distilling from events a philosophical
meaning linked with the author's personal preoccupations dates from the
first version rather than from 1910–11. The master work of this period, *The
White Peacock*, shows the writer's first timid attempts to introduce himself
into his work, as he begins to formulate his problems and trace back to their
deep-seated origins the difficulties of his adjustment to life.

Lawrence told Jessie that he had put the whole of himself into his novel.[9] This perhaps explains why his intentions are often difficult to unravel. So dense a work is impossible to summarize, atmosphere being at least as important as the story. There is however a central plot which serves to guide the reader through the maze.

Lettie Beardsall, whose social situation remains somewhat vague (she has been to university, and her mother appears to be a person of modest independent means), is engaged to Leslie Tempest, son of the great Erewash mine-owner. She is also carrying on a flirtation with George Saxton, a dreamy and irresolute farmer. Hesitant, mostly inarticulate, the young man cannot bring himself to speak or act at the right moment to win the flighty Lettie, who is far from insensitive to his manly beauty and his love. He lets her marry the insignificant Leslie and falls back on courting and marrying his cousin Meg, granddaughter and heiress to the landlady of the Ram Inn. For some time George maintains friendly relations with Lettie, who becomes a narrow, dictatorial, self-centred bourgeois wife, transferring on to her children her own disappointed hopes. He "goes" socialist, leads a polite political campaign against Leslie and continues to cultivate his mind, but in the end he gives up completely. Unhappily married, despising his wife, a stranger to his own children, out of place and at sea in the modern world, he seeks oblivion in alcohol, finally sinking into delirium tremens.

The story is told by Cyril, Lettie's brother, a friend of George and of his sister Emily. Cyril is Lawrence himself. Lettie, at least in the early chapters, is a close portrait of his sister Ada, one of whose names was in fact Lettice. Emily recalls Jessie Chambers, and George her brother Alan. Strelley Mill, their farm, is the Haggs, transplanted some 200 yards from the original. All the other characters are taken from Lawrence's own immediate background. As Bert was not personally acquainted with the mine-owners, he installed in their mansion, under the name of Leslie, his own friend George Neville.[10] The major part of the book is taken up by a series of pictures of life in the Eastwood neighbourhood: the farm, the mutual visiting between the younger generation, the family life of the Beardsalls – a much idealized version of that of the Lawrences minus the father – the conversations, the allusions to the university, walks through the woods, all these stem directly from the author's everyday experience.

The idealization consists mainly in raising the social status of the characters, no doubt corresponding to Leslie's elevated rank and, perhaps, the author's secret aspirations. There are beflannelled picnics; private dances (perhaps glorified versions of one once organized by Bert at Walker Street);[11] endless discussions on art, literature and music. Only an occasional passing reference evokes the existence of the near-by pits and the men who work in them.[12] But the reality underlying this transfiguration is to be found at every step: the mother who cannot forgive Cyril his ambiguous friendship with Emily;[13]

Mrs Lawrence's old piano;[14] life and work on the farm; innumerable
detailed traits of character and background that give the book that psychological truthfulness that is one of its main merits. More often than not the
author sees life with a fresh, accurate and penetrating eye.

Lawrence's starting-point seems to have been the conviction that a novel
should above all describe the middle classes and the aristocracy. It was to be
some time before he began to give an unembellished picture of his own
immediate surroundings. The plot summarized above was thus a purely
conventional framework which he proceeded to fill in gradually with
descriptive matter and episodes designed to extract a symbolic meaning.[15]
It is interesting to note that in the original manuscript George married Lettie,
abandoned by Leslie. In the final version Lettie gives herself to Leslie before
marriage,[16] but marries him almost despite this and partly out of pity. This
change seems to correspond to Lawrence's contemporary discovery that
"it is the man who needs the woman, and who suffers when she will not
have him".[17]

The intrinsic banality of the love story itself is in contrast with two incidents
which, at first sight, might appear almost superfluous. There is no obvious
aesthetic justification for the introduction of either the father or the gamekeeper: it seems due to a renewed access of realism, combined with the
author's effort to give significance to the novel. It is as if Lawrence, unable or
unwilling to state an explicit view of life, had chosen to draw attention to its
unpleasant aspects by an accumulation of disturbing facts.

Beardsall, who had long since abandoned his family, returns to die in the
neighbourhood, leaving a small legacy to his children. Cyril and his mother
attend the funeral.[18] This estranged father is clearly John Arthur Lawrence,
slightly raised in social status. If Lawrence found it necessary to include him
in this work of fantasy, it was no doubt in order to sound, at the beginning
of the novel, a note which is taken up and amplified towards the end: George
Saxton, too, will live in isolation in the midst of his own children who
despise his vulgar drunken habits. Man, in fact, vowed to solitude, is excluded
from the closed circle formed by the mother and her offspring. If we except
Mr Saxton, who plays a sympathetic but minor role, Lawrence seems unable
to imagine normal, affectionate relations between a father and his family. Or,
indeed, between a husband and a wife: George and Meg, Leslie and Lettie
are no more capable of mutual understanding than were the Beardsalls.
Lettie keeps her distance from a husband who "does not seem real to her"
and whom she treats as a retainer whose very devotion is repaid by increased
scorn.[19] Marriage is less a duet than a duel; and victory is always to the
strong, that is to say the woman, whose alliance with her children makes her
a formidable enemy.[20]

The woman, whose children are a mere projection of her own ego, tends
with all her being towards the purely selfish goal of social advancement.

Lettie marries a rich man, without really loving him; even simple Meg presses good manners upon her children, dresses opulently and dominates her "ruffled and dejected" husband.[21] Elegance, distinction, riches, these are the feminine ideal, together with the satisfaction of the powerful urge towards maternity. The man is no more than the instrument for the realization of these ambitions and desires, at the most a privileged type of servant.[22] He, for his part, requires of the woman no more than the satisfaction of his sexual instincts which she rejects, preferring her lover's soul and mind:

> A woman is so ready to disclaim the body of a man's love; she yields him her own soft beauty with so much gentle patience and regret, she clings to his neck, to his head and his cheeks, fondling them for the soul's meaning that is there, and shrinking from his passionate limbs and his body.[23]

And once she has her children, and her position is assured, it only remains for the man to keep quiet or, if he causes her embarrassment, to disappear. Thus civilization, or progress towards an ever-higher social standing, runs the risk of completely suppressing the very instinct which drives a man towards a woman and renders her desirable to him. And his sex is driven underground into a zone of scarcely admissible physical need.

In this novel, the problem is not, of course, presented in such abstract form, but is conveyed entirely by suggestion, by action, and by an occasional and still enigmatic half-admission. But Lawrence insists strongly on the rights of nature and of natural instincts. And right through this would-be refined society, in a novel mistakenly thought by several critics to have been written by a woman,[24] runs a streak of brutality, almost as if already love and suffering were inseparable in the author's mind. Already in the second version of "A Fragment of Stained Glass" the love scenes had a taste of blood and tears. The serf, master groom in the manor stables, has been kicked on the mouth by a vicious horse and at his first kiss the reopened wound brings tears to his own eyes, while blood from his lips smears the maiden's mouth; blood flows again, though less profusely, in the final version, when he grasps his fragment of stained glass. In the snow the bloodstained lover and the red-haired girl "swoon together"; with eyes, cheeks and hair wet with tears he clasps his mistress in the final scene.[25] In *The White Peacock*, violence rears its head as early as the second chapter, where the Saxtons find one of their cats caught in a snare and George is forced to put the poor creature out of its agony. The daily life of the farm is constantly bringing home to Leslie, whom it shocks, to Cyril, who seems to find in it some strange enjoyment, and to the girls, who protest against the inevitable, the physical realities of birth and death. George "feeling the gristles" of the red heifer to see when she will calve;[26] the rabbit hunt, in which the great brute of a man, armed with a rake, throws himself passionately upon the "little mite of a rabbit", warm, brown and palpitating, yet in a second lying dead and bleeding. Blood again becomes the symbol of sexual instinct when a red gash across George's thumb makes Lettie cling almost convulsively to his outstretched hand.[27]

The gamekeeper Annable is both sum and symbol of this primitive vitality, of nature's ironic indifference towards the veneer with which civilization cloaks the brute in man. His profession predestines him to assume this symbolic value, for of all country dwellers the gamekeeper is closest to nature in the raw, to those animals which must at once be protected, killed and propagated. Lawrence's marked interest in gamekeepers cannot however be explained entirely by the contrast between their robust animal nature and his own overcivilized, intellectualized debility. It is possible that they called into play his sensitivity over social class. The question of trespassing in certain parts of High Park Woods belonging to the mine-owner's family was evidently a thorny one. One day when he was a pupil-teacher Lawrence and one or two companions were accosted by young Philip Barber, who ordered them off his property. When one of them tried to reply, he was called a "young counter-jumper", to Lawrence's intense humiliation.[28] On another occasion, when gathering primroses in Annesley Woods, Lawrence, then about seventeen, his sister Ada, Jessie Chambers and her brothers, were obliged by a burly gamekeeper to give their names and addresses, to throw away their flowers and to leave the woods. Lawrence was "white-faced and still" with shame.[29] This would seem to be the origin of the scene described below, for neither Mrs Clarke nor Jessie remembered any other encounter between Lawrence and a gamekeeper. It may well be that Lawrence resented the unwarranted authority wielded by such crude types over his own doings; at the same time, perhaps, unconsciously inclined to admire them as representatives of power and riches as well as the guardians of nature and its secrets of life and death. Richard Jefferies may also have inspired certain characteristics of the Lawrentian gamekeeper.

Annable's first appearance is extremely violent: two blows of his fists send George and Cyril reeling to the ground in an incident over a rabbit snare. Another time, coarse and sardonic, he breaks in upon Lettie and Leslie, Cyril and Emily, seated in a flowery glade among the trees, discoursing on eternal truths. He apologizes when he recognizes Leslie, and begins to speak with pride of his woman and his "brats", his "pretty little bag of ferrets", offering the two young couples some very unlooked-for advice:

> Be a good animal, says I, whether it's man or woman. You, Sir, a good natural male animal; the lady there,—a female un—that's proper—as long as you enjoys it.[30]

Cyril soon becomes friends with this odd character, attracted by his magnificent physique, his misanthropy, his belief in the decadence of humanity and his contagious pessimism.[31] One evening, in an abandoned churchyard by a ruined church, Annable tells Cyril the story of his life.[32]

His father was a big cattle-dealer, whose bankruptcy interrupted the son's Cambridge studies; he had to leave the university and take orders. As curate in a rich country parish, he was inveigled into proposing marriage to the rector's cousin, Lady Crystabel, in romantic circumstances expressly arranged by her to catch him. She gave him a living on her estates and her Hall became their home until the day when she grew tired of him. She refused to have children, fell in love with a poet and despised her husband as her "animal, son bœuf". After a year of such treatment he went off, ostensibly to Australia, where he was supposed to have died. Crystabel remarried. Annable became a gamekeeper, married a woman of the people and learned to become "a good animal", proudly producing a fine brood of healthy children. Yet he retains a nostalgia for things of the mind. A feeling of fatality overcomes him on learning of the death of his first wife. No one can be sure whether his own death, shortly afterwards, is due to a poacher's act of vengeance, to an accident, or even to some sort of suicide. He is found in the quarry, crushed by fallen rock: the typical miner's death, yet another touch of realism.[33]

Jessie Chambers remembered that Annable "did not appear in any shape or form in the first writing of The White Peacock" and was no more than crudely indicated in the second draft. Only in the third was he fully worked out. His first appearance shocked Jessie, but Lawrence insisted that Annable must be there as a contrast, and she felt from his manner that Annable was a vexed and difficult problem to him.[34] While one detail of his story is taken from Octave Feuillet's Roman d'un jeune homme pauvre,[35] its main source appears to be an incident borrowed from George Moore's Esther Waters. Jessie's testimony fully confirms the internal evidence of the novels:

> During the final writing of the latter part of the story L. sent Esther Waters to me, and told me that George Moore became a groom in order to pick up the "local colour". About the same time he sent me Evelyn Innes and Sister Teresa and was extremely enthusiastic over the former.[36]

From Esther Waters, too, Lawrence seems to have borrowed the local colour of the public-house (not, according to Jessie, figuring in the first two versions) and stable scenes (George sets up as a horse-breeder). Esther Waters and her husband, William Latch, having formerly been servants in the establishment of a rich horse-breeder, keep a public-house in London. It was there that William had met his first wife, his master's niece, who took him as her lover and, when this was discovered, married him. After a period of travelling, he tires of being no more than the instrument of the aristocratic lady's pleasure. He would like to have children and regrets Esther Waters by whom he has previously had a son. His wife takes up with a dubious group of artists and is unfaithful to him with a young man of her own class. William leaves her to return to Esther.[37]

Nor does Lawrence's debt end there: in the churchyard where Cyril listens to Annable's adventures, a white peacock alights on the head of an old carved angel, and "showing the full wealth of its tail" in the moonlight "glimmers like a stream of coloured stars" around the angel's face, simultaneously fouling the statue with its excrement. Annable at once sees in this bird the image of woman: "all vanity and screech and defilement".[38] On the last page of *Esther Waters*, the heroine and her former mistress, now her friend, walking in an overgrown garden near the ruined stables, come upon a solitary peacock lamenting the loss of its mate:[39] symbolic, too, no doubt, in Moore, but only of the sad note on which the story closes. In a similar setting probably taken from real life (there was an abandoned churchyard not far from Underwood), the peacock becomes the symbol of Lawrence's deep disturbance when faced with woman's dual nature: high aspirations and low bestiality. The scene subsequently assumed such significance in his eyes that he took from it the title for his book. Thus Lawrence would take up suggestions contained in the work of other writers, supplementing his own still inadequate experience, at the same time trying to blend all the elements together into a new and personal synthesis. Here we see him forcefully, if clumsily, transforming an image gathered from George Moore into something completely new. From the story of William Latch he extracts a more precise, if narrower, meaning, by insisting on Annable's detestation of *the lady*.[40]

The gamekeeper's story thus brings out the idea of the passionate brutality of life, as well as Lawrence's reaction against that ideal of spirituality and refinement he attributes to women, simultaneously accused, for no apparent reason, of soiling true and spontaneous passion.

An undercurrent of apprehension of woman runs almost throughout the book. No other theme is so insistent, and its predominance is confirmed by the title, making the vainglorious bird the symbol of the whole meaning of the book.

The sexes are at war: has humanity then lost some vital secret? Such is the question Lettie asks herself as she fingers the sad and mysterious snowdrops, "dim, strange flecks among the dusky leaves", symbols of some wisdom forgotten by humanity.[41]

Cyril denies that man has lost anything of value, but nothing in his behaviour, except perhaps his friendship with the gamekeeper, suggests that he possesses the lost secret so haunting to his sister.

The tragedy of George implies a reply to Lettie's question: humanity has strayed from the path of primitive simplicity: the endless adjustments required by modern conditions prohibit a way of life in which consciousness is reduced to a minimum and instinct is the surest guide to action. From the very beginning of the book George stands for the old rural world, dormant and close to nature. True son of Rousseau, he needs no watch to tell him it is time for dinner. But the education he acquires, stimulated by his love for a

woman "of superior culture", will rouse him from his slumbers, leaving him
half-civilized. Music, art, conversations with Cyril on chemistry, botany,
psychology, sex and its origins, Schopenhauer or William James, might
perhaps have given him some kind of happiness had the development of his
will kept pace with that of his intelligence. Failing this, George becomes one
of the wrecks of the modern world.

And around him crumble the foundations of an ancient culture: the old
farm no longer pays, the Saxtons emigrate to Canada, George becomes
successively milkman, publican, horse-breeder and gambler: a less and less
productive cog in the economic machine. He is rootless and torn from his
native earth. Without undue insistence, without a trace of theorizing,
simply by observing life around him, Lawrence here touches on one of the
gravest problems of his time, with all its distressing consequences on individual lives: the displacement of the centre of gravity of economic life, brought
about by progressively easier production of essential goods, and the consequent creation of leisure.

But *The White Peacock* is the work neither of an economist nor of a
sociologist: what preoccupies the author is the suffering of individuals.
Cyril's life in London does, however, represent the new civilization which
has come to replace that of the old agricultural era. We are shown something
of its wrecks, such as beggars on the embankment; crowds in search of
pleasure; the solitude of countless men and women torn from their roots;
but also the kaleidoscopic whirl of this new world which, while destroying
natural rhythms, creates new, broken, accelerated tempos of its own.[42]

All this goes to Cyril's head but does not stir him to action; the pleasure
he takes in this modern life is rather that of the artist who observes than that
of the man of action or the organizer. Suffering remains the dominant note
of the book: suffering in marriage and in love, in family and social relationships; the suffering of being severed from one's natural environment, torn
away from beloved places, the pain of departure, the disillusionment of
return. The titles of the chapters are heavy with foreboding: "A Shadow in
Spring", "The Irony of Inspired Moments", "The Dominant Motif of
Suffering", "The Scarp Slope", "A Prospect among the Marshes of Lethe";
such are the perspectives offered to the reader of *The White Peacock*.

The entire work is a poem of inevitable change, of the terrible and
poignant mutability of the universe, source of pain but also of ecstasy. Indeed,
beyond the general impression of despair (in which more than a little literature may perhaps be suspected, in particular an overdose of Schopenhauer)[43]
and an attempt at achieving a kind of *fin de siècle* art not yet quite played out
in 1910, the main impression left by this early work is an acute and lively
feeling for nature's passing beauties, doubly precious to the writer for their
very transience. It is a constant pleasure to reread his descriptions of the
sleeping valley, nature's careless prodigality, the sudden revelation of spring

heralded by a thousand secret signs, the rich harvest of September, the gorgeous reds and golds of autumn turning to "balls of rottenness" and death, the ruined church and abandoned graves, the great city with its vivid colours, strange lights and busy crowds.[44] Every page reveals some fresh and delicate note, an intimate knowledge of some unlooked-for aspect of wood and field: the string of green beads on the poplars; the golden saxifrage varnished by its minister, the snail; the last trembling ecstasy of the harebells falling before the scythe.[45] The unfolding of each flower is observed and described with a precision which might prove wearisome were the detail not invariably apt and touched with the poetry of natural beauty perceived afresh by the writer's sharp and loving eye.

Lawrence weaves a web of threads between nature and his characters, or rather the problems with which they are obsessed: the snowdrops become mysterious symbols of primitive creation, of nature's closely-guarded secret of happy fecundity; the repeated complaint of the peewit is a cry of anguish and despair.[46] Birds and flowers speak magically of a world of poetry, the playground of supernatural forces far superior to our vain human flutterings. Certain rare moments of supreme harmony culminate in ecstasy. When George and Cyril walk together in the fields, the rhythmic movements of their bodies, their shared friendship, the wheeling birds, merge into one of those miraculous moments when the individual is one with the whole universe:

> I took a fork and scattered the manure along the hollows, and thus we worked, with a wide field between us, yet very near in the sense of intimacy. I watched him through the wheeling peewits, as the low clouds went stealthily overhead. Beneath us, the spires of the poplars in the spinney were warm gold, as if the blood shone through. Further gleamed the grey water, and below it the red roofs. Nethermere was half hidden, and far away. There was nothing in this grey, lonely world but the peewits swinging and crying, and George swinging silently at his work. The movement of active life held all my attention, and when I looked up, it was to see the motion of his limbs and his head, the rise and fall of his rhythmic body, and the rise and fall of the slow waving peewits.[47]

But such joys are short-lived; soon the inexorable law of change and decay will separate the friends, sending Cyril to his new life in London and George to his sad destiny. For this, Lawrence blames civilization, but without any attempt at rising to a philosophy of eternal change; his poetic vision remaining subjective and restricted, concentrated on the two or three essential problems which constitute the kernel of his thought. As an antidote to a modern world too harsh for tender natures, glimmers the back-to-the-land illusion of Arcadian happiness. The schoolmistress, Emily, marries a farmer and finds in the daily life of the farm, with a good and simple man, her place in the universal order of things. Of all the characters in the novel, she alone is happy: "she has escaped from the torture of strange, complex, modern life".[48] Soon she will be a mother. And Cyril, "living his life" in London, is distressed by a feeling of "ephemerality and fragility" in the presence of this incarnation of continuity and natural harmony. Faced with the mystery of womanhood, he feels nostalgia and a sense of envy.[49]

Thus the various motifs are intertwined, linked and developed in Lawrence's first full-length work. It would be possible to show in detail how he projects into each of the characters certain traits of his own personality: to George he gives his indecision; to Lettie his nostalgia, his tendency to play-acting; to Cyril his ambiguous attitude to woman, his artistic talent.[50]

His own youthful problems have found expression in this first novel: his social uprooting, his apprehension and hesitation when faced with the necessity to adjust to change, and the unresolved problem of his relationship to women, which, combined with his complex social problems, casts a shadow of gloom over the whole work.

Other qualities are evinced: a keen understanding of the perturbations which modern life entails for innocent people; a sense of the poetry of life; the ability to enjoy fugitive beauty. The writer's ego is ever-present in this book. But that ego does not yet openly occupy the whole stage: it pervades the scene without obtruding itself, it seeks objective forms of self-expression. Though not yet fully self-aware, by probing around certain elements of his plot, he has already uncovered two great Lawrentian themes: that of civilization versus instinct, and that of woman, wife and mother, as opposed to man, son and lover. *The White Peacock*, like the Lawrence of 1910–12, is a rich and seething mass of often contradictory emotions and ideas, impossible to fuse into a harmonious whole because the writer's own personality is made up of such contradictions, much in the same way as the fleeting themes of a modern symphony oppose and succeed one another to the end, no single theme emerging finally triumphant: its modernity lies in the sincerity and contradictions of the artist.

II. THE TRESPASSER

Lawrence's earliest works showed an effort to build on a basis of objective facts. In relation to purely descriptive scenes, plot and setting play an important role. Clearly the novelist sought to cast his experience in a formal mould. But his personality overflows the mould to the point of making it unrecognizable. The essential merit of *The White Peacock* springs precisely from the true lyricism of his poetic nature. Whenever he allows himself to forget his awkward affectations, his culture and his polished manners (all of which, incidentally, throw interesting light on some aspects of the working-class intelligentsia of the time), whenever he reveals without bravado or false shame the things he loved: work on the farm, talk and play with George, philosophical walks with Emily, the subtlest shades of nature, in short, whenever his spontaneous self appears beneath the veneer of the new-fledged "gentleman", then indeed Lawrence charms his readers. All that is best in *The White Peacock* is also to be found in the poems he was writing at this time.

With *The Trespasser* the theme he tackled was more simple: a true-life story, the heroine of which provided him with both a plot and, to some extent, its interpretation.[51] The subject was perhaps more suited to a short story than a novel: a violinist spends a week's holiday with a girl pupil, returns to his wife and children, and perceiving their unconcealed contempt for him after this escapade, hangs himself. The notes on which Lawrence based the 300 pages of his novel take up no more than thirty-two pages in Helen Corke's later version of the story, *Neutral Ground*.[52] Yet all the main data were already there: the journey to the Isle of Wight, the evenings in the cottage where the lovers stay; their bathes and seashore explorations; sunscorched and moonlit walks; Helena's emotion at the carved Christ on his cross in a Catholic graveyard; their anguish at the thought of the morrow; the last goodbye on Wimbledon station; Helena's departure to complete her holiday in Cornwall; her anxiety at not receiving a letter; the news of the suicide in the evening paper; Helena's illness and delirium. Everything, even the smallest incident such as an electric light bulb found unbroken on the seashore or a misshapen invalid in his bathchair,[53] passes directly from Helen's notes into Lawrence's novel.

Lawrence's role has been above all to amplify and develop the original. If we except Sections I and XXXI, a prologue and epilogue in which Lawrence, under the name of Byrne, appears in his self-appointed role of bringing back to earth this new Persephone, and Section XXX, a second epilogue showing how Siegmund was soon forgotten by his family, and how his widow used this tragedy to impress her lodgers—the remaining 260 pages of the book are an expansion of the story of Helena and Siegmund.

The amplification consisted mainly in extracting from Helen Corke's diary, already very consciously "literary", anything that was likely to throw light on the characters and the causes of their tragedy. Every incident assumes symbolic value; no detail is allowed to remain insignificant. Hence the sense of strain and exaggeration when the book is read from beginning to end, whereas in small doses it is not without poetic charm.

A single extract will show how surely and sensitively Lawrence was able to draw from Helen's brief indications their full psychological and poetic meaning:

> We find a safer shore. Three children are here, searching for treasures. Domine gives them an electric bulb, which he has found, unbroken, in a little sea-weedy pool.[54]

From this short jotting of the diary, Lawrence draws the following:

The tide was creeping back. Siegmund stooped, and from among the water's combings, picked up an electric-light bulb. It lay in some weed at the base of a rock. He held it in his hand to Helena. Her face lighted with a curious pleasure. She took the thing delicately from his hand, fingered it with her exquisite softness.

"Isn't it remarkable!" she exclaimed joyously. "The sea must be very, very gentle—and very kind."

"Sometimes," smiled Siegmund.

"But I did not think it could be so fine-fingered," she said. She breathed on the glass bulb till it looked like a dim magnolia bud; she inhaled its fine savour.

"It would not have treated *you* so well," he said. She looked at him with heavy eyes. Then she returned to her bulb. Her fingers were very small and very pink. She had the most delicate touch in the world, like a faint feel of silk. As he watched her lifting her fingers from off the glass, then gently stroking it, his blood ran hot; he watched her, waited upon her words and movements attentively.

"It is a graceful action on the sea's part," she said. "Wotan is so clumsy— he knocks over the bowl, and flap-flap-flap go the gaping fishes, *pizzicato*!— But the sea . . ."

Helena's speech was often difficult to render into plain terms. She was not lucid . . .[55]

They come across three children on the beach, and Siegmund, to whom Helena has handed back the bulb, gives it to a little girl and falls to thinking of his own favourite youngest daughter, Gwen. A thin glass bubble has served to reveal two characters: the lovers have been first drawn closer, then separated by this trifling incident which serves to bring home to them their destiny.

But this method leads Lawrence into an unceasing and therefore too-elaborate effort of revelation of his two characters, who not only are momentarily living in a social vacuum but who do not even provide the spectacle of happy and triumphant love.[56]

In several tortured and obscure scenes[57] he makes an interesting attempt to study the mutual reactions of their two personalities; to analyse hour by hour, and even minute by minute, the changing and therefore inevitably contradictory[58] feelings of each of the lovers. There is, however, no perspective to allow our impressions to become organized into any sort of overall view of these two persons, their natures and their relationship. The superabundance of analysis and symbolism too often destroys direct perception of the psychology of Helena and Siegmund, no doubt in part because they were far from simple. Helena, in particular, could not be otherwise.

Glutted with literature, German romanticism and Wagnerian music, "preferring fancy to imagination",[58] she was incapable of seeing things with ordinary eyes. For her, the sound of the foghorn was Tristan's trumpet; pink convolvuli became fairy telephones; the rippling sunlight on the sea was the Rhine maidens spreading their bright hair to the sun.[59] Her nature was not passionate: clothing everything in fancy, she had little taste for reality, whether in the form of flowers, ships or love.[60] "Physically . . . she shrank from anything extreme. But psychically she was an extremist, and a dangerous one."[61] Giving herself to her fancies only,[62] little by little she led Siegmund to despair, if not to madness, impossible as it was to take possession of this nymph-like incarnation of the eternal female mystery, who dreamed of an ideal lover and awoke beside a man of flesh and blood.[63] Self-sufficient and careless as the sea, like the sea she spent her passions on herself, plunging into solitude all who would approach her.[64]

This portrait, developed by a long succession of small touches, by a cumulative process reminiscent of impressionist painting,[65] fits in pretty well with that given of herself by the author of *Neutral Ground*. But Lawrence certainly contributed something of his own. This solitude, this predisposition to a romanticism peopling the universe with creatures of fantasy, this hesitation before the ultimate acts of love, all this must have been the common ground on which Helen and "David" met—"*Neutral Ground*", as Helen Corke was to put it revealingly in the title of her novel. Certainly these traits accord with all we so far know of Lawrence. However important the role of Helen Corke in the drafting of the initial manuscript, it is clear that the shadow of the writer slipped in between the portrait and the model.

Into the portrait of Siegmund, quite apart from the purely external circumstances of his real-life model, Lawrence has put himself even more. The family life of the violinist tallies with the description given in Helen's manuscript.[66] It required little effort of the imagination for Lawrence to describe a lower-middle-class household and the state of mind of a husband and father lacking contact with his family, despised by his own children, conscious of an atmosphere of hostility rendering repentance impossible.[67] He was also all too familiar with the weakness and irresolution of the artistic temperament, only too willing to be guided by a woman, or by events.

But above all the lover so long kept at a distance by Helen, and finally accepted without warmth, seems to have increasingly become one with the violinist he was trying to describe. He writes his novel "almost mechanically", under the dictation of a "second consciousness":[68] as if hypnotized, he becomes the *Doppelgänger* of the first lover, who now haunts his thoughts; he is jealously aware that the shadow of Siegmund-Domine will always come between them. As Helen puts it, "Domine first, me second. The primitive part of me couldn't bear it."[69]

But as well as jealousy, there is a sort of identification with his model.

Married too young, revolted at thirty-eight by a vulgar wife and a slatternly household, Siegmund had found in Helena a sister-soul whose imagination could fire his own. But during their brief interlude she gives herself to him without passion, playing at love while he risks all, and he soon feels isolated and incapable of reintegrating himself into life through her. He knows it is the end. Lawrence has tried to make the reader understand Siegmund's suicide. He has not succeeded, because the reasons he gives are contradictory. On the one hand he suggests a kind of cerebral fever contracted by sleeping in the August sun.[70] At the same time he stresses the despair that drives Siegmund to death, but without relating it sufficiently to this physical cause, which therefore remains vague and superfluous. Siegmund kills himself because his escapade, like his marriage, had led nowhere: despite what he assures himself was complete amatory success. Against all reason, and almost in spite of himself, he "feels himself a failure as Helena's lover" and sinks into a feeling of irreparable defeat.[71] Is not this Lawrence substituting himself for Siegmund, whose despair and suicidal drive recall the poems Lawrence was writing at this time? The feeling of fatality always present in the mind of the violinist, the wheels of the train beating out the "Ride of the Walküre", the deep horror which grips him at the thought of Helena who wants "to explore him like a rock pool", the decision to die which comes to him in sleep,[72] all this brings to mind the Lawrence of 1911 and early 1912. The two images mingle and interact upon each other. The novelist attributes to Siegmund his own reasons for despair, and in him seems tempted to imitate his suicide.

Gradually there emerges, as the *leitmotif* of this symbolist tragedy, the idea that it is Helena who drives Siegmund, and with him the writer, towards death. Helena not only invites tragedy, but feeds on it like a Shakespearean witch. Her mind must always be occupied with presentiments, auguries, sinister suggestions which become rooted in the devitalized souls of her lovers.[73] But in this respect Siegmund is just as bad: he has "a preference of death",[74] and dwells on the thought of it with a kind of joy. The perverse tendencies already noticeable in Lawrence's earlier works here find full development. His Helena never touched anyone without hurting:

> She had a destructive force; anyone she embraced she injured. Faint voices echoed back from her conscience. The shadows were full of complaint against her. It was all true, she was a harmful force, dragging Fate to petty mean conclusions.[75]

As for the final scenes, the terrible deliberate preparation for the hanging, the discovery of the corpse, which has to be hauled down "from the door 'ooks" by a window cleaner, everything denotes an irresistible fascination with death.[76]

Further insistence on the parallels between Lawrence's feelings and the tenor of the story is unnecessary: the interaction of his own character and his subject is evident enough. It may perhaps be more profitable to point out the importance of Wagnerian music in this work, of which the chief protagonists are both musicians. Helen Corke and some of her musician friends probably revealed Wagner to Lawrence in the course of his rewarding London years. But the Wagnerian atmosphere may also be appropriately linked with the name of George Moore, particularly the Wagnerian evocations in Evelyn Innes.[77] Like Evelyn, Helena *lives* her Wagner; like Ulick Dean, the Irish composer who becomes the lover of the primadonna after the performance of *Tristan and Isolde*, Siegmund is driven by a feeling of some fatality separating him from Helena for ever. Down upon her knees, Evelyn plays the role of Brünnhilde in the reconciliation scene. On rising she is amazed to find not Wotan, but her dear old music-loving father. Similarly Helena is continually playing a role: Isolde or the Valkyrie; Siegmund, her symbolically named lover, is a Wagnerian hero for ever seeking his way with her through a mystic fog.[78] Through Wagner, through Maeterlinck,[79] and no doubt through George Moore, symbolism, with its chosen themes of tragic passion, fatality and heroes seeking their souls in the dim Twilight of the Gods, has penetrated *The Trespasser* and set upon it, more than upon any other work by Lawrence, the seal of a *fin de siècle* mood surviving in England until well after 1914.

One thing, however, Lawrence fails to borrow from the Irish writer, for while he tries to imitate the aristocratic negligence with which Moore scatters his pages with literary and artistic echoes (Lawrence's first two novels are studded with allusions to his recently-acquired culture), while he imitates from Moore the idea and even sometimes the style of the symbolist novel, he is far from possessing the same degree of audacity and detached candour in the portrayal of the love scenes. Lawrence is still swaddled in the stiff shyness of the working-class youth, for whom love is not an artistic and spontaneous expression of the self, but a dreaded mystery, wellnigh impossible to penetrate.

With *The White Peacock*, Lawrence might possibly still be taken for one of the innumerable authors whose simple stories, delicate sentiments and poetic descriptions of the English countryside have long delighted French mothers in quest of suitable reading for their daughters. Except for a few minor audacities of thought or of expression, mostly advanced by Annable and presumably added in the final version, the novel is completely anodyne. *The Trespasser* is a definite step forward, and with it its author takes his place among the great craftsmen of the English language. Into this work Lawrence has successfully absorbed the very essence of symbolism, and his descriptive talent is well set on the way to what were to prove his greatest triumphs, the fine counterpoint of the great natural rhythms leading to those rare and sublime moments when, finally united in perfect harmony, they reach consummate ecstasy. Helena lays her head on Siegmund's breast, watching the sea and listening to his heart-beats, so near and yet so far. Fascinated by the throbbing pulsations she asks herself whether there is not "deep in the world a great God thudding out the waves of life, like a great heart, unconscious".[80] Or again, the muffled sound of cannon saluting the Tsar at Osborne, the mounting tide, the roaring thud of the waves, the strong heaving warmth of Siegmund's passion, to Helena as wild and savage as the ocean: so many motifs blended and orchestrated with great skill.[81] This is pure Lawrence: all influences fused in a new and unique synthesis centred on personal impressions, all literary themes fully assimilated into direct observation of actual experience.

III. SHORT STORIES AND PLAYS 1910-12

The study of the short stories and two plays written by Lawrence at this time seems suitably placed at this point, between *The Trespasser* and *Sons and Lovers*. The former, by virtue of its subject and perhaps also of its style (which Lawrence seems to have tried without great success to render less "florid" and less *chargé* in his revision of 1912),[82] represents no more than an incident in Lawrence's literary career, whereas all the rest of his contemporary writing undoubtedly leads up to *Sons and Lovers*, the great achievement of his youth.

Lawrence was not anxious to publish *The Trespasser*: he feared that this work, judged "erotic", might harm his reputation.[83] When in June 1911 the publisher Martin Secker asked him for a volume of short stories, he replied that he had only six already written, but "several sketched out and neglected".[84] He set to work at once and his letters thereafter record the progress of the "Secker volume".[85] For the most part, the short stories considered in the present chapter would seem to have been written or revised in 1911 and early 1912. They are to be found in *The Prussian Officer and Other Stories* (1914) and in the posthumous volume *A Modern Lover* (1934),[86] in which an editor's note dates all six stories 1910-11. Some of the stories in both collections, which bear signs of later rewriting, are discussed in later chapters.[87] The precise dating of the 1910-12 stories being impossible, they are here grouped according to subject-matter.

As for the first of the two plays, Edward Garnett, who, in his introduction to *A Collier's Friday Night*, bases his dating on a pencilled marginal note by Lawrence, mistakenly calculates that the play was written in 1906 or 1907, for it was in November 1909 that Jessie Chambers was urgently called to Croydon to read it.[88] It also contains an allusion to "Letter from Town: Almond Tree", one of his own poems, obviously first written in Croydon,[89] and also to Francis Thompson's "Shelley", which appeared for the first time in the *Dublin Review* of 1908[90] and in volume form in London a year later.

The Widowing of Mrs Holroyd dates from 1911. Before being published in America in 1914, the play had been in Edward Garnett's hands for nearly two years, and the author had almost forgotten it when in August or September 1913 he hurriedly revised it immediately before printing.[91] A letter to the publisher indicates a number of changes which, even if they arrived in time, cannot have greatly affected the plot.[92] Neither of these two plays having been envisaged by him as theatrical innovations, but as realistic "slices of life", they can be considered together with the corresponding short stories, as part of the cycles linked to one or other of the Lawrentian themes of that period.

"The Witch à la Mode"[93] must be classed with *The Trespasser* in the "Helen cycle"; the same woman violinist wanders lost in the same "fog of symbols".[94] She is the modern witch whose incantations fascinate this hero, who asks nothing better than to be unfaithful with her to his Yorkshire fiancée. Annoyed at his own weakness, and even more irritated with this vampire whose passion always stops short at the preliminaries, he knocks down the lamp and flees after putting out the beginning of a fire. The themes are all familiar: the destructive force of this new *femme fatale*, the violence of the frustrated lover, the weakness of the man who burns himself against her flame like a moth against a candle. No doubt this story dates from the months when Lawrence was still seeking from Helen the satisfactions refused by his fiancée; he could not understand Helen's cold irony and the temptation to tantalize him by mocking his incredible marriage plans. The only thing that might suggest a later date or a rewriting is the unerring sureness of the narrative, and the firm precision of the style.

Nothing need be added to what has already been said of "A Modern Lover", a story clearly belonging to the "Jessie cycle", one of the richest and most significant.[95] To this cycle also belongs "The Fly in the Ointment",[96] a slight and unimportant story first published in 1913 in the *New Statesman*. A first approach to the problems of his relations with Jessie can be found in "Second Best" in *The English Review* for February 1912 and qualified by Lawrence as "a story I don't care for".[97] Frances, a farmer's daughter, returns from Liverpool where her friend Jimmy has become engaged to another, "now he's a Doctor of Chemistry". She falls back on a local peasant, Tom, whom she courts by killing a mole, no doubt to prove that she is not afraid of the facts of life. In the final version in *The Prussian Officer* volume, Lawrence has touched up the dialogue, and quickened the pace of the story. Less happy is the introduction into the last few lines of such phrases as "the blood came up in him, strong, overmastering", "a thrill of pleasure in this death", in contradiction with the characters as previously shown,[98] Tom, in particular, being an irresolute lover waiting for the woman to make the advances.

"The Soiled Rose" has become "The Shades of Spring" after a rehandling which completely modifies its meaning.[99] A young writer, John Adderley

Syson, married for some years, returns to visit the scene of his adolescence; he finds his friend Hilda engaged to marry a gamekeeper, whose mistress she confesses to have been since Syson's own wedding night. Syson suffers to see how completely he has succeeded in killing Hilda's love "at last, as he had often wished he could". She had been the guardian of his conscience; now he is alone, lost in the wide world (his wife apparently forgotten!):

> He began to count his losses. In spite of himself, he was unutterably miserable, though not regretful. He would not alter what he had done. Yet, he was drearily, hopelessly wretched. After a while he had got it clear.
>
> She always knew the best of me, and believed in the best I might be. While she kept her ideal "me" living, I was sort of responsible to her; I must live somewhere up to standard. Now I have destroyed myself in her, and I am alone, my star is gone out. I have destroyed the beautiful "me" who was always ahead of her, nearer the realities. And I have struck the topmost flower from off her faith. And yet it was the only thing to do, considering all the other folk . . .
>
> He lay quite still, feeling a kind of death.[100]

This and several similar passages, as well as many naïvetés, are suppressed in the 1914 edition. Now it is Syson who has been mistaken in Hilda; she, hard and arrogant, has never really loved him. He sees her at last for what she really is, as he had never previously been able to see her.[101] But this literary revenge upon his youthful sentiments is subsequent to the final break with Jessie.[102] When he wrote "The Soiled Rose" during his engagement to Louie, he was far from being so sure that he was not suffering from their first estrangement.

"A Modern Lover", "Second Best", "The Soiled Rose", all three raise the problem of the rival. He is invariably a simple, athletic man, usually a sturdy man of the soil, sometimes a gamekeeper. They also formulate a feeling of responsibility on the part of the hero towards the woman he has abandoned: the idea that she has suffered a wrong.[103] Syson, feeling it is his duty, comes to release from his influence the girl he loved and is somewhat piqued to find himself already replaced in her affections. This theme of jealousy is not present in "Second Best" where Jimmy does not appear; it is only briefly indicated in the momentary anxiety of Cyril Mersham at the sight of his rival in "A Modern Lover";[104] it grows in importance in "The Soiled Rose": Syson is jealous of the keeper who, in turn, is jealous of him.

Lawrence's family life furnished him with many subjects, all of which are grouped in *Sons and Lovers*. *A Collier's Friday Night* describes the uncouth manners of the collier; the splitting of the pay between the butties; the hostility of the mother and her children, Nellie the schoolmistress and Ernest the student, against the vulgar, drunken father; the friendship of Ernest Lambert and Maggie Pearson (another Jessie figure); the hatred of Mrs Lambert for the girl; the nastiness of Nellie and of Ernest's friends towards

Maggie, held responsible for all the student's peccadilloes; finally the return
of the drunken father, when his son almost comes to blows with him; the
implacable hold of the mother who weaves round the heart of her son a web
of pity and devotion. Every character in these realistic scenes is clearly
identifiable in Lawrence's immediate circle. Taken as a whole, the value of
this little sketch is photographic rather than dramatic, for while certain scenes,
as Edward Garnett pointed out, are forcefully presented,[105] their juxtaposition
is governed by no real necessity, unless it be by the character of Ernest; and
this character, in 1909, was too special a case, too involved in a network of
over-complex circumstances, to come across theatrically. The recent success
of this play on the stage corresponds to a change in the public's sense of
dramatic values, and to its psychological education by such books as *Sons and
Lovers*. A pure slice of life, the play contributed neither to drama, nor, once
Sons and Lovers is taken into account, to a better understanding of its author.
But it does prove that even in 1909 Lawrence was capable of producing a
realistic rendering of his own milieu.

A whole new series of realistic scenes culminating in *Sons and Lovers*
revolves around Lawrence's family, particularly his mother, and the colliers'
way of life. The theme of the mother's misalliance also links these creations
with those of the "Jessie cycle".

"Odour of Chrysanthemums"[106] begins with the description of a little
house (in reality that of Lawrence's aunt) near a branch railway leading to
Brinsley colliery.[107] Some of the details of its opening passages, such as the
conversation of Elizabeth Bates with her father, an engine driver who stops
his train outside the house to have a cup of tea, are pure concessions to reality
without any apparent relation to the subject of the story. The action begins
only on page five. On coming up from the pit, Walter Bates is in the habit of
slipping furtively past his own door to the pub. One evening his wife and
two children wait for him; it grows late; Elizabeth is sure he will soon be
carried home drunk. To the children she speaks harshly of their father before
putting them to bed. At eight o'clock she goes to a neighbour's house in
search of news of Walter. Rigley, the neighbour, has not seen him since the
close of work, when he had left him at the bottom "finishin' a stint".
Alarmed, the man goes off to find out what has happened. Back home,
Elizabeth waits anxiously, suddenly startled to hear the sound of the winding
engine at the pit at such an unaccustomed hour. Walter's old mother arrives
lamenting: there has been an accident. The body is brought in, quite
untouched; the gallery roof had caved in behind the miner, trapping and
asphyxiating him. The distraught mother, the wife dignified in her grief,
together wash the black coal-dust from the body. Elizabeth's heart bursts
with grief and pity for this man she had tried to wrest from his bad habits.
And suddenly Lawrence the schoolteacher breaks into Elizabeth's silent
soliloquy in quite characteristic contempt of artistic verisimilitude:

He had come from the discipleship of youth, through the Pentecost of adolescence, pledged to keep with honour his own individuality, to be steadily and unquenchably himself, electing his own masters and serving them till the wages were won. He betrayed himself in his search for amusement. Let Education teach us to amuse ourselves, necessity will train us to work. Once out of the pit, there was nothing to interest this man. He sought the public-house, where, by paying the price of his own integrity, he found amusement, destroying the clamours for activity, because he knew not what form the activities might take.[108]

Elizabeth is happy at the thought that her husband is restored to her free of any hideous and disfiguring wound. She loves him still despite their incessant quarrelling and deep discord.

Reading the text in *The English Review*, it is impossible not to see that Lawrence has expressed in this story his feelings on the death of his mother:

> He seemed to be dreaming back, half awake. Life with its smoky burning gone from him, had left a purity and a candour like an adolescent's moulded upon his reverie. His intrinsic beauty was evident now . . . It was grief unutterable to think that now all was over between them . . .[109]

The final version, the end of which is almost entirely rewritten, stresses only the harshness of Elizabeth, who reflects that she has never really known the husband now isolated in death, cold, inert, eternally remote.[110] She cannot weep for a body which to her signifies nothing but the abyss that had always separated her from him in life.[111]

The Widowing of Mrs Holroyd[112] is a dramatic adaptation of this story. Drunken and fickle, Holroyd is also jealous. His wife Lizzie, tired of the life he leads her, has a suitor, the young electrician Blackmore. The first act presents this situation: in the course of a long scene quite out of proportion to its importance and clearly introduced by Lawrence to justify Lizzie's behaviour, Holroyd brings home two drunken women. In the second act, Blackmore, a kind of guardian angel, brings the drunkard home. Holroyd drowses off, but suddenly wakes up to accuse the electrician and his wife of adultery. He tries to strike Blackmore but the latter trips him up and he goes sprawling into the yard, where he once more falls into a drunken stupor. They carry him to the kitchen sofa. Both wish him dead. Blackmore makes Mrs Holroyd promise that she and the children will go to live with him in Spain where he can get a job. The next day the collier is killed in the mine in the same circumstances as Bates. His wife is convinced it was suicide, and feels responsible. Had she not wished him dead, in connivance with the man she has agreed to take as lover? This does not, however, prevent her from tacitly agreeing to meet Blackmore the next day.

This is the first time we encounter in Lawrence this idea that the woman's wish has killed the husband: is it, perhaps, a heritage from *The Trespasser*? "He'd have come up with the others if he hadn't felt me murdering him," says Lizzie.[113] Lawrence has almost reached the point of denying accident altogether: a man's destiny is determined by some mysterious working of another's will, an idea he will explore more deeply and to which he constantly returns. Already Annable, George Saxton, Siegmund and Holroyd have all died semi-suicides, varying only in the degree to which purely physical forces contributed to their deaths.

Lawrence seems to have been seeking by this process to regain the spirit of the Greek tragedies, or at any rate that of Synge's *Riders to the Sea* which he admired to the point of calling it, in 1911, "about the genuinest bit of domestic tragedy, English" since Shakespeare.[114] The lamentations of the old mother seem to be a faint echo of the words of Maurya, towards the end of that play,[115] but here we find no trace of the verbal beauty of Synge, whose characters also possess a dignity worlds away from the platitudes proffered by Mrs Holroyd, Blackmore and the old woman. A discordant note of squalid realism is continually creeping in: arguments about money, the old woman's recriminations against Lizzie, the triteness of the mother's final words. And how far removed from Synge's original and poetical Anglo-Irish idiom is the rough Nottinghamshire speech! As for the theme of death caused by the wish of the two accomplices, Lawrence does not succeed in giving it the impact it might have made at the hands of a dramatist capable of creating a real atmosphere of horror and tragedy, in which anything becomes possible. Holroyd does not attract sympathy, and indeed never seems sufficiently sensitive for his suicide to seem even remotely plausible.

Lawrence's fundamental realism makes it impossible for him to abandon himself to the emotion his subject might have evoked. The writer could not escape the personality of his mother, a practical and unpoetical woman, and the real subject of both story and play is the marriage of Mrs Lawrence to a man "below" her, her life in a milieu she detested, her hatred for the father of her children. Her son fails to raise this subject to a universal level and to convey that feeling of real and profound fatality which is the stuff of tragedy.

The portrait of the proud and socially-displaced mother blends also with that of the fiancée who, abandoned by a young man making his way in the world, turns to a peasant or a workman. This problem of social inequality between couples, already present in "A Prelude", "A Fragment of Stained Glass" (the serf and the miller's daughter), and "Goose Fair" (Lois is richer than her fiancé, whose father had been a working man) also dominated *The White Peacock*: Lady Crystabel-Annable, Leslie-Lettie, George-Meg, Cyril-Emily, each pair suffers to a certain extent from a dissimilarity of social background. The stories of the "Jessie cycle" all raise in some degree the question of class differences in love and marriage. The "superior" woman compares two men, one introspective and cultured, the other rough and simple, and, though sometimes also violent and vulgar, always a fine strapping fellow. "Odour of Chrysanthemums" and *Mrs Holroyd*, as well as the short sketch "A Sick Collier",[116] contrast a woman of higher moral standards and greater refinement with her collier husband, whose mental development is rudimentary. Similarly, in "Two Marriages", Mrs Durant, a burgher's daughter from Nottingham, does not use the "vernacular", as does her husband.[117]

The problem is never solved one way or the other. Often, like Muriel in "A Modern Lover", the heroine returns to the more refined, *gentlemanly* type. At all events, the other is never accepted as anything but *second best*.

"Two Marriages", the first version (12,000 words) of a very long short story later entitled "Daughters of the Vicar" (19,000 words),[118] hints at a solution in the contrast between the marriages of Mary and Louisa Lindley. The final text, however, contains important additions, including the most categorical solution to the dilemma, which can only date from between 1913 and 1914 and to which we shall return.[119] For the moment only the indications given in "Two Marriages" will be considered.

Mr Lindley, vicar of the mining village of Aldecar, and his wife, who, worn out by "poverty, worry and insult" and eight consecutive years of childbearing, has "retired to an invalid's sofa", have the utmost difficulty in managing to rear their large family. The villagers are hostile, or at best ironical, and continue to treat them like strangers. A scene in the Durants' haberdashery shop illustrates well the relation between the clergyman and his plain-spoken parishioners. Mr Lindley breaks his leg. He is replaced by a distant cousin, the Reverend Edward Massey, a hideous little abortion of a man, a Cambridge graduate with a precise mind and an "indomitable little ego". He is about to take up an excellent living, and the Lindleys do nothing to discourage Mary from marrying him. She is the eldest; possible suitors are rare; she understands that she has no alternative. But to Louisa her brother-in-law is abhorrent, a man "without the full range of human feelings", an inflexible abstract automaton who does his duty coldly, without the least feeling for the true pathos of life. In the course of a visit from the Masseys, Louisa, irritated by Edward, goes off to the Durants. The father has died and old Mrs Durant is keeping house for her son Alfred, who, after several years in the Navy, has gone back to the mine. Alfred has no girl-friend. He does not drink. He is proud of his naval training and perfect physical condition. He is as "naïve as a boy of fourteen" and an expert on the flute.

Louisa finds Mrs Durant dying; she looks after her and, at her request, prepares Alfred's dinner. Then the old woman begs her to help the returned collier soap his back. This is accomplished with great shyness on both sides; but Louisa's blushes do not prevent her from noticing the "opaque solid whiteness of Alfred's shoulders". And before she dies Mrs Durant makes her promise to marry her son. Louisa consents, though somewhat apprehensive at the thought of marriage with a man who, "though keen-sighted", can't "see into things", and "is not introspective".[120]

The story is still imperfectly worked out. Lawrence lays too much stress on unnecessary details: the marriage of the elder Lindleys (which, like the character of Massey, owes something to Butler's *The Way of all Flesh*); the teasing talk of the colliers waiting their turn after "loose-all" to take the cage up to the surface. The various incidents are not sufficiently welded into the plot and it is impossible to see why Louisa goes to the Durants rather than anywhere else. All this has been put right in "Daughters of the Vicar". Above all, Louisa does not know if she really *wants* to marry Alfred. She resigns herself to doing so to please Mrs Durant, and in a spirit of revolt against Massey and everything he represents: it is hard to believe in such a marriage. Lawrence, too, seems to be indicating his disgust at all that made it possible to condemn a fine girl like Mary to the "badly little gudgeon" of a clergy-man, rather than his real belief in Louisa's marriage.

Lawrence's attitude towards the strait-laced Christian middle class to which the Lindleys belonged is already very clear. Mr Lindley loved his flock as was right and proper, but he loved them collectively; individually, he feared them almost without exception. A religious ideal of self-sacrifice went hand-in-hand with a cold and abstract intellectual attitude,[121] which led the family to expect Mary to sacrifice herself and "practically cut herself off from the rest of the world". As for Massey, he is a synthesis of all that Lawrence most detested: a man of principle, ostensibly self-sacrificing but in reality an unbearable domestic tyrant. His religion is accompanied by a hypocrisy all the more formidable for being totally unconscious. Nietzsche's influence here reinforces that of Samuel Butler, and both concur in re-inforcing Lawrence's hatred of middle-class stiffness and reticence in family relationships,[122] of the naïve belief of this class in its own moral superiority. He shows the clergyman's daughters isolated by a false sense of social prestige, cut off from the only eligible suitors in their village, so that Mary comes to accept a repugnant marriage as the only possible course. Revolted by all this, and in order to escape the horror of an existence like that of Mary, Louisa turns towards the simple life of the working class, with its sheer physi-cal closeness. Already one of the basic principles of Lawrence's social criticism of the Midlands is clearly stated; all that remains is for him to drive home his attack on the morality of self-sacrifice and to give adequate artistic expression to this theme.

The scenes in the mine and at the Durants' belong to the group of portraits of working-class life in the Midlands. "A Sick Collier",[123] again, is a simple sketch of a wounded collier driven mad by pain and the reactions of his young wife, a stranger to mining manners and mentality alike. In "Her Turn",[124] the woman spends her husband's savings on furniture and kitchen utensils, forcing him to give her the whole of his strike pay to feed the family; "Strike Pay"[125] portrays groups of colliers on strike: a young man returns home after a day of idle and childish distractions; his mother-in-law reproaches him violently with having spent part of his strike pay. These three studies probably date from Lawrence's stay in Eastwood during a strike, early in 1912.[126] The same applies to "The Miner at Home",[127] a still-life of the familiar scene of the woman washing the collier's back, and a domestic quarrel about a proposed strike. All these minor scenes are noted with precision, every significant detail well observed, each character marked by an unerring touch of dialogue. These sketches present no new problems: every one is to be found again merged into *Sons and Lovers*.

"The Old Adam"[128] plunges us into a very different atmosphere. While there is no knowing whether the story dates from 1911-12 or 1912-14, its setting is clearly that of Lawrence's Croydon years as lodger in the home of Mr and Mrs Jones, where relations with his landlord seem finally to have become somewhat strained. Edward Severn, an elegant young man "wearing white flannels and carrying a tennis racket under his arm", comes home to his lodgings at the Thomases. He plays with their little girl, helping the mother to put her to bed. He is not insensitive to the beauty of Mrs Thomas, who, for her part, is not averse to certain admiring looks. Together they await the return of the master of the house. The young woman is on edge because of an impending storm; an undercurrent of hostility pervades the room, both between the two men and between husband and wife. Several times they are on the brink of quarrelling. Before going to bed Severn helps Thomas to bring downstairs a trunk belonging to the maid, Kate, who is due to leave the following day. Mrs Thomas lights them from above; the husband goes down first, bearing the brunt of the trunk's weight; Severn remarks laughingly that if he slipped the trunk would squash his landlord. One step from the landing, he does slip, accidentally. Thomas is flung backwards across the landing, his head striking the banister. No one is hurt, but seeing Severn laughing Thomas lashes out at him. Severn defends himself and starts to strangle him. Mrs Thomas stands by petrified, and Kate, awakened by the noise, has to pull them apart. Remorseful, Severn then helps Thomas to his feet, bathes the blood from his face and temples, and puts him to bed, filled with tenderness for the man he has just tried to kill. The next day, both men are rather proud of having shown they have "got some fight" in them.[129] They become firm friends, whereas Mrs Thomas remains distant and polite, treating Severn as a stranger.

This adventure, which in *Sons and Lovers*, with a few modifications, becomes the fight and reconciliation with Baxter Dawes, is a development of a theme already observed but now growing in importance: that of the relationship between violence and tenderness. Cyril Beardsall made friends with Annable after having been almost knocked out by him; Ernest Lambert raised his hand to his own father; Blackmore good-heartedly accompanied the drunken Holroyd home, fought with him, undressed him and bathed his face, all the time wishing he were dead.[130] No doubt this theme is linked with the sadistic trend already noted in several of Lawrence's early works. Was there any real-life incident, except perhaps for certain scenes of paternal brutality witnessed as a child,[131] behind this story? Jessie Chambers was convinced that "Lawrence never fought any man. He was not that kind of fighter."[132] If, as is possible, the story dates from 1912, after his "marriage", this particular theme of violence might be explained by some of Lawrence's dreams about Weekley.[133] But the theme itself certainly existed before his flight with another man's wife.[134] Yet Severn, like Paul Morel, is a portrait of the author.[135] Lawrence's imagination seems in some way to have demanded violence in whichever character most represents himself, a need expressed in literary fantasies in which "the old Adam" breaks out in the hero for an instant, transforming him into a man of action and of violence. But reality returns triumphant to redress the balance, and to separate the combatants in time to unite them in a friendship based on a sense of their common power. But is it not possible that a certain common hostility towards the woman also draws the two men together, such as that which had attracted Lawrence towards "Siegmund" and possibly towards Harry Dax?

This same theme, combined with others already familiar to us, reappears in "Love Among the Haystacks", a long short story, the first version of which is mentioned in a letter to Edward Garnett of 7 January 1912.[136] The date of July–August 1912 advanced by David Garnett in his "Reminiscence" published in the posthumous volume in which this story first appeared in 1930, must therefore refer to a revision made soon after Lawrence's departure for Germany. At all events, the character of Paula undoubtedly owes much to Frieda, or at least to Lawrence's first stay in Germany.

Geoffrey and Maurice Wookey are stacking hay. Their father, their elder brother Henry and a labourer cart the hay to the foot of the stack and the father then pitches the hay to Geoffrey, who passes it on to Maurice who builds the stack. In the intervals of their work they discuss Paula Jablonowsky, the German governess at the neighbouring vicarage. Both boys are interested in her, but Maurice, the younger, has recently made rapid progress in her favour and Geoffrey is secretly mortified and jealous. His ill-humour culminates in his wrestling briefly with Maurice, who falls over backwards and slithers over the edge of the stack. Paula, the vicar and the other haymakers rush up to the young man, who remains unconscious. Geoffrey keeps quiet, half hoping that Maurice is dead and that his death will be taken for an accident.

Maurice comes to and says nothing; the whole family accepts the version of an accidental slip. After this access of violence the two brothers are "entirely amicable, almost affectionate":

They had both been deeply moved, so much so that their ordinary inter-course was interrupted: but underneath, each felt a strong regard for the other.[137]

The wrestling has somehow relieved Geoffrey, has rid him of his resent-ment towards Maurice. Nevertheless he remained "sullenly hostile to the most part of the world" from which he felt isolated:

> He was a man who could not bear to stand alone, he was too much afraid of the vast confusion of life surrounding him, in which he was helpless. Geoffrey mistrusted himself with everybody.[138]

Maurice insists it is his turn to sleep outside to protect the stacks and tools, taking advantage of this imposition to advance his courtship of Paula. They gambol recklessly together in the fields, but as night falls it comes on to rain and the haystack has to be covered with a heavy stack-cloth. When this task has been completed, the young lovers hear the ladder fall: prisoners on the giant stack, they reconcile themselves willingly to their fate. It was, in fact, Geoffrey, coming out to help Maurice, who had accidentally knocked the ladder over; hearing the lovers, he does not replace it but goes off to brood in a near-by shelter where the tools are kept. Here he is joined by the wife of a seedy tramp who had already come begging for work in the hay-field that same morning. Cold, wet through, young and pretty, abandoned by her worthless husband, she inspires the sensitive Geoffrey with self-confidence and pity. He feeds her, dries her clothes, refusing to let her wander off again into the rain. These two lonely souls comfort each other as best they can and plan to go off together to Canada, that welcoming haven for illicit couples.

In the morning Geoffrey puts the ladder back without a word. The lovers have not slept too well in the hay, and Paula picks a quarrel with Maurice, convinced that the ladder has never been removed. Geoffrey explains every-thing as they breakfast together in the shed. Later Paula marries Maurice and Geoffrey and Lydia emigrate as planned.

The descriptive scenes which form the major part of "Love Among the Haystacks" are in the always successful vein of some descriptions in *The White Peacock*: the haymaking, in fields belonging to the Chambers opposite Greasley church; the stack-building, reminiscent of a similar scene in Querido's *Toil of Men*,[139] a book much admired by Lawrence and which may well have inspired him to make literary capital out of a familiar piece of farm-labour; the picnics in the fields, which Lawrence had so often shared with Mr Chambers and his sons; Maurice's bathing in the spring-filled trough, the delight of his race with Paula through the fields and their dare-devil bareback ride after the dip; the thumbnail sketches of a vicar, a farm labourer, etc. As for the German Fräulein, she will turn up later.[140] But

Geoffrey's adventure throws interesting new light on Lawrence's idea of the circumstances likely to free a young man of his excessive shyness with women. Both Maurice and Geoffrey are "virgin but tormented"; to them "the whole feminine sex had been represented by their mother", a proud stranger to the county, "who spoke pure English and was very quiet"; thus they had been brought up to despise the "loud-mouthed and broad-tongued" local girls.[141] The foreigner thus represents a different type of woman and, as such, acceptable.[142] Yet Maurice goes ahead, or rather lets himself be chosen by Paula. Geoffrey remains alone: the wife of the tramp attracts him, above all because he recognizes in her an unhappy soul, like himself, driven hard "by stress of life". Even at their first encounter they exchange an understanding glance. Yet to bring Geoffrey to the point of decision exceptional circumstances such as darkness and rain are necessary. When Lydia creeps into the shed where he lies awake, he grasps her tender arm, feels her rain-soaked sleeve and, recognizing her, gives her a horse blanket in which to wrap herself while her clothes are drying. When they have become a little better acquainted, he offers to warm her feet with his hands:

> He warmed her feet as best he could, putting them close against him. Now and again convulsive tremors ran over her. She felt his warm breath on the ball of her toes, that were bunched up in his hands. Leaning forward, she touched his hair delicately with her fingers. He thrilled. She fell to gently stroking his hair, with timid, pleading finger-tips.

Putting out a hand to find hers, his fingers encounter her face:

> He touched it curiously. It was wet. He put his big fingers cautiously on her eyes, into two little pools of tears.[143]

Lydia takes Geoffrey in her arms, clasps his head to her breast, covering his hair with tears. Soon they are locked in what is for Geoffrey "his first love kiss".

Once more, love can only be manifested, shyness overcome by a sudden upsurge of instinct, when accompanied by tears, rain, cold, and, to do Lawrence justice, by a mutual feeling of tenderness, born of the realization by two outcasts of their own distress. It is as if a timorous soul like Geoffrey, who must wait "till a woman would come and take him for what he was worth",[144] can break the chrysalis of his virginity only under the onset of a sudden impulse, often encouraged by contact with water, tears, frozen feet, a strange and ambiguous blend of sadism and pity, of maternal tenderness and desire.[145] It seems as if the man always needed an excuse to touch the body or limbs of the woman. The question should perhaps be asked if feet had not for Lawrence some special erotic significance, whether as a symbol or as a true fetish. Without wishing to draw conclusions, comparison may be

IV. SONS AND LOVERS

made between the poem "A Baby Running Barefoot",[146] particularly the verse:

> I long for the baby to wander hither to me
> Like a wind-shadow wandering over the water,
> *So that she can stand on my knee*
> *With her little bare feet in my hands,*
> *Cool like syringa-buds,*
> Firm and silken like pink young peony flowers. [*Italics added.*]

and the scenes between Severn and the baby in "The Old Adam".[147] In both cases the baby is the Jones baby Hilda May in Croydon, and there is something both innocent and equivocal about these games—equivocal as is indeed the whole atmosphere of this short story.

IV. SONS AND LOVERS

Some of the short stories analysed above were no doubt preliminary sketches for *Sons and Lovers*, and, since the substance of the novel is essentially auto-biographical, it is possible to restrict ourselves here to a relatively succinct account of a work including so many scenes largely explained by what has been said in previous chapters.

Of all Lawrence's works *Sons and Lovers* is that which most contributes to the accepted image of its author. It is, therefore, all the more necessary to make an effort to distinguish between factual data and the ideological and emotional patterns constantly coming between real life and its literary image.

The basis of the novel is well known: the story of the mother, her social demotion, her growing indifference to and subsequent hatred of her husband; the birth of Paul, dearly loved and cherished son; the youthful successes, engagement and death of his elder brother, William; Paul's adolescence, his innocent childhood friendship with Miriam; the slow growth of love between the two young people; the struggle between filial devotion and a deep affection; the defeat of a love which nevertheless lives on in the depths of their shattered hearts. The rest of the novel treats freely certain auto-biographical facts which the Lawrence of 1912 had his own reasons for concealing, but which correspond quite faithfully to his experiences. Paul makes friends with Clara Dawes, a factory hand living apart from her husband. It is Clara who tells him Miriam loves him and who persuades him he should ask her to give herself to him. A disillusioned Paul returns to Clara and there follow a few months of passion, some moments of ecstasy. The illness and death of his mother interrupt this brittle happiness, which, in any case, contains the seeds of its own death. Meanwhile a violent fight between Paul and Dawes has linked the two men in a strange bond of friendship. Paul reunites Clara with her husband. An attempted reconciliation with Miriam fails miserably and the novel ends on a note of darkness and uncertainty.

Sons and Lovers is more ambitious than any of Lawrence's preceding works: Lawrence is here attempting much more than in *The White Peacock*, in which the changing mutual relationships between a small group of characters is based on relatively simple principles and a conventional technique. More also than in *The Trespasser*, a prose poem celebrating a single brief experience.

In *Sons and Lovers* Lawrence tackles his own fundamental psychological problem and, what is more, a problem to which he has no solution when he starts describing it. He immediately brings into play characters whose story covers a long period, without any obvious link to ensure the continuity of his plot. In the initial conception of his work, what link is there between such episodes as the marriage of Mrs Morel, the youth of William and the loves of Paul?

We can for the moment forget the Foreword sent to Garnett in January 1913,[148] outcome rather than starting-point of the writing of *Sons and Lovers*. A letter of November 1912,[149] following closely upon his finding (in late October) a title which underlines the novel's true significance, is the first text clearly defining the guiding principle which links the three subjects of the book.[150] Must we then accept the view that the significance of the facts related was only revealed to the writer as he proceeded to redraft and revise, as ideas and interpretations of the action crept imperceptibly into a straightforward recording of events? A similar process of composition seems already to have been in operation for *The White Peacock* and for many of the short stories. Information provided by Jessie Chambers on the first version, entitled "Paul Morel", confirms this impression.

When, in October 1910, Lawrence tells Sydney Pawling that he has already written one-eighth of "Paul Morel", he expresses satisfaction with the interesting way in which it has "plotted out". But it is clear that he is here referring to the tone and structure of the novel rather than to its meaning. Only just emerged from what he himself recognizes as the excessive symbolist poetry of *The Trespasser*, he proposes to make "Paul Morel" "a restrained, somewhat impersonal novel". He also seems to distrust his own realism, or at least his tendency to alternate between symbolic heights and down-to-earth realism.[151] Jessie Chambers remembers the first (or was it rather the second?[152]) manuscript as "far behind the reality in vividness and dramatic strength", "story-bookish" and quite lacking in the spontaneity she had come to regard as the distinguishing feature of Lawrence's writing. Neither the mother nor Miriam was portrayed convincingly against her real background. The characters were locked together in a "frustrating bondage"; and the absence of Ernest from this version indicates that Lawrence was not then prepared to extend to an older brother his interpretation of

Paul's dilemma. Jessie realized the possibilities of such a novel, if Lawrence were only able to bring himself to make a rigorously exact picture of his youth and hers:

. . . I thought what had really happened was much more poignant and interesting than the situations he had invented. In particular I was surprised that he had omitted the story of Ernest, which seemed to me vital enough to be worth telling as it actually happened.

She therefore suggested that he should write the whole story again and keep it true to life. Knowing his gift for accurate and vivid description and his "miraculous power of translating the raw material of life into significant form", she also hoped that by going over his past without illusions, with all the integrity of which she thought him capable, he might rid himself for ever of his "strange obsession with his mother".[153]

But Lawrence had not yet attempted direct and realistic autobiography, at least in the works he had so far thought worth publishing. And such progress, apart from that of style and technique, as is distinguishable between *The White Peacock* and the last in date of the short stories already studied, lies in the author's growing ability to come to grips with problems directly concerning himself. From a series of attempts at fanciful and more or less conventional literary inventions, he moves forward to a growing boldness in the direct representation of himself and those around him. The sympathetic young man, always more or less reminiscent of Cyril in *The White Peacock* or Byrne in *The Trespasser*, had appeared more and more frequently in the short stories of 1911: Severn in "The Old Adam", Coutts in "Witch à la Mode", Mersham and Syson in "A Modern Lover" and "The Soiled Rose". The backgrounds too became more and more exact and true to life: compare, for example, "A Modern Lover" with "A Fragment of Stained Glass", or with the scenes of social life in *The White Peacock*, or the cameos of colliery life in "A Sick Collier", or "Odour of Chrysanthemums", with the almost complete absence of any suggestion of mine or miners in *The White Peacock*. Jessie's suggestion in fact probably did no more than encourage a tendency already becoming more and more pronounced.

Accurate background description and a straightforward picture of his childhood thus place the first half of *Sons and Lovers* among Lawrence's realist works. The method once established and the author quite decided to stick closely to facts, life itself provided an untold wealth of detail, as well as many great descriptive scenes destined to enrich the heritage of English realism. The novelist's technique was based on a reasonably long apprenticeship, as well as on the study of his English and French predecessors, from Balzac and Zola to George Moore, Gissing and Rutherford. He opens with a brief history of the village of Bestwood and the working-class quarter in which the Morels lived. Then comes a great Flaubertian description of the local wakes: steam horses, barrel organs, shooting booths and peepshows, men swilling beer and shouting in the pubs, drunkards reeling home at night, etc., all perceived through the senses of Mrs Morel, the central figure of the opening chapters.[154] Passages of this kind recur frequently, especially in the first half: the collier's courting at the Christmas party; his outing to Nottingham the day after the wakes; all the scenes of working-class life: birth, sickness, pit accident, pay day, unemployment, the children's games and squabbles in the alley. Then comes the description of life in Jordan's factory, and at the farm, the long rambles of the local lads and girls, Friday evenings at the Morels' when the children are grown up. Every aspect of the daily life of a working-class family, the whole social background, become part and parcel of the novel, solidly enclosing the characters in a framework of concrete reality which reveals them bit by bit, like people encountered in the course of daily life.

Against this background the characters stand out vividly and clearly: the father and the mother; the children at different stages of their development, each indicated, as and when the story demands, in some short phrase or revealing episode. By much the same process we also come to know the Leivers family, though with the difference that Lawrence introduces them less by action, as with the Morels, and more by a static external analysis of their personalities. All these pictures are so real that it is often difficult to conceive the originals as in any way different from their portraits. Indeed it has happened that, looking further into incidents in which some literary embellishment was suspected, we found contemporary witnesses quoting the novel as their point of reference, as though literature rather than experience had in fact inspired their memories.[155]

These characters owe their vividness to exact observation, to an astonishing sureness in the choice of the familiar and revealing gesture, the typical, accurate, conversational touch: Mrs Morel spitting on her iron to see if it is hot, then rubbing it against the lining of the mat; Morel in good-humoured mood, speaking gently to his children, telling them of Taffy the pit pony, or of how a mouse had hidden in his pocket and nibbled at his snap: the awkward talk and gestures of the colliers sharing out their week's wages at the Morels' house, or again Miriam's characteristic postures, the slight lift of Clara's upper lip "that did not know whether it was raised in scorn of all men or out of eagerness to be kissed".[156]

Three characters stand out above the rest: Paul, Miriam and Mrs Morel. Naturally Paul stands at the very core of the book, and it is in an effort to account for his character that Lawrence retraces events as far back as the marriage of his parents. As an autobiographical novel *Sons and Lovers* may be measured by the extent to which it enables us to understand the hero, and helped Lawrence to understand himself.

He seems to have aimed at first at being objective: he wanted to distinguish himself from his hero, never removing Paul from his original working-class background and making him continue, even after his pneumonia, as a humble clerical employee in a factory. Could this have been so as to face the problem of his love in a setting where no social considerations would interfere between Paul and Miriam? This flimsy veil of fiction, however, does not prevent Paul from being in every important respect identified with his creator, who even endows him with his own talent: Paul is an artist, whose gift receives early recognition. But while Lawrence was able to see Paul's childhood dispassionately, and from a sufficient distance, the nearer he got to his actual "self" the more closely Paul's character became fused with his own, the relatively objective realism of the earlier pages giving way to a passionate and partial interpretation of reality. With the result that, as the novel moves further and further away from the external course of Lawrence's life, it becomes more and more coloured by the emotions of its author.

Nothing could be more significant of this evolution than the account of the long-drawn-out conflict with Miriam. The ambiguity of Lawrence's attitude is due to his reluctance or inability to choose between Jessie and his mother. Not yet having reached the point of blaming the latter, he becomes more and more convinced that his destiny does not lie in marrying Jessie.[157] Whereas in speaking and writing to her he was occasionally able to admit the baleful role played by his mother,[158] this did not mean that he ever thought it possible to put back the clock to efface the years of suffering or dissipate the cruel misunderstanding which had separated them so profoundly. It is as if he no longer wanted to love the girl he had so long been accustomed to trying not to want to love, and who, no doubt, recalled too vividly a period of his own development not particularly pleasant to remember. This period, as we can see from "The Shades of Spring" and "A Modern Lover", he now feels he has put behind him. No doubt the exhilaration of his success, and the morally emancipated London literary circles in which he moved, combined to make him feel he could not link his life with Jessie's: he could not bring himself to accept the conditions of a woman of strict moral standards, who refused to condone his hankering after other women. Moreover, by the time he received the proofs of *Sons and Lovers* for correction, he had already linked his fate irrevocably, in his own eyes, with that of Frieda, whose feelings towards his Nottingham past were inspired by mingled jealousy and scorn, and who proceeded to "document" him on her own modern German reading of Miriam's innermost feelings.[159]

Thus the presentation of this character suffers throughout almost all the book from a distortion similar to that inflicted on Hilda in the revision of "The Soiled Rose".[160] It is not so much a distortion of Paul's feelings as of the actual character of Miriam: we no longer see her in herself, obeying the laws of her own internal evolution, nor even as Paul saw her at each step of their love, but instead with a deliberate hostility, a blend of bitterness, guilt and commiseration. In contrast to the dynamic development of Paul's character and destiny, the girl is presented statically, as seen by the Lawrence of 1912, and even, occasionally, as seen by Frieda. Instead of living and developing as Jessie did, Miriam remains transfixed in certain attitudes: and Jessie, that great enigma of Lawrence's youth, both loved and feared, to whom he feels bound by bonds of heart and conscience, is continually concealed behind a more or less appropriate label, which provides Lawrence with an alibi and assuages his sense of guilt. It is easier to throw off responsibilities towards a label than towards a living woman. Thus Miriam is shown either jealous of Paul or "romantic in her soul"; moved by the "will to power" as she "drenches" Paul or her small brother with her love; stroking flowers with a selfish passion. She is a priestess, a Botticelli nun, never a woman of flesh and blood, a woman who suffers at seeing herself caught in the inextricable psychic embrace of a man incapable either of loving or of leaving her.

Images of Miriam most flattering to the author's delicate self-respect are continually being substituted for the observed "otherness". Incapable of giving herself in love, yet continually demanding it of him, she drives Paul towards the abstract, the spiritual, away from the realities of the flesh. As previously he reproached her for her romanticism, Lawrence now attributes to her his own inability to face up to the new conditions of adult life. In comparison the moments of lucidity when he understands and expresses his own impotence are rare indeed.[161]

In the decisive chapters comes the "test on Miriam".[162] On Miriam, not on Paul, to whom it never occurs that his own tact, his delicacy and his capacity to stir physical desires might also be in question. The girl is condemned for not giving him the perfect sensual satisfaction he is seeking. He tells her he will break with her. She replies with some vehemence that he is still a child, irresponsible and inconsequent. She had always felt him struggling against his love, pulling against a chain. Whereupon, oblivious to the end, it is the man who dares feel flouted! Miriam has deceived him, pretending to love him when all the time she was judging him. He hates her because she has treated him as a hero while considering him a child. He closes his embittered heart to all pity for the girl who has so grievously offended, so undeservedly duped him.[163]

By thus venting his spleen on Miriam, Lawrence reveals his secret need to justify his behaviour and liquidate the past: his self-respect, still suffering from recently inflicted wounds, made it impossible for him to maintain the objectivity of the first part of his novel. *Sons and Lovers* did not have the result Jessie hoped for, because for the immature chance alone provides solutions. Unless it serves to trace a line of action, literature can only mirror life or explain it. A work like *Dominique* or *L'Education Sentimentale* can only be written in the calm resulting from the passage of time. For Lawrence the old conflict remained unresolved: to marry Jessie would have been, by some curious subtlety of the mind, to remain under the influence of the dead woman who, within himself, still struggled with the living Jessie.[164]

Yet, in the course of successive versions, above all during the last revision, after his conversations with Frieda had revealed to him the first rudiments of Freudian psychology,[165] the meaning of his novel became clearer to him: the influence of the mother in the destiny of her sons became apparent, and the juxtaposition of the story of William and that of Paul took on its full value; so that, once the novel was finished, he could define for Garnett its main lines more clearly than they actually appear from a reading of the work itself. The mother absorbs the whole of her sons' capacity for love because she had not found with her husband the spiritual union she desired:

> As soon as the young men come into contact with women, there's a split. William gives his sex to a fribble, and his mother holds his soul. But the split kills him, because he doesn't know where he is. The next son gets a woman who fights for his soul—fights his mother. The son loves the mother— all the sons hate and are jealous of the father. The battle goes on between the mother and the girl, with the son as object. The mother gradually proves stronger, because of the tie of blood. The son decides to leave his soul in his mother's hands, and, like his elder brother, go for passion. He gets passion. Then the split begins to tell again. But almost unconsciously, the mother realizes what is the matter and begins to die. The son casts off his mistress, attends to his mother dying. He is left in the end naked of everything, with the drift towards death.[166]

This is an attractive interpretation because it lends the novel unity, and sheds light on the conflict between Mrs Morel and Miriam, who both strive for the soul of Paul. But it fails to take into account the full complexity of the circumstances which, in real life, forced Lawrence and Jessie into a platonic friendship from which all physical contact was excluded. It is impossible to reduce all these circumstances to a single cause, his mother's jealousy. Nothing explains why Paul, like Lawrence, is sickly, subject to bronchitis and pneumonia, weak in body and in will. Would a physically stronger boy, less slow to reach puberty, have allowed himself to become enmeshed in this net? Or would he not rather have broken his bonds sooner, without the continual shilly-shallying between his mother and Miriam, Miriam and Clara?

For Paul soon wearies of his "passion" for Clara. He finds that he cannot love her: she occupies his thoughts only when they are together, and not always even then![167] Their few fleeting moments of ecstasy soon leave them both unsatisfied, further apart than before.[168] Clara, a woman of the people, is no mate for the artist Paul Morel.[169] His mother's agony, which results in Paul seeking in his mistress no more than a kind of opiate, completes the break. Here, the novel follows the real life of its author more closely than

Jessie was aware,[170] ignorant as she was of the truth about Alice Dax, and therefore seeing in certain scenes only allusions to Helen Corke,[171] combined with certain features attributable to Frieda. Yet in Paul's break with Clara Lawrence is in fact combining all the reasons which made him flee not only Helen, but also Louie and Alice, laying bare his solitude and inability to love. Paul cannot bear Clara when she "talks and criticizes": this applies to Helen, but also to Alice, the suffragette; and when he reconciles Clara to Baxter, it is Lawrence abandoning Helen to the ghost of Siegmund, but perhaps also Lawrence visiting the Daxes in March 1912 and leaving Alice to the husband to whom she was soon to bear a second child, after deciding she could not leave him and her son for Lawrence. Paul feels that even if they married and were faithful to each other, he would still have to follow his own way, go on alone, her role being only to look after his physical needs. Lawrence here probably had in mind not only Louie, but all the other loves of his early years from whom he then felt he had finally parted to follow a higher destiny.[172]

The over-simple argument discovered by Lawrence after the event, the "split" produced by filial love, does not contain the whole truth; reality is more complex than this Freudian view and includes other aspects of his personality, in particular his sense of having risen above his Nottingham surroundings.

William's story suggests similar reserves. At the time of his brother's death Lawrence was too young to understand its underlying causes. As for the immediate causes, pneumonia and erysipelas, surely few medical authorities would go so far as to link these with Ernest's love for his mother? And why does William Morel, son of an intelligent mother, get engaged to a "fribble"? Probably less because of his mother's influence than as a result of his social displacement in the great city where he "seemed to spin rather giddily on the quick current of the new life".[173] This flighty brunette, *Louisa Lily Denys Western*, whom William calls *Louie* or *Gypsy*,[174] has more than one point of resemblance with Lawrence's one-time fiancée, whom he describes to Garnett as "big and swarthy and passionate as a Gypsy".[175] William's exasperation at her shallowness and "weasel-brain" re-echo that of the poet with "the woman of 'Kisses in the Train'".[176] Does Lawrence, in fact, give a picture of William's engagement largely inspired by his own? If so, he is merely following his usual method of projecting his own feelings into those of his characters.

His generalization is thus based no longer on two cases, but one. There is nothing to prove the mother's responsibility in William's story. We are led to suppose it; indeed Lawrence suggests it to us by adding the case of Paul. But to assert with Lawrence that such is "the tragedy of thousands of young Englishmen"[177] is to go much further. The psychological value of *Sons and Lovers* lies essentially in the portrait of Mrs Morel, and in the detailed and exact study of the character of Paul himself, with his contradictions, his immaturity, his obliviousness, but also his kindness, his filial piety, his talent, his passionate feeling for the power of fleeting beauty. Miriam is falsified by Lawrence's own sense of guilt and indecision. Clara we see only rarely as a living individual, as something more than a variety of disconnected moral and physical attributes. William, except as a child, is most convincing when Lawrence is using him as his own mouthpiece. The other characters—Morel, Paul's sister and younger brother, the factory girls, all less complex personalities—are brought to life by apt annotations of their gestures, their physical appearance. But wherever Lawrence puts his own soul into his work, he communicates to his characters and to the world about them a vibrancy creating an illusion of direct contact with reality.

In the long run it is the lyrical quality of *Sons and Lovers* that most impresses. Particularly when expressing himself through Paul or his mother, Lawrence uses his lyric gift to reveal their inmost feelings. But it is always *he* who feels, who is what he says his characters feel and are: whether it is Mrs Morel waiting for her husband on the day of the wakes, reflecting how life sometimes "takes hold of one, carries the body along, accomplishes one's history, and yet is not real, but leaves oneself as it were slurred over",[178] Paul's sensations during his bouts of bronchitis or pneumonia,[179] or Miriam's romanticism, her tendency to live in a world of fantasy,[180] it is invariably Lawrence's own ego which slips into his characters, quickening them with his own life.

Every sensation, every perception of nature, of flowers, light or feeling attributed to the characters of *Sons and Lovers*, all that in addition to simple, elemental, everyday act and gesture constitutes the very substance of the psyche, everything that transcends mere observation of ear and eye, comes from Lawrence himself. But the true Lawrentian lyric gift is to be found above all in moments of semi-mystical exaltation: when Paul threads daisies into Lily's hair, lays a bunch of crimson berries in Miriam's curls, or covers Clara's head with cowslips; when he gives himself up completely to the rhythm of swinging or haymaking; experiences moments of sudden contact with the soul of Miriam; or again in the strange scenes by the seashore, or the happy hours Paul and his mother spend together. The sensual ecstasies, the loss of all self-control in the homicidal struggle with Baxter Dawes; the revelation of the body of Miriam or of Clara; the long outdoor evenings with Clara when they come together in communion with all the great natural forces of love, earth and life, "the thrust of the grass stems, the cry of the peewit, the wheel of the stars", and the swirling waters of the river Trent, symbol of eternal change[181]—such scenes are the climax of that lyrical intensity which is never absent from this essentially poetic work, every detail of which bears the stamp of the real or imaginary experience of a personality supremely interested in its own workings.

And we recognize here the very principle of literary creation in *Sons and Lovers*. Starting out from concrete events, the broad lines of his own life, factual details, portraits, gestures, all that depicts and delineates, Lawrence nevertheless succeeds in quickening people and things with spiritual life. This he does by means of that symbolic process with which he reproaches both Miriam and Helena, but which he himself constantly employs: the injection of his own psychic life into everything he describes. The weakness of this process in a novel so closely linked to his own life is a flagrant lack of objectivity with regard to problems and personalities worthy of more detached appreciation. Its great richness on the other hand is to create before our eyes a living world, at once true and poetical, a world recognizable as our own, but which suddenly comes to life at the call of mysterious, unknown currents and forces. Despite Paul's despair, despite the spiritual vacuum of the industrialized world and the dying peasant order in the mining country-side, Lawrence gives from time to time a fleeting but vivifying vision of the eternal cosmos in which the threads of all our destinies are darkly inter-twined. In a book in which discord is almost the rule, the reader is rewarded by supreme and rare moments of perfect accord between man and the mysterious creative rhythms of the universe.

As it progresses, however, *Sons and Lovers* takes on an increasingly acrid flavour. Scenes of violence and of death grow more important. Already the brutality of Morel, the hatred of his children, the ever-dreaded threat of accidents in the mine, combined with the feeling that the suffering of the father might indirectly bring a kind of happiness to his family, all lead up to a theme fully developed only later in the novel.

As a small child, Paul Morel had organized the symbolic sacrifice of a doll, watching "with wicked satisfaction" the drops of wax melt off Arabella's forehead and face "like sweat" into the flames. "He seemed to hate the doll so intensely because he had broken it."[182] This confession (which may also owe something to Lawrence's recollection of Rossetti's "Sister Helen") sheds some light on Lawrence's inherent sadism and on Paul's hatred of Miriam after he has destroyed their love. For years Paul tortures both his mother and the girl, and even while suffering himself seems to enjoy this cruelty, rather in the way one can enjoy the twinges of an aching tooth.[183] All this contained, repressed violence explodes in the pages where, after a passionately jealous scene between Paul and his mother, the father comes home drunk and vicious. Picking a quarrel over nothing, he and Paul are about to come to blows when Mrs Morel faints away with horror and exhaustion.[184] Could anything be at once more poignant and more repulsive than these family relationships perverted into such a magma of brutality and spiritual incest?

From this point onwards violence and hatred underlie every emotion: Paul's savage onslaught on Miriam's beliefs; the equivocal attraction of Clara, who, to Paul, is "an angel full of bitterness and remorse"; the fear and disgust of Miriam and of Paul at male bestiality. As Paul feels himself more and more irresistibly drawn to Clara he is haunted by the thought of Dawes. Tortured by a lewd mixture of jealousy and unhealthy curiosity, he must at all cost penetrate the most intimate secrets of Clara and her husband, just as Lawrence would rake over the sexual relations of Helen and her violinist.[185]

The first quarrel between the two men breaks out in a pub, followed by a second at the factory. Finally, just when Clara, not satisfied with Paul's love, returns in imagination to her husband, at the very moment when their passion is dying out in mutual irritation, Dawes attacks Paul in the darkness. The two men wrestle wildly, with savage blows and kicks. For several days Paul retreats into sickness; something in him seems broken.[186] In the fight with Dawes Lawrence seems to have infused something of his own delirious and imaginary battles with his "double", Siegmund, in 1911, and Paul's illness recalls his own subsequent collapse with pneumonia, immediately before he breaks off his engagement.

A mysterious "feeling of connexion", a "painful nearness" then draws Paul to Dawes, whereas Clara understandably enough develops a kind of horror for this lover and returns to her husband, encouraged by Paul.[187] Meanwhile the agony of the mother has again introduced the theme of suffering and death, henceforward inseparable from those of hate and love. Mrs Morel dies by slow degrees, but too slowly for Paul, who seeks to inspire her with the desire to be done with it all, setting them both free.[188] In the end he tries to kill his mother, in an appalling cowardly way, by adding water to her milk. But the sick woman keeps her hold on life, yielding at last after a final night of ghastly rasping agony to an overdose of morphia administered by Paul.[189]

Here Lawrence is elaborating on fact in the same way we saw him do in *The Trespasser*. Should these morbid pages be viewed as the realization of a deep, long-repressed wish, manifesting itself in the creations of a deranged imagination? Such is the commonly accepted interpretation, which fits in perfectly reasonably with all that we already know of Lawrence. But had not the whole school of the unconscious, above all the Symbolists and the Russians, tried to emphasize the secret motives of our most gratuitous actions, to translate into deed and gesture the inner impulses of the human heart? Was not this the technique of Wagnerian drama, beloved by the Symbolists, by George Moore and by Helen? Lawrence is following in the steps of a school which postulates as aesthetic principle the exteriorization of inner depths, the physical manifestation of the unconscious. Before Freud, before Frieda, his personal experience, combined with the literary heritage he had received, sufficed for the creation of *Sons and Lovers*, a tragedy of repression and impotence, of the fatalism engendered in the soul by the habit of submitting everything to the will of the mother. The symbolist technique was admirably adapted to an unstable temperament inclined to seek realization in fantasy rather than in action. The metaphysical explanations offered after the event, in the Foreword, add little that throws light on the novel as a work of art, nor do they really help us to understand either Paul Morel or his creator.

6

LIFE AND THE ARTIST

Thus, as far as literature is concerned, Lawrence's youth resulted in a novel in which are interwoven and expressed his deepest tendencies: everything, in fact, that had contributed to the moulding of his personality through the twenty-seven years of his existence. Yet other men live and suffer without feeling impelled to write a book about it. Others again write to earn their daily bread or as a pastime, or for other reasons which seem highly superficial compared with the painful exploration of himself and others undertaken by Lawrence in *Sons and Lovers*. How then did it come about that, after seeking for some time subjects outside his immediate experience, Lawrence placed his own ego at the very centre of his book? How can we account for his strange compulsion to transcribe on to paper the very essence of his being? How, in the first place, does he conceive this "self" of his, the centre of his universe? What principles does he adopt to guide himself through life? An attempt to reply to these questions, at a moment when we must soon follow Lawrence into an entirely new phase of his existence, may help to assess the turn he was suddenly to take both in life and in his literary adventure.

Literary vocation

Some hints may be discovered by returning for a moment to that period when, as an avid reader, he passed from the receptivity of childhood to a desire for self-expression, then manifested by constant commentaries on his reading, and quotation from his favourite authors. At a very early age he perceived in literature a guide to the discovery of those personal and emotive truths concealed by life under a layer of habit and of prejudice. He read rather like Montaigne, explaining his author by continual comparison with his own experience, at the same time using him to explain the world in which he lived.

Writing was for him above all a means to self-understanding, a way of interpreting the characters of those around him, of expressing all that he dimly felt within himself. It also gave him an opportunity to make allusions without revealing himself completely: when he insisted on reading *Coriolanus* from end to end with Jessie, for example, was it in the hope that she might apply to himself Volumnia's words?

> There's no man in the world
> More bound to's mother . . .[1]

And was he not thinking of his parents, and seeking from the poet an explanation of their ill-assorted union, when he asked Jessie if she agreed with Longfellow that:

> As the bow unto the arrow,
> So is woman unto man;
> Though she bends him, she obeys him,
> Though she draws him, yet she follows,
> Useless each without the other . . .?[2]

After reading in the life of one writer that every great man depends upon the love of a woman, he proceeds to model on this his relations with Jessie. In the course of a long walk they "live with Blake and his wife".[3] He loses himself completely in reading: Rochester and Jane Eyre, Swift and Stella are as real to him as the world around him, which he goes so far as to interpret in the form of his favourite literary characters; the smooth trunks of the beeches *are* to him the white arms of Maggie Tulliver,[4] a character whom he in turn *sees* as a dryad of his own northern forest.

From earliest adolescence literature was thus for Lawrence an imaginary world in which the beauty of field and wood played an evocatory role: there he was able to isolate himself with Jessie, to forget poverty and family opposition, the sordid industrial world, the drudgery of teaching, the endless studying to pass exams. He long allowed his imagination to wander in "a wistful dream of *Lorna Doone*"; and later would look back upon these idyllic days as "the old romance of Dora and David",[5] thus blurring the boundaries between the real and the imaginary. Before his character had time to become tempered by contact with real life, the boy found in books not only an interpretation of what he knew, but a sort of vicarious experience, all too often leading to disillusion. Lawrence thus became accustomed to perceiving reality through a veil of literature, attributing meaning to it only if it was connected with an inner universe motivated not by any determinism, but by sheer desire. Thus he could never see Jessie simply as the straightforward girl she was: he kept comparing her to stereotypes existing only in his own mind: to Emily Brontë, a holy nun, a Pre-Raphaelite woman, a Botticelli angel. As if driven by an irresistible need to transmute the real into the imaginary, he must always see her through a legend, express their relationship in symbols, meaningful to himself, but which neither explained nor resolved any of their problems.

"You are Psyche, you are the soul," he told Jessie, "and I leave you as I *must*."[6] The influences of Schopenhauer and of the Symbolists, themselves imbued with the psychology of *The World as Will and Representation*, could only confirm a basic tendency long since predisposing him to express reality in its most subjective and imaginative forms. We have already seen the same attitude in his studies: botany and French opened up to him worlds in which fantasy could spread its wings, freed from the constraints of reality. His reactions to works of art was also totally subjective. In the philosophers he sought above all an explanation and justification of his own ideas. All this is the antithesis of the scientific approach, patiently trying to reconstitute the universe according to a plan satisfying reason and respecting the evidence of the senses. In reading, as in life, Lawrence proceeds by intuitive comparisons, perceiving each scrap of truth as though revealed in a flash of illumination and delving frantically around to try to extend his revelation. But he never transcends the personal aspect of his problems, incapable as he is of escaping from the incoherence of facts. Where cool analysis might help him, as in the creation of the character of Miriam, he remains passionate and biased: the lyric poet prevails over the psychologist.

Everything in the philosophy then in vogue encouraged him in this path. In Schopenhauer, Nietzsche and William James he finds justification for subjectivism, for the denial that objective truth exists. He found in their works arguments to convince him that each man has the right to his own truth, his own morality, his own God, thus opening up the primrose path to intellectual laziness and a new form of dogmatism, but also to magnificent flights of the imagination. Is not all Lawrence's work in fact a passionate search for *his* truth, which he will preach dogmatically, but also a poetic expression of problems constantly envisaged in their concrete and personal aspects?

Certain problems reappear again and again in these early works: woman and class. And since his literary vocation is the main cause of his personal uprooting, the problem of class would naturally arise in connexion with the idea of the artist's destiny.

Predestination of the artist

On the fly-leaf of a book sent to Jessie shortly after their break in 1910, Lawrence copied out a verse of Baudelaire:

> *Soyez béni, mon Dieu, qui donnez la souffrance*
> *Comme un divin remède à nos impuretés*
> *Et comme la meilleure et la plus pure essence*
> *Qui prépare les forts aux saintes voluptés.*[7]

The poem "Bénédiction", like the sonnet "L'Albatros", seems to have stirred deep and various echoes in Lawrence. The whole of the beginning of *Sons and Lovers*, the birth and childhood of Paul Morel, might be an elaboration of the first and fourth stanzas of "Bénédiction":

> *Lorsque, par un décret des puissances suprêmes*[8]
> *Le Poète apparaît en ce monde ennuyé*
> *Sa mère épouvantée et pleine de blasphèmes*
> *Crispe ses poings vers Dieu qui la prend en pitié.*
> . . . .
> *Elle ravale ainsi l'écume de sa haine*
> *Et, ne comprenant pas les desseins éternels,*
> *Elle même prépare au fond de la Gehenne*
> *Les buchers consacrés aux crimes maternels.*

Baudelaire may not have been thinking of the incestuous love of a mother. But what is important is what Lawrence may have read into or unconsciously added to these verses. As to the role of woman in the life of the artist, he may well have taken up another hint from Baudelaire:

> *Et mes ongles, pareils aux ongles des Harpies,*
> *Sauront jusqu'à son cœur te frayer un chemin.*

While Lawrence may not have considered himself *"un fort"*, he certainly thought of himself as exceptional, burdened with a difficult, painful but heaven-sent task. This conception of the nature and the predestination of the poet was based on the romantic tradition certainly known to him, in its French form, through Baudelaire: a tradition maintained even in the naturalist movement by the "art for art's sake" school, and reaching full impetus in Verlaine and the Symbolists. But there is also an English tradition, from Milton to Blake, from Carlyle to Ruskin, from Shelley to Francis Thompson, which holds the poet to be at once an inspired prophet and the scapegoat of humanity. It is hardly necessary to recall here the close link uniting this conception and the proud individualism of the English puritans, as well as with the Nietzschean concept of the Superman.

The poet, the artist, lives an intense spiritual life, and his whole physique is adversely affected. Such is the Lawrentian interpretation of the curse he bears:

> If you have acquired a liking for intensity in life, you can't do without it. I mean vivid soul experience. It takes the place, with us, of the old adventure, and physical excitement ... A craving for intense life is nearly as deadly as any other craving. You become a "concentré"; you feed your normal flame over with oxygen, and it devours your tissue.[9]

But the artist's mission cannot be denied: of this Lawrence was very early aware. If he writes it is because an irresistible force drives him to do so. Paul Morel paints without any clear knowledge of what he is doing, stimulated by his mother's presence: Miriam interprets to him the meaning of his pictures after they are painted. He is no more than the executor of his artistic drive. Lawrence himself refused to raise a finger to put his more serious work before the public: it was Jessie who sent his poems to Hueffer. To Lawrence commercial dealings with publishers were always the worst possible chore, an intolerable humiliation to his ego: surely it was for the public to take the first steps to seek out the man of God?

> This transacting of literary business makes me sick. I have no faith in myself at the end, and I simply loathe writing. You do not know how repugnant to me was the sight of that *Nethermere* MS.[10]

His mission was to open new horizons to men, to extend their consciousness to its utmost limits:

> I can open the blue heaven by looking and push back the doors of day a little, and see—God knows what! One of these days I shall slip through. Oh, I am perfectly sane; I only strive beyond myself!—"Don't you think it's wrong to get like it?" asked Siegmund. "Well, I do and so does everybody. But the crowd profits by us in the end. When they understand my music, it will be an education to them; and the whole aim of mankind is to render life intelligible."[11]

But men are not yet ready to understand: the artist is a whipping-boy, isolated and rejected by men:

> Exilé sur le sol au mileu des huées ...

The hostility of the public is taken for granted, an attitude, incidentally, little calculated to conciliate it: the English will not like what he wants to write: "the British public will stone me if it ever catches sight" of *Sons and Lovers*.[12] Lawrence seems almost to take a secret pleasure in knowing he can arouse irritation and thus attract attention.

The artist is a nervous, hypersensitive type: Sarah Bernhardt, in *La Dame aux Camélias*, so upset Lawrence that he let himself be shut in the theatre.[13] Music can disturb him deeply.[14] His suffering is out of proportion to its cause: hence his pessimism, his disgust with life. His literary vocation is a malediction which saps his vitals, corroding the whole of life, and inspiring the poet with nostalgia for animal simplicity:

> I wish, from the bottom of my heart, the fates had not stigmatized me "writer". It is a sickening business . . . The literary world seems a particularly hateful yet powerful one. The literary element, like a disagreeable substratum under a fair country, spreads under every inch of life, sticking to the roots of growing things. Ugh, that is hateful! I wish I might be delivered . . .[15]

Woman and morality

From his earliest youth, Lawrence was convinced that woman was the intermediary between the artist and life. She was therefore as essential to him as a public and it was through her he suffered most. Having a double role, she caused double suffering.

In the first place she was the companion, the source of inspiration: "One part of my nature needs you deeply," he told Jessie. "Some parts of one's nature are always changing but another part never changes, and that part will always want you." "I, its creator, you its nurse," he wrote to her of his first novel, telling her again she was "the anvil on which I have hammered myself out". Without her he felt incapable of writing.[16]

But woman also represents sex life; it is through her that men may rediscover "the lost wisdom" of the snowdrops.[17] If modern man is indeed deprived of divine simplicity, of a direct and naïve vision of the universe, of pure and unadulterated physical enjoyment, this must be even more true of the artist. To retreat into animality like Annable, like George Saxton, is a form of abdication, of suicide. To seek a sister-soul is to indulge in a more refined but equally cruel form of torture. Miriam and Helena are true harpies, tearing to the very marrow of their bones Paul Morel and Siegmund:

> The best sort of women—the most interesting—are the worst for us. By instinct they aim at suppressing the gross and animal in us. They are super-sensitive—refined a bit beyond humanity. We, who are as little gross as need be, become their instruments. Life is grounded in them, like electricity in the earth; and we take from them their unrealized life, turn it into light or warmth or power for them. The ordinary woman is, alone, a great potential force, an accumulator, if you like, charged from the source of life. In us her force becomes evident. She can't live without us, but she destroys us. These deep, interesting women don't want *us*; they want the flowers of the spirit they can gather of us; we, as natural men, are more or less degrading to them

and to their love of us; therefore they destroy the natural man in us—that is, us altogether.[18]

Lawrence must at all costs explain his failure, his disillusionment: sometimes he does so in more generous terms; sometimes, as here, he links his frustration to his sense of predestination as a poet. But always his desire to understand is mingled with an unpleasant aftertaste of hatred or at least resentment, probably not unconnected with the sadism often associated with what Havelock Ellis calls the "somewhat feminine organization" of cruel men, less apt than the strong to know how to restrain any impulse to cruelty.[19]

Woman must not be allowed to forget all the blood and brutality of animal nature. She must be made to weep, to regain contact with the deep realities of instinctive life, and with the physical emotions which the organization and coldness of modern life eliminate, weaken or disguise. She must be made to admit her carnal self, torn from her indifference, even if this means torturing her: not unlike the reaction of the spoiled child, who, feeling himself abandoned, draws attention to himself by scratching and biting.

A constant craving for emotion and sensation is here evident: the artist must experience everything, must sacrifice none of the infinite possibilities of his nature. But while Lawrence has a strong leaning towards animality, he does not feel obliged to abandon the general direction of human progress, the path of consciousness and differentiation. He does not want simply to turn back:

Like a beast with lower pleasures, like a beast with lower pains.

On the contrary, he wants to preserve and extend the consciousness which is the mark of civilized man, not to let himself go like George Saxton. Paul Morel is driven by the deep conviction that his destiny is somewhere further on in human development, in a world more highly evolved than that of Nottingham and Eastwood.[20] The artist is an intense being, whose life is "fierce experience and hot destruction";[21] an eternal adolescent incessantly on the move, he also has something of the romantic man of destiny, of de Musset's "Don Juan". No woman can hope to keep for herself alone the love of such a man. His profession, his mission also have their exigencies: in order to write Helen's story, he must become her lover. With should and ought Lawrence has nothing to do: how can he bind himself when he can never know where the spirit will carry him? Jessie Chambers found that he "assumed the rights and privileges of the 'superman'", arguing that as an exceptional man he met with exceptional difficulties and should be allowed a larger latitude of conduct.[22]

The logical result, as well as probably the initial cause, of this assumption is total moral instability, particularly evident at a time when Lawrence, already fully adult, still seems in need of consolidating a fluid, fluctuating, variable ego.

Learning from Jessie that Helen was in Nottingham, he suddenly changes from "tender and wistful" to "hard and flippant".[23] Miriam often sees in Paul Morel an unstable, changeable child, a leaf floating on the breeze; and to Jessie Lawrence quotes Verlaine's "Chanson d'automne", likening himself to the leaf blown by the autumn wind.[24]

He is well aware of his own impotence:

I *must* run away from my battles. I fight a bit, and run away, and then fight again. *You* are strong, and can fight to the end, but I *must* run away.[25]

Important decisions are always taken in his dreams:

My dreams make conclusions for me. They decide things finally. I dream a decision. Sleep seems to hammer out for me the logical conclusions of my vague days, and offer me them as dreams. It is a horrid feeling, not to be able to escape from one's own—what?—self-daemon—fate, or something. I hate to have my own judgments clinched inside me involuntarily. But it is so.[26]

Seeing Jessie to the station on a tram after one of their last meetings, he exclaims:

If only we could run away on this.[27]

He would like the rails to take the initiative: such are the limitations of his will-power.

In 1910, to explain to Jessie his conduct with Helen, he made her read Barrie's *Sentimental Tommy* and *Tommy and Grizel*, telling her that he was "in exactly the same predicament" as Tommy.[28] He has indeed certain affinities with Barrie, like Lawrence a son deeply devoted to a mother ravaged by the loss of an elder son. Like Lawrence, Barrie came from the common people and a calvinistic background, but by dint of talent and hard work opened all doors before him. In Tommy Sandys, a Scotch urchin who becomes a famous novelist, Barrie intended to portray one aspect of his own nature, as well as of the artistic temperament in general. Morbidly sentimental, Tommy has lost all notion of the boundary between the real and the imaginary. He refuses to choose, since choice involves self-restriction, destroying a whole world of attractive possibilities. This incorrigible egoist thinks he can please everyone. Hence his attitude to women: agreeing with each in turn, always charming, he allows himself to be led into declarations of a love almost always totally imaginary. While he is with her, each girl in turn is the best, the only beloved.[29] His imagination invariably carries him beyond all idea of restraint:

The most conspicuous of his traits was the faculty of stepping into other people's shoes and remaining there until he became someone else; his individuality consisted in having none.[30]

Tommy tortures the practical and courageous Grizel, whom he loves, without ever being sure that this genuine emotion is not as imaginary as the others: no doubt this was what Lawrence was trying to explain to Jessie. Like Barrie's hero, he redeems himself by his charm. He had all the seduction of imaginative irresponsibility, reconciling contradictions with an ease which great men of action might well begrudge him. From the age of seventeen or eighteen he dreamed of gathering all his friends round him in a great house big enough to contain them all. Jessie, for once recalcitrant, suggested they might not agree among themselves: "But he brushed my objection aside: it would be all right, he was sure, and wouldn't it be fine?"[31]

A mere dream could thus inflame his imagination, and provided he had a sympathetic listener he was happy. His mobility, his gift of sympathy made him a delightful companion, a charming friend, provided no one expected from him either decision or responsibility. His real genius was his gift of seeing "into the very essence of life".[32] At first he was surprised that women found him pleasing, since he seemed to lack the animal vigour so much envied in his imaginary rivals. But he soon found the explanation: like Barrie's hero he had the gift of persuading them that "black is green or purple". He could make the stars "flash and quiver".[33] He was an excellent actor: charades, at which he excelled, remained a favourite amusement, even after he was married, and all his friends remember with admiration his irresistible miming of other people's individual foibles and characteristics. Is this not one more sign of that talent for observation, that intuitive discernment, which are the very basis of the art of pleasing?

Too sensitive, too delicate for the world of action, inevitably suffering if not protected against the constant pricks of daily life, he was amply compensated by the possession of all the great artistic qualities: a feeling for the subtlest shades, imperceptible to coarser natures; an intuitive imagination which gave him the key to character and won him fervent friends; the gift of illusion, making up for the inadequacies of this world and effacing sorrows. For those around him he could open up the gates of imagination, exploring with them the infinite kingdom of hopes and possibilities, ruled by no law other than that of desire. Beside such an enchanter, Barrie's Peter Pan, with whom he has so much in common, was no better than a parlour conjurer.

The realist

Yet with his mother, that tireless worker and courageous character, Lawrence had learned to face reality. He could, when necessary, show tenacity in pursuit of some essential aim. Remembering his precarious health, we must not in all fairness underestimate the constant effort he made to progress in a world in which he had to pass examinations, study, teach, and build up a literary reputation by dint of racking his own brain and covering reams of paper. His temperament had an obstinate and realistic side which both he and Jessie related to his mother's influence. If, with Jessie, he generally drifted in a world of dreams, he also recalled the cold and practical lessons learned from his mother: all our actions are inspired by self-interest;[34] passionate love does not last—"small showers last long", as Mrs Lawrence put it.[35] When he is in this mood, Jessie trembles at his sarcasms. She dare not ask him to reread the lines of Shakespeare:

> Let me not to the marriage of true minds
> Admit impediments . . .

for fear of hearing him say in the glacial tone she knew so well: "But *are* we true minds?" This is the same Bert who, like Browning's Andrea del Sarto, is convinced that a man is what he makes himself, with his own fierce energy, and that he, Lawrence, owes no man anything:

> Besides, incentives come from the soul's self;
> The rest avails not . . .[36]

The critical spirit of this puritan is not exempt from the sin of pride, but this does not prevent him from perceiving from time to time what it is he lacks. George, content to hope that life will soon decide his destiny for him, is advised by Cyril to "make things happen". Like Siegmund, George is accused of lacking the "dispassionate intelligence" to control himself and "economize".[37] Lawrence himself was certainly not without such intelligence. But on his own he was incapable of the effort of will required to execute its orders. Such incapacity may have been due in part to his ill-health, for as his success in his studies and his teaching prove, in the world of action he was well able, when necessary, to hold his own. But his recriminations show clearly what the effort cost him.

Talent and intelligence apart, instability and irresolution remain his most characteristic traits. And this is how he has shown himself in *Sons and Lovers*, torn between Miriam and his mother, floating from one to the other, his heart bleeding at each wound he inflicts. He would like to let all his loves co-exist, as well as all his selves, however incompatible, even at the risk of seeing his soul lacerated in the fearful struggle. He burns the candle at both ends, indifferent to his imminent collapse. A beautiful obsessive image expresses this state of mind: "a tree that flowers until it kills itself".[38] "Life is beautiful, so long as it is consuming you."[39] Paul Morel fiercely rejects the conception of happiness desperately held out to him by his anxious mother:

> Struggles of this kind often took place between her and her son, where she seemed to fight for his very life against his own will to die . . . At this rate she knew he would not live. He had that poignant carelessness about himself, his own suffering, his own life, which is a form of slow suicide.[40]

We have seen Lawrence plunged by the death of his mother and his own failures in love into a despair culminating in a very serious illness and the threat of an untimely death. We have seen his work haunted by the thought of suicide. There still remains a God, but not a personal God:

A vast, shimmering impulse which waves onwards towards some end, I don't know what—taking no regard of the little individual, but taking regard for humanity. When we die, like rain-drops falling back again into the sea, we fall back into the big, shimmering sea of unorganized life which we call God. We are lost as individuals, yet we count in the whole.[41]

The best the individual can hope from this God is a fleeting sense of happiness when he finds himself in harmony with the vague overall design ordering the world.[42] For the most part Lawrence feels himself alone, isolated, incapable of getting into rhythm with humanity. Sensuality is indeed the expression of God, of Life, among all living things:

I think there's more in the warm touch of a soft body than in a prayer. I'll pray with kisses.[43]

Already he has made with two or three women "the great experiment of sex",[44] without finding that which he is seeking and which only a woman can give him. But they are too perverse; they insist on loving all that is best in him, and which he most despises: his intelligence, his radiant personality. They attach less importance than he to what he trembles at the thought of lacking: physical vigour. Does he really know himself what it is he asks of the woman?

Surely, surely somebody could give him enough of the philtre of life to stop the craving which tormented him hither and thither, enough to satisfy for a while, to intoxicate him till he could laugh the crystalline laughter of the star, and bathe in the retreating flood of twilight like a naked boy in the surf, clasping the waves and beating them and answering their wild clawings with laughter sometimes, and sometimes gasps of pain.[45]

This is an even more subtle form of refusal to live, of that fear of the endless march towards the unknown—which for Lawrence goes hand in hand with a love of intense, dangerous and destructive living. What Lawrence unknowingly seeks in women is the source of life, the Mother. He wants to play like a child in the sun of a protective love which, bathing him in the warm contact of reality and smoothing the stones along his path, preserves him from the cruelty of decision. He is ready to embark desperately in the first adventure likely to provide such happiness, and at the same time offering the prospect of a passionate existence capable of assuaging his thirst for strong emotion.

PART TWO:

THE EXILE: 1912–19

7

A NEW START

The swiftly-moving chain of events which bore Lawrence away from his own country and past into a new life with Emma Maria Frieda von Richthofen demands clear analysis. Lawrence's own letters reveal a part of the truth; another part emerges from the Memoirs of Frieda Lawrence; while the letters published in her two books make it possible, by a step-by-step review of the principal stages of the drama, to elucidate the attitudes of the two main protagonists.

Elopement with Frieda von Richthofen

In the early months of 1912 Lawrence was still steeped in despair.[1] Anxious to get away from everything, it occurred to him that he might well follow up the suggestion of Fritz Krenkow, his German uncle by marriage, and apply for a lecturership in a German university. To this end he made inquiries of his former teacher, Professor Ernest Weekley of Nottingham University College. In the second half of March, Weekley invited him to lunch. Lawrence refused: but Mrs Weekley sent a note urging him to accept. It was she who received him when he arrived, and talked with him for half an hour before lunch, clearly eager to make the acquaintance of this young writer whose budding reputation had preceded him. Immediately they felt drawn to each other and almost at once he was writing to tell her she was "the most wonderful woman in all England".[2] On 17 April Edward Garnett was assured, "She is ripping—she's the finest woman I've ever met ... she's splendid ... the woman of a lifetime."[3]

The visit was renewed, and soon followed by excursions into the countryside with Mrs Weekley's two small girls. It was on one of these rambles that Frieda realized that she loved this long, thin man with light, sure movements, who was capable of forgetting her completely as he squatted playing with her children by the brook.[4] Whereupon, one Sunday, in her husband's absence, she asked him to stay the night with her. "No," replied Lawrence,

> I will not stay in your husband's house while he is away, but you must tell
> him the truth and we will go away together, because I love you.[5]

The next day Mrs Weekley left home, leaving her son with his father but
taking the two little girls to their grandparents in London.[6] Lawrence's own
letters here take up the story: on 23 April he asked Garnett whether he might
come to The Cearne for the weekend on the following Saturday with Mrs
Weekley, who was due to leave for Germany on 4 May to celebrate her
father's "fifty-two-years-of-service jubilee".[7] After spending the weekend of
27–8 April with Lawrence at The Cearne, Frieda returned to Nottingham
with the intention, according to Lawrence, of "telling" her husband that
very day.[8] On Friday 3 May they left England together.

Lawrence could muster only £11 in cash; another £25 was owed to him.[9]
The rest of his fortune consisted entirely of hopes—articles or short stories
written or planned, and his almost-completed novel "Paul Morel". He had
no idea how he would be received in Metz by Frieda's family. Yet Jessie
Chambers, seeing him for the last time by chance about this time, found him
"a different man": his "look of despair" had gone, and he was more normal,
though "subdued and gentle" with her family and herself.[10] Clearly his
confidence in life had been restored.

The woman who had wrought this change was a luxuriant Germanic
beauty of a type rarely met with in England: flaxen-haired, with green eyes
"that would contract, catlike, into a curious half-smile at once direct,
penetrating and averted", ample curves, proud shoulders, and "a face borne
up by a fierce, native vitality".[11] Her leonine profile, haughty manners, her
passionate and almost brutal frankness, seduced Lawrence to the point of
making him forget that, in fact, he knew nothing of this woman. Only that
she was of Prussian origin, "daughter of Baron von Richthofen of the ancient
and famous house of Richthofen",[12] that she was thirty-one years old, the
mother of three children, and wife of a man to whom he himself was bound
by a certain degree of gratitude and whose position in the world was far
securer than his own.

Mrs Weekley had grown up in the aristocratic cum military circles of the
garrison city of Metz. A local convent education had failed to tame this wild
and boisterous child. Indeed her character had been moulded less by her
detested schooling than by influences totally foreign to any experienced by
Lawrence: the joyous freedom of the garden round her father's official
residence, her happy, teasing exchanges with the friendly soldiers temporarily
quartered just outside the house, games among the huts and trenches of the
Metz fortifications with boys of her own age, her preferred companions. She
herself suggests that a corporal impatiently counting the days till his release
from a bullying, unjust and stupid service may have encouraged her

unexpressed revolt against the social order, symbolized in conquered Lorraine by military rank. On the whole, adolescence seems to have left her puzzled and unsatisfied, waiting for something indefinable, "something more" to fill the void of a perhaps over-free existence.[13]

Her marriage in 1899 to an English professor, a distinguished gentleman, well known for his scholarly works and popular with his colleagues, transplanted her at the age of eighteen to Nottingham, a busy industrial and commercial centre, into a narrowly puritan environment: a drastic change indeed from open-handed life in a family which, though relatively not well off (in fact, her branch of the family was of the minor Prussian landowning nobility, impoverished by an unfortunate grandparental investment in sugar beet),[14] led in occupied Lorraine the life of conquerors and overlords.

How could she have foreseen the dreariness of the Midland town, its rows of identical little houses, its interminable Sundays?

Gossip later retailed by Mabel Luhan, confirmed not only by Lawrence's *Letters*, but by Frieda's own *Memoirs and Correspondence*, and her affirmation to the present author in 1932 that "everything Lawrence wrote really happened", suggests that Mrs Weekley sought and found compensations, sometimes on the spot, but above all during annual holidays in Germany, affording her ample opportunity to satisfy her need for pleasure. Meanwhile, under the influence of one of her German lovers, the psychoanalyst Otto Gross (whom she calls Octavio in her autobiographical sketch), she was beginning to realize that her life was an empty shell totally unrelated to her natural temperament.[15]

Frieda von Richthofen was certainly not made to fit into the narrow life of provincial England. Though capable of generosity and tenderness, as well as pity for the suffering inflicted by her conduct, the strictures of a moral sense as it is commonly understood were absolutely foreign to her impulsive nature. There was nothing narrow or conventional about her. Lawrence attracted her: therefore she would take him for her lover. But the curious creature refused, insisting that she should confess to her husband her previous infidelities and commit herself immediately to him:

> I was frightened. I knew how terrible such a thing would be for my husband, he had always trusted me.[16]

She struggled against the imperious sway of this young writer, so frank as to be almost insolent, who pierced her to the very core, revealing the deep dissatisfaction of a woman used to playing with men.[17] Must she then give up her comfortable life, the joy of having her children about her, in order to follow his still uncertain career? It would seem that at first Mrs Weekley entertained only the idea of a brief escapade with Lawrence.[18]

But this was not what Lawrence had in mind. At last he had found the woman of his dreams: beautiful, free from the inhibitions imposed upon a Miriam or a Helena by an excess of spiritual life or by the age-old pressure of middle-class morality; a woman who made advances, who took the initiative in love-making. Moreover, not only was she a *lady*, the daughter of a baron, descendant of a noble family, but also a foreigner, thereby facilitating for the miner's son the leap across the barrier of class. Could he, in fact, have overcome his social inhibitions with a woman of the English aristocracy?[19] Who can tell how heavily such considerations may have weighed in Lawrence's sudden decision? Certainly he was never able to resist talking of his wife's aristocratic origin.[20]

Scruples of conscience or practical considerations might have made other men hesitate. What were they to live on? What would her husband do? All this Lawrence brushed aside. She must tell Weekley her decision before it was even taken; afterwards, once they were irremediably committed, they could worry about the rest.

They arrive in Metz on 4 May. Frieda has warned no one:[21] her parents' house is full of guests. She goes to the same hotel as Lawrence, letting only her sisters into the secret. But Lawrence, taken for an English spy, is threatened with arrest, the baron's influence has to be invoked and "the cat is out of the bag". Not unnaturally the Richthofens try to dissuade their daughter from wrecking her life for a poor devil of a writer who cannot even afford to buy her shoes. She should go back to her husband: she herself begins to talk of returning to Nottingham; she calls her lover "Mr Lawrence".[22]

Lawrence's tactics are simple: to remove her as much as possible from the influence of her family, if necessary preventing her from reading her own letters from home;[23] to convert her to a policy of frankness. His first step is to write to Weekley, a letter received by the husband on 10 May and subsequently read out in the divorce court:

> Mrs Weekley will have told you everything, but you do not suffer alone. There are three of us, although I do not compare my sufferings with what yours must be. It is really torture to be in this position. I am here as a distant friend, and you can imagine the thousand lies it all entails. Mrs Weekley hates it, but it had to be. I love your wife, and she loves me. I am not frivolous or impertinent. Mrs Weekley is afraid of being stunted and not allowed to grow, so she must live her own life. Women in their natures are like giantesses; they will break through everything and go on with their own lives . . .
>
> Don't curse my impudence in writing to you; in this hour we are only single men. However you think of me, the situation still remains. I almost burst my heart in trying to think what will be the best. At any rate we ought to be fair to ourselves. Mrs Weekley must live largely and abundantly: it is her nature. To me it means the future. I feel as if my effort to live was all for her. Cannot we all forgive something?[24]

He follows this with a passionate outburst to Frieda against the ambiguity of their position:

No more dishonour, no more lies. Let them do their —— silliest but no more subterfuge, lying, dirt, fear. I feel as if it would strangle me. What is it all but procrastination? No, I can't bear it, because it's bad. I love you. Let us face anything, do anything, put up with anything. But this crawling under the mud I cannot bear . . . I will stop in Metz till you get Ernest's answer to the truth. But no, I won't utter or act or willingly let you utter or act, another single lie in the business . . . You are clean, but you dirty your feet . . . If I didn't love you I wouldn't mind when you lied.[25]

The next day he leaves Metz, and waits at Trier for Frieda.[26] She joins him there on 11 May, but almost at once he leaves again for Waldbröl in the Rhineland, to stay with his young relative Hannah Krenkow. What then happened in Trier between the lovers? Lawrence destroyed the first letter he wrote to Frieda from Waldbröl; clearly it was too unkind. Yet en route from Trier, at Hennef-am-Sieg, he had overcome his doubts and anger:

I know I love only you. The rest is nothing at all. And the promise of life with you is all richness. Now I know.[27]

Frieda seems to be nearing a decision:[28] she is preparing to leave for Munich where he is to join her.[29] But many things are still unsettled. Will her husband consent to a divorce? This is what Lawrence hopes, though later it appears that he will consent only to a legal separation, seriously considering divorce only in December.[30]

Where will they live? Alfred Weber, brother of the economist Max Weber, and lover of Frieda's eldest sister Else Jaffe, offers them his apartment; if necessary they can borrow money.[31] Lawrence's plebeian soul revolts: somehow they must ensure the future on a firmer basis, all the more so since Frieda has expressed the fear (for him almost a hope) that she may be pregnant.[32]

They must wait, not spoil anything by being overhasty. Lawrence takes his responsibilities very seriously: now that the suspense is over he feels that they should "be still awhile and let themselves come to rest". After all, it is his marriage,

. . . not a thing to be snatched and clumsily handled. The love is there, then let the common sense match it.[33]

All at once he seems overcome by the majesty of the occasion: before being united with Frieda, he would like to have "a kind of vigil", like the knights of old. For a time he behaves like a bride trembling at the altar, not daring to say "Yes".[34] He almost seems to be seeking excuses, to be no longer sure of himself: both of them are "shaky" and need time to recover; they must not risk starting off their life together by a failure or a quarrel.

Frieda grows impatient, does not understand. Perhaps with the intention of rousing the jealousy of this strange lover, she tells him of a rival, H . . . At first Lawrence does not respond:

> If you want H— or anybody, have him. But I don't want anybody, till I see you. But all natures aren't alike. But I don't believe even you are your best, when you are using H— as a dose of morphia—he's not much else to you.[35]

All the same his jealousy has been pricked: how hard it is to defy convention to the bitter end! His next letter tells her, though without great enthusiasm, that his young relative Hannah is "getting fonder and fonder" of him.[36]

Moreover he is anxious to achieve the respectable and permanent state of matrimony, and dreams of an open, honourable and fertile union which will be the "great thing" in his life:[37]

> . . . we can wait even a bit religiously for one another . . . When I have come, things shall not put us apart again . . . Henceforth, dignity in our movements and our arrangements, no shufflings and underhandedness . . . It's a marriage. not a meeting.[38]

The "wandering" sexual desire which had so long tormented him is now transformed by the certitude of "real love" into "a calm, steady sort of force". He will come to her "solemn", full of greatness, intending to observe "dignity in our movements and arrangements".[39]

These daily letters to Frieda, preserved thanks to Frau von Richthofen, come to an end on 17 May, with Frieda's departure for Munich. Others would seem to have been lost. A week later their "honeymoon" begins: on 24 May Lawrence arrives at Munich[40] and on the 25th they leave together for Beuerberg on the Isar. Henceforward the story of their life can be read in the series of poems *Look! We Have Come Through!* and in the correspondence. All that will be necessary in this chapter will be to summarize their movements and try to distinguish the birth of those feelings and ideas that led the writer to formulate the "philosophy" of the relations between man and woman expressed in his works after 1912.

Chronology: 1912–14

After a week in Beuerberg and some six weeks in Alfred Weber's apartment at Icking, near Munich, Lawrence and Frieda, accompanied part of the way by David Garnett and his friend Harold Hobson, walked up the Isar valley, pausing for several days at Mayrhofen, near Innsbruck, and crossing the

Brenner early in September. After staying a month at Riva, at the then Austrian end of Lake Garda, they settled for the winter at the Villa Igea, at Gargnano, on its western shore.[41]

Early in 1913, they began to think of coming to England to negotiate the divorce, see the children and try to obtain custody.[42] But in mid-April they first went for a time to Irschenhausen in Bavaria to a chalet belonging to Frieda's sister Else. By 21 June they were in England, staying with the Garnetts. Then, Frieda having been refused permission to see the children, they went to Broadstairs till the end of July.[43] New friendships began: with Edward Marsh, who had published Lawrence's poem "Snap-Dragon" in his *Georgian Poetry*, and who introduced them to Herbert and Lady Cynthia Asquith, son and daughter-in-law of the Prime Minister, to W. H. Davies and to several other poets. Lawrence had already been in touch with Katherine Mansfield, and through her with her lover John Middleton Murry. The two couples quickly formed a "spontaneous and jolly" friendship, their mutual sympathy perhaps enhanced by the similarity of their matrimonial situations.[44]

The Lawrences then returned together to Bavaria: in mid-September Frieda remained with her family while Lawrence went off alone on foot to Italy by way of Switzerland, via Lake Constance, Lugano and Milan.[45] The great romantic tradition drew them towards Leghorn and the Gulf of Spezia, where they met again, subsequently settling at Lerici[46] from late September 1913 till June 1914. They then returned separately to England, Frieda by way of Baden-Baden, Lawrence walking through Switzerland and France. Frieda's decree nisi, pronounced on 18 October of the previous year, having been made absolute on 27 April, they were married in London shortly after their arrival, on 13 June 1914.[47]

Life with Frieda

From 1912 onwards, neither the life nor the work of Lawrence can be understood without knowledge of the intimate story of his "marriage", which, moreover, he never attempted to conceal. His very sincerity, which some might judge excessive, forces us to look closely at an experience which colours the whole Lawrentian concept of existence.

At Beuerberg, in the Bavarian highlands, they spent eight idyllic days. Lawrence was intoxicated by so many new experiences: unknown flowers, jade-green mountain torrents, a Mystery played by peasants, walks with Frieda, everything enchanted him. Even the most childish games were touched with magic:

> One day we went into the mountains, and sat, putting Frieda's rings on our toes, holding our feet under the pale green water of a lake, to see how they looked.[48]

The first letters written from Icking exhale a total happiness, a confidence in life, a love both self-assured and unreserved:

I love Frieda so much, I don't like to talk about it. I never knew what love was before . . . The world is wonderful and beautiful and good beyond one's wildest imagination. Never, never, never could one conceive what love is beforehand, never. Life *can* be great—quite god-like.[49]

This new love has two facets: it is both a feeling of unity so perfect that it transcends physical desire, making Frieda cry out "I'm so happy I don't even want to kiss you",[50] and a wild and "shameless" enjoyment of all the pleasures of the flesh. Lawrence had never before lived in constant intimate contact with a woman's body: the revelation was so overwhelming that he felt impelled to regale his correspondents with pictures of his mistress in her nightgown, and to describe her for them, and in his poems, a Teutonic Rubens beauty, her breasts "swaying like full-blown *Gloire de Dijon* roses".[51] His own sensuality took him by surprise: he scarcely recognized his tame English nature in the barbarities of the *Hinterland der Seele* into which he plunged with Frieda, and advised those "blasted fools", his fellow-countrymen, to follow his example.[52] In the poem "Frohnleichnam", in which the Corpus Christi of the title is the lover's body, he expresses the utter shamelessness of their love, of a physical passion triumphant over all difficulties, asserting itself by total repudiation of social taboos, perhaps, in fact, requiring certain powerful ritual and semi-blasphemous stimulation to achieve its full expression.[53]

But into all this physical intoxication soon crept a discordant note. Before the end of June Lawrence had discovered that "the real tragedy is in the inner war which is waged between people who love each other, a war out of which comes knowledge and —". Does the dash already stand for "hate"?[54]

Why war? In the first place because he was not a free man, capable of giving himself up completely to his love: this was brought home to him the very first night:

The night was a failure
  but why not—?
In the darkness
  with the pale dawn seething at the window
  through the black frame
  I could not be free,
  not free myself from the past, those others—
  and our love was a confusion,
  there was a horror,
  you recoiled away from me.[55]

Who were "those others"? Those who had already troubled his dreams, haunted his poems and his novels? His mother, Jessie, Alice, Louie, Helen, "Siegmund"; perhaps the husband and former lovers of his mistress?[56] For a man as psychically unstable as Lawrence, it was easy for these ghosts to come between himself and his desire, and make him wish for annihilation deeper than death.[57] In his dreams he raved deliriously and Frieda was afraid, feeling in him a force which sought to break and to destroy her.[58]

He was indeed seeking to extirpate one whole aspect of her inner self: her yearning for her children. She had been told that they were unhappy, and were asking for her. Her husband would have taken her back on their account. And she had been at least "half-contemplating" going to England to see Weekley. In spite of Lawrence's repeated assurances that Frieda's nose was "nailed to his waggon" and that she could no longer leave him, however painful the loss of the children, he was clearly tortured by jealousy.[59] Why must she, like Lot's wife, turn round to look behind her, towards England, weeping tears of salt? He cursed her "base motherhood", the mother-love that was once more destroying his happiness. He longed for the time to come when the curse against her would have left his heart, but meanwhile found no salve for the deep corrosion of tears not shed for him.[60]

Renewed efforts were made to get her to return to England. Frieda would have liked Lawrence to implore her to stay. But Lawrence had his own strategy: let her choose freely between him and the children. At heart he knew it was already too late: she knew he needed her more than did the children. But when, after breaking a dish on Lawrence's head at Irschenhausen, Frieda left him for two days and sought refuge with her sister Else at Wolfratshausen, perhaps with the idea of going back to England without him, he soon found he could not bear to be away from her, "even for hours".[61] What would he do without her? The thought of his being "cut off"[62] from her filled him with terror and in his poem "Mutilation" he invoked the dark Gods, Powers of Night, to carry off her decision in sleep, making her choose him and not the children. He was reduced to humiliating himself before her, begging her not to abandon him, for without her "neither life nor death could help".[63]

In the little apartment on the Isar, on the way to Italy, then at the Villa Igea, the struggle was waged constantly, quarrel following quarrel with such incredible regularity[64] that Lawrence ended by referring to them euphemistically as "the trouble about the children".[65] Yet the children were not their only cause. They were rather one of a number of pretexts to explain the bottled-up resentment which exploded whenever the differences between their characters aggravated them to madness, or when Frieda gave Lawrence cause to doubt her faithfulness, according to one eye-witness swimming off even on their unmarried "honeymoon" to spend long hours with a woodcutter on an island in the Isar. So many potential points of friction were bound to exist between two such totally different characters. They were poor, their money barely sufficient to pay for rent and food. The £50 received in October had to last till March.[66] Frieda was disorderly, indifferent to considerations of economy and the petty details of material life, totally lacking in respect for other people's work, the simplest household tasks remaining incomprehensible mysteries to her. Lawrence was orderly, hard-working, economical, scrupulously attentive to detail; he liked her to have a drawer for cottons, a drawer for woollens and a drawer for silks; Frieda's wastefulness exasperated him. It is he who was obliged "to watch the money, Frieda doesn't care".[67] She liked to stay in bed all morning, leaving it to him to get the meals and clean the rooms while she, Bovary-like, lay smoking cigarette after cigarette.[68] The common people, with whom Lawrence felt at ease, Frieda treated "*de haut en bas*" and to his annoyance had made the class-distinction felt in her first contact with his sister Ada.[69]

He was jealous of her previous lovers and feared he might last no longer than they. But when he questioned her too closely about her past life as an emancipated woman, Frieda, perhaps involuntarily, made him feel her aristocratic superiority, her scorn for vulgar suspicions, for his requests for superfluous details: how could *she* be capable of half-measures in love? The jealous lover was made to realize the vulgarity of such uncouth and plebeian sententiousness, such clumsy moral qualms.[70]

Frieda, for her part, was jealous of his work, feeling that something in him was beyond her reach and left her quite outside. When he was writing, he was no longer entirely hers, but a machine for turning everything into literature, interested in her only in order to transform her into copy; some-times she thought of him as "a big fountain pen which was always sucking at my blood for ink".[71] On one occasion, probably in Italy, she scribbled on a poem dedicated to his mother, whose memory still haunted him, her disgust for the emotional thraldom in which he was still held; while she had proved that *she* could love, this was entirely beyond him:

> . . . I have nearly killed myself in the battle to get you in connection with myself and other people, early I proved to myself that I can love, but never you. Now I will leave you for some days and I will see if being alone will help you to see me as I am, I will heal again by myself, you cannot help me, you are a sad thing. I know your secret and your despair, I have seen you ashamed—I love you better, that is my reward.[72]

Were there deeper causes for these mutual recriminations? It is unwise to try to read too much between the lines, and so fall into the error of trying to construct an interpretation of the physical life of an author on quotations from his works. John Middleton Murry, for example, insinuates Lawrence's sexual impotence, without perhaps distinguishing sufficiently between different periods of his life and varying states of health; he also makes no distinction between physiological and psychic impotence. When he wrote

Son of Woman, Murry may have had information the source of which he was not then willing to divulge; but he was satisfied to rest his case on interpretations of the works (such as his reading of the poem "Rose of All the World"), which in themselves prove nothing.[73]

The short story "New Eve and Old Adam", almost certainly written during the first year of the "marriage", can, however, help our understanding of these quarrels and their causes. The two protagonists, who have been married a year, wage "almost continuously that battle between them that so many married people fight, without knowing why".[74]

The plot is of no importance; it merely serves to thinly disguise Lawrence and Frieda. What counts is the description of the quarrels between Peter and Paula, and of their efforts to understand what is behind this relentless struggle.

Their grievances are many and complex. On a purely abstract plane, they might perhaps be reduced to the inevitable opposition between two totally unrestricted egoisms. Peter nor Paula are unable to give themselves up completely to each other: each desires the total submission of the other to his own invading personality. Such at least is the impasse they reach after striving to arrive at an explanation of their mutually inflicted sufferings.[75]

They do, however, give voice to some pointed accusations: Paula makes fun of her husband for coming back to her sooner than she would have liked, without carrying out his threat of staying on in Paris to amuse himself with other women. Nowhere does she openly throw doubt on his virility; on the other hand she makes no attempt to hide a certain irritation, a suppressed contempt for this bashful lover, "too palky to take a woman".[76] She reproaches him for strewing the path of their love with reservations and difficulties.[77] While she pours herself out to him without reserve, all she finds is a total void—he simply isn't there. He, on the other hand, is always asking, demanding all her attention, he follows her everywhere, like a jealous shadow. She can no longer stand it:

> I must rest . . . from you . . . who use a woman's soul up, with your rotten life. I suppose it is partly your health, and you can't help it . . . But I simply can't stick it,—I simply can't, and that is all.[78]

He is always holding something back, as though he were afraid of trusting himself completely. He loves her, he cannot stay away from her; but he denies this love and hates her because he finds himself dependent on her.[79]

Peter cannot understand what she is driving at and can only reply by counter-accusations of his own. He is jealous, he suspects her, he suffers to see her taking too great an interest in a workman installing telephone wires,[80] or in a total stranger. She is heartless, unstable:

> There was no core to the woman. She was full of generosity and bigness and kindness, but there was no heart in her, no security, no place for one

single man. He began to understand now sirens and sphinxes and the other Greek fabulous female things. They had not been created by fancy, but out of bitter necessity of the man's human heart to express itself.[81]

She takes a man only for her own egotistical satisfaction: "You treat me as if I were a piece of cake, for you to eat when you wanted."[82] As a husband he hates to be a mere thing for his wife to play with at her pleasure. (In the short story "Once", Lawrence carries this analogy even further: "I lay wondering if I too were going into Anita's pocket, along with her purse and her perfume and the little sweets she loved.)[83] Whenever Paula humbles herself before him and treats him as her lord and master, Peter knows it is no more than a sensual, egoistic game and he feels his insignificance more than ever, knowing himself to be no more than "something like her lordliest plaything", the instrument to satisfy the need to love which comes over her from time to time.[84] A wife, at least, he feels, should be more submissive. Never would it be peace between them:

> She would never belong to him as a wife. She would take him and reject him, like a mistress.[85]

But he too loves only with that impersonal desire that ignores the partner, seeking only blind self-satisfaction:

> He seemed, often, just to have served her, or to have obeyed some impersonal instinct for which she was the only outlet, in his loving her.[86]

Was his own love, then, in some way defective, incomplete?

> Did he only want the attributes which went along with her, the peace of heart which a man has in living to one woman, even if the love between them be not complete; the singleness and unity in his life that made it easy; the fixed establishment of himself as a married man with a home; the feeling that he belonged somewhere, that one woman existed—not was paid but *existed*—really to take care of him; was it these things he wanted, and not her? Yet he wanted her for these purposes—her, and nobody else. But was that not enough for her? Perhaps he wronged her—it was possible . . . She said he did not love her. But he knew that, in his way, he did . . . Was there something wrong, something missing in his nature, that he could not love?—He struggled madly as if he were in a mesh and could not get out. He did not want to believe that he was deficient in his nature. Wherein was he deficient? It was nothing physical. She said he could not come out of himself, that he was no good to her, because he could not get outside himself. What did she mean?[87]

What, indeed, did she mean? Lawrence passionately denies any physical incapacity on his part. At approximately the same time (1913) he returns to the subject in "Daughters of the Vicar",[88] amplifying with evident sympathy the character of Alfred Durant. Before allowing himself to be married to a "young lady" at the age of thirty, this miner had been a sailor, and in the course of his voyages had remained "almost quite chaste". Like Tom Brangwen, like the Birkin of the Prologue to *Women in Love*, Alfred prefers the "idea of women" to the reality.[89] Can it be that his *relative* chastity corresponds to some form of masturbation, of which there is more than a faint suggestion in the Prologue?

> There were two things for him, the idea of women, *with which he sometimes debauched himself*, and real women, before whom he felt a deep uneasiness, and a need to draw away. He shrank and defended himself from the approach of any woman. And then he felt ashamed. In his innermost soul he felt he was not a man, he was less than the normal man. [*Italics added.*][90]

In a low drinking-house in Genoa, he had watched with curious envy "the swaggering, easy-passionate" Italians who, by "instinctive impersonal attraction", could go with women who aroused in him only pity and disgust. When drunk he had dared approach such women, but the "sordid insignificance" of the experience had appalled him: "It had been nothing really: it meant nothing." "He felt as if he were, not physically, but spiritually impotent: not actually impotent, but intrinsically so."[91]

It is difficult not to suspect that the Lawrence who wrote these lines in 1913 is harbouring a certain anxiety concerning his sexual prowess. The following passage from "New Eve and Old Adam" seems to shed some light on this:

> Since she had begun to hate him, he had gradually lost that physical pride and pleasure in his own physique which the first months of married life had given him. His body had gone meaningless to him again, almost as if it were not there. It had wakened up, there had been the physical glow and satisfaction about his movements of a creature which rejoices in itself; a glow which comes on a man who loves and is loved passionately and successfully. Now this was going again. All the life was accumulating in his mental consciousness, and his body felt like a piece of waste.[92]

The first blaze of passion triumphant seems then to have subsided, making way for the difficulties of former days. Nowhere does Lawrence repeat his first astonishment at his own amorous feats: "You don't know how surprised I am, considering the rate we go at it."[93] He settles down to marriage and seeks in it stability and peace with a woman who is indisputably his for ever:

> I want to be able to look ahead and see some rest and security somewhere. By the time I am thirty I shall have had my bellyful of living, I think, and shall have either to slacken off or go to the devil.[94]

Whatever the causes of this change, he soon asks Frieda for material care as well as sensual satisfaction: his expectations in this respect, however, were doomed to disappointment. In the poem "Lady Wife" he bursts out in eloquent verses against this mistress whom he would reduce to the role of wife:

> Put ashes on your head, put sackcloth on,
> And learn to serve.
> You have fed me with your sweetness, now I am sick
> As I deserve.
>
> Queens, ladies, angels, women rare,
> I have had enough,
> Put sackcloth on, be crowned with powdery ash,
> Be common stuff.[95]

Nor is this all: away from a woman, Lawrence is haunted by a feeling of utter isolation; he feels lost and incomplete. The protective touch of a body is like an opiate which soothes the agonies of "the man who is not loved":

> The space of the world is immense, before me and around me;
> If I turn quickly, I am terrified, feeling space surround me;
> Like a man in a boat on very clear, deep water, space frightens and
>   confounds me.[96]

The man who is loved, however, finds, if not confidence, at least oblivion like that of the infant cradled by its mother:

> Between her breasts is my home, between her breasts.
> Three sides set on me space and fear, but the fourth side rests,
> Warm in a city of strength, between her breasts . . .
> And I hope to spend eternity
> With my face down buried between her breasts
> And my still heart full of security
> And my still hands full of her breasts.[97]

Such oblivion, foretaste of eternity, bears some analogy to religious ecstasy. It cannot, for instance, be reached without effort, for the conscious ego protests and refuses to accept annihilation. All Lawrence's lovers experience this struggle between consciousness and total surrender of being. When Paula, after a quarrel, comes back and lifts her arms to him, Peter cannot resist her, but even in the ensuing ecstasy he suffers bitterly:

> They clasped each other closer, body to body. And the intensity of his feeling was so fierce, he felt himself going dim, fusing into something soft and plastic between her hands. And this connection with her was bigger than life or death. And at the bottom of his heart was a sob.[98]

The plunge into darkness is both sinister and divine, at once death of the self and entry into eternal life. Certain additions to the stories appearing in the *Prussian Officer* volume, made in 1914, show how important this concept had become for Lawrence since he began to live with Frieda. In "Second Best", the simple Tom, having accepted the symbolic mole offered by Frances, asks her to marry him:

> The blood came up in him, strong, overmastering. He resisted it. But it drove him down, and he was carried away.

In Frances, too, the ego is annihilated: she can now respond to the call of the flesh and marry a man less cultured than the husband of her dreams. She laughs nervously and replies in "a dead voice", "But there was a thrill of pleasure in this death."[99]

Alfred Durant, driven by necessity to kiss Miss Louisa, suffers agonies of martyrdom, but finally lets himself go:

> Then clumsily he put his arms round her, and took her, cruelly, blindly, straining her till she nearly lost consciousness, till he himself had almost fallen.
>
> Then, gradually, as he held her gripped, and his brain reeled round, and he felt himself falling, falling from himself, and whilst she yielded up, swooned to a kind of death of herself, a moment of utter darkness came over him, and they began to wake up again as if from a long sleep. He was himself.[100]

The violence of this dissociation, or rather dissolution, of consciousness, suggests a relatively simple explanation of the psychological impotence admitted by Peter and by Alfred Durant. We know that at the end of 1911 Lawrence felt himself to be a sexual failure, but at this point it was still possible for him to blame the woman, to believe she was frigid, her instincts inhibited by excessive spirituality. Above all, he seems to have feared that he would never be able to win a woman for himself, that he lacked the power to subjugate another.[101] We also know his vacillating temperament, his difficulty in openly envisaging the sexual act with any individual woman.[102]

We do not know whether this had physiological causes. His health was delicate; shaken by two bouts of pneumonia, he was, if not tubercular, at least predisposed to tuberculosis. Against this must be set the evidence of one of his mistresses—possibly tinted by the glow of memory many years after the event—who after his death confided to a friend that he could "come back to a woman time after time".[102a] This pleads in favour of psychological maladjustment rather than of physical weakness. Doctors do not agree on the psychic and sexual effects of pulmonary consumption, some even venturing to suggest that it may be the result, not the cause, of unresolved psychic conflict. In a study of "The Psychology of the Consumptive", S. Vere Pearson, Physician to the Mundesley Sanatorium, has concluded that it would be erroneous to ascribe to pulmonary tuberculosis "the peculiarities of Lawrence", which he would rather attribute to his family environment, love experience etc.[103] Lawrence was certainly a nervous type, highly psychosomatic, with oversensitive reactions and psycho-physiological mechanisms easily affected by emotional disturbances.

Inhibitions acquired in early life were probably liable to interfere with his sexual life: an association of physical passion with the brutalities of his father; a hatred or fear of the flesh inculcated from infancy by his puritan environment and by a secret maternal belief that anything to do with love was shameful, unclean and socially unsafe. The influence of such unconsciously-acquired ideas on a shy, sensitive boy can scarcely be exaggerated. Then, closely linked with these early repressions of instinct, came his mother's prohibition of his spontaneous love for Jessie, the suppression of any carnal aspect of that love, resulting in a split of the ego. Nor had his conscience ever been able entirely to sanction the carnal attraction of Louie or his liaison with Alice Dax.

With every woman he approached, Lawrence experienced this same split: he found himself incapable of loving those he respected and of respecting those he dared desire. Small wonder he believed himself doomed to a kind of impotence, his sole issue being to find a woman who would respond at once to his passion, before the judgment of his conscious self could intervene. A woman who would make him forget this self and its repressions. Ideally she should be a foreigner, since a woman of his own kind and background would inevitably recall the self he abhorred.[104]

But a new complication now arose: the sin against society. The woman he carried off triumphantly was married and the mother of a family, and her lover had to bear the weight of her responsibilities. They could find happiness only in forgetting or completely repudiating not only the hostile world outside but, as far as Lawrence was concerned, his religious nature as well.[105] The innocent and pure joys of love were spoiled by the memory of "those others"[106] they had left behind:

> At last, as you stood, your white gown falling from your breasts,
> You looked into my eyes, and said: "But this is joy!"
> I acquiesced again.
> But the shadow of lying was in your eyes.
> The mother in you, fierce as a murderess, glaring to England,
> Yearning towards England, towards your young children,
> Insisting upon your motherhood, devastating.[107]

The only solution was to plunge into that *Hinterland der Seele* revealed at Icking. All they had in common was the world of the flesh, in moments when both could simultaneously deny moral responsibility, and all sense of past and future, annihilating the self, with its insistence on continuity through successive states of consciousness. Carnal love seen as mystic experience was entirely consistent with Lawrence's psychological nature and behaviour.[108] The only hope of complete union was to abandon oneself for a moment to the sudden and brutal impulse of the flesh. So they would come together, anywhere and any time, regardless of external circumstances:

> We whispered: "No one knows us.
> Let it be as the snake disposes
> Here in this simmering marsh."[109]

"The Primrose Path", a short story written before the end of 1913,[110] recounts an incident which, taken alone, seems insignificant and obscure, but becomes clear as soon as it is seen as a true reflection of the early period of the Lawrences' own life together. At Victoria Station, Nottingham, young Berry meets a long-lost uncle, Dan Sutton, now a taxi driver. In the past Sutton had left his first wife, Maud, for the path of adventure; quite recently he has set up house with a young girl, Elaine Greenwell, whose mother lives with them. After driving his nephew to his destination, he invites him home. On the way they visit Maud, who is dying of consumption. Both men are heavily affected by her agony. Sutton then drops Berry at his home while he goes off to park his taxi. Deep in a kind of daydream, Elaine seems to come to life only on the arrival of her lover. Dan eats his soup standing before the fire, without removing his rain-soaked overcoat. His eyes never leave Elaine, who goes to take off his heavy coat. As she thus symbolically undresses him, he alternates between seeking the girl's eyes and turning away from her as he recalls "the death-horror" of his wife. Step by step Lawrence brings us to understand what the woman's gesture in trying to unclothe the man means to them:

> She was playing with passion, afraid of it, and really wretched because it left her, the person, out of count.[111]

Gradually, on the man's face, a "curious smile of passion" replaces the expression of horror caused by the memory of the dying woman. His eyes meet those of Elaine "in a flame of passion" and, without regard for the unfinished meal or for the embarrassment of Berry and Mrs Greenwell, they abruptly leave the room[112]—a mode of conduct which witnesses of the Lawrences' life have assured the present author was characteristic of the couple.

The end of the story foreshadows a return to a sense of social obligation and personal dignity: the awakening will be disappointing and cruel. Elaine, so Berry tells himself, will end up by detesting Sutton and go off with someone else: "and so she did".[113]

Lawrence, too, knew what it is to awaken from ecstasy, his heart full of hatred:

A kind of blind helplessness drove them to one another, even when, after he had taken her, they only felt more apart than ever. It had seemed to her that he had been mechanical and barren with her. She felt a horrible feeling of aversion from him, inside her, even while physically she still desired him.[114]

Here Lawrence is recording experience, not interpreting and evaluating it as he was to do later, for instance in *Women in Love*. When the conscious self takes over after the oblivion in the contact of the flesh, his lovers remain separate, hostile, consumed with mutual hatred. Each separation seems more inevitable, more definitive than the last. Then follow quarrels innumerable, battles as blind and as hurtful to mind and body as the duel of the flesh itself. A "love so full of hate" also found expression in sadistic brutality:

> What?—Your throat is bruised, bruised with my kisses?
> Ah, but if I am cruel what then are you?
> I am bruised right through.[115]

The lovers evolved a rhythm of their own, a regular cycle: ecstasy of being together, sure of each other and of mutual desire; passionate union, followed by a return to consciousness—depression, jealousy and reproaches, an onslaught of words, a battle reaching a paroxysm of hatred; the return to peace, all shame forgotten, all bitterness dissolved. Waves of passion, love and hate washed over the two lovers, leaving them in a state of "purity" which, for the poet, was an ideal to be desired:

> Now the hate is gone,
> There is nothing left;
> I am pure like bone,
> Of all feeling bereft.[116]

For Lawrence this cycle was dictated by a psychological necessity. We have already seen how the image of love is, for him, closely linked with violence. It is not impossible that this alternation of blows and caresses, of annihilation of the conscious self in amorous ecstasy and in hatred, may have corresponded to some profound requirement of his being. In any event it is clear he was unable to do without Frieda: she strengthened his personality, for him she was a source of life; eternally young, with what he calls "a genius for living".[117] Similarly, for Frieda too, Lawrence soon became a necessity, an overpowering habit. It was he who brought her the revelation of her true nature. The intense and dangerous way of life that the romantic and Nietzschean Lawrence so ardently desired before discovering it, Frieda provided; and he, in turn, stimulated her own desire for it. The amorality he sought so eagerly to achieve was Frieda's natural state. At first she swept before her all his puritanic scruples. Alone against the world, they rejoiced in their isolation, savouring their freedom, *vogelfrei*. Living only in the present, intensely, ardently, they "rejected immortality" and delighted in the fullness of their being, oblivious of yesterday and of tomorrow.[118]

To Lawrence this way of life offered both a maximum of nervous exaltation and, through the fulfilment of his sexual needs and his profound conviction that the whole of his being now found satisfaction, a maximum of self-preservation, at least at the beginning. He was happy, and he put on weight.[119] Both had the courage to live according to what they believed to be the laws of their own natures, to reject the mean existence of those who seek to save their psychic capital. Monotony was unknown to them. Emerging from the depths of despair, Lawrence's eagerness for life was renewed by an existence which might well have exhausted healthier constitutions than his. Both were convinced that they were following their predestined course, and that, with the forces of love and hatred in constant equilibrium, their lives, linked one to the other like the orbits of twin stars, were destined eternally to "circle on their fate in strange conjunction".[120]

The scene was set for tragedy, but in real life the action was often nearer to burlesque. Neither lover dared to make the supreme gesture, so that instead of the single tragic crisis we find a succession of minor "scenes" and a tragi-comedy which reached its *dénouement* only with the exhaustion of the weaker protagonist, eighteen years after the honeymoon at Beuerberg. The wheel of fate turned with the precision of a well-oiled machine:

> The conflict of love and hate goes on between the man and the woman, and between these two and the world around them till it reaches some sort of conclusion.[121]

Its course sometimes slowed down, sometimes speeded up by adventitious causes, it pursued its inexorable and consuming rhythm.

And indeed fatality does seem to have been at work: the inherent fatality of character. Lawrence was already repeating a familiar pattern. The old conflicts, the struggle against Jessie, against Helen, against Louie, against his mother, the estrangement from Alice-Clara, seem to have determined for ever the cadence of his life. Even his hatred for Frieda's maternal instinct echoes the old jealousy of the frustrated lover for the caresses freely lavished on the younger members of their families by Emily and Miriam[122] and his old conviction that marriage is a duel in which woman and children are invariably pitted against the man.[123]

Lawrence's earlier works sometimes seem to have forecast his own destiny, an impression perhaps due to his power of self-penetration and to its accompanying weakness; his ability to foresee the possibilities open to his personality, but inability or refusal to react, to mould his own character for persevering action. He meets the woman of his dreams:[124] a being completely different from all those who, tormented by a need for moral and psychological continuity, are unable to forget the wounds of battle in the pleasures of the flesh; one who lives entirely in the present, forgetful of yesterday, careless of tomorrow. Far more than Lawrence, himself poorly equipped for a life of adventure and constantly haunted by a longing for spiritual and moral values, she personifies that philosophy of discontinuity and of the fleeting moment he wished to make his own, that renunciation of moral continuities which will mark his conception of character in his new novels. This she makes abundantly clear in her own book of reminiscences, a masterpiece of direct and spontaneous expression of her own nature. The choice of the title, taken from one of Lawrence's poems,[125] is in itself a stroke of self-revelatory genius.

It is difficult to imagine a contrast more absolute than between the German "lady", born to live in the present to the cry of "*après moi le déluge*", and the farmer's daughter from the Haggs, aspiring to be her young lover's conscience and the keeper of his ideal.[126] Surely guided by her instinct, Jessie was able to build up a balanced and sensible personality which enabled her to weather the blow of what she felt to be her lover's final cruelty. As for Lawrence, he found all that he was seeking, in a most unlooked-for combination: the seed that had sprouted on the slag heaps of Eastwood, fortified by transplantation to the fertile soil of Haggs Farm, suddenly let itself be borne away at the whim of the passing wind.

New ideas in the making: the social self

This new turn in Lawrence's life is accompanied by an adjustment of some of his ideas. To what extent the new trends of thought came from Frieda and the German circle, or were the continuation of certain changes already in progress when he first met her, is not certain. But it is clear that his attempt during 1912–13 to construct a "philosophy" is partly intended to explain and justify his conduct. And no sooner had he conceived this justification than he saw it as a rule of life for others, and started to preach it.

Despite all the acrimony, Italy immediately became for Lawrence the land of all delights. His health improved rapidly. The absolute unconstraint of the life enchanted him. After the great trip on foot from Munich to Riva[127] came the revelation of the South, of the mountains round Lake Garda and, later, the Mediterranean itself. Countless descriptions scattered through the letters of the period show us the village of Gargnano, with its miles of red and golden autumn vineyards, its olive and lemon groves, the ever-changing face of the lake with its sails and little steamer, its new moon and rose-coloured mountain tops.[128] The letters from Lerici are permeated by the friendly presence of the sea, the village rising sheer out of the black rocks,[129] the perpetual fruit and flowers, all the luxuriant vegetation that so rejoiced his poet's heart. The effect of a London almond tree in bloom on this child

MR. D. H. LAWRENCE

1. D. H. Lawrence's birthplace, 8a Victoria Street, Eastwood, Nottinghamshire. (*By courtesy of the Central Library, Nottingham.*)

2. The Lawrence family in about 1893. *Left to right, standing:* Emily, George Arthur, William Ernest; *seated:* Ada, Lydia Lawrence, D. H. Lawrence, John-Arthur Lawrence. (*By courtesy of the Humanities Research Center, The University of Texas at Austin.*)

3. D. H. Lawrence, King's Scholar, 1905. From *The Teacher*, 25 March 1905. (*By courtesy of the Trustees of the British Museum.*)

4. Lawrence in 1908. (*By courtesy of Mrs Margaret Needham.*)

5. Haggs Farm, Underwood, Nottinghamshire. (*By courtesy of the Central Library, Nottingham.*)

6. Jessie Chambers in about 1913. (*By courtesy of J. R. Wood Esq.*)

7. Louie Burrows. (*By courtesy of Professor J. T. Boulton.*)

8. Alice Dax and her daughter in about 1916. (*By courtesy of Mrs. W. E. Hopkin.*)

9. (*Right*) Helen Corke in about 1912. (*By courtesy of Humanities Research Center, The University of Texas at Austin.*)

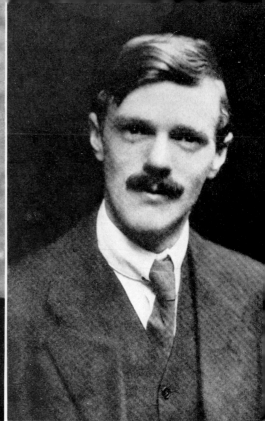

10. Frieda von Richthofen, aged eighteen. (*From the personal collection of Professor Warren Roberts, Director of the Humanities Research Center, The University of Texas at Austin.*)

11. D. H. Lawrence in about 1913. (*By courtesy of Professor Warren Roberts. Photograph by Walter Barnes Studio.*)

12. (*Left*) David Garnett in 1916. (*By courtesy of the Mansell Collection.*)

13. Portrait of Lady Ottoline Morrell by Augustus John, 1909. (*By courtesy of Mrs J. Vinogradoff.*)

14. D. H. Lawrence at Garsington Manor in 1916. (*By courtesy of Mrs J. Vinogradoff.*)

15. Phoenix rising from its flames. From a thirteenth-century bestiary in the Ashmole Collection, M.S. 1511, folio 68R. It was seen by Lawrence in Mrs Jenner's *Christian Symbolism.* (*By courtesy of the Bodleian Library.*)

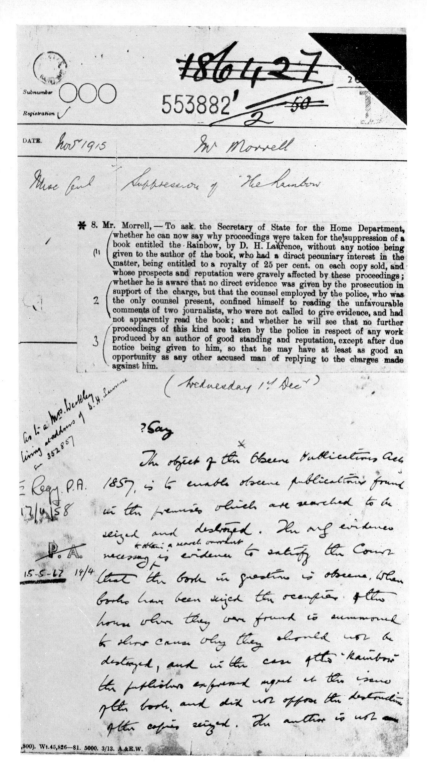

~~186427~~

553882' ~~/50~~

DATE. nov 1915

Mr Morrell

Misc Genl | Suppression of The Rainbow

✳ **8. Mr. Morrell,** — To ask the Secretary of State for the Home Department, whether he can now say why proceedings were taken for the suppression of a book entitled the Rainbow, by D. H. Laurence, without any notice being given to the author of the book, who had a direct pecuniary interest in the matter, being entitled to a royalty of 25 per cent. on each copy sold, and whose prospects and reputation were gravely affected by these proceedings; whether he is aware that no direct evidence was given by the prosecution in support of the charge, but that the counsel employed by the police, who was the only counsel present, confined himself to reading the unfavourable comments of two journalists, who were not called to give evidence, and had not apparently read the book; and whether he will see that no further proceedings of this kind are taken by the police in respect of any work produced by an author of good standing and reputation, except after due notice being given to him, so that he may have at least as good an opportunity as any other accused man of replying to the charges made against him.

(Wednesday 1st Dec)

?Say

The object of the Obscene Publications Acts 1857, is to enable obscene publications found in the premises which are searched to be seized and destroyed. The only evidence necessary is evidence to satisfy the Court that the book in question is obscene. When books have been seized the occupier of the house where they were found is summoned to show cause why they should not be destroyed, and in the case of the "Rainbow" the publishers expressed regret at the issue of the book, and did not oppose the destruction of the copies seized. The author is not

16. Home Office minutes concerning *The Rainbow*: (1) Philip Morrell's written question in the House of Commons and the draft reply (*continued in Plate* 20). Note, in the left margin, handwritten minute relating to Frieda. It is in red ink in the original. (*Crown copyright. Public Record Office Document No* HO45/13944.)

accused, ~~nor~~ nor is he any
party in the case. The Police
acted in accordance with the
law, and I cannot give any
instructions of the nature
suggested.

[initials]
26. 11 . 15

To Commr of Police for
Observations. *[initials]*
29-11-15.

The proposed reply seems
quite correct

[initials]
30/11

It is correct but
rather avoids answering
the questions.
Draft reply A herewith
[initials]
30-11-15

S. of S. dictated reply.
R.

17. Home Office minutes concerning *The Rainbow*: (2) The Draft reply
to Philip Morrell continued; minuted "for observations" to Scotland
Yard by Sir Edward Troup, Permanent Under-Secretary. Note, at the
end, "S[ecretary] of S[tate] dictated reply" (i.e. Sir John Simon). (*Crown
copyright. Public Record Office Document No HO45/13944.*)

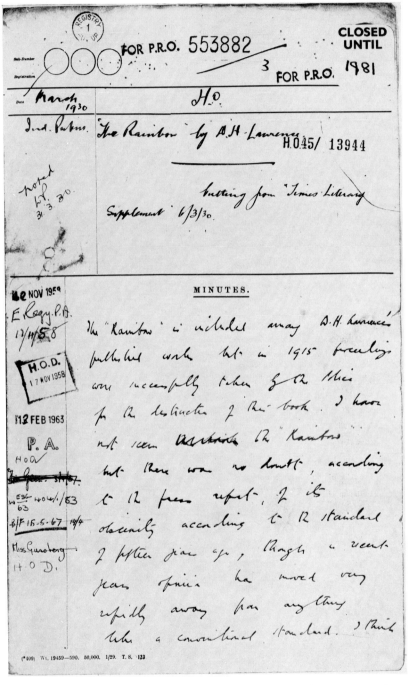

March 1930   *H.O.*

The Rainbow by *D.H. Lawrence*

H.O.45/ 13944

cutting from "Times Literary Supplement" 6/3/30.

MINUTES.

The "Rainbow" is included among D.H. Lawrence's published work but in 1915 proceedings were successfully taken & the thing for the destruction of the book. I have not seen the "Rainbow" but there was no doubt, according to the press report, of its obscenity according to the standard of fifteen years ago, though in recent years opinion has moved very rapidly away from anything like a conventional standard. I think

(*409) Wt. 19459—590. 50,000. 1/29. T.S. 123

18. Home Office minutes concerning *The Rainbow*: (3) The March 1930 minute by Sir Sidney Harris, calling the attention of the police to the reissue of *The Rainbow*, as advertised by Martin Secker in the *New Statesman*. (*Crown Copyright. Public Record Office Document No HO45/13944.*)

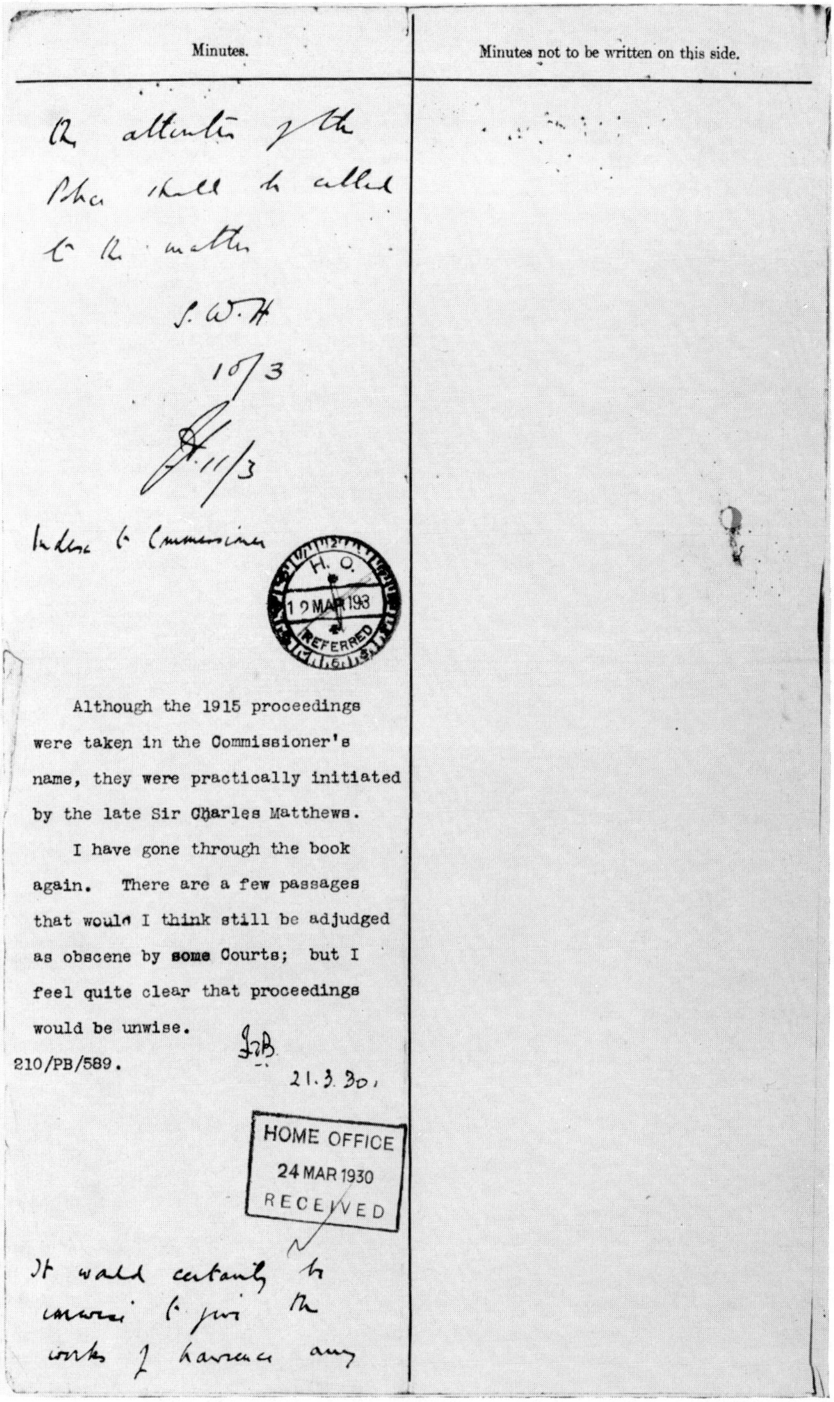

[handwritten, upper left]

The attention of the
Police shall be called
to the matter

J. W. H.
10/3

[initialed] 11/3

Letter to Commissioner

Although the 1915 proceedings
were taken in the Commissioner's
name, they were practically initiated
by the late Sir Charles Matthews.

I have gone through the book
again. There are a few passages
that would I think still be adjudged
as obscene by **some** Courts; but I
feel quite clear that proceedings
would be unwise.

210/PB/589.   *[initialed]*

21.3.30.

HOME OFFICE
24 MAR 1930
RECEIVED

[handwritten, lower left]

It would certainly be
unwise to give the
works of Lawrence any

19. Home Office minutes concerning *The Rainbow*: (4) The second page
of Sir Sidney Harris's minute, initialed by Sir John Anderson, Permanent
Under-Secretary, and forwarded by him to Scotland Yard. The reply by
the Prosecutions Branch of the Metropolitan Police, laying the onus for
the initial prosecution on the Director of Public Prosecutions, Sir Charles
Matthews. (*Crown Copyright. Public Record Office Document No HO45/
13944.*)

20. Lady Cynthia Asquith. (*By courtesy of Bassano and Vandyk Studios.*)

21. Bertrand Russell in 1916. (*By courtesy of the Russell Estate and Features International, London.*)

22. Lawrence and Frieda with Katherine Mansfield and John Middleton Murry. (*By courtesy of Professor Warren Roberts, The Humanities Research Center, The University of Texas at Austin.*)

23. Botticelli's "Mystic Nativity". See p. 355 of the present text and *Phoenix*, p. 461. (*By courtesy of the Trustees of the National Gallery.*)

24. "Madonna degli Ansidei" by Raphael. See pp. 313, 355 and *Phoenix*, p. 461. (*By courtesy of the Trustees of the National Gallery.*)

25. Ducks swimming among lotus flowers, from a pavement in the villa of Amenothes III at Medinet-Habu, from Maspéro, *Egypte, Ars Una*, figure 278 and p. 165. See p. 391 of this text and *Women in Love*, p. 91. (*By courtesy of Librairie Hachette.*)

26. The Meidum Geese, Cairo Museum, as reproduced in Maspéro, *Egpyte, Ars Una*, pp. 92, 95. See p. 391 of this text and *Women in Love*, p. 91. (*By courtesy of Librairie Hachette.*)

Abb. 13

27. Wrestlers at Beni-Hassan, in Maspéro, *Egypte, Ars Una*, p. 197. Could this wrestling scene have contributed to the chapter "Gladitorial" in *Women in Love?* (*By courtesy of Librairie Hachette.*)

28. The chakras: a diagram from *The Apocalypse Unsealed* by J. M. Pryse, p. 26. See pp. 392, 407–8, etc. of the present text. (*By courtesy of the Trustees of the British Museum.*)

29. Mark Gertler, "The Merry-Go-Round", 1916. See p. 390. (*By courtesy of the Ben-Uri Gallery, London.*)

of the north was multiplied a hundredfold by the spell of the Mediterranean. The spirit of pure delight engendered by these letters reveals the full charm of a Lawrence whose passion for life's every magical detail is his greatest quality.

After the country, the inhabitants. Lawrence delighted in their mere existence. He saw them with enraptured eyes and makes us see them too. The warm life of the local wineshop, the old lady who keeps the little mountain inn and who tells him her daughters have all trained to be teachers, bring back his own boyhood: these are his sort of people, and as he talks to them of familiar matters, he is both delighted and delightful.[130] Felice, the old servant in Lerici, her daughter Elide with her recaptured hen, a peasant wedding feast, all spring to life in these letters, living proof of the infinite joys the universe offers at every instant to a man knowing how to look for them. From the "flying jump" of the flea caught while writing a letter to Edward Marsh, to the black and shiny flies that will insist on keeping the sunlight from his drying figs—every detail is perpetuated in these letters.[131]

This is Lawrence at his best: spontaneous, simple, accessible to every passing influence, a child playing carelessly beside Mother Nature, every pore open to the faintest fleeting impression. He immortalizes the evanescent and the irreplaceable. Such flashes of beauty make these Italian letters delightful reading despite the tortured doubts of the bad days.

Thanks to the combined influences of a sun-drenched countryside, of love, and liberty at last achieved, Lawrence was writing copiously, chiefly poems, most of which were to appear, after various revisions, in *Look! We Have Come Through!*, *Love Poems* or *Amores*. As soon as he was installed at Riva, and again at Gargnano, he tackled the revision of *Sons and Lovers*. On 14 November the novel was finished; it only remained for Edward Garnett to cut out a few details which he felt might shock some readers.[132] Lawrence then dealt with the volume *Love Poems and Others* which appeared in February 1913.[133]

At Icking he had written three short stories but found that, under Frieda's influence, their "moral tone" would not have pleased his countrymen.[134] Needing to raise money quickly, he proposed writing another six, but the London magazines failed to greet his output with enthusiasm.[135] He then proceeded to write three plays, not published until after his death: "The Fight for Barbara", "The Merry-Go-Round" and "Married Man".[136]

As soon as *Sons and Lovers* was off his hands, he began almost at once on two new novels, one of which was destined eventually to become *The Lost Girl*, the other *The Rainbow* and *Women in Love*.[137] The genesis of the main ideas of these works is studied separately below.[138] At Irschenhausen, in 1913, he wrote three short stories set in Germany: "Honour and Arms" ("The Prussian Officer"), "Vin Ordinaire" ("The Thorn in the Flesh") and "Once".[139]

A large part of his correspondence with Garnett deals with his literary affairs: work submitted to magazines and publishers, contracts, payment of author's royalties, and so on. The financial situation was not bright: *Love Poems* did not sell well,[140] and while *Sons and Lovers* made it possible for him to return to Italy in 1913 money was still far from plentiful. The question crops up frequently in the letters, and on one occasion at least he was down to his last 50 francs.[141] None of which prevented him from showing generosity, sending pocket money to Frieda's son through Katherine Mansfield, or offering to lend £5 to Murry.[142]

During the first year his correspondents were relatively few: Edward Garnett and his son David; his former colleague McLeod, who kept him supplied with books and newspapers;[143] his old Eastwood friends the Hopkins, and his sister Ada.[144] When Ernest Collings, a young engraver, sent him a book he had illustrated which had shocked the booksellers by its daring, Lawrence showed himself touched by this first confraternal homage. He replied at length, embarked on a friendly correspondence, criticizing with sincerity and penetration Collings's own poems and praising his engravings rather more generously than in his correspondence with McLeod. Before long he was making him his confidant, telling him of his novels and his philosophy, asking him for a drawing for the wrapper of *Sons and Lovers*.[145]

The brief stay in England in 1913 added the names of new friends to the list of correspondents: the Murrys and, above all, Edward Marsh and Lady Cynthia Asquith, to whom letters soon became increasingly numerous and friendly, despite a small disagreement with Marsh over poetic rhythm.[146]

At Gargnano, isolation began to pall upon the Lawrences; the rhythm of their own loving and quarrelling was no longer enough:

> We've had a hard time, Frieda and I. It is not so easy for a woman to leave a man and children like that. And it's not so easy for a man and woman to live alone together in a foreign country for six months, and dig out a love deeper and deeper.[147]

This was followed by repeated appeals to all his correspondents to leave everything, get away from their jobs, their social obligations, and come to spend a few days with the runaways and taste with them the intoxicating joys of freedom.[148] None of them, however, arrived and Lawrence, impatient, reproached them all for their indifference.

Harold Hobson in 1912, Constance Garnett, Marsh and a friend in 1914, did bring some diversion, but Frieda seems to have found Harold Hobson too attractive.[149] A group of "Georgian" poets descended on Lerici one day, putting them in touch with the small local English colony, including a clergyman who took a fancy to the Lawrences: "When our dark history comes out, I shall laugh." Since they felt obliged to reveal they were not married, a slight coolness seems to have ensued.[150] Ivy Low, the future Mrs

Litvinov, also spent some time at Lerici, her friendship miraculously surviving the ordeal.[151]

Social contacts were probably more necessary to this couple than to many others and, at least at first, the temptation to quarrel was less great in company. But for many reasons such contacts were difficult to establish. At Irschenhausen, with Frieda's relatives, this was brought clearly home to Lawrence:

It is queer, but nobody seems to want or to love, *two* people together. Heaps of folks love me alone—if I were alone—and of course all the world adores Frieda—when I'm not there. But together we seem to be a pest. I suppose married people ought to be sufficient to themselves. It's poverty which is so out of place.[152]

Poverty was, indeed, an important element in the embarrassing circumstances then isolating the Lawrences from the rest of the world. Lawrence himself was happy with the ordinary Italians around them, the servants and peasants who to his gratified astonishment greeted Frieda and himself as *Signori*: a miner's son treated as a gentleman![153]

Nor did his wife's attitude make things easy. More from habit than out of arrogance, she treated the local people haughtily. Playing for a time with the idea of applying for a headmastership in a small English country school, Lawrence soon realized that Frieda's involuntary disdain for the common run of humanity must inevitably rule out such a project.[154]

In society, the boot was on the other leg, and it was he who found it impossible to be completely natural. It took him several days to get over the effect of meeting Lady Cynthia Asquith, so surprised and delighted was he that an earl's daughter should condescend to converse pleasantly with him:

There seems to be a big change in England, even in a year: such a dissolving down of old barriers and prejudices.[155]

Lawrence needed the moral support of his fellow-creatures and was ready to take his place in society and seek recognition from it. Reading *The Morning Post* in Lerici he was overcome with nostalgia for good form:

By the way, what a frightfully *decent* paper the *Morning Post* is. The more I read it, the more I think it is worth while to be a gentleman and to have to do with gentlemen. Their reviews of books, their leaders, and all, have such a decent, honourable tone, such a relief after the majority of newspaper filth.[156]

After the hard winter of 1912–13, he became anxious to settle down once and for all to a regular mode of life, to put an end to wandering and incertitude:

If there is a divorce, we shall stay out here till it is consummated, then come to England married. Frieda says she's not keen on marrying me—but I want some peace.[157]

Even in his beloved Italy he dreamed of "furnishing a little house in England", of friends receiving Frieda and himself as a respectable married couple.[158] Even when, by his behaviour, he was vehemently asserting the rights of the individual, he remained at heart a prisoner of his social self. While rejoicing in freedom from the bonds of his old profession, he sometimes seemed bitten by remorse and a sense of duty unfulfilled. In a frequently recurring nightmare, he finds himself back in England teaching.[159] The humour with which he treats this dream does not entirely succeed in concealing his preoccupation. Indifference would have been more convincing.

He could not get quite used to the idea that he was sinning against society by "the wickedness of waiting for another man's wife". He suffered at having to hurt others, and was "driven crazy" by the severe censure contained in letters from England. Why couldn't people let them alone?

I am sick to death of the bother. It's the rotten outsiders who plant nettles in paradise.[160]

With Frieda's family he was at once conscious of his isolation, of a slight feeling of reprobation. He trembled to think it might be the same in England and wrote pathetically to Garnett:

I hope you will stand by me a bit; I haven't a man in the world, not a woman either, besides Frieda who will. Not that anybody else has, I suppose, who goes his own way. But I haven't yet got used to being cut off from folks—inside: a bit childish.[161]

The publicity given to the divorce at first upset him, but only for a time, or so he says:

As for the divorce, it is curious how at first it upsets me and then goes off, and matters no more. I have found that one has such a living social self. I am sure every man feels first that he is a servant—he is a martyr or what—of society. And if he feels that he has trespassed against society, and it is adverse to him, he suffers. Then the individual self comes up and says, "you fool!"[162]

This, however, was not enough to kill the "social self": he had not confessed to Marsh and the Asquiths that he was living with another man's wife, but had introduced Frieda as Mrs Lawrence. When the divorce was reported in the press, he wrote to apologize for this impropriety, expressing the fear that they might feel displeased.[163] Once more he was dividing his personality into two: an "English feeling" which made him ashamed, and a far more brazen Italian "self".

Life was indeed a bed of nettles to his sensitive soul. People, places, even countries, he found pleasant or disagreeable according to whether they seemed to approve or censure his way of life. In Bavaria, home of Frieda's relations, he felt crushed, and smothered by the "tightness, the *domesticity* of Germany".[164]

In Italy, on the contrary, he found his spiritual home: "It broke my heart to leave Italy ... One must love Italy, if one has lived there. It is so non-moral. It leaves the soul so free. Over these countries, Germany and England, like the grey skies, lies the gloom of the dark moral judgment and condemnation and reservation of the people. Italy does not judge. I shall want to go back there." "I like Italy, which takes no thought for the morrow neither fear nor pride." "That is why I like to live in Italy. The people are so unconscious. They only feel and want; they don't know. We know too much."[165]

In Italy, indeed, away from Frieda's children, far from all those who might reproach them for their conduct, far from any specific social duties in the modern world, the Lawrences could best relish such happiness as they were capable of enjoying. Towards the end of 1913 and early 1914, with the help of the good climate, good health and Frieda's approaching liberation, "the trouble about the children" appears less often in the letters. Some kind of peace has been established and recriminations concerning the difficulties of marriage become more rare. The personality of each gradually working on that of the other, some sort of *modus vivendi* has been reached: "We are gradually getting near again, Frieda and I." At about the same time letters grow rather less frequent and the lovers are described as "really very deeply happy".[166] Calm had descended once more on the little "pink-washed" villa in Lerici and literary preoccupations take their place in the foreground of the correspondence.

The photograph published in *The Bookman* in February 1914 shows a Lawrence less thin, and with a certain assurance both in his expression and the way he holds his head. The outline of the mouth is strengthened by a thick moustache, but there remains something vulnerable and tender about the outer corners of the eyes. It is the portrait of a man content both with himself and others, the smile suggesting gentle amusement. The great "crisis" of marriage was over; it was possible for Lawrence and Frieda to believe they had "come through" triumphant. Lawrence was feeling sure both of himself and of the future.

The ideas and the mission

Little by little a conviction had been born in him, namely that he had found the remedy to all the ills of humanity. It is as if, unable to do without moral and intellectual sanction, he could find no better way of getting himself in harmony with society than to generalize on his own case, inviting everyone else to follow his example. The first, rudimentary expression of this attitude dates from August 1912:

Let every man find, keep on trying till he finds, the woman who can take him and whose love he can take, then who will grumble about men or about women. But the thing must be two-sided. At any rate, and whatever happens, I do love, and I am loved. I have given and I have taken—and that is eternal. Oh, if only people could marry properly. I believe in marriage.[167]

But what if there is no reciprocity? And how to reconcile this "belief in marriage" with adultery? A more logical mind might well have boggled at such considerations. Lawrence, however, did not hesitate to follow this idea to the very end. A letter to Collings, dated 17 January 1913, contains the clearest summary of a line of thought which finds more complex expression in the works of this period. In it he announces his belief in the blood, the flesh, as being wiser than the intellect. What the blood "feels and believes and says", is always true:

What do I care about knowledge. All I want is to answer to my blood, direct, without fribbling intervention of mind, or moral, or what-not.

Knowledge of the external world is of no importance: what matters is to look at ourselves, and say "My God, I am myself." That is why he likes to live in Italy: the people are so unconscious. To be is not to go in "for Humanitarianism and such like forms of not-being": to be is to answer to one's own wants, to do as one likes:

For the living of my full flame, I want that liberty, I want that woman, I want that pound of peaches, I want to go to sleep, I want to go to the pub and have a good time, I want to look a beastly swell to-day, I want to kiss that girl, I want to insult that man,

so speaks the man who wants only to be himself.[168]

Yet this is not the language of a truly amoral man, who would be content *to be*, and nothing more. This Lawrence saw clearly for himself: "I am like Carlyle, who they say, wrote fifty volumes on the value of silence."[169] He is preaching immorality with the conviction of a Methodist who has seen the Light of God.

What is more, this "passionately religious man" formulates his doctrine in a vivid language heavily inspired the Bible. The new St John has found his Patmos on Lake Garda. It remains only for him to convert his compatriots, in spite of themselves, since they do not know what they want:

I think, do you know, I have inside me a sort of answer to the *want* of to-day: to the real, deep want of the English people, not to just what they fancy they want. And gradually, I shall get my hold on them.[170]

He has in fact just sent Garnett his Foreword to *Sons and Lovers*. This truly apocalyptic piece, possessing its own logic once the premises are accepted, and written in a style which combines the most appalling jargon with subtle and persuasive poetry, heralds a series of "philosophical" essays on similar themes and in a similar style. It reveals Lawrence's passionate search for a new morality which can assuage his sense of having sinned against God and man. It is part of the slow process of self-understanding which starts with the writing of *Sons and Lovers* and leads to *Women in Love* and the character of Birkin.

St John said, "The Word was made Flesh." But this, comments Lawrence, is to reverse the natural order of things. The Flesh came first. Gradually, in his laborious biblical language, he works round to stating two equations:

(1) The Father = The Flesh = the eternal and infinite, the unutterable;
(2) The Son = the Word = the Spirit, the individual form adopted by the Flesh!

The Father was Flesh—and the Son, who in Himself was finite and had form, became Word. For form is the uttered Word, and the Son is the Flesh as it utters the Word, but the unutterable Flesh is the Father.[171]

The second equation must therefore be somewhat modified: the Son, in his lifetime, was Flesh, but he uttered the Word. All that now remains of him is the Word, his flesh being dead. He is the intermediary between the Father and the Word: and so it is with all men.

On this play of words Lawrence builds a psychological and ethical system. The "self" which says "I" *is* mere Word; the Flesh, the substance of a man's being, remains unutterable:

We are the Word, we are not the Flesh . . . We are the Word, we know the Word, and the Word alone is ours. When we say "I", we mean "The Word I am". This flesh I am is beyond me.[172]

Henceforward, therefore, the personal pronoun designates only the separate and distinct "self", which is the Word. The word Flesh expresses both the Father and that which in the individual is directly of the Father.

In terms of psychology this amounts to saying that the conscious, personal life, is inferior to the instinctive, unconscious life, which is divine because it is of the Father. Ethically, it is the divine justification of instinct, of the impulse of the flesh, the denial of the guidance of the intellect and conscious self over impulse.

From that starting-point Lawrence sets out to solve two of his theoretical difficulties: Christian charity and the Law of marriage. The latter condemns adultery. The former ordains that we should love our neighbour as ourselves and therefore refrain from stealing his wife; tender the other cheek instead of striking back: clearly two vulnerable points on which he needs the protection of an ethic of his own forging. No analytical exposition of his thinking can follow the passionate confusion of his detailed arguments: to render it accessible some rearrangement is essential. Lawrence distinguishes between love, which is of the Flesh; and charity, which relates to the Word alone:

> For the Word hath neither passion nor pain, but lives and moves in equity. It has charity, which we call love. But only the Flesh has love, for that is the Father, and in love he begets us all, of love are we begotten.[173]

Only the Flesh has love; of the pageful of none too coherent arguments which lead to this statement only the following need be remembered here: the "self" which is Word can only love "as itself" the Word its neighbour, i.e. a conscious "self". Charity ordains that we should suffer the pain of our neighbour; but only the flesh suffers; thus charity condemns my flesh to suffer the pain of others, which is tantamount to making the Word supreme over the flesh, thus denying the Father, the Almighty: "and pain is a denial of the Father". The Word, which is less than the Flesh, usurps the supremacy of the Flesh, thus reversing the natural order. This explains, in his letter to Collings, the reference to "humanitarianism" as a form of "not-being".

Charity is therefore a lie and a blasphemy. Worse still, it is bound to engender hatred: this idea, not yet clearly developed, is nevertheless apparent:

> So that if we love our neighbour, we love that Word, our neighbour, and we hate that Lie, our neighbour, which is a deformity.[174]

Lawrence had recently discovered an allied truth which a little psychological introspection on his part might well have made him perceive earlier, namely that "Cruelty is a form of perverted sex".[175]

Proceeding by a series of dogmatic assertions, the style of which owes as much to Zarathustra as to the Book of Revelation, he arrives gradually at a theory of marriage, incidentally condemning birth-control as though to give expression to some idea then in the back of his mind: who, in the name of the Word, can forbid the Flesh to reproduce itself?[176]

Thus marriage has only one divine basis: mutual attraction of the flesh. The Word may say "This woman is Flesh of my Flesh", but it must submit to the decree of the Flesh or it will deny God.[177]

Thus there exists a living, natural law, and a dead law:

> The Father is the Flesh, the eternal and unquestionable, the law-giver, but not the law . . . And each law is a fabric that must crumble away, and the Word is a graven image th t is worn down, and forsaken, like the Sphinx in the desert.[178]

The law which says "they shall be one Flesh" is of the Word: it is valid only if consecrated by the "unquestionable sincerity" of the attraction of flesh for flesh. This throws light on his affirmation to Mrs Hopkin: "*I believe in marriage.*" Marriages, or at least perfect physical marriages, are the work of God. Lawrence has taken the Christian idea of the union of souls in marriage and neatly turned it inside-out.

He who says "This woman is flesh of my flesh" must beware of blaspheming against the Father: only the will of the Father and not that of the Word can make her so. This means that marriage is valid only if the partners have attained perfect physical harmony. The first man to achieve such harmony with the wife of another has the right to take her away and make her his wife, since her marriage with the other is founded only on the Word. Thus the adulterer succeeds in putting himself right in the eyes of the Lord.

But he must have yet another justification: he may be doing wrong to the man whose wife he takes, and to the children of this woman; his marital struggles with Frieda are also casting their shadow over the picture:

> But if in my passion I slay my neighbour, it is no sin of mine, but it is his sin, for he should not have permitted me.[179]

Violence and wrong inflicted on others are justified provided they are inspired by passion, that is to say by the need of the flesh. The only unpardonable crimes are those committed in cold blood, by an impassive decree of the Word.

> And yet, if a man hath denied his Flesh, saying, "I, the Word, have dominion over the flesh of my neighbour", then shall the Flesh, his neighbour, slay him in self-defence.[180]

The criminal is thus he who tries to bind another in the name of the law.

None of this has much to do with *Sons and Lovers*: it is above all a justification for the conduct of the two lovers in conflict with society. These are the very arguments that Lawrence used with the Richthofens to prevent Frieda from "sacrificing" herself to her children,[181] and doubtless also those he marshalled against Frieda herself, and against her husband. No one could have tried harder to put justice on the side of might, or, in this case, on that of frailty, of the superior need; "he needed me more", said Frieda, echoing Candida.[182] The Nietzschean argument sounds hollow coming from so weak a man, eternally dependent on his woman, incapable of bearing separation even for a few hours. Most characteristic of all is his need to develop an ethical doctrine with the aid of the very images, style and phraseology of the Methodist chapel. Nothing is more significant of the struggle raging in a mind suddenly disturbed by a behaviour and by ideas foreign to his oldest habits of life and thought. In exactly the same way as he uses subtle intellectual argument to deny the mind, so, in order to assert the rights of Might against Law, he resorts to the oldest argument of all jurists, natural law.

The second part of the Foreword, on the whole clearer and more poetic, explains *Sons and Lovers* on the basis of an original conception of the creation of mankind and the relationship of Man, Woman and God.

Man believed that he was created by the Word, and that from his flesh woman was created. This is wrong: "We know that Woman lay in travail, and gave birth to Man, who in his hour uttered his Word."[183] Woman is identified with God: she is the Flesh and the source of all flesh "including the intermediary pieces called man", pieces which are like stamens, capable of turning into exquisite-coloured petals but remaining always sterile. By flowering, man lowers his vitality to become Word, a petal of the perfect Rose, the ultimate product of the rose tree. The true essence of the "Rose" is not the flower, but the eternal, infinite, unquestionable substance or life-stream, "the infinite of the Rose, the Flesh, the Father—which were more properly, the Mother".[184]

Thus the true sequence is: Mother (= God) produces the Son (= Man) who utters the Word: thus forming "the eternal Trinity". The Holy Ghost is the "moment of consciousness" in which the Son becomes Word, the stamen becomes a petal, the "Snip of Flame" of consciousness. And God the Father, the Unknowable, is known to man only in the Flesh of the Woman:

> She is the door for our ingoing and our outcoming. In her we go back to the Father; but like the witnesses of the Transfiguration, blind and unconscious.[185]

Like bees flying in and out of the hive, going and coming from their work to the hive and the queen, man must establish a relationship between the Eternal, which is Woman, source of all life, and the Word, which is expression of the Moment. With woman he is full of reverence and humility; in his work he is proud and masterful. The woman renews his being, and sends him out again inspired into the world to expend the energy thus absorbed, by giving himself to the task of self-expression. This philosophy leads to an aesthetic theory which shows how deeply Lawrence had reflected on the principles of his art: every work of art is a "fixing into stiffness and deadness" of a moment of being, for the sake of the glad cry of ecstasy, the revelation of the Holy Ghost: "This is I—I am I."[186]

Only the last page of this Foreword is directly related to *Sons and Lovers*: Lawrence had found a system which explained to him his childhood, the conflicts of his adolescence and young manhood, even the difficulties of his adaptation to his new way of life.

In order to express herself, he tells us, every woman needs a man to serve as intermediary between herself (representing the Flesh, the Father) and the world of utterance, ultimate product of individual life (the Holy Ghost). The man must return to steep himself in the source of life through her. But if, on leaving his work, he does not abandon himself to her entirely, "becoming simply her man of flesh", she will reject him like a drone. If he holds back or is too weak, then she will seek another. But if the law perpetuates their ill-assorted union, they are vowed to mutual destruction: the man driven to consume his own flesh in some form of artificial stimulation, such as alcohol; the woman wearing away her flesh in sickness or in the pursuit of some obsession. Or, if she has a son, she will turn to him and say, "Be you my Go-between."

Now any man who is his mother's go-between becomes spiritually her lover. But his flesh, finding no regeneration in woman, will wither and waste away. If he takes a mistress, he can give her his body only: his whole being is "torn in twain" and his wife in her despair will hope for sons, to serve in turn as *her* intermediaries.[187] Such was the tragic fate of the Morels, and herein lay the explanation of the "psychological impotence" of so many Lawrentian characters.

These ideas are no doubt the result of much reflection on Lawrence's own problems, but they also result from his recent reading, and literary sources can be traced. Among the most obvious: Schopenhauer, Nietzsche, Bergson, Whitman, and the latter's English disciple, Edward Carpenter, with possibly some echoes of psychoanalysis through Frieda. Either directly or through Edward Carpenter, one of the basic ideas can be traced to Schopenhauer: that the individual is the expression in time of the species which is timeless. The influence of Carpenter is everywhere in this text.[188]

Whitman he misquotes in "uttering glad leaves". "Joyous leaves", is what Whitman wrote.[189] He also paraphrases him: "You are the gates of the body, and you are the gates of the soul", says Whitman. The Foreword makes woman "the door for our ingoing and our outcoming".[190]

From Nietzsche, Lawrence has inherited the criticism of Christian ethics, of charity, and of the law of the weak by which the weak protect themselves against the strong.

Bergson may easily have inspired Lawrence, through the very theme of his 1911 Huxley Lecture, published in the *Hibbert Journal* for October 1911, with the thought on which the Foreword begins: the idea that the Word is *not* the beginning but that consciousness arises from matter. As for psychoanalysis, a sentence such as this may be an echo of its phraseology: "The old son-lover was Oedipus. The name of the new one is legion."[191]

But more important than all these sources are those personal preoccupations we have tried to establish earlier in this chapter. The "philosophy" of the Foreword is inspired by the problems of Lawrence's own life: it tries to justify his conduct by linking it to a metaphysical concept which he sees as reaching beyond the vacuous forms of social life and common morals. It is also an attempt to explain Lawrence's subjection to women without wounding his masculine self-respect; it culminates in a wholly personal, highly poetical conception of the relations between God, woman, man and the creative activity of the male. In it, there is a relative balance between the desires for immersion of the self in the great Whole, and the vital instinct of individual development and personal expression. Remarkably enough, it sets out from the idea of the divinity of the flesh to culminate in that of the spirit. Lawrence's God has undergone a new avatar. He is no longer, as in 1911, only "a vast shimmering impulse which waves towards some end". He has become both polarized and divided into a dual entity: He is Flesh (source of life) and Word (the individual's purpose and utterance in the world of action). But will not man, divided as he is between the tendency to return to his source, and that towards differentiation which drives him to the isolation of the self, ultimately be torn asunder?[192] And will this dual God, in Lawrence's own likeness, not succumb to the temptation to allow one half to devour the other?

As for woman, identified with the flesh, is she then no more than a non-differentiated form of life? Is she not an individual just as much as man? Does she not also want to express directly, without the intermediary of the other sex, that personality developed by the modern world? Certainly her sole function is not to reproduce the species. In the contemporary poem "Rose of All the World" this problem is tackled in highly characteristic fashion.

> I am here myself, as though this heave of effort
> At starting other life, fulfilled my own;
> Rose-leaves that whirl in colour round a core
> Of seed-specks kindled lately and softly blown
> By all the blood of the rose-bush into being.

Thus the sexual act is for the poet a confirmation of his own being as well as the possibility of creating another life. That being so, must he believe that "the seed is purpose, blossom accident"? Or is the supreme reality not rather the consummation of pleasure attained by the man and woman?

> Or are we kindled, you and I, to be
> One rose of wonderment upon the tree
> Of perfect life, and is our possible seed
> But the residuum of the ecstasy?

What is it then that counts, the flower or the fruit? Lawrence opts for the rose, and defines his ideal of the female role:

> Blossom, my darling, blossom, be a rose
> Of roses unchidden and purposeless; a rose
> For rosiness only, without an ulterior motive,
> For me it is more than enough if the flower unclose.[193]

It is possible, as J. M. Murry has suggested,[194] that the rose may desire to become fruit, the woman want to have children; and what would happen if, instead of flowering in sensual ecstasy, she prefers to express herself in the way Lawrence defined for man in the Foreword? What if she too desires to create with her hands or with her mind, to become worker, writer, artist? This is one of the problems he begins to face in works begun about 1913, but with limitations fully expressed by "Rose of All the World". This poem contains his answer, that of a man convinced that the supreme expression of the woman is the love ecstasy.

Most of the post-1913 works would be clear to any careful reader of the Foreword familiar with Lawrence's life, were it not that the writer's philosophy will in fact undergo many modifications in detail and expression in accordance with his changing moods. The balance expressed in the Foreword will not be maintained. There is nothing abnormal in conceiving, as Lawrence does, self-annihilation in sensual ecstasy as an entry into true being. Such an idea certainly goes back to the very origins of human thought, and has been expressed by many poets and thinkers.[195]

But when he is expressing the reality of his own life rather than his ideal, Lawrence adds to this poetical concept something at once original and dangerous: a denial of the metaphysical existence of all that is not Flesh. So that annihilation of the conscious self in love becomes the sole reality. Reversing normal terminology, he calls "non-being" active and conscious life and "being" the moments when consciousness is obscured or obliterated:

> To him now, life seemed a shadow, day a white shadow; night, and death, and stillness and inaction, this seemed like *being*. To be alive, to be urgent and insistent—that was *not-to-be*. The highest of all was to melt out into the darkness and sway there, identified with the great Being . . . To be rid of our individuality, which is our will, which is our effort—to live effortless, a kind of conscious sleep—that is very beautiful, I think; that is our after-life,—our immortality.[196]

This passage from *Sons and Lovers* provides the key to a new series of equations:

> Being = shadow, darkness, death of consciousness, inaction, immobility = warmth, blood;[197]
>
> Non-being (Word) = light, whiteness, clear consciousness, intellectual, mechanical, social activity = coolness, ice.[198]

But these equations do not always apply, Lawrence's use of the terms being far from consistent. For example, he sometimes makes light synonymous with true being: the daylight is then a "white shadow", and shadow synonymous with non-being: or in the poem "In the Dark", where he equates non-being with darkness, with mystery and that "conscious sleep" so tempting to the poet and defined by him in *Sons and Lovers*.[199] This being the major cause of obscurity in his symbolic use of light and shadow, with a little practice one soon comes to understand the language of the poems in *Look! We Have Come Through!* in which these images appear. A world of darkness looms around the luminous centre of pure consciousness; a black or grey zone surrounds each brilliant object, rendering it mysterious and strange.[200] The red twilight glints, synonymous of warmth and blood, symbolizing a certain balance between consciousness and desire, and intermediary states which may lead to regeneration and happiness. A new poetry now enters Lawrence's work, a whole set of complex symbols superimposed upon the obscurity of the language forged in the Foreword, and subsequently adopted in both poems and novels. His new system is largely based on personal but obscure uses of current terms, of which he transforms into a language of his own both immediate meaning and hidden implications.

Towards the new novel

Out of the joys and troubles of the new life and the accompanying changes of outlook, but very gradually, several new and more ambitious novels were to be conceived in a process of further self-discovery. Uprooted, the child of the Midlands now dared to face his old self, not with serene detachment, but rather in such iconoclastic rapture as finds expression in the Foreword to *Sons and Lovers*. In the prolonged crisis of the years 1912 and 1913 are to be found the germs of the double novel *The Rainbow* and *Women in Love*, begun at the end of 1912 under the title "The Sisters". Another novel, *The Lost Girl*, is, at least in its original idea, contemporary with "The Sisters" and very often it is impossible in Lawrence's letters to determine to which of the two he refers.

In a way he was looking for a subject, rather than for ideas to express. By December 1912 he had begun a novel with Robert Burns as hero—but the poet was to be turned into a Midlands figure, a sort of self-portrait of Lawrence in the mood expressed by his poem "Don Juan".[201] At the same time he was "simmering a new work", the thought of which filled him "with a curious pleasure—venomous almost".[202] Could this have been "The Sisters"? Or was it the satire of Eastwood in "The Insurrection of Miss Houghton", later to become "Mixed Marriage" and finally *The Lost Girl*? Two letters to Sallie Hopkin at the end of December 1912, announcing "a novel about Love Triumphant" and promising that he would do his "work for women, better than the Suffrage",[203] would now seem to point to "The Sisters" as the work he was then "simmering", although one cannot be absolutely sure. Indeed several letters assert a preference for "Miss Houghton", as opposed to the short, morally impeccable novel which he intended "for the *jeunes filles*"[204] and which does seem to be "The Sisters": "Miss Houghton", of which 200 pages were written by April 1913, lies "next to his heart" but is "too improper".[205] However "The Sisters", at one time conceived as a "potboiler", also soon "falls from grace" and definitely becomes centred on "the relation between men and women":

After all, it is *the* problem of today, the establishment of a new relation, or the readjustment of the old one, between men and women.—In a month "The Sisters" will be finished.[206]

In spite of the obscurities of the correspondence the reader can roughly perceive what is happening: there are of course similarities in depth between "The Insurrection of Miss Houghton" and the story of Ursula Brangwen in *The Rainbow* and *Women in Love*: both owe something to Wells's *Ann Veronica*; what matters to Lawrence however is not his "story", but the ideas he wants to illustrate by it, and by April 1913, while *The Lost Girl* is fairly well advanced, he is still struggling to discover the real subject of "The Sisters", i.e. presumably of that part, written first, which was to become *Women in Love*:

> I am doing a novel which I have never grasped. Damn its eyes, there am I at page 145, and I have no notion what it's about. I hate it. F. says it's good. But it's like a novel in a foreign language I don't know very well. I can only just make out what it's about.[207]

Gradually a fusion takes place between this new novel and the themes uppermost in his mind at the end of 1912: "sticking up for the love between man and woman", finding the answer to the unconscious need of the English people. The messianic urge is there, and the sense of power and of a mission. He knows he can "write bigger stuff than any man in England",[208] and that he writes for the future:

> . . . for men like David [Garnett] and Harold [Hobson]—they will read me, soon. My stuff is what they want: when they know what they want. You wait.[209]

In this conviction Lawrence soon finishes his first draft of "The Sisters" between March and June 1913, leaving at Irschenhausen the manuscript of "The Insurrection of Miss Houghton", which he will not see again and complete until the beginning of 1920.

Even the correspondence offers little direct evidence of the mental processes of the creative artist during those months as applied to the works in hand; the ideas which will find tumultuous expression in the autumn of 1914 in the "Study of Thomas Hardy" are, however, taking shape, concurrently with the writing of "The Sisters". It is clear that the whole problem of the relations between man and woman is a major preoccupation, and evidence has been found of his familiarity at this time with the recently published book of Edward Carpenter, *The Drama of Love and Death*. *Women in Love* contains definite echoes of *Love's Coming of Age*, which suggest not only detailed knowledge but a recent rereading of Carpenter's works.[210] For the first time, homosexuality is explicitly mentioned in a December

1913 letter to Henry Savage.[211] Lawrence has travelled far since his 1912 discovery that "Cruelty is a form of perverted sex". The fascination and repulsion exercised on him by homosexuality also finds veiled expression under the more general terms of a later letter to Savage on Whitman, foreshadowing the final Whitman essay of *Studies in Classic American Literature*. Writing about Richard Middleton's suicide in the earlier letter, he says:

> I should like to know why *nearly every man that approaches greatness tends to homosexuality, whether he admits it or not*: so that he loves the *body* of a man better than the body of a woman,—as I believe the Greeks did, sculptors and all, by far. *I believe a man projects his own image on another man, like on a mirror.* But from a woman he wants himself re-born, re-constructed. So he can always get satisfaction from a man, but it is the hardest thing in life to get one's soul and body satisfied from a woman, so that one is free from oneself. And one is kept by all tradition and instinct from loving men, or a man—for it means just extinction of all the purposive influences. And one doesn't believe in one's power to find and to form the woman in whom one can be free—and one shoots oneself, if one is vital and feels powerfully and down to the core.
>
> Again I don't know what I am talking about.[212] [*Italics added*.]

He may not know what he is talking about, but this letter reveals an association of ideas between his claim to greatness and to a mission, and homosexuality; as well as a deep connexion between his attitude to woman as the Mother, and the attraction exercised upon him by men as "projections" of his own image. This is perhaps his clearest admission of his inability to love a woman except as a mother.

Thus some of the themes of the "Hardy", and the character of Birkin as described in the Prologue to *Women in Love*, already seemed to be shaping in his mind—soon after the time when he promised Edward Garnett to rewrite "The Sisters", putting it "in the third person", and admitted that it had done him good to "theorize myself out" in "this first crude fermenting of the book"; all of which suggests that the book is largely one of self-revelation.

Garnett had read that first version and made his comments, which led Lawrence to rewrite it during the summer and autumn of 1913. By 30 December 1913 he had written what was now "The Wedding Ring", i.e. the first part of the double novel later to become *The Rainbow*.[213]

This manuscript Garnett did not approve. Lawrence rewrote it once more between the end of January and the beginning of May 1914. By then he is sure of what he wants to do, he fights back his mentor's criticism, and in a famous letter of June 1914[214] explains the ethical and psychological conceptions underlying his treatment of characters. He is more interested in "that which is physic—non-human, in humanity" than in "the old-fashioned human element—which causes one to conceive a character *in a certain moral scheme and make him consistent". [Italics added.]* In other words, he is reacting, even more definitely than in the Foreword, against the tradition of nine-teenth-century morality and educational psychology, which aimed at character-building and consistency in thought and action. He emphasizes his antinomianism by adding: "*The certain moral scheme is what I object to.*"

Quite in accordance with his new moral philosophy, beyond the conscious *ego* of his characters, beyond *feelings* of which they may be aware, he looks for an ill-defined, underlying, deeper reality:

> I don't so much care about what the woman feels—in the ordinary usage of the word. That presumes an ego to feel with. I only care about what the woman is—what she IS—inhumanly, physiologically, materially—according to the use of the word: but for me, she is a phenomenon (or as representing some greater, inhuman will), instead of what she feels according to the human conception.

Thus beyond the artificial continuities of the classical *ego* he is looking for something fundamental; he has already expressed his belief in "the blood", "the flesh". Yet the word materialism does not quite describe what he is after, and while he uses some of Marinetti's language to express what he is seeking, he takes care to criticize the Futurist's "pseudo-scientific", mechanistic positions, his preoccupation with "making diagrams of certain physic or mental states".[215] The old dichotomy, spirit *versus* matter, does not satisfy him. He partly acknowledges his own debt to Maeterlinck and the Symbolists when he says that the Futurists go "beyond" them in being "ultra-ultra intellectual" while the Symbolists are "intellectual". Yet how close his conception of the subconscious states of his characters is to Maeterlinck's somnambulists:

> You mustn't look in my novel for the old stable *ego*—of the character. There is another *ego*, according to whose action the individual is unrecogniz-able, and passes through, as it were, allotropic states which it needs a deeper sense than any we've been used to exercise, to discover are states of the same radically unchanged element. (Like as diamond and coal are the same pure single element of carbon.) The ordinary novel would trace the history of the diamond—but I say, "Diamond, what! This is carbon." And my diamond might be coal or soot, and my theme is carbon.[216]

How directly this conception of the evanescent ego proceeds from the techniques used in the description of the characters in *The Trespasser*, and is thus in line with the development of Lawrence's art in his Croydon days, has perhaps never been stressed enough; critics tend instead to insist on the novelty of this statement on "the carbon of character". Nor has it been seen how close this conception is to the theosophist and Hindu-inspired thinking of Edward Carpenter, as expressed in his *Drama of Love and Death*. This notion of an underlying, unpredictable ego is of course illustrated by *The Rainbow* and *Women in Love*, but also by the behaviour of Alvina Houghton in *The Lost Girl*. Lawrence has raised to the level of a literary theory his own insurrection against his own, too consistent past, and with sure artistic instinct he has carried one step further the lesson of the Symbolists. As much as a new departure in the aesthetics of character delineation in the novel, this marks a breaking point in his view of his own past life, as well as a new stage in his artistic evolution towards the expression of the depths of the unconscious.

This letter marks, too, the breaking point in his relations with Edward Garnett. Duckworth, having published *The Trespasser*, *Love Poems* and *Sons and Lovers* on Garnett's advice, hesitates over "The Wedding Ring", for reasons which have not been stated anywhere, so that Lawrence accepted, through J. B. Pinker the literary agent, a promise of a £300 advance for the book from Methuen. He undertook to make some changes at the publisher's request, in all likelihood to make the book safe for the lending libraries.[217]

His self-confidence had increased enormously during those two years preceding the First World War: he asserted that "The Wedding Ring" was "a big and beautiful work";[218] his ambition was to "re-source" and "re-vivify" art by making it "more the joint work of men and women". But not all his friends followed him in this sense of a divine and androgynous mission: several 1914 letters show him to be hypersensitive to criticism.[219] He "cruelly" felt the need of "friends who will believe in [him] a bit".[220] "There isn't a soul cares a damn for me except Frieda—and it's rough to have all the burden put on her":[221] an ominous admission, a few weeks before the War which was severely to test his friendships and his love for a German woman. With "his heart in his boots" he took Frieda to Kensington Registry Office on 13 July 1914 and opened a new chapter in his life.[222]

8

FROM *SONS AND LOVERS* TO *THE RAINBOW*

Between *Sons and Lovers*, in which Lawrence reviewed his early years, and *The Rainbow*, where he attempts to fuse into an overall conception the experience of those first twenty-seven years with the acquisitions of his new life, a highly varied series of stories and essays leads to the ambitious synthesis of 1915. The fact that many of these works underwent profound modification during this period makes them all the more revealing of the changing mental attitudes of their author.

The new personal themes emerging from these two years are already familiar: the joys and difficulties of life with Frieda; the impressions made by his travels, particularly the revelation of Italy. For the moment we shall deal only with the transposition of these themes into literature, and their utilization in creative works, which, though stemming directly from experience, are nevertheless already in the process of breaking away into their own separate existence, distinct from the changeable personality of their author. This chapter will therefore trace, through the rewriting of the short stories and the literary exploitation of new ideas, a progressive crystallization of themes and subjects for *The Rainbow*.

I. TRAVELS

As soon as he reached the Continent Lawrence began to think of turning his travels to financial gain. As early as August 1912 the *Westminster Gazette* published two of his articles, entitled "German Impressions".[1] Two others would seem to have been rejected as too "anti-German".[2]

"French Sons of Germany" describes the hostility of the French population of Lorraine to German hegemony. The French encountered by Lawrence—a barber and his wife, a couple running a small café, a group of "keen, naïve" schoolboys—all won his sympathy, whereas his hatred was aroused by German militarism, in particular the brutal way in which he saw soldiers treating a fine and delicate mare, a scene which foreshadows a passage of *Women in Love*.[3]

In his reaction against militarist, Protestant and nordic Germany, he makes the ordinary Frenchman the prototype of his ideal of humanity:

> A Frenchman has the same soul, whether he is eating his dinner or kissing his baby. A German has no soul when he is eating his dinner and is beautiful when he kisses the baby. So I prefer the Frenchman who hasn't the tiresome split between his animal nature and his spiritual, in whom the two are fused.[4]

This role was soon taken over by the Italians, and Lawrence was to become less tender towards the French.[5]

"Hail in the Rhineland" recounts with a great deal of exaggeration intended to be humorous a walk taken by Lawrence in the company of his young relative Hannah Krenkow. Transformed into a curious mixture of peasant and bourgeoise, Johanna, the heroine of this incident, may perhaps owe something to the character of Frieda's younger sister, Johanna von Richthofen, whom Lawrence once described as "in a large, splendid way— cocotte".[6] Lawrence here shows himself in a playful and spontaneous mood. The young man's flirtation with Johanna, his ambiguous, half-cautious, half-surrendering attitude to love, the great hailstorm with stones "as big as pigeon-eggs", the conversations with the Rhineland peasants, make an attractive though superficial mixture, of a kind which might have been immediately successful with the newspapers.

On the way to Italy Lawrence continued at first to work in the same vein. The crucifixes encountered along the Alpine paths inspired an article entitled "Christs in the Tyrol",[7] first version of the sombre opening essay of *Twilight in Italy*.[8] Although humorous reflections still abound, the tone is already different from that of the German sketches. Struck by the diversity of the endless succession of Christs upon the Cross which line the mountain roads of Upper Bavaria and the Tyrol, the traveller launches into a series of meditations on the authors of these lugubrious images. Two main traits emerge from this preliminary sketch: a preoccupation with the problem of human suffering, and a critical attitude towards his native country, manifested by unfavourable comparisons between the naïvely expressive Bavarian and Tyrolean Christs and the sentimental, anaemic images of "strange neutrals with long hair" which represented Jesus to English children.

In these Alpine Christs Lawrence discovers the souls of their creators. The mountaineer is afraid of physical suffering and by making a crucifix beside the high road he is obscurely attempting to "decipher the riddle of pain":

> And so they try to get used to the idea of death and suffering, to rid themselves of some of the fear thereof. And all tragic art is part of the same attempt.[9]

The "fearfully florid and ornate" crucifixes of the Italians seem to him unreal after the sincerity of the German peasant Christs: once over the Brenner, vulgarity sets in. But Lawrence does not linger to criticize Italian conventionality. His thoughts return to England, which he is now seeing with new eyes. Can it be that "we have carved no Christs, afraid lest they should be too like men, too like ourselves . . .?"[10]

In his darkest wartime hours Lawrence was to return to these thoughts and, without effacing the precise material details which had served as his point of departure, he was to extract from them a kind of lyrical hymn to pain and death. The interest of "Christs in the Tyrol" lies in showing how close his original version remains to the material facts, and how little he sought at first to extract symbolical meaning from those facts. Several years were to pass before he developed the "Lawrentian" theme inherent in this first sketch, seeking to relate it to a whole philosophy of pain.

Two Tyrol sketches, "A Chapel Among the Mountains" and "A Hayhut Among the Mountains",[11] belong to the same period and, like the above works, combine descriptive meditation and autobiography. Lawrence and a certain Anita, clearly none other than Frieda, get lost among the Tyrolean Alps, laugh heartily at their misadventures and at nightfall come upon a tiny wooden chapel. In the flickering light of the candles he has lighted, Lawrence examines the ex-votos, the "naked little pictures, all coloured" hanging on the walls: thank-offerings made to God by the simple peasants who could trust Him to understand their pictures "because they are His own language. How should He read German, and English and Russian" like a schoolmaster?

With sympathetic amusement Lawrence describes the scenes inspired by accidents or domestic crises. Like the crucifix carvers, the authors of these ex-votos had suddenly felt the hand of death:

> Deepest of all things, among the mountain darkness, was the ever-felt fear. First of all gods was the unknown god who crushed life at any moment, and threatened it always. His shadow was over the valleys. And a tacit acknowledgement and propitiation of Him were the ex-voto pictures, painted out of fear and offered to Him unnamed.[12]

These reflections are interrupted by Anita: she has discovered "a gorgeous hay hut, a little farther on" where, after further misadventures, and much good-natured badinage, the two lovers pass the night. Awakening next morning they see the peaks covered with fresh snow. Its whiteness seems to bind together earth and sky, leading straight into the world beyond. In this snow-transformed world, a mountain dweller and his wife appear to the poet as symbols of the immobility and solitude of the mountain peaks:

> The woman was going up the steep path in a mechanical, lifeless way. The brilliant snow glistened up above, in peaks. The hollow green cup that formed the farm was utterly still. And the woman seemed infected with all this immobility and silence. It was as if she were gradually going dead, because she had

no place there. And I saw the man at the cow-shed door. He was thin, with sandy moustaches; and there was about him the same look of distance, as if silence, loneliness, and the mountains deadened him, too.[13]

The menacing Alpine peaks had already made their deep impression on Lawrence; but a long time was to pass before he extracted the whole of their symbolic content, before high mountains and eternal snows became the scene of a triumphant spirit of death and dissolution. Yet already in these sketches the poet's eye perceived more than the simple material details. Already the landscape is lit with a strange malevolence, already there is something quite arbitrary in the way he explains the mental slowness of the mountain dweller. In his introduction, David Garnett has pointed out other and more obvious exaggerations resulting from the author's deliberate attempt at humour.[14] On to the plain data of direct experience, or at least on to average, commonplace perception of the outside world, are grafted ideas which transform and restructure it. Between the bare fact and the reader falls the shadow of the innermost preoccupations of the author: the German divorce between body and soul; the Tyrolean religion of fear; the gradual deadening of the man and woman in the silence of the Alps. These are the first faint burgeonings of the ideas which later come to dominate Lawrence's descriptions of the same objects. But no systematic effort is yet perceptible in the few comments that sometimes raise these descriptions above the level of the purely matter-of-fact.

"Italian Studies", three sketches appearing in *The English Review* of September 1913,[15] already mark a transition towards the method of Lawrence's future travel studies. But how sober they remain when compared with the three corresponding chapters in *Twilight in Italy*! There the original sketches have become no more than a thin excuse for Lawrence's theoretical and symbolic dissertations. The wartime versions speak much more of Lawrence's state of mind in England in 1915–16 than of Italy in 1913. But even the original versions are not made out of absolutely first impressions; these studies already differ considerably from corresponding passages in his letters of the period. A search for literary effect is occasionally apparent, particularly, for instance, in "The Theatre".

The various descriptive scenes in "The Spinner and the Monks" may at first seem almost unconnected with one another; Lawrence paints splendid Alpine landscapes such as his letters could evoke in a few lines. Yet the title links the two main themes. Lawrence talks for a moment to an old Italian woman spinning wool in the bright sunshine of Lake Garda, a symbol of a bygone age, a vestige of a humanity scarcely awakened to consciousness, for whom time does not exist.[16]

Soon after, he sees two monks pacing backwards and forwards the garden of their monastery, beneath a clear blue sky, in which a frail crescent moon is already visible. The quietude of the twilight hour, the spectacle of the calm, silent motion of the monks, elevate the tone to a meditation on the meaning of monastic life. At one point the monks look "forward to the white moonlight of eternity".[17] At another they look "backward to that frail white body on the Cross, that was murdered":

> They were not here, they were there: there away back with the murdered body, there away in front with the free white spirit, either in the past or the future, in the death of the tortured body, in the death of the glorified soul, but never here. They were like a bridge that is built from either side of the stream, that leaps out but does not meet: ends in a gap in mid-air.[18]

Having launched out into an image of some beauty, Lawrence falls to earth clumsily, almost as though seeking by platitudes to make amends for a lyrical flight of fancy. His monks return to the monastery: "I hoped they would have a pleasant meal," he says, thankful that he is not a monk. True, he then takes the trouble to explain his title briefly: the old woman symbolizes the present moment, in contrast to these men who, remaining outside life,

> . . . look before and after
> And pine for what is not.

Humour and poetry are the dominant notes of the two other Garda studies: "The Lemon Gardens" and "The Theatre". The first describes the proprietor of the Villa Igéa, with its terraces of lemons and oranges on the mountainside, the second, a troupe of strolling players come to Gargnano in carnival time, to act Ibsen, d'Annunzio and Shakespeare; the audience is keenly observed, and Lawrence notes how the peasants, village shopkeepers, *bersaglieri*, etc., gather together without mingling.

A number of ideas later developed at greater length in *Twilight in Italy* make their first appearance here and there in these sketches. Personal preoccupations become apparent, such as a keen interest in the private life of couples: for instance, his landlords, the Di Paoli, the man elderly, the woman still young and childless. Or a remarkable trio glimpsed at the theatre: a peasant, his wife and child, a Holy Family with a young and untamed Joseph. Lawrence the northerner is astonished by the lack of any comradeship between the sexes.[19]

His attitude towards the Italians lacks clarity for the uninitiated; certain reactions are well in the national tradition: he hates the "sepulchral" houses, the stuffy interiors of a supposedly sun-loving people; he makes a discreet allusion (later developed in *Twilight in Italy*) to filth in the narrow streets. He is annoyed by the caricature of *Hamlet* presented by the peasant actors. He smiles when his host expresses envy of British wealth and of Anglo-Saxon mastery over the machine.[20]

While noting the Italian cult of the child, and the passionate desire of the

Latins to perpetuate themselves in a son, Lawrence does not yet pass judgment on it. Only a knowledge of his later works makes it possible to perceive the inner significance of this message:

> The man seems not to be able to believe in himself till he has a child. His whole pride is based in this fact—that he can beget a son. It is his children who justify him. Unless he be an artist, he feels that his only real claim to being a man is that he has children, that he is himself is nothing. For his soul is nothing to him.[21]

"His soul is nothing to him": hence the physical grace, the animal flexibility of the Italian. The Englishman walks aggressively, convinced his body is the repository of a precious particle of the Almighty:

> But the Italian feels, no matter what he believes, that he is made in the image of God, and in this image of flesh is his godliness and with its defacement and crumbling, crumbles himself. Which is why he often gives one the feeling that he has nothing inside him.

The puritan in Lawrence cannot surrender to so exclusive a cult of the body. He reconciles in the following theory his new ideas on love and his need for the spiritual:

> I suppose a passionate people is of necessity unhappy: because passion is an instrument, a means; and to mistake the means for the end is to leave oneself at last empty. And the northern races are the really passionate people, because theirs is the passion that persists and achieves, achieves everything, including that intimacy between a man and a woman which is the fruit of passion, and which is rarely seen here: the love, the knowledge, the simplicity, and the absence of shame, that one sometimes sees in English eyes; and which is the flower of civilization.[22]

We know of whose eyes he is speaking, and that the flower of civilization was at that moment being cultivated at the Villa Igéa by an Englishman and a German woman: hence possibly the allusion to the northern races, unless Lawrence had already been reading Houston Stewart Chamberlain.

A little further on he is moved to the following tirade by the Hamlet of the Italian actor Persivalli:

> I tried to imagine any Italian in the part: he would not have been a Hamlet. Because every Italian I have seen lives by the human ties which connect him with his neighbours. But Hamlet had no neighbour, and no bond held him to anybody. He could not love, he could only judge . . . He had no feelings. He never had any. And the whole of *Hamlet* seems to me like a gleam of decay.[23]

Thus between the unfeeling Hamlet who could judge but not love and the physical passion of the Italian who has no soul, Lawrence puts forward a balanced "northern" ideal of passion in which spirituality absorbs and accepts desire: that is the ideal which he will attempt to illustrate in the early conception of *Women in Love*.

But so far these ideas remain vague and tentative, and Lawrence seems to hesitate between the Italian cult of the flesh and his "northern" ideal. The performance of *Ghosts* inspired the following reflection:

> Ibsen is the mind, recognizing that itself is of no avail against the flesh. Hence his despair. But what was the root of his despair holds the root of our hope. For of the flesh all things are possible. It holds all things within itself, both the discovered and that which will be discovered . . . I believe everybody hates Ibsen. He denied the universality of the blood, of which we are all cups. He owned the universality of the mind, to which we all subscribe, as to the wearing of clothes. Then he showed how the mind is overthrown at any moment by the body. But why shouldn't it be? And if the son of *Ghosts* must die, still I live, who am the flesh and the blood, the same as he . . . We are tired of going rigid with grief or insane, over a little spilt life. The sun will lick it up.[24]

This is very close to the Foreword to *Sons and Lovers*. Already it is possible to measure the distance travelled between the summer of 1912 and the spring of the following year, when these sketches must have been first composed.[25] More and more it is the author's personal preoccupations, barely perceptible in the impressions of Germany, that command the reader's attention, transforming the whole style of writing. From the playful tone of "Hail in the Rhineland" we pass to dogmatic assertions reminiscent of Nietzsche or of Blake, but without the cohesion or precision of thought which might provide a semblance of justification for such dogmatism.

There is no record of an earlier and more direct version of the four last chapters of "On the Lago di Garda" in *Twilight in Italy* and the two studies ("Italians in Exile" and "The Return Journey") that follow them. What matters in these studies is the ideas they reveal, and the descriptive skill they illustrate. The descriptions are in a style more mature and more lyrically exalted than anything Lawrence wrote in 1913, suggesting that if they were, in fact, first written at this date, they have probably undergone a transformation at least as radical as that imposed on "The Spinner and the Monks", "The Lemon Gardens" and "The Theatre". As for the ideas, they are clearly related to moods and thoughts reaching full development in the autumn of 1915.

What then should be our final judgment of these first travel sketches, forerunners of the numerous books of travel which stand high in Lawrence's total output?

In his first attempts at the genre Lawrence opted clearly for "impressions" rather than for a detailed and faithful description of things seen. He also sought to give these impressions a personal touch; first by humorous exaggeration of anything that could draw a smile; then, as he grew bolder and more sure of his "mission", by revealing more and more openly the ideas inspired in him by what he saw, selecting for preference, as in "The Spinner and the Monks", subjects which lent themselves to symbolic interpretation.

In the three studies published in *The English Review*, a certain balance is maintained between a purely descriptive style and the symbolic interpretation of things described. The intrinsic value of his landscapes and sketches of people remains at the high standard set in *The White Peacock*. As for the ideas, the necessary reserves have just been made. But those who love Lawrence for the spontaneity of his first impressions, the charm of his descriptive passages and the youthfulness of character that so endeared him to his friends of 1912–13, should seek his real and immediate impressions of Italy in the September number of *The English Review* and in the letters of the period rather than in the wartime essays, where often obscure ideas intrude into descriptions of Italian scenes which had become a distant and inaccessible mirage.

II. THE EVOLUTION OF LAWRENTIAN THEMES

Between 1912 and July 1914, with a view to publication in volume form, or revised for periodicals, Lawrence prepared a certain number of earlier short stories. Reworking data which had already undergone a first literary transposition, he often interpreted them afresh in the light of recent experience; characters are thus illuminated by reflections of his new life, and simple incidents from daily life take on a deeper meaning.

Going over the past

The popular, puritan social background of Eastwood no longer found any grace in Lawrence's eyes when, in August 1913, he planned "to do a bookful of sketches" on his native town. He called upon his old friend William Hopkin to provide the material; and Hopkin did indeed send him "good old crusty Eastwood gossip".[26] From the same period dates "The Christening", published in *The Smart Set* in February 1914, and relatively little revised.[27] This story describes with biting humour the christening at home of the illegitimate baby of Emma Rowbotham, daughter of a dictatorial old miner. The picture of the family group sitting down to high tea is painted with incisive strokes, utterly unsparing of these provincial figures: the eldest daughter Hilda, a college-trained schoolmistress determined "to keep up the prestige of her house in spite of blows" by her "dry distinction"; Emma herself, sulky, gauche and violent; the imperious Bertha, with a weakness for the baby, cause of the family disgrace; the "big-boned, thin and ugly" minister, embarrassed by the whole performance, hopelessly bullied by his old parishioner. Rowbotham's spirited harangues, inimitable jumbles of pride and hypocrisy, his prayer during the actual baptism of the child, are punctuated off-stage by the muttered oaths and ironical grimaces of his son returning from the mine. Lawrence is here fully successful in the satirical presentation of things and people. "The Christening" would be artistically perfect if, towards the end, the author had not seen fit to graft on to his mocking sketch a somewhat theoretical and irrelevant discourse, possibly inspired by notions of psychoanalysis acquired from Frieda and without any real link to the subject, but related to Lawrence's personal preoccupations.

The problem of his first love was certainly still haunting his mind: *Sons and Lovers*, and "The Shades of Spring", the latter revised before mid-July 1914,[28] are ample evidence of this. But uppermost in this connexion is a new attitude to his mother, revealed almost as soon as he had put the final touches to *Sons and Lovers*. We have noted in the Foreword a vital change: Lawrence invoking for the first time the relationship between mother and son to explain the characters in the novel. In "The Christening" he simultaneously satirizes the background of his childhood and attacks the accepted idea of the role of parents in their children's lives. In his truly extraordinary prayer, Rowbotham accuses himself of unjust domination over his children. He is conscious of having deformed their characters by abuse of paternal authority:

> Lord, take away from us the conceit that our children are ours. Lord, Thou art Father of this child as is fatherless here. O God, Thou bring him up. For I have stood between Thee and my children; I've cut 'em off from Thee because they were mine. And they've grown twisted, because of me. Who is their father, Lord, but Thee? But I put myself in the way, they've been plants under a stone, because of me. Lord, if it hadn't been for me, they might ha' been trees in the sunshine . . . It would ha' been better if they'd never known no father . . . For I've been like a stone upon them, and they rise up and curse me in their wickedness.[29]

A very similar conception has found its way into the final and considerably expanded version of "Daughters of the Vicar"[30] in which the character of Alfred Durant, rather skimped in "Two Marriages", becomes the object of detailed analysis. If throughout his youth the miner had never been able to escape from himself sufficiently to love, if Louisa Lindley's advances were necessary to overcome his reserve, it now appears that his mother is responsible: she had unconsciously so overwhelmed his timid nature that the whole of his deep need for affection had been transferred to her:

> His feeling for her was deep and unexpressed. He noticed when she was tired, or when she had a new cap. And he bought little things for her occasionally. She was not wise enough to see how much he lived by her.[31]

She, on the other hand, finds him somewhat effeminate: this over-devoted younger son of hers does not give her satisfaction, and in her heart of hearts she is even a little contemptuous of him.[32]

At the age of twenty Alfred escapes from the fold to join the Navy. In this type of flight from home of children stifled by a too close family atmosphere, psychoanalysts see a secret revolt of a repressed personality. In *Sons and Lovers* Arthur Morel, Lawrence's imaginary younger brother, leaves home in similar circumstances. Consciously or not, the novelist is on the track of something fundamental to the psychology of his young men. Naval life has not taught Alfred Durant to break the psychological bonds which render him shy and impotent with women. He even wishes he could change selves with some unthinking brute in order to break away from the man he is. This vague desire to escape his own ego is constantly with him and finds satisfaction only in the first kiss that Louisa tears from him.

To give Lawrence his due, theoretical considerations here remain in the background and can scarcely be said to interfere with the description of the characters. Alfred Durant is alive because he unmistakably expresses an aspect of Lawrence's own self, and not because he was conceived in accordance with any psychological theory. A close comparison of the two versions of this long short story shows clearly to what extent the deeper exploration of character was achieved through a toning down of the didactic aspect of some earlier judgments, and through presenting the main characters in action. In so far as this short story still contains any passages suggestive of bookish theorizing, the emphasis has shifted from the earlier attack on Christianity to the analysis of the character of Alfred's psychology. Whereas the earlier version still recalls Samuel Butler, the final text belongs already to the novel of the twentieth century.

Love and the new women

At the same time, as more light is thus thrown upon the figure of the Lawrentian hero, shy with women, and in psychoanalytical language "mother-fixated", after 1912 a new type of woman makes her appearance in his works. Physically and morally she certainly owes much to Frieda von Richthofen. Her attitude to love is of a kind so far totally unknown in Lawrence's works.

More often than not a foreigner, she suddenly erupts into the life of some

young Englishman, winning him with a single look. The series begins with
Paula Jablonowsky, the German-Polish governess in "Love Among the
Haystacks". Although Lawrence has endowed her with freckles, she has
many points of resemblance with the prototype. A blonde with "Slavonic"
cheekbones, speaking English with a pronounced foreign accent, she is
"swift and light as a wild cat".[33] There is something feline, too, about her
smile. There is a hint of the runaway filly in her personality and we are told
that she had left her father's house to "seek life" in a school for young ladies
in Paris. Somehow or other she has turned up in a Midlands vicarage as a
children's nurse. The indifference with which she treats her employer the
vicar is perhaps the most typical of all the features which make of her a
barely disguised version of Frieda von Richthofen.[34]

This resemblance shows that Lawrence modified a 1912 version of "Love
Among the Haystacks"; this is confirmed by David Garnett's introductory
statement that he was writing the stories included in the volume of the same
name in August 1914.[35] There are other indications; the name of Lydia, the
tramp's wife with whom Geoffrey falls in love, might or might not be one of
those which remind one of Frieda, but Geoffrey pronounces her married
name, Mrs Bredon, with a bitterness not unlike that felt by Lawrence for
Frieda's undissolved first marriage.

"Once"[36] belongs to the same period. This story is written in the first
person, with an ease and freedom that are entirely new. The narrator is
travelling in the Tyrol with Anita, the daughter of a German aristocrat.
At eighteen she had married an officer "stupid as an ass", a great worker, too
devoid of romantic appeal ever to satisfy her flighty temperament. Anita
spent her wedding night counting the flowers on the wallpaper, and she
lost no time in seeking outside marriage the satisfaction denied her at home.
She now condescends to give the narrator a little love, in spite of his lack of
self-confidence, and of his fears that he may be reduced to a mere attribute of
his too charming companion. A serious young man, with a tendency to
moralize, he is ready to try to convert her and, through love, to give her
"more than pleasure".

As her lover lies on the bed, musing on their relationship, the door opens
and in bursts Anita, dressed in "a transparent, lacy chemise, that was slipping
over her shoulder, high boots, upon one of which her string-coloured stocking had fallen", and an enormous new hat from Berlin covered with "a
tremendously creamy-brown feather", exactly like the lady on a typical
English "French postcard". Her warm flesh glistens, and through the fine web
of her chemise "the light runs in silver up her lifted arms". At once the man
slips off his dressing-gown, seizes a silk hat and, stark naked save for that and a
pair of gloves, goes forward to her. Their fit of laughter over, he asks Anita
on how many more men she has played this trick. He knows that for the moment he is like the other lovers, and fears he will not last as long as most. Anita

meanwhile pensively passes in review her former lovers, asking herself what they have meant in her life. A sudden recollection, and the title of the story is explained: shall she tell him something she *once* did?

In Dresden, a young officer almost ran into her in the street and apologized, but not before a glance had been exchanged. Meeting him later on the terrace of an elegant café she gave him the number of her hotel room. Without the least sense of shame she recounts to her present lover her perfect night of love with the impetuous yet tender stranger she was never to see again. Nostalgically she recalls the easy gestures of the young officer, even to the way he unfastened his sword-belt and flung it on the bed: "With him, she mused, everything felt so inevitable."

While Anita is thus searching into her past love life, the narrator is "burning with rage" and jealousy. He bitterly attacks Anita, accusing her of seeking only sensation. But his heart stands still when she confesses she has yet to find happiness in love: might he not be the one to bring it to her?

However much fantasy is here mingled with autobiography, it is a fact that in this story Lawrence portrays a new type of woman and poses a problem of his own. The attitude of the two characters to one another is indeed that of Lawrence and Frieda at the beginning of their liaison, and the real-life significance of the lover's jealousy in this story has already been noted. His anxiety, however, here remains latent and under control: for once Lawrence's deliberate humour makes it possible for him to turn a quizzical eye upon himself. Perhaps it is this gay tone that makes it possible for him to exaggerate certain details without offending his own sensibility. In this story deliberate exaggeration constitutes the essential difference between mere autobiography and the finished work of literature.

The same heroine reappears under the name of Paula Moest in "New Eve and Old Adam".[37] All her familiar gestures are abundantly described: now weaving flowers into her hair braided in Bavarian fashion, now turning her feline gaze upon her husband and lifting her golden arms to him in ecstasy . . . When angry, Peter sees her entirely without sympathy, and we have seen in the preceding chapter what he thinks of her total lack of heart. Nowhere has Lawrence painted so realistic a portrait of his wife as in these pages, in all probability written in the hour of their gravest difficulties:

> She was a beautiful woman of about thirty, fair, luxuriant, with proud shoulders and a face borne up by a fierce, native vitality. Her green eyes had a curiously puzzled contraction just now.

Her eyes light up as she bends to put her arms around him:

> She was smiling into his face, her green eyes, looking into his, were bright and wide. But somewhere in them, as he looked back, was a little twist that could not come loose to him, a little cast, that was like an aversion from him, a strain of hate for him.

Paula is beautiful and generous but there are certain aspects of her character that Peter loathes.

> Through all her warmth and kindliness, lay, he said, at the bottom, an almost feline selfishness, a coldness.

Her clothes, "her untidy, flimsy, lovable things" always "a little bit torn", make his heart go hard with hate, even while he loves her.

Jealousy

In addition to elements already analysed—the inability of Peter and Paula to love simply and without torturing each other, their reciprocal accusations of egoism, of hatred and of the lack of a capacity to love—jealousy is a major theme of this confusing story in which literary creation fails to triumph over autobiography: the very absence of order and direction reveal it as a slice of Lawrence's life rather than a construction of his imagination.

The couple are living in a London flat, and Peter has already looked askance at Paula's swift exchange of looks with a workman mending telephone wires on a neighbouring roof. His jealousy finds stronger grounds with the arrival of a telegram signed "Richard" and addressed to "Moest", fixing a rendezvous for the same evening. Knowing no Richard, Peter is sure that this must be for Paula, and refuses to believe her jeering disclaimers. On top of all their many reasons for quarrelling, this mystery gives rise to a scene in which the unfounded suspicions of the husband arouse in his wife a flood of revulsion and contempt. The next day she triumphantly reveals to Peter that she has discovered another Moest, a young German writer staying in the same block of flats, the cousin of the mysterious Richard.

Lawrence does not paint Peter in a flattering light: his jealousy makes him appear vulgar and gauche with Paula, who has no difficulty in making him feel an uncouth and ill-mannered fool. The interest she takes in the young German soon becomes another cause of suffering for her husband, as always the prisoner of his own emotions and well aware how easily the merest stranger can excite Paula's interest.

Published posthumously and never revised for publication, "New Eve and Old Adam" is conspicuous for its lack of literary invention. But certain of its elements, and in particular the study of jealousy, reappear in two far more objective tales revised in 1914. To themes dating from his early youth, Lawrence has added interpretations and scenes suggested by his 1913–14 experience with Frieda and seems to have tried subsequently to efface anything that might suggest the personal character of certain details. These two works also give considerable emphasis to the irremediable conflict between two beings bound to one another by alternating love and hate. As in "New

Eve", the woman, by her manners and upbringing, or simply by virtue of her natural refinement, is the man's superior.

"The Shadow in the Rose Garden" first appeared in March 1914 in *The Smart Set*.[38] Jessie Chambers had never heard Lawrence mention this story: she was inclined to think it might have been written after the spring of 1912. On the other hand she thought the rose garden described at length was probably a garden she and Lawrence had visited at Robin Hood's Bay during one of their holidays. This impression is corroborated by the "soft Yorkshire accent" of the old lady in whose cottage the hero and heroine of the story are lodging.[39] Therefore if, in writing for *The Smart Set*, Lawrence was not working over an existing sketch, he was certainly making use of pre-1911 memories; the reminiscences of *Jane Eyre*, one of his adolescent enthusiasms, also argue in favour of an early draft: the principal scene of this story is very like that in which Jane discovers Rochester blind and disfigured in a flower garden. There is also an echo of the well-worn early theme of the mother who has come down in the world.

A newly-married couple are spending their honeymoon in an English seaside village. The woman is distinguished, well turned out, evidently used to a life of refinement: the husband is a mining electrician, coarser than his wife; countless small details place him at once as "working class".

The young woman goes off alone to revisit places where she had previously lived and loved. In the rectory garden she meets face-to-face the lover she believed dead of sunstroke in Africa: alive, but insane, he does not recognize her. Shaken to the core, she returns to their lodgings. Her husband, tormented and "silent with fury" to find her so remote and strange, so shut away in her cultured female superiority, brutally forces her to confess her past. At the thought that she married him as second best on learning of the other man's supposed death, his fury reaches a climax and he is "mad with anguish". The story ends as he comes to realize what an abyss of pain and incomprehension separates them, and both remain shocked, impersonal, "locked in silent thought".

Several Lawrentian themes are clearly recognizable: the jealousy of a husband conscious of being only second best; the contempt of a superior woman for the common workman she has married; the spectre of the first love, possibly a reminiscence of the ghost of Siegmund imposing itself between Helena and Byrne in *The Trespasser*, but reinforced by fresh experience of jealousy. The narrative is clear-cut and swift-moving, the characters revealed in dialogue. The choice of words matches the characters admirably: the man's uncouth and stumbling phrases when trying to speak of passion; the woman's dignity and frankness in avowal; her prostration at the brutal revelation so suddenly encountered. Lawrence conveys most forcefully the moral isolation of these two beings.

The *Smart Set* version shows signs of hasty writing: the madness of the lover—an English officer—is due not to sunstroke in South Africa but to an attack of dysentery in Tripoli, which is unlikely on medical as well as historical grounds.

Moreover the early version ends flatly, as if Lawrence fails to achieve the tragic atmosphere he sought:

> Her husband watched her. She was pale and silent. And he had nothing to do with her. He lifted himself, trying to ease himself, and sighed, "We can't stop here then," he said.

The opposition of the two main characters never rises above the commonplace. Their quarrels sometimes evoke echoes of those of Gargnano. When the husband reminds his wife that dinner is ready: "How she hated him and his dinners." Frieda had already upbraided Lawrence with eating too much to love much![40] At a critical moment, the woman's wedding ring draws the jealous attention of the lover: as long as Frieda wore the wedding ring of her first marriage, Lawrence regarded it as a symbol of infidelity. Finally, as in "Once", jealousy is provoked by an army officer. Slender as such indications may seem, they do show the storyteller in the process of filling out his subject with details doubtless often in his mind in 1913.

These details are attenuated or suppressed in the final version. No more wedding ring, no more dinners, no more suggested contrast between the honesty of the man and the duplicity of his wife. Above all, the end has been entirely recast and has gained both in dignity and in tragic value. The flatness of the *Smart Set* ending has been replaced by this:

> He stood and looked at her. At last he had learned the width of the breach between them. She still squatted on the bed. He could not go near her. It would be a violation to each of them to be brought into contact with the other. The thing must work itself out. They were both shocked so much, they were impersonal, and no longer hated each other. After some minutes he left her and went out.

"The White Stocking", in its original form, now lost, dates from 1907, the year of "Prelude" and "A Fragment of Stained Glass".[41] It was suggested to Lawrence by a misadventure which happened to his mother at a dance in Nottingham. The *Smart Set* version certainly contains traces of this earlier text. As in "Goose Fair" the events are set in 1870; the men come to the Christmas party wearing trousers strapped under their boots and long, full-skirted overcoats; they dance Scotch reels and quadrilles; and Sam Adams, the local dandy, likes to speak French to his Nottingham neighbours in the manner of the young Lawrence and of Lettie in *The White Peacock*.

This text differs considerably from the final version, into which an entirely new type of scene has been incorporated. In July 1914, Lawrence rates "The

White Stocking" at 8,000 words; the *Prussian Officer* version contains at least 10,500.

One St Valentine's Day, Elsie Whiston, who has been married for two years, receives a letter containing a white stocking. In the toe is concealed a pair of earrings. These she quickly hides, showing her husband only the stocking, which, she says, must have been sent by her former employer, a lace manufacturer called Sam Adams. Jealous, Ted Whiston questions his wife about her relations with Adams. She admits having recently encountered him on a tram. When Ted has gone off to work (he is a commercial traveller), Elsie puts on the earrings, and postures simperingly before her mirror, happy to be rid of her spoil-sport husband.

We are then told how, two years earlier, Sam Adams, a hard drinker and wencher, had invited Ted and Elsie, who were then engaged, to a Christmas party given by him for his factory staff. He had danced attendance on the pretty Elsie until, half-drunk, he spilt over his own leg a cup of coffee Whiston was carrying to a lady. Quite badly burnt, and having made himself ridiculous in the eyes of his guests, Adams had then avoided Elsie for a short time.

But when the music sounded for the quadrilles, Elsie stooped to pick up her pocket handkerchief, shook it out as she rose, and found she had taken by mistake a long white stocking. Not knowing what to do she had let it fall back to the floor and Adams, seizing it as a trophy, showed it triumphantly to the whole assembly amid shouts of laughter. Whiston had snatched the stocking from him and led Elsie away in great embarrassment. Soon after the incident they were married, and each year on St Valentine's Day Sam Adams sent Elsie a white cotton stocking as a souvenir.

Wearing her earrings, Elsie goes off deliberately to meet Adams, dallies pleasantly with him and then, suddenly afraid and disgusted, returns home deeply depressed. On his return from work Whiston continues his interrogation. What is she going to do with the stocking? Wear it, she says, and confesses to having received its pair the year before. She puts on the two white stockings and, pulling up her skirts to reveal her pretty legs, capers insolently before her husband. Defiantly, she tells him how she has met Adams that very day. Whiston cannot understand how she can play around with such a man. His irritation reaches such a pitch that he has to leave the room to stop himself from striking her. Soon she calls him back, and, calming down, he returns and takes her silently in his arms. Their reconciliation is complete, and the next day Elsie sends back to Adams not only the stockings, but also the earrings of which her husband knew nothing.

This relatively mild *Smart Set* version is evidently still pretty close to the preliminary sketch. The party scenes, the provincial posturings, the grotesque incidents are in the very early Lawrence manner. Only a few phrases here and there indicate some degree of revision based on life with Frieda: the stress laid on Elsie's untidiness, which, however, serves here to increase her husband's love; certain half-dressed bedroom scenes that Lawrence could scarcely have written before 1912.

In the final text the "handsomely strapped" trousers still take us back to the nineteenth century, but the false provincial airs and graces, the spilled coffee, the unpardonable caddishness of Sam Adams brandishing the white stocking have completely disappeared. Two new elements, on the other hand, are strongly stressed: Elsie's sensual turmoil while dancing with Sam Adams, and the violent jealousy driving Whiston to the point of striking his wife across the mouth in an access of blind brutality.

Elsie is transformed into an original blend of feminine guile and weakness: an ingenious liar, a creature without character or conscience, telling part of the truth only to hide the rest more effectively, and driven by sudden and unreflecting impulses. In her own way she loves Whiston, but rather the way one loves a faithful dog, whereas Sam has for her the attraction of forbidden fruit.

The woman's sensual rapture is entirely new. In the *Smart Set* version Elsie was also stirred by the dance, but in a confused, more naïve way: "Everything seemed vague and there was a delicious conflagration in her blood."[42] Now, however, she lets herself be carried rhythmically away by Adams, who is an excellent dancer: hypnotized by the movement and by the gleam in the man's eyes, just like Frieda in the "San Gaudenzio" scenes of *Twilight in Italy*. Oblivious of all around them, she is conscious only of the "large, voluptuous body" of her partner who whirls her round the room, fused with her in "perfect unconsciousness".

But Whiston is there watching, and a dim perception of her fiancé somewhere in the back of her mind restores her to some sort of consciousness. In a way she is repelled by the sheer bestiality of Adams. The incident of the white stocking, which Adams still snatches up as a trophy, quickly slipping Elsie a handkerchief in exchange, gives Whiston the chance to lead her away completely overwrought by the evening's emotions.

The Valentine's Day episode understandably upsets Whiston much more than would have been plausible in the *Smart Set* version. Elsie begins by telling him the stocking is a sample; little by little she reveals that it comes from Adams, and that she had received a similar one the year before. Finally, he tells her furiously to burn the stockings. Regardless of his jealousy she dances provocatively round the room, holding up her skirts, performing high kicks and chanting, "I shan't backfire them stockings, I shan't, I shan't, I shan't," insinuating slyly that she would like Sam to see how prettily they fit. Incapable of grasping her husband's uncontrollable anger, she continues to jeer scornfully at all his threats. In the end "with a queer chirrup of mocking laughter" she throws in his face the fact that Sam has previously sent her an amethyst brooch and a pair of earrings. Ted strikes her, flinging her against the wall. She crouches there, with open, bleeding mouth and wide, staring eyes, her "two hands clutching over her temples" to ward off further blows.

After extracting the last details of her weak and foolish deceptions, Whiston's "passion suddenly goes down". Sick and tired of the responsibility of it, the violence, the shame, he makes the jewels up into "a careful little package" to return to Adams, and the story ends on a note of tearful reconciliation.

In this last scene, the obsession with violence, the savage desire for blood and tears is crudely and deliberately shown. Rewriting his rather characterless earlier draft, Lawrence extracts from it all he now considers worthy of attention. As in the previous scene of Elsie's sensual rapture in the arms of her dancing partner, Lawrence here attempts a far greater realism then ever before. In both cases it seems certain that only personal experience could have enabled him to convey with such conviction physical details of sensuality and brutality entirely unknown in his early work.

"The Old Adam" probably dates from 1913, and the fight with Baxter Dawes in *Sons and Lovers* was revised, if not first written, during the winter of 1912–13. The scenes of violence in *Sons and Lovers* and "The Old Adam" are intermediary between those in "A Fragment of Stained Glass", "Love Among the Haystacks" and *The White Peacock*, and those described above. Lawrence has apparently moved on from the plane of psychological predispositions to that of practice.

A link is now established between violence and sensuality: it is jealousy that makes Whiston brutal and breaks down for a moment the barriers civilization has built round animal instincts. Moreover his blows are, as so often with Lawrence, a step on the way to reconciliation.

He seems, in fact, to have discovered, in this autumn of 1912, a principle which dominates several of his other works dating from this period, above all the title story in the 1914 volume published in 1914: "The Prussian Officer". "Cruelty is a form of perverted sex", is its keynote.[43]

A real-life incident in Austria may have given Lawrence the original idea. In 1912, either on his way through Austria or during his stay on the Italian-Austrian border, Lawrence may have heard of a sensational trial: a captain who had kicked his orderly to death was acquitted on the grounds that it was "only the second time".[44] Incidentally, as Harry T. Moore has pointed out, Frieda's father used to beat his orderly.[45] Lawrence clearly had in mind the theme when, in the autumn of 1912, he wrote to Garnett:

> And soldiers, being herded together, men without women, never being *satisfied* by a woman, as a man never is from a street affair, get their surplus sex and their frustration and dissatisfaction into the blood, and *love* cruelty.[46]

By 11 June 1913, the story was finished, written at one sitting. "The best short story I have ever done," Lawrence told Garnett.[47] First published in

The English Review in August 1914 under the title "Honour and Arms", it reappeared practically unaltered in the volume, entitled by Garnett (against Lawrence's wishes) *The Prussian Officer*.[48] *The English Review* seems to have imposed a fair number of cuts which were restored in volume form.

A Prussian infantry captain, who has never married for lack of money and prospects, and also because "no woman had ever moved him to it", is dissatisfied by his occasional mistresses and finds himself driven to bouts of sadistic frenzy by the sight of his orderly. This madness is increased by the fact that the soldier has a sweetheart, "a simple girl from the mountains", as "independent and primitive" as the man himself; he finds with her a simple happiness. All the captain's pent-up jealousy, all his sexual frustration, finally explode. He beats his servant with his belt and kicks him brutally. The next day, being alone with him for a while, in the course of field manœuvres, the orderly breaks the captain's neck. Panic-stricken and fevered, he wanders aimlessly about the "sun-blazing" countryside, finally dying delirious in an access of brain fever.

With relative, and for him remarkable, sobriety of narrative and expression, Lawrence has succeeded in making credible, if not absolutely comprehensible, the brutal passion which suddenly overcomes the officer, as well as the instinctive and purely animal vengeance of the soldier. The actions of the two characters spring from the depths of their being without emerging into actual consciousness. On the psychological plane on which Lawrence places them, they seem to issue directly from the realm of dreams. Moved by obscure forces, the characters do not even allow their conscious selves to realize the acts performed by their bodies. A mere detail can thus assume intense significance, unleashing reactions as unforeseen as they are revealing. A bottle of red wine, suggestive of blood, upset by the orderly, suddenly unleashes the officer's hatred; a scar across the knuckle of the soldier's left thumb exacerbates this hatred and increases out of all proportion the captain's desire for violence.

The brutal details are deliberately selected, forcefully described and driven home: the heavy kicks, the dark bruised flesh and aching limbs of the orderly, the long agony of the next day's march and, above all, the hallucinating scene of the murder itself—the little "cluck" and crunching sensation of the breaking neck, the blood which fills the dead man's nostrils and, brimming over, trickles down the upturned face into the eyes. It is the same, almost repulsive realism Lawrence had already used to describe the suicide of Siegmund.

The thread of the story is never interrupted by theoretical discussion; yet Lawrence clearly indicates the causes of the brutality he describes. The officer is the victim of repression, forced to become a mere machine for giving orders, endeavouring to have only impersonal relationships with his men. But human nature irrepressibly reasserts its rights. The source of the hatred he feels towards his orderly lies in the young man's instinctive, balanced personality, his "dark expressionless eyes that seemed never to have thought, only to have received life direct through his senses, and acted straight from instinct". The officer envies his sureness of movement, his calm and equilibrium, and is forced despite himself to see the man behind the soldier, to abandon his deliberately impersonal attitude. The orderly, on the other hand, takes refuge in impersonal service, submitting easily to the mechanical discipline of military life which only brushes the surface of his deep and primitive nature without causing harm.

At one point, his passionate nature continually suppressed to conform with military principle, the captain tries to cure himself by one of those casual affairs from which he always returns "his brow still more tense, his eyes still more hostile and irritable". Once again his temporary mistress has served only to aggravate the instincts which precipitate the violent scene around which the story is constructed.

Love and the conscious self

The captain and his orderly both seek in love, or at least in woman, in characteristic Lawrentian fashion, oblivion from an ill-defined but tormenting sense of inadequacy. Consciously and deliberately the officer gives himself up to a "mockery of pleasure"; blindly, the soldier goes out with his sweetheart "not to talk, but to have his arm round her, and for the physical contact. This eased him, made it easier for him to ignore the Captain."

Since *Sons and Lovers*, a recurrent theme in Lawrence's work has been momentary oblivion, a plunge into a sometimes beneficial, sometimes harmful darkness, usually induced by erotic contacts of diverse and often very ill-defined nature. Certain love scenes expressing this notion have been studied in the previous chapter in their biographical aspects. We may now consider them for the light they throw on the none too evident differences seen by Lawrence between various aspects of "love", which will be developed in *The Rainbow* and *Women in Love*. Indeed they provide us with some clues as to the criterion by which Lawrence will approve or disapprove various manifestations of "love".

The two versions of his second military story set in Germany, "The Thorn in the Flesh",[49] reveal a first and useful distinction. This work is more interesting for what it tells us of the role and nature of the Lawrentian idea of love than for its implicit criticism of the brutalities of military life.

First published in *The English Review* in June 1914, under the title "Vin Ordinaire", it was completely recast for publication in volume form by December of the same year.[50] There can be little doubt that the original text was written in 1913, the same year as "Honour and Arms".

Bachmann, a young soldier stationed in Metz, turns giddy when, in the course of a military exercise, he has to scale the fortifications of the city by means of a long, unsteady ladder which swerves about above the moat. His loss of control is demonstrated to all and sundry when his urine trickles down his leg. Brutally bawled out by his sergeant when he is finally hauled to the top, with an instinctive gesture originally intended as self-defence, Bachmann half-accidentally sends his superior reeling back over the ramparts. In the ensuing confusion the young soldier panics and deserts.

Instinctively he seeks refuge with his friend Emilie, a maidservant in the family of a German baron living near the barracks. The girl, of whom the first version tells us little, hides him in her room, while she spends the night with the children's governess. All she allows Bachmann is a stolen kiss which stirs her to the depths. Subconsciously she is vexed with him for having gone no further than the kiss; tormented by unsatisfied and unadmitted desire, disturbed by an obscure feeling that Bachmann has let her down, she cannot sleep, and next morning looks on almost unconcerned as the deserter is arrested. Her main preoccupation is that the baron should not continue to suspect that she spent the night with a man. The soldier returns to the barracks feeling that to the previous day's shame has been added failure in love.

While "Vin Ordinaire" thus insists on the discord provoked by unsatisfied passion, "The Thorn in the Flesh" on the contrary develops the idea of liberation by successful love. In this version Emilie gives herself unreservedly to Bachmann, sharing his conviction that the two of them now form a new being and that they are "one, complete". Satisfied, and knowing he has given satisfaction as a lover, Bachmann is able to forget both the agony of his shame and the threat of military discipline, becoming once more indifferent to the outside world.

In his instinctive flight from the ramparts to Emilie, the soldier had been seeking to escape not only the rigid automatism of military life, but also the shame of having revealed in public a weakness he would have preferred to keep secret: he was not his true self. Only when he had put himself in Emilie's hands, and submitted to the action of a kind of "secondary will" driving him to make love to her, could he become fully himself. Emilie is a foundling, a "naïve, poignantly religious" being, brought up in blind obeisance to the social class she was called upon to serve. She has no independent self. At first, upset by Bachmann's intrusion into the normal discharge of her daily duties, she recovers her balance and self-assurance once satisfied passion has made her "a new being". A first erotic scene, rather obscure, as is often the case with Lawrence, shows her losing "consciousness", then "translated in the peace of satisfaction", full of reverence and gratitude towards Bachmann, who for his part is "restored and completed" and filled with "unconquerable" pride:

They loved each other, and all was whole. She loved him, he had taken her, she was given to him. It was right. He was given to her, and they were one, complete.

Any precise-minded reader wondering exactly what had taken place between them in this scene will still be asking himself the same question when he finds that she loses her virginity only in the night of love which follows. Emilie emerges from the test of love "curiously changed", transported into "a new world of her own, that she had never even imagined and which was the land of promise for all that. In this she moved and had her being." All her activity now radiates from this new centre of her being, and no longer exclusively from her loyalty to her employers and their class. Similarly, Bachmann had "won his own being, in himself and Emilie; he had drawn the stigma from his own shame, he was beginning to be himself".[51]

Love has washed away his imperfections, so that when he is arrested he has no need to exchange even a glance with his mistress: "They knew each other. They were themselves." For the first time in Lawrence's work, love appears to bring to two lovers something positive, a consecration and a confirmation of their being which makes them independent of hostile outside forces.

Since 1912, Lawrence has indeed modified both his concept and his portrayal of physical love. In particular he has extended and deepened his knowledge of feminine reactions, so as to include those of a new type of woman. Never before had he depicted an unsatisfied woman, suffering obscurely but intensely to find herself abandoned either because she is not understood by the man who has awakened her senses, or because she is betrayed by adverse circumstance. Such is Emilie tormented by Bachmann's kiss; such is Elsie in "The White Stocking", stimulated by her dance with Adams, bursting into tears in the arms of the totally uncomprehending Whiston.[52] What a far cry from the reserve of Miriam, the coldness of Helena, whose passion was slaked by a mere kiss!

While the boldness and perspicacity of the men have not greatly increased since the hesitating and gauche lovers of the early works, the women on the contrary now know how to take the lead. The first to do so is Louisa Lindley in "Daughters of the Vicar". Unhappy to feel Alfred Durant building up a barrier of social caste between them, and driven by some obscure instinct beyond her control, she finally offers herself boldly to the miner's son, inviting him to marry her. The conquest of this shrinking male by the vicar's daughter is no meagre victory for them both: in each case the individual has to surrender to something more fundamental than the conscious self. Both pay dearly for this triumph of instinct. Alfred has to conquer his sexual timidity, his fear of infringing the class barrier; Louisa has to overcome that social prejudice revealed in its full horror by her sister's marriage, and the age-old convention according to which initiative is a male prerogative.

For them, as for so many of Lawrence's characters, love involves first and foremost the death, the disappearance, the destruction of an artificial self, tending to suppress instinctive life. Sometimes there is a new birth, when love unlocks the door of a new world, recreating the selves of the two lovers in communication with a superior reality partaking of the divine. But such a renaissance is a rare thing, conditioned by certain hidden factors for which we must seek further.

The last chapters of *Sons and Lovers*, those which probably underwent most alteration in the course of Lawrence's final revision and under Frieda's influence, offer a series of love scenes which are relevant here and were probably written at the time when Lawrence's new ideas were in the process of development.

Over-spirituality, any intervention of will or consciousness, can prevent this re-creation of the couple through love, arresting them on the brink of the quasi-religious revelation, the transmutation of their being which is love's objective. One of the causes of the failure of the love relationship between Paul and Miriam, as conceived by Lawrence, is that the girl is incapable of letting herself go, of forgetting her separate self and that of Paul:

> Not for an instant would she let him forget. Back again he had to torture himself into a sense of his responsibility and hers. Never any relaxing, never any leaving himself to the great hunger and impersonality of passion; he must be brought back to a deliberate, reflective creature. As if from the swoon of passion she called him back to the littleness, the personal relationship.[53]

Paul, asserting his love of a "good, thick darkness", is almost unaware of her as a person, to him she is "only a woman". But while he "melts into the darkness", oblivious of his own self and at one with the great Being, Miriam never leaves the plane of conscious personal relationship. Paul invariably leaves her with an aftertaste of failure and of death, and a "dull pain in his soul".[54] Much might still be said concerning the source of these feelings, which is not only psychological and to which Lawrence refers only in vague terms. Without going into psycho-physiological detail, the net result of these pages on "the Test on Miriam" is that the lover feels a taste of death when his mistress fails to join him in the great plunge into the mystical Beyond. No rebirth is possible unless the two egos let themselves be carried away simultaneously into this beyond where they are merged and whence they eventually return together. Only then can true transmutation take place. Paul explains this to Miriam at the time when his liaison with Clara, at first wholly satisfactory, has taught him this great secret. He has been telling her of the bond uniting two beings who have experienced a "real, real flame of feeling" through another person, even if "it only lasts three months":

> "What has happened exactly?" asked Miriam.
> "It's so hard to say, but the something big and intense that changes you when you really come together with somebody else. It almost seems to fertilize your soul and make it that you can go on and mature."[55]

For some time Clara's love provides Paul with that deep mystical experience that satisfies his soul. One evening, in particular, while they are walking across the fields, troubled by a conversation about their uncertain future Paul pleads, "Don't ask me anything about the future . . . Be with me now, will you, no matter what it is?"[56] Losing oneself in the present is a second condition of perfect union: Paul will not think of tomorrow, any more than Bachmann, lost in Emilie's arms, will plot his escape to France.

The two selves thus united are annihilated. It is not Clara that Paul holds in his arms, but anonymous, unidentified "woman", the incarnation of all the mystery of the universe:

> And after such an evening they both were very still, having known the immensity of passion. They felt small, half-afraid, childish, and wondering, like Adam and Eve when they lost their innocence and realized the magnificence of the power which drove them out of Paradise and across the great night and the great day of humanity. It was for each of them an initiation and a satisfaction. To know their own nothingness, to know the tremendous living flood which carried them always, gave them rest within themselves. If so great a magnificent power could overwhelm them, identify them altogether with itself, so that they knew they were only grains in the tremendous heave that lifted every grass blade its little height, and every tree, and living thing, then why fret about themselves? They could let themselves be carried by life, and they felt a sort of peace each in the other. There was a verification which they had had together. Nothing could nullify it, nothing could take it away; it was almost their belief in life.[57]

"Immensity of passion" has here opened the gates of the soul to a sense of participation in the vital forces of the universe, awakening in Paul a sort of cosmic consciousness in which is recreated not an abstract idea of the universe but a direct, spontaneous perception of things about him. The momentary ecstasy is thus prolonged to colour all existence. In these moments when time ceases to exist Paul achieves full mystical experience and at the climax of ecstasy he is aware of partaking in eternity. But even here the shadow of discord creeps in between himself and Clara. She cannot "keep the moment". To plunge into the absolute is not enough for her: she needs something permanent. Rather than the ecstasy, she imagines that she wants the *person* of her lover: "She had been there, but she had not gripped the—the something—she knew not what—which she was mad to have." From the cosmic she descends to the individual plane. Gradually the first harmony of their love-making gives way to a feeling of physical maladjustment. Finally, during his mother's illness, Paul asks of Clara no more than moments of oblivion and death. From then onwards their liaison is doomed to failure.

All these scenes contain the same elements: the death of the "self" which represses perfect sensual enjoyment and constitutes an obstacle to awakening into cosmic consciousness; the rebirth of a more impersonal "self" steeped in the creative springs: or, on the contrary, a return to the old "self", an after-taste of death, a disintegration that follows on imperfect love. The first "self" that must die is that normally operating on the plane of social and individual concepts: the self of Louisa Lindley, of the heroine of "Second Best", to some extent of Miriam when, with clenched teeth, she consents to give herself to Paul. It is also the self which Paul Morel, bound to his mother by bonds of intense spiritual passion, seeks vainly to destroy; the inhibited selves of Paul and of Alfred Durant, the ashamed self of Bachmann with the brand of military servitude upon his soul.

All is well if, in this conflict between instinct and idea, the social self, the individual, goes under to become submerged as it does in the great scenes of passion between Paul and Clara, between Bachmann and Emilie; perhaps also between Louisa and Alfred Durant, although in this case the future of the couple is not revealed. More numerous are the cases where the self reclaims its rights and drives out love. Passion then becomes a distintegrating force, as when Paul asks of Clara only a momentary suppression of conscious-ness. If the annihilation of the self in the fertile darkness of cosmic experience is imperfect or short-lived, if the will intervenes either to force an eclipse of the self or to hold the conscious self back at the very moment of submersion, then the soul returns from its journey into love bruised and irritated. That is what happens to Paul first with Miriam, then with Clara during his mother's last illness; that is the cause of the exasperation of the Prussian officer, deliberately seeking in a casual affair an annihilation which cannot lead to a rebirth. In "Vin Ordinaire" Bachmann and Emilie both suffer for allowing convention to thwart the call of instinct. The self which attains mystic reality without complete submergence remains nostalgically drawn towards death, which it confuses with the true impersonal and profound life of those whom passion has carried over the borderlines of the self. Having almost reached the goal, mental and purposive activity seems to them as to Paul Morel a death, a non-being; whereas merging with the Great Being is the true aim of all existence.[58]

Thus in his works of 1913–14 Lawrence finds wisdom in the abandonment of the self to obscure forces: as soon as will or consciousness, as soon as any specific practical objective or deliberate purpose intervenes, love is doomed to failure. Each individual must, like Bachmann, allow his or her self to be taken over by a "secondary will", which is the unconscious expression of the underlying reality. In the works we have studied here, no abstract ideas are ever directly expressed: were they indeed clearly formulated in the writer's mind, except in the apocalyptic form in which they appear in the Foreword to Sons and Lovers, and in one or two highly personal letters? Nevertheless the basis of a complete ethical and psychological system can be discerned in the modifications made to his earlier drafts between 1912 and 1914: both ethic and psychology are expressed in the study of relations between lovers, the author's own major preoccupation during 1913 and 1914. As for the general background of ideas and probable sources, we have stressed in another study the immense debt of Lawrence to the works of Edward Carpenter.[59]

Technical progress

Around this central problem are grouped a number of secondary themes later taken up and amplified: a marked anti-militarism, already apparent in *Sons and Lovers* and "Daughters of the Vicar",[60] and firmly expressed in the two German stories; certain elements of a social philosophy or social criticism contained in the portrait of Emilie and seeming to presage those pages of *Women in Love* where the writer analyses the changing relations between worker and employer.[61] Lawrence is constantly concerned with the relationship between the deep self and the outer world envisaged either on the social, mechanistic plane, the army, discipline, etc., or on that of the personal loyalty of the servant towards the revered master class.

Quite apart from a constant preoccupation with the problem of love, this period is marked by definite technical progress. This is particularly visible in a comparison between "Daughters of the Vicar" and its earlier version, "Two Marriages". While the subject remains the same, Lawrence has done far more than merely correct the style and lengthen the story. The study of the principal characters, and in particular, as we have already seen, that of Alfred Durant, has been considerably amplified and deepened. The influence of Samuel Butler has been partly shaken off and the work has taken on an unmistakably Lawrentian tone. The hostility towards Christianity, the satirical portrayal of the Eastwood *milieu*, the caricatures of the clergy are all toned down a little. The Lindleys remain an impoverished lower-middle-class family, hidebound by the prejudices of their class, coldly performing their Christian "duties", preoccupied by the sordid details of material life, irritated by the forced contact with their parishioners. Lawrence has also softened the tone of certain dialogues between Lindley and Durant, leaving the secret hatred of the vicar for his flock to be expressed in action, whereas in "Two Marriages" this is baldly stated in didactic terms.

The character of Massy loses nothing of its forcefulness, and remains a vivid incarnation of a cold and theoretical form of Christianity, which manifests itself in everyday life not by gestures of human sympathy but by the mathematical application of guiding principles dictated by the mind. Here again Lawrence must be credited with translating into terms of art, without too obvious an exaggeration, the ideas formulated in the Foreword, the falseness of a certain conception of Christian charity, and the horror of a marriage founded on anything but true feeling. The portrait of Mary Lindley also shows remarkable dexterity of touch; Lawrence succeeds in explaining the generous motives, the real sympathy for the moral qualities of Massy, which persuaded her to accept a union repugnant to her deepest feelings.

In thus filling out the earlier version Lawrence shows artistic objectivity; above all he has sought to explain and bring to life the characters of Louisa and Alfred Durant to such an extent that this couple now occupy the front of the stage. He has tried to contrast with Mary's marriage, based on spiritual considerations and charity, that of her younger sister, in which a frank and healthy physical attraction plays the major role, though the possibility of spiritual contact between the partners is not excluded. We get to know Alfred Durant better and to recognize beneath the layer of coal dust covering his face his real sensitivity and human potentialities. The character of Louisa also becomes more intelligible: ever since her adolescence, Alfred's smile, the memory of his musical voice in the choir of the little church, have haunted her daydreams. She has dimly sought to lower the barriers that stand between them. From being a docile instrument to the will of Alfred's mother, she has become a free spirit acting spontaneously in response not only to the voice of instinct, but also to a large extent to that of reason, which conveys to her the full horror of Mary's fate. Her open defiance of her parents is finely portrayed in the final scenes when she takes the miner home to ask for her hand in marriage. Intelligible and acceptable from beginning to end of this novella, Louisa Lindley has become a consistently developed, broadly human character.

Detailed comparison of the texts of many other 1914 stories with their earlier known versions would demonstrate similar progress. Everywhere Lawrence has sought to achieve a more objective perspective, to efface those personal traits he subsequently found too obvious or too naïve; he has worked over his dialogue to make it more natural, less verbose ("The Shadow in the Rose Garden", "The Shades of Spring", "Second Best", etc.); he has developed the characters and made the incidents more probable, elaborating the detail and placing it more firmly in context ("The White Stocking", "The Thorn in the Flesh"). It is therefore scarcely surprising that *The Prussian Officer and Other Stories* was considered by critics as placing its author in the front rank of contemporary English short-story writers.

But technical progress aside, what does Lawrence's work during these first two years of conjugal life contribute that is new? Considerable elaboration of old themes; the appearance of a new feminine type; the impact of living in Germany and in Italy and a great effervescence of thought centred upon certain moral questions, particularly sexual problems. No attempt to synthesize all this was made before *The Rainbow*, on which Lawrence was still working in 1915, and which is, in fact, a transposition into novel form of the ideas then teeming in the author's mind. Indeed, the whole of this important section of his output gravitates round this master work in which Lawrence was to assert himself as never before.

9

FROM MISSION TO ALIENATION

I. LAWRENCE IN 1914:
HIGH HOPES AND SOCIAL PROSPECTS

By July 1914 Lawrence was riding on the crest of the wave of his early success. *Sons and Lovers* having made him a leading figure of the younger generation, no hope seemed too high for the future. Spurred by undoubted ambition, he could be seen as a potential conqueror of the literary scene. Such signs as he had shown of his sense of mission, supported by obvious talent, might, given the necessary skill in handling people, have developed positively and compelled the allegiance of his contemporaries and fellow-countrymen. Yet five years and three months later he left England alone, an embittered and lonely figure, his novels unpublishable; and, indeed, since the end of 1916, without a book of any size even ready for submission to a publisher.

Lawrence has given his own version of this calvary in the "Nightmare" chapter of *Kangaroo*. But when considering the man as he appears in his letters and in the eyes of his contemporaries, and the artist as revealed in the works written during these same years, one senses inadequacy in the existing explanations of this downfall. The bitterness of the man, his isolation, the incomprehension, tolerant at best, with which he met, present problems no critic, no biographer has so far solved or even fully faced. The nature of the crisis through which he passed may best be understood by a study of his mental universe during this crucial period, the works, the ideas they contain, the questionings they reveal, filling out the gaps in the biographical material.

While there is no lack of purely external biographical data, much of what went on in his mind still remains obscure. His own letters, the memoirs of many of his contemporaries, the works of H. T. Moore and Edward Nehls, provide factual accounts, sometimes suggest interpretations, usually based on the shock of the war. While it is true indeed that the Lawrence who left England in 1919 was no longer the same man who had come home to it in 1914, it is also a fact worthy of consideration that the works completed between 1914 and 1919 develop themes and ideas already present in his mind well before his return, and are very often the elaboration of earlier plans. As always with the Lawrentian method of literary creation, present mingles with past, and the incidents of today are woven into the fabric of yesterday. Rather than give a chronological account—which can be found in the books of Catherine Carswell, Richard Aldington and Harry T. Moore, and in Edward Nehls's *Composite Biography*—we shall concentrate on the interplay between life and work during the war years. Certain pre-1914 themes are developed, in conjunction with new elements contributed by the experience of the period from 1914 to 1919. To what extent are the new works the direct result of life-experience, or do they express a vision of life which antedates the war years?

One *leitmotif* of these war years was the refusal to participate in society; the flight from social obligation only partially concealing a half-admitted failure to face up to full human responsibilities. Most characteristic was the shrinking of the social environment around the writer, accentuated by the fact that the war denied him even the illusions permitted by physical exile. In the end the only remaining refuge for his starved and wounded spirit were nature, household and rural work, literary creation whenever its source was not dried up, and a ceaseless quest for friendship, often doomed to cruel disappointment. The beauty of some of the prose and poetry written during these years reveals a cleavage between the artist and the socially maladjusted man, a haunting sense of deep loneliness and despair, which is different from the pre-1914 period. Something in Lawrence had broken finally by the time he left for Italy in November 1919. His departure from England marks the end of a whole phase in his life. But did war conditions, by detaining him forcibly in England, do more than aggravate a crisis latent in his character, and alter its outward manifestations? In other words, was the role of the war determinant, or largely coincidental?

In 1914, the upward turn of Lawrence's career may to some extent have masked his inner conflicts, the deep dualism of his nature, his social maladjustment. Were it not for the war, might he not, like others, have achieved some sort of balance, have learned to keep up a façade without coming so near to tragedy? In the early summer of 1914 his situation may well have seemed enviable to Murry or Katherine Mansfield, as well as to enthusiastic young readers of *Sons and Lovers* such as Ivy Low, Catherine Jackson (Carswell) or Viola Meynell. Was he not greeted as a pioneer by the circle of psychoanalysts revolving round Ernest Jones, Dr Eder, and Mrs Eder's sister Barbara Low? His desertion of Duckworth for Methuen had led to an almost complete break with Edward Garnett, but his interests were immediately placed in the hands of the competent literary agent J. B. Pinker, while David Garnett was busy introducing him to his young and brilliant Bloomsbury friends, Francis Birrell, the Olivier girls, the Stracheys and the Stephenses.[1] Eminent American cosmopolitans such as Hilda Doolittle, Amy

Lowell, Harriet Monroe, were interested in his poetry. Through Edward Marsh, private secretary to Cabinet Ministers and patron of the arts and letters, or through the Herbert Asquiths, he had access to those in power. Left-wing liberal circles were as open to him as he might wish. The purchase of tails to dine at the house of H. G. Wells in August 1914 was a consecration of his new status, and he attached considerable importance to this "initiation into the dress-suit world".[2] Among his new friends were the novelist Gilbert Cannan and his wife Mary, formerly married to Sir James Barrie; the Irish lawyer Gordon Campbell, future Lord Glenavy; the painter Mark Gertler; and an important new name in his life is that of the young Russian translator S. S. Kotelianksy.

Social glitter and titles exercised a curious attraction for Lawrence, who proudly drops names in his correspondence, excusing himself for not waiting to see Garnett on the grounds that he "had to lunch with Lady St Helier".[3] Even when completely rejecting any form of compromise with society and homeland, he never neglected to call upon his influential friends for help, for intervention in high places, even for favoured treatment.

What are the main causes of Lawrence's social maladjustment, and how do they rank in order of importance? The most that one can do is to list and describe certain permanent or durable features of his behaviour towards his country, friends, family and Frieda. The predominant trait, manifested in a thousand different ways, was his almost compulsive inability to maintain any kind of human relationship. His moments of peace, of contentment, sprang from contact not with men but with nature. Lawrence could be unreservedly himself only when alone, with some chosen friend, or in the company of a child. It seems useless to look to the events of these five years for a coherent, simple, factual explanation of the evolution of his character. In the conflict opposing him to society, there can be no such thing as objectivity: the incomprehension was tragically mutual, and all facts become distorted by subjective interpretation. But a methodical investigation of certain aspects of his life and of the interaction of the misunderstood individual with the national and administrative circles with which he clashed may at least make it possible to place the conflict in perspective, and to begin to appreciate its true nature.

II. MATERIAL AND PSYCHOLOGICAL CIRCUMSTANCES

Poverty, lack of a fixed abode, a constant irritability in his contacts with others, forced the writer to lead a wandering existence which, after the war, became his normal way of life. Abortive plans, changes of mind, hesitations plot the course of moves from place to place, only one of which was, in fact, dictated by the intervention of an external authority. To what extent less unstable, more methodical behaviour, better conjugal relations, might have spared the Lawrences many of their moves, remains an open question.

Against a background of ill-health, quarrels with Frieda, stormy friendships, frequent removals, a few important events stand out: a period of mystic illumination in late 1914 and early 1915; the publication and suppression of *The Rainbow*; the recurrent quarrels with Murry and Katherine Mansfield (1915–16); the attempted collaboration and subsequent break with Bertrand Russell (1915); the writing of the final version of *Women in Love* and the friendship and quarrel with Lady Ottoline Morrell (1916); the stay in Cornwall, ending in expulsion by the military authorities (1917); the army medicals (1916, 1917, 1918); the attempts to leave for the United States and the dream of a free community in the New World or on some distant island. On the positive side may be noted a lasting friendship with Lady Cynthia Asquith, and that persistent personal charm of Lawrence, thanks to which he retained some faithful friends even after his final break with England.

Poverty

In 1914, Lawrence seemed relatively affluent to John Middleton Murry, also of humble origin and without private means (though, as time was to prove, far better equipped for the battle of life). Tempted by Methuen's higher offer for *The Rainbow*, Lawrence had decided, not without a momentary qualm, to break with Duckworth[4] and deposited in a newly-opened London bank account Pinker's first cheque; this was the first instalment (£100, less the agent's commission) of Methuen's advance, due in full on receipt of the revised manuscript.[5] At no time throughout the war and up to the time of his voluntary exile, when he began to be able to live on American royalties, did Lawrence have in his possession any sizeable sum of money. His reiterated appeals to Pinker or to literary trusts, which constantly recur in his letters, show him as a careful and economical man, counting every penny, to whom the humiliation of begging for money did not come easily:

> I am very sorry to worry you again about money. Do you think Methuen will pay up the £150 to you? I can last out here only another month— then I don't know where to raise a penny, for nobody will pay me. It makes me quite savage. Extort me my dues out of Methuen if you can, will you?[6]

Despite the arrival of small sums, the urgency of the appeals increased, particularly when Lawrence was ordered to pay £145 divorce costs, which he had no intention of paying:

> The Literary Fund gave me £50. I have got about £70 in the world now. Of this I owe £145 to the divorce lawyers, for costs claimed against me. This

I am never going to pay. I also owe about £20 otherwise. So I've got some £50. If you think the other fund would give me any more—benissimo, I'll take it like a shot. Have I not earned my whack—at least enough to live on—from this nation?[7]

The lawyers' costs worried him seriously; not that he felt in any way obliged to pay them, but because the bankruptcy proceedings instituted by Weekley's solicitor, Goldberg, involved a legal obligation to declare all sums owing to him, thus risking the loss of the last instalment of Methuen's advance. On 3 May 1915 he was obliged to make his declaration before the Registrar at Somerset House. To this end he had accepted from "an unclean creature" twenty-five shillings "conduct money" to pay his fare to London, and declared roundly that no one "should have a penny" out of him.[8] The visit to the Registrar, however, seems to have somewhat calmed him down and before long he was asking his solicitor, Robert Garnett, "to compound with the detestable Goldbergs". He feared that if his novel was handed over

> ... the Goldbergs ... will serve a summons on me and on Methuen, ordering Methuen to pay them the £50 due to me. They can't serve the summons— or at least it is null if they do—until the debt is due.

So Robert Garnett was asked to come to terms with Goldberg before Lawrence gave Methuen the revised manuscript:

> Because the debt to me does not fall due till I hand in the MS. to you ... You see I can't pay this £144, or I shall starve for ever. This money for *The Rainbow* is all I have to look forward to at all—and Mrs Lawrence can't get any money from Germany now.[9]

At this particular moment he was living on lessons given to a niece of Viola Meynell. Did he in fact compound with his creditors, before handing over the manuscript in response to a wire from Edward Garnett? Except in a letter to Ottoline Morrell, in which he says that "they didn't make me a bankrupt" but that it was "still in the air", he makes no further mention of the matter.[10]

The evidence suggests that in fact he had agreed to compound, since in August he was renting a flat and furnishing it, with the help of friends, at the same time embarking with Murry on a quasi-commercial venture, in which, so he told Russell, he was prepared, if necessary, to lose money; this project was the publication of a little fortnightly paper, *The Signature*, which ceased after three numbers for want of subscribers. Lawrence, then preparing to leave for the United States, borrowed £20 from Edward Marsh at the very moment that he learned of the seizure of the copies of *The Rainbow*.[11] The Morrells had sent him £30, in return for which he sent off to Garsington a "pack of MS", and his letters to Pinker speak of possible gifts from Henry James and Arnold Bennett. Bernard Shaw gave him £5, and Pinker advanced another £40, at least part of which (£25) came from Arnold Bennett;[12] so that when he postponed his departure for the United States "to fight out this business of *The Rainbow*", Lawrence possessed in all about £100.

In Porthcothan, where he and Frieda lived on £2 a week, money worries were less pressing. In February 1916 he calculated that their money would last another three or four months; "then I think we may as well all go and drown ourselves". At the same time, although they had already quarrelled, he wrote to ask Bertrand Russell to leave him "enough to live on" in his will. By July a new appeal went out to Pinker: "Do send me some money then, for I have only six pounds in the world . . . Thank you very much for keeping me going." A few contracts, notably one with Duckworth for *Twilight in Italy*, helped to keep the pot boiling. The Zennor cottage cost only £5 a year, and in fact the stay in Cornwall, where the Lawrences could "manage on about £150 a year", corresponded to a lull in their financial troubles. In December 1916, Lawrence replied to Gertler's offer to lend him something by saying they now had £60, "which solves the money difficulty for the time being", adding that "it is a principle with me to borrow from the rich as long as I can, not the poor". In fact Amy Lowell, to whom Frieda had appealed, had just sent the £60, for which Lawrence thanked her quite tactfully.[13]

By early 1917, when he was trying to get passports for America, the situation had taken a turn for the worse: nobody would print his work, he complained to Cynthia Asquith, "the public taste" was "averse" to him; his books were not selling:

> It is quite useless trying to live and write here. I shall only starve into ignominy . . . I shall have just enough money to take us to New York if we can go on the first of March with our friends; and I can't go on living on the miserable pittance which Pinker will allow me . . . it is too insulting.[14]

On 25 June he told Pinker he was coming to the end of his resources, but did not want to ask him for further advances. The next day he received from Marsh £7 15s. representing royalties from *Georgian Poetry*, which may perhaps explain the truculent tone of a letter to Kot014 in which, before launching into a tirade against the Jews, he speaks of breaking with his agent, "that little *parvenu* snob of a procurer of books", to whom, however, he was far more conciliatory when writing about the future publication of his *Look! We Have Come Through!*[15]

While working, to try to earn some ready money, on what was to become *Studies in Classic American Literature*, he was expelled from Cornwall and left virtually penniless. Through Cynthia Asquith he received an anonymous gift from Charles Whibley.[16] Not until February 1918 did he again appeal to Pinker in writing, possibly having seen him in London in the meantime:

I am sorry to tell you that I am coming to the last end of all my resources, as far as money goes. Do you think that Arnold Bennett or somebody like that, who is quite rich out of literature, would give me something to get along with . . . Do try and tempt a little money out of some rich good-natured author for me, will you—or I don't know what I shall do. And really, you know, one can't begin taking one's hat off to money at this late hour of the day. I'd rather play a tin whistle in the street.[17]

A fortnight later, having had no reply, the appeal was repeated, but this time Pinker was only asked to try to get payment of moneys due, or an advance on work accepted. Through Gertler, Montague Shearman sent £10, and Koteliansky, hearing of Lawrence's hard straits from Gertler, "went and sent" a similar amount to Lawrence, who at this point also borrowed from his well-to-do aunt, Mrs Krenkow.[18]

In March he told Lady Cynthia he was "very willing to accept £100 from any fund whatsoever", though contemptuously rejecting Whibley's suggestion that he should in exchange accept an obligation to go on writing:

... as for obligation, I shall certainly go on writing and I am not married to the censor ... Tell my well-wisher to get me £100, which will be a great boon to me, as being a mere necessity, and not to mind about any obligation, which is surely *infra dig* on the part of gentlemen. Why has the world become so ambidextrous that the left hand must always be implicated in what the right hand does! Pah—people—pfui.[19]

At this point his sister Ada came to the rescue by lending him £20 and paying a year's rent in advance (£65) on a house in Middleton in Derbyshire, whereupon Lawrence encouraged Gertler to "go on borrowing" while he could from *his* brother, a modest artisan: "One rather hates taking money from one's hard-worked people. But this is a peculiar and crucial time and one must get through it somehow—it doesn't seem to matter much now."[20] In June he resumed contact with Mary Cannan after several years of silence to ask her to speak in his favour to members of the Royal Literary Fund to which he had applied for a grant:

For months and months and months, now, we have lived from shilling to shilling—and a £10 from Shearman—and so on. I am very tired of it, and *irritated* by it—terribly irritated. And it is not the slightest use my trying to write selling stuff, in this state of affairs.[21]

Before 19 July, according to a letter from Gertler to Koteliansky, the Royal Literary Fund had paid him £50.[22]

By the end of 1918 things were looking up; the Lawrences were certainly poor, badly dressed and ill-nourished, like most of 1918 Britain; but they were able to travel, to visit friends and renew relations with the Murrys.

Lawrence was able to earn his living by his writing, publishing several of his Studies in Classic American Literature in *The English Review*, and grumblingly compiling for Oxford University Press his *Movements in European History*, for which he was paid £30 early in 1919. On 5 May he acknowledged receipt of £50 from Pinker. On the 10th, Edward Marsh sent him £20, sparing his pride by telling him it came from Rupert Brooke. The nightmare of poverty was over, though his German brother-in-law Jaffe, then Bavarian Minister of Finance, was apparently unable to prevent the Allies from "swallowing" an expected legacy from Frieda's godfather.[23]

A comparison with the careful accounts of the Woolf *ménage*, provided by Leonard Woolf in his autobiography, helps to put Lawrence's financial situation in perspective. Virginia Woolf, then regularly writing for *The Times Literary Supplement*, earned £95 9s. 6d. in 1917 and £104 5s. 6d. in 1918. Between 1919 and 1929 she earned on an average £170 a year.[24] Only her private income of £400 a year gave her greater financial security than Lawrence, in spite of the fact that her publisher was her half-brother, Gerald Duckworth. This suggests that during the war years Lawrence suffered from his total lack of other means of support rather than any form of persecution or special harshness of fate towards misunderstood genius.

Vagrant life

Apart from frequent minor journeys and short intervals between longer stays in borrowed or rented dwellings, the list of the various Lawrence establishments between 1914 and 1919 is as follows:

1. Chesham, Bucks, from the end of August 1914 to 21 January 1915 (five months, cottage rented furnished);
2. Greatham, Sussex, from 21 January to end of July 1915 (six months, cottage lent by Viola Meynell);
3. Hampstead, London, from August to the end of December 1915 (five months, flat rented unfurnished);
4. Porthcothan, Cornwall, from the end of December 1915 to the end of February 1916 (two months, house lent by J. D. Beresford);
5. Higher Tregerthen, Zennor, Cornwall, from March 1916 to 15 October 1917 (nineteen and a half months, cottage rented unfurnished);
6. London, from 16 October to the end of December 1917 (two and a half months, accommodation lent by various friends);
7. Hermitage, Bucks, from the end of December 1917 to April 1918 (four months, cottage lent by Dollie Radford);
8. Middleton-by-Wirksworth, Derbyshire, from May 1918 to the end of April 1919 (cottage rented for a year by Ada Clarke);

9. Hermitage, Bucks, from May to November 1919 (cottage again lent by Dollie Radford).

No one who has witnessed the family upheavals of two world wars will find these displacements in any way extraordinary or dramatic in themselves. The only one involving any outside intervention, other than the perfectly reasonable requirements of those lending accommodation, was the expulsion from Cornwall in 1917. The Murrys, for example (to say nothing of countless active soldiers and their families), led equally disrupted lives during the same period, without becoming the object of any romantic legend. Poverty was certainly one cause of their wanderings, but several unwise choices for a man with so weak a chest as Lawrence were another, and the constant impression of instability is due quite as much to the personalities and conflicts of the Lawrences themselves as to external elements.

The Triangle, the house at Chesham rented by Lawrence when all idea of leaving once more for Lerici had been abandoned, was, according to David Garnett and Compton Mackenzie, ugly and very badly furnished. There Lawrence was continually "seedy", morose, and quarrelsome; neither the proximity of the Cannans at Cholesbury or of the Murrys at Missenden, nor frequent visits from various friends, succeeded in cheering him up. On the contrary friends of the three couples were treated to classical scenes of violence and rupture with Frieda, as well as to demonstrations of Lawrence's talents as handyman, housekeeper and cook. The severe climate, the lack of amenities in the house, the meagre landscape and the people, all depressed Lawrence, while Frieda "jumped at the thought" of leaving Chesham.[25]

At Greatham, the atmosphere was very different: there was hot water and even a bathroom in Viola Meynell's cottage, one of the barns and other out-buildings of the old farm, transformed by Wilfred Meynell into houses for his children. At first Lawrence was enchanted by this literary family phalanstery, though Frieda was less enthusiastic: he soon began to complain of the "danger of invasion from the other houses" and in April was already preparing to "decamp". Viola Meynell found the couple happy but "quarrelsome"; Lawrence felt cramped when his hostess and her friend Ivy Low came down at Whitsun to occupy part of the flimsily partitioned cottage. He consented to stay until the end of July in order to give lessons to two of Viola's nieces, Sylvia Lucas and Mary Saleeby. While his experience of this phalanstery may have helped to discourage him from accepting Ottoline's offer of "some monkish buildings" on her estate, Lady Cynthia Asquith has suggested that a more cogent reason was that this offer did not include Frieda. At this same time, Frieda herself seems to have entertained the idea of going alone to Hampstead for a time to be nearer to the children. The "cloistral" quality of Greatham, however, genuinely appealed to Lawrence, and his "thank you" letter shows real appreciation for the interlude:

I am *very glad* you lent it to us. It has a special atmosphere, and I feel as if I had been born afresh there, got a new, sure, separate soul; as a monk in a monastery, or St John in the wilderness.[26]

Lawrence was not happy in their London flat: according to Frieda "he did not like the *Vale of Health* and he didn't like the little flat and he didn't like me or anybody else". The Hampstead months were marked by the suppression of *The Rainbow*, and by preparations to leave first for New York, then for Key West. Lawrence sold or deposited with friends the secondhand furniture acquired in August and his own personal belongings, and gave up his lease on the Byron Villas flat before learning that he could not leave the country without a visa. He then accepted J. D. Beresford's offer of a "biggish house with big, clear rooms" at Porthcothan on the north coast of Cornwall, looking upon this departure for the Celtic west as a first stage on the road to the New World. Since the house had to be restored to its proprietor on 9 March (minus a precious bottle of sloe gin drunk one night with Heseltine), the Lawrences soon began looking for alternative accommodation in Cornwall which Lawrence "liked so much". A furnished house at Gurnard's Head proved too expensive and in the end they rented at Higher Tregerthen, Zennor, a two-room cottage overlooking the approaches to the Bristol Channel, where they stayed until expelled from Cornwall. The low rent— £5 a year—made it financially attractive, and Lawrence was able to reduce living expenses by growing his own vegetables. The indefatigable Dollie Radford collected and dispatched from London furniture, crockery and other belongings they had left scattered among their friends, and the couple made a real effort to settle down at last. At Zennor Lawrence rewrote *Women in Love* and, spurred by his reading of Melville's *Moby Dick* in Beresford's library (he had also very probably found in Carpenter's *The Intermediate Sex* references to *Omoo* and *Typee* and read both books), he embarked on his studies in American literature. For nearly two years, in this wind-lashed cottage on the Celtic moors, the battle with Frieda was waged continuously, either as a solitary duel, or in the fairly frequent presence and hearing of visiting friends and neighbours.[27]

The forced return to London was a time of increased uncertainty and wounded self-respect. Dollie Radford, Cecil Gray's mother, and Hilda Doolittle-Aldington each put them up for a time. But when the Aldingtons needed their room back, a letter to Amy Lowell shows Lawrence's spleen spreading even to such benefactors:

When one has no money, it's no joke to be kicked out of one's house and home at random and given nowhere to go.

Fortunately at this very moment Dollie Radford offered to let the Lawrences borrow or rent, at a nominal price, her daughter Margaret's cottage at

Hermitage, where Lawrence established himself in mid-December, just before leaving for Ripley on a visit to his sister Ada.[28]

By January the Radfords' cottage was felt to be cold and comfortless, even by 1918 English standards, and Lawrence was already casting his eye around prior to another flight; he made no attempt to conceal his ill-temper when either Dollie Radford and her husband, or their "impossible" daughter Margaret, needed their own house for a few days.[29] Lawrence's nerves were so raw that the mere idea of another move drove him to distraction. When the Radfords came down to Chapel Farm Cottage he was obliged to take rooms at the village grocer's, or at Grimsbury Farm, run by the two young women on whom he based "The Fox". In January he tried to negotiate the exchange of the Zennor cottage against Leonard Woolf's house in Richmond.[30]

Lawrence's stay at Middleton from 18 May 1918 to April 1919 corresponds exactly to the duration of the lease taken by Ada Clarke: there he immediately felt "very lost and queer and exiled".[31] He had several visitors, and in August 1918 went to stay with the Carswells at Lydbrook in Gloucestershire, followed by a trip to London in October and November. As soon as the Middleton lease ran out, the couple returned to Hermitage, where, except for brief absences, they remained until November.

In fact, after the Zennor catastrophe, poverty alone accounts for Lawrence's failure to reconcile the exigencies of his health, his literary contacts, his personal relationships and his stormy life with Frieda; in more prosperous circumstances, surely, they would have been able to find a satisfactory solution to their housing problem, if not to those difficulties due to ill-health and their conflicting personalities.

Tuberculosis

Between 1914 and 1919 Lawrence's health was consistently poor, but the state of medical knowledge at this time has combined with the patient's own aversion to obtaining any clear definition of his illness to obscure such information as is available. Nevertheless, it is clear that much of Lawrence's instability of character, his irritability, his misanthropy and periodic phases of deep depression bear some relation to his state of health. A brief chronological account shows how constant a preoccupation this was.

In 1914, his friends found him "looking radiantly well", transfigured by his stay in Lerici. In late July he was in sufficiently good form to set out on an all-male walking tour lasting several days. Catherine Carswell and Aldington speak of his sparkling "jewel-like" eyes and "lithe, springing step". He was thin, but in good health; but by October he was "seedy" enough to grow a beard while confined to bed; he decided to keep it permanently because it was "so warm and complete, and such a clothing to one's nakedness".

Murry remembers that at this time "two things were preying on him together: one was the war, the other his struggle with his wife; the two strains seemed to be making a sick man" of him. In January 1915 he complained of a "long, slow, pernicious cold" from which he was still suffering at Greatham on 22 February. This chill coincided with a visit from Murry during which Lawrence nursed his friend through a bad bout of influenza. On 11 February he asked Barbara Low, who was a doctor, to come to Greatham on a visit: his heart felt "like a swelling root that quite hurts". In March he could not talk to anybody, feeling inescapably oppressed by "the whole universe of darkness and dark passions . . . the subterranean black universe of things which have not yet had being". Some three weeks later he was still in bed, with "a sort of cold in my inside—like a sore throat in one's stomach. Do you understand? I am going to stay in bed till it is better." While his spirit had emerged from the powers of darkness, his body was still in thrall. On the other hand, in the same letter he thanks God that Barbara Low, who had just left after a visit, is no longer there to nag at him, probably about the treatment that he should have followed. About this time he consulted another psychologist, her brother-in-law, Dr Eder, for a complaint not specified in the relevant letter to Koteliansky:

I got up today—this afternoon—very limp and weed-like. I wrote to Dr Eder all my symptoms and my ailments—he must cure me. I am weary in heart and head, in hands and feet. And surely more than all things sleep were sweet, than all things save the unconquerable desire which whoso knoweth shall not faint nor tire. I am so limp I could recite Swinburne.

About 20 April he was able to tell Koteliansky that he was at last "on the mend".[32]

His psychological reaction to the war was no doubt closely linked with his state of health, and no one can describe this better than Lawrence himself: in a letter to Cynthia Asquith, written in January 1915, he summed up what the five preceding months had meant to him:

I feel as if I had less than no history—as if I had spent those five months in the tomb. And now, I feel very sick and corpse-cold, too newly risen to share yet with anybody, having the smell of the grave in my nostrils, and a feel of grave clothes about me. The War finished me: it was the spear through the side of all sorrows and hopes.[33]

In May he had arrived at the state of hating men and wishing he were a blackbird, of hoping the Lord would send down another Flood and drown the world. He was not even sure that he would cast himself for the role of Noah:

I am not sure. I've got again into one of those horrible sleeps from which I can't wake. I can't brush it aside to wake up. You know those horrible sleeps when one is struggling to wake up, and can't. I was like it all autumn—now I am again like it. Everything has a touch of delirium, the blackbird on the wall is a delirium, even the apple-blossom. And when I see a snake winding rapidly in the marshy places, I think I am mad. It is not a question of me, it is the world of men. The world of men is dreaming, it has gone mad in its sleep, and a snake is strangling it, but it can't wake up.[34]

After the sinking of the *Lusitania*, he would have liked to "kill a million, two million Germans". Such bouts of fury and moments of black depression seem to have alternated with periods of greater serenity, especially when he was writing to Lady Cynthia. Moreover, the lessons he gave Mary Saleeby seem to have been entirely normal and well adapted to his pupil.

In November he felt so sick "in body and soul" that he thought he would "die" if he didn't "get away" (to America); he dreaded the coming winter. Robert Nichols, who made his acquaintance at this point, thought he had just been going through "a bad patch of the tuberculosis which eventually killed him" as well as suffering from some kind of "nervous condition". Heseltine told Delius he was afraid Lawrence was "rather far gone with consumption", which suggests that among his friends, if not actually in his presence, the name of his illness was openly mentioned. In November he was again examined by Dr Eder, who advised against the New York climate in winter. A few days before giving up the Hampstead flat, he was once more "laid up in bed with a violent cold", and had been incapable of writing a line "these many weeks".[35] On 7 January 1916 he wrote gloomily to Ottoline:

> Two days ago a bad cold came on, which makes me feel queer as if I couldn't see any further, as if all things had come to an end, and one must only wait for the new to begin. But it is rather terrible this being confronted with the end, only with the end.[36]

By 15 January he was feeling better, but "still inclined to tremble, and to have pains in my limbs and a raw chest".[37] Was it to give Lawrence a medical examination that Dollie Radford, to whom this letter was addressed, sent her son, an army doctor home from France, to Cornwall to see him? At all events, Dr Maitland Radford came down to Porthcothan some time before 16 January and seems to have tried to reassure Lawrence concerning some curious new symptoms:

> Now I've got neuritis in my arm, and my left hand feels paralysed— but it is all part of the game. It was very good of Maitland to come down . . . he says my nerves are at the root of the trouble and I think it is true. I must lie and rest—always lie and rest, at present, I know. I begin to feel ill when I sit up.[38]

Maitland Radford told him reassuringly that "the pain and inflammation is . . . all referred from the nerves, there is no organic illness at all, except the mucous in the bronchi, etc. are weak".[39] Lady Cynthia received a more detailed analysis:

> He says the stress on the nerves sets up a deferred inflammation in all the internal linings, and that I must keep very quiet and still and warm and peaceful. There was a sort of numbness all down the left side, very funny— I could hardly hold anything in my hand . . . Now I can walk to the sea again and all that fever and inflammation and madness has nearly gone. But I feel very queer after it—sort of hardly know myself.[40]

Frieda was sufficiently alarmed to write to Bertrand Russell to ask him to share her responsibility. "He might just die because everything is too much for him. But he simply mustn't die. It's not as if it concerned me alone." By mid-February Lawrence was on the mend but felt "quite anti-social, against this social whole as it exists. I wish one could be a pirate or a highwayman in these days." After a few weeks of relatively better health, he sent Barbara Low a letter expressing "utter disgust and nausea" for humanity, but recognizing that renewed "seediness" might partly explain his depression.[41]

The whole of this period is marked by misanthropy and bitter hatred of society; the quarrels with Frieda reached a new pitch of violence: "desperate and frightening". To Murry arriving at Zennor Lawrence seemed to be subject to "the raging of some awful mania". To judge from the more balanced tone of the correspondence, the summer months calmed him down to some extent, but when Frieda returned from seeing the children in London in October she found him so ill and depressed that she was seriously worried and wrote to Dollie Radford telling her "a dryer place" was essential to Lawrence's health, asking when they might have the cottage at Hermitage, and inviting Maitland to "come and see L" on the pretext of their interest in his "health reform". In fact he had been unwell and in and out of bed ever since Catherine Carswell's departure in September. On 11 November he talked of going to London "to consult a good doctor—if there is such a thing—and learn how to make the best of this bad job of health".[42]

He was writing nothing, and felt as if he were passing through "a kind of interval" in his life, "like a sleep"; he read, cooked, looked out at the sea, as if he too were "hibernating, like the snakes and the dormice", his mind obsessed with a vision of a "most beautiful brindled adder" seen in the previous spring, "asleep in the sun, like a Princess of the fairy world".[43]

Torpid, violent, depressed, misanthropic, stirred to poetry only by non-human manifestations, such was Lawrence's state of mind in Cornwall. Some at least of these characteristics were surely directly attributable to his state of health. The declaration "I am much better" runs like a refrain through his letters, but it carries no more conviction that his reiterated affirmations of having at last found true love and peace with Frieda. And in claiming exemption from military service, he openly mentioned his tuberculosis:

> I got my complete exemption because I was able, spiritually, to manage the doctors. Usually, in a crisis like that, one has a certain authority. I said the doctors said I had had consumption—I didn't produce any certificate, I didn't think it fair to [Ernest] Jones.[44]

This is the first and so far the only reference to the fact that Ernest Jones had given him a medical certificate, probably in 1915.

In April 1917 Lawrence fell ill while in London, went down to the Radfords' to recuperate and then back to Cornwall. In May, while writing "The Reality of Peace", he suddenly felt "as if I were going dotty, straight out of my mind, so I left off. One can only wait and let the crisis come and go." In February 1918, he began a cold in London which turned into "the very devil of a sore throat", lasting for three weeks, giving him "a queer feeling", as if he were blind and making him talk "in a senile, fluty squeak, very ignoble". Another succession of colds started in Middleton the following autumn: early in November he went to London, went down with 'flu and again took refuge with Dollie Radford at Hermitage. On Armistice Day David Garnett found him "sick and unhappy", and on 6 December Lawrence suspected himself of having 'flu again, though admitting "it may only be temper". In January 1919, according to Murry, he developed near-pneumonia. The doctor found him enfeebled and very ill, and for two days "feared the worst". Frieda wrote to Koteliansky that only his own will to live had pulled him through.[45] His sister Ada took him to her own house at Ripley, and as soon as he was better went to Middleton to look after him herself:

> My sister goes with us to Middleton. I am not going to be left to Frieda's tender mercies until I am well again. She really is a devil—and I feel as if I would part from her for ever—let her go alone to Germany, while I take another road. For it is true, I have been bullied by her long enough. I really could leave her now, without a pang I believe. The time comes, to make an end, one way or another. If this illness has not been a lesson to her, it has to me.[46]

Lawrence's last illness before his departure for Italy was certainly the most serious until the grave pulmonary crisis in Mexico in 1925. When he left England in November 1919 at the age of thirty-four, he was both physically and morally exhausted; his survival until 1929 and the renewal of his creative energy are equally remarkable. Once more, as in 1901 and in 1911, a critical period of his life ended with a serious illness. It is an open question whether Lawrence's psychic conflicts, of a depth and violence of which we have seen no more than the outer surface, were a cause or an effect of the tuberculosis, which was undoubtedly an important factor in Lawrence's wartime history.

An opinion expressed by Dr Edmund Clark, Jr, given by Harry T. Moore in *The Intelligent Heart*, is worth quoting again here:

> I should suspect Lawrence was the type of individual who had very chronic, very indolent, so-called "fibroid" tuberculosis, which, with or without treatments, underwent little or no change for better or worse, with the exception of periods when he might have been discouraged and depressed, at which time, he probably demonstrated some worsening of disease. He sounds like the type of fellow we see frequently in our research patients who seldom die of tuberculosis, but who likewise seldom get well and who have a high level of adrenal activity.

Moore also refers to hormonal tests carried out on 190 tubercular patients at Firland Sanatorium, showing that high levels of adrenal activity, manifested in sudden fits of anger, corresponded to stubborn, localized infections, predisposing patients to anxieties, conflicts, and rapid alterations of blood pressure: he advances the hypothesis that "Lawrence's frequent spells of irascibility . . . were unconscious attempts to protect himself", the outbursts of anger, during which the endocrine glands produced steroid hormones, being, in fact, a kind of physical defence mechanism.[47]

An interesting comparison with this text is provided by an extract from the *Journal* of Katherine Mansfield, herself a victim of tuberculosis, aptly cited by Edward Nehls:

> 20 September, 1918. My fits of temper are really terrifying. I had one this . . . morning and tore up a page of the book I was reading—and absolutely lost my head. Very significant. When it was over J. came in and stared. "What is the matter? What have you done?" "Why?" "You look *all dark*." He drew back the curtains and called it an effect of light, but when I came into my studio to dress I saw it was not that. I was a deep earthy colour, *with pinched eyes*. I was *green*. Strangely enough these fits are Lawrence and Frieda over again. I am more like L. than anybody. We are *unthinkably* alike, in fact.[48]

Had Lawrence not been so poor, might his health have received better attention? It is striking to note that most of the medical consultations of which any trace remains were given by friends: by Ernest Jones, David Eder, Barbara Low (all psychoanalysts) and by Maitland Radford. Only two exceptions are known: a doctor in Cornwall who certified him unfit for military service in June 1917, just before the official army medical, and a doctor or doctors in the Middleton/Ripley area in 1919, in all probability the Clarkes' family doctor, Dr Feroze, a Parsee on whom Lawrence later based a character in *Aaron's Rod*. Lawrence's own attitude towards his illness on the one hand, and towards society and the authorities on the other, makes it unlikely that he would have consented to enter a sanatorium. From 1911 onwards doctors were legally obliged to report all cases of tuberculosis:

was this perhaps one reason why Lawrence preferred to consult only doctors who were also personal friends? In 1934, following some rather unsympathetic remarks about Frieda, Barbara Low confided to the author her view that Lawrence's premature death was attributable largely to "mismanagement".

To what extent may the gloom and the depression in which he was so frequently plunged have been related to psychotic troubles—for instance when he felt himself going "dotty"? Clinical evidence is lacking. Yet in later chapters of this study, an analysis of Lawrence's preoccupation with homosexuality, as revealed in his works, viewed together with the evident changes in his attitude to love and to Frieda during these years, suggests, to say the least, that between the autumn of 1914 and the end of the war he may have searched further into the psychological causes of the failures of his love life and discovered in some anguish leanings of which he was ashamed. This would partly explain the increasing gloom which began at Chesham at about the time Lawrence grew his beard, and at the height of his quarrelling with Frieda; this being also the time when he wrote "Study of Thomas Hardy", in which new views on sex and its failures are revealed.

Frieda

Ever since they had first started living together, Lawrence and Frieda had been caught up in a cycle of alternating love and hatred, of bitter struggles and passionate reconciliations. War, poverty, ill-health, insecurity and the sense of failure served only to exacerbate the rhythm and increase the bitterness. Their mutual attraction and repulsion being a matter of character rather than of circumstance, any new element brought in by the war merely fell into the existing pattern of their relationship, without adding anything decisively new to their lives. In their relations, in fact, the war is but an aggravating circumstance, not a determining factor.

No one who knew the Lawrences well at this time could help asking himself questions about their relationship, and most of those who did so remained convinced of the depth and indestructibility of the bond uniting them. Sir Walter Raleigh saw in Frieda "a first-rate poet's wife"; Cynthia Asquith, who, on the whole, thought well of "the Hun", stressed her "spontaneousness and warm cleverness", her adoration and understanding of Lawrence. Aldington remarked that only a woman of such intense vitality could have borne life with a difficult and sometimes perverse "genius": "anyone who thinks those two weren't in love with each other is crazy. How else could they have endured one another?" Katherine Mansfield expressed to Koteliansky her disgust at the "loving and playing with each other" that invariably followed their frenzied fights.[49] The long-term judgments ultimately reached by such close witnesses as Catherine Carswell, Ottoline Morrell or Middleton Murry probably show in proper perspective the quarrels and conflicts which would certainly have destroyed unions less solidly established on mutual frankness and, when all is said and done, on what seems an essential compatibility between the partners.

These, however, are judgments formulated in tranquillity after a lapse of years, following Lawrence's death. At the time their behaviour was a source of continual astonishment to witnesses of their daily life. In London and at Chesham, the relative proximity of Frieda's children seems to have reawakened her husband's jealousy and provoked the scenes described by Murry, Katherine Mansfield and others. At any mention of the children, Frieda would burst into tears. At this Lawrence would explode:

> He had had enough, he said; she must go, she was draining the life out of him. She must go, she must go now. She knew what money he had; he could give her her share—more than her share. He went upstairs, and came down again, and counted out on the table to me sixteen sovereigns. Frieda was standing by the door, crying, with her hat and coat on, ready to go—but where?[50]

When Koteliansky lectured Frieda on the necessity of choosing between husband and children, Frieda went off and Katherine Mansfield came to tell Lawrence she had gone for good: "Damn the woman," shouted Lawrence in a fury, "tell her I never want to see her again."[51]

During this period, at Chesham and at Greatham in 1914 and 1915, Lawrence's friends often showed hostility to Frieda, some even attempting to separate her from him. Murry certainly entertained this idea but, recognizing the impossibility of such a separation, wisely decided against giving Frieda shelter in his own home, on the grounds that this would have transformed his cottage into "an anti-Lawrence camp". In 1915, at Littlehampton, Frieda confided to Cynthia Asquith the difficulties attendant on being the wife of a genius: "People, above all women, and one woman in particular [Ottoline Morrell] treat her as a simple appendage and try to 'explain' her husband to her." According to Catherine Carswell, Frieda sometimes thought Lawrence was mad, would announce that she must leave him, proclaiming that she "detested" everything he wrote.[52] A letter written by Frieda to Murry in 1951, looking back over the years, vividly evokes the atmosphere of this period:

> I believe my deepest feeling for L. was a profound compassion. He wanted so much that he could never have with his intensity. I felt so terribly sorry for him or I could never have stood it all. Sometimes he went over the edge of sanity. I was many times frightened but never the last bit of me. Once, I remember, he had worked himself up and his hands were on my throat and he

was pressing me against the wall and ground out: "I am the master, I am the master." I said: "Is that all? You can be master as much as you like, I don't care." His hands dropped away, he looked at me in astonishment and was all right.[53]

Not all the violence was on Lawrence's side: both recounted "in concert" to Catherine Carswell a typical Zennor scene, when, after a quarrel "fought out to what Lawrence took to be a finish", Frieda, emerging from the living-room with a stone dinner plate, furious to hear him singing quietly to himself at the sink after what had happened, suddenly brought down the dinner plate on his head. "That was like a woman," he said, turning on her viciously, but too much astonished to strike back. "But as you are a woman, you were right to do as you felt. I was only lucky you didn't kill me. These plates are hard and heavy." Frieda refers to a similar scene having taken place in 1913 at Irschenhausen. In *Women in Love* Lawrence attributes to Hermione Roddice a very similar gesture, the plate being changed to a paperweight. Moreover Murry has described the subtle provocation offered by Frieda who, for example, would deliberately undertake the defence of Shelley, Nietzsche, or other prophets repudiated by Lawrence. Murry goes so far as to suggest in Frieda's conduct a certain element of masochism; the same suggestion is implied in Compton Mackenzie's description of the "grin of exultation" with which Hildegarde (Frieda) would rejoice in the violence and fierceness of Rayner (Lawrence).[54]

It is clearly in the light of these incessant quarrels, followed by the billing and cooing of tender reconciliations, that we must interpret the half-hearted idea of a final break with Frieda, of which Lawrence informed Koteliansky in 1919. Their fates seem, however, to have been irrevocably linked and Lawrence's perpetual dualism found expression in this union, as it did in his creative work. In December 1914, after a visit from Koteliansky, Lawrence asked his friend not to judge Frieda "lightly":

> There is another quality in woman that you do not know, so you can't estimate it. You don't know that a woman is not a man with different sex. She is a different world. You do not understand that enough. Your world is all of one hemisphere.[55]

Inseparable from Lawrence, almost always at his side, Frieda is an integral part of the psychological record of these years: her personality, whether acting as irritant or as sedative, her judgments, her ideas, all affected the history of Lawrence's relations with the authorities. Apart from the actual quarrels and exchanges of blows, she caused or at least occasioned constant tension between him and his friends, many of whom considered her an evil influence. That her bitterest and most outspoken enemy was no doubt Koteliansky is shown by the letters she wrote him in self-defence, and by a letter from Kot to Gertler in which he wishes she would "disappear".

E. M. Forster protested at finding her written comments scrawled all over a letter he received from Lawrence, commenting wryly that he would "have no dealings with a firm".[56] Ottoline Morrell and Bertrand Russell both tried to rescue Lawrence from her influence.

Reference is frequently made to their most intimate relations in connexion with his writings. *The Rainbow* and *Women in Love* were, of course, both written under the influence of the hopes and conflicts of 1913 to 1916, and the scenes between the various couples in these two works owe much to his experience of life with Frieda. Except for his excessive irritability, fatigue and recrudescence of ill-health, the war years add little to what we already knew. Lawrence's 1914 to 1919 works are in many respects the fruit of a reflection on his relations with Frieda prior to the period under consideration, and while they contain a great deal of autobiographical material, little of it is strictly speaking new, except in the poems of *Look! We Have Come Through!* written during the war, and the related scenes in the novels.

A certain number of facts are nevertheless reasonably well established. In spite of their frequent quarrels, Lawrence's love for Frieda did not vary greatly during 1914 and, so it would seem, 1915. It cooled down considerably, however, in Cornwall, where both partners in this stormy union seem to have sought distractions, each according to his nature. The year 1918 marked the nadir, and in 1919 Lawrence was prepared to leave Frieda for good; yet did not do so. Did some kind of sexual incompatibility develop or confirm itself between Lawrence and Frieda? While the works may suggest that this may have been the case, nothing so far published on their relationship proves it conclusively.

Moreover, throughout this period, it is important to avoid falling into the error illustrated by Middleton Murry, which consists in seeking in sexual experience alone the explanation of an evolution in which mystical experience and philosophical reflection also played their part. To reduce Lawrence to the dimensions of a psycho-physiological problem is certainly to underestimate his intellect and his emotions, and to distort his thinking: it is to perpetuate, in fact, the "treason" of which he accuses Murry.

On the strictly episodic and factual level, what was the role of reciprocal sexual jealousy in the conflicts and quarrels with Frieda?

The correspondence, which is the principal source of information on their relationship, is silent on this point. It is, however, difficult to believe that Lawrence was not violently jealous. He was indignant to find Murry indifferent when, miming a love scene at a Christmas party at the Cannans' in 1914, Katherine and Gertler, slightly drunk, somewhat overplayed their parts. This scene partly inspired the "Crème de Menthe" chapter in *Women in Love*; Murry's tolerance may well have suggested that of Halliday towards Minette. Gertler, on the contrary, who refused to attach any importance to this incident, wrote to Dora Carrington that "the Lawrences were most

anxious to weave a real romance out of it". This suggests that either Lawrence, or Frieda, or both, made different comments on this scene to Murry
and to Gertler.[57] Other episodes, in particular those recounted by Hilda
Doolittle in *Bid me to Live*, show that Lawrence was in the habit of using the
charades, in which both he and Frieda delighted, either to suggest amorous
intrigues to his friends, or to reveal to participants their subconscious
desires. There seems no doubt that Lawrence, that repressed puritan, allowed
himself to be pushed by Frieda's avidity for sexual liberty into concocting
plots and intrigues concerning the love-lives of their friends.[58]

In 1922, Frieda is alleged to have confided to Mabel Luhan that in Cornwall in 1917 Lawrence, in her absence, conducted an affair with the American
Esther Andrews, the result of which was highly discomforting to his male
pride. Frieda may even have turned Esther Andrews out of the house; at
all events the letters of spring 1917 contain echoes of an emotional crisis
centring on the person of this young journalist.[59] Frieda also apparently
confided to Mabel Luhan her jealousy of the farmer William Henry Hocking, with whom Lawrence spent much of his time in 1917. And Hilda
Doolittle, in *Bid me to Live*, suggests that, on their return to London, Frieda
encouraged a liaison between Hilda and Lawrence, in order to leave the field
clear for herself and Cecil Gray, whom she used to visit in Lawrence's
absence when he was their neighbour in Cornwall. Lawrence also seems to
have used a game of charades to attract Gray to Hilda Doolittle and vice
versa. According to Lawrence's letters to Gray in 1917–18, both Frieda and
the young musician misunderstood what the novelist expected from his
female friendships. Gray, for his part, has suggested that these were not
strictly platonic, and may have explained certain of Lawrence's trips to
London; Gray's motives, however, may in this case have been mixed and his
evidence therefore may not be entirely reliable.[60]

None of this is either clear or conclusive: a vague impression of malaise
nevertheless persists, confirmed by the veiled confessions of Hilda Doolittle
in *Bid me to Live*. It should not be forgotten that the period with which we
are dealing, the wartime period of late 1917 and early 1918, was one of
extreme moral laxity in England. The effects of such dissoluteness on
Lawrence's instinctive puritanism are clear in his poem "Frost Flowers"
as also in *Women in Love*, particularly in Birkin's reprobation for Bohemian
London. According to Hilda Doolittle Lawrence's reaction towards her was
one of fierce reserve, explicable either by his character or by a fear of repeating the recent failure with Esther Andrews. Be that as it may, it is certain that,
in the interplay of friendships and quarrels with other couples, the effect
of Lawrence's jealousies now of one sex, now of the other, and particularly
of Frieda's jealousy of women, although not always clearly manifested,
must not be underestimated. Frieda's provocations in all probability grew
more marked in 1917 and 1918, when ill-health and a sense of failure under-

mined Lawrence, forcing him into ever-increasing isolation. In 1919, Aldington, who saw Lawrence after Frieda's departure for Germany, asserts that he "seemed not to care if he never saw her again".[61]

III. AN EXILE IN HIS OWN COUNTRY

Legend has it that Lawrence was a great misunderstood and persecuted genius, and that the 1914-18 war provided an occasion for the demonstration of this incomprehension by the vulgar herd. He himself helped to give credence to this legend, particularly by the "Nightmare" chapter in his Australian novel *Kangaroo*, in which he summarizes, synthesizes and stylizes his wartime experience. He reveals himself exactly as he was, that is to say as a virtually asocial being, outside all the movements of his own time, an individual refusing to associate with the mind of the mass, for fear of losing "his own centrality, his own manly isolation in his own integrity, which alone keeps life real".[62] In his life as in his works, Lawrence asserts the principle that integrity of the individual can be safeguarded only by his isolation. He was to suffer intensely, to feel himself "torn off from the body of mankind", so that "the oneness of mankind" was destroyed in him.[63] This suffering is genuine, and we are in no way underestimating it when we seek to analyse the painful misunderstanding which opposed him to official Britain, in order to ascertain to what extent, in this particular instance, the "persecution" was not largely self-inflicted.

Lawrence's first open clash with the authorities relates to the suppression of *The Rainbow*; he also came up against them every time he tried to obtain an exit visa or a passport; he was several times obliged by law to appear before Army medical boards; and in the end he was expelled from Cornwall by the military authorities, i.e. those responsible for security. In all these clashes with the authorities, how did Lawrence behave, and with whom do the responsibilities lie? The more tenacious the legend, the more important it is to make sure that the facts are clearly established, the obscurities stated.

Certain factual elements are still missing: the exact origin and real motivation of *The Rainbow* prosecution remain subject to conjecture; reports made about Frieda, as an alien—a matter of routine in wartime—and any records of a watch kept on Lawrence himself, at least from 1917 onwards, have either been destroyed, or remain protected by the secrecy observed over any counter-intelligence records that might exist. Were the authorities aware of Lawrence's ideas, for instance through postal censorship or other intelligence reports? His works themselves suggest that he was influenced by Houston Chamberlain,[64] probably in the autumn of 1914, i.e. when Chamberlain had become the Number One enemy of the British and French counter-propaganda services. It may well be—but we cannot prove it—that such sympathies were known to the authorities at the time of the suppression of *The Rainbow*. Nor can Lawrence's subversive intentions manifested in the agitation around *The Signature* have passed unnoticed by the police.

Lawrence and the war: the personal issue

Up to 1915, the real nature of the conflict opposing his country to that of his wife was no more apparent to Lawrence than to most of his fellow-country-men. For him, as for most Englishmen, the watchword was at first "business as usual", and although he knew through Edward Marsh as early as 30 July that England could not avoid being drawn into the conflict,[65] he set off as arranged on a walking tour in the Lake District on the 31st. "I am very miserable about the war. *Auf Wiedersehen*," he wrote to Koteliansky immedi-ately after his return, adding a few days later: "We can't go back to Italy as things stand."[66] But before long he was reacting strongly to events, and writing to Edward Marsh:

> The war is just hell for me. I don't see why I should be so disturbed, but I am. I can't get away from it for a minute: I live in a sort of coma, like one of those nightmares when you can't move. I hate it—everything.[67]

By September, like some of the liberal pacifists, he saw in "this" war a "colossal idiocy" which provoked him to "sheer rage"; but, and this shows the extent of his unconcern, he hoped it might perhaps have a salutary effect on literature: "I am glad of this war . . . It sets a slump in trifling."[68] As his misanthropy grew more pronounced he cared not for those who were being killed, but for the psychology of the living,

> . . . those who, being sensitive, will receive such a blow from the ghastliness and mechanical, obsolete, hideous stupidity of war, that they will be crippled beings further burdening our sick society . . . The war doesn't alter my beliefs or visions.[69]

Although not in the least shocked by the idea that anyone should enlist to go and fight, he affected a flippant note when refusing to send a war poem to Harriet Monroe for the special number of *Poetry* she was preparing:

> I am not in the war zone. I think I am too valuable a creature to offer myself to a German bullet gratis and for fun.[70]

On the whole, as regards the Anglo-German conflict, he seems to have identified with Frieda, even though he occasionally cursed the German in her, even calling her "you bloody Prussian". His letters do not show to what extent he may, in 1914, have sympathized with those who believed, with Bertrand Russell, that England should have left Germany alone and taken no part in the war; or with Carpenter for whom the war was inspired by the British industrialists' fears of competition from German industry. While this was precisely one of the themes of German propaganda, and particularly of the brochures Houston Chamberlain was then writing in Bayreuth for the edification of neutrals, it was a view largely held among pacifists in Britain, and such a belief, combined with personal loyalty towards Frieda, would explain his perturbed state in the early months of the war. There were, however, other feelings—which Murry no doubt makes even more complex when he notes a double dualism in Lawrence's attitude: in the first place a repudiation of war, allied to a feeling of deep affinity with war, which itself in turn assumed two aspects: on the one hand a primitive, racial solidarity with "his own people", and on the other a savage desire for destruction. Sometimes, according to Murry, Lawrence even hated the war because it failed to destroy as completely and as swiftly as he would have liked.[71]

Lawrence's attitude to the war was, in fact, emotional, never rationally thought out, and in constant evolution. Before long, his letters began to evoke the horror of the slaughter, exacerbated by news from Germany telling of the death of Frieda's friends: "She and I hardly quarrel any more," he told Garnett when reporting deaths in her family circle. The death of Rupert Brooke, of their Greatham maid's brother, and other acquaintances, made him feel "like wringing the neck of humanity".[72] The man who, in 1913, felt himself destined to show the English nation the way, seems to have taken upon himself the sins of both belligerents. After several months of silence, he wrote to Cynthia Asquith:

> The war finished me: it was the spear through the side of all sorrows and hopes . . . And since then . . . things have not existed for me. I have spoken to no one, I have touched no one, I have seen no one. All the while, I swear, my soul lay in the tomb—not dead, but with a flat stone over it, a corpse, become corpse-cold. And nobody existed, because I did not exist myself. Yet I was not dead—only passed over trespassed—and all the time I knew I should have to rise again.[73]

Sometimes he would let off steam in all directions, for example when, after the sinking of the Lusitania in May 1915, there were outbreaks of rioting by the London mob:

> Soon we in England shall go fully mad, with hate. I too hate the Germans so much, I could kill every one of them. Why should they goad us into this frenzy of hatred, why should we be tortured to bloody madness, when we are only grieved in our souls, and heavy? . . . I am mad with rage myself. I would like to kill a million Germans—two millions.[74]

He "would like to be a bus conductor at the front—anything to escape this".[75]

Thus he was carried away, as it were, in spite of himself, by the current of opinion in England, and at the same time tortured by his dual loyalty. It was at this point he drew nearer to the pacifists, in particular to Bertrand Russell, with whom he entertained for a time the idea of joint political action. How then did he stand in relation to the various pacifist movements of the time?

When England declared war, two pacifist ministers resigned: the Liberal Lord Morley and the Independent radical John Burns. Many left-wing Liberals were hostile to the use of force and to war of any kind, among them Bertrand Russell as well as other intellectuals not necessarily as resolute or as courageous as he. In the Liberal Party there existed a tendency, persisting all through and after the war, which, without going so far as to approve the Prussian general staff or the policy of the Kaiser, considered that England's entry into the war was a regrettable concession to the "*revanchard*" spirit of the Poincarists in France. Within the Asquith Government itself there raged a struggle between opposing tendencies which culminated in the 1915 coalition giving increased powers to Lloyd George, and in the departure of Lord Haldane, whose titles to national gratitude as the reorganizer of the British Army did not prevent certain propagandists holding him in suspicion on account of his philosophical studies at the University of Göttingen. Asquith himself was to be the object of vicious attacks, accusing him for instance of excessive benevolence towards enemy prisoners of war, which even found an echo after the war in Lawrence's "Ladybird".

A strong current of pacifism also existed among the socialists, friends or members of the Second International, notably Keir Hardie, Ramsay Mac-Donald, Philip Snowden, and several influential trade union leaders, faithful to their internationalist principles. A Fabian socialist like Edward Carpenter wrote articles in *The English Review* expressing a fundamental socialist pacifism, later directed towards the organization of peace and those ideas which culminated in the establishment of the League of Nations; his concern was to combat the dangers of commercial imperialism and to defend civil liberties against abuse by military authorities and wartime legislation, such as D.O.R.A., which restricted traditional liberties.

There were also the conscientious objectors, numerous among non-conformists, but some of them to be found among the non-religious intelligentsia, for instance Lytton Strachey. Others, like David Garnett, chose to serve in an ambulance rather than a fighting unit, without registering as objectors.

Although never voiced by more than a minority even from the beginning, pacifist opinion was nevertheless strong enough and articulate enough to cause concern to a Government anxious not to move more quickly than public opinion allowed, and to wait before taking radical measures such as conscription or rationing, until the majority of the country was convinced of their necessity.

In relation to these different pacifist circles, Lawrence remained essentially a freelance, his position being individualist and negative. He did, however, have contacts with several of these groups, if only through his friend William Hopkin at home, and the Philip Morrells, whose London house, and later Garsington Manor, soon became gathering places for pacifists.

Conversely, those in favour of a vigorous prosecution of the war attacked the pacifists relentlessly, feeling that they compromised the national effort, sapped the morale of the population, and encouraged strikes in the munitions industry.

Neither Lawrence's correspondence, nor his novels, nor his poems, ever touch on this aspect of the question, for the simple reason that never at any time did he see any argument in favour of the pursuit of hostilities, and that it was a matter of complete indifference to him whether the war, as such, were won or lost. His works over those five years show that his thoughts were elsewhere, and the echoes of the external world affected him but little; in so far as he does refer to the war and its problems, he is closer to sheer defeatism than to any of the conflicting propagandas, but where he does express views they are of the type that would attract vehement reactions from war-minded patriots.

Spy mania and indiscretions

Lawrence never seems to have paid much attention to the risks run by himself and his wife, who was not only German-born but a member of a well-known military family, sister-in-law of an aide-de-camp to the Crown Prince, and moreover thoroughly imbued with German ideas she never hesitated to express with complete spontaneity. As early as August 1914 David Garnett invited them to meet his friend Newth in his parents' flat. Frieda spoke gaily of her cousins in the German air force, and of her sister Johanna, exciting a certain sympathy by telling the company she already realized that her origins and personality were causing her to be cold-shouldered in certain English circles. Newth exchanged loud and "guttural" goodbyes in German with Frieda as she went down the stairs. Before long, plain-clothes policemen made several visits to the flat inquiring how many Germans lived there. From the fifth such inquirer, Garnett learnt that Scotland Yard was overwhelmed with denunciations, each of which led to an inquiry.

No doubt, confident in her innocence, Frieda took umbrage, as Lawrence was to do later in the face of threats or opposition. Compton Mackenzie's portrait of her at Chesham, in the guise of Hildegarde Rayner, is hardly overdrawn: she speaks proudly of "our German trees", of "our army" which has just forced the English to retreat; she might be describing a football match, until launching into a tirade against English hypocrisy and refuting the accepted idea that Germany began the war.

The Lawrences' departure from Chesham was locally attributed to malevolent rumours accusing them of poisoning berries in the hedges.[76] In March 1915, Ford Madox Ford, formerly Hueffer, whose own father was a German, was sent, so he asserted later, by the "Minister of Information" to see what could be done for Lawrence, who "was supposed to be a good deal persecuted". As there was then no Minister of Information, and as Ford seems to have had some kind of a job in counter-propaganda (in 1915, he employed Richard Aldington and later Sir Alec Randall to write booklets replying to enemy propaganda), it is conceivable that he had rather been entrusted with some sort of investigatory mission for the Foreign Office propaganda service, itself closely linked with counter-intelligence. There may be a connexion between this mission and another piece of almost contemporary evidence: in early February, E. M. Forster had "brought down a ghastly rumour" of possible police intervention to stop the sale of *The Prussian Officer*. It may be, of course, that the two first stories were not felt to be good for army morale: the suggestions of homosexuality in the (German!) army and the idea of an orderly killing his captain may have been considered potentially harmful in time of war. The same might apply to the portrayal of desertion for combined reasons of physical weakness and love in "The Thorn in the Flesh".[77] Whatever the motives, an intervention of this sort could only have taken place on a Home Office decision. What seems certain is that the attention of the authorities had been drawn to Lawrence shortly before Ford's visit.

In any event, in early March, when Mrs H. G. Wells took Ford and Violet Hunt to Greatham in her car, Lawrence, as it happened, was away at Cambridge. This incident has given rise to several different and partially contested versions. Even if Frieda did not say, as she denied in 1955, "Dirty Belgians! Who cares for them?", referring to the refugees then fleeing before the German armies, she has admitted welcoming Ford-Hueffer with the unfortunate salutation *"Wir sind auch deutsch?"* Violet Hunt remembers having a "regular mill" with "the Valkyrie" on the subject of the Belgian refugees, whose fate was then very much in the public mind.[78]

The Lawrences' sense of discretion did not increase as the war continued. In Cornwall, Catherine Carswell found Frieda "loudly provocative and indiscreet". Knowing that they were spied upon by neighbours thought to be malevolent, and that they were under surveillance by the coastguard, the couple nevertheless sang German songs at the top of their voices in the evening. When a German submarine was being hunted off the Cornish coast, Frieda remarked to a neighbouring farmer, "What an awful thing war is! In that submarine may be some of the boys I went to school with." Back in London, the Lawrences were several times invited to the opera by Cynthia Asquith; one evening they were in a box with the painter Augustus John and "a very young Guardsman" (Ivo Grenfell, son of Lord Desborough) who showed pained surprise when Frieda, "looking every inch a Richthofen, told him how very much smarter she thought the Prussian Guards than the Household Brigade".[79]

It is not impossible that on his return from Greatham Ford may have made a report on Frieda Lawrence. David Garnett, in a lecture given in the United States after working in Air Intelligence during the Second World War, expressed the conviction that an unfavourable report from Ford must have figured in the Lawrence file, which indeed would be scarcely surprising.[80] This report, he has told the author, must, in his opinion, have been "dictated" by Violet Hunt; he did not say on what he based this opinion. On a minute-sheet from the Home Office concerning a question asked in the Commons on the suppression of The Rainbow, there figures in red ink a note referring to a numbered file on "a Mrs Weekley living at address of D. H. Lawrence". In 1967 the author made two inquiries about this file. On the first occasion he was told that the contents of Intelligence files were never disclosed since the sources had to be protected; on the second occasion, he was assured that the particular file would have been destroyed since it was no longer needed. Did it contain the alleged Ford-Violet Hunt report? At all events, and however moderate the terms of such a report, any Security service having access to it would be obliged to give it careful attention and might well have set up a watch on an Anglo-German couple with no visible means of support, and who were receiving letters and newspapers from Germany.

This is all the more probable if one considers that Lawrence was then in close touch with pacifists such as Bertrand Russell and the Morrells, and that his words and deeds were hardly calculated to reassure the authorities. A self-proclaimed revolutionary, he was preaching his own form of communism, proposing to undertake collective action, to give lectures, to publish with Murry a more or less subversive review, to "smash" the social frame, to nationalize land, industries, transport, the means of communication and the public amusements.[81] One shudders at the thought that one of his letters to Russell might have been read by a junior official of the Home Office, let alone a higher authority, at a time when social agitation constituted the gravest possible danger to the vital supply of munitions.

Nor was it only to Russell that Lawrence wrote. Mary Cannan was urged to enrol her husband (then a civil defence volunteer) in the revolutionary battle to kill "the money spirit", to provide "free eating and sleeping" and "bring down" the barriers. Lawrence warned Ottoline that, like the hero of "The Prussian Officer", the soldiers would "murder their officers one day". Enraged by the threat of bankruptcy, he conceived an "utter hatred of the whole establishment—the whole constitution of England as it now stands . . . I will do my best to lay a mine under their foundations . . . I am hostile, hostile, hostile to all that is, in our public and national life. I want to destroy it."[82] A German greeting ends this letter!

Writing to Cynthia Asquith, after talks in Littlehampton during which she seems to have tried patiently to exercise a moderating influence, he did show slightly more prudence, postponing the social and political revolution until "after the war"—"during the next ten years"—and outlining an anti-democratic form of government prefiguring certain aspects of fascist paternalism.[83] If there did indeed exist a security file on Lawrence and Frieda, the writer may quite well in 1915 have figured in it as a revolutionary agitator, all the more dangerous to the national effort for the fact that his talent was already known, as were his relations with the entourage of the Prime Minister and certain pacifist milieux.

However this may be, Lawrence was shortly to provide ammunition to public opinion and to the authorities by publishing *The Rainbow*, that is to say one of the "mines" he was proposing to lay under the foundations of public order. He himself has stressed that this novel was conceived as an indissoluble whole, as the full statement of his thinking of the time; indeed, in the years to come, it was to be nearer to his heart than any other. At the time he was confident that it would bring him fame and "pots of gold".[84]

His social criticism centres on the character of Ursula, on her intellectual development, and on her disappointment with the established order of things; she serves to proclaim his own anti-militarist and anti-imperialist convictions. At sixteen, Ursula talks to her friend Anton Skrebensky, a subaltern in the sappers, about his life as a soldier and about the Omdurman campaign. This English soldier has a somewhat German idea of this colonial campaign: he speaks of the Sudan in terms of *Lebensraum*, asserts that the nation needs him to get "room to live in". Where would the nation be if no one were a professional soldier? Like Frieda (for whom she may be speaking?) writing to Cynthia Asquith about military service, Ursula protests:

"But we aren't the nation. There are heaps of other people who are the nation."

"They might say *they* weren't either."

"Well, if everybody said it, there wouldn't be a nation. But I should still be myself," she asserted brilliantly.

"You wouldn't be yourself if there were no nation."

A little further on Ursula concludes: "I hate soldiers: they are stiff and wooden."[85] Lawrence's sympathies are obviously with Ursula. The effect of such a passage on some readers can be imagined at the very moment when the voluntary recruitment campaign was at its height, when the newspapers were full of obituaries of young men, and the posters pointed an accusing finger at young girls asking them:

Is your "best boy" wearing khaki? . . . If your young man neglects his duty to his King and Country, the time may come when he will NEGLECT YOU![86]

Skrebensky leaves for the Boer war, and Lawrence analyses as follows his servitude to a national, social, human ideal:

> He could not see, it was not born in him to see, that the highest good of the community as it stands is no longer the highest good of even the average individual . . . the "common good" becomes a general nuisance, representing the vulgar, conservative materialism at a low level.[87]

Skrebensky sacrifices his individual "self" to the community and to a sense of duty. For him this results in a sort of nullity which strikes and troubles Ursula. When he returns from Africa, she feels "they were enemies come together in a truce", which is ended when he goes off to India in the service of the inhuman concept of Empire, imposed on an ancient civilization.[88] Ursula finally rejects him, like a ghost out of the past.

It is one thing to read today, after two world wars and twenty years of decolonization, passages like these which may be taken as inspired by an anti-imperialist and pacifist tradition. It is quite another to read them in the context of a merciless war and of the reactions of a public opinion only then beginning, in 1915, to understand the desperate nature of the conflict opposing Britain to Germany.

The Rainbow crisis

Had Lawrence any idea of the forces to be unleashed by the publication of his novel? It seems unlikely. He was too deeply immersed in his individualism, too scornful of the "crowd", the "mob", the "canaille"; he believed too much in his predestined mission. Another man might perhaps have heeded such warnings as he had received. The Trespasser had shocked some readers, and E. M. Forster had recently brought to Greatham rumours of police action against The Prussian Officer. At this very time Lawrence was busy reassuring Methuen, via Pinker, concerning the love scenes in The Rainbow.[89] In July, he consented to change certain terms at proof but refused to cut or modify passages and paragraphs marked by the publisher: "feeling as he did that they were living parts of an organic whole":

> Those who object, will object to the book altogether. These bits won't affect them particularly. Tell Methuen, he need not be afraid. If the novel does not pay him back this year, it will before long. Does he expect me to be popular? I shan't be that. But I am a safe speculation for a publisher.[90]

He certainly had no sense of timing, seeking a head-on clash with public opinion, even going so far as to ask Pinker to have the dedication to his sister-in-law Else printed not only in German, but in Gothic characters, adding optimistically, "We shall have peace by the time this book is published."[91]

It is thus easy to imagine the effect on Lawrence and Frieda, as described by Murry,[92] of the first review of *The Rainbow* signed by Robert Lynd in the Liberal *Daily News* under the title "The Downfall".[93] Lynd, finding the novel "windy, tedious, boring and nauseating", reproached it for being "largely a monotonous wilderness of phallicism"; he regretted seeing the author's powers so wasted, and warned the reader against scenes "which are reminiscent of Diderot's *La Religieuse*". James Douglas in the *Star* (also Liberal) and Clement Shorter in the *Sphere* followed up with reviews practically inviting police intervention.[94]

On 5 November Lawrence learned from the novelist W. L. George that his novel had been seized at Methuen's. George had noticed the advertisement had been dropped and had telephoned the publisher to ask why.[95]

From this point onward it becomes important to try to sift facts from gossip and interpretation, if we are to obtain a clear picture of what actually happened, and of possible explanations of the course of events.

First of all, how did Lawrence react to the *Rainbow* crisis? His letter of Saturday, 6 November to Pinker is clearly a reply to a communication from his agent, his only means of communication with Methuen: "I had heard yesterday about the magistrates and *The Rainbow*." On 17 November he confirmed that his first intimation had been through W. L. George, before be received Pinker's letter.[96]

At first he was "not very much moved", he felt "beyond that", and he postponed a luncheon meeting with Pinker because he had to go to Garsington; his letters give one the impression that he was not preparing to fight a legal battle. His main aim was apparently the mobilization of powerful friends, the Morrells, Bernard Shaw through Dollie Radford, and possibly the Prime Minister through his son and daughter-in-law.[97] He informed Edward Marsh, then assistant private secretary to H. H. Asquith. His reactions on the whole were defensive, even when he showed pride in his novel, as when telling Marsh "you jeered rather at *The Rainbow*, but notwithstanding it is a big book, and one of the important novels in the language. I tell you, who know." And to Lady Cynthia: "You know quite well the book is not indecent, though I heard of you saying to a man that it was like the second story in *The Prussian Officer*, only *much worse*. Still one easily says these things." Middleton Murry had reported to him the result of his eavesdropping on Lady Cynthia's conversation at an exhibition.[98]

There is no record of any meeting with Pinker, or of Lawrence taking any legal advice as to his right of intervention before the magistrate. His only hope seems to have been of having "the decision reversed" by the intervention of the Asquiths.[99] The Lawrences' idea of what was feasible in such matters may perhaps be gauged from a December 1916 letter from Frieda to Lady Cynthia, showing her surprise that Herbert Asquith could not be exempted from field service:

What is the good of being the Prime Minister's son and you can't be any different from other people . . . if you have some advantages over other men's wives, do take them. I know it seems low, but it isn't.[100]

Not only was the Prime Minister not readily accessible to family intervention in affairs of State, but he was then engaged in perilous political negotiations over the impending withdrawal from Gallipoli.

The chances of intervention by the Prime Minister or even his private secretary were certainly much slighter than the Lawrences could imagine, in their total ignorance of legal procedure and of the political climate. November 1915 was scarcely a time when Asquith could have intervened in such a matter, had he even thought fit to do so. The supposition, voiced many years later by Aldington, that the prosecution against *The Rainbow* was a political manœuvre against the Prime Minister,[101] would hardly commend itself to the historian, in the absence of any proof that the Director of Public Prosecutions may have been acting, consciously or not, in a manner disloyal to Asquith. But the history of the J. R. Campbell case in 1924 stands as a reminder of the dangers which may beset a British Cabinet when interference with legal proceedings seems to be suggested.

Lawrence's lack of any will to fight the legal battle was, indeed, puzzling until 1969, when certain information from the files of the Society of Authors became public. The full facts of the case, as distinct from what emerges from the records of the police court action, are not yet known, but enough is now established to suggest that this was no ordinary obscenity police court case and that whoever initiated it intended to bring it to the attention of the public in no uncertain fashion.

The sources for what follows are: the accounts of the proceedings in *The Times* and the *Daily Telegraph* for Monday, 15 November 1915; Home Office documents now in the Public Records Office; and a recent article by Mr John Carter in *The Times Literary Supplement*, to which should be added the present author's inquiries from Sir Stanley Unwin and from the son and successor of Mr Herbert Muskett, the solicitor who acted for Scotland Yard in the *Rainbow* case.

On 3 November Detective-Inspector Draper of the Criminal Investigation Department, New Scotland Yard, called at Methuen and Co. with a warrant from the chief magistrate at Bow Street Police Court, under the "Obscene Prints Act, 1857", to seize all copies of *The Rainbow* on the grounds that it was an obscene work.[102]

Here it is essential to quote from Methuen's letter to the Society of Authors in reply to an inquiry made on 15 November by its secretary G. H. Thring:

The solicitors, in consideration of the reputation of our firm, kindly suggested that we might prefer to hand over the books rather than submit to actual search, and this we did.[103]

Who were "the solicitors" who were thus ready with this suggestion, presumably through the mouthpiece of Inspector Draper? Clearly not Methuen's solicitors, to whom the word "kindly" would not apply, but Scotland Yard's solicitors, Messrs Wontner and Sons, of Bow Street, whose senior partner, Mr Herbert Muskett, was prosecuting for the Commissioner of Metropolitan Police ten days later, and clearly was already in full charge of the case.

Having informed Pinker, Messrs Methuen seem to have been under the impression that provided they avoided "any fuss" the book would be seized but there would be no public prosecution. This is, at any rate, what their second letter to G. H. Thring (16 November) conveys:

> On Thursday, November 11, Inspector Draper called with a summons to show cause why "the said books should not be destroyed, and to be further dealt with according to the law". We understood from Inspector Draper that this was merely a formal matter to obtain our formal consent on the destruction of the book; *the impression we received was that it would not be heard in a public court*, and we did not therefore obtain legal assistance or arrange to be legally represented.
>
> We asked Inspector Draper if the author could have a voice in the destruction of the books, and understood him to say that the action of the Police Court was taken against us and *the author had no right to appear in the matter*.
>
> We were very much surprised on Saturday, the 13th, to find, on attending at the Police Court, *that the case was to be heard in open court*. You will no doubt have seen the report in many of the papers; these reports are substantially correct.[104] [*Italics added.*]

In his letter to G. H. Thring of the same date (16 November) Pinker stressed two points. Whereas Methuen assert that they informed him on 3 November but "have had no communication *from* Mr Pinker since then", he refers to several telephone conversations with members of the firm, in which Methuen expressed their wish to hush up the affair. Not only did they discourage a proposal by Clive Bell to write in defence of Lawrence, but they expressed the hope that Pinker would do nothing to get the magistrate's order reversed.

Methuen and Co. thus seems to have played the game of the authorities, either consciously (the evidence for such an assertion is insufficient) or under skilful manipulation, and in the hope of saving their own reputation from any slur, by complying with the suggestions of Inspector Draper. The net effect of their malleability was that neither they nor Pinker nor Lawrence were represented in court on 13 November, the field thus being clear for the prosecution.

In such circumstances and in the absence of any opposing views, why did Mr Muskett and Sir John Dickinson go out of their way to express their horrified virtuous endeavours to protect British homes from obscenity and "filth"? The proceedings read, in retrospect, especially in the light of the recently published facts, like a ritual execution, performed in accordance with an arranged scenario. Although it is still not possible to conclude without the shadow of a doubt that it had been so prearranged, a great deal of the evidence points that way.

Mr Muskett, the prosecuting solicitor, was senior partner of Wontner and Sons, a firm then acting for the Commissioner of Metropolitan Police in all Bow Street prosecutions. He "handled the cases of most public importance" as his son and successor has kindly stated in answer to our inquiries.[105] He had specialized in suffragette cases, and in 1917 it was he who was to prosecute E. D. Morel for a technical offence involving communication with Romain Rolland in Switzerland concerning pacifist propaganda.

In his statement on behalf of the Commissioner of Police, Mr Muskett "said he had also been in communication with the Director of Public Prosecutions in the matter", a clear signal to the magistrate and Press that the prosecution had the backing of this high legal authority. These words assume their full significance when read in conjunction with a Scotland Yard minute of 1930 (when the question was raised by the Home Office as to whether or not to prosecute Martin Secker for republishing *The Rainbow*), which the Home Office have kindly allowed us to quote:

> Although the 1915 proceedings were taken in the Commissioner's name, they were practically initiated by the late Sir Charles Matthews.[106]

Sir Charles Matthews was the Director of Public Prosecutions from 1908 to 1920.

In the light of the above, none of which Lawrence or Pinker could have known, the proceedings begin to make sense. Methuen had been deliberately misled into thinking that they would escape without publicity. Their docility was duly rewarded: Mr Muskett referred to "the defendant company" as "a publishing house of old standing and the highest repute", who had "dealt with the matter with the strictest propriety"; and Sir John Dickinson, the magistrate, using exactly the same words to describe the firm, added that their name "on the title page of a book justified anyone in taking it into their home". Apart from ordering all copies to be destroyed, he did not (as has often been mistakenly reported) inflict a *fine* but merely ordered Methuen to pay £10 10s. *costs*. Recent inquiries suggest that the total cost to Methuen, apart from their disbursements to Lawrence and the printer, were of the order of £40.[107]

The venom of the prosecuting solicitor and of the magistrate was thus saved for the absent author. Although nobody was opposing the summons, Mr Muskett, immediately after mentioning his reference to the Director of Public Prosecutions, said that "it was considered advisable in the public interest that a statement should be made". And this is the essence of the statement as summarized in the *Daily Telegraph*:

> To him personally it was a matter for the most profound regret that it should have been necessary for the protection of public morals and public decency in literary productions to bring this disgusting, detestable and pernicious work under the notice of the Court. Although there might not be an obscene word to be found in the book, it was in fact a mass of obscenity of thought, idea, and action, wrapped up in language which in some quarters might be considered artistic and intellectual. It was difficult to understand how Messrs Methuen could have lent their great name to the publication of this bawdy volume.

Mr Muskett proceeded to quote from two notices of *The Rainbow*, one of the critics being Mr Clement K. Shorter, who wrote:

> "Zola's novels are child's food compared with the strong meat contained in this book.'[108]

The magistrate having particularly singled out for a brief reference the chapter entitled "Shame", which contains the lesbian bathing scene between Ursula and Winifred, Mr Muskett went on to state that any booksellers holding copies, who might "persist in selling them after this warning", "would run the risk of prosecution". Having made sure the public libraries had not taken the book, Sir John Dickinson then joined in the execution:

> . . . he had never read anything more disgusting than this book, and how it could ever have passed through Messrs Methuen's hands he failed to understand . . . It was appalling to think of the harm that such a book might have done. It was utter filth, nothing else would describe it. He was very glad to hear that the libraries refused to circulate it.

Virtuous indignation of this order, without ulterior motives, even if it leaves one sceptical, is not absolutely out of the question: Lawrence himself was soon to be led to believe that his troubles were due to "a ridiculous affair instigated by the National Purity League, Dr Horton and Co., nonconformity".[109] Later on, Aldington was to attribute responsibility for the prosecution to the Public Morality Council.[110] Whether or not either of these religious bodies drew the attention of the Home Office or of the Director of Public Prosecutions to *The Rainbow* as an objectionable book, it has not yet been possible to ascertain. The evidence at present available points to considerations other than obscenity as the main motivation.

A first indication, and an important one, is to be found in Home Office papers relating to the parliamentary questions put to the Home Secretary by Philip Morrell.

A first question was asked on 18 November, when Philip Morrell received from Sir John Simon an evasive answer: the police had taken action "in the pursuance of their ordinary duty" (a statement on which the 1930 Scotland Yard minute to the Home Office now casts a doubt). Sir John Simon went on to say that "the publishers and not the author were the defendants, and they had the customary opportunity to produce such evidence as they considered necessary in defence"; but "so far from resisting the proceedings they said they thought it right that the order should be issued".[111] In other words, the Home Secretary in this first answer had sheltered behind the Metropolitan Police and Methuen.

On 1st December, a second, this time written, question from Philip Morrell was due for reply. It had received attention at the highest level in the last days of November, and Sir Edward Troup, Permanent Under-Secretary, had asked for the observations of Scotland Yard on a proposed answer which, according to his own handwritten comment, was "correct" but "rather avoided answering the question". He had attached his own draft reply, but page 2 of the minutes bears the annotation: "S. of S. [Secretary of State] dictated reply", which clearly indicates that Sir John took the matter in hand personally. Immediately below the printed text of the question, on page 1, his attention had been drawn to what might seem a quite irrelevant but highly important handwritten marginal note, in red ink, which reads: "As to a Mrs Weekley living at address of D. H. Lawrence, see 352857." This numbered document, which at the time must have been appended for the Minister to see, cannot now be found in the files of the Home Office for the reasons stated above.[112]

The marginal note on the Home Office papers makes it difficult to believe that obscenity was the only or main consideration in the high-level official action taken against Lawrence. German affiliations through Frieda were evidently felt to be relevant by the Director of Public Prosecutions. Sir John Simon's skilful handling of embarrassing questions, in full knowledge of the background to the affair, thus appears to have been the equivalent of throwing a smoke-screen over the real motives.

While this much seems clear today, it is hardly surprising that Lawrence and Pinker and their friends were left in the dark. The radical M.P. Sir William Byles may have been nearer the truth when, following Philip Morrell's question on 1st December, he asked the Home Secretary whether the proceedings had been taken under the Defence of the Realm Act—D.O.R.A. then being considered as increasing far too widely the discretionary powers of the government. As for Lawrence, he was left with the idea that the congregationalist minister Dr Horton was to blame; Aldington was to state many years later that he knew "in his bones" that the real reason for the attack was that [Lawrence] denounced war";[113] he had heard this stated both by Lawrence and by May Sinclair.[114]

For a short time Lawrence thought he could fight to have the magistrate's decision reversed. He joined the Society of Authors on 11 November, only to be informed on 7 December that "after hearing the opinion of the solicitors in regard to the legal aspect, the Committee came to the conclusion that in the present circumstances they could not take any useful action on the general principles involved".[115] He had for a while entertained Donald Carswell's idea of a re-trial (arising from Sir John Simon's statement that it might be possible "for another copy to be seized by arrangement", in order that he might defend the book),[116] but his spirit "did not rise to it": "I am not going to pay any more out of my soul, even for the sake of beating them."[117]

What then was really behind the *Rainbow* prosecution? A similar attempt publicly to discredit another writer may provide a clue. A few days after the successful proceedings against *The Rainbow*, Sir Stanley Unwin informed the author in 1967, he received a visit from a detective who showed him a marked copy of Edward Carpenter's *The Intermediate Sex* and asked that the book be withdrawn on the grounds of obscenity. Sir Stanley listened to him, asked if he might note the marked passages, then went to the Commissioner of Police and threatened legal action for slander. He heard no more about it.

Carpenter, like Lawrence, was not happy about the war: during 1914 and 1915, he had contributed to *The English Review* outspoken articles which were later published under the title *The Healing of Nations and the Hidden Sources of their Strife*. Lawrence had been far less balanced and controlled in his statements, and had been attempting to run subversive meetings at 12 Fisher Street, London, just before the *Rainbow* case. Both men were probably marked down by the police as leftist agitators. The reported intention to stop sales of *The Prussian Officer* in February 1915, the peremptory statements of Mr Herbert Muskett, the attempt to have Carpenter's name brought before the public as an objectionable writer on homosexuality, the leakage of the alleged Roger Casement diaries in 1916, and the prosecution of E. D. Morel by Mr Herbert Muskett for attempting to communicate with the pacifist Romain Rolland—all these facts suggest the operation of secret services responsible for the control of pacifist tendencies and propaganda. In Lawrence's case, such intervention was undoubtedly successful; as a potential leader of public opinion he was effectively silenced. Whether this can be put down to the "persecution" of a misunderstood genius is another matter. He saw it as such, but his published views about the war in *The Signature* were such that Lady Cynthia Asquith wrote in her diary: "I am not sure that technically it doesn't amount to treason."[118] He was easier game than a Carpenter or a Bertrand Russell for the defenders of the national war morale.

Passports, military service, medical examinations

Lawrence and Frieda had received their passports for America early in November, thanks to the intervention of a friend of Cynthia Asquith in the Foreign Office. Such intervention may well have been necessary to dispel doubts as to the wisdom of letting loose in the United States a naturalized German woman and a talented writer hostile to the very idea of war, at a moment when the support of American opinion was becoming more indispensable than ever. Lawrence was then in the process of discussing with Lady Cynthia (whose brother had just been killed) his own attitude towards the war and to the Allied cause: he was ready to "give the Germans England and the whole Empire"; she found "his feet quite leave the ground" when he tried to persuade her "that we ought to down tools". From this note in her diary, as well as Lawrence's next letter, the reader can guess what objections could be opposed to his request for passports.[119]

The *Rainbow* crisis led Lawrence reluctantly to postpone his departure, and when he decided to leave, it was only to learn, after a fresh intervention by Lady Cynthia at the Foreign Office, that in order to obtain an exit visa a certificate of exemption from military service was now necessary. Although revolted at the idea of "swearing to serve his King and Country" or "being stripped naked before two recruiting sergeants", he resigned himself to it, in order to leave his abhorred country. He went to the Battersea Recruiting Office, queued up for two hours, then suddenly "broke out of the queue, in face of the table where one's name was to be written, and went across the hall away from all the underworld of spectral submission". He felt that he had "triumphed, like Satan flying over the world and knowing he had won at last, though he had not come into a fragment of his own".[120]

In January 1917 he was once more to ask his influential friends to help him leave the country. Shortly before Asquith resigned the premiership, Frieda had actually told Lady Cynthia that she felt she must "go to Germany and see what terms they would give. I suppose nothing can be done or is being done."[121] Lawrence, perfectly well aware of the possible objections to his request for passports, set about refuting them in his own way, in letters to Edward Marsh and Cynthia Asquith. He saw the war as lost, England on the edge of collapse and national disaster, "trodden under the feet of swine and dogs" who preferred "Messrs Lloyd George and Lord Derby" to Asquith. For him the "débâcle", the "great smash up" could not come quickly enough; he only hoped it might give rise to a republic based not on equality and fraternity, but on "intrinsic inequality".[122] He did, however, try to control himself, and to justify his departure on grounds of "definite" reasons "as convincing as possible":

I shall give: 1. Ill-health. 2. Failure to make any money at all over here. 3. Necessity to place short stories, and literary articles, and poems, and to arrange with a publisher the publication of *The Rainbow* . . . and of the novel *Women in Love*.

But he added that he hoped to go "not so much for business", but because he "felt he could not breathe in England".[123] When Lady Cynthia gently admonished him, probably retailing doubts expressed by the Foreign Office, he tried to convince her of his innocence, succeeding only in demonstrating his defeatism:

> I don't want to write or talk about the war at all—only stories and literary stuff: because I think the war will end this year, and even if it doesn't I can't help it any more. I feel there is disaster impending for England . . . I know one ought not to ask for anything from you. But I believe it is quite legal for us to go to America. I am medically exempt, we are not spies, and I will neither write or talk about the war to the Americans—they have nothing to do with it, it is our affair, alas! So just confer a little with Eddie about it, will you?[124]

What official with any knowledge of this attitude could possibly have taken the responsibility of authorizing Lawrence's departure? On 12 February, Lawrence was informed that the exit visas had been refused. He immediately envisaged a renewed request, and sought new reasons to justify it. England was "only a tomb" for him. "Do you think I don't know what it is to be an Englishman?" he asked Lady Cynthia. "There is one thing, America won't come into the war. If she does, that will be a most fearful blow, which I don't know I shall recover from."[125]

His futile visit to the Battersea Recruiting Office dated from the time of the Derby Scheme which preceded conscription. As more and more families of volunteers were plunged into mourning, abuse of the loopholes of the Derby Scheme caused widespread public indignation. In 1916 conscription was adopted after bitter debate. Religious and trade union opposition to the principle of conscription was such that the Liberal Home Secretary, Sir John Simon, resigned when Parliament passed the law making military service obligatory for all men from eighteen to forty years old, except for conscientious objectors or those engaged in essential national service.

According to Aldington, himself a volunteer, it was the "threat of conscription" which, from 1915 onwards, forced Lawrence to "face up to the reality of war". In support of this conviction he quotes a letter written by Lawrence to Ottoline Morrell in May 1915, the incoherent style and syntax of which clearly betrays his troubled state of mind. His heart is "very cold" with fear at the mere thought of a coalition Government:

> It is as if we were all going to die . . . Why does even the coalition of the government fill me with terror? Some say it is for peace negotiations. It may

be, because we are all afraid. But it is most probably for conscription. The touch of death is very cold and horrible on us all.[126]

He must have known that he ran no risk being passed fit for active service, though later he made out that he had deceived the doctors as to the state of his health on the occasion of his first Army medical at Bodmin, where he was exempted in June 1916. The medical examination scenes in *Kangaroo* are realistic and faithful enough, though the "Nightmare" chapter does, to some extent, rationalize after the event his reasons for opposition to all forms of military service. At the time he stuck mainly to the *Rainbow* arguments, sheltering behind the individualist standpoint which he shared with Frieda:

And what duty is it, which makes us forfeit everything, because Germany invaded Belgium? Is there nothing beyond my fellow-man? If not, then there is nothing beyond myself, beyond my own throat, which may be cut and my own purse, which may be slit: because I am the fellow-man of all the world, my neighbour is but myself in a mirror. So we toil in a circle of pure egoism.[127]

This idle outpouring, expressing no more than his impotence in the face of the social and military machine, at least throws some light on the "deaths" and "annulments" which Lawrence sprinkles so lavishly both in his works and letters: "I am sure I should *die* in a week, if they kept me," he tells Catherine Carswell; "it is the annulling of all one stands for." At a time when the holocaust of Verdun was drawing to a close, when the British offensive on the Somme was just beginning, what worried Lawrence, as he describes himself in *Kangaroo*, was that they might shave off his beard, symbol of his "isolate manhood", and force him to participate in any way in the national effort; or that the Cornish farm hands called up for a medical at the same time as himself should see him naked or in his woollen pants "with patches on the knees".[128]

Summoned to Bodmin once more in June 1917, he was classified C.3, which meant he was in principle liable to light non-military duties. He justified his non-participation on the grounds that there were "thousands of C. men—men who wanted to have jobs as C. men", and that "he would only be a nuisance anyhow".[129]

Expulsion from Cornwall and capitulation

By 1917, England had no more illusions concerning the nature of the war; she had undergone aerial bombardment, and suffered the merciless submarine war fought out on the high seas, including the southern approaches to the Bristol Channel below the cliffs of Higher Tregerthen. Public opinion turned indignantly against "shirkers" and conscientious objectors. A minority of pacifists persisted, some (like Bertrand Russell, Clifford Allen or E. D. Morel) going to prison, others (like Ramsay MacDonald) risking their political careers. Strict rationing was enforced. Trade union or revolutionary opposition continued to foment strikes in the munitions industry and the railways.

Lawrence and his wife, very probably unaware of the facts, had come to live in a theatre of naval operations, in a forbidden military zone of the Salisbury Command. Both were notably unrestrained in language; she was German-born, he had a German uncle; the company they kept may well have surprised the local people: American visitors, young men like Heseltine and Cecil Gray, for no apparent reason not in uniform. They received letters and newspapers from Germany. Cecil Gray has reported how Lawrence talked to all and sundry of going to the industrial North to campaign for pacifism and to bring the war to a speedy end.[130] It is almost certain that letters warranted to make the hair of the most benevolent postal censor stand on end were in fact read by the censorship.[131] How would an official react to Lawrence's letter to Edward Marsh, at that time Private Secretary to Winston Churchill, Minister of Munitions, in which he said: "I should like to flourish a pistol under the nose of the fools that govern us"?[132] He was in contact with Koteliansky, a Russian anti-tsarist, with Ivy Low, who had just married Maxim Litvinov, then a refugee in London after being in jail, and shortly to become Lenin's ambassador.

After the entry of the United States into the war and the Russian Revolution, Lawrence's references to America grew somewhat cooler: he seems to have entertained the idea of going to Russia to get his work published, and Frieda thought of submitting his "Peace" articles for the Nobel Prize.[133] It is not clear at which Nobel Prize she aimed, but it is interesting to note, in this connexion, that on 20 December 1917, commenting on the award of the Nobel Prize for literature to the Danish writer Karl Gjellerup, Sir Edmund Gosse expressed, in an article in the Times Literary Supplement, his regret that "the Nobel Prize for imaginative literature should thus have been annexed by that pro-German 'activist' party which is still so prominent in Stockholm".[134] Lawrence's outraged protestations of innocence in Kangaroo and in his letters reveal not only his complete failure to understand the impression he might have made on anyone responsible for security, but also a distinct propensity for provocation. Despite his great gift for plumbing the depths of the subconscious, he failed signally to perceive the immediate and natural reactions of his own neighbours.

The circumstances ending in his summary expulsion from Cornwall are fully documented: the old piano that served to accompany their German sing-songs, the warnings of neighbours who knew that they were being watched; the arrest and search by the police in London of the American Mountsier after his visit to the Lawrences in Cornwall at Christmas 1916;[135] the various occasions on which either soldiers searched a knapsack full of groceries, or coastguards watched outside their windows at night; the incident of the badly blacked-out light at Cecil Gray's house at Bosigran, the irruption of armed men into the sitting-room where Gray and his friends were singing in German; Gray's sentence to a heavy fine for this offence; the subsequent search of the Lawrences' cottage in their absence.

There is perhaps more than a touch of Cornish folklore in the "stupid, shifty, small and sly" eyes of the Cornish women as seen by Katherine Mansfield and in many reports of the prevailing atmosphere of malevolence.[136] The statements of the neighbouring farmers interviewed by the B.B.C. in 1953 were balanced and anodyne, certainly more convincing than the almost psychopathological intensity of *Kangaroo*.[137] On the whole it is Catherine Carswell who gives the most sane and sober picture of this period: she mentions only the probability of a malicious denunciation, and the reported spying of a "half-demented" and self-appointed unpaid temporary charwoman. She does not, on the other hand, underestimate frequent instances of carelessness and provocation offered by her friends.

The day after the cottage was searched by the police, an officer and two civilians arrived, accompanied by the local police sergeant, armed with a search warrant and an order from Sir William Western, major-general in charge of administration, Southern Command, Salisbury, enjoining the couple to leave Cornwall within three days. The whole scene is photographically rendered in *Kangaroo*, where Lawrence depicts himself as "unconscious that the other people were real human beings". To him they were not: they were just *things*, obeying orders.[138]

Such alienation from the human scene, which Lawrence grasped with perfect retrospective lucidity when writing *Kangaroo* in Australia, was a phenomenon he frequently experienced during the dark years of the war. It did not, however, preclude a certain false ingenuousness, a shade of insincerity to which even the tolerant Harry T. Moore has drawn attention, as for instance, when Lawrence wrote to Lady Cynthia:

> I cannot even conceive how I have incurred suspicion—have not the faintest notion. We are as innocent even of pacifist activities, let alone spying of any sort as the rabbits in the field outside.[139]

Or again to Montague Shearman, lawyer son of a High Court judge, associate of the Bloomsbury circle so abhorrent to Lawrence: "We don't know in the least why this has taken place. Of course my wife was corresponding with her people in Germany, through a friend in Switzerland—but through the ordinary post."[140] To Lady Cynthia, however, "their exclusion" from Cornwall seemed "so very reasonable".[141]

In London (and afterwards at Hermitage), Lawrence continued to be the object of police surveillance, described in measured terms by Aldington and Cecil Gray, but which to Lawrence conveyed "an atmosphere of terror all through London, as under the Tsar, when no man dared open his mouth".[142]

To Aldington, with his experience at the front and behind the lines in France, such indignation could only seem faintly ridiculous.

Lawrence's last skirmish with the authorities, prior to the later battles over *Lady Chatterley's Lover* and his pictures, took place in September 1918, on the occasion of his last Army medical. Classified C.3 in 1917, he should, in principle, have sought an occupation useful to the nation. In February 1918, he thought of offering his services to Maxim Litvinov, and in September he told Koteliansky he wanted to meet the trade union leaders Mary MacArthur and Margaret Bondfield, and the pacifists Robert Smillie and Philip Snowden.

He does not seem to have followed up this idea, which coincided with his receipt of a third summons to appear before a medical board. In the same letter, however, he was still asserting that he would "rather be hanged or put in prison than endure any more. So now I shall move actively, personally, do what I can. I am a desperado."[143] He would submit to nothing, with the possible exception of another medical examination. Moreover he had already sent back his papers, saying "how could they expect me to do anything, if I am still a black-marked person".[144] Having thus drawn official attention to himself, he went to Derby as summoned and underwent the humiliations of a prolonged medical examination under the sneering and sceptical eyes of the doctors and of their assistants. He was classed C.2 (Class 3), fit for non-military service. He "knew" that "they would like to seize him and make him empty latrines in some camp".[145]

However, he soon swallowed his anger and forgot his promises of non-co-operation. Whereas in 1916 he would rather have been "a soldier than a schoolteacher", he at once reminded Lady Cynthia of his past career:

> I want a job under the Ministry of Education: not where I shall be kicked about like an old can: I've had enough of that. You must help me to something where I shall not be ashamed. Don't you know that man Fisher?[146] He sounds decent. Really try and get me introduced and started fairly. I need a start—and I'm not going to be an under-servant to anybody; no, I'm not. If these military *canaille* call me up for any of their filthy jobs—I am graded for sedentary work—I shall just remove myself, and be a deserter.[147]

Fortunately for his self-respect, the war ended without his having either to execute these threats, or to face the consequences of a total capitulation by accepting some sort of educational work.

10

INTEGRATION—THE DREAM AND THE FAILURE

With Lawrence's refusal to co-operate in national life, to participate in society, went an intense desire for integration into an elect group. Soon after a characteristic call to W. D. McLeod to "escape" in 1912,[1] a need to mitigate his moral exile had showed itself by many pressing invitations to friends to join him in Italy. Similarly, his wartime alienation from organized society went hand in hand with a yearning to belong to a group, but to one led by himself, in which he as demiurge would interpret the secret of the gods. Inside the "circle of pure egoism" in which he toiled, the more he rejected his own people, the more he sought for some principle of communal life. For a time he even entertained, and communicated to others, the illusion that he might play a national role in reforming the entire structure of society.

How could such contradictory tendencies thus co-exist? The question is relevant to the significance of his works; for he gave up his dreams of group integration only when, after having travelled round the world in vain in search of the "good society", he had reached the limit of his strength. All the works germinating in his mind during the war years, from *Aaron's Rod* to *Kangaroo*, and even *The Plumed Serpent*, deal with this problem of the individual in relation to society. These were also the years when he hovered on the brink of the belief in autocracy which was to turn other revolutionaries of his time into dictators. In the essentially ambiguous nature of his relations with others, in the failure of his friendships, inseparably bound up with his yearning for leadership, we find the underlying causes, for instance, of his break with Bertrand Russell, one of the significant events in this period of his life.

I. LAWRENCE'S PERSONAL MAGNETISM

During the 1914–19 period, Lawrence's circle divides into two categories: those who, captivated by his charm, became his lifelong friends, and those who, while originally attracted by his personality, ended regretfully, but more or less finally, by cutting him out of their lives. Both camps agree on the fascination exercised by him on all he met. Significantly enough, the first group consists mostly of women, the second mainly of men. The exceptions, Koteliansky and Gertler among the men, and Lady Ottoline Morrell among the women, deserve particular attention.

The immediate effect of a first contact with Lawrence has been well described by Lady Cynthia Asquith, not only a level-headed and dispassionate witness, but one who, having moved from childhood in the brilliant aristocratic world centred on her mother, Lady Elcho, was used to the company of men eminent in the arts, letters and politics. "The moment a slender, lithe figure stepped lightly into the room," she writes, she and her husband "realized almost with the shock of a collision that something new and startling had come into their lives."[2] Between Lawrence and other men she found not a difference of degree but of kind: even before he grew his beard, to her he looked "half-faun, half-prophet". She also notes that he was very much more of a Jeremiah in his letters than in his talk. Another aristocrat, Lady Ottoline Morrell, stresses his magnetic gift of inspiring the enthusiasm of his interlocutors, combined with a great gentleness in human contacts.

He appeared to a Chesham neighbour as "an attractive-looking young man whitewashing a bedroom"; to her husband as "full of humility and gentleness . . . really Christ-like". Natural, spontaneous, alive, flamelike, are adjectives which seem to spring to the pen of those who, like Catherine Carswell and Ottoline Morrell, made his acquaintance at this time. To Dollie Radford he was "a sweet man,—so simple and kind, touchingly childlike, and brimful of sensibility and perception". He seemed to her to "understand most human matters at a first glance".[3]

Though at first astonished at his "uncontrolled irritabilities", Eleanor Farjeon soon realized that "one must know Lawrence all-of-apiece or not at all" and remembered, too, "his angelic, childlike" moods.[4] Katherine Mansfield has left several touching descriptions of him at his best:

> He has begun to write to me again and quite in the old way—all about the leaves of the melon plant "speckled like a newt", and all about "the social egg which must collapse into nothingness, into non-being". I am so fond of him for many things. I cannot shut my heart against him and I never shall.

And in October 1918:

I loved him. He was just his old, merry, rich self, laughing, describing things, giving you pictures, full of enthusiasm and joy in a future where we become all "vagabonds"—we simply did not talk about people. We kept to things like nuts and cowslips and fires in woods and his black self *was* not. Oh, there is something so lovable about him and his eagerness, his passionate eagerness for life, that is what one loves so.[5]

Most of such ecstatic portraits have been drawn by women; yet it must not be forgotten that John Middleton Murry, Richard Aldington, E. M. Forster, Bertrand Russell, John Maynard Keynes and many other eminent men also felt his charm, falling to some extent under his spell and treating him as a peer or a superior. If Russell was struck and attracted by his "energy and passion and his feelings", by what seemed to him at first to be a deeper intuitive insight into human nature,[6] one can well imagine his immediate influence on younger men, less well prepared to be critical of their own perceptions, or on artists such as Philip Heseltine or Cecil Gray. In his *Reminiscences* Murry has described the joy Lawrence inspired in all those that came within his orbit and how he seemed to communicate to them the fullness of life.[7]

To this personal magnetism must be added a mutual attraction between the rising young writer and the radical aristocracy of 1914–15. Ottoline Morrell here played a highly characteristic role, as the focal point of encounter and clash between Lawrence and Cambridge and Bloomsbury intellectualism.

Born in 1873, Ottoline Bentinck was descended from the ancient family of the Dukes of Portland and, through her paternal grandmother, from the Wellesleys. She was reared in the pre-Victorian atmosphere of Welbeck Abbey, becoming "Lady Ottoline" when her brother succeeded to the Duchy of Portland. Her relative emancipation from aristocratic taboos was early illustrated by her brief period of study at St Andrews University. After a visit to Italy, where she fell in love with Axel Munthe, in 1902 she married Philip Morrell, an Oxford solicitor, who later became a Liberal M.P. From 1905 their house in Bedford Square, and later their country estate of Garsington Manor near Oxford, became fashionable meeting places for the artistic, literary, radical and socialist élite; in 1914 and 1915 Ottoline's salon was one of the centres of opposition to the war. In her very much edited memoirs, she provides a disorderly but graphic picture of her circle, considerably wider than the group of writers, artists, critics, politicians and Cambridge figures which were to be known as Bloomsbury; a rationalist, intellectualist and progressive élite, of which Bertrand Russell was one of the rare survivors into the sixties. He himself has candidly related in his memoirs the tale of his passion for Ottoline not long before Lawrence met her.

In that world of clear-cut ideas, Ottoline's memoirs show her intelligence to have been curiously clouded by a form of intellectual myopia, characteristic of so many rich women in the first quarter of this century: barred by social conventions from a full-scale higher education, but at the same time cultivated, they had acquired from their menfolk a familiarity with ideas, but not much power of analysis, so that fact and ideas tended to blur in their minds like outlines in a Turner painting. Today, with her extraordinary clothes, her dogs, her dramatic poses before so many famous painters, Ottoline tends to be seen as a grotesque. Yet she was nothing of the sort to Lawrence, to Frieda, to Russell, Murry or Gertler, to the painters Augustus John, Charles Conder, Henry Lamb, or to Aldous and Julian Huxley, Sidney and Beatrice Webb, and a host of others for whom her house, her regalia, her receptions were part of the natural framework of the period. The Ottoline of 1914 should be seen in the atmosphere of her time, rather as a symbol of post-Victorian liberation, of the opening up of a new world, and not as some fantastic image of a bygone age.

By December 1914, she was anxious to meet the author of *The Prussian Officer*; before David Garnett could arrange it, they met through Gilbert Cannan. Lawrence's first letter to Ottoline is dated 3 January 1915, and in it, chameleon-like as always, he immediately assures this aristocratic wife of a Liberal M.P. that "life itself is an affair of aristocrats", and that he is "no democrat, save in politics". He at once found her "really nice", and included her in his New Jerusalem: though he did not appreciate "her parties"! Nor did he approve of all those he met at her house; in particular the abstract painter Duncan Grant provoked a violent diatribe to his face, and "a spate of verbiage" to Ottoline on the art of painting.[8]

II. JEALOUSY AND INDISCRETION

The scene in Duncan Grant's studio was one first sign of the incipient rift between the puritan prophet risen from the people and the affranchised intelligentsia of Bloomsbury and Cambridge. Lawrence certainly felt ill at ease among these men whose detached intellect seemed to him frivolous and superficial. Looking back over the years in his *Memoirs*, and remembering the "brittle" quality of their worldly discourse of 1915, Lord Keynes was to wonder in later years whether there was not "something true and right in what Lawrence felt" at the time.

Lawrence's hostile reactions towards Bloomsbury soon cost him valued friendships, to begin with that of David Garnett. "Dear Bunny" had been one of the first gay companions of Lawrence's voluntary exile, one of those "young Englishmen" for whom he felt he was writing in 1912 and 1913— with a definite suggestion that his novels would help save them from sexual deviation. From 1914 to the end of the war, Garnett's friends formed a large part of the Lawrence circle, as his three-volume memoirs amply testify.[9] But Lawrence was as jealous and exclusive in friendship as in love. He soon felt Bunny slipping from his grasp into the alien milieu of his own childhood and youth: the Olivier girls, the Stracheys, Francis Birrell. On two occasions Garnett took Birrell to visit the Lawrences, each time provoking crises; the second, at Greatham, was exceptionally violent. Garnett has described how Lawrence brooded silently while Birrell, quite unconscious of what was going on, chatted gaily with Frieda of their mutual friends the Lichnowskys, and other aristocratic Berlin acquaintances. The growing tension, which Garnett has verbally attributed to Lawrence's gnawing feeling of exclusion, was followed by Birrell's strange sudden seizure, treated by Lawrence as if "his Dark Gods" had sent this mischievous sign to blast his enemy. In two venomous letters written immediately after their departure, Lawrence told Ottoline how Birrell had made him "dream in the night of a beetle that bites like a scorpion", while Garnett was adjured never to bring the nasty, black-beetle-like Birrell to see him again:

> I feel I should go mad when I think of your set, Duncan Grant and Keynes and Birrell. It makes me dream of beetles. In Cambridge I had a similar dream. I had felt it slightly before in the Stracheys. But it came full upon me in Keynes and in Duncan Grant. And yesterday I knew it again in Birrell—you must leave these friends, these beetles. Birrell and Duncan Grant are done forever. Keynes I am not sure—when I saw Keynes that morning in Cambridge, it was one of the crises of my life. It sent me mad with misery and hostility and rage.

And in a postscript: "You have always known the wrong people. Harolds [Hobson] and Olivier girls."[10]

Frieda's added comment, "You always admire others too much", suggests that she knew what ailed Lawrence. J. M. Keynes thinks these quarrels were due to intense jealousy on the part of Lawrence, then a prey to two causes of emotional disturbance, one centring on Ottoline, the other on his first contact with the world of Bloomsbury and Cambridge:

> As always, Ottoline was keeping more than one world. Except for Bertie, the Cambridge and Bloomsbury world was only just beginning to hold her. Lawrence, Gertler, Carrington were a different strand in her furbelows. Lawrence was jealous of the other lot; and Cambridge rationalism and cynicism, then at its height, were, of course, repulsive to him. Bertie gave him what must have been, I think, his first glimpse of Cambridge. It over-whelmed, attracted and repulsed him—which was the other emotional disturbance ... Now Bunny had come into his life quite independently, neither through Ottoline nor from Cambridge and Bloomsbury; he was evidently very fond of Bunny; and when he saw *him* being seduced by Cambridge, he

was yet more jealous, just as he was jealous of Ottoline's new leanings that way. And jealousy apart, it is impossible to imagine moods more antagonistic than those of Lawrence and of pre-war Cambridge.[11]

Without any documentary evidence, but with his own memories of the Bloomsbury in which he grew, Quentin Bell has more recently attributed Lawrence's reaction to sexual jealousy and the discovery in himself of homosexual passion,[12] an explanation which becomes more and more plausible the closer one looks at Lawrence's behaviour at this time and considers the profound implications of the Prologue to *Women in Love*, written in 1916. Moreover the revelations made in Michael Holroyd's biography of Lytton Strachey concerning the homosexual affections prevalent in Bloomsbury, particularly that between Strachey, Duncan Grant and Keynes, give added significance to the latter's insistence on the "jealousy" of Lawrence.

David Garnett was so angered by Lawrence's letter that, in spite of his affection for both Lawrence and for Frieda, he decided never to see them again. Whether they ended in a complete break or merely in alternating periods of coolness and reconciliation, many of Lawrence's deepest friendships were similarly spoiled by his own intolerance and jealousy, by his barbs and shafts, all the more wounding in that he showed deep insight into the characters of his friends, without seeing any reason ever to spare their feelings.

While jealousy of one kind or another is certainly the key to his break with Garnett, gross tactlessness was responsible for an equally typical rupture with the Meynells. While enjoying their hospitality at Greatham and giving lessons to Sylvia, a daughter of Madeleine Meynell and Percy Lucas, lamed by an accident two years earlier, he had occasion to observe the whole family carefully. A few months later he published in *The English Review* a cruel and clearly recognizable psychological portrait of the family. In this first version of "England, My England", the father, deprived of all reason to go on living because he is morally exiled from the family circle, joins the army and is killed in action. The distress of the Meynell family at the publication of this portrait was intensified by the intervening death in France of the wounded Percy Lucas. Lawrence did express a moment's remorse, writing to Catherine Carswell that he wished his story "at the bottom of the sea", but only to eat his words a few lines later: "I don't wish I had never written that story. It should do good at the long run."[13]

Not unnaturally, Viola Meynell's friendship did not survive this breach of trust, and Lawrence's personal reputation suffered in those literary circles in which the Meynells and the Lucases commanded affection and respect.

Against this unprepossessing background of petty jealousies and merciless literary exploitation must be set a constant search for disciples, which goes with the sense of a divine mission, of being predestined to make some revelation to mankind.

The tone of certain letters and some passages in "The Crown" and the "Study of Thomas Hardy" show a genuine mystical exaltation mingled with a confused desire for a form of leadership, much more destructive of the present than genuinely constructive. Violent opposition to egalitarian and humanitarian ideology combines in Lawrence's mind with some aspects of traditional revolutionary socialism.

Did he seriously think of political action, or aim at the exercise of power? He flirted with this idea with Russell in 1915; according to Cecil Gray he talked about it in 1917; and in 1918 he certainly thought of contacting trade union leaders; enough, probably, to incur suspicion, but not to become a focus of genuine agitation. Not only was he held back by a personal rectitude which his occasional pettiness should not be allowed to obscure, but there are also signs of a distaste for sustained and organized action. He must have been aware of his lack of any gift in that direction, of his timidity, of his instinctive shrinking from the inevitable human contacts. He saw himself rather as the precursor of a new faith, whose temple disciples such as Russell or Murry would establish: one can scarcely imagine Lawrence facing a crowd, or even group discussion of his ideas; his attitude in the *Rainbow* crisis is revealing: he felt that he could not descend to the level of his opponents and face a retrial. The thin-skinned, timid Lawrence was apt to expend such nervous energy as he possessed on the spoken and written word. In social action as in love he was better able to conceive than to execute.

Could he have become, as Cecil Gray has suggested, "a British Hitler"? Gray thinks we were saved from this by the fact that Lawrence was an artistic success, and not, like Hitler and Mussolini, an artistic failure.[14] The artist certainly prevailed in him over the man of action. But his frustrations, his impotent anger, his undirected revolutionary tendencies, did contribute to the expression of ideas on which hindsight throws for us a sinister light. It is significant that these ideas, as we shall subsequently try to show, are part of a mystic tradition and reaction against rationalism, and were formed between 1912 and 1915 partly through the absorption of themes encountered in the works of Houston S. Chamberlain—mystic ideas of blood and race, violent reactions against humanitarian and egalitarian democracy, linked with Hegelian romanticism and theories of aesthetics of German origin. While it cannot be said that Lawrence was ever a serious candidate for dictatorship, his search for a new society and for disciples with whom to found it leads to concepts closer to those of fascism than to democratic socialism; the mental attitudes which it reveals are those on which the twentieth-century dictatorships were able to establish themselves in the minds of men, not those on which democracies can thrive. The dream of leadership and the ideas that cluster around it take shape in 1914 under the name of *Rananim*.

Rananim: focus for a social fantasy

The quest for integration of the self in a social environment, for the achievement of "complete being", such dreams of revolutionary action as Lawrence entertained, are all contained in that code word, which means different things to different people, and tends to become a symbol rather than an idea. Its importance lies precisely in what it tells us of Lawrence's social dream and in the light it throws on his major works.

The idea takes shape towards the end of 1914, at the time of writing "Study of Thomas Hardy". As an adolescent Lawrence had dreamed of an imaginary community of friends. In his Italian exile the existence of a "social self" had given him food for thought. While Frieda could ask herself "What is civilization? What is it, this man-made world that I don't understand?"[15] Lawrence was concerned with a man's social role, his communal activity independent of but related to woman. In his self-inflicted wartime exile, thrown back more than ever into isolation with Frieda, he sought to escape this solitude and to achieve wholeness of thought and action in the creation of a new society. Rananim, a name taken from one of Koteliansky's Hebrew chants, stands for the different levels at which this effort towards social integration was conducted: the artistic and philosophical level in his writings from 1914 to late 1917, the level of intended action and of attempts to influence public opinion in 1915, and the level of escapist daydreams and social play in his conversations in mixed company.

Frieda never thought of Rananim as anything but a game invented at Chesham by Katherine Mansfield, Lawrence and Murry. Mrs Carswell on the other hand sees in it something that Lawrence desperately wanted to achieve. For Katherine Mansfield it certainly was never more than verbal play: "Dined at the Lawrences and talked the island," she wrote in her diary on 3 January 1915. Lawrence, writing to Koteliansky the next day, was on the contrary preparing most seriously to found "the Order of the knights of Rananim", with FIER as its motto, for emblem "an eagle or phoenix argent, rising from a flaming nest of scarlet, on a black background", and for a flag a "blazing, ten-pointed star, scarlet on a black background". The same day he was telling Ottoline "the time has come to wave the oriflamme and rally against humanity and Ho, Ho! St John and the New Jerusalem".

By February, Murry, after crystallizing his own daydreams on Rananim, was realizing that he was out of his depth when Lawrence seriously strove to enlist him "under the banner of the Revolution". His *Reminiscences* are clear proof of the complete mutual incomprehension that characterized their conversations at the time. Murry accepted Rananim as "an island on which I should have had no need to fear",[16] while Lawrence was seeking a fundamental reformation of society. Exactly what kind of reform, he never seems to have confided clearly or fully to Murry, or, for that matter, to anyone else. His ideas remained confused, dominated by his subjective vision of a religious and sexual rehabilitation of man.

The idea of Rananim was to fluctuate between the daydream and the vague plans for revolution and social regeneration: the climax of those plans coincides with the visit to Greatham of Russell and Ottoline in February 1915. At that time the seat of the new community shifts from "the island" to "England": when Russell and Ottoline came on 6 February it was to "struggle with [Lawrence's] island idea"—Rananim: "But *they say*, the island shall be England, that we shall start our new community in the midst of this old one, as a seed falls among the roots of the parent."[17] [*Italics added.*] In the months that followed, after the visit to Cambridge and the attempt to define a joint programme with Russell, they were to clash over the latter's draft of *Principles of Social Reconstruction*, and it became clear to them both that their preoccupations were essentially divergent and their methods of thinking incompatible. The hope of effective social action receded with the *Rainbow* prosecution and the break with Russell. For most of his friends Lawrence's Rananim then became little more than a conspiracy of kindness towards him.

It is in the period of religious and social ferment, from the autumn of 1914 to the summer of 1915, that we may seek for aspects of this dream which have permanent reference to Lawrence's creative work. That is the time when a new orientation, manifest in his works from 1916 to *The Plumed Serpent*, begins to make itself felt—namely the transition from the early Christian symbolism of the Foreword to *Sons and Lovers*, still present in the "Hardy" essay, to the ethnological primitivism of later works. The crisis of Rananim in 1915 marks this passage, which is noticeable in certain differences between *The Rainbow* and its sequel *Women in Love*. It is the passage from Christian imagery to the search for strange gods, coinciding with the collapse of Lawrence's short-lived attempt at social reconstruction.

A communist colony

Rananim also marks the transition from the vague but fairly orthodox English socialism of Lawrence to other political formulas closer to post-war developments. Evidence of the starting-point is found in a letter to William

Hopkin, the socialist Eastwood friend who belongs to Lawrence's ideological past. It is worth recalling here that Hopkin was a friend of Edward Carpenter, of whose early connexion with the Fellowship of the New Life Lawrence may have been aware and from whose *Intermediate Types Among Primitive Folk* (1914) he appears to have freely drawn ideas at the time.[18] Lawrence's original idea for Rananim is indeed very similar to the old phalansteric plans of the Fellowship, and not at all estranged from the themes of Carpenter's first Fabian lecture, "Civilization, its Cause and Cure".[19] He writes to propose the gathering together of "about twenty souls" who would "sail away from this world of war and squalor", in order to found

> . . . a little colony where there shall be no money but a sort of communism as far as necessaries of life go, and some real decency. It is to be a colony built up on the real decency which is in each member of the community. A community which is established upon the assumption of goodness in the members, instead of the assumption of badness.[20]

Very soon after this he writes to Ottoline a letter full of enthusiasm for "the child in [his] heart", outlining a programme evidently discussed with her during her stay at Greatham. Ottoline is to form "the nucleus of a new community which shall start a new life amongst us—a life in which the only riches is integrity of character". It seems clear towards the end of the letter that this will be a community of leaders to rule over the common herd, even if it is organized to provide for the fullest accomplishment of its own members. Was he already thinking of Ottoline as the "Dictatrix" of the community? This letter, and another in which he sees her, following suggestions of Carpenter's latest book, as "the priestess, the medium, the prophetess", as belonging to "a special type, a special race of women"—tends to suggest it.[21] The religious, prophetic element is sustained throughout the letter to the "priestess". The aim is that "each one may fulfil his own nature and deep desires to the utmost"; in the new life each one will find "ultimate satisfaction and joy . . . in the completeness of us all as one":

> Let us be good all together, instead of just in the privacy of our chambers, let us know that the intrinsic part of all of us is the best part, the believing part, the passionate, generous part. We can all come croppers, but what does it matter? We can laugh at each other, and dislike each other, but the good remains and we know it. And the new community shall be established upon the known, eternal good part in us. This present community consists, as far as it is a framed thing, in a myriad contrivances for preventing us from being let down by the meanness in ourselves or in our neighbours . . . I hold this the most sacred duty—the gathering together of a number of people who shall so agree to live by the *best* they know, that they shall be *free* to live by the best they know. The ideal, the religion, must now be *lived, practised*. We will have

no more churches. We will bring church and house and shop together . . . It is no good plastering and tinkering with this community. Every strong soul must put off its connection with this society, its vanity and chiefly its fear, and go naked with its fellows, weaponless, armourless, without shield or spear, but only with naked hands and open eyes. Not self-sacrifice, but fulfilment, the flesh and the spirit in league together not in arms against one another. And each man shall know that he is part of the greater body, each man shall submit that his own soul is not supreme even to himself. "To be or not to be" is no longer the question. The question now is, how shall we fulfil our declaration, "God is"? For all our life is now based on the assumption that God is not—or except on rare occasions.

Having admitted the necessity of going "very, very carefully at first", the "great serpent" to destroy being the will to power, personal magnetism, the desire to save one's own soul, this extraordinary epistle continues by a definition of the role of the new aristocrats:

It is Communism based, not on poverty but on riches, not on humility but on pride, not on sacrifice but *upon complete fulfilment in the flesh of all strong desire, not in Heaven but on earth. We will be Sons of God who walk here on earth,* not bent on getting and having, because we know we inherit all things. We will be aristocrats, and as wise as the serpent in dealing with the mob. For the mob shall not crush us nor starve us nor cry us to death. We will deal cunningly with the mob, the greedy soul, we will gradually bring it to subjection. *We will found an order, and we will all be Princes, as the angels are.*[22] [*Italics added.*]

Such was to be the New Jerusalem, the Order of St John: that it was no mere fantasy is attested by the fact that Lawrence then spent some time elaborating a long Constitution of his community, and gave it to his lawyer friend Campbell to study and comment upon. Campbell put it aside, forgot it, and finally lost it altogether. The question arises here, and is taken up below, whether or not he may have based this draft on a model such as the Constitution of Oneida. The only thing which is certain is that the role of women was to be important: an undated letter to Campbell, certainly written before February 1915, stated that for Rananim, "this thing at which I stutter so damnably", Lawrence wanted

. . . to form a league—you and Murry and me and perhaps Forster—and our women—and anyone who will be added on to us—so long as we are centred around a core of reality, and carried on one impulse.[23]

Forster was then still thought to be redeemable.

The sex element in this religious community under the aegis of early Christianity was not outspokenly emphasized in those first letters, and indeed remains throughout important though ambiguous. A prominent feature of the correspondence bears on the necessity of achieving sexual adjustment before any social reform can succeed. This is always characteristically associated with religious symbolism and the themes of crucifixion and resurrection. Those are the days when Lawrence identifies himself with Christ, in more than poetic image, so it would seem: he writes to Cynthia Asquith that he has risen from the dead; symbol and reality fuse into one idea, he has indeed become the Messiah. Not long before this he had written Campbell a long letter on Christian symbols, largely inspired by Mrs Jenner's little book *Christian Symbolism*.[24] In it he spoke of the Father and the Hierarchies of Angels, of "the mutual love of the Father and the Son" from which "proceeds the Holy Ghost, the Reconciler, the Comforter, the Annunciation": in fact much the language of parts of "Study of Thomas Hardy", continuing in the style of the Foreword to *Sons and Lovers*. "It is .. a very great conception", he goes on, "which, when we feel it, satisfies one, and one is at rest . . . Give us the Resurrection after the Crucifixion."[25]

Already, a few months earlier, he had shown in another letter to Campbell the close association in his mind of a return to the origins of mankind and of his preoccupation with sex and "raw philosophy". Denying that he was in any way a Freudian, he had asserted the pre-eminence of sex in the establishment of any kind of "vision"; this applied to his art, but also to his social conceptions.

> I believe there is no getting of a vision, as you call it, before we get our sex right: before we get our souls fertilized by the female. I don't mean the feminine: I mean the female. Because life tends to take two streams, male and female, and only some female influence (not necessarily woman, but most obviously woman) can fertilize the soul of man to vision or being. Then the vision we are after, I don't know what it is, but it is something that contains awe and dread and submission, not pride or sensuous egotism and assertion. I went to the British Museum—and I know, from the Egyptian and Assyrian sculptures—what we are after. We want to realize the tremendous *non-human* quality of life—, it is wonderful. It is not the emotions, nor the personal feelings and attachments that matter. These are all only expressive, and expression has become mechanical. Behind in all are the tremendous unknown forces of life, coming unseen and unperceived as out of the desert to the Egyptians and driving us, forcing us, destroying us if we do not submit to be swept away.[26]

The same priority of "getting our sex right" is asserted on 12 February 1915 in relation to his programme of social reconstruction, in a letter to Russell following close upon a visit of E. M. Forster. As in a short passage of "Study of Thomas Hardy",[27] Lawrence then shows a new interest in sexual deviations, which he thinks are due to egotism, the "fear of life", and capitalism. He accepts that there must be an economic revolution, but he sees it neither as an end in itself, nor as the essential or primordial condition of freedom of spirit. His thoughts bear rather on the relationship of mind and body—that is to say, sex: "The freedom of the soul *within the denied body* is a sheer conceit."

"Denial of the body", it is clear from the context, consists for him in being unable to "take a woman" in order to be "up against the unknown". "Going to a woman" is for Lawrence the first and fundamental social act, an act of self-discovery and discovery of humanity. Inability to love a woman amounts to a refusal of the social challenge:

> And a man prefers to have nothing to do with a woman than to have to slink away without answering the challenge. Or if he be a mean souled man, he will use the woman to masterbate himself [*sic*].[28]

So the sexual connexion, if properly approached, is an answer to a challenge:

> So then, how shall I come to a woman? To know myself first. Well and good. But knowing myself is only preparing myself. What for? For the adventure into the unexplored, the woman, the whatever-it-is I am up against.[29]

"Shame" comes from refusing the spiritual adventure, from treating the sex experience like "a curio-hunter", or selfishly only "repeating the experience" in order to "get a sensation":

> This is what nearly *all* English people now do. When a man takes a woman, he is *merely* repeating a known reaction upon himself, not seeking a new reaction, a discovery. And this is like self-abuse or masterbation. The ordinary Englishman of the educated class goes to a woman now to masterbate himself. Because he is not going for discovery or new connection or progress, but only to repeat upon himself a known reaction.
>
> When this condition arrives, there is always Sodomy. The man goes to the man to repeat this reaction upon himself. It is a nearer form of masterbation. But still it has some *object*—there are still two bodies instead of one.[30]

In the letters which refer most directly to the complex theme of Rananim, we thus find Lawrence preoccupied simultaneously with the setting up of a community of the elect, and with some form of personal salvation or resurrection or rebirth connected with sexual adjustment, his favourite themes relating to early Christian doctrine. Many would put down his remarks on sex and shame merely to his sexual obsession. The question which arises, however, is whether or not they relate to a general scheme or system for which he might have found precedents in the works of other writers.

An American precedent: Oneida

The first name that springs to mind is Carpenter, whose share in the foundation of a perfectionist community, the Fellowship of the New Life, in 1883, may have been known to him through W. E. Hopkin. Through its principal founder Thomas Davidson, the Fellowship, the Constitution of which, *Vita Nuova*, had many features borrowed from American communist societies, had links with New England and the ethical societies which still flourished there towards the end of the nineteenth century.

Lawrence's Rananim may have been indebted to New England. In a letter to Edward Nehls written in 1952, Aldington stressed the spiritual affinities between Lawrence and Hilda Doolittle. Unfortunately he sees this as a matter of heredity rather than searching for clues to the passing on of ideas. "The New England type", he says, "is your clue to Lawrence, who came from much the same stock":

> . . . note how proud he was at having been brought up in Oliver Cromwell's sect, the Congregationalists . . . H.D. and L. had the same passion for flowers and used them as symbols for beauty. Of course, behind both is the ancient Norse-Teuton-Saxon strain, hating big cities, and crazy about ideal little "communities". I was always having to crawfish out of the schemes for them.[31]

This at least suggests that Lawrence did discuss New England communities with his American friend H.D.

Supposing he "documented" himself on them, where would he find most information? It is not clear when he first read Hawthorne's *Blithedale Romance*, which takes place at Brook Farm, one of the many American socialistic ventures. Allusions to Brook Farm in the *Studies in Classic American Literature* were possibly written after 1922. But in the earlier version of the Hawthorne essay in *The Symbolic Meaning*, he speaks of Brook Farm in terms suggesting that as early as 1917 he had pondered on the psychological motivations of the foundation of American socialist communities.[32]

Two American books are the most informative. One is the result of an inquiry conducted by Charles Nordhoff and published in 1875 under the title *The Communistic Societies of the United States*. The other, in some ways more enlightening on their ideas, their history, and the causes of their failures, is John Humphrey Noyes's *History of American Socialisms* (1870); this remains by far the most complete and sympathetic study, and the closest in style and spirit to Lawrence's own manner. An English writer, W. H. Dixon, had also described at length in his *New America* (1867) the socialist and religious communities of the New World; in *Spiritual Wives* (1868) he had examined the romantic Germanic origins with the pietists, with Goethe and Swedenborg, of the idea of spiritual marriage as a complement to physical marriage. He had followed its applications in the polygamic American communities, especially Salt Lake City and Oneida. It is noteworthy that the trend of thought of "spiritual brides" is present in Lawrence from the "Study of Thomas Hardy" down to *The Boy in the Bush*, and that this phrase was one with which Frieda used to taunt him.

In most of those communities one notes a return to the ideals of the primitive Christian Church, often with a pietist or nonconformist bias, as well as the influence, among early socialists, of Robert Owen, and later of Fourier. In most communities the problems of sexual relations, of birth control, and of free love, or communism applied to wives, play a large part. Noyes has better than anyone else followed the evolution of the guiding ideas, their ramifications and consequences, from the early influences of Godwin, Mary Wollstonecraft and Owen, through Fourier, to the influence of Harvard Transcendentalism, of Swedenborg, and of the spiritualism of Andrew Jackson Davis. He recounts the history of New Harmony, of Channing's Brook Farm, of the Pennsylvanian communities and various Fourierist phalansteries, then of the Shakers and of Brocton. This analysis of their failures naturally leads him to an exposition of his own Bible Communism, already developed in a pamphlet of that name, as elaborated and applied in the Perfectionist community of Oneida.

While it is not possible to state definitely that Lawrence had read either the *History of American Socialisms* or the shorter doctrinal pamphlet *Bible Communism*, there are striking resemblances between his 1914-15 ideas of Rananim, and the religious and social doctrine of Noyes. This hypothesis of a direct influence of Noyes on Lawrence is strengthened by the latter's obvious preoccupation with sex, which has its counterpart in the Oneida practice of what Noyes called "Male Continence" and his insistence on the regeneration of man through "complex marriage". The probability is increased by the fact that Havelock Ellis had described favourably the Oneida sexual practics in "The Art of Love", i.e. Chapter XI of Volume Six of his *Studies in the Psychology of Sex* (1910); Carpenter makes several references to this particular passage in Ellis's book. In any case it would have been difficult for anyone to hold any conversations on either American communities or sexual matters without Oneida being discussed. H. G. Wells had also briefly described the recent history of the community in *New Worlds for Old* and in *The Future in America*. Lawrence may conceivably have become interested in the practice of male continence, since he told Compton Mackenzie in 1920 of having experienced some sense of humiliation from his inability to contain himself in order to "attain consummation simultaneously with his wife".[33]

Bible Communism

Noyes had formulated his Perfectionist creed in the little family congregationalist church where he preached at Putney, Vermont. He had combined his religious belief in the ability of man to attain moral perfection, with a Unitarian form of socialism. On the basis of these beliefs he had founded in 1847 the Perfectionist community at Oneida, at the time when Brook Farm was breaking up. It would be difficult to find among Lawrence's known or suspected reading a combination of ideas which evokes so many echoes in his 1914-15 writings as the doctrine of Bible Communism expounded by Noyes.

At least for the purposes of exposition, the doctrine stems from Christian belief, freely interpreted according to Gnostic and Swedenborgian tradition. As in the Foreword to *Sons and Lovers* and "Study of Thomas Hardy", Hebraic and early Christian theology is the starting-point. God has created man male and female in his own image. Disease and death proceed from the Devil, but by Second Birth man can be saved from sin, and death can be abolished on earth. Innumerable biblical references are used in support of Noyes's opinions, which soon lead to his exposition of what marriage will be like when the Kingdom of God is achieved on earth. St Paul is called upon to uphold the idea of "complex marriage", as in the Foreword to *Sons and Lovers* St John was invoked at the beginning of what amounted to a defence of adultery. In the Kingdom of Heaven "the institution of marriage which assigns the exclusive possession of one woman to one man, does not exist", so that it must not exist in the earthly paradise: is it not written that "all mine are thine, and all thine are mine"? Similarly, egotism "is abolished by the Gospel relation to Christ . . . the merging of self in his life; the extinguishing of the pronoun I at the spiritual center". The unredeemed self is bound up in the "I-spirit", but in the true community "reigns the We-spirit".[34] We may recall that in Lawrence's Rananim each was to find "ultimate satisfaction and joy" in "the completeness of all in one".

Having derived from St Paul[35] the idea that man must love "not by pairs, as in the world, but *en masse*", in fact "in all directions", Noyes announces that all restrictions temporarily put by the Church on love for reasons of expediency, will cease "in the final state" when the marriage system has been abolished on earth. "Sexual love is not naturally restricted to pairs." Such restriction is the cause of such evils as secret adultery, the tying together of "unmatched natures", and the sundering of those that are matched; also of sex starvation, diseases of women, "prostitution, masturbation, and licentiousness in general".

The emphasis on sex is as definite as with Lawrence: a prerequisite of the establishment on earth of the Kingdom of God is indeed "the restoration of true relations between the sexes". The attempt "to redeem man and to reorganize society" depends first of all on "reconciliation with God", and next on the bringing about of "a true union of the sexes. In other words, religion is the first subject of interest, and sexual morality the second, in the great enterprise of establishing the Kingdom of Heaven on earth."[36]

Here Noyes disagrees with Fourier, who concentrated on reforming working conditions:

> The sin-system, the marriage-system, the work-system, and the death-system, are all one, and must be abolished together. Holiness, free-love, association in labor, and immortality, constitute the chain of redemption, and must come together in their true order.[37]

He then expounds a theory of which the theme of Lawrence's "Rose of All the World" may well contain poetic echoes: the sexual relation has two "branches", the "amative" and the "propagative"; and the first is the one which answers to God's initial design, before the Fall. Woman was made by God "for social, not primarily for propagative purposes". There was no question of propagation in Eden, where "conception would have been comparatively infrequent": was it not after the Fall that God said to Eve "I will greatly multiply thy sorrow and thy conception"? The union of the sexes is divine, since "Adam was the channel specially of the life of the Father, and Eve of the life of the Son". But it need not lead to procreation, considering especially that seminal discharge weakens the male, and that maternity taxes the woman's health. On this chain of mystical arguments and pseudo-medical considerations Noyes builds up the justification of his practice of male continence, which is not fully presented in the *History* but is explained in the pamphlets *Male Continence* and *Bible Communism*.

The exercise of the amative function—i.e. sexual connexion without male orgasm or seminal discharge—becomes "the natural agency of the distribution of [the] two forms of life" represented by male and female, the Father and the Son. "Each excites and develops the divine action in the other."[38]

Thanks to this liberation of love—each member of the community being free to have sexual relations short of procreation with any of the other sex—shame disappears; "each is married to all", there is no jealousy, social reform becomes possible. Labour is equally remunerated, each doing freely as much as he can do, and work becomes attractive because men and women work freely together. The limitation of births reduces poverty and labour, "thus removing the antecedents of death".[39] Sin and shame being abolished, the curse of maternity reduced, and the curse of labour brought within bounds, the happy community sees the prospect of "arriving at the tree of life".

But the Oneida paradise is not a democracy of equals. It remains a theocracy, just as will the various communities invented by Lawrence down to "Education of the People" and *The Plumed Serpent*. Noyes formulates an important *caveat* at the end of his exposition. The new society must "look to God, not only for a Constitution, but for Presidential outlook and counsel; for a Cabinet and corps of officers". Indeed "the men who are called to usher in the Kingdom of God" must be guided "by the Spirit of God and specific manifestations of His will and policy, as were Abraham, Moses, David, Jesus Christ, Paul, etc."

> This will be called a fanatical principle, because it requires *bona fide* communication with the heavens, and displaces the sanctified maxim that "the age of miracles and inspiration is past". But it is clearly a Bible principle; and we must place it on high, above all others, as the palladium of conservatism in the introduction of the new social order.[40]

In *Bible Communism* Noyes explains more amply "how the sexual function is to be redeemed, and the relations between the sexes restored"—and uses language which is very close indeed to some of the already quoted statements in Lawrence's letter to Russell of 12 February 1915. He asserts that "the relation of male and female was the first social relation".[41] The main act of sexual intercourse is not the discharge of semen:

> Sexual intercourse, pure and simple, is the conjunction of the organs of union, and the interchange of magnetic influences, or conversation of spirits, through the medium of that conjunction.[42]

We shall find evidence of similar beliefs in Lawrence both in "Study of Thomas Hardy" and in a later letter to Russell.[43]

The reader may compare the letter of 12 February, written at the height of Lawrence's excitement over Rananim[44] with the following reasoning of Noyes: seminal discharge can be both "voluntarily withheld in sexual connection" and "be produced without sexual connection, as it is in masturbation". Neither it nor the pleasure connected with it is "essentially social, since it can be produced in solitude; it is a personal and not a dual affair". Far above such a pleasure Noyes places "the amative function—that which consists in a simple union of persons, making of twain one flesh", and giving a medium of magnetic and spiritual interchange.[45]

In contrast with this, "ordinary sexual intercourse" is "a momentary affair, terminating in exhaustion and disgust" and leading to shame; it is "properly to be classed with masturbation" and is only less injurious to health "simply because a woman is less convenient than the ordinary means of masturbation". The reader will remember Lawrence's reference to "two bodies instead of one" in the passage quoted. Noyes concludes that lovers "who use their sexual organs simply as the servants of their spiritual natures, abstaining from the procreative act . . . may enjoy the highest bliss of sexual fellowship for any length of time, and from day to day, without satiety or exhaustion".[46]

A summary of similarities

This analysis of the doctrines of Noyes reveals striking similarities both in general preoccupations and in ideas and language. Whether or not Lawrence ever became an adept of "amative" intercourse, beyond the expression of ideas found in the poem "Rose of All the World", it might be worth while studying in detail his references to "frictional" love, to repetitive and reactive sex, in the works of that period, to see whether contexts suggest any other points of comparison with Noyes. This does seem to be the case for the letter to Russell dealing with the pre-eminent role of sex in social reconstruction. The vitalistic attitude, the assimilation of sex with religion, are very much the same, just as the Christian symbolism of the early texts on Rananim, the references to St John and the New Jerusalem, recall Noyes's biblical references and argument based on the Gospels and the primitive Church.

Lawrence's dream also runs parallel to that of the founder of Oneida when they both aim at a small integrated socialist community which will "bring church and house and shop together". They both want to fight egotism and the separate *I*, to assert the We-spirit; both are after "complete fulfilment in the flesh of every strong desire"; both want an earthly paradise, a community of free men and women who will be like angels, "Sons of God who walk the earth". Lawrence remains a pioneer, like Noyes, of a system of thought theocratic rather than humanistic. And there are concordant details as well: the principle of mutual criticism, as applied by Noyes at the Oneida daily meeting, is echoed in Lawrence when he admits that his "angels" can "laugh at each other", but that "the good remains as we know it" and that by this process of mutual criticism they will build their community on "the known, eternal good part of us", upon the statement "God is". Like the Perfectionists, he also wants to live *now* according to his redeeming faith, i.e. to create the Earthly Paradise.

The theocratic, authoritarian doctrine of divine counsel received by the leaders of the community, the "fanatical principle" enunciated by Noyes, also seems to find an echo in the last paragraph, quoted above, of the 1 February letter to Ottoline, in which the "Princes" will "bring [the mob] to subjection". Even the Oneida practice of having a leader for the men, Noyes, and one for the women, Mary Cragin, has its parallel in later letters where Lawrence decides there shall be a Dictator, himself, and also a "Dictatrix", probably Ottoline, who shall control "the things relating to private life".[47] The aspiring Dictator feels directly inspired by God: "It is not *I* who matter—it is what is said through me," he writes to Barbara Low.[48]

The end of Rananim

The dream of Rananim, even when it approaches the field of action in England, is thus closely linked to the messianic tendencies which, having developed in Lawrence between the end of 1912 and the war, reached their climax about the time of the final writing of *The Rainbow*. During those months, and until Russell suggested some other reading, he remained obsessed by themes derived from Christian symbolism mixed with his own sexual symbolism and personal search for sexual values. As the idea of the new community was put to the test of planning social reform for England, the inadequacies of the poetic imagination to cope with political and economic realities must have become clear to his new friends if not to himself. This climax is in fact the turning point, the beginning of the bitter quarrel with Russell, and of the disappointments of 1915.

Under Russell's guidance Lawrence soon turned to other primitives than the early Christians; to begin with he read Burnet's *Early Greek Philosophy*. By then he had begun to realize that he was unable to communicate his personal vision:

> Sometimes I am afraid of the terrible things that are real, in the darkness, and of the entire unreality of these things I see . . . The subterranean black universe of the things which have not yet had being has conquered for me now, and I can't escape. So I think with fear of having to talk to anybody, because I can't talk.[49]

> My world is real, it is a true world, and it is a world I have in my measure understood. But no doubt you also have a true world, which I can't understand.[50]

And the seer strove to understand the world of Russell the thinker, to incorporate into his own mental universe other interpretations than those of Christian mysticism which had supplied a structure to the vision during the winter of 1914–15:

> I shall write all my philosophy again. Last time I came out of the Christian Camp. This time I must come out of these early Greek philosophers.[51]

> I have been wrong, much too Christian, in my philosophy. These early Greeks have clarified my soul. I must drop all about God. You must drop all your democracy . . . I am rid of all my Christian religiosity. It was only muddiness. You need not mistrust me.[52]

Soon he will turn to *The Golden Bough* and to *Totemism and Exogamy*, listed in Burnet's footnotes: he was ready to move on to other reading, some more scientific, some more alluring, exercising the fascination for his poetic mind of magic and of symbolic fantasy.

Whatever its "sources", Rananim is certainly central to his desperate search for completeness of being, for a system that could reconcile his dualism, justify his emotions to his own judgment. The failure to translate the idea of Rananim into political action, the estrangement from new friends, contributed to the bitterness of 1916. In a way there were by then two Lawrences: the poet and prophet who expressed his meaning in esoteric "philosophy", poetry and novels; and the ordinary man, mostly isolated in a savage solitude from which he emerged only to curse mankind. Rananim by then had become a mere game, which he pretended to treat lightly, or a brotherhood from which he excluded people in bitter disapproval after first considering them for adoption. The search for disciples went on, but without the early self-confidence of the self-appointed redeemer of mankind.

John Middleton Murry: a comedy of errors

At one time Lawrence's relations with John Middleton Murry bade fair to become a major theme of the literary history of the early 1900s. They are best seen in the perspective of the preceding pages and of Lawrence's relations with Russell. It was an intermittent friendship, constantly renewed by vague ideas of joint action. Tendentious affirmations were made on both sides, for both men sought to escape blame for a failure wounding to their pride as writers and as would-be apostles. The episodic jealousies between the two couples, the complexity of relationships with one another and with others, have tended to embitter quarrels of interest mainly in so far as they served as models for certain scenes of *Women in Love* and *Aaron's Rod*.

Murry has given his version in his *Journal*, in two works devoted to Lawrence and in *Between Two Worlds*. His biographer, F. A. Lea,[53] has told the whole story, or at least as much of it as matters: the mutual sympathy springing up between two illicit couples; the feeling shared by both men of being excluded by their social origins from those upper-class and literary circles with which their talent brought them into contact; Murry's sexual naïveté compared with Katherine's experience, Lawrence's concern for Murry culminating on the day when Katherine, drunk, and on the point of leaving Murry to rejoin Francis Carco, responded publicly at the Cannans' to the advances of an equally drunken Gertler. The whole story is sufficiently well documented to call for no more than an attempt at interpretation.

Up to 1919, two episodes stand out. In February 1915, after Katherine's desertion, Murry arrived ill at the Greatham cottage, at the height of Lawrence's great mystic crisis over Rananim. He was nursed by Lawrence, as, in *Aaron's Rod*, the hero was to be nursed by Lilly.[54] Did Lawrence's motherly care for Murry lead to a possessive passion in the true maternal tradition? At any rate he sowed seeds of jealousy in Murry's mind: Katherine had left him, Lawrence said, because of Jack's friendship for Campbell, because of her resentment at their interminable "confabulations" over Dostoevsky, then one of Lawrence's great bugbears, archetype of the sin of egotism and of "reduction" of the self. He also told Murry that Campbell had confided to him a week before that these "intellectual probings" between himself and Murry were "the most regrettable part" of each of them. This was a clear attempt to isolate Murry by dealing a swift right and left at the two objects of his love and friendship; after which Murry could turn only to Lawrence. That he almost succeeded is admitted by Murry: "From that time onwards whatever capacity I possessed for affection towards a man was turned towards Lawrence himself." "And that, I suppose," concludes Murry, "was what he wanted."

Lawrence was, then, convinced he had drawn Murry into his revolutionary camp, whereas during the previous autumn he had felt a certain reticence similar to that shown by Campbell and Marsh in April 1914.[55] Murry was quite ready to accept Lawrence the man, and Lawrence the writer, but he rejected Lawrence the prophet, whose "thought and writing had begun to be incomprehensible" to him. At the same time he had a deep need for affection. In expounding his ideas on social and economic reform Lawrence combined the messianic and the personal in an appeal Murry failed to understand, suggesting that he, Lawrence, was a forerunner, and that Murry was in some way destined to succeed him, "to build up the temple" if Lawrence "carved out the way".[56]

At such moments, possibly retrospectively echoing Frieda, Murry says he felt "like a woman instinctively humouring her husband by accepting his arguments and principles, although in fact they are quite indifferent to her";[57] whereas Lawrence, shrinking from the idea of having to go out and win men's allegiance, seemed to count on Murry to apprehend and interpret his ideas. For the sake of the "personal bond" between them, which he supposed "far more valuable" to himself than to Lawrence, Murry acquiesced, though well aware of the insincerity inherent in such submission.[58] In Son of Woman[59] he shows his total failure to understand Lawrence's mystic doctrine of unity with God, triumphing over the dualism of human nature. He saw Lawrence as a fallible, at times almost a demented, person. He could make sense of his friend's ideas on resurrection and love only in relation to Lawrence's personal experience of love and sex, which he himself did not understand, let alone admitting the desirability of its general application. He thought the love struggle of Will and Anna in The Rainbow, inspired by that of Lawrence and Frieda, was intended as a shining example, whereas for Lawrence it is an illustration of the many earthly imperfections to be overcome by those who seek but fail to find redemption. Inspired visionary or near-paranoiac, Lawrence was at all events quite unable to communicate to his chosen disciple tne splendour and inspiration of his own mystic vision. The disciple could only acquiesce uncomprehendingly. He was convinced that Frieda had an execrable influence on Lawrence:

> Whenever Frieda announced to us that something which Lawrence was writing was magnificent and wonderful, our hearts promptly sank; when, in Lawrence's presence and with his evident approval, she told us that such and such a chapter was really hers, we felt uncomfortable, and in secret sighed and shook our heads. Was sex really so important, could it be? Or was it important in that particular way?[60]

Their short-lived collaboration in *The Signature*, their desultory attempt to organize meetings in London, their projected co-operative publishing venture in 1916, are only minor incidents in the stormy course of their relationship. *Reflections on the Death of a Porcupine* (1925) contains Lawrence's disillusioned and tendentious version of this abortive collaboration.[61] The spiteful "Note to the Crown" no doubt reflects the festering of the wound inflicted ten years earlier and aggravated by the intermittent affair between Murry and Frieda which began in 1923.

A further instalment of this tale of repeated misapprehension took place in Cornwall in 1916 and was once more amply documented by the two protagonists.[62] Only one aspect of this episode is of any real interest: Lawrence's psychological attitude in regard to Murry. After his Porthcothan illness, Lawrence was evidently in one of his periods of deep depression. The Murrys were embarrassed by the violence of his quarrels with Frieda, and Katherine had taken a dislike to the wild Cornish countryside. Lawrence repeated to Murry the offer of *Blutbrüderschaft* already made to Russell and refused by him. He had recently been reading Frazer, and was showing interest in primitive man; Carpenter's *Intermediate Types* and *The Intermediate Sex* had probably renewed his interest in male comradeship, and he had fresh in his mind the friendship rites practised by the Polynesian Queequeg in *Moby Dick*. He seemed to want to proceed to some ritual destined to consecrate his friendship with Murry. Exactly what form of ritual, Murry had no idea; he seems to have reacted in true public schoolboy style to Lawrence's wild suggestion that "their blood should mingle".

In the strange wrestling scene between Birkin and Gerald in *Women in Love*, Murry later saw an image of what Lawrence was seeking. This scene is certainly most ambiguous, especially in the light of the Prologue to *Women in Love*. It is possible to see in it a symbolic figuration of the free and glad acceptance of all desires, such as was advocated by Edward Carpenter.[63] That is to say, Birkin accepting his own body and self absolutely without reserve and without any *fear* of homosexuality: the episode is otherwise almost meaningless. Murry admits to not having understood. He may well have feared, as Gerald does in the wrestling scene, the manifestations of Lawrence's love, on which the Prologue throws more light. In this uncomprehending state, he assured Lawrence of his love, telling him he saw no need of any kind of sacrament, and received the vehement response: "I hate your love, I hate it."[64] Like Gerald he had failed in the test on his sincerity.

He demonstrates this again in his attempted explanation in *Between Two Worlds*, when he never rises above a personal, commonplace level. Lawrence, however equivocal his attitude, seems to have been convinced that he was acting on a higher level of sanctity and search for the "tree of life". How much evasion of the true emotional issues there was on either side is a matter for speculation. The pattern is no doubt to be found in the almost pathological hesitations of Birkin between Gerald and Ursula. Lawrence was probably seeking a world of men from which women were momentarily excluded, except Frieda, already turned into the Great Mother.

The curious structure of this conception, Murry goes on, is evident:

> The foundation of it all is the relation between Lawrence and Frieda. That is, as it were, the ultimate reality. That foundation secure, Lawrence needs or desires a further relation with me, in which Katherine is temporarily but totally ignored. By virtue of this "mystical" relation with Lawrence, I participate in this premental reality, the "dark sources" of my being come alive. From this changed personality, I, in turn, enter a new relation with Katherine.[65]

In the face of Murry's embarrassment and empty protestations, Lawrence's mystical call for absolute sympathy and trust fell flat. It is easy to see how, seized with delirium as on the occasion of Birrell's visit to Greatham, and probably for similar reasons, Lawrence cried out in the night accusing Murry of being "an obscene bug" sucking his life away.[66] For Lawrence insects were the symbol of narrow, constricted selves, prisoners of their own egotism, incapable of giving themselves spontaneously. On the other hand, Murry's reservations in the face of what seemed to him demential or equivocal demands are equally comprehensible.

Bertrand Russell: opposition to the war and social reform

Lawrence's short friendship with Bertrand Russell was a far more significant factor in his long-term evolution. Begun under the double sign of Ottoline, then Russell's mistress, and of opposition to the war, it ended with the simultaneous discovery by both men of the mental chasm which divided them. Both, however, remained conscious that it had brought them something.

Ottoline introduced them to each other, and, because she admired them both, made them think that they should therefore admire each other.[67]

They were drawn together by a common opposition to the war, which Russell regarded as a criminal folly. A partisan of English neutrality, which, according to him, would have assured that early German victory of which he enumerates the advantages in *Portraits from Memory*, Russell maintained not only that progressive forces in the Kaiser's Germany had every chance of succeeding, but that there was "more freedom in the Kaiser's Germany than in any country in the world now [1965], with the exception of Great Britain and the Scandinavian countries".[68] In Lawrence's attitude towards the war he detected two factors: he could not be wholeheartedly patriotic because his wife was German; on the other hand, he had such a hatred of mankind that he tended to think that both sides were right in so far as they hated each other.[69] Lawrence saw in the war a vital mystical impulse towards a "waste and squandering of life", the aim of which was "to prove that we are not altogether sealed in our own self-preservation as dying chrysalids". Man goes to war because he "cannot live", he "cannot *be*", because he needs "sensation", and "perhaps, after all, the value of life is in death".[70] He discovered in himself what he abhorred in others, "a deep and total satisfaction" at the thought of war. Thus while Russell's attitude was in the tradition of Condorcet and Godwin, Lawrence was nearer to Joseph de Maistre, or to the Shelley of *Prometheus Unbound*. Whereas Russell believed in democracy, Lawrence sought to found a republic in which the freedom of the slaves was immaterial, as it had been to Plato. His sole preoccupation was, in fact, to save the souls of the elect.

It took them nearly eight months fully to realize the irremediable incompatibility of their points of view. Lawrence was flattered by the attention of the mathematician and philosopher. He was greatly impressed by the social and academic standing of this "Fellow of Cambridge University [*sic*], F.R.S., Earl Russell's brother". When Russell invited him to Trinity to meet J. M. Keynes, Lowes Dickinson, and G. E. Moore, he felt "frightfully important", "horribly intimidated", and inquired whether he should "bring an evening suit".[71]

Unaccustomed to discussing ideas with his intellectual equals, Lawrence was afraid of seeming impertinent, and he treated Russell with a certain deference to his intellectual achievement; he admits to being "saddened" by a feeling that Russell was sometimes "tolerant"—no doubt he dared not say condescending—when listening to his ideas. Russell "liked Lawrence's fire", shared his conviction "that something very fundamental was needed to put the world right", and agreed with him "in thinking that politics could not be divorced from individual psychology". Above all, he recognized the power of his "imaginative genius" and even when "inclined to disagree with him" thought his insight into human nature deeper than his own.[72]

It is in his letters to Russell that Lawrence has expressed the essence of a political and social ideology, in some respects very rudimentary, the more psychologically stable elements of which are also to be found in the "Study of Thomas Hardy", "The Crown", and later, with certain post-war ideas incorporated, in *Aaron's Rod*, *Kangaroo*, and even *The Plumed Serpent*. His analysis of economic problems was that of an early nineteenth-century socialist, embellished with a few ideas derived from Ruskin and William Morris: the machine, a means of production devoid of artistic value, can serve to reduce man's labour but must not serve the unrestricted appetites of the few.[73] The State was for him a "vulgar institution" and life itself "an affair of aristocrats". His revolutionary motto was *Fierté, Inégalité, Hostilité*.[74] The "solution" of the economic question, unfortunately necessary to achieve "real life", lay in the nationalizing "in one fell blow" of industries, means of communication, land and public amusements, and in paying a man his wages, "whether he is sick or well or old", which, concluded Lawrence, "practically solves the economic question for the moment".[75] In fact, economics held no interest for him: what he wanted was to make it possible for everyone to "create the work of art, the living man, achieve that piece of supreme art, a man's life".[76]

His visit to Cambridge, just as he was embarking on rewriting his "Study of Thomas Hardy", under the title "Le Gai Savaire" (a play upon the words "*Le gai savoir*", The Gay Saver or Saviour), was catastrophic: neither Lawrence nor the philosopher G. E. Moore, next to whom he was placed at dinner in Trinity, could find anything to say to each other. After dinner Lawrence seems to have been somewhat more forthcoming with the mathematician G. H. Hardy, but at breakfast the next day, in Russell's rooms, Keynes found him "morose" and silent, apart from "indefinite expressions of irritable dissent", despite all efforts of his host and Keynes to get him to join in the conversation.[77] Back in Greatham, Lawrence confided to Frieda his disappointment:

> Well, in the evening they drank port and they walked up and down the room and talked about the Balkan situation and things like that, and they know nothing about it.[78]

The cold, intellectual atmosphere of Cambridge, so he told Russell a few days later, had made him "very black and down",[79] though he admitted to being very much interested "in God and the devil, particularly the devil—and in immortality"—the very themes of his "philosophy", Le Gai Saver. Lawrence then pursued his ideas of political and social reform simultaneously with the writing of his "philosophy", but almost at once these ideas began to take a turn incompatible with those of Russell: he began to assert that his reasoning came "from the knowledge of God and the truth",[80] recommending to Russell "entire separation" from the social body, exhorting him to leave Cambridge forthwith, and refusing to acknowledge the existence of more than five or six of his own "peers" in the whole world.[81] They met once more to prepare a joint series of lectures to be given in the following autumn: the war was bound to end in a conflict between labour and capital, and it was essential that "real leaders" should come forward to prevent the revolution from degenerating into "another French Revolution muddle". Neither labour nor capital must be allowed to seize power. While yielding to Russell on religion, Lawrence insisted on having his own way on the subject of democracy:

> You must drop all your democracy. You must not believe in "the people". One class is no better than another. It must be a case of Wisdom, or Truth. Let the working classes be working classes. That is the truth. There must be an aristocracy of people who have wisdom, and there must be a Ruler: a Kaiser: no Presidents and democracies.[82]

His slogan is taken (misspelled) from Heraclitus, quoted by John Burnet: "And it is law too to obey the Council [Counsel] of one."[83] His new State, in which he wished to interest Shaw and the editor of *The New Age*, A. R. Orage, was to have as its aim "The highest good of the soul, of the individual, the fulfilment in the Infinite, in the Absolute."[84]

What he wanted was "wholeness of movement, Unanimity of Purpose, Oneness in Construction", an echo, perhaps, of Jane Harrison's remarks on Unanimism,[85] but a foretaste of much fascist and "integrationist" literature. The "great falsity of subjectivitism" on which the State is based had to be killed at the root. Russell protested, but Lawrence returned to the charge: the electoral law must be utterly revised: "The working man shall elect superiors for the things that concern him immediately and no more. From the other classes, as they rise, shall be elected the higher governors." This corporatist State must culminate in one man: "No foolish republics with foolish presidents, but an elected King, something like Julius Caesar." Like Mary Wollstonecraft he believed that women must take part in political life: but for him there was to be "a rising rank of women governors, as of men, culminating in a woman Dictator, of equal authority with the supreme man". "The whole thing" must be living, but, above all, "there must be no democratic control—that is the worst of all. There must be an elected aristocracy."[86]

The question where, if anywhere, Lawrence may have picked up the germs of a corporatist ideology which led others to Fascism and Nazism is still obscure. While such an ideology recalls the anti-humanitarianist ideas of Houston Chamberlain, it has not so far been traceable to any definite source. It is of course not very different from the political doctrine expressed in the *caveat* in Noyes's *History of American Socialisms*. Russell and Ottoline at any rate seem to have reacted strongly, for on 3 September Lawrence felt "a bitterness in his soul", as if they had turned traitor. "They say I cannot think."[87] In July, he had already violently accused Russell of inexperience "in matters of life and emotion". The trouble between Frieda and Ottoline had grown worse. Ottoline had sent Russell to try to separate Lawrence from Frieda, who reached the point of wondering whether she should not withdraw in favour of Ottoline for the sake of England.[88] Lawrence sensed that his relationship with Russell had entered a "winter" phase and that the time had come for them to part "for a little while".[89] Next came an open breach, Lawrence charging Russell with total insincerity, with being "really the super-war-spirit" and "full of repressed desires, which have become savage and anti-social". Since Russell was "the enemy of all mankind", he concluded, "better we become strangers again".[90]

Despite this decision, Lawrence still seemed to find pleasure in denouncing Russell and for some months continued "to write letters containing sufficient friendliness to keep the correspondence alive". In the end their association "faded away without any dramatic termination". While Lawrence later scored off Russell by caricaturing him as Sir Joshua Matheson in *Women in Love*, Russell lived long enough to win the last round by denouncing Lawrence's political ideas of "blood consciousness" as distinct from mental consciousness, as a doctrine which "though I did not know it then . . . led straight to Auschwitz".[91] Russell does not seem to have been aware of the probable origin of certain of Lawrence's ideas on blood and race which did, indeed, lead others straight to Auschwitz. Or if he did, he attached no importance to it. H. S. Chamberlain was at this time a natural ally of the English pacifists, since he, like themselves, accused England of commercial imperialism; it was only much later that the dangers of his mystic racialism and anti-humanitarian doctrine became apparent.

All along, Russell was struck by the purely verbal character of Lawrence's affirmations: he had, Russell observed, "no real wish to make the world better, but only to indulge in eloquent soliloquy about how bad it was".

Lawrence's relations with E. M. Forster were even shorter-lived. After two visits to Greatham, Forster, a man of far greater tact than most of his literary contemporaries in 1915, was embarrassed by the Lawrences' brutal frankness and total lack of discretion, and deliberately disappeared from their lives, though not before evoking from the great reformer of humanity a number of extremely hostile and censorious remarks.[92] The gossip, the petty jealousies, the *chassés-croisés* of their Greatham circle were evidently little to his taste, and complex marriage held no more attraction for him than the ordinary brand.

Lawrence had originally been attracted to Forster as to Russell and other Cambridge figures by their common opposition to the war; such friendships, however, failed to survive the test of a fundamental incompatibility of minds and personalities. A democratic conception of social progress lay at the root of the anti-war convictions of Russell the liberal as of Forster the humanist. As Aldington, Murry and Russell all came to understand, Lawrence in fact did not condemn war as such. His reactions were instinctive, and the justification he subsequently sought for them was reached *a posteriori*, not based on any social considerations but on a superhuman and entirely pre-mental plane. The war actually satisfied that Nietzschean nostalgia for tragedy and catastrophe which he shared with Frieda. He perceived in it an expression of an eternal curse inflicted on man, from which only a chosen few could escape. He was, in fact, a prisoner of his own idea of Grace. For him the war became part of his own dualist universe, and was accepted by him as a permanent condition of that dualism.

Russell, like Forster, also perceived the authoritarian and egoistic nature of his ideas, which he stresses in *Portraits from Memory*: in his dreams, as several letters show, Lawrence saw himself as Caesar; he would accept direction from no one, he believed he was the direct interpreter of God's intentions for the benefit of mankind.[92a] Between 1914 and the end of 1915 he lived through a great visionary crisis, but failed in his effort to relate this vision to any possibility of direct action upon men. Male companionship became more and more difficult to achieve; his messianism inspired only minor saints, and his own tragic isolation became more and more apparent.

Some minor apostles

Several new friendships burgeoned in the autumn of 1915, at the time of the *Rainbow* crisis: potential recruits for the colony of the elect in America followed one another in quick succession during the fateful weeks when Lawrence continued to hope against hope. The poet Robert Nichols, home from the front, was sensitive to his strange charm, but refused to capitulate, deploring Lawrence's "obsession" and "obscurity". Nichols's friend Philip Heseltine, who was later to achieve high recognition as the composer Peter Warlock, before a tragic suicide in 1930, was a great admirer of *Sons and Lovers*. He met Lawrence in November 1915, at the age of twenty-one, at once becoming an enthusiast for the "colony of escape". He immediately tried to persuade the composer Delius to provide a home for Rananim in an orange grove he owned in Florida. According to Lawrence, Lady Cynthia Asquith and her sons were also to be in the party, perhaps without her husband. The idea was evidently to people the colony with members of both sexes grouped in happy couples, for Lawrence and Frieda seem to have tried to marry off both Robert Nichols and Heseltine. Aldous Huxley, also aged twenty-one, whom Lawrence met at the Morrells', at once received and accepted an invitation to join the Rananim party: luckily for the course of a friendship which blossomed many years later, his undertaking was not put to the test and he subsequently chose a wife for himself in the person of Maria Nys, a Belgian refugee living at Garsington Manor, while his brother Julian married Juliette Baillot, Swiss "Mademoiselle" at Garsington, later to figure as the Fräulein of *Women in Love*.[93]

Armed with a medical certificate declaring him unfit for military service, Heseltine followed the Lawrences to Cornwall, where he was joined by his friend Kouyoumdjian, the future novelist Michael Arlen. Conscious of the "utterly wild and irresponsible nature of the enterprise, unthinkable to the cautious", Heseltine nevertheless felt he must plunge into a "whirlpool of alternating excitement and depression". By 6 January, his enthusiasm had already waned: Lawrence had become "hard and autocratic in his views and outlook". Heseltine's letters to Delius are full of images and symbols from "Study of Thomas Hardy" and "The Crown", in spite of his reserve concerning Lawrence's "metaphysical" aspect. He also seriously envisaged setting up a publishing firm, The Rainbow Books and Music, specializing in private printing and circulation, its first proposed publication being *The Rainbow*, and the second "Mr Lawrence's philosophical work, *Goats and Compasses*".[94]

Lawrence introduced Heseltine to Ottoline, though judging him "backboneless" and in need of "stiffening up". He appears to have been greatly preoccupied with his young friend's love-life, in which he meddled quite unwarrantably in his letters to Ottoline. Her gossip, combined with that of Frieda, and the Murrys' jealousy at Heseltine's sudden intrusion into the proposed co-operative publishing venture, made matters worse. After a short stay at Higher Tregerthen, Heseltine concluded that though Lawrence was "a fine artist and a hard, though horribly distorted thinker", any personal relationship with him was impossible—"he acts as a subtle and deadly poison". His attempt to have out with Lawrence the reasons for the breach in their friendship was met by the odd request "Do not talk about me in London."

In fact the break seems to have concerned Heseltine's relationship with Minnie Channing, who shares with Dora Carrington the doubtful honour of having served as model for Minette in *Women in Love*. Heseltine left for Ireland, subsequently marrying Minnie Channing. In 1917 he returned to Zennor where he "re-established friendly relations with Lawrence".[95]

Lawrence's 1916 quarrel with Murry took place soon after his first break with Heseltine, to whom he had at one point suggested "the fantastic project that all five should live together as one happy family". After this, the only remaining disciple in Cornwall was Cecil Gray, whose biography of Peter Warlock leaves no doubt to what extent he shared his friend's final judgment on Lawrence. His relationship with the couple, close and friendly at first, became more complicated when, in 1917 and 1918, Gray clearly sided with Frieda against Lawrence.[96] At this time Gray's life was intimately linked with that of the Aldingtons, and the complexities of the relations between himself and Frieda, Aldington and his wife Hilda Doolittle, Hilda and Lawrence, Aldington and Dorothy Yorke, can be read between the lines in such letters as are published. It is therefore not surprising to find Gray and Hilda suddenly figuring together in 1917 among the latest recruits for Rananim. Musician and musicographer, Gray (1895–1951) was a relatively objective witness of Lawrence's life in Cornwall. He was never profoundly influenced by the writer's tormented personality, and has passed severe judgment on his inability to make and keep friends.

Back to the land

Gray was Lawrence's neighbour at the time of his still unexplained friendship for the young Cornish farmer William Henry Hocking, an episode of which the true version may possibly be that given by Lawrence in *Kangaroo*. Why then did he give this young farmer the phallic name John Thomas when, according to his own story, his interest in the Hockings was based on no more than nostalgia for the atmosphere of Haggs Farm and the delight he took in working in the fields in the wild and primitive Cornish countryside?

> Somers loved these people. He loved the sensitiveness of their intelligence.
> They were not educated. But they had an endless curiosity about the world,
> and an endless interest in what was right.[97]

Lawrence often worked like any farm labourer, to help the Hockings with the haymaking or the harvesting. On many occasions he would go over to the farm and spend his evenings talking to William Henry or giving French lessons to his brother Stanley, leaving to her own devices Frieda, incapable as ever of coming into contact with simple people without making them feel her own superiority. Lawrence, on the contrary, found himself at once on their own level, smiling when his friend observed "You've getting more like one of us every day, Mr Lawrence."[98]

To people like Murry, Aldington and Frieda, who had never worked on a farm, this period of Lawrence's life was incomprehensible. They saw in it a kind of deliberate masochistic self-abasement, a mystic seeking after some strange pre-mental brotherhood. Frieda herself diagnosed it as the fascination Lawrence felt for the "Celtic natures" of the Hockings at a time when he was reacting against "the bit of German" in her.[99] In fact this "regressive" impulse on the part of the writer towards the simple life of his childhood was probably due to many different factors. Lawrence specifically denied to Catherine Carswell any suggestion of pederasty with William Henry. The denial is noteworthy: together with the description in the Prologue to *Women in Love*, of the attraction exercised on Birkin by dark-eyed "Cornish" types of men, it contains an element of admission. The real drama lay both in this attraction, against which Lawrence fought, and in the fierce desperation of a man who, in his most lucid moments, questioned his own sanity, and had come to the conclusion that he was wrong to try to found a colony with other people, that one must learn to live alone. Conscious of his social alienation, wounded by the failure of so many friendships, and possibly of his love for Frieda, aware of the futility of his attempts at social and moral reform, he seems to have sought refuge in farm labour and in a warm, human contact with simple, honest people, at a time when, in any case, poverty and strict rationing had led him literally to cultivate his own garden, and to rejoice in the "nice green rows" of young vegetables William Henry helped him raise, which sometimes looked to him, amid the surrounding gloom, "like a triumph of life itself".[100]

The faithful few: Gertler, Koteliansky

This rapid succession of friendships and quarrels had by 1918-19 reduced Lawrence to almost total isolation. The enthusiastic welcome he extended to each new disciple was almost invariably succeeded by disillusionment on his part, and prudent withdrawal on the part of those approaching him too closely. Not even Richard Aldington could wholly stomach the gratuitously offensive remarks made in Lawrence's letters during H.D.'s stay with Cecil Gray at Bosigran. It is almost as if Lawrence wanted to isolate himself, to cut himself off from the world: writing to one person concerning his plans and at the same time begging his correspondent not to mention them to others, as if afraid people were discussing him behind his back. References to the colony of the blessed were reduced to a kind of incantation. The list of participants alone changed, and sometimes "other people" were excluded altogether: "I am willing to give up people—they are what they are, why should they be as I want them to be," he told Koteliansky in January 1916. Rananim was quite right, he assured Catherine Carswell in November, "all save the people. It was wrong to seek adherents. One must be single." As for republics, "they are the imaginary chickens of an addled egg". He was no longer seeking redemption in men, but in the soil, the sky "which may feed a new mind in one". He believed "in Paradise and in Paradisal beings, but humanity, mankind—*crotte*!"[101]

During 1917 and 1918 new friendships or the renewal of old ones occasionally kindled fresh hope: candidates for Rananim changed from month to month: Dr and Mrs Eder, Cecil Gray, Hilda Aldington, Dorothy Yorke, Koteliansky, William Henry Hocking, Catherine Carswell and her husband, followed by Gordon Campbell, his friend Shearman, and Mark Gertler. Starting out with the idea of a colony capable of becoming a State, Lawrence came to think more in terms of a Pacific island, or a small band of friends escaping to Italy or elsewhere. Later the whole aim became evasion, escape with Frieda or alone: "I do so want to get out—out of England—really out of Europe. And I *will* get out."[102]

During these last two years of the war two faithful friends stand out:

Gertler and Koteliansky, one a young Jewish painter of Austro-Polish descent, the other a Russian Jew earning a modest living in London by his excellent translations. Both were from many points of view "outsiders", strangers on the fringe of English wartime society. Both were attractive and outstanding personalities. Both remained friends with Lawrence despite his moodiness and remarks to which others might have taken violent offence.

Gertler, youngest son of a Jewish furrier turned innkeeper at Przemysl, was born in London in 1891 on the occasion of his family's first migration, returning to live there permanently at the age of five. Brought up in the direst poverty in Shoreditch, apprenticed at sixteen to a firm of glass painters, he was able to study at the Slade School of Art thanks to the intervention of Sir William Rothenstein. Under his patronage and later that of Edward Marsh, he became an important painter of his generation. He never made money, he contracted tuberculosis, and after the war repeatedly underwent sanatorium treatment. After attempting suicide in a bout of despair in 1936, he finally succeeded in taking his own life in 1939. His unrequited love for Dora Carrington, Slade School student friend of Dorothy Brett, marked him for life, her bourgeois background making him miserably conscious of his own origins. He was deeply affected by Carrington's passion for Lytton Strachey, her marriage to Ralph Partridge and her suicide following Strachey's death. Gertler remained a tortured, maladjusted figure, seeking to drown his doubts and humiliations in drink and dissolute living. Like Lawrence, he was perpetually short of money, borrowing from benefactors or living on advances on his work, accepting also money from his own working-class family despite his growing estrangement. His fate was, in fact, sadder and more tragic than that of Lawrence, who, however, recognized something of Gertler in himself, even when analysing him mercilessly or turning him into the Loerke of *Women in Love*.

Gertler, a regular guest at the Morrells' since 1914, moved in the same world as Lawrence, but without his arrogance and sense of mission. He remained shy, reserved, never sure of himself even when producing his best works, always ready to renew his sensitive and intelligent art which, whether romantic or resolutely and harshly Post-Impressionist, always revealed the contradictions and deep conflicts of his personality.

On the whole Lawrence seems to have retained a feeling of friendly kinship with Gertler, who may have been partly responsible for launching, or at least encouraging him in, his search for a pre-mental art in Africa and Egypt. Was it not Gertler who, taken to the British Museum by Jacob Epstein in 1912, discovered an Egyptian art so wonderful that his "inspiration knew no bounds"? "Egyptian art", he concluded, "is *by far, by far, by far* the greatest of *all* art. We moderns are but ants in comparison, but ants."[103]

Two years later, Lawrence, who at this time often saw Gertler at Chesham, was re-echoing this same thought, after a visit to the British Museum, perhaps in Gertler's company.[104] It is possible that Gertler's "Creation of Eve" (1914), in which reminiscences of Blake combine with the face of a Rabbi from another of his paintings, may bear some relation to Lawrence's gnostic preoccupations of that period, as well as to Will Brangwen's efforts to sculpt a birth of Eve. In 1916, Gertler's picture "Merry-Go-Round", in which soldiers, sailors and women career madly round and round, vividly struck Lawrence's imagination. He found it "great and true", "horrible and terrifying" in its "soul-searing obscenity", which reminded him of Pompeii. For him this was the only possible form of art, "a real and ultimate revelation", and he informed the painter that he was "all absorbed in the violent and lurid processes of inner decomposition". Only a Jew could have painted such a picture: a race to whom it was left to utter "the final and great death-cry of this epoch", the Christians "not being reduced sufficiently".[105]

Did Lawrence see Gertler's first sculpture, "The Acrobats" (1917), inspired by primitive African art, before *Women in Love* was completed? Gertler was working on this in September 1916 when Frieda visited him in London in his studio.[106] From Koteliansky Lawrence received a description of this work which, even if it did not directly influence *Women in Love*, certainly demonstrates an interest in primitive art, also shared by Heseltine.[107] Gertler illustrates a common trend, an attempt to find a way out for modern art beyond the Impressionists and the Symbolists. To this extent the friendship between Lawrence and Gertler was significant and important, opening up to the writer certain new contemporary vistas. In Bloomsbury, with its relative affluence and intellectual assurance only faintly disturbed by doubt, Lawrence and Gertler, because of their working-class origins, both remained outside the pale; to which they both adopted ambiguous and essentially dualistic attitudes.

Of all the members of the Lawrence circle, Koteliansky probably possessed the greatest gift for friendship. His portrait by Gertler, Leonard Woolf's description, his representation as the Australian leader Benjamin Cooley in *Kangaroo*, all lay stress on his tall and strong figure and show him as "a remarkable and formidable man". Physically, says Leonard Woolf, he was "a Jew of the Trotsky type" with thick black bristly hair, and eyes which, from behind thick glasses, "looked at, through, and over you, sad and desperate, and yet with resigned intensity": a handshake reminiscent of the Commendatore and a delightful smile that transformed his ugly, heavy features. Born in 1882 in a ghetto village of the Ukraine, Koteliansky helped Leonard Woolf understand "what a major Hebrew prophet must have been like 3,000 years ago"; capable of absolute love for those whom he considered "real persons", but not hesitating ruthlessly to condemn all those who seemed to him false or "swindlers".[108]

Koteliansky had come to London with a scholarship from the University of Kiev shortly before the war, and became a translator in the Russian Law

Bureau, earning his living by translating Tolstoy, Chekhov, Gorki, Ivan Bunin, Dostoevsky, etc. Throughout the war years, and indeed right up till Lawrence's death, Kot remained a faithful, disinterested friend, often depriving himself in order to help Lawrence, though resolutely opposed to Frieda, convinced that she was devouring her husband bit by bit and that if she disappeared Lawrence "would be saved".[109] Lawrence introduced him to the Murrys, and his esteem for Katherine was equalled only by his dislike of Jack. He later became a close friend of both Gertler and Leonard Woolf.

In any evaluation of Lawrence's human relationships his unclouded friendship with Kot must be placed on the credit side: possibly because no woman was involved, and because Kot persistently took the offensive against Frieda. As early as 1915, the latter recognized that "L. would be fonder of you if I were not there"; she remained on the defensive,[110] though never hesitating to turn to Kot when Lawrence was in need of help. Kot typed his manuscripts, or got them typed, bought or borrowed books, unearthed the necessary cheap Jewish tailor or printer, and indeed, for five years, served as a tireless and ever-willing friend-in-need. It was he who initiated Lawrence into Russian literature, which he certainly saw more objectively and with less violent enthusiasm than Murry. From the letters we can easily imagine the long friendly discussions, the constant dialogue which must have taken place between them whenever Lawrence went to London. In the gossipy, back-biting literary circle they frequented, Kot's presence certainly constituted an element of sincerity and calm. But as in his relations with Gertler, one is always conscious of a shade of condescension in Lawrence's attitude to Kot: his insistence on their Jewish origins seems tinged with a national prejudice openly expressed in other contexts. For Lawrence, Kot and Gertler remained for ever outside the inner circle of his revered "aristocracy", and certainly below him in the pecking order. Koteliansky remains loyal though clear-sighted. Douglas Goldring quotes him as follows: "If you don't want to lose Lawrence's friendship, you must be careful never to let him guess that you are doing anything for him."[111]

Lawrence's female friends

From adolescence onwards Lawrence was always surrounded by women, except for the period of his Italian exile with Frieda. His few quarrels with women were far less resounding than with men. During this period of his life Ottoline Morrell was the only woman deliberately to sever relations, and even she was persuaded to make it up in 1928. We have seen how Katherine Mansfield, for instance, was always ready to make friends again with Lawrence, to fall once more under his charm.

What did he ask of women? Catherine Carswell has testified to his fiercely puritan strain, and to a prudery too ferocious to be altogether convincing.

She has emphasized his "strongly working-class . . . distaste of anything that could be regarded as indecent". In Cornwall, having just begun to undress for bed, she found she had left her book in the sitting-room. Returning downstairs "in an ankle-length petticoat topped by a long-sleeved woollen vest", she was severely reprimanded by Lawrence for appearing in her underclothes!

In her largely autobiographical novel *Bid me to Live*, Hilda Doolittle is even more revealing. When she put up the Lawrences on their return from Cornwall in October 1917 "Arabella" (Dorothy Yorke, the Bella of *Bid me to Live* and the Josephine Ford of *Aaron's Rod*), then living on the floor above, came down to share Hilda's room with Frieda, while Lawrence slept alone upstairs. Poet and poetess had recently exchanged "fiery" letters, revealing a strong mutual attraction, apparently encouraged by Frieda, who murmured that this would leave her free for "Vanio", alias Cecil Gray. "Our love is written in blood for all eternity," Lawrence had told Hilda. Temporarily alone with him, and feeling his gaze upon her, she went up and placed a hand on his sleeve. Lawrence started and drew back like a wounded animal, leaving H.D. for ever uncertain whether this reaction was due to physical revulsion or to a sudden presentiment of Frieda's return. She had however a sudden vision of him as a satyr "chained to Frieda's totem pole", making sudden excursions round and about, browsing on the flowers and grass, secure in Frieda's absolute permanence, occasionally changing meadows but never leaving his pole! For him, she realized, the fiery love letters had been no more than a mental game![112]

Having thus stimulated and disappointed Hilda, Lawrence seems to have taken peculiar pleasure in pushing her into the arms of Gray. In *Bid me to Live*, the deliberate reserve of a confession woven of past memories and contemporary stream of consciousness does not entirely conceal the devastating effect of the poet's retreat from the love offered by a beautiful, talented woman, distressed by her husband's infidelity with "Arabella". Like Jessie Chambers before her, H.D. was to realize the immeasurable distance separating Lawrence's thoughts of love from any will to action.

But certainly the thought was constantly in his mind: with or without Frieda, he pored over the love lives of his friends in his own imagination, setting himself up as confessor, revealer of hidden feelings and as matchmaker. He never tired of giving advice to Catherine Carswell, the Murrys, or Cynthia Asquith on the psychology and conduct of their respective married lives. When Ivy Low was about to marry Maxim Litvinov, he told Catherine Carswell how she should arrange her life:

> It is a mistake for Ivy to have children (*don't tell her*). For her, that is clutching at the past, the back origins, for fulfilment. And fulfilment *does not lie in the past*. You should be glad you have no children: they are a stumbling-block now. There are plenty of children, and no hope.[113]

He never missed an opportunity to use his charm on women: in 1917, for instance, he chose the right moment to compliment a hostile landlady on her Venetian glass necklace: "That fetched her," he said. And H.D. understood: "So he was 'fetching' people, was he? No fish was too small for his net, was it?" She felt "repelled" by the satyr's mask "he seemed suddenly to clap on his face . . . The flame of the red beard, aggressive, horn symbol, horn of plenty. The mouth showed the teeth, not remarkable in any way for symmetry or lack of symmetry, but teeth to tear, to devour."[114]

But for one perceptive Hilda Doolittle, Lawrence's own equal on the plane of lyric creation, a "beautiful, reckless" poetess, whose work moved him to "fear" and "wonder",[115] how many women simply surrendered to his charm? Esther Andrews, the American journalist, or Dorothy Yorke, were probably no more than small fry for his net. Catherine Carswell, secure in her own marriage, was able to preserve her independence and the friendship of both Lawrences, though noting that "his marriage with Frieda was a step which inevitably created a morass about the paths of friendship", in which "one person after another" was to "flounder".[116]

As doctor and psychoanalyst, Barbara Low clearly impressed Lawrence. While plainly sensitive to his charm, she maintained a certain scientific detachment, with the result that Lawrence's attitude to her (as well as Frieda's) was rather ambiguous. Lawrence often used her as a source of information and of reading matter (particularly in 1916–18) and spoke of her in a not unkindly way, though complaining that she "harassed" him with her questions and constant pursuit of clarity of thought. To Katherine Mansfield, however, he described her as a chattering "Jewish magpie" liable to settle on his roof.[117]

The minor poetess Dollie Radford was constantly at his beck and call, getting little thanks even when providing him with accommodation in London or in Berkshire. In *Kangaroo* she received shabby treatment in the person of Hattie Redburn, a demonstration of ingratitude as remarkable, if not as flagrant, as that previously shown to Viola Meynell.[118]

Ottoline Morrell was a case apart. By her Lawrence was triply impressed: first by her aristocratic origins, secondly by her personality, and thirdly by her familiarity with his native countryside. If a member of the lesser nobility in the form of Frieda had not got in first, might not Ottoline have been a candidate to fulfil Lydia Lawrence's dream of her son's marriage to a great lady?

Lawrence certainly fell under her spell, as his first letters show. Did he go so far as to reproach Frieda with barring his road to success through women? She, at any rate, seems at one time to have wondered whether she ought not to leave the field clear for Ottoline, and was certainly responsible for several minor incidents disturbing their relationship prior to the major break at the end of 1916. Characteristically enough, Lawrence almost at once made a distinction between Ottoline and her immediate circle: in the first flush of enthusiasm of February 1915, he was delighted at the idea of the possible donation of "some monkish buildings" on the Garsington estate by the woman who was to be "the nucleus" of the new community.[119] Soon he was following his usual tactic of separating the chosen disciple from others, the better to exercise his full powers of domination:

> Why don't you have the pride of your own intrinsic self? Why must you tamper with the idea of being an ordinary physical woman—wife, mother, mistress. Primarily, you are none of these things. Primarily, you belong to a special type, a special race of women: like Cassandra in Greece, and some of the great women saints. They were the great media of *truth*, of the deepest truth: through them, as through Cassandra, the truth came as through a fissure from the depths and the burning darkness that lies out of the depth of time. It is necessary for this great type to reassert itself on the face of the earth. It is not the *salon* lady and the blue stocking—it is not the critic and judge, but the priestess, the medium, the prophetess.

He saw Ottoline as the Cassandra of Aeschylus and of Homer, concluding:

> It is not your brain you must trust to, nor your will—but to that fundamental pathetic faculty for receiving the hidden waves that come from the depths of life, and for transferring them to the unreceptive world. It is something which happens below the consciousness, and below the range of the will—it is something which is unrecognized and frustrated and destroyed.[120]

This letter was written at the height of the mystical crisis of February–March 1915: how far was it sincere, how far may he not have been merely going through the motions of mystical experience, deluding even himself? Other letters written at this same time are perfectly matter-of-fact, full of humdrum daily happenings. With Lawrence, however, mystic exaltation never excluded interest in the everyday trivia of his professional life. Whether such outpourings proved little to the taste of Lady Ottoline, or whether Frieda kept watch, the temperature of Lawrence's letters soon dropped sharply. But this letter, like those he wrote to H.D. in 1917, as revealed in *Bid me to Live*, is characteristic of his method of attracting female sympathy.

His friendship with Ottoline was to last through minor clashes and rumpuses until the end of 1916. But long before the break, the respectful appellation "Lady Ottoline" became "the Ottoline" (from the German *Die Ottoline*) or simply "the Ott", and while both she and her husband were somewhat ineffectually mobilized in defence of *The Rainbow*, their relations were never as cordial as before the quarrel with Russell. In a 1915 letter to Cynthia Asquith, Lawrence described Ottoline bluntly as "an old tragic queen who knows her life has beeneds nt in conflict with a Kingdom that was not worth her life".[121] He remained, however, ready to accept her occasional patronage, albeit ungraciously. During his stay in Cornwall distance lent her friendship a certain charm: Ottoline bought or borrowed books to send him, and let him use her subscription to the London Library; she also dispatched clothes, blankets, nourishing foods. He replied with gossip about Heseltine's love life, and occasional notes on what he had been reading. Meanwhile he was busy writing *Women in Love*, with its caricature of Ottoline, dedicating to her his book of poems, *Amores*, pressing her to come and see them at Tregerthern, all the while endeavouring to ensure that she did not see the manuscript of his novel.

By 27 November, however, the cat was out of the bag, and Ottoline wrote "saying she hears she is the villainess of the new book".[122] "Poor old vindictive Ottoline" threatened a libel suit, to which Lawrence replied that there was no more than "a hint" of her in Hermione; he found her "disgusting", "contemptible", and called her an "old carrion". Yet, when in desperate need of money and shelter in 1917, he tried to get back into grace: in June he made a formal overture by inviting himself to Garsington through Gertler. The reply, "vague and conditional like Mr Balfour discussing peace terms", provoked this outburst: "To Hell with Ott—the whole Ottlerie—what am I doing temporizing with them."[123]

The story of Lawrence's relations with Ottoline thus ended in the usual way: brazen literary exploitation of physical and moral traits, base ingratitude followed by capitulation. It is particularly important for the light it sheds on Lawrence's ambiguous approach to women. What did he hope to gain? Puritanical, loath to make any gesture liable to impinge on his essential isolation, why, in fact, did he feel an urge to seduce at all? What was the "fear" mingled with his "wonder" at H.D.'s poetry? Was it in any way related to his desire to make use of Ottoline as a medium in Blithedale Romance style? Such questions arise also in connexion with Cecil Gray's insinuations on the subject of his "Orphic maenads":

> At this distance of time I am more inclined to suspect that there was a certain element of sour grapes in my denunciation of his acceptance of adoration and homage from an adoring circle of attractive female disciples, whom Frieda had painted for me in glowing and slightly venomous colours.[124]

Gray suggests that this "Cornish Saint Anthony" may have found "the burden of chastity excessive" and even deliberately sought occasions to go up to London to reconnoitre, thus causing "a certain disarray and havoc in the ranks of the Orphic maenads before he returned to his hermitage". In Gray's mind there was clearly a link as late as 1918 between these veiled hints and the idea of Rananim, against which he was then turning: he accused Lawrence of "allowing himself to become the object of a kind of esoteric female cult, an Adonis, Atthis, Dionysos religion of which he was the central figure, a Jesus Christ to a regiment of Mary Magadalenes".

Lawrence replied that "the pure understanding between the Magdalene and Jesus went deeper than the understanding between the disciples and Jesus or Jesus and the Bethany women", and that Jesus "was frightened" (cf. his own "fear" of H.D.'s poetry) by the knowledge that subsisted between the Magdalene and him, a knowledge deeper than the knowledge of Christianity and "good", "deeper than love anyhow". He accused Frieda and Gray of Pharisaism, of not having penetrated a whole new, "deeper", "lower", world of knowledge:

> And your hatred of me, like Frieda's hatred of me, is your cleavage to a world of knowledge and being which you ought to forsake, which, by organic law, you must depart from or die. And my "women" represent, in an impure and unproud, subservient, cringing, bad fashion, I admit—but represent none the less the threshold of a new world, or underworld, of knowledge and being . . . You want an emotional sensuous underworld, like Frieda and the Hebrideans: my "women" want an ecstatic subtly-intellectual underworld, like the Greeks—Orphicism—like Magdalene at her feet-washing—and there you are.[125]

It is clear that, at this particular moment in the autumn of 1917, Gray and Frieda, like H.D., felt an ambiguity in Lawrence's relations with "his women" which his talk of a "deeper knowledge", his rejection of H.D. and his sending her into Gray's arms on the rebound did nothing to resolve.

It is impossible not to wonder how, in peopling his Rananim with men and women of his choice, Lawrence envisaged their mutual relationships. Did he ever have in mind a community practising "free love" in the Oneida manner? The enigma remains: his attitude is no clearer to us than it was to Hilda Doolittle. Did he vaguely hope to escape at least in part from Frieda's all-powerful grasp? There is no documentary support for such an affirmation. One thing alone is certain: from 1914 to 1919, until the moment when he came to reject the idea of any companion, even Frieda, it was his intention to people his ideal island with women with whom he felt some kind of spiritual communion, some deep bond of sympathy lacking in his marriage and which, in 1915, he believed for a moment he had found in Ottoline. During the war years Lawrence never expressed himself clearly on the subject of complex marriage, though in a passage of "Study of Thomas Hardy"[125a] he went so far as to try to make a place for Sue at the side of Jude and Arabella. But an incident recounted by Beatrice Campbell suggests that something very like escape was in his mind: one day at Koteliansky's, irritated by some chance remark, Lawrence, who had just delighted everyone by making a splendid omelette, suddenly burst out furiously: "'Everyone must change wives. Kot can have Beatrice and Gertler can have Frieda.' In a minute Frieda was attacking Lawrence and everything was spoilt."[126]

A place of honour was always reserved in Rananim for the woman of Lawrence's dreams, Lady Cynthia Asquith, against whom the only complaint in the whole of his correspondence is that she "wearies" him a bit.[127] Lawrence paid her the same honour as to Ottoline, confiding his mystical ideas, revealing himself in terms of his favourite symbols, borrowed from the myth of the Resurrection, and expressing his ideas on the redemption of the soul. His letter of late January 1915,[128] already quoted, is typical of her special place in his mind: she had consulted him about her autistic son John: he was replying, he said, because he felt "a sort of love for your hard stoical spirit— not for anything else".[129] When he despaired of converting to his mystical beliefs "Frieda, Russell, Lady O", he continued to confide them to Lady Cynthia, but with calm and moderation, carefully weighing her objections. In 1915 he wrote "The Thimble", of which the heroine is a portrait of Lady Cynthia, and in which he sought to express the all-important "fact of the resurrection . . . whether we dead can rise from the dead and love, and live, in a new life, here".[130]

It was also to Lady Cynthia that he tried to explain as convincingly as he could the deep reasons for his opposition to war:

> If war prevails, I do not love. If love prevails, there is no war. War is a great and necessary disintegrating autumnal process. Love is the great creative process, like spring, the making of an integral unity out of many disintegrated factors.[131]

Although saddened by her very reasonable objections, he invariably replied with restraint. His appeals to her in difficult moments were always marked by a reserve which shows how much he respected the intelligence and character of his correspondent, whom he certainly feared to offend by ill-timed remarks on the war or military service, and who could make even him realize how ludicrous were some of his affirmations.[132]

Naturally, it was to Cynthia Asquith that Lawrence turned most often in his entanglements with the authorities. At the very darkest moments she remained for him a tenuous but firm link with social and national reality: some of his letters to her show an awareness of other people's legitimate points of view.

He felt "some sort of connection between our fates—yours and your children's and your husband's, and Frieda's and mine" and hoped to be able one day to repay the services rendered. He had frequent dreams in which she or her "aura" played a part. Cynthia Asquith was certainly never one of Lawrence's maenads (unless perhaps in his most secret dreams), yet at the time when he was thinking most clearly of complex marriage in his free community of men and women, it is significant that he automatically included her and her sons, though ready to abandon to "this decompositing life" Herbert Asquith, in whom he thought "the true living was already defeated".[133]

No review of Lawrence's relationships with women, which, after 1916, gradually took the place of his frustrated attempts at male companionships, can be complete unless we face the question of what, exactly, was Lawrence's concept of "complex marriage". If he had read and absorbed the works of both Carpenter and Noyes, and had borrowed from Oneida some of the basic ideas of Rananim, some such concept must have been fundamental to his dream of a community of chosen men and women. The idea of free love, of "wide excursions" apart from each other permitted to the married, is part of the social reconstruction dreams of both writers. Carpenter sets no limits to the bonds of affection which married people may thus enjoy with others of either sex.[134] Noyes established free love at Oneida, the only strict rule being that certain couples alone enjoyed the right to procreate, under the eugenic guidance of the elders.

Notwithstanding his puritanic inhibitions, it would seem that Lawrence's thoughts ran on similar lines, at least in 1915. A link with Carpenter's ideas is present in his letter written to Hopkin on 18 January 1915, in which he founds his new society of communism on "the assumption of goodness" and "real decency which is in each member of the community".[135] "Real" seems to be the operative word in what must surely be interpreted as an understatement, when one remembers that his programme was based on the concept that "each one may fulfil his own nature and deep desires to the utmost", "the flesh and the spirit in league together", men and women meeting "on natural terms instead of being barred within so many barriers". The association with American communities is present in his wish to create in America "a new school, a new germ of a new creation there: *I believe it exists there already. I want to join on to it.*"[136] [*Italics added.*] Up to the beginning of 1916, one can scarcely doubt that the idea of a community such as Oneida played any important role in his thoughts. In July 1916, when he was about to finish writing *Women in Love*, a letter to Catherine Carswell expounded a doctrine in which one can trace elements of Carpenter's cosmic consciousness, as well as Noyes's idea of the dual nature—spiritual and physical, and the accompanying idea of complex marriage:

> What we want is the fulfilment of our desires, down to the deepest and most spiritual desire. The body is immediate, the spirit is beyond: first the leaves and then the flower: but the plant is an integral whole: therefore *every* desire, to the very deepest. And I shall find my deepest desire to be a wish for pure, unadulterated relationship with the universe, for truth in being. My pure relationship with one woman is marriage, physical and spiritual: with another, is another form of happiness, according to our nature. And so on for ever.[137]

Can it be that the transition from this concept to that of the maenads, predominant in late 1917 and 1918, was linked either to the failure of Lawrence's male friendships, or to some crisis in his sex life suggested by Lawrence's odd behaviour in Cornwall when he deserted Frieda to spend so much of his time with William Henry Hocking? In 1918, when he had drained to the dregs the cup of disillusionment, he wrote to Katherine Mansfield after reading Jung (lent by Barbara Low):

> In a way, Frieda is the devouring mother. It is awfully hard, once the sex relation has gone this way, to recover. If we don't recover, we die. But Frieda says I am antediluvian in my positive attitude. I do think a woman must yield some sort of precedence to a man, and he must take this precedence. I do think men must go ahead absolutely in front of their women, without turning round to ask for permission or approval from their women . . .
>
> Secondly, I do believe in friendship, I believe tremendously in friendship between man and man, a pledging of men to each other inviolably. But I have not ever met or formed such a friendship. Also I believe the same way in friendship between men and women, and between women and women, sworn, pledged, eternal, as eternal as the marriage bond, and as deep. But I have not met or formed such friendship.[138]

This letter brings to a close the cycle of his mystical search for love and friendship: by this time Lawrence was alone, having abandoned hope of realizing on earth, in the flesh and in the spirit, his dream of complex marriage. But the dream recurs in his works, from *Women in Love* to *The Boy in the Bush* and even *The Plumed Serpent*, in what appears to be a constant effort to escape the loneliness *à deux* of his marriage with the "devouring mother".

II

THE QUEST FOR SYNTHESIS:
"STUDY OF THOMAS HARDY",
"THE CROWN", *TWILIGHT IN ITALY*

I. THE AESTHETICS AND ETHICS
OF "LIVING EXPERIENCE"

Lawrence's works from 1914 to 1919 for the first time include what he called "philosophy": "Study of Thomas Hardy", "The Crown", the "Reality of Peace" essays, and the early versions of *Studies in Classic American Literature*. Over these relative lowlands tower the high literary peaks, *The Rainbow* and *Women in Love*. Taken together, the novels, such short stories as were actually finished during the period, and the "philosophy" show us a man searching for an ethical and aesthetic synthesis, endeavouring to form a comprehensive view of human character and destiny.

Differences of emphasis between the novels, or between them and the "philosophy", should not obscure their common rejection of certain values, or their common attempt to formulate certain positive beliefs. In the novels, the artistic form on the whole clarifies, or filtrates, for the reader, the confusion and profusion of the "philosophy"; the presentation of ideas in narrative form makes them more acceptable, as their mythical content is taken over and enacted by the various characters. But a study of the exact relationship between the "theoretical" writings and the artistic creations is essential to the full understanding of the latter.

This study indirectly raises the question of Lawrence's sources in the years 1912 to 1916. It might seem easy today to dismiss most of the "theoretical" writings of 1914–17 as wild lucubrations produced in the course of a quest for myths. But the man who wrote *The Rainbow* and *Women in Love* did not, could not, have towards myths and myth-making the detached philosophical attitude of the historian of today. He was *living* his own myths, even as he was making them. And he was not ready to distinguish between myth and scientific, historical knowledge. He was often naïvely anxious, as we shall have occasion to note, to find "scientific" authority for some of his wildest ideas, and therefore to hammer out his beliefs on the anvil of other men's statements: indeed he *believed*, in the full sense of the word, what he was saying. It is therefore important to trace to their sources the main beliefs which, especially in the "Study of Thomas Hardy", lead to the formation of Lawrence's personal mythology in its purer post-war form.

According to him, and even more according to Frieda after his death,[1] his creative genius functioned by a sort of spontaneous generation, entirely exempt from "influences" and innocent of "sources"; the creative process in works of imagination was, so we are told, *followed* rather than *preceded* by an effort at rationalization, leading *a posteriori* to such theoretical works as *Fantasia of the Unconscious*. This idea is advanced with some show of nonchalance in the Foreword to the said *Fantasia*, written in 1921. It will be seen that this contention requires qualification. It fits a little too cosily with Lawrence's quest for pre-mental forms of psychic life—and with the anti-intellectualism he cultivated with considerable skill and intelligence—not to arouse our suspicion, especially coming, as it did, at a time when the Messiah had lost his apostles and, having re-entered his role of professional writer mindful of his critics, was adjusting his public image for the post-war world, and showing himself more detached from his earlier myths.

Lawrence casually throws the reader of the *Fantasia* "one last weary little word" to explain the origin of his "pseudo-philosophy", which, he says,

> . . . is deduced from the novels and poems, not the reverse. The novels and poems come unwatched out of one's pen. And then the absolute need which one has for some sort of satisfactory mental attitude towards oneself and things in general makes one try to abstract some definite conclusions from one's experiences as a writer and as a man. The novels and poems are pure passionate experience. These "pollyanalytics" are inferences made afterwards, from the experience.[2]

The notion that artistic creation as "experience" precedes *in time* (as it does in value) the "pseudo-philosophy" is, however, not sustained. Practically in the same terms as in the more truly spontaneous "Hardy", Lawrence goes on to state the dependence of creation upon ideas:

> And finally, it seems to me that even art is utterly dependent on philosophy: or if you prefer it, on a metaphysic. The metaphysic or philosophy may not be anywhere very accurately stated and may be quite unconscious, in the artist, yet it is a metaphysic that governs men at the time, and is by all men more or less comprehended, and lived. Men live and see according to some gradually developing and gradually withering vision. This vision exists also as a dynamic idea or metaphysics—*exists first as such. Then it is unfolded into life and art.*[3] [*Italics added.*]

While in 1914 Lawrence saw in Hardy, in Dostoevsky, in the later Turner, in Mallarmé and Debussy, the end of an artistic and mental epoch, he then hoped to break new ground by means of a new synthesis, based on the union of the male and female principles.[4] In 1921 he still proposes to "rip the old veil of a vision across" and emerge on the other side, but no longer holds out to the reader any prospect of a new revelation. In other words, the philosophic revelation has receded into the background with the messianic fervour: the artist has come to the fore, and must be shown as pre-eminent over the "thinker"; and to some extent it is true that the artist by then dominates and controls his myths.

The truth lies somewhere between the two attitudes defined in the *Fantasia* Foreword. In *Sons and Lovers*, Lawrence had revealed, in auto-biographical and realistic form, the very essence of his directly communicable experience. He could not do this again without risk of repetition. Yet he went on drawing on this experience, interpreting it into narratives of events no longer strictly autobiographical. Two fundamental elements of his creative process are thus displayed: the utilization of incidents or events implicating others, and the interpretation of such incidents in the light of the writer's own "passionate experience", itself seen and explained by what he calls an overall "vision", a *Weltanschauung*, which we might call a mythology of experience.

This means that the theory of spontaneous artistic creation directly out of experience is not strictly according to fact; as indeed is more than suggested by a careful examination of the chronology of Lawrence's works from 1913 to 1916 and after. *The Rainbow* and *Women in Love*, and, to an even greater extent, certain short stories begun during this period and later deliberately charged with symbolic meaning, are conditioned by aesthetic, moral and psychological attitudes, quite as much as these attitudes in their turn derive from the writer's reflection on his personal experience and earlier writings: the process has to be considered as a continuing one over the years. No doubt the stress on spontaneity, rather than on reflection, fitted in better with the *persona* Lawrence was trying in 1921 to put before the world: it also made it possible to deny the existence of any embarrassing "sources", as Frieda did in her review of W. Y. Tindall's book, in a statement on "living experience" which shows her to be steeped in the very sources of which she contests the influence![5]

In these four years, during which Lawrence wrote and rewrote *The Rainbow* and *Women in Love*,[6] he also wrote, at intervals coinciding more or less with periods of renewed illumination, a series of "philosophical" works concerned with ethics and aesthetics, that is to say, developing ideas first expressed in the Foreword to *Sons and Lovers*. "Study of Thomas Hardy", written in September and October 1914, was quickly followed by the draft constitution of Rananim. "The Crown", a new presentation of some of the themes of the "Hardy", was written immediately after the completion of

The Rainbow, between March and September 1915; in the second half of 1915 came the additions made to *Twilight in Italy* prior to its publication in volume form in 1916. In all these works we find the same moral preoccupations, the same personal mythology, a fairly uniform use and interpretation of symbols. It is in this vision, rather than in the detail of scene or incident in novels and poems, that we must look for an underlying unity in the works of the war years, and the vision is made of ideas and of images of living experience. Any doubt as to which comes first, experience or myths, may be due precisely to Lawrence's refusal to analyse the nature, value and meaning of his symbols: his very sincerity making him, it would seem, unaware of the extent to which they arose, already charged with meaning, in his own subconscious, not only as the fruit of personal experience, but also as the expression of artistic and literary conceptions intuitively perceived, of his intellectual reactions to paintings and to books. His symbolism is, in fact, an intellectual structure, the abstract nature of which is disguised, so to speak, as "vision" and "direct experience".

His quest for pre-mental representations, underlying mental consciousness, may have caused him to ignore the role of the latter in the formation of his own personality, to deny the role of abstract ideas in the structuring and interpretation of "experience". Whatever he may say, any honest analysis of his works in relation to his life must stress the pre-eminence over direct, crude "experience" of what are, when all is said and done, intellectual representations—the peculiar form of ideas underlying myths. The interpretation of experience in the light of myths, and the creation of myths out of experience, was with him a complex but single process, it being true for him as for others that, without intelligence, experience cannot produce anything of value. This makes it all the more important to try to discover where his ideas came from, and by what process certain ideas encountered in other writers were assimilated, appropriated and fused into his own "experience".

Lawrence himself has stressed the unity of his creative process in a 1917 letter to Waldo Frank affirming that *The Rainbow* was entirely written before the war, though "revised" in September and October 1915. His memory was, however, not quite accurate on this point, for he was actually still at work on it in February 1915. The war, he says, did not alter its pre-war statement and the revision "only clarified a little":

> I knew I was writing a destructive work, otherwise I would not have called it *The Rainbow*—in reference to the Flood ... And I knew, as I revised the book, that it was a kind of working up to the dark sensual or Dionysic ecstasy, which does actually burst the world, burst the world-consciousness in every individual.[7]

The problem is to determine what exactly constitutes *creation*: the moment of first drafting, or that of revising to bring out and clarify the main ideas?

Or the marriage of "ideas", wherever they may come from, with "passionate experience"? When he said of Gilbert Cannan's *Mendel* that it was "statement without creation",[8] was he not implicitly admitting the pre-eminence of what he called "philosophy" in literary creation?

As far as the very first version of "The Sisters" is concerned, Lawrence put us on the path of discovery when, announcing to Edward Garnett this new novel, he described it as "quite different in manner from my other stuff— far less visualized" and susceptible of being well received by "the Meredithy public".[9] Soon after, he reiterated that the novel was "all analytical", quite unlike *Sons and Lovers*, "not a bit visualized".[10] Was he not then aware of having passed from direct experience to experience processed, interpreted, transposed?

Thus it is both legitimate and desirable to begin by the study of the ideas expressed in essays roughly contemporary with the two great novels—essays which are astonishingly free from the atmosphere of the war, but rather reiterate themes dating from late 1912 and early 1913. "Study of Thomas Hardy", "The Crown", and the 1915 additions to *Twilight in Italy*, thus partially explain the conception of the two novels, by revealing the nature of Lawrence's "vision" at the time he wrote them, while the intentions in the novels become more perceptible thanks to the sources revealed in the essays.

II. "STUDY OF THOMAS HARDY"

Published posthumously in *Phoenix* in 1936, this work seems to have been written in one go just before November 1914: entrusted to Murry for publication, it would seem subsequently to have been forgotten by its author.[11] The original intention, traces of which appear in Chapters III, V and IX, had been to make a study in depth of Hardy's characters. Other themes, however, intruded themselves, and were never moulded into a homogeneous whole. The intrinsic interest of the essay lies precisely in showing us the sedimentation of successive layers of the writer's interpretation of his experience, and of his reading and thinking from 1913 to the end of 1914.

Starting out from themes and symbols already present in the Foreword to *Sons and Lovers*, he began his book "about Thomas Hardy" in "sheer rage" at the "colossal idiocy" of the war. To his surprise, it turned out to be "about anything but Thomas Hardy, I'm afraid. Queer stuff, but not bad."[12] "A sort of Confessions of my heart", he called it to Amy Lowell.[13] "A sort of Story of my Heart", or a "*Confessio Fidei*", for which he feared the critics would "plainly beat" him.[14] The fact that he re-used its main themes in "The Crown", and again in various other pieces in the following years, may explain why he "forgot" it and never attempted to publish it as such. As a posthumous work, very probably in its primitive form as it came straight from the pen in October 1914, it is in many ways less elaborate than any other contemporary work by Lawrence, and more revealing of his effervescent state of mind shortly before rewriting *The Rainbow* and just before the Rananim climax.

A work such as "Study of Thomas Hardy" could be approached analytically from many angles, none of which would lead to complete understanding of the links between its different aspects. Lawrence has poured out into it, in a relatively short time, themes, images and ideas mentally associated and partially synthesized by him, but without that rigorous, formal expression of relationships of which he sometimes felt the need, though tending to prefer the form of parable or apologue made up of images and symbols. Only occasionally does he attempt rational exposition of his "vision". The ideas, and the symbols which often stand for them, remain confused, their very abundance being the enemy of clarity. Yet they provide a valuable mirror of the author's mental turmoil. Our analysis aims at extracting from the "Study" as much guidance as possible to the understanding of the intentions behind *The Rainbow*, and to some extent *Women in Love*, these novels being the translation into action and character-creation of ideas in the "Hardy" essay.

The title itself is a poor guide to the full intentions: the study of Hardy's characters is neither the main subject, nor, since the whole essay serves as pretext for a general outpouring of Lawrence's "philosophy", is it by any means the only one. The "Study" is in fact the revelation of a complex vision, an attempt to give voice to an illumination, coinciding in part with the beginning of the war, but also proceeding directly from the messianic attitudes of the 1912–14 period. The real subjects are sometimes indicated by sub-titles: "The Angel and the Unbegotten Hero" (V), "The Wheel of Eternity" (VI), "Being and Not-Being" (VII). The argument leads to the expression of Lawrence's belief in the advent of a new epoch of art which will reconcile "the Epoch of the Law and the Epoch of Love". The book is also the confession of an angry man, pouring out his hatreds and his hopes, and of a divided man trying to formulate beliefs which might heal his dualism. No analysis carried out from the outside can hope to do more than extract and bring to light certain major themes, and show how they interact one upon the other.

H. S. Chamberlain and "Study of Thomas Hardy"

This admitted "confession" of Lawrence's is naturally unusually revealing of the sources of certain of his ideas and of the use made of his reading since the end of 1912. As we shall have occasion to show, ideas and actual formulations can be traced to Jane Harrison, Edward Carpenter, Blake, Nietzsche, and to Otto Weininger. But among all the traceable sources, Houston S. Chamberlain assumes special significance if one remembers that, in September 1914, Lawrence was in violent reaction against a war which Chamberlain was at that same moment denouncing in Bayreuth as a manifestation of British imperial commercialism: "Study of Thomas Hardy" is in part an expression of Lawrence's sense of alienation from English life in October 1914. At the same time it both reveals influences from his recent cosmopolitan experience, and demonstrates how remote his preoccupations really were from the problems of war and day-to-day human affairs. The essay on Hardy reveals his concentration on a personal ethic and aesthetic, on the formulation of artistic and sexual theories, according to a mode of thinking which follows lines laid down in Chamberlain, one of the oracles of the Symbolist movement, and, where religion, sex and race are concerned, in his disciple Otto Weininger.

That Lawrence read Houston Chamberlain either between the end of 1912 and the autumn of 1914, or in the weeks immediately following the outbreak of war, appears from a number of striking similarities of thought and phrase between passages of the "Hardy" and of Chamberlain's *Foundations of the XIXth Century*. This book, first published in German in 1899, had met with immediate success in Germany, and Frieda and her sisters were bound to have known it. The Kaiser had purchased two thousand copies for distribution to members of his Court. By 1915 100,000 copies of the original German were in circulation. Married to Wagner's daughter, Chamberlain was then living in Bayreuth, whence he had some years previously participated with Dujardin in the creation of the *Revue Wagnérienne*. He had also collaborated in the *Mercure de France*. In the realm of art and literature, he was one of the leaders of the mystical romantic revival of the late nineteenth century, culminating in Symbolism, a movement which led straight to Lawrence's personal artistic and literary evolution from *The Trespasser* onwards.

The English translation of the *Foundations of the XIXth Century*, published in 1911 with an enthusiastic Introduction by Lord Redesdale (1837–1916), had been acclaimed as "one of the rare books that really matter".[15] Theodore Roosevelt had been one of the few Anglo-Saxon critics to express reservations. In *Fabian News* George Bernard Shaw had recommended it wholeheartedly, with no more than a passing second thought for its Teutonic racialism, as a "notable book" to "be read by all good Fabians"; "a masterpiece of really scientific history" which would "show many a Fabian what side they are really on".[16]

Chamberlain's propaganda services to the Kaiser were to be rewarded with the Iron Cross in 1915, and the granting of German nationality in 1916. Immediately after the outbreak of the war, he was very much in the public eye as a renegade Englishman writing pamphlets, published in 1915, on

England and *Germany*, intended for the neutrals. The British counter-propagandists, among them Ford Madox Ford (at the moment of his visit to the Lawrences at Greatham), and for a time Richard Aldington working as his "secretary", were at pains to counteract his potential influence abroad. The socialist Edward Carpenter, discussing "The Roots of the War" in *The English Review* for October 1914, took great care to dissociate his own analysis from Chamberlain's arguments on British responsibility for the conflict. His name must have been a subject of discussion by the Lawrences whenever responsibility for the war was debated.

But apart from this wartime actuality, there are many common features in the interests of the two writers: Wagnerian and Symbolist aesthetics, in the Germanic and Goethean tradition, the attraction of nineteenth-century mysticism, of Indian thought and religion, a mystical belief in race and blood, anti-humanitarianism and the criticism of eighteenth-century rationalism in science and politics; a common passion for botany and plant biology and for metaphors drawn therefrom. There is indeed room for a detailed analytical study of the "Hardy" in relation to the favourite themes of Chamberlain, extending the comparison to other works of the Bayreuth mystic.

That neither Lawrence nor Frieda should ever have named Chamberlain is highly understandable: his name had become anathema in Britain after 1914.[17] It was even less possible to acknowledge him as a source after Lawrence's death, by which time Hitler had honoured him, and Nazi propagandists were giving his racial supremacy theories those sinister applications which ended in war and genocide. Yet a study of Chamberlain in 1913 or 1914 seems the main explanation of the striking similarities between Lawrence's ideas and "recent German ideologies", detected as early as 1936 by Ernest Seillière in a highly perspicacious book, the only short-coming of which was that it failed to trace these resemblances to Chamberlain, their common source.[18]

Professor Armin Arnold has since shown how sensitive to possible accusations of pro-Nazi tendencies Frieda, or whoever edited Lawrence's German letters for her, showed themselves in 1935, when extracts of those letters were published in *Not I . . . but the Wind*.[19] The public image of D. H. Lawrence would certainly have suffered gravely, had it then become known that as early as 1914 he had come under the influence of the main propagator of the theories of Teutonic racial supremacy which inspired both Wilhelm II and Hitler.

Weininger, whom Lawrence, like all those of his generation, had certainly read,[20] was a vehicle of many ideas openly borrowed from Chamberlain, and especially of that brand of mystic anti-Semitism common to all three authors. But Weininger's undoubted influence does not explain everything. There is distinct evidence that Lawrence had read and remembered *Foundations of the XIXth Century* as well as *Sex and Character*. Some of it is given

below at its natural place in the analysis of "Study of Thomas Hardy".
Meanwhile, it may be appropriate to quote here some of the most direct
links associating this particular work with Chamberlain.

In a letter to Henry Savage, Lawrence had expressed, in the same breath
as his admiration for Jane Harrison's *Art and Ritual*, his passionate interest in
"raw philosophy" and "books about Greek religions and rise of Greek
drama, or Egyptian influences",[21] indicating a taste for historical works in
the Nietzschean and Wagnerian tradition to which the *Foundations of the
XIXth Century* belong. Many parallels come to mind between that book
and the "Study of Thomas Hardy", passages of *Twilight in Italy*, and certain
remarks in *The Rainbow*; all of which suggest a recent reading but in themselves prove nothing.

Specific proof, indeed, is not to be found in the main line of argument,
which is Lawrence's own, so much as in episodic details, where coincidence
cannot be fortuitous, and in the general theory of inner experience. Here is an
interesting case of the first type of proof. Lawrence wants to demonstrate
that "the division into male and female is arbitrary, *for the purpose of thought*".
His symbol for the male is the Indian wheel, and for the female, the hub;
"the rapid motion of the rim of a wheel", he says, "is the same as *the perfect
rest at the centre of the wheel . . . motion and rest are the same when seen completely*". [*Italics added.*]

> How can one say, there is motion and rest? If all things move together in
> one infinite motion, that is rest. Rest and motion are only two degrees of
> motion, or two degrees of rest. *Infinite motion and infinite rest are the same thing.*
> It is obvious. Since, if motion were infinite, there would be no standing-ground
> from which to regard it as motion. And the same with rest . . . So there is no
> such thing as rest. There is only infinite motion. *But infinite motion must contain
> every degree of rest. So that motion and rest are the same thing. Rest is the lowest
> speed of motion which I recognize under normal conditions.*[22] [*Italics added.*]

Chamberlain had illustrated in similar terms the "fundamental principle"
of "Teutonic science", which he had found stated in a letter from Leibniz to
Bayle of July 1687:

> *Rest can be regarded as an infinitely slow speed* or as an infinitely great retarda-
> tion, so that in any case the law of rest is to be considered merely as a special
> case within the laws of motion. Similarly *we can regard two perfectly equal
> magnitudes as unequal (if it serves our purpose)*, by looking upon the inequality as
> infinitely small.[23] [*Italics added.*]

The strictly mathematical argument of Leibniz had been advanced by
Chamberlain to justify some of his more debatable reasonings; Lawrence
uses it in precisely the same way to show that the same phenomenon can be
viewed as either negative or positive "according to the point of view".

Not only is the play on the ideas of "speed" and "retardation", "motion" and "rest" the same, but the rhetorical uses made of them are identical.

Apart from this and one other piece of textual evidence, to which reference is made later, it is clear that both writers have remarkably similar attitudes to nation and to race.[24] Chamberlain expresses a "mystical belief" in race which "lifts a man above himself . . . endows him with extraordinary—I might almost say supernatural—powers, so entirely does it distinguish him from the individual who springs from the chaotic jumble of peoples drawn from all parts of the world".[25] He considers it essential to understand "the organic relation of race to its quintessence, the hero or genius . . . The richer the blood that courses invisibly through the veins, the more luxuriant will be the blossoms of life that spring forth."[26] The Teutons, by preserving racial purity, have before them a great future, thanks to their traditions of "freedom and loyalty . . . the two roots of the Germanic nature", but thanks also to their ability "to make room for themselves, slaughtering whole tribes and races, or slowly killing them by systematic demoralization"; laying "by this very means the surest foundation of what is highest and most moral".[27]

Lawrence's analysis of race and religion in the "Hardy", his attempt to outline national psychologies in *Twilight in Italy*, do not differ greatly from this idea of Teutonic supremacy. And even in his early American Studies, written in 1917 and 1918, there will be faint echoes of this idea of conquest.

But the religious, mystical approach to nature and art, and the historical analysis on which it rests in the "Hardy", recall Chamberlain's attitude even more precisely. For the Wagnerian mystic "the so-called Renaissance" is a "misfortune". It has provided "not a stimulus but laws", rules imitated from Antiquity. Faced with the ravages of the Renaissance, of the "chaos of peoples", of "the empty phrases of the *droits de l'homme*, a parliamentary clap-trap", and with the destruction wrought by "*le peuple souverain*"— in brief, of the eighteenth century—he asserts that "only one human power is capable of rescuing religion from the double danger of idolatry and philosophic Deism, that power is art. For it is art alone that can give new birth *to the original form, i.e. original experience*." Art indeed is seen as "*a pulsing blood-system of the higher spiritual life*".[28] [*Italics added.*]

Lawrence we find seeking to reconcile in a new, revivified, re-sourced art, the *Law* and *Love*: Chamberlain says the *Law* and *Grace*, and he also associates those with the *masculine* and *feminine* principles.[29] With Lawrence this reconciliation, to be achieved through a mystical-sexual approach to artistic creation, leads to an art which spontaneously finds its *original form*, just as life does in creating beasts or flowers. His aesthetic theory opens out on to a vague promise of a new creation that shall save man from the dead ends of contemporary art. Hardy, Dostoevsky, Mallarmé and Debussy, as in their day Plato or Dante, are the apocalyptic manifestations of the end of an era, of the exhaustion of the resources of the old forms.

After them, the artist has to discover new sources of inspiration. Thus Chamberlain:

> If . . . we regard this age as the end of the world, we are almost oppressed by the near splendour of the great Italian epoch, but if we take refuge in the arms of an extravagantly generous future, that wonderful splendour of plastic art will perhaps appear as a mere episode in a much greater whole.[30]

The same promise of a new age is to be found in a 1914 letter, and in the concluding pages of "Study of Thomas Hardy". Lawrence, having reversed the terms of the equation, and made the Law female, merely insists more than Chamberlain on the embodiment in Man and Woman of Love and the Law, and on their joyful reconciliation in the Great Peace, from which "shall come [man's] supreme art": an art which "it will take a big further lapse of civilization to exploit and work out".[31] For Chamberlain, it is Teutonic genius which will provide that "extravagantly generous future" of a new age. For Lawrence, this will be accomplished by the co-operation of man and woman in the free Germanic tradition of the relations of the sexes. The Joachite origin of the whole apocalyptic conception is clear, but within the Joachite tradition Chamberlain appears to be the most likely link with Lawrence. He may also be a link with the German romantics on aesthetic theory.

Chamberlain founds his aesthetics on a *Weltanschauung*, a term which he defines as the "perception of the problems of life . . . *Welt* means mankind; *anschauung*, intuitive perception."[32] Lawrence says "a metaphysic", by which he means the same thing. Artistic creation expresses the values and problems of life, and is a check on, and a criticism of, the "metaphysic": this metaphysic should express "the artistic purpose beyond the artist's conscious aim",[33] it is an abstract expression of the contents of the vital subconscious. According to Chamberlain, "the idea of Time and so of History" having been destroyed by the German mystics, "it was the task of the Humanists to build up true History anew" by relinking spiritual life, with the help of Germanic philology, to the pre-Hebraic and pre-Hellenic sources of European spiritual life, i.e. the true Aryans.[34] It was the mystics, for whom "eternity was like the present moment",[35] who identified nature with God, and made possible both the revolution in the science of nature and the romantic reaffirmation of man's love of nature.

For Chamberlain, art is an intuitive, mystic perception and re-creation, based on "seeing" rather than "thinking"—on experience rather than abstract ideas:

> The relative value of a *Weltanschauung* depends more upon power of seeing than upon abstract power of thinking, more upon the correctness of the perspective, upon the vividness of the picture, upon its artistic qualities . . . than upon the amount seen . . .[36]

Comparing Rembrandt's "Landscape with the Three Trees" and a hypothetical photograph taken from the same point, he goes on to say: "Beauty is *man's addition*: by it nature *grows into art, and chaos into intuitive perception*." [*Italics added.*]

Lawrence's opinion of Cannan's novel *Mendel*: "statement without creation", responds to the same aesthetic conception, developed in his mind at the same time as his notions of blood and race, and of national differences as expressed in *Twilight in Italy*. It may well stem from the same combination of ideas and mystical intuitions as Chamberlain's.

Did *The Foundations of the XIXth Century* play a major part in the evolution and crystallization of Lawrence's ideas between 1912 and 1915? Internal evidence not only in the "Hardy" but in his letters of that period points that way, and so does the "sheer rage" which he felt about England's declaration of war. That anger was likely to reinforce on political grounds a current of general sympathy with the Wagnerian Chamberlain: the two men swim in the same romantic stream, that of post-Wagnerian aesthetics and Nietzschean anti-humanitarian mysticism, of an anti-Hebraic and anti-Hellenic search for primeval, non-abstract sources of human perception, for a direct, spontaneous, naïve interpretation of the universe. Much of Chamberlain's general mystical orientation was shared by him with Carpenter and other late-nineteenth-century romantics; Carpenter's theosophical leanings, like Chamberlain's lucubrations, were influenced by nineteenth-century studies of Indian thought. But from 1914 onwards, Lawrence is closer to Chamberlain than to Carpenter on many subjects, especially political philosophy. The key to the resemblances noted between his ideas and some of those which led to Nazism is to be found in the influence of Chamberlain, who at the vital moment seems to have catalysed tendencies inherent in Lawrence's romantic heritage. The main point of application of this influence will be found in the "Study of Thomas Hardy".

Flower, Seed and Eternity

The first germs of the mythology of "Study of Thomas Hardy" exist in the Foreword to *Sons and Lovers*, and in the idea of a perfect consummation, raising the individual out of time and identifying him with the Divine; a consummation achieved in the completeness of love, which unites the Flesh and the Word, putting an end to the dualism of "male" and "female" principles.

The symbols of the Foreword reappear in the "Hardy". A single symbol, the flower, created by the Father "for a moment wasting himself that he might know himself" in "a moment of joy, of saying 'I am I' ",[37] expresses those two aspects of creativeness, love and art. The notion of "excess", or "waste", in the creation of the beautiful, is linked in both essays, as in the poem "Rose of All the World", with the idea that what matters is not the seed, not the preservation of the species, but the consummation of the individual, the flower.

In the "Hardy" this theme is taken up and amplified: man, to ensure his self-preservation, has evolved industry, government, nation, so many "futile" activities, divorced from the "passionate purpose that issued him out of the earth into being". But he also has a gratuitous, artistic activity. The yearly outburst of the red petals of the poppy symbolizes this "excess", this "waste", this beauty. So does the eternal phoenix which "escapes away into flame". The flame is "all the story and all the triumph". What matters is to have seen the red blaze of the flower "in all its evanescence and its being".[38]

Thus self-preservation and all that goes with it have a subsidiary place in the divine order: but each individual is new, unique and the waste, the excess accompanying the reproduction of the species is "the thing itself at its maximum of being".[39] Existing outside time, it is altogether superior to the vulgar "tick-tack of birth and death, monotonous as time". "Children and good works are a minor aim" the final object of every living thing is "the full achievement of itself . . . The world is a world because of the poppy's red."[40]

While the distinctly Nietzschean tone of the apologue with which the "Hardy" opens reveals one source of Lawrence's thought, and while echoes of Carpenter are still discernible, a number of new elements are also evident. One is the symbol of the poppy, which, together with the fact that in 1915 Lawrence thought of calling his rewritten "philosophy" "Morgenrot", suggests echoes of Boehme as well as of Nietzsche.[41] Another is the symbolic phoenix: not only does it appear in the "Hardy", but Will Brangwen sculpts one for Anna, and a phoenix which was to be the emblem of Rananim is described and drawn in a letter to Koteliansky. Both descriptions, in *The Rainbow* and in the letter, clearly reveal the source: Mrs Jenner's *Christian Symbolism*, where a full-page illustration reproduces a thirteenth-century phoenix from the Ashmole Collection in the Bodleian Library.[42] Both the "Hardy" and *The Rainbow* owe other debts to Mrs Jenner's little book. Lawrence found it helpful in putting his symbolism "more into order", and in grasping "something of what the mediaeval church tried to express".[43]

The symbols of the rose, the poppy, the phoenix are synonymous throughout the "Hardy". The inspiration for another symbol, the wheel, may also have come from the same source. Apropos of the cross, Mrs Jenner sketches the passage from the solar wheel to the swastika: ⊕卐卍. For Lawrence the flower becomes a wheel, the four petals forming the spokes: the centre, where "the pollen stream clashes into the pistil stream, where the male clashes into the female", becomes the hub or pivot; and the corolla the "transcendent flame", the "red fall" of the two converging streams. Little by little the image is transformed into that of the male wheel whirling "in incredible speed upon the pivot of the female, where the two are one, as axle and wheel are one, and the motions travel out to infinity".[44] The wheel may, of course, have been borrowed from theosophy, since recent evidence from Mrs Enid Hilton tends to show that as a young man Lawrence had discussed with her father the theosophic lectures of Edward Carpenter.[44a] It is also to Carpenter, and above all to Weininger, that we must look for the sources of Lawrence's ideas on the existence of male and female "principles".

Onto the symbols of the flower and the phoenix, above all onto that of the flower, Lawrence grafts his theory of the ego, which is fundamental to his conception of the novel, while the symbol of the wheel is developed into a specifically Lawrentian theory of sexual union, foreshadowing "The Crown". On this he builds an aesthetic and a psychology, both based on a theology, each of which helps in the understanding of the novels.

The "fulfilled" ego: the hero

In "Hardy", as in *The Rainbow*, the theory of the fulfilled ego is practically inseparable from social criticism, the latter being, however, but a subsidiary aspect of the psychology. The Lawrence of 1914 summarily dismisses "the earnest people" who waste their time seeking for social reform, trying to right wrongs by means of law, serving in vain before the "old, second-rate altar of self-preservation". To these people, he opposes his idea of the true hero, boldly attempting to attain true Being. According to Blake, those who do not follow their sexual desire "are vegetable, only fit for burning".[45] Lawrence's doctrine is expressed in the same symbol: men, he says, dare not seek absolute fulfilment of being, but are content to vegetate, concerned with self-preservation, instead of letting themselves be consumed in the flame of Being; like cabbages, instead of struggling into flower, they bind up their buds tightly inside a bunch of leaves, so that the heart can only rot and perish.

The pure, unfettered ego (this may well be an echo of Blake, critic of moral law, as well as of St Paul) will refuse to claim "rights", "as if any external power could give us the right to ourselves",[46] but will live his life like an artist, seeking only the fulfilment of his own being. From this point onwards two terms recur again and again in Lawrence's writing: *consummation* and *reduction*.[47] The poppy, the Bodleian Phoenix lighting the ten-point star, this star itself, emblem of Rananim, all symbolize this consummation, which is at once the fulfilment of being, its marriage and perfection, as well as the end of time. "Consummation" is thus conformity with the deepest aim of existence, the achievement of beautiful form, of perfect being. The hide-bound cabbage, stifling its flower, rotting slowly at the heart.

is the symbol of "reduction", which separates an individual being from its divine consummation, restraining and preventing the perfect fulfilment of form.

This gives a first clue to Lawrence's scale of values as applied by him to the characters of the novels: "to them that have shall be given, and from them that have not shall be taken away even that which they have".[48] The Lawrentian universe is henceforward subdivided into a thickly populated Hell and a Paradise reserved for a few, as in the Memling "Triptych of the Last Judgment",[49] the central panel of which figures as frontispiece to Mrs Jenner's little treatise. Certain forms of "consummation" are for the elect.

The pure and unadulterated individual, the perfect "ego", capable of "consummation", is no egoist. Being "completely himself, he will desire only what is his own". The fulfilment of desire is not egoistic: "A selfish person is an impure person, one who wants that which is not himself."[50] The finer, the more distinct the individual, the more finely and distinctly he is aware of other individuals in their purity or impurity. Several times Lawrence calls Hardy's characters *aristocratic*, without explaining the term. In fact, he seems to be referring above all to that quality of distinctness, of self-knowledge and purity, singleness of desire: "like angels . . . each one himself, perfect as a complete melody or a pure colour".[51] Thus Tess, who possesses "the aristocratic quality of respect for the other being" and "does not see the other person as an extension of herself, existing in a universe of which she is the centre and pivot".[52] The Lawrentian aristocrat is a Nietzschean and Wagnerian hero, being his true self and living beyond good and evil.

In contrast to these "aristocrats" Lawrence describes the "egos" that in his novels appear as incomplete and impure: Will and the second Tom Brangwen, Winifred Inger, Skrebensky, Halliday, and even Gerald Crich. Although by nature "intrinsically an individual", each one of them appears to us in life as "an impurity, almost a nonentity". They have not succeeded in fusing their individuality with their "knowledge":

> To each individuality belongs, by nature, its own knowledge. It would seem as if each soul, detaching itself from the mass, the matrix, should achieve its own knowledge. Yet this is not so. Many a soul which we feel should have detached itself and become distinct, remains embedded, and struggles with knowledge that does not pertain to it. It reached a point of distinctness and a degree of personal knowledge, and then became confused, lost itself.[53]

Such souls seek to purify themselves by work, by knowledge, by "re-enacting some old movement of life's"; they seek in vain a "second birth", that of the spirit, looking for the utterance to fertilize them and set them free, whereas it may be that the word, the idea has never yet been uttered; they take refuge in good works, hoping these will deliver them into their own being:

So we struggle mechanically, unformed, unbegotten, unborn, repeating some old process of life, unable to become ourselves, unable to produce anything new.[54]

Having thus defined the "unbegotten hero", typical of the doomed or damned in his own novels, Lawrence proceeds to a somewhat unconvincing classification of Hardy's characters, attributing to the novelist a "*prédilection d'artiste*" for the aristocrat, the passionate being "who must act in his own particular way to fulfil his own individual nature".[55]

What then is the role of these liberated personalities, ready to live to the full their life as aristocrats? By what activity shall man free himself from work? Like a flower, he shall free himself for love, not the vulgar form of love, which aims at procreation, but for the total and gratuitous fulfilment of his own being:

> But the act, called the sexual act, is not for the depositing of the seed. It is for leaping off into the unknown, as from a cliff's edge, like Sappho into the sea.[56]

"Everything . . . is male or female"

After two pages taking up once more the theme of "Rose of All the World" and affirming that the flower, i.e. happiness, exists when "the pure male stream meets the pure female stream in a heave and an overflowing",[57] Lawrence develops the symbol of the male wheel whirling upon its female pivot, and then proceeds to extend to the whole universe the male and female principles. They do not find expression only in the flesh and in reproduction: sex pervades everything. While not actually saying that God is male and female, he makes this clear by his contention that:

> The physical, what we call in its narrowest meaning, the sex, is only a definite indication of the great male and female duality and unity.

The two sexual principles extend far beyond man and woman, beyond the reproduction of the species. Sexual differentiation is part and parcel of temporal existence and, therefore, of Divine Creation:

> Man is man, and woman is woman, whether no children be born any more for ever. As long as time lasts, man is man. In eternity, where infinite motion becomes rest, the two may be one. But until eternity man is man. Until eternity, there shall be this separateness, this interaction of man upon woman, male upon female, this suffering, this delight, this imperfection. In eternity, maybe, the action may be perfect. In infinity, the spinning of the wheel upon the hub may be a frictionless whole, complete, an unbroken sleep that is infinite, motion that is utter rest, a duality that is sheerly one.

But except in infinity, everything of life is male or female, distinct. But the consciousness, that is of both; and the flower, that is of both. Every impulse that stirs in life, every single impulse, is either male or female, distinct, except the being of the complete flower, of the complete consciousness, which is two in one, fused. These are infinite and eternal. The consciousness, what we call the truth, is eternal, beyond change or motion, beyond time or limit. But that which is not conscious, which is Time, and Life, that is our field.[58]

Since sexual differentiation is in "everything of life", Lawrence will base on it both his aesthetics and the history of art. But first he must explain *how* it shows itself in art and in religion. This he does by asserting boldly that "In life no new thing has ever arisen, or can arise, save out of the impulse of the male upon the female, the female upon the male." Is it not their interaction that "begot" the wheel and the plough, and which gave birth to the "first utterance that was made on the face of the earth"?[59] From what treatise on the phallic origin of all man's inventions can he have derived this doctrine? The peremptory character of his affirmation, presented as self-evident, is significant, and it is difficult not to see in it the influence of one of the key books of his generation: Otto Weininger's *Sex and Character*, published in English in 1906.[60] "Weininger, we had all read him," David Garnett assured the author in 1967. Havelock Ellis, Carpenter, Weininger, Whitman, Richard Jefferies, Nietzsche—such were the masters of Philip Heseltine, Robert Nichols and their Oxford generation. In one of his very last works, a review of the English translation of V. V. Rozanov's *Fallen Leaves*, Lawrence, discussing Rozanov's "struggle to get back to a positive self", comments on his "strange and self-revealing statements concerning Weininger", admitting familiarity with Weininger's views.[61]

Lawrence was certainly not the only one to be impressed at the time by the scientific pretensions of this violently anti-Semitic Austrian Jew, disciple of Nietzsche and of Chamberlain, who committed suicide at the age of twenty-three. According to Weininger, in every individual there are, in varying proportions, male and female "plasmas". Lawrence goes further, carrying the generalization to its utmost limits, possibly influenced by some current reading on phallic symbolism in art and religion, and by such a secondhand smattering of Freud as he had acquired from Frieda. According to Barbara Low, his own reading of Freud, and above all of Jung, did not begin until about 1916.[62]

In the "Hardy" Lawrence next plunges into metaphysics, oblivious of his own warning apropos of Tolstoy, some thirty pages later, that "a sense of fault or failure is the usual cause of a man's making himself a metaphysic, to justify himself".[63]

The female principle being stability, the axle or pivot, whereas the male principle is motion, the wheel, what man first seeks in woman is the female principle, and vice versa. Perfect, "frictionless" motion, "man upon woman, woman upon man" being impossible in this world, man nevertheless strives towards this perfection: he wants "the woman of his body", to "beget" his "whole life" and motion, including his spiritual and active working life. If he fails to achieve this, he will "look at his work" and suffer "an agony like death which contains resurrection".[64] Similarly the woman, looking at her children "begotten in her by a strange man, not the man of her spirit" will "know what it is to be happy with anguish, and to love with pain". These ideas are very close to those of the Foreword to *Sons and Lovers*; what is new, is the addition of Weininger's pseudo-science and of the symbol of the wheel.

The ideal total union of body and soul not being given to all, sex becomes "functional, a matter of relief or sensation" and man starts seeking for the female principle elsewhere than in woman: "to fertilize him and make him try with increase", he makes himself a "vision, his God", being conscious of a need "to find a symbol, to create and define in his consciousness the object of his desire".[65] God is the inexpressible, eternal, infinite, he is the "unrealized complement" of man; man, the male, is essentially "a thing of movement and time and change"; he is stirred into thought by dissatisfaction; consciousness is the result of this quest for one's "complement":

> Consciousness is the same effort in male and female to obtain perfect frictionless interaction, perfect as Nirvana. It is the reflex both of male and female from defect in their dual motion. Being reflex from the dual motion, consciousness contains the two in one, and is therefore in itself an Absolute.[66]

The idea of God is thus according to Lawrence a form of the male consciousness seeking its female complement: "The attributes of God will reveal that which man lacked and yearned for in his living. And these attributes are always, in their essence, Eternality, Infinity, Immutability." These attributes, he goes on to say, are the qualities that man seeks in woman. That this was true of himself is attested by the fact that he restates here the very terms of a letter to Ernest Collings of 1913. His metaphysic does indeed stem from his own weakness.[67]

Historical psycho-theology

Having thus postulated, though without stating it in so many words, a bisexual God or First Principle of Being, and a separation of the sexes in the imperfection of Creation, Lawrence's formal reasoning leads him perfectly naturally, via the detours summarized above, to the exposition of a theology based on this postulate, for which he then tries to find historical justification. This he presents entirely as his own, but while it does, indeed, tally in many respects with the preoccupations revealed in his letters of 1913, it is improbable that his reading played no part in its elaboration.

One of the foundations of his system is the conviction that the male and female principles are not equally actively distributed either in all individuals or in all races. He could have read in Carpenter's *The Intermediate Sex*, arguments and quotations from Krafft-Ebing, Havelock Ellis and, above all, from the American Charles G. Leland and the German Dr Jaeger, maintaining that certain great men—Goethe, Shakespeare, Shelley, Byron, Darwin—had highly developed "female souls", whereas others—Alexander, Socrates, Plato, Julius Caesar, Michelangelo, Charles XII, William of Orange—were, on the contrary, "supervirile" types. Lawrence lists more or less the same names, with the same attribution of sexual characteristics. One exception is Shelley, with whom he tended at times to identify, and whom he transfers from the female to the supervirile category. Since Weininger, though seeking a mathematical formula for such admixtures, never considers their effect on specific persons or artists, it seems most likely that in this case the source was Carpenter's *The Intermediate Sex*. There are definite indications that Lawrence was more or less simultaneously influenced by another book by Carpenter on a closely related subject, published not long before the "Hardy" was written and reviewed by Havelock Ellis in the July issue of *The Occult Review*: *Intermediate Types among Primitive Folk: a Study of Social Evolution*.

At this point in the "Hardy", however, Lawrence does not linger over application of his theory to *individuals*, but passes on the idea of a greater or lesser degree of virility or femininity as applied to different *races*. "Everything we see and know" being "the resultant" of two wills, the male "Will-to-Motion" and the female "Will-to-Inertia", each "race's" theological idea of the "unthinkable" One Will, i.e. God, is bound to stress either the female or the male aspect of the Creator, by "enlarging the attributes which are lacking or deficient in the race".[68]

Lawrence does not attempt to define this concept of race, which, with the exception of one passage speaking of the Italian, Nordic and English "races", he here applies above all to the Jewish people. Like Chamberlain, he generalizes on "the race conception of God" according to "whether the Will-to-Inertia or the Will-to-Motion has gained the ascendancy".[69]

Though widespread, the idea of race often remained vague in the early years of this century, among writers who failed to distinguish between its biological and cultural content. This is typically the case with Carpenter in his *Drama of Love and Death* and his *Art of Creation*; writers such as H. G. Wells and G. B. Shaw use it in an evolutionist context, but also with a national connotation. What is interesting is that Lawrence's notion of race, of the "race conception of God", is both biological and mystical, and that he struggles with it in a context manifestly reminiscent of Chamberlain's and Weininger's discussions on the "religious instincts of race".

Having spoken of "the soul of the race", and of a "Will-to-Motion" and a "Will-to-Inertia", one of which inevitably predominates and enlarges "the attributes which are lacking or deficient in the race", he proceeds to analyse the Jewish idea of God, "the God of the body, the rudimentary God of physical laws and physical functions".[70] In the Jewish people the female "Will-to-Inertia" predominates; but, Lawrence suddenly adds, "this will to inertia is not negative, and the other positive. Rather, according to some conception, is Motion negative and Inertia, the static geometric idea, positive. That is according to point of view."[71]

Chamberlain here appears clearly as the source: for him the Jewish race is "the negative race", its monotheism (or rather "unvarnished monolatry") is "fictitious" and "negative", a sign of spiritual indigence, whereas true monotheism, such as that of the Aryans, possesses "the organic unity of a superabundant religious richness".[72] He does, however, admit that the Jewish influence on Christianity contained some degree of positive male value. In the religious dilemma, the choice between the Law and Grace,

Nothing would be falser than to regard the Jewish influence in the creation of the Christian religion *as merely negative*, destructive and pernicious ... For in this marriage the Jewish spirit was the masculine principle, the generative element, the Will.[73] [*Italics added.*]

From the idea of God held by a given race, Lawrence asserts, "we can say whether the Will-to-Inertia or the Will-to-Motion has gained the ascendancy",[74] in other words, whether the male or female principle predominates. He attributes Jewish "monism" (a term probably inspired in this context by Weininger rather than Haeckel) to the female nature of the Jew. The jealous One God of the Old Testament is a "female conception". The Jew, "the servant of his God, the female, passive", lived on "in physical contact with God", the "god of the body, the rudimentary God of physical laws and physical functions" (the Jewish nature is in opposition to the "active male principle" and lives in "scrupulous physical voluptuousness"). Had not Chamberlain asserted that the Old Testament expressed "the triumph of the materialistic conception of the world"? Jesus was not a Jew, but an Aryan who was to become "the God of the young Indo-European peoples, overflowing with life".[75]

Similarly, according to Lawrence, Christ "rose from the suppressed male spirit of Judea": he repudiated Woman, ordaining "Thou shalt love thy neighbour as thyself", that is to say asserting his opposition to "monism" while compromising with it: the Jews, according to their "female" conception, saw their jealous God as "the One Being", essentially female, in which the male was merged. Christianity asserts the separateness of the male. To see God as a "manifold Being" is a male conception:[76]

The great assertion of the Male was the New Testament, and, in its beauty, the Union of Male and Female. Christ was born of Woman, begotten by the Holy Spirit. This was why *Christ* should be called the Son of Man. For He was born of Woman. He was born to the Spirit, the Word, the Man, the Male.[77]

It was therefore necessary for his body to be destroyed, for "that part of Him which was Woman" to be put to death, in order to testify that "He was Spirit, that he was Male, that he was Man, without any womanly part".

Humanity has thus known two great movements: the Fall, "the consciousness through Woman, of the flesh, the body", and the Redemption or Resurrection through Christ, with his affirmation "That which is Not-Me, that is God. All is God, except that which I know immediately as Myself. First I must lose Myself, then I find God."[78] And Resurrection is rebirth "unto knowledge of his own separate existence". Here Lawrence's argument is that advanced in a December 1941 letter to Campbell,[79] and clears the way for the main theme of "The Crown", i.e. the Trinity. The One God of the Jews becomes threefold: "The Father, the All-Containing; . . . the Son, the Word, the Changer, the Separator; . . . the Spirit, the Comforter, the Reconciliator between the Two."[80]

Henceforward, according to the predominance in the "race" of the male or female principle, the various Christian peoples were to worship the Father rather than the Son, or vice versa. In mediaeval Europe, still imbued with the passive spirit of Judaism, "the suppressed, inadequate male desire, both in men and women, stretched out to the idea of Christ, as a woman should stretch out her hands to a man". This produced a sensual, female art, the art of the cathedrals, symbols of stability and unity. Meanwhile Greece, where the female element had always been neglected, fell silent. Despite some signs of a denial of monism in the addition of mocking gargoyles, imps and human figures to the cathedrals, perfection in art came only with the Renaissance, that is to say with the stimulus of the male influence through a return to the art of Greece. We may note here that, according to Chamberlain, the Mediterranean *Völkerchaos* passing under Roman domination failed to disengage the true message of Christ from the clutch of Judaism, so that German Christianity was unable to assert itself until the fourteenth century. Thus, while differing from that of Chamberlain in matters of detail, Lawrence's mind nevertheless can be seen to follow the same general direction.[81]

Approaches to an aesthetic theory

Lawrence's general theory of race and religion, when applied to aesthetics, soon begins to crack. In his spontaneous outpouring of ideas, he seems to have been blind to certain obvious inconsistencies, and the long analyses of the evolution of painting from Botticelli to the Futurists and to abstract art into which he launches, are memorable mainly for the keen sensitivity to painting they reveal. Thanks to his practice of copying pictures, of going deeply into the intentions of the artists, the detail of what he has to say of Botticelli, Correggio, Dürer, Raphael, Rembrandt, Turner, and even Michelangelo, bears the stamp of exceptionally fine artistic perception. But the system into which he tries to force them breaks down under the weight of inner contradictions, from which he seeks to escape by further application of the male and female principles. As soon as he tries to accommodate to it Raphael or Michelangelo, his over-ambitious attempt at generalization falls completely to the ground. Apart from the subtlety of his remarks on certain paintings, two essential ideas emerge from his aesthetic considerations: they are found at the beginning and at the end of his argument, and they tell us something of what he was seeking in artistic creation. In other words, they reveal his intuitions, whereas his reasoning strikes one as forced and artificial. Certain of the details, however, do throw light on the novelist's intention in such scenes, for example, as the chapter in *The Rainbow* entitled "The Cathedral", in which the general theory is eclipsed by the psychology of living characters and their intuitive reactions to mediaeval art.

Lawrence starts from a conception of artistic creation, expressed on the very first page of the "Hardy". He aims ultimately at defining a new supreme art such as can avoid the scientific abstractions of Futurism, which, he says, originates from a sterile, mental process. The geometric abstraction of Raphael was the end of all art in Italy, just as Plato spelled the end of Greece. The Italian conception of inviolable marriage, in which the manifestation of divinity is the child, and which refuses to admit the man and the woman as two separate identities, results in a withdrawal of the male, in a "denying of consummation", which, he thinks, characterizes the scientific attitude and the Futurists.[82] To this negation of life, he opposes his own ultimate solution (the idea on which the "Hardy" concludes), that is to say an art proceeding from knowledge of natural law, of the complementary laws of the separate natures of man and woman: an art 'which recognizes his own [law] and also the law of the woman, his neighbour", and which is possible only after the artist has died and been born again.[83] This art "utters the glad embraces and the struggle between the two conflicting laws, and knows the final reconciliation, when both are equal, two in one, complete".[84]

The culminating point of Lawrence's "Hardy" is this definition of the art of the future, already expressed by him in letters of the early summer of 1914.[85] In fact he probably started from that idea, and from it proceeded to build up, from ideas gleaned here and there, an ambitious general system. Certainly his aim was partly to explain certain aspects of the Wessex novels, but, more importantly, to put some order in his own interpretation of life.

Sex, artistic creation, religion, race and blood being uppermost in his mind, he found congenial material in Chamberlain, in Nietzsche, and also in Jane Harrison, whose little book on ancient art and ritual he has acknowledged as a vital influence on his ideas.[86]

Ancient Art and Ritual, a remarkably modern book for its time, studies the psychological and historical sources of artistic creation in relation to the role of art in contemporary civilization, particularly stressing the seasonal, rhythmic character of rites and primitive festivals, the origins of Greek drama and sculpture, and the social function of art; it concludes with the Post-Impressionists, the Futurists, Expressionism, Tolstoy and the Unanimism of Charles Vildrac. Indeed its contents correspond very closely to Lawrence's main aesthetic preoccupations of 1913–14, which were, by and large, those of his contemporaries. One remark in particular: "Spiritual creation *à deux* is a happening so rare as to be negligible", would seem to have acted as a kind of challenge to Lawrence to advance his own conviction that an entirely renovated art could, on the contrary, spring only from profound collaboration between man and woman.[87]

A number of textual parallels can be found between *Ancient Art and Ritual*, and certain passages of the "Hardy" essay. In particular, Lawrence may well have imbibed from this work the idea that art and religion, "though not perhaps wholly ritual, spring from the incomplete cycle, from unsatisfied desire, from the perception and emotion that have not found immediate outlet in practical action".[88] This idea is taken up by him and developed on several occasions, although he introduces this distinction, that artistic effort is a backward glance, a repetition of the known, while religious effort is the expression of a need or an aspiration. The dualism of the male and female principles, protean, takes the form of an opposition between the "God of Aspiration" and the "God of Knowledge", whose accord shows itself in Botticelli's "Mystic Nativity" in the National Gallery, "the perfect union of male and female".[89]

What matters in this aesthetic theory is the predominant belief in a creative flux, a superabundance of life giving birth to those gratuitous things of beauty, the flower, love, or a work of art: the emphasis placed on the idea that art flows as sheer "excess" from the source of life, is a "consummation" of the creative flux. From Jane Harrison he borrows the idea that Beauty is not the aim of the artist. Beauty is the result of the intensity of his emotion, the purity of his vision; the artist is opposed to the aesthete, who can only feel pleasure whereas the artist creates in joy: the artist is truly a man, the aesthete an outsider, a parasite, watching from outside the flow of life, doomed to death and to corruption.[90] In *Ancient Art and Ritual* Lawrence found not his main inspiration, but a substantial part of his dialectic and the sounder basis for his historical ideas on art.

Where aesthetics meet ethics and sex-psychology

As the "Study of Thomas Hardy" proceeds, Lawrence links his aesthetic more closely with his theory of the Hero and also therefore with his ethic. This attempt at synthesis is most clearly demonstrated by the, for him, new form in which the great duality of sex is now presented: "In the Father, we are one flesh, in Christ we are crucified and rise again, and are One with Him in Spirit. It is the difference between Law and Love",[91] between the old religion and the new.

His definition of love makes no pretence at being historically Christian, but corresponds to Lawrence's personal religion, to his own inmost interpretation of the Christian symbols,[92] to a "mythology of personal experience" which also owes much to Chamberlain:

> The old symbols were each a word in a great attempt at relating the whole history of the soul of Man . . . The Crucifix, and Christ, are only symbols. They do not mean a man who suffered his life out as I suffer mine. They mean a moment in the history of my soul, if I must be personal. But it is a moment fixed in context and having its being only according to context.[93]

For Lawrence, love is the desire for consummation, for the

> . . . momentary contact or union of male with female, of spirit with spirit and flesh with flesh, when each is complete in itself and rejoices in its own being, when each is in himself or herself complete and single and essential. And love is the great aspiration towards this complete consummation and this joy; it is the *aspiration of each man that all men, that all life shall know it and rejoice. Since, until all men shall know it, no man shall fully know it. Since, by the Law, we are all one flesh.*[94] [*Italics added.*]

These ideas may contain, if not the explanation, at least the justification in Lawrence's eyes of his messianic tendencies going back to early 1913. While it is highly possible that they owe something to the Unanimism expounded by Jane Harrison, they are also remarkably close to ideas expressed by Carpenter in the chapter entitled "Love's Ultimate Meaning" in *Love's Coming of Age*. Love, says Carpenter, is an art, to which self-consciousness is fatal, for "it is the true expression of the soul":

> Regeneration is the key to the meaning of love—to be in the first place born again *in* someone else or *through* someone else; in the second place only, to be born again through a child.[95]

But the statement which we have italicized above also expresses a typical cabbalistic concept closely related to an idea, latent surely in Lawrence's mind, of the original Unity of Being, followed at the Creation by a division into male and female.[96] This is, as far as we know, the first explicit appearance in Lawrence's work of an idea so clearly occultist in origin, to which he might have been introduced by Blake.[97]

Much more is here involved than the mere romantic conception of regeneration through love. What Lawrence has in mind is a whole coherent system, a kind of illumination of which the "Hardy", alone of all his work, provides not only the elements but also a nearly explicit synthesis. Lawrence had promised Sallie Hopkin, friend of both Carpenter and himself, that he would always be a "glad" priest of love.[98] In the "Hardy" he tries to fuse the Christianity of his childhood, from which he had broken away intellectually, but not emotionally, with his new religion of love. He sees it as his mission to contribute, by sexual education, to the increase and universal spreading of the joy of living and loving, and to attune men and women to the great natural rhythm of life. Following Weininger very closely for a moment, he then advances a theory of sex which explains how this is to be achieved.

The division into the two sexual principles is never perfect in any given creature:

> Sex, as we call it, is only the point where the dual stream begins to divide, where it is nearly together, almost one. An infant is of no very determinate sex: that is, it is of both. Only at adolescence is there a real differentiation, the one is singled out to predominate . . . For every man comprises male and female in his being, the male always struggling for predominance. A woman likewise consists in male and female, with female predominant.[99]

Thus sexual union is at one and the same time a process of reunion of dissimilar beings, of separation of the sex mixture in each, and of mutual penetration, of momentary return to original oneness, when individuals are once more wholly identified with the creative principle. Here Lawrence deviates sharply from Weininger in formulating a theory which is either his own, or drawn from some cabbalistic source:

> In Love, in the act of love, that which is mixed in me becomes pure, that which is female in me is given to the female; we rejoice in contact perfect and naked and clear, singled out unto ourselves, and given the surpassing freedom. No longer we see through a glass, darkly. For she is she, and I am I, clasped together with her, I know how perfectly she is not me, how perfectly I am not her, how utterly we are two, the light and the darkness, and how infinitely and eternally not-to-be-comprehended by either of us is the surpassing One we make. Yet of this One, this incomprehensible, we have an inkling that satisfies us.[100]

This intuitive psycho-physiology of sexual union, so characteristic of Lawrence, would seem to spring from a true mystical illumination, though based on meditations on his own sexual experience and on ideas and themes gathered from his reading. Together with his theory of the twice-born hero, with his aesthetic of joy, and with a certain biological conception of the *Gestalt* of plant and flower, this cluster of intuitive ideas is central to any interpretation of Lawrence as literary creator—a focal point in his mental development.

If one can look beyond its turgid, often obscure, critical and historical argumentation, the "Hardy" is, in fact, his most thorough, most sincere, most candid confession. By the end of 1914, Lawrence reached a high peak of mental activity in which the main currents of his artistic inspiration and of his reflection on personal matters converge, so that he sees unity in his mission, before the onset of failure, disappointment and bitterness. In the evolution of his conception of himself as artist, this moment marks the completion and culmination of his youth. His aesthetic and his programme of work converge with his sense of having understood his own sexual nature and aspirations.

The "Hardy" consists essentially in a clearing of the ground, a search for solid foundations on which to base current and future works—first and foremost the two great novels. In the essay Lawrence's mystique of sex occupies a vital though not yet disproportionate place: not so much an obsession as a genuine and passionate attempt to discover the basic unity of a deeply divided mind and ego. It remains for us to analyse those important elements of the "Hardy" marking an effort either to surmount his fundamental dualism, or to establish the difference, then more and more clearly felt, between his own ethic and aesthetic and those of others. Painting, the denial of sex and the consequent perversions, society, the war, and Hardy himself are the main points of application of this attempt at self-understanding.

Lawrence's discussion of painting comes naturally to him: in the semantics of his dualist system, Male and Female, Light and Shadow, Love and Law, the Word (or Son) and the Father are synonymous oppositions; and it is a discussion of the Law and Love that leads him to treat of love in the joint context of Christian symbolism and of painting, always as significant to him as was poetry. To Lawrence painting is a test of the degree of vitality of individuals and of races. Following his attack on futurist abstraction, he therefore opens his Chapter VIII, entitled "The Light of the World", with the affirmation that England had never known "the great embrace, the surprising consummation, which Botticelli recorded and which Raphael fixed in a perfect Abstraction".[101]

Lawrence sees the evolution of painting as an opposition between the Law (and the predominance of form and geometrical Abstraction proceeding from the Law) and Love, or new law; the latter, denying the creator, denies the flesh, thus sinning against the Holy Ghost which indissolubly unites flesh and spirit, Law and Love: in the abstraction of Love, in mystic marriage, Christianity abjures the flesh. The old law being that of the Body, the new law is the Law of the Spirit, resuscitated after the crucifixion of the body. But the new law was only really followed after the Renaissance—when Christianity began to exist and "Christ's great assertion of Not-Being, of No-Consummation" prevailed.[102]

And Christianity is to blame for the denial of sex. To the man not satisfied by the sexual act, who finds it null, sterile, and has no desire for paternity, the new law brings the consolation of mystic marriage, which is a form of denial of the Holy Ghost, mediator between the Father and the Son, between the flesh and the spirit. "Races" have thus become divided by the deep schism of the churches, Rome being the Church of the Father, and the "Protestant Church" that of the Son:

> And since the Renaissance, disappointed in the flesh, the northern races have sought the consummation through Love; and they have denied the Father . . . Northern humanity has sought for consummation in the spirit, it has sought for the female apart from woman.

The Italian race is "fundamentally melancholic" because it has "circumscribed its consummation within the body". And the Jewish race, for the same reason, "has become now almost hollow, with a pit of emptiness and misery" in its eyes. As for the "English race", has it not become indifferent, like a thing that eschews life?

> The body at last begins to wilt and become corrupt. But before it submits, half of the life of the English race must be a lie. The life of the body, denied by the professed adherence to the spirit, must be something disowned, corrupt, ugly.[103]

Elsewhere Lawrence speaks of certain "passionate nations"; while he does not name them, it is clear from an explicit allusion to Nietzsche and *The Will to Power* that he was, in fact, thinking of the Teutonic capacity for pure, fearless, passionate love.

The Nordic Protestant races, on the other hand, set about looking for a marriage which would be not corporeal, but of body with spirit, or even spirit with spirit, completely incorporeal. Instead of proclaiming with Rome that "God is God", they affirm that "Light is come into the World": St John, representing in paintings the Spirit, the Word, or Love, stresses the antagonism between the spirit of Christ and that of the Father. Lawrence here harks back to the argument of the Foreword to *Sons and Lovers*, strengthened and clarified by his study of Christian symbolism and of painting: he defines more accurately his position concerning the symbolic meaning of light, still somewhat confused and impenetrable in *Sons and Lovers* and its Foreword.

> It is light, actual sunlight or the luminous quality of the day, which has infused more and more into the defined body, fusing away the outline,

absolving the concrete reality, making a marriage, an embrace between the two things, light and object.[104]

To Lawrence, Rembrandt provides "the finest great evidence" of the new conception: the struggle of light and shadow, of object and mind, the desire for "pure spirit of change" free from all laws and conditions of being". His painting expresses the eternal non-marriage of the flesh and the spirit, which are always two: "never Two-in-One"; Rembrandt symbolizes the "great northern [above all Germanic] confusion" of the spiritual bride, of the marriage of flesh and spirit. As when he himself courted Louie for the flesh and Jessie for the spirit, he accepts two distinct marriages: flesh with flesh and spirit with spirit, but not flesh with spirit. In this he is close to Carpenter, who also accepts complex marriage, in the form of tolerance by the loved one for other, secondary, subsidiary loves.[105] This prepares the way for his explanation of the characters in *Jude the Obscure*.

But, says Lawrence, we reach the climax and consummate revelation of light with Turner: he is the perfect expression of the opposite abstraction to that of Raphael, "the abstraction from the spiritual marriage and consummation, the transcending of all the Law, the achieving of what is to us almost a nullity". The bride of Turner was light, or rather, "he was the Bride himself, and Light—the Bridegroom". His "Norham Castle, Sunrise" is "the last word that can be uttered, before the blazing and timeless silence".[106]

Therefore, concludes Lawrence, Turner, like Raphael, is "a lie": the only true marriage is that of body with body, spirit with spirit, two-in-one. To renounce either is to blaspheme against the Holy Ghost: "But the two must be for ever reconciled, even if they must exist on occasions apart one from the other."[107]

This line of argument is of special interest to a critic. Lawrence had absorbed Mrs Jenner's little book, including a passage in the introduction stressing the difficulty of expressing spiritual reality by words, and the consequent necessity of symbolism and metaphor as means of expression for the esoteric and mystic elements of early Christianity. Not only has Lawrence retained this lesson, but he has used artistic criticism as a means of expressing his own aesthetic and moral ideas, as well as the esoteric and mystic elements drawn from various sources, not all of them identifiable.

In the "Hardy" he thus asserts himself as an occultist and a symbolist; these gifts will find their full development in the creation of his two great novels; the explanation of their hidden and symbolic content, however, can be clearly and unequivocally discerned in the "Hardy" by anyone prepared to extract the essence of a work as remarkable for its richness as for the apparent disarray of its main trends of thought.

Above all, the "Hardy" is revelatory of Lawrence's aesthetic theory and of the genesis of his ideas on art. For him, form in art is a revelation of the exact balance, in the artist's ego, between Love and the Law; conflict and mediation, "active force meeting and overcoming and yet not overcoming inertia"—the conjunction of which "makes form". And, because this equilibrium is always subject to fresh conditions, "each work of art has its own form, which has no relation to any other form".[108] In poetry, the Law is adherence to rhyme and rhythm, a concession to "the being and requirements of the body". And Lawrence, in a passage vital to any understanding of his own method of literary creation, speaks straight from his experience as an artist:

> When a young painter studies an old master, he studies, not the form, that is an abstraction which does not exist: he studies maybe the method of the old artist: But he studies chiefly to understand how the old great artist suffered in himself the conflict of Love and Law, and brought them to a reconciliation. Apart from artistic method, it is not the Art that the young man is studying, but the State of the Soul of the great old artist, so that he, the young artist, may understand his own soul and gain a reconciliation between the aspiration and the resistant.[109]

This passage is of major importance, both for what it reveals concerning Lawrence's working method, including his predilection for visualization through symbols, and for the pertinence of its reply to all those who deny or underestimate the degree to which he accepted literary influences or used models without forfeiting his originality. It enables one to gauge the role played in the development of his art both by the copying of paintings, from an early age, as well as the role of sources in his theory and practice of spontaneous creation.

Social criticism

Little need be said here concerning such social criticism as is contained in the "Hardy" essay. Not that its role in it is not vital; but it does not differ from the social criticism developed in later works, particularly *Women in Love*. All that is necessary at this point is to note how Lawrence links it to the main argument of the essay, and to identify possible sources.

"Earnest people", says Lawrence, perhaps thinking of his Eastwood friends, the Hopkins, Alice Dax, Jessie Chambers, and so on, "serve at the old, second-rate altar of self-preservation." His attitude to the feminists, not unlike that of Weininger, is to reproach them for trying to change by law the social exploitation of women. Like St Paul and Nietzsche, he refuses to admit the power of any human law over himself, accepting only natural law; and he would tolerate Parliament only "for the careful and gradual unmaking of laws". And like Noyes to Fourier, he quotes Christ's challenge, "Physician, heal thyself!" Such evils as capitalism, sexual perversion or abuse, the degradation of man and woman, can only be attacked in the depths of human nature. Social and political reforms will only leave the human "cabbages" secure till their "hearts go rotten", saying all the while "how safe" they are.[110] The social vision is much nearer to Blake than to Carpenter; Lawrence would probably classify the latter, poet of democratic education and of tolerance, among his "earnest people". Summary as it is, his rejection of institutions and reformers clearly leads to an archaic system in which the chosen few seek in dangerous living the fulfilment of their being.

For most of humanity, work—justified only because man must have food and clothing—is a form of non-being, from which they crave freedom. The good workman is a machine, a perfect instrument, whereas his aspiration is to be, to escape the eternal repetition of "the old, habitual movements". The machinery which has now taken the place of the human machine, is acceptable in so far as it produces simple, utilitarian goods. But machines cannot be expected to make beautiful objects: their production should be restricted to supplying needs, and there must be no middlemen exploiting them as "muck-rakes" for "raking together heaps of money".

In the industrial system, poor and rich are "the head and tail of the same penny": the only conscious ideal of the poor is riches. Only a few elect, having experienced riches "in fact or imagination", are capable of moderating their appetite and putting away "the whole money tyranny of England". Lawrence seems here to be following a conservative line rather in the tradition of Mallock and the later Gissing, but he soon diverges from it by making his élite reject the State and leave "the walled city" to go out and pitch their tents in the wilderness.[111] Nor does he carry to any depth his own synthesis of disparate ideas, with its echoes of Shelley and Godwin, and perhaps of Noyes. Indeed he dismisses the whole economic problem with the thought that man, once outside the social system, could work "three or four hours a day, according to his kind". This childish programme shows Lawrence at his weakest, incapable of considering social relations in constructive terms.[112]

The war

Remembering how Lawrence began this study in sheer rage at the thought of the "idiocy" of the 1914 war, it is surprising to see what a very minor role the war actually plays in its 119 pages. While aesthetic, religious, racial, sexual and moral considerations play a part out of all proportion to current events, barely one page is, in fact, devoted to the war. This does not prevent him from taking up a position as regards both the war and its aftermath prefiguring certain attitudes leading to the birth of Nazism. Like Chamberlain in Bayreuth, he challenges British "war aims": his compatriots are fighting

not against Prussian militarism, or for the freedom of man, but to free themselves from the "sluggish greed of security and well being", from "the grip"
of their own caution. Men and women alike "draw deep and thorough
satisfaction" from the war: the English should "be grateful to Germany that
she still has the power to burst the bound hide of the cabbage".

For the post-war period he foresees a need for a renewed fight against
mediocrity and the outcry of the war-weakened for security:

> . . . this is the only good that can result from the "world disaster": that we
> realize once more that self-preservation is not the final goal of life: that we
> realize that we can still squander life and property and inflict suffering whole-
> sale. That will free us, perhaps, from the bushel we cower under, from the
> paucity of our lives, from the cowardice that will not let us *be*, which will only
> let us exist in security, unflowering, unreal, fat, under the cosy jam-pot of the
> State, under the shelter of the social frame.

According to Lawrence, the true elect, the hero, the aristocrat, will have
to take responsibility for the maintenance of social order:

> And we must be prepared to fight, after the war, a renewed rage of activity
> for greater self-preservation, a renewed outcry for a stronger bushel to shelter
> our light.[113]

No matter if we die fighting, he concludes, so long as "there is alive in the
land some new courage to let go the securities and to be, to risk ourselves".
He has assimilated the Nietzschean hostility to vulgarity of mind, to the love
of one's neighbours, and to all forms of humanitarianism. Scorning as he
does organized mediocrity, in this autumn of 1914 he is not far from the
idea of "*frischer und fröhlicher Krieg*".

Hardy and the quest for grace

To Hardy, ostensibly the pretext for the whole work, he gives some fifty
pages; many of the judgments expressed are remarkable for their penetration, but they matter to us far less for the author's study of the Wessex
novelist than for what they reveal about Lawrence himself.

The leading idea in his analysis of Hardy's characters is announced early on:
"none of the heroes and heroines care very much for money, or immediate
self-preservation, and all of them are struggling hard *to come into being*".[114]
[*Italics added.*] Love between the sexes, the only way to "being", is the principal factor in this struggle into existence. Hardy's novels are thus "about
becoming complete or about the failure to become complete". His heroes
"are always bursting suddenly out of bud and taking a wild flight into
flower", acting "quite unreasonably" and defying convention. And from

such outbursts the tragedy develops, for none of Hardy's heroes succeeds in freeing himself from the grip of "the greater idea of self-preservation, which is formulated in the State, in the whole modelling of the community". Lawrence is interpreting the Wessex novels in the light of his own problems, so intensively explored in retrospect in 1912 and 1913.

After a summary analysis of five of the early novels, he finds in *The Return of the Native* a theme particularly close to his own heart and one which expresses his own deep affinity as Englishman and poet with the genius of Hardy. All the characters of this great novel are seen by him as exceptional beings, but each *reduced* in his being by a struggle against social convention.

Behind these characters looms the great vital symbol dear to Lawrence's imagination: Egdon Heath "the primitive, primal earth, where the instinctive life heaves up", the reality that "works the tragedy". In a passage strangely reminiscent of Jane Harrison, the heath becomes the "tremendous background of natural happenings . . . that preceded man and will outlast him", the "deep, black source" from which the "small lives" of the characters are drawn.[115] Egdon is the symbol of the eternal creative power, the characters embodying the futility of conscious human objectives:

> Man has a purpose which he has divorced from the passionate purpose that issued him out of the earth into being.[116]

After five pages devoted to Clym and above all to Egdon Heath, Lawrence defines the beauty of this work as follows:

> The vast, unexplored morality of life itself, what we call the immorality of nature, surrounds us in its eternal incomprehensibility, and in its midst goes on the little human morality play, with its queer frame of morality and its mechanized movement.[117]

When, weary of the stage, one of the protagonists chances to look out of the charmed circle "into the wilderness raging round", then he is lost, and the "stupendous theatre" outside goes on enacting "its own incomprehensible drama, untouched". But although this is a quality which Hardy shares with Shakespeare, Sophocles and Tolstoy, his tragedy, like Tolstoy's, is played out on a different plane from that of Greek and of Elizabethan drama. For in it only "the lesser, human morality", the mechanical system, is actively transgressed, and not "the greater, unwritten morality". Punishment comes to the heroes of Hardy and of Tolstoy not from God but from social convention. In his attempt to define his own absolute quest for unadulterated Being, for the Grace which singles out the Elect—and which goes with the rejection of society—Lawrence uses Hardy as the touchstone of his own renewed art of the novel.

In his criticism of *The Return of the Native*, he somewhat overstates his case, with the result that the picture he conveys, while not untrue, is certainly exaggerated and distorted in order to fit in with his own pre-occupations.

While the tone of the passage of Chapter V, also devoted to Hardy's characters, is less exalted, the analysis is far less convincing, and sometimes definitely beside the point, as, for instance, when he sees Sergeant Troy of *Far from the Madding Crowd* as a "passionate nature" and one of Hardy's favourite "aristocrats", whereas he is, in fact, little more than a callous adventurer. And the application of his previous ambitious generalities to Hardy's characters here peters out in a series of unconvincing repetitions.[118]

Lawrence, however, gets well back into his critical stride when, fortified by his definition of the opposition between love and the law, he devotes Chapter IX entirely to Hardy. The novel, he says, must create its own form, must reconcile the law and love, find a balance between an author's *theory* of being and his individual, living *sense* of being. Every novel must have "the structural skeleton" of some theory of being, some metaphysic, subservient to "the artistic purpose beyond the artist's conscious aim".[119] And Lawrence proceeds to blame both Hardy and Tolstoy for trying to apply the world to their metaphysic instead of applying their metaphysic to the world.

Hardy's novels proclaim that there is no reconciliation between the law and love: the spirit of love always succumbs before the "blind, stupid but overwhelming power of the law". This assertion, according to Lawrence, amounts to an attempt by Hardy to explain his own sense of failure. But, despite his constantly uttered curse against the flesh and creation, the artist in Hardy being far superior to the metaphysician, he has created strongly instinctive and passionate characters. Here Lawrence launches out into a highly personal thirty-page study of the principal characters of Hardy's novels, analysed from the angle of the distribution in each of male and female principles.

While this analysis is far from negligible as an interpretation of Hardy, its main interest lies in showing to what extent the Lawrence of October 1914 is still involved in the old conflict between spiritual and carnal love dating back to his Eastwood entanglements. His descriptions of Jude, Tess, Sue and Arabella are veritable portraits of himself and of the women of his youth. No less self-revealing is his theorizing:

> And a man who is strongly male tends to deny, to refute the female in him. A real "man" takes no heed of his body, which is the more female part of him. He considers himself only as an instrument, to be used in the service of some idea.
>
> The true female, on the other hand, will eternally hold herself superior to any idea, will hold full life in the body to be the real happiness. The male exists in doing, the female in being. The male lives in the satisfaction of some purpose achieved, the female in the satisfaction of some purpose contained.[120]

Whatever the value of such a generalization, no one can fail to recognize in it a striking portrait of Frieda: the "strongly male" man with whom she is contrasted being, presumably, Lawrence himself. Similarly for "pure maleness", Shelley is rated superior to Plato, Raphael and Goethe, whereas to Leland and to Carpenter he is essentially a man in whom female traits predominate.[121] The question must be asked whether Lawrence was not to some extent here identifying with Shelley, seeking to compensate for the femininity of his own nature by asserting the pure maleness of his idol.

His interpretation of Angel Clare, with his "ultra-Christian" inability to understand woman, and of Tess, "the acquiescent complement to the male", in whom "the female has become inert", are, in fact, new analyses of Bert and Jessie. And his masterly study of *Jude the Obscure* is another piece of self-confession, a continuation of the eternal argument with and within himself concerning his adolescent loves. In October 1914, living again on English soil, trying to get back to his own artistic roots, to reassess his personal values in preparation for the synthesis of three generations in *The Rainbow*, Lawrence was reliving his early loves, his contradictions, while engaged in violent quarrels with Frieda, "the true female". Jude, who is both male and female, is placed between Arabella—physically female, just as Alec d'Urberville is "physically male"[122]—and Sue, the counterpart of Angel Clare, the "pure thing" recognizing in herself only the "spirit" or "male" element. If Sue is Jessie Chambers, who then is Arabella in Lawrence's personal mythology? She cannot be either Alice Dax, Helen or Jessie: is she perhaps a composite portrait of Louie and of the Frieda of his blackest moods, when to Lawrence she was the companion of the body and not of the spirit, to his friends the only woman in the world capable of putting up with him:

> Few women, indeed, dared have made Jude marry them . . . And no ordinary woman would want Jude. Moreover, no ordinary woman could have laid her hands on Jude . . . A coarse, shallow woman does not want to marry a sensitive, deep feeling man . . . She wants a man to correspond to herself.[123]

Thus Lawrence, anticipating, as it were, some forms of the new criticism, undertakes to correct Hardy and to prove that Arabella was by no means as superficial a creature as her inventor wished to make out! Despite her "pig-fat and false hair", she is "in character, somewhat an aristocrat", amazingly but splendidly lawless,[124] *vogelfrei*, as Frieda might have said! She makes Jude a man, a male, and Hardy no doubt exaggerated her "coarseness" in order to satisfy his moralizing tendency!

Without her, Jude might indeed have remained "monkish, passionate, mediaeval", refusing to "know woman", stultifying and perverting the physical side of his nature (as Birkin might have done without Ursula in *Women in Love*); his tragedy is that Arabella "hated his books, and his whole attitude to study", rejecting his being and occupied only with her own, neither willing nor able to "combine her life with him for the fulfilment of a purpose".[125] How literally should this Lawrentian confession be taken? These passages contain the clearest and most precise textual indications we possess of that deep *moral* divergence between Lawrence and Frieda, strongly stressed by David Garnett in his *Golden Echo*.[126]

While Jude has much in common with Lawrence and Birkin, Sue is seen as an early prototype of Hermione Roddice in *Women in Love* as well as a reflection of Jessie Chambers. Like Jude, like Miriam, she wants to live "partially, in the consciousness, in the mind only", wanting no experience in the senses, only "to know". The vital female is atrophied in her. Her *will* is male. She is not the virgin type but the "witch type, which has no sex". All of which leads Lawrence to what seems almost an echo of Carpenter's *Intermediate Types among Primitive Folk*, a note re-echoed in a letter to Ottoline Morrell:

> She belonged, like Tess, to the old-woman type of witch or prophetess, which adhered to the male principle, and destroyed the female. But in the true prophetess, in Cassandra, for example, the denial of the female cost a strong and almost maddening effect.[127]

Mutatis mutandis, Sue (i.e. Jessie) is the Cassandra or Aspasia of the north, but without the gift of prophecy, without the mystic marriage of her female spirit to the male spirit of Apollo. She wants satisfaction through the mind, she stimulates and invigorates Jude; she is "physically impotent, but spiritually potent".[128] For Jude, she and Arabella together make "One Bride".

Pursuing this analysis, Lawrence relives his own youth and conflicts, rewriting Hardy's novel in the process, with an almost hallucinatory intensity of detail. He shares the "horror" of the moment when "because of Jude's insatisfaction, he must take Sue sexually", when they "exhaust their lives, he in the consciousness, she in the body".[129] Seeking the causes of their tragedy, he recapitulates and passes judgment on his own adventure, "result of overdevelopment of one principle of human life at the expense of the other", gratefully and even reverently accepting the "special and beautiful" being of the composite Sue-Jessie. Why in our present civilization does this type of humanity no longer have a place of its own, respected and revered? Deliberately, within the concept of complex marriage, Lawrence effects the reconciliation between himself and Jessie, his spiritual bride, in a reformed society:

> If we had reverence for what we are, our life would take real form, and Sue would have a place, as Cassandra had a place; she would have a place which does not yet exist, because we are all so vulgar, we have nothing.[130]

"Study of Thomas Hardy", while containing many revelatory passages on the background of ideas to Lawrence's novels of the years 1912–16, is not one of the high points of his literary production. It is, above all, a document on the genesis of his works, a sketch-book for his literary creations. It stands to these in very much the same relationship as his *Letters*. And it is a document to which the critic of the novels will always return with profit for insights into Lawrence's meaning and intentions. The analysis attempted here emphasizes mainly Lawrence's sources—the climate of ideas in which he lived—some of his psychological motivations, and some of the directions followed by his ideas on aesthetic theory. To try to derive from all this a Lawrentian doctrine of ethics or aesthetics would amount to misrepresentation. Ideas contributed to his passionate interpretation of experience, to his "vision" of what characters represented in a visionary universe, but they never constituted a system, an abstract, coherent structure. And when he rewrote what he had begun as a "philosophy", the poetic, symbolic images took over to become a kind of concrete embodiment of such abstract ideas as had found their way into the "Study of Thomas Hardy". This long essay remains as a proof that, for better or for worse, ideas from diverse sources, some of which were later to prove tainted, played a part in the imaginative conception of the moral universe which finds expression in the war-time novels.

III. "THE CROWN" 1915 AND 1925

A stable vision

Lawrence's second "philosophical" text, which is, in fact, a third or fourth "rewrite" of the "Study of Thomas Hardy", consists of a more personal and poetic elaboration of the basic themes of the earlier version. The first half appeared in *The Signature* for October/November 1915. The second is known only under its final form as part of the complete text published in the *Reflections on the Death of a Porcupine and Other Essays*, in 1925. The letters, however, show that the whole text was written between July and September 1915. A great deal of the material from the "Hardy" has been jettisoned in the course of rewriting. The main themes which subsist include the Lawrentian trinity; the artist-hero and his entry into paradise; the varieties of damnation and "uncreation" of the individual; scorn for men and for society, all of which are synthesized into an aesthetic and ethic of the individual and unique.

In this much more personal synthesis, many of the influences visible in the "Hardy" survive, notably echoes of Nietzsche; of Blake's aesthetic and mystic occultism; of the animal symbolism of both Blake and Nietzsche; something of Chamberlain's aesthetic theory and analysis of the Old Testament, together with persistent traces of racialism.[131] But while Lawrence's tendency to use and elaborate Christian symbols still persists, a recent reading of Burnet's *Early Greek Philosophers* introduces new images.

The text of "The Crown" is indeed contemporaneous with Lawrence's move away from the "Christians" and towards the "primitive Greeks", particularly Heraclitus, under the influence of Ottoline and Russell.[132] After the massive dose of romantic German ideology evident in the "Hardy", "The Crown" represents a genuine effort to formulate a personal philosophy, as well, perhaps, as a temporary return to more specifically English sources, especially Blake.

Thus, while it is in the "Hardy" that we find evidence of Lawrence's formative reading between 1912 and the end of 1914, it is in "The Crown" that we can begin to see what permanent effects those early influences have had; all the more so for the fact that subsequent emendations and slight additions made in 1925 suggest that Lawrence had not by then significantly modified his 1915 views. These textual variants are found in the earlier chapters, published first in *The Signature* and later in *Reflections*. The last three chapters include allusions to post-war events and American references, while in the Lawrentian bestiary appear hyenas, condors and baboons, seeming to belong to the American period, treated as they are in the new and different manner of *Birds, Beasts and Flowers*. There is also an obvious change in style, a marked contrast between the rhythmic, pulsating prose of the beginning, very similar to that of *The Rainbow*, and the bold, brittle style of certain passages in the last three chapters: for instance the short, broken sentences describing the vultures, reduced to absolute simplicity of structure. Faith and mystic hope begin here to give way to the satirical, ironic tone characteristic of his American years.

Between 1915 and 1925 Lawrence's beliefs undergo no important change: Jewish monotheism is still felt to be proof of sterility, and the Chamberlain-inspired doctrine of a religion of "inner experience" still holds good. True, his psychological vocabulary is somewhat modified: *hate* being replaced by *power*, *wrath* by *strength*, "*intact virginity*" by "*virgin spontaneity*", and so on. Similarly the synonymous coupling of *flesh* and *senses* is replaced by that of *blood* and *power*. The very superficiality of such amendments constitutes further proof of Lawrence's fidelity to themes and ideas which stem directly from the mood of late 1914.

The last three chapters, and an important addition to Chapter II, introduce not only new animals but also a series of historical characters to complete the gallery of heroes and traitors of the writer's personal mythology. Saul, David, Solomon, Shelley, St Francis of Assisi, Leonardo and Michelangelo belong to the mythology of history common to Chamberlain and Lawrence. To them are added Don Juan, Sardanapalus, Julius Caesar, d'Annunzio, characters from *The Idiot* and *The Brothers Karamazov*, and from Edgar Allan Poe, most of which seem to belong to the post-war Lawrence; Pericles and Plato, typical of the 1915 batch, are replaced by a less committed reference to Assyria and Egypt.[133]

By stressing in his otherwise somewhat hypocritical Introductory Note to "The Crown" that this essay had been "only a very little" altered, Lawrence on his return from Mexico in 1925 admits his fidelity to the themes and ideas of his younger years and, by and large, to the ideology forged for himself in late 1914.

The Lawrence trinity

As in the "Hardy", the presentation opens with an apologue, this time based on symbols drawn from Mrs Jenner and from British heraldic folklore: in the battle of the lion and the unicorn for the crown, the lion symbolizes the Origin, the beginning, the flesh, the source, and also night, darkness; while the unicorn is the Goal, the end, the spirit, aspiration, day, and light. And since Lawrence's dualism involves a yearning for a third, reconciling term, the battle of the lion and the unicorn represents that of the two complementary tendencies of the Perfect Being; their reconciliation beneath the crown of the Holy Ghost stands for the entry into Paradise, the perfect consummation of the elect, those who know how "to be and to be different", as the title to Chapter VI proclaims.

The Lawrentian trinity is thus reaffirmed in "The Crown", in a language which, while clearer and more forthright than that of the "Hardy", yet remains poetic and wholly symbolic: the creature issuing from the Eternity of the Flesh, from the Darkness of the Beginning, but not yet completely "begotten" or "reborn", travels towards a second Eternity, that of the Spirit, Life, Faith. He may worship either one only of these two Eternities, but in so doing he mutilates and "reduces" his being: the exclusive worship of either the Origin or the Goal can give him a consummation, but through the sacrifice of a part of his full Being. Such a consummation into only one of the two Infinites is symbolized by the placing of the crown over the head of one or other of the two heraldic beasts; the crown should remain poised above both, as a symbol of mediation and reconciliation by the Holy Ghost. Whether like David and Solomon, Egypt and Assyria, man gives himself up to ecstasy, to the Bacchic delirium, the dance before the Ark, within the warm shadow of the womb, or whether, like St Francis or Shelley, he burns with the white gleam of universal love, he can never know the reconciliation of opposites, but only live the lie that denies either of the two. Perfection exists only in absolute opposition and absolute balance between "Love and Power" ("Love and Hate" in the 1915 version), light and darkness. The supreme sin, the unforgivable blasphemy, is "to make the lion lie down with the lamb", which is "the creation of nothingness", says Lawrence, revealing his close familiarity with *The Marriage of Heaven and Hell*. The crown is "upon the perfect balance of the fight"; it is not the "prize of either combatant", not the "fruit of either victory". Three short sentences added in 1925 here sum up the whole idea:

Anything that *triumphs*, perishes. The consummation comes from perfect relatedness. To this a man may *win*. But he who triumphs, perishes.[134]

This admirable summary of the essence of "The Crown" already responds to different concepts, different reading; neither in substance nor in form do these staccato sentences bear the stamp of the Lawrence of 1915.

The false ego

The Lawrentian hell contains two kinds of "uncreated heroes", those of the Flesh, of Inertia, in whom triumph hate and power, and whose spirit remains sterile; and those of the Spirit, of Motion, in whom triumph love and self-assertion.

Rather than in hell itself they move in a kind of limbo, they are the shades of those unable to enter into full being, myriads of "uncreated lives" wavering and tossing in confusion and nothingness, never achieving immortality, always on the "fringe of time".[135] A partial, sterile, uncreated soul, who establishes the part for the whole, proclaiming "one God, one Creator, one Almighty": such is the soul of the heroic tyrant, Sardanapalus or Caesar (1925), David, Agamemnon, Caesar or Napoleon (1915), devouring lions, "Dionysic" tigers, whose light is the light of darkness.

But equally fatal is the assertion of a "false ego", a "self-conscious ego", the apotheosis of the self. This is truly hell, the self asserting itself as having absolute temporal existence, whereas existence in time is an illusion:

This I, which I am, has no being save in timelessness. In my consummation, when that which came from the Beginning and that which came from the End are transfused into oneness, then I come into being, I have existence. Till then I am only a part of nature; I am not.[136]

Any assertion of one's own temporal existence as absolute is a usurpation and a lie. The phoenix and the poppy exist in the absolute; the ash of the bird and the stem of the plant belong to the "temporal flux of corruption". To affirm the permanence, the endurance of the self in time is an imposture, "a nice fat lie" like the cabbage: "The soul does not come into being at birth. The soul comes into being in the midst of life, just as the phoenix in her maturity becomes immortal in flame."[137] Myriads of "framed gaps", men unable to enter into being, are the democratic equivalent of that other lie—the lie of the "heroic tyrants": they are the cabbage "threshed rotten inside" with the effort to preserve their nullity and their lying; vowed to the angels of corruption, to Blake's symbolic newt and snake; they are the water-lily, symbol of civilization and of the cold and inevitable destruction of the false "ego".[138]

The false ego, usurping the Crown, glorifies itself, destroying itself by *analysis*, which "presupposes a corpse"; by aestheticism, mistaking statement for art; by sentimentality, which usurps the place of feeling; by the lie of humanitarian and egalitarian democracy, and by science, which "kills the mysteries and devours the secrets"; by introspection, and by mechanical war and destruction.[139] Dimitri Karamazov, Rogogine, and the heroes of Edgar Allan Poe symbolize this form of damnation, of that *reduction*, that living death, the different aspects of which are described in Chapter IV, "Within the Sepulchre". There we come near to what Lawrence has in mind in his frequent references to *reduction* of being. It is, so to speak, a disintegration, a corrosion of the true ego by self-consciousness, and one of its manifestations is sensuality in love, and what Lawrence calls "frictional" love, a notion not clearly defined here but on which a letter to Russell already quoted throws some light.[140] This passage on love, very different in its clarity and poetic style from the prosaic tone of the corresponding pages of the "Hardy", may have been added in 1925.

War and civilization

Naturally war and society come in for bitter comment; the satirical tone is raised even higher in passages known, or presumed, to have been added in 1925. The war is the insensate battle of the lion with the unicorn, both "gone mad" and fighting for the Crown, a frenzy of blind things dashing themselves and each other to pieces" without rhyme or reason.[141] Lawrence does not say which of the two combatants, Germany or England, is "the unicorn of virtue and virgin spontaneity", driven mad by "extremity" of light and consciousness, and which the "lion of power and splendour" roaring in an "agony of imprisoned darkness"! But he presents the war as the collective, mechanical manifestation of the process of *reduction*: rotten within, men seek in sensation, as in sudden spurts of sexual perversion, the only form of life left to them. Such sensationalism is our form of "lust":

> It became at last a collective activity, a war, when, within the great rind of virtue we thresh destruction further and further, till our whole civilization is like a great rind full of corruption, of breaking down, a mere shell threatened with collapse upon itself.[142]

This "closed shell" is "the Christian Conception", within which humanity "lapses utterly back, through reduction, back to the Beginning. It is the triumph of death, of decomposition."[143]

The war is an upsurge of desire on the part of a civilization grown too fond of security, too "complacent" about its own triumphs of will: "Sex seems exhausted, passion falls flat", the soul wearies of everything, even of analysis. The war is a quest for "a final satisfaction", a playing with death, "a sort of self-inflicted Sadism" (would the 1915 Lawrence have used this word?).[144] A maimed soldier encountered in Bognor in May 1915 becomes the symbol of the sexual, sadistic fascination exercised by death and destruction.[145]

Lawrence was to remain faithful to this fatalistic, mystical concept of war, which reappears in the conclusions to *Movements in European History*: for him, history is a blind succession of destructive and creative urges.[146]

While war which is pure, creative in intention, has, like corruption, a divine function, Lawrence sees nothing divine about the social structure, refuge of myriads of "uncreated lives", of false egos, devoid of any vitality, condemned to the cult of the "glassy envelope of the established concept". Rare are those who have immortal souls; most men are "just transitory natural phenomena" and it matters little whether they live or die:[147] they are fat cabbages, self-satisfied lies, victims of the will to possess and to persist in their nullity. Lawrence is here giving free rein to an ideology hostile to humanitarianism and to the doctrine of human rights: the text of the third and last issue of *The Signature* expresses a purely anti-democratic doctrine, a contempt for the human individual, a negation of majority rights in the name of a brand of sacred superhuman egotism.[148]

The ideas on society expressed in the "Hardy" are briefly recapitulated, in more forthright style: rich and poor are all alike; there are no masses and middle classes or aristocrats—quite a different line from that taken in the first letter to Ottoline. There are only "myriads of framed gaps", and a few "timeless fountains", from which spring life and art. To the nullity of society, Lawrence opposes his vital, dynamic experience, but his vision isolates the hero even more completely than in 1914, making him a supernatural creature unrelated to human society. Whereas the Chamberlain heroes—Homer, Jesus, St Francis, Luther—spring from the race, and draw their strength from it, Lawrence's hero, as early as 1915, is drawn in upon himself, neither understood nor understandable. His isolation already strongly foreshadows the lonely contemplation of nature in *Birds, Beasts and Flowers*.

An aesthetic of the unique

Lawrence's social paradox is paralleled, if not indeed inspired, by an aesthetic paradox: to be and to be different is the positive programme proposed in 1915 to the English at war by the man who would have led them to a better peace. And this programme is based on an aesthetic of the individual and the unique, the aesthetic of the Phoenix; one which recognizes only the artist and his creation, taking into account neither the origins nor the public of the work of art. "*Art for my sake*," as Lawrence was to proclaim some few years later: a perfect summary of the Lawrentian conception of artistic creation, which excludes the indispensable partner, reader or spectator.

The object of art, as of life, is to escape into timelessness and attain to immortality: the only real existence is intemporal just as "the flower is timeless and beyond condition". Rebirth can be achieved in sexual love by the annihilation of the conscious self in "primal, creative darkness", in fusion with "the dark Almighty of the beginning".[149] A consummation can also be achieved by breaking open the ego to "the spurt of destruction", whether through sex (Aphrodite) or through spirit (Dionysos).[150] Alternatively it may come about by the achievement of an "utter" relationship between the two eternities, the beginning and the end, darkness and light, by consummation "into a spark of oneness, the gleam of the Holy Ghost", an immortal spark which "is not swept away down either direction of time". Rebirth is thus the attainment of immortality, "attainment to absolute being", a fulfilment "supremely difficult" for the individual, realized in suffering and in joy:

> It is not a question of time. It is a question of being. It is a question of submitting to the divine grace, in suffering and self-obliteration, and it is a question of conquering by divine grace, as the tiger leaps on the trembling deer, in utter satisfaction of the Self, in complete fulfilment of desire.[151]

Once again ethic and aesthetic are merged into one: but the ethic is anti-social, an ethic of the beast of prey, a divine law of the jungle, where, as with Blake, each animal is obedient only to its own law, and it would be vain to hope that the lion might lie down with the lamb. Perfect creation demands the merging of the artist's personality with his work. In a letter on Van Gogh, written in March 1915, Lawrence affirms that "to live one's animal would be to create oneself, in fact be the artist creating a man in living fact", art thus becoming "the final expression of the created animal or man".[152] Similarly in "The Crown" he scarcely distinguishes between the life of the artist and his work.

He does, however, foresee one objection: if art is timeless creation, how can the work of art preserve its beauty over the centuries? If the manifestation of the "God-Quick" alone is timeless, how can the image of the gleam of the Holy Ghost in the artist survive universal dissolution? For "perpetuation is sin": and "we must not think to tie a knot in Time and thus make the consummation temporal or eternal". The answer is that matter flows slowly on the eternal flux; solid matter is a slow wave of the eternal decomposition of forms; on it the artist who "belongs to Time" engraves the image which he has conceived, "the form that was attained at the maximum of confluence between the two quick waves" of his living. On slow-moving matter he thus fixes

> ... the revelation of a pure, an absolute relation between the two eternities. Matter is a slow, big wave flowing back to the Origin. And Spirit is a slow,

infinite wave flowing back to the Goal, the ultimate Future. On the slow wave of matter and spirit, on marble or bronze or colour or air, and on the consciousness, we imprint a perfect revelation, and this is art: whether it reveals the relation in creation or in corruption, it is the same, it is a revelation of God ... Because the revelation is imprinted on stone or granite, on the slow, last-receding wave, therefore it remains with us for a long, long time, like the sculptures of Egypt.[153]

All the perfect, timeless revelations of past artists are "established" in our souls, just as every time a true love relationship is established, love is made fuller, nearer to perfection for all; the true God

... is *created* every time a pure relationship, or a consummation out of twoness into oneness takes place. So that the poppy flower is God come red out of the poppy plant. And a man, if he win to a sheer fusion in himself of all the manifold creation, a pure relation, a sheer gleam of oneness out of manyness, then this man is God created where before God was uncreate. He is the Holy Ghost in tissue of flame and flesh, whereas before, the Holy Ghost was but Ghost.[154]

We find here merged together the ideas of mystic and cabbalistic writers ranging from Paracelsus to Blake, through Boehme and Swedenborg, ending with Chamberlain's aesthetic of inner experience. But while it is permissible, indeed divine, to fix the timeless moment, *repetition* of that moment is wrong: "there is no revelation of God in Memory. Memory is not truth." God is gone, until next time; the revelation of God is "always different". Man must ever seek a new revelation, his "one glorious activity" being "the getting himself into a new relationship with a new heaven and a new earth".[155]

In the name of spontaneous creation, as in the name of spontaneous love, Lawrence cuts the artist off from society: memory means either the artist on the morrow of creation, or someone else remembering his created work; hence it means imitation. And yet he accepts History, without perceiving that without society, without the social group, the artist has neither roots nor springboard. Lawrence's vitalist and *Gestaltist* aesthetic exalts the individual and the "never twice seen", cuts off the artist from his social and human roots, and leads inevitably, as Lawrence himself was led, to the animalist and botanical solitude of *Birds, Beasts and Flowers* and to the satire of *Women in Love*. The establishment of a "new relation" between the individual and the cosmos, in the absence of any communication with others, can only be another form of human solitude. And history, so testifies the "Hardy" and even more "The Crown", becomes no more than a vast bestiary in which the symbolic hero-beasts, David, Sardanapalus, Napoleon or Caesar, as well as characters from fiction like Dimitri Karamazov, Rogogine and Ligeia, mingle with heraldic lions and unicorns, Blakean tigers, pascal lambs, fleas, vultures, condors, eagles, hyenas, newts and snakes. Art itself becomes an intense, mystic, momentary, symbolic vision, the creative act giving simultaneous birth to form and content.

When Lawrence says *perpetuation is sin* and *memory is not truth*, traditional form is his target. His aesthetic of the unique and of the spontaneously creative spark is an aesthetic of the discovery of the unique, distinctive form of each work. But it is also a static theory, rejecting any social role for art, and freezing inspiration into a series of artistic prototypes or stereotypes: whether he likes it or not, his poppy is bound to end up in a herbal, his hero in a picture-book and his phoenix in the bestiary from which he borrowed it. Since he denies society and accepts history, the history of art appears to Lawrence as a series of peaks emerging from an ocean in which the collective springs of creation have been lost for ever.

In the process of constant effort towards poetic expression made by Lawrence between the "Hardy" and "The Crown", his aesthetic has gradually moved closer to that of Blake and other English sources. While deep and lasting traces of Weininger and Chamberlain linger on, and while Nietzsche's arrogant messianism still remains, it is the poetic genius of Blake that wins the day, making "The Crown" a prose poem both in the great tradition of English writing, and in that of the hermetic mystics.

The Christian inspiration of the "Hardy", in the winter of 1914–15, with which were combined the influence of Blake, of Chamberlain, possibly of Noyes, and certainly of his own nonconformist education, has passed out of the foreground in accordance with the plan announced after his first reading of Burnet in 1915.[156] The most that can be done here is to draw attention to the more evident traces of his reading, notably in Chapter III, "The Flux of Corruption", in which the sense of becoming, of change, of the decomposition of all that is temporal, the term *flux* itself, are all reminiscent of Heraclitus. The comparison can be carried much further to show how Lawrence has appropriated the doctrine of the "struggle between opposites", which is in reality harmony and wisdom, for, as Philon says, "that which is composed of two contraries is one: and when one is divided, the contraries appear".[157] Not only is the idea of the "correlation of contraries" substituted for the rudimentary opposition between male and female found in Weininger, but the antithetical images of Heraclitus recur throughout "The Crown", in explanation not of the mystic beasts but of the components of their being: the upward and the downward paths; fire as a primitive substance; exhalations, either luminous and pure or dark and wet; day and night, summer and winter, the single and the multiple, strife and harmony, all these are found in the language of "The Crown", elevating the level of thought by giving greater coherence to symbol and to image. The opposition of fire and water, the idea that those who die by fire become immortal gods, whereas those who die by water return to earth, belong to the basic imagery of "The Crown". While the Heraclitan tradition was certainly incorporated into gnostic and mystic legend, it is nevertheless clear that Burnet enabled Lawrence to discover it independently, through the 130 passages from Heraclitus quoted in his book, and the accompanying commentaries. It is also clear that "The Crown" represents a highly personal synthesis of various forms of mystic tradition to which the author had had access. And there can be little doubt that the decisive influences behind his most poetic passages are those of Blake and of Heraclitus.

What strikes us most forcibly about "The Crown", even in the parts undoubtedly dating from 1915, is the quality of the synthesis, the complete fusion of the various influences into a highly individual work. Blake and Heraclitus, Chamberlain and Nietzsche, Mrs Jenner, Dostoevsky and Lawrence's own 1914 discussions with Campbell on the subject of the "self" and egotism, make way for Lawrence, poet of spontaneous creation, contemplator of the great creative and destructive processes of life, symbolized in images combining the many and various sources of his own psychic experience: the cohorts of cherubim and of angels of destruction truly "palpitate about the Presence".158 The processes of corruption and creation are touched with poetic dignity, and the whole essay seems inspired by a religious inspiration of the same order as that of Memling's "Last Judgment" or Dürer's "Assembly of Saints", both of which are reproduced in Mrs Jenner's *Christian Symbolism*. Even the satire is not without dignity, and at times the tone approaches the poetic serenity of Lawrence's *Last Poems*. In "The Crown", he expresses himself almost without bitterness, revealing a matured religion corresponding to his deeper poetical instincts, conveyed in a style purified by the elimination of almost everything adventitious or extraneous to the mainstream of his thought. "The Crown" remains one of his major poetic works; and while analysis of its sources and its composition certainly facilitates fuller understanding, it is possible to read and appreciate it as it stands.

IV. ADDITIONS TO *TWILIGHT IN ITALY*

"The persistent nothingness of the war makes me feel like a paralytic convulsed with rage. Meanwhile I am writing a book of sketches, or preparing a book of sketches, about the nations, Italian, German and English, *full of philosophising and struggling to show things real*."159 [*Italics added.*] These words, written to Cynthia Asquith in September 1915, at the time of his first break with Russell, refer to Lawrence's revision of the text published by Duckworth in June 1916 under the title *Twilight in Italy*.

This revision of texts published in reviews in 1913 was thus contemporaneous with his attempt "to do something" with Murry, and with his short-lived ambition to become a national leader with an anti-democratic, anti-egalitarian, anti-humanitarian platform. He wants to "have done with this foolish form of government and this idea of democratic control" and proposes that England should "submit to the knowledge that there are aristocrats and plebeians born, not made. Some are born to be artisans and labourers, some to be lords and governors." It is not a question of "heritage and tradition" but of "incontrovertible soul". His aim is to build a nation

> . . . according to a living idea, a great architecture of living people, which shall express the greatest truth of which we are capable . . . It is a question of spirit even more than of intelligence. A bad spirit in a nation chooses a bad spirit in a governor.[160]

The temptation is therefore to address himself directly to the public; art "after all is indirect and ultimate", his aim is "more immediate . . . to initiate, if possible, a new movement for real life and real freedom". He is eager to speak "for life and growth", and to work for "a new heaven and a new earth", "the beginning of a new religious era".[161] He wants to bring about "a great utter revolution, and the dawn of a new historical epoch".[162] Germany is "the child of Europe", provoked into a "purely destructive mood" by senile and decadent Europe, with her "conventions and arbitrary rules of conduct of life and very being". The mother should have yielded to the "paroxysm" of the child, trusting "to the ultimate good".[163] The politically propagandist attitude is evident, and so are the similarities with Chamberlain's contemporary positions.

At about the same time Sir James Frazer's studies in totemism provide him with arguments in support of his theory of "blood consciousness" tyrannized by a mental consciousness originating in the nervous system. Not only will Lawrence's state of mind on these subjects scarcely vary between October 1915 and February 1916, when he corrected the proofs of *Twilight in Italy*, but he will write that this book "contains a plainer statement of a 'message' " than *The Rainbow*.[163a]

What then are the themes superimposed on the straightforward travel impressions of 1912 and 1913? Naturally they appear most clearly in the sketches previously published in quite different form: "The Crucifix across the Mountains", and the three first studies of the series "On the Lago di Garda"—"The Spinner and the Monks", "The Lemon Gardens" and "The Theatre". No such comparison is possible for the last six studies, of which no first drafts are extant; but it is not difficult to distinguish in these a number of themes clearly contemporary with other undisputable 1915 additions.

The essential merit of *Twilight in Italy* lies in its high literary quality, its sincerity, the simplicity of the character sketches and travel impressions. But on the narrative and direct observation Lawrence has superimposed a series of historico-philosophical digressions, in which, as also in certain completely rewritten passages, it is easy to detect a somewhat forced effort at interpretation, corresponding to the deliberate attempt to "show things real" announced in the letter quoted above. Thanks to its intrinsic narrative and descriptive quality, this little book will no doubt survive when the pretentious philosophical and religious homilies and political digressions have long since been relegated to the scrap-heap of obsolete ideas. It is nonetheless useful, for the light they shed on the rest of the works, to trace to their various sources the themes which so mar the naïve, spontaneous charm of the earlier sketches.

Lawrence is deliberately writing "about the nations", and his theme is clearly Europe and the war, beginning with Germany, the "aristocrat" of nations. The road to the Brenner is the "imperial German road"; and while admitting the megalomania inherent in the German soul, the author is clearly prepared to cut his losses, and recommends robbing the aggressor of his consummation by non-resistance.[164] "If only nations would realize that they have certain natural characteristics," he sighs, in connexion with what he discreetly calls German *grossenwahn*, "if only they could understand and agree to each other's particular nature, how much simpler it would be."[165]

True, occasional expressions of disapproval of German militarism can be found here and there,[166] his own preference being clearly for the Wagnerian manifestations of the German soul. A Bavarian crucifix moves him to rapturous description of "the only race with the souls of artists", the race of the Bavarian highlanders, with their keen blue eyes, full-moulded limbs and erect bodies which are "distinct, separate, as if they were perfectly chiselled out of the stuff of life, static, cut off"; a race "that moves on the poles of mystic, sensual delight, every gesture a gesture from the blood, every expression a symbolic utterance".[167] It would be hard to improve on this as a description of the Wagnerian Teuton, as seen by Chamberlain, mystic and pure-bred, source of all European art, on whom the religious and artistic life of the future will be founded.[168] For such a people "everything is of the blood, of the senses. There is no mind." Whether it be play-acting or the physical transport of love, vengeance or cruelty, work or sorrow or religion, "everything is, once and for all. Hence the strange beauty and finality and isolation of the Bavarian peasant."[169]

After this hymn to the mystics of Bayreuth and Oberammergau, Lawrence finds that the crucifixes encountered further south gradually lose their artistic quality, either because the artist has become conscious, or because he is expressing the cult of death, or simply because of the vulgarity and love of the sensational intrinsic to the Italian sculptor.

The writer's intention is here ethical and political as well as aesthetic. He is trying to mark the contrast between the true civilization of Upper Bavaria and the artistic and social decadence of countries dominated by a Renaissance culture. Typical of this determination to prove, to impress forcibly upon the

reader, is the expansion into over four hundred words of the seventy originally devoted to the startlingly sensational Christ in the St Jakob valley.[170] In
the original text three adjectives suffice to set the tone: ghastly (twice),
criminal and shocking. Other adjectives evoke colour: bloodshot, scarlet,
purpled, bloody. In *Twilight in Italy*, the colour contrasts are heightened and
a veritable orgy of adjectives is used to convey violence: hulked, defeated,
terrifying, killed, horrible, terrible, sinister, gruesome, violated, finished,
conquered, beaten, broken, etc.

Happily for the reader, instead of rewriting in detail the "Lago di Garda"
sketches, he adopted the method of inserting developments, most of which
are so totally extraneous to the subject that they can be largely disregarded,
and do not greatly impair the humour and freshness of the 1913 texts.

His attitude to the Italians is ambivalent: he is both attracted by and
envious of their insouciance, their freedom from moral and metaphysical
preoccupations. By and large his interpretation remains true to the line
taken in the "Hardy", which differs significantly from his 1912 reactions.
Italy is the country of phallic obscurity, its people are "Children of the
Shadow", hence of the Flesh, even the "tiny, chaotic backways" of their
villages becoming "lairs and caves of darkness".[171] Yet it is also a country
of blue-eyed men and women, a mixture of ethnic elements, which, according to Chamberlain, are "outwardly latinized but inwardly thoroughly
Teutonic".[172] In the old spinner of Gargnano, an Italian with "eyes clear as
the sky, blue, empyrean, transcendent", Lawrence finds the same un-self-
consciousness, the same sublime identification with the cosmos, as in the
peasants of the Bavarian highlands. As for the two monks pacing up and down
the monastery garden, they are neutral, between blood and spirit, as they
tread continually between light and shadow. They symbolize "the neutrality
of the law", "the abstraction of the average", "the flesh, neutralizing the
spirit, the spirit neutralizing the flesh", the official religion of Rome, "the
triumph of dogma and of law".[173] They stand for the law of democratic
average, the denial of ecstasy, a prudent isolation from the consummation
and adventure of the two eternities.

In blaming the devastation of the Renaissance for driving "the southern
nation, perhaps all the Latin races", towards Aphrodite, queen of the senses,
towards the luminous night, the "Mosaic ecstasy" of the divinity of the
flesh, Lawrence is faithfully following Chamberlain for whom the official,
sixteenth-century Renaissance is a retrogressive step following upon the real
renascence, the great romantic and Teutonic creative urge of the thirteenth
century.[174] He then pursues his own idea, introducing elements from Blake,
Nietzsche and Weininger, interpreting in his own way the general theory of
the *Foundations of the XIXth Century* in terms of sex and phallicism. An
eleven-page addition takes up once more themes familiar from the "Hardy"
and "The Crown": to the Mosaic and Latin ecstasy of the flesh is opposed

another partial ecstasy, that of the spirit, of abnegation, the ecstasy of the northern races, the affirmation of the "God which is Not-Me". The last great attack on the God who is Me was made by the Puritans when they beheaded Charles the First, and symbolically destroyed the supremacy of the "Me who am", the image of God and of the flesh, the Lord, the aristocrat, the incarnation of God.[175] In 1915, Lawrence is already following that thread of ideas which was to lead him from Rananim and Brook Farm to his *Studies in Classic American Literature*. He takes a stand against the classicism of Pope's insistence that "The proper study of mankind is man", against Shelley's empirical and idealistic philosophy and faith in the perfectibility of man, against the ideas of freedom, against science and the machine, that "selfless" substitute for the genuine power destroyed by the Puritan revolution; against the selfless world of equity.[176]

At the end of this eleven-page exposé of an anti-egalitarian, anti-humanitarian, nationalist doctrine, Lawrence returns to Blake's tiger, symbol of the true warlike spirit, and shows the absurdity of mechanized warfare, which tries to harness the tiger to the machine, resulting in "a chaos beyond chaos, an unthinkable hell"; he pictures "the transcendent self" of the warrior endeavouring to embrace the opposite extreme of "mechanical selflessness". Modern warfare is condemned, not as war or as conquest, but as being contrary to the poetic logic of natural conflict, as conceived by Lawrence.[177]

The enemy of man, of true culture, indeed, is intelligence: mind, education, science, are all forms of non-being, of the denial of the self; to Lawrence "mindless" has become the very highest form of compliment.[178]

He witnesses with mixed feelings the awakening of the Italians to consciousness, to science and technology: they aspire to "this last reduction", to an ultimate histrionic conquest of power through the machine.[179] Some of the finest pages of *Twilight in Italy* are devoted to studying, in portraits drawn from reality, the fascination exercised by modern life and machinery on the minds of simple Italian peasants and tradesmen. Lawrence invariably excels when content to observe without generalizing: his models spring to life, and his characters, unburdened with symbolic meaning, are as those encountered at every turn of the road in Switzerland and Italy.

When he comes to write of England, he can at first only describe his dilemma: he detests "the great mass of London, and the black, fuming, laborious Midlands and North country"; but when he compares them with the fatalism of Italy, irremediably fixed in the past, he prefers "to go forward into error".[180] This was perhaps his 1913 reaction but, in 1915, he sees England "conquering the world with her machines and her horrible destruction of natural life". She is conquering "the whole world". Attention has never been drawn to the impudent, and to what must have seemed to many contemporaries almost treasonable, character of such language, during the autumn of 1915, probably just before the *Rainbow* prosecution. Nobody has stressed the parallel between the apocalyptic vision of the last paragraphs of "The Lemon Gardens" and the themes of German propaganda then emanating from Chamberlain in Bayreuth, accusing England of undertaking the commercial and industrial conquest of the world. Lawrence has been seen as an anti-imperialist pacifist, and not as an irresponsible propagandist advancing, under cover of studies "about the nations", the very arguments of the Kaiser's Germany, writing that England, "replete with the conquest of the outer world, satisfied with the destruction of the Self", must either "cease", turn round, or else expire!

What was the "great structure of truth" which Lawrence was offering his country as an alternative in the last paragraph of "The Lemon Gardens"? That same society based on "wholeness of movement" and led by a "supreme man", an "elected King" chosen by "aristocrats fit to govern", that he had already proposed to Russell the previous July and to Cynthia Asquith a month later. At this time he seems to have considered England beaten, and was warning Ottoline to prepare for the "war between Labour and Capital", and for the emergence of "real leaders" capable of preventing, "in the light of a wide-embracing philosophy", another "French Revolution muddle"—a programme with undertones since then made familiar by Fascism, the very terms employed being reminiscent of Chamberlain.[181]

A digression inserted into the excellent sketch on the visit to Gargnano of the travelling company of Italian players completes the series of his reflections on themes of the *Foundations of the XIXth Century*. Using a criticism of their naïve performance of *Hamlet* as a pretext, he returns once more to a theme recurrent in the "Hardy", "The Crown" and *Twilight in Italy*: "To be, or not to be." Hamlet is for him the repulsive symbol of self-hatred and of the spirit of disintegration. In Renaissance art, in Shakespeare, in Leonardo, Lawrence sees a strain of self-dislike, "a corruption of the flesh" and "a conscious revolt from this". Michelangelo, on the contrary, "stands by" the flesh; but Hamlet represents "the convulsed reaction of the mind from the flesh, of the spirit from the self, the reaction from the great aristocratic to the great democratic principle".[182] According to the aristocratic principle Hamlet would "either have set about murdering his uncle" or else "gone right away". There would have been no need for him to murder his mother. Gertrude, Lady Macbeth, Lear's daughters, all "murder the supreme male, the ideal Self, the King and Father. This is the tragic position Shakespeare must dwell upon. The woman rejects, repudiates the ideal Self which the male represents to her".[183]

But with Hamlet the murder of the Father is only the symbol of a deeper "suicidal" decision, "that the Self in its supremacy, Father and King, must die". "The great religious, philosophical tide, which had been swelling all through the Middle Ages", had culminated in the "inevitable philosophic conclusion of all the Renaissance": the decision "not to be". If my fulfilment is "the fulfilment and establishment of the unknown divine Self which I am", then "my order of life will be kingly, imperial, aristocratic" and I shall desire "a king, an emperor, a tyrant, glorious, mighty, in whom I see myself consummated and fulfilled". With the Renaissance the "great half-truth" of death, of abnegation, has replaced the Pagan Infinite. With Savonarola and Luther, the Church was transformed, abandoning the pagan path of Rome for the path of the new Infinite, reached through renunciation and merging into Others. Henry VIII replaced the Church by the State; after which disintegration reached the State as well. The King, the Father, passed away in the human soul, and with Cromwell, the actual regicide, the old way of life was brought to an end. Henceforward the *"vital*, governing idea" in the State has been the "Common Good". And to Lawrence this new principle is a failure: either "we are tempted, like Nietzsche, to return back to the old pagan Infinite, to say that is supreme."

> Or we are inclined, like the English and the Pragmatist, to say, "There is no Infinite, there is no Absolute. The only Absolute is expediency, the only reality is sensation and momentariness."

But, says Lawrence, while we may say this, and even act on it, we never believe it.

And to this contradiction he once more opposes the Absolute of the Holy Ghost, the "mystic Reason which connects both Infinites", and proposes to "make a living State", built on the idea of the Holy Spirit, "the supreme Relationship".[184] *The Plumed Serpent* is the ultimate outcome of his attempt to do so.

It is perhaps not surprising that Rolf Gardiner should have loved and admired *Twilight in Italy* and found in it "all the germ" of Lawrence's thought. The 1915 views "on leadership and community, on discipline and power", which Gardiner found "remarkably akin to those exemplified by the German *Buende* after the war" and to the Spirit of National Socialism,[185] did indeed constitute a platform for a corporatist, authoritarian and mystic State, not exempt from latent philo-Teutonic racialism. Despite certain superficial changes in his thought after 1916, the main social ideas of Lawrence's post-war work are all contained in some thirty pages of the little volume published by Duckworth in 1916. These pages also show that, despite the effort made in "The Crown" to arrive at a personal poetic synthesis, the historical and political ideas of Houston Chamberlain had made a deep and lasting mark on Lawrence's tortured personality: and his abortive desire for political action in 1915 bears the stamp of a totalitarian, anti-progressive, anti-intellectualist policy—an ideology based on contempt for man and on the cult of the hero.

Twilight in Italy proves conclusively the misleading nature of the affirmation contained in the Preface to *Fantasia of the Unconscious*, according to which the work of art comes first, the philosophy only later. The 1913 sketches are fresh and straightforward—the travel notes of an intelligent poet and excellent observer of persons and places. In 1915, an ideology was superimposed upon these notes, resulting in deliberate symbolical distortion of observed reality. Nothing shows this more clearly than the passage briefly discussed above, describing the Christ of St Jakob: the determination to achieve expressionism at all costs, the swamping of reality by interpretation, the distortion of the object of observation in an attempt to wring out meaning. Lawrence was not altogether immune from the influence of Van Gogh,[186] from a tendency to paranoiac distortion of objects under the influence of structures imposed by a system or *Weltanschauung*. But *creation* added to *statement* is more revealing of the sufferings and torments of the poet than of the innate nature of the object. The moments of beauty in *Twilight in Italy* are to be found, almost invariably, in the passages taken straight from the 1913 text. Biographically, the additions are of the utmost interest: their literary value is slight.

By the end of 1915, Lawrence's philosophy has been finally established: it demonstrates his alienation, his relative isolation from the mainstream of life and thought in his own country. Dreams and lucubrations of a sick man and a poet, it may be objected. But the trace of these dreams and lucubrations runs deeply through both works and correspondence. And the impotence of the dreamer can only have served to intensify both desire and dream.

12

THE RAINBOW

TOTAL ARTISTIC CREATION

The Rainbow is Lawrence's first attempt at total artistic creation. He is no longer, as in *The Trespasser*, embroidering imaginatively on the canvas of an experience lived by someone else, nor, as in *Sons and Lovers*, slowly exploring the meaning of an almost exclusively autobiographical story. *The Rainbow* aims at synthesis, at the imaginative construction of a world illustrating certain conceptions; the author's own experience is transposed and serves to interpret imaginary events lived by characters of his own invention. An undertaking made all the more ambitious by the length and luxuriance of a book originally conceived as the first part of a double novel, the full meaning of which would normally become apparent only after a reading of the second half.

Reduced to its simplest expression, the real subject of this double novel, though enormous in scope and ramifications, is simple enough: the accession of the individual to full consciousness, with all that this entails. And this, to Lawrence, means consciousness, awareness, of *self*, with the Lawrentian sense of the evil aspects of self-consciousness; but also awareness of others, and ultimately a search for vital equilibrium, in another and superior form of consciousness—different from "cerebral" or "nervous" consciousness. This form of consciousness, however, is not clearly and finally defined by Lawrence in the double novel: to call it "mystical" simplifies language but does not really describe it accurately. Lawrence himself tries to localize it first in the blood, then in sex, and finally, in *Women in Love*, in certain dark, vital centres beyond sex, where the use of words such as darkness may amount to a subterfuge disguising vagueness or reticence.

In *The Rainbow*, the supreme vital relationship is that between the two partners in the human couple. In *Women in Love*, Birkin will conceive and seek other forms of association, but from the first Tom Brangwen to Ursula, the way to consciousness lies in frank recognition by man and woman of their own desires, in knowledge and acceptance of the partner, full acceptance both of the self and the other in complete fullness of being. If we consider only its broad outline, the development of Lawrence's thought from the beginning of *The Rainbow* to the end of *Women in Love* is perfectly clear. It is obscured only by incidentals, by the description of the society in which the main characters must necessarily live and move, though refusing and condemning it. The real centre of interest of the double novel is in the "adventure in consciousness" of the various generations of Brangwens, that march towards consciousness which so obsessively preoccupied Lawrence because of his dissatisfaction with his own conscious self, and his conviction that humanity could not return to the old, unconscious state: his search for "another form" of consciousness is a quest for a remedy to his own suffering. This advance into consciousness and beyond does not concern the individual only: for Lawrence the human unit is the couple; the problem was thus to achieve some unity of consciousness without either partner dominating, or being in any way subject to the other. In one scene in *The Rainbow*, Tom Brangwen recalls that a man and a woman who have found true love, together form "an angel": the conscious "self" must "die" to make way for the regenerated "self", i.e. that half of an angel, the individual that loves. The characters of the two novels are either half-angels united for transfiguration in love, or fallen pieces of angels, abortive creatures, impure and incomplete. Together the two novels form a sort of Divine Comedy, or Last Judgment separating the blessed from the damned, the immortals from those doomed to stay in limbo.

An exhaustive critical commentary of *The Rainbow* is completely outside the scope of this study; only a carefully annotated critical edition can hope fully to elucidate a work in which invention and memory are so intricately interwoven. For while the intensity of actual experience contributes greatly to the dynamics of literary invention, any reader who knows his Lawrence is in continual danger of having his attention distracted by bits of autobiographical detail, some of which run contrary to the declared intentions of the author; *The Rainbow* has to be approached in its broad outlines, so that the detail may sink to its true proportion and not monopolize attention.

Yet *The Rainbow* is a work which cannot be fully understood without some critical knowledge not only of certain of the author's earlier works, notably the "Study of Thomas Hardy" and "The Crown", and a number of directly and indirectly relevant passages of the correspondence, but also of such of Lawrence's own reading—admitted or unadmitted—as throws some light on the intentions and ideas behind the novel, both in outline and in detail. But while Lawrence's philosophical texts illuminate *The Rainbow*, they remain fundamentally different. The "Hardy" and "The Crown" are confessions, or expositions of theoretical ideas, whereas *The Rainbow* is an attempt at total artistic creation, an endeavour to summon up a universe corresponding to his ideas, in which he also paints the world in which he lives, interpreted in the light of these ideas. In so doing he inevitably asks of the reader an effort of intuitive perception and penetration; but he does not always know how to elicit this effort at the right moment, by guiding the reader to an understanding of his own vision. Thus any reconstruction of Lawrence's intentions in *The Rainbow*, as is proved by the abundance and subtlety of the criticism it has evoked, necessitates much rereading and retrospection, and even after fifty years of the modern novel the majority of readers are not yet ready to understand *The Rainbow* at first reading. This may be due to Lawrence's deliberate choice of an esoteric and symbolic method of exposition; but it is also related to the fact that his main idea was to make it poetic, and hence slow to reveal its deepest meaning.

What Lawrence wanted to do; how far he succeeded, particularly in communicating his intentions to the reader; to what extent these intentions remain constant throughout the composition; what makes *The Rainbow* one of the great novels of this century: such are the main themes studied in the present chapter.

Genesis of The Rainbow

The genesis of the novel is complex, and Lawrence's own explanations are far from simple, partly because they date from several different periods and refer to several different planes or levels of creation. Nor are they complete. They do, however, provide valuable indications, to which must be added other interpretative elements. All Lawrence's explanations, whether dating from the time of writing *The Rainbow* or from after its completion, are true and valid in themselves; for what altered, between 1914 and 1917, was not so much the author's intention as his vision. His earlier explications tell us what he was seeking when he began; others show where his creative work led him, and refer to *The Rainbow/Women in Love* considered as a whole.

In September 1913, "The Wedding Ring", first draft of *The Rainbow*, was conceived as a "new beginning" added to "The Sisters", on which Lawrence had been working since the beginning of the year: he had found it necessary to provide Ursula (then called Ella) with some experience of men before meeting Birkin, with whom he intended her to form the perfect liberated couple. It would be interesting to know, but unfortunately no evidence of any kind is available, at what point Lawrence conceived the idea of going back two generations to illustrate the relations of earlier couples, some of whom had failed to achieve the full liberation of each partner's self. All we know is that *The Rainbow* was undertaken in the thick of a quarrel with Frieda; the result satisfied neither her, nor the author, nor Edward Garnett, and in February 1914 he started out again, this time with the promise of Frieda's collaboration.[1]

Woman becoming individual

Soon he was sure of his theme, the germ of which, he tells us, was already in "The Sisters": "woman becoming individual, self-responsible, taking her own initiative".[2] The theme was topical enough at the height of the agitation for women's suffrage. *The Rainbow* thus sets out from an optimistic conception of the development of the feminine personality, a conception which should be compared with a letter written by Lawrence to Sallie Hopkin, herself a suffragette, on Christmas Day 1912, with "The Sisters" already in mind:

> Once you've known what love *can* be, there's no disappointment anymore, and no despair . . . I think folk have got sceptic about love—that's because nearly everybody fails. It's their own fault. I'll do my life work sticking up for the love between man and woman . . . I shall always be a priest of love, and now a glad one—and I'll preach my heart out. Lord bless you.[3]

The theme of the individualization, the enfranchisement of woman, of the need for a corresponding evolution and liberation of man, are expressed in *Love's Coming of Age* by the Hopkins' friend Edward Carpenter, a book to which *Women in Love* bears certain striking resemblances which we shall have occasion to point out. Lawrence's intentions in *The Rainbow* become clear only if one bears in mind the continuity of subject between the two novels, and that he was concerned not only with woman, but with the human couple. The titles of Carpenter's chapters practically constitute a plan for the novels: Man, the Ungrown; Woman, the Serf; Woman in Freedom; Marriage: a Retrospect; Marriage: a Forecast; Love's Ultimate Meaning; the Free Society. One is almost tempted to assert that the original plan of the two novels conceived as a whole closely follows Carpenter's ideas, and that only the evolution of Lawrence's own character and views made him renounce to some extent in the final drafting the optimism of late 1912.

Carpenter puts great emphasis on the immaturity of man in the face of love, the need for an intelligent adaptation to the various needs of the female personality if love is to play its true regenerative role in a society of free individuals. In *The Rainbow*, particularly on the subject of Ursula's studies, we find reflected something of the disappointments of 1915; in *Women in Love* we see the bitterness of the author's failures on the human level in 1915 and 1916. The fact that the composition of the two novels spread from 1913 to 1916 has to some extent adversely affected the blending of details into the original basic idea; so that the reader may often have difficulty in seeing the main outline through the mass of details. The whole double novel becomes clear if the reader bears in mind both the declared intentions of the author, which condition its whole structure, and the climate of his letter to Sallie Hopkin. Lawrence is concerned not with woman, but with the couple, not with the fight for feminine emancipation, but with the emancipation, defence and illustration of regenerative love.

Regeneration through love

With emancipation goes another important idea relatively new in Lawrence: partly as the result of life with Frieda, partly from his reading of Carpenter and of Weininger, he has become keenly aware of the deep psychological differences existing between men and women. He has also assimilated the idea, of which great case is made in the "Hardy", of the unequal distribution of masculinity among men and of femininity among women. Not only is Weininger quoted by Carpenter, but there is every reason to believe that Lawrence had read him for himself, though doubtless rejecting much of the pseudo-scientific nonsense of this young misogynist. It is probably from Weininger that he takes the idea of a profound, quasi-cellular difference between the psychic and physical natures of male and female. Weininger speaks of the unequal distribution of male and female *plasmas* in different individuals.[4] Through Frieda, and the Lows, Lawrence had already acquired some slight acquaintance with the ideas of Freud, faint echoes of which are discernible in the psychology of *The Rainbow*. But Weininger, who was also a vehicle for Wagnerian themes Lawrence had already absorbed from George Moore, Maeterlinck and Nietzsche, was surely the main influence on the development of his ideas on sex psychology during the crucial shaping of *The Rainbow*.

In a letter to McLeod, the friend-disciple to whom he was more inclined to confide new ideas than to his mentor Garnett, Lawrence had defined in 1914 one of the themes of his current aesthetic of the novel. The "re-sourcing" of art will come about not through science nor through Marinetti's Futurism, but through its becoming "more the joint work of man and woman". Men must have the courage "to draw nearer to women, to expose themselves to them and be altered by them" and women must "accept and admit men" as they are; as a result, both will gain "great blind knowledge and suffering and joy", and this will result in a new art which it will take "a big further lapse of civilization to exploit and work out":

> Because the source of all living is in the interchange and the meeting and mingling of these two: man-life and woman-life, man-knowledge and woman-knowledge, man-being and woman-being.[5]

This is the very basis of the aesthetic doctrine expounded in the "Hardy", where is also proclaimed a new art founded on mutual knowledge and understanding of the male and female principles.

A molecular ego

But while the general line of this leads him to reject Futurism, Lawrence nevertheless uses Marinetti to illustrate a materialistic rather than psychoanalytical conception of character. He is looking for concealed elements underlying the conscious, deliberate, socially-disciplined self. He "sees something" of what he is after in Marinetti's theory that "the profound intuitions of life added one to the other, word by word, according to their illogical conception, will give us the general lines of an intuitive physiology of matter". Lawrence, however, is thinking not of inanimate matter, but of "that which is physic—non-human, in humanity", a concept which may be compared both with Weininger's *plasmas* and with a chapter of Carpenter's *Drama of Love and Death*, "The Beginnings of Love". This discusses not only Weininger's plasmas, but also the more scientifically established cellular phenomena of nutrition and reproduction among protozoa and multicellular organisms. This non-human "physic" interests Lawrence more than "the old-fashioned human element which causes one to conceive a character in a certain moral scheme and make him consistent".[6]

The "certain moral scheme" is indeed what he objects to, in full accord with Frieda who, for her part, never understood what people meant by "civilization"—and also in accord with a contemporary concept of the atomization of the individual, developed by both Carpenter and Weininger in their psychology of the mutual attraction of the sexes. In Turgenev, in Tolstoy, and in Dostoevsky, the moral scheme into which the characters fit is, according to Lawrence, "dull, old, dead"; and Marinetti is wrong to see a difference between "the heat of a piece of wood or iron" and "the laughter or tears of a woman". What interests Lawrence in this laughter is "the same as the binding of the molecules of steel or their action in heat":

> It is the inhuman will, call it physiology, or like Marinetti, physiology of matter, that fascinates me. I don't so much care about what the woman *feels*— in the ordinary usage of the word. That presumes an *ego* to feel with. I only care about what the woman *is*—what she IS—inhumanly, physiologically, materially—according to the use of the word: but for me, what she is as a phenomenon (or as representing some greater, inhuman will), instead of what she feels according to the human conception.[7]

It should be noted that Lawrence rarely employs words such as "unconscious" or "subconscious": he is looking for deeper elements of a cellular and material, not a psychological or psychoanalytic, order. He is nearer to the psychological materialism of the late nineteenth century than to twentieth-century methods of analysis of the psyche and its formation. For all that, he no longer wishes to show in his novels the traditional, "stable ego" of old. His characters answer to a different conception of being:

> You mustn't look in my novel for the old stable *ego*—of the character. There is another *ego*, according to whose action the individual is unrecognizable, and passes through, as it were, allotropic states which it needs a deeper sense than any we've been used to exercise, to discover are states of the same single radically unchanged element.[8]

He does not yet speak of the unconscious, but he is looking for something which is very close to it.

The form of the novel

To discover the plan of *The Rainbow*, we must therefore look elsewhere than in the evolution of the characters as individuals: "the characters fall into the form of some other rhythmic form, as when one draws a fiddle-bow across a fine tray delicately sanded, the sand takes lines unknown".[9] The three fundamental elements of this book are thus indissolubly linked: the simultaneous expression of "man-knowledge and woman-knowledge"; the quest for underlying, pre-mental, elements of this knowledge; and a construction of the novel conditioned not by the evolution of characters, but by the deeper and secret rhythms of their being. The conscious, intelligent, social being is deeply influenced by forces operating on the physiological and cellular plane: Lawrence's psychology of 1913–14 is thus essentially materialist and determinist.

Lawrence was to remain faithful to this conception all the time he was writing the final version of *The Rainbow*: but what may have started out as an aesthetic method, without any mere precise ideological basis than the "belief in the blood" exposed to Collings in 1913,[10] fairly soon took on a more theoretical turn. Intellectual impurities of every kind soon find their way into this intuitive alloy, both in the elaboration of detail and whenever Lawrence seeks greater depths and looks for "scientific" backing for his intuitions. His starting-point is both intuitive and artistic:

> We want to realize the tremendous *non-human* quality of life—it is wonderful. It is not the emotions, nor the personal feelings and attachments, that matter. These are all only expressive, and expression has become mechanical.[11]

But ethical values are also at stake: beyond the conscious, mechanical self and its "expressive" emotions, he is looking for something which is "sane and healthy and original", the discovery of which will give a novel new and unique form. Already for Lawrence the novel expresses the whole of life, is a living organism: "a novel, after all this period of coming into being, has definite organic form, just as a man when he is grown".[12] He thinks he may find in the pre-Hellenic past in Egypt and Assyria those "non-human" forms which will fascinate him in *Women in Love*. But he also seeks "non-human" truths in a conception of symbolism which, so he thinks, "avoids the I". Wagnerian romanticism, and Chamberlain's aesthetic mysticism, are very close to this search for the "non-human" underlying the conscious ego, and in point of fact, apart from an increasing awareness of his own aesthetic, none of this is very different from the aims and techniques of *The Trespasser*.

Theory of blood consciousness

The logical and historical link between these ideas as expressed in 1914, and Lawrence's evolution at the time of writing *Women in Love* and even later, appears clearly in a letter to Russell which, although written in December 1915, i.e. after *The Rainbow* was finished, nevertheless throws some light on its conception. The "non-human" elements which Lawrence was trying to express are mainly associated with love and even more (and this is what so struck readers of *The Rainbow* in 1915) with sex. This, however, is scarcely surprising, since his concept of character is partly based on Weininger's idea of male and female *plasmas*. In late 1915 he went so far as to confide to Russell, apropos of his recent reading of Sir James Frazer, a theory dating, he says, from when he was about twenty, for which he thinks he has found justification in *The Golden Bough* and *Totemism and Exogamy*. Reading these has convinced him "that there is another seat of consciousness than the brain and nerve system". There is a "blood consciousness" which exists in us "independently of the ordinary mental consciousness". Whereas mental consciousness perceives through the eye, blood consciousness perceives through "the sexual connexion"; so that his quest for another form of consciousness, too, bears a materialistic stamp:

> One lives, knows, and has one's being in the blood, without any reference to nerves and brain. This is one half of life, belonging to the darkness. And the tragedy of this our life and of your life, is that the mental and nerve consciousness exerts a tyranny over the blood-consciousness and that your will has gone completely over to the mental consciousness, and is engaged in the destruction of your blood-being or blood-consciousness, the final liberating of the one, which is only death in result. Plato was the same.[13]

This blood relationship being "active in the darkness", the "blood-percept" is weakened by seeing. "On the other hand, when I take a woman, then the blood-percept is supreme, my blood-knowing is overwhelming. There is a transmission, I don't know of what, between her blood and mine, in the act of connexion." This is an idea already present in a passage of the "Hardy" essay demonstrating that sexual union separates the male from the female in each partner, purifying and "singling out" man and woman.[14]

In fact, Lawrence merely takes from Frazer examples of primitive totemic beliefs which he proceeds to interpret in his own way prior to adoption. He then sees in them confirmation of his own beliefs, and asks Russell "what science says" about blood consciousness. In point of fact, this sudden mutation into theory of a previously purely mystic combination of blood and sex may well owe less to Frazer than to Weininger, with his male and female plasmas, and his theory of the "impregnation" of the woman resulting in the children of a second marriage resembling the first husband;[15] and perhaps to Rudolph Steiner. Not only does this letter show Lawrence in search of academic backing for beliefs which were already either implicit, or stated in the "Hardy": it also suggests that, at the time *The Rainbow* was written (i.e. between the "Hardy" and this letter), his intellectual balance was more precarious than his declared intentions lead one to expect, being in fact at the mercy of a sudden sprouting of certain mystic and occultist ideas which had been germinating in his mind since the beginning of 1913.

The attempt to find support in Frazer for the idea of a "blood-consciousness" testifies to this, as do also some echoes of similar beliefs in the novel itself—with its often hesitant psychology.

The foregoing is one example of how certain adventitious ideas intrude upon and obscure a main theme. *The Rainbow* is less pure in its genesis, less monolithic in its form, than is suggested by the author's original declarations. He knows well enough what he wants to do, but the scientific basis of his thought is shaky, and his psychology, while intuitively sound, is linked up with some very confused and mixed theoretical concepts.

Some a posteriori explanations

His aesthetic of the work which creates its own form naturally limits the application of any pre-established plan, and explains the divergencies between intentions proclaimed in advance and certain *a posteriori* judgments:

> You ask me about the message of *The Rainbow*. I don't know myself what it is: except that the older world is done for, toppling on top of us: and that it's no use the men looking to the women for salvation, nor the women looking to sensuous satisfaction for their fulfilment. There must be a new world.[16]

What a difference between his April 1914 summary and this declaration dating from just before the final drafting of *Women in Love*! In a 1917 letter to Waldo Frank, written just after the completion of this draft, Lawrence stresses the continuity of thought throughout the two books: but here again he considers his novel with hindsight, rather than from the angle of his original intention. In spite of the fact that some scenes of *The Rainbow*, such as a description of Greatham,[17] cannot have been written earlier than 1915, we must accept by and large Lawrence's statement that the work was "all written" before August 1914. He did not think the war "altered it from its pre-war statement", nor did he think he had done more than "clarify a little in revision".[18] On the other hand in the same letter he attributes to his 1914 draft of *The Rainbow* certain central themes which are much more characteristic of *Women in Love* and of his 1916 moods:

> I knew I was writing a destructive work, otherwise I couldn't have called it *The Rainbow*—in reference to the Flood. And the book was written and named in Italy, by the Mediterranean, before there was any thought of war. And I knew, as I revised the book, that it was a kind of working up to the dark sensual or Dionysic or Aphrodisic ecstasy, which does actually burst the world, burst the world-consciousness in every individual. What I did through individuals, the world has done through the war . . . There is a great *consummation* in death, or sensual ecstasy, as in *The Rainbow*.[19]

This judgment was pronounced in the pessimistic mood of *Women in Love*, in which the destructive, negative elements won out over the optimism of 1913–14. It is scarcely applicable to the first two tableaux of *The Rainbow*, the stories of Tom and Lydia, and of Will and Anna. When he comes to Ursula's education, his negative and bitter criticism of society grows more frequent. Certainly there is some basic contradiction between Ursula's intellectual development (in any case cut short by her affair with Skrebensky), a prerequisite for her social and economic emancipation, and her quest with Birkin for a balance based on pre-mental harmony. Thus the negative and asocial aspects of Ursula's ideas in the last chapters of *The Rainbow* are not entirely consonant with Lawrence's initial purpose, but rather seem to echo Lawrence's reactions to the war, and his revulsion from English life in 1914–15.

It is thus essential to stress the complexity of the gestation of *The Rainbow*, due both to the long period over which its writing stretched and to the evolution in its author's ideas between 1913 and 1915. Emotionally these were heavy years, and what should really strike us about *The Rainbow* is the relative unity of its construction, particularly of the first half, rather than those diversities largely explicable by the long lapse of time between conception and completion.

STRUCTURE OF *THE RAINBOW*:
TRIPTYCH AND CYCLES

Painting: Botticelli

Every critic is struck by the rhythmic structure of this novel, symbolized by its two successive titles: "The Wedding Ring" and "The Rainbow". The "Hardy" essay shows clearly that by 1914 Lawrence had given much thought to the question of the structure of a work of art, and that he had also given some attention to the specific form of the novel, rejecting traditional linear development for reasons inherent in his conception of character. His previous experiments in form, style and development, following in the track of Flaubert, George Moore and the Symbolists, led directly to this development. But painting, and particularly Botticelli, also played an important part in his search for the right structure for his subject.

Besides showing his concern for form in general and the form of the novel in particular, the "Hardy" also testifies to an intense interest in Italian Renaissance painting, at the very moment he was preparing to rewrite *The Rainbow*.

Will Brangwen is fascinated by certain pictures, particularly Raphael's "Dispute of the Sacrament" and Fra Angelico's "Last Judgment", both of which, like the phoenix motif he sculpts for Anna on a butter stamper, are all reproduced in Mrs Jenner's *Christian Symbolism*.[20] The phoenix is a symbol of instantaneous passage from non-being to absolute, perfect being, from birth to the last judgment. The nativity and the last judgment are, then, favourite themes with Lawrence, and the works of this period contain constant reference to "rebirth" and salvation. His theory of the "begotten" or "unbegotten" hero concerns birth and salvation, the passage of the individual to a higher plane of being. In *The Rainbow* he will show how, in each generation, individuals and couples try more or less successfully to "become complete": in other words to solve what he considers the central issue of all Hardy's novels: the problem "about becoming complete or about failure to become complete".[21]

The supreme aim of the new art, he asserts, will be to reveal and express the law of man and woman, "the glad embraces and the struggle between them", and the final reconciliation, "two in one, complete".[22] The novel being a free genre, it is more difficult for it than for poetry to formulate its own "law", to achieve balance between the law (form) and love (creative force). For Lawrence an instance of perfect balance between the law and love, of the expression of the living union of the male and female spirits, is to be found in the paintings of Botticelli, particularly in the "Mystic Nativity" in the National Gallery.

His observations on this picture constitute a perfect expression of his conception of the overall structure of *The Rainbow*, of the relations of the parts to the whole, and of the artistic construction of the novel. Whereas Raphael expresses the same subject (the Nativity, which is in a way the subject of *The Rainbow*) by rigorous geometrical "symbols", Botticelli is all motion:

> To express the same moment [union between the male and the female] Botticelli uses no symbol, but builds up a complicated system of circles, of movements wheeling in their horizontal plane about their fixed centres, the whole builded up dome-shaped, and then the dome surpassed by another singing cycle in the open air above. This is Botticelli always: different cycles of joy, different moments of embrace, different forms of dancing round, all contained in one picture, without solution. He has not solved it yet.
>
> And Raphael, in reaching the pure symbolic solution, has surpassed art and become almost mathematics. Since the business of art is never to solve, but only to declare. There is no such thing as solution. Nietzsche talks about the *Ewige Wiederkehr*. It is like Botticelli singing cycles. But each cycle is different. There is no real recurrence.[23]

It is evident, incidentally, that by "symbol" Lawrence here means geometrical abstraction. In the Botticelli, the angels flying under the vault of heaven carry little golden crowns evoking both the wedding ring and the crown of thorns. The analogy with the imagist symbolism of the titles successively given to *The Rainbow* is evident. Lawrence's analysis of Botticelli's "Nativity" could not be improved upon as a description of the imaginative freedom of his own symbolism, and of its relationship with the structure of his novel. It defines exactly the creative spirit which animates his work, refusing to be forced into any predetermined concept of form, to conform to any external rule. The overall plan of his novel, like that of Botticelli's picture, allows very great liberty in the elaboration of detail, and of secondary or minor cycles. The co-ordination of these cycles into the whole is a matter of taste and inspiration, not of a rigid preconceived plan.

The Rainbow is thus constructed like a triptych: the main, central panel is devoted to Ursula, the other two being given to Tom and Lydia, and to Anna and Will, respectively the grandparents and parents of the heroine. All three parts are strongly linked together, not by any repetition from one cycle to another—Lawrence's idea of the form of his novel excludes this—but by chapters in which time passes, vital events occur, and the characters are able to draw the lesson of their lives. Such are the chapters relating Anna's marriage, the flood and the death of Tom, Will's change of employment just when Ursula is entering university—all typically either linking two of the descriptive panels of the triptych or introducing a new subject in the central panel. The rest is essentially description, dialogue, and descriptive action.

The general lines of the novel's structure are clear but unobtrusive: the very first pages outline the conflict between the warm, intimate but confined life of the farm and the aspirations of the Brangwen women towards something different, towards "another form of life" based on the spirit, on knowledge, on the Word. This outside life, previously symbolized for the women by the vicar and the squire, intrudes upon the farm with the progressive advance of industrial civilization: first the high canal embankment "trespasses" across their land, and it is soon followed by the railway and the mine, bringing to the quiet valley the disturbing noises of the world of machines. In six pages Lawrence sets the tone and marks the crucial ambivalence of his position: on the one hand the desire for human consciousness, for a broader life; on the other the invasion of human consciousness by the civilization man himself creates. Acceptance and necessity of change for the promotion of the individual, the disastrous effects of this change on others, these are the twin poles of this ambivalence. And Lawrence recommends neither an impossible return to a bygone Golden Age nor the acceptance of all the impositions of the present, but, at least at first, a search for some kind of adaptation worthy of the human personality: less an ambivalence, perhaps, than a neutrality.

As in the Botticelli painting, each scene, each little tableau lives by its own movement, obeys its own particular rhythm. The development is neither linear nor spiral, but proceeds by a succession of scenes, occasionally overlapping in time but juxtaposed rather like the scenes of a stained-glass window. ("The Cathedral" chapter for instance follows after "Anna Victrix", though its action actually takes place in the middle of the period covered by this chapter.) And each chapter is in turn composed of a succession of short scenes, conveyed in narrative, or dialogue, or a close mixture of the two. The technique is not that of "interior soliloquy", or of the stream of consciousness. The author intervenes positively, nearly always discreetly, to present fact or to interpret action. In this respect the technique remains very similar to that of the more closely structured of the novels of the previous century. Lawrence has not chosen between purely dramatic presentation and explanatory commentary. We are struck not so much by any revolutionary change in the style of the novel as by a radical change of ordering, a new combination of the various parts, and above all a predominance of those rhythmic movements answering but never re-echoing one another, already heralded by *The Trespasser* and *Sons and Lovers*.

The lives of each of the two couples, and that of Ursula, each form one main cycle, each episode generally forming a secondary cycle. Each of the great scenes, such as the harvesting of the corn by moonlight, is marked by its own particular rhythm. Ursula's life takes the form of concentric circles, like ever-widening waves. A complete rhythmic infrastructure can be perceived in the play of words and images.

This is particularly marked not only in the opening pages, with their evocation of the Brangwen farm, the pulsing beat of creation, of nature and of season, but also throughout the cycle of Tom and Lydia and in the early life of Anna, who, till adolescence, is still closely enfolded in the animal warmth of the farm, as witness the telling details of her first love scenes with Will. With the changing generations and the irruption of the outside world, difficulties and discordancies increase. The rhythmic passages grow rarer, but return to mark, if no longer a true union of individuals and vital instincts, at least the strength and pull of these instincts at important moments.

The interplay of scene, dialogue and symbolic suggestion thus remains complex and subtle, never ordered to comply with any abstract system, but tuned to life and to creative imagination. The essential "message" of the novel as revealed by its structure is not didactic, but intentionally artistic and alive, respectful of the sense of life rather than of any preconceived idea or theory.

Such was Lawrence's conception of *The Rainbow*, and his success in carrying it out is one of the most convincing proofs that his apprenticeship as an artist had borne fruit. He did not so much revolutionize the structure of the novel as carry forward the structural patterns of his great predecessors: the structure of *The Rainbow* is not, when all is said and done, widely different from Flaubert.

Symbolism as a structural element

Symbol, like cyclic and rhythmic elements, is used by Lawrence as an integral part of the structure and overall conception of his novel and of the ordering of its various parts. As we have already seen, his symbols are free, not bound by any systematic spirit: the rainbow appears to Anna as an arch, a door opening on to the unknown and on to hope; at the end of the novel it appears to Ursula as the symbol of truth and of the creation of a new world. Because Lawrence wanted to depict instinctive, pre-mental states of his characters, he was structurally impelled to use symbol, in the same way that Will Brangwen, the art teacher, was driven to seek in religious art the expression of a self unable "to be and to be different". Lawrence showed his concern with this problem of symbolism and its function in a letter to Campbell written at the time he began to write *The Rainbow*. The novelist, he says, may look at things in two ways: either we can proclaim "I am all", all other things are but "radiation out from me", or we can

> . . . try to conceive the whole, to build up a whole by means of symbolism, because symbolism avoids the I and puts aside the egotist; and, in the whole, to take our decent place. That was how man built the cathedrals. He didn't say "out of my breast springs this cathedral!" But "in this vast whole I am a small part, I move and live and have my being" . . . The old symbols were each a

word in a great attempt at formulating the whole history of the soul of Man. They *are unintelligible* except in their whole context.[24]

Lawrence makes a dual use of symbol. His characters, particularly Will and Anna, use them unconsciously, obscurely, to express their aspirations and their beliefs, Will's blindly accepted symbols becoming subject to the sarcasm of the more perspicacious, more demanding Anna. The novelist, for his part, deliberately uses symbols, stars, meteors, light and shadow, rhythms and cycles for the evocation of feelings and aspirations deep in the pre-mental consciousness of his characters, concerning which they are either unaware, or inarticulate. The symbolist form of the novel is conditioned both by an effort towards objectivity and by Lawrence's "physiological" and molecular conception of character; it is an integral part of the structure of *The Rainbow*.

TWO BRANGWEN COUPLES

The non-linear novel

The deliberate non-linear structure of the novel, corollary of a certain conception of character, based on an intuitive psychology without a very firm theoretical basis, contributes considerably to masking the main lines of the destiny of the two Brangwen couples, Tom and Lydia, Will and Anna, to whom the first half of the novel is devoted. The painter-novelist no longer has the ultimate resource of the painter working in two dimensions, the spatial juxtaposition of scenes, so that, without either a definite linear development or explicit reminders to guide the reader, each scene inevitably tends to assert its own autonomy. *The Rainbow* precedes the "stream of consciousness" novel, and differs from it more distinctly than does the best of Flaubert. It does not occur to Lawrence to use the soliloquy, which in any case would be unlikely to help express psychic or physio-psychological states of which the characters themselves are not fully aware. He is often obliged to intervene, like the narrator of the conventional novel, and comment discreetly by image or comparison, or by introducing a symbolism of his own, instead of letting the characters express themselves by dialogue and gesture only.

Putting his finger on a weak point in Lawrence's experiment, Professor H. M. Daleski gives an excellent example of what he ingeniously calls the "stream of half-consciousness". Tom Brangwen, to whom "love is the most serious and the most terrible thing", is bidding his guests goodbye on his wedding night:

His heart was tormented within him, he did not try to smile. The time of his trial and his admittance, his Gethsemane and his Triumphal Entry in one, had come now.

Where does commentary begin, where does physical description of behaviour end? Which words correspond to Tom's state of mind, to soliloquy and which to the introduction of Lawrence's personal symbolism and favourite images? Tom cannot express in words states of his being which are not articulate nor even near the surface of consciousness; so that Lawrence intervenes as a sort of commentator.

A hesitant psychology

Moreover, being unsure both of the basis and vocabulary of his psychology, still hesitating between the vocabulary of traditional psychology and his intuitions of an "unconscious" or of a molecular ego, Lawrence often pursues false trails, leaving the reader to distinguish as best he can between physiology and old-fashioned notions of psychic life. Thus Tom Brangwen, who has just met Lydia for the first time, discovers in himself "another centre of consciousness", another centre of activity "in his breast, or in his bowels, somewhere in his body", as if "a strong light were burning there", a kind of "transfiguration between him and her": at the same time he feels bound to her by some "inner reality, a logic of the soul": the vocabulary is not adequate either to fulfil the author's descriptive ambition or to express his materialist psychology.[25]

Nor can Lawrence fully explain certain guiding principles: on several occasions he shows us Tom and Lydia in the process of "transfiguration" or "rebirth".[26] Thanks to a series of "second births", Will Brangwen also accedes in three or four stages to fuller integration of being, without the reader ever really being informed of what has happened to him or being enabled to understand why, after these successive changes, Will still remains "uncreated", incapable of fullness of being.[27]

The explanation of these four lives thus often remains obscure, buried in detail from which only an attentive examination of key scenes can help to disinter it. For in his anxiety to show his characters in action, not only does Lawrence allow minor incident to proliferate, but, in describing Tom's married life or Will's quarrels with his wife, he sometimes lets memories of his personal struggle with Frieda dominate his overall plan. Since the key scenes are drawn from his own life, but without his always daring to reveal the whole of his mind, or bringing the action of his characters entirely into the open, the basic structure of the story inevitably suffers.

Tom and Lydia

Tom is the last of the Brangwens in close touch with the teeming earth. Generations of Brangwens have cultivated their land, without seeking knowledge of the outer world. But while this "blood-intimacy" was enough for the men, the women wanted something different. They look outside to the symbols of the activity of man in the "spoken" world beyond, where men move "dominant and creative".[28] They want to give their sons the power of learning, the knowledge of what happens far from the Brangwen farmland. Their imagination is first fired by the "superior" life of the vicar, of the squire and his lady. Then, without completely disrupting the life of the farm, the encroachment of industry upon the countryside comes as a perpetual reminder of "other activity going on beyond them".

Tom Brangwen, forcibly dispatched to a grammar school in Derby by an ambitious mother, is an "unwilling failure" from the first. This unsuccessful venture in the paths of learning is not unlike that of Tom Tulliver in *The Mill on the Floss*: both Toms have the same generous character, the same natural sensitivity. His elder brothers having chosen other careers, at the age of seventeen Tom Brangwen takes over the farm following the accidental death of his father. An experience with a prostitute at nineteen, an adventure at Matlock at twenty-four with the young and unsatisfied mistress of a distinguished foreigner, a shyness touched with religious awe leave him hard to please, haunted by the dream of a voluptuous woman different from those he knows, who would bring him something of the atmosphere of a wider world. This portrait of Tom before his meeting with Lydia—a mixture of literary souvenirs and personal experience—is painted in exact and striking detail, conveying a sense of reality and psychological truth.

Lydia Lensky, Polish housekeeper to the local vicar, is thirty-two to Tom's twenty-eight. Of aristocratic origin, the widow of a doctor who died a refugee in London, she had lost two children before the birth of her daughter Anna. Her personality is, of course, a skilful transposition of that of Frieda, from whose behaviour and past life Lawrence has borrowed widely for his heroine. More experienced, less shy than Tom, free of all the conventional scruples which trammel him, she accepts open-eyed his proposal of marriage. This gives Lawrence an opportunity to depict a first instance in *The Rainbow* of masculine immaturity in face of the surer vital instinct of the woman. The first two years of their married life show the generous and sensitive Tom learning the role of the male in face of the female, acquiring a male understanding of the "law of the woman".

This picture of the cycles of love, of attraction and repulsion, its moments of perfect harmony or of mutual withdrawal by the two partners, its alternating periods of incomprehension between their two conscious "selves" and of their passionate union in physical unconsciousness, owes much to the personal experience of Lawrence and Frieda. But certain passages lead us to wonder whether the novelist may not have sought other sources of information, if, for instance, he may not have been to some extent illustrating certain pages of Havelock Ellis, notably those of the third volume of *Studies in the Psychology of Sex* devoted to sexual impulse. A passage describing Lydia's periodicity of desire is very close to the corresponding description in Chapter 3 of that volume: "The Sexual Impulse in Women".[29] It is not impossible that the theories exposed in the "Hardy" on the "law of the man" and that of the woman, and their illustration in this novel, were based on Lawrence's study of the most famous and effective of contemporary English sexologists.

Viewed as the story of the gradual initiation of the good, simple Tom, little used to expressing his feelings and ideas, into a respect for the rhythms of Lydia's personal life, this part of the novel is most successful. Lawrence is as frank as contemporary conventions permitted, and as the subject requires. He hides nothing of the awkwardness, the clumsiness, the hesitancy of Tom's slow discovery of his role of husband to a partner previously married to a man of greater refinement than himself. And if the novelist did, indeed, seek in Havelock Ellis or elsewhere a more clinical observation of sexual psychology, he certainly adapted it with taste and tact, successfully merging his reading with his own experience.

The transfiguration

The love of Tom and Lydia reaches a climax after some two years of marriage. The importance of this climax in Lawrence's mind is made clear by its presentation as a final "transfiguration" or "baptism", an accession to a higher plane of being, which also results in Lydia's daughter Anna becoming Tom's spiritual daughter. Moreover this transfiguration scene is the first in a series; it is repeated, *mutatis mutandis*, between Will and Anna, Ursula and Birkin, and Mellors and Constance Chatterley. It is also the subject of "Manifesto", one of the most important poems in *Look! We Have Come Through!* We are clearly faced with a major theme in the Lawrentian concept of the couple.[30]

Tom Brangwen has already learned, as Will will later learn with Anna, to "abate himself", not to impose himself on Lydia when she does not desire him. "She was Woman to him", but she could not "want him as much as he demanded that she should want him".[31] Therefore he must find "other centres of living". He is excited by a visit to his brother Alfred's mistress, a cultured woman who reads Browning and Herbert Spencer, and who brings home to him his own inferiority to a form of life outside his experience. Lydia and he then feel obscurely that something is lacking in their life, and when they discuss this together Tom is indignant to hear Lydia speaking to him "as if she were a stranger". She has once more become "the active unknown facing him". In other words he perceives that she is not part of himself, that she exists by and for herself. Suddenly he perceives that she may be lonely, isolated, unsure, and this Lydia confirms:

> Why aren't you satisfied with me?—I'm not satisfied with you. Paul used to come to me and take me like a man does. You only leave me alone or take me like your cattle, quickly, to forget me again—so that you can forget me again . . . I want you to know there is somebody there besides yourself . . . You come to me as if it was for nothing, as if I was nothing there. When Paul came to me, I *was* something to him—a woman, I was. To you I am nothing—it is like cattle —or nothing—

"You make me feel as if *I* was nothing", Tom replies. After a long silence, she calls him to her. She puts her arms round him as he stands before her: "and her hands on him seemed to reveal to him the mould of his own nakedness, he was passionately lovely to himself". She is still "the awful unknown", but transfigured, wonderful. He would have liked to kiss her feet but was "too ashamed for the actual deed, which were like an affront":

> She waited for him to meet her, not to bow before her and serve her. She wanted his active participation, not his submission. She put her fingers on him. And it was torture to him, that he must give himself to her actively, participate in her, that he must meet and embrace and know her, who was other than himself . . . But he let go his hold on himself, he relinquished himself and knew the subterranean force of his desire to come to her, to be with her, to mingle with her, losing himself to find her, to find himself in her.[32]

This is the moment of final transfiguration, the baptism into another life, the discovery of a new world which it remains only to explore.

Although dated from Zennor, the poem "Manifesto" clearly refers to the same experience, the same theory, the same symbolism. The poet is tortured by "the hunger for a woman", for any woman, indiscriminate woman, mere "female adjunct of himself", by a "threatening, torturing, phallic Moloch" of hunger, "a thing to be afraid of". One woman only has fed this hunger. But even knowing himself loved by her he is still "ashamed, and shameful and vicious". He has learned to know his wife as the "not-me", to know "his own limitation against her", to know that, "ultimately, she is all not me". She meanwhile treats him as though they were "one piece", as though he, like Tom, were nothing:

> She touches me as if I were herself, her own.
> She has not realized yet, that fearful thing, that I am the other,
> She thinks we are all of one piece.
> It is painfully untrue.

And so the poet cries his need:

> I want her to touch me at last, ah, on the root and quick of my darkness
> and perish on me as I have perished on her.
> Then, we shall be two and distinct, we shall have each our separate being.
> And that will be pure existence, real liberty.
> Till then, we are confused, a mixture, unresolved, unextricated one
>   from the other.
> . . . .
> When she has put her hand on my secret, darkest sources, the darkest
>   outgoings,
> when it has struck home to her, like a death, "this is *him*!"
> she has no part in it, no part whatever,
> it is the terrible *other* . . .

And he insists that she lay her hands on his "secret, darkest sources, the darkest outgoings", that she shall recognize, like a death, that "this is him", that which is in him and in which she has no part, "it is the terrible *other*". This mystic gesture puts an end to all confusion:

> then I shall be glad, I shall not be confused with her,
> I shall be cleared, distinct, single, as if burnished in silver,
> having no adherence, no adhesion anywhere,
>
> one clear, burnished, isolated being, unique,
> and she also, pure, isolated, complete,
> two of us, unutterably distinguished, and in unutterable conjunction.
> Then we shall be free, freer than angels, ah, perfect.[33]

This poem is of capital importance in Lawrence's 1914–17 output because it develops a theme haunting the writer throughout this period. In his remarkable attempt at interpretation of the wartime novels, Daleski makes no mention of it. He gives, of the mystic gestures designed to bring home to the woman the fact that the man is "other", not belonging to her, certain physiological explanations which no critic can altogether exclude. Yet, taking things on a relatively simple plane, it seems possible to put forward a literary explanation of these scenes of *The Rainbow*, independent of any suggestion of sexual anomaly.

The key words to the scene between Tom and Lydia and between Will and Anna, which reappear in "Manifesto" and in *Lady Chatterley's Lover*, are *shame* and *ashamed*. Sometimes the man, sometimes the woman, refusing to accept unreservedly the sexual relation with the other, hesitates and struggles. The sexual act has not fully entered into consciousness but remains something obscure, something animal, rejected by the social self. Lydia's gesture in putting her arms around Tom's thighs as he stands before her, pressing him against her breast, symbolizes and reveals her conscious acceptance of the whole being of the man she loves; and he interprets it as such. He ceases to "be nothing" to her in the sexual act, she accepts him completely, freely, knowing that after their union he will once more become "other", free. The fact that in other novels Lawrence embroiders on this theme, introducing anal contacts, is no doubt significant in terms of Freudian psychology, but it changes nothing in the essential interpretation of this scene. Lydia's chaste caress, an invitation to participate actively, to forget herself, simply shows that henceforward, for both of them, their conscious life and their sex life is one and the same, in a way it had not been before this scene. They have acceded to the last stage of sexual initiation, in which the conscious self accepts the other, in the fullness of his being and admitting all his instincts, each treating the other with deep respect for his or her own separate and distinct existence. With Birkin and Ursula we shall see the importance Lawrence attached to total acceptance of the physical being of the loved one, including the eliminatory functions, and the special role these play in his philosophy of being. To accept these functions is to recognize that the universe is subject to a dual process of creation and destruction and to admit the "flux of corruption" which is part of all life.

Because as a couple they do not possess the same human quality, the corresponding scene between Will and Anna is on a different level, culminating in partial liberation, but not in a "transfiguration" into a kind of sanctity.

In the scene between Tom and Lydia we find the same element of mysticism so strongly stressed in the last line of "Manifesto":

We, the Mystic NOW.

Acquaintance with *Love's Coming of Age* or *The Drama of Love and Death*, in both of which Carpenter expresses, in increasingly mystic terms, the idea of regeneration through love, would have been enough to initiate Lawrence to this line of thought.

In the first of these works Carpenter quotes Ellen Key to stress that "two beings through one another may become a new being, and a greater than either could be of itself alone".[34] In the second, he declares that love creates a new soul, quoting Swedenborg: "Those who are truly married on earth are in heaven one Angel."[35] At Anna's wedding to Will, Tom Brangwen harangues the company at large, proclaiming that man and woman are made for each other and that "If we've got to be Angels, and if there's no such thing as a man nor a woman amongst them, then it seems to me as a married couple makes one Angel . . . they rise united at the Judgment Day as one Angel."[36]

After Tom's death, showing her granddaughter Ursula her wedding rings, Lydia tells her of her two husbands, of how, after serving Lensky as a slave during her first marriage, she gradually discovered she had a life of her own, and she expresses her gratitude to Tom for having given her her true place in life and immortality.[37] Transposed into the register of nineteenth-century farm life, this is the exact equivalent of the "mystic moment" of "Manifesto" which, however, brings additional proof of Lawrence's 1916–17 preoccupation with occultism.

Will and Anna

Will and Anna differ from Tom and Lydia in their total lack of love experience. At the time of their meeting and short courtship prior to marriage, Anna is eighteen and Will twenty. Up to the moment Ursula becomes the central character, the novel shows four stages of their love life. Their adolescent love culminates in the moonlight harvesting and marriage proposal. With their honeymoon begins a cycle of quarrels and reconciliations. The pregnant Anna's ritual dance, naked before God, marks the end of this stage and the triumph of her "ego" over that of Will, who, for his part, acquires an "absolute ego" and some degree of independence. To Anna child-bearing then becomes the main object of existence, while Will, having failed to dominate her, seeks refuge in amateur artistic activities and in the company of his little daughter Ursula. After his attempt to seduce a Nottingham working girl, he and Anna reach, in their own way, some sort of liberation, in mutual acceptance of the partner's ego and in unbridled sensuality. This fourth stage is attained in a scene similar to that of the transfiguration of Tom and Lydia. Will's social ego is then freed, and he establishes his utility by seeking appointment as a teacher of handicrafts, a career in which he achieves some success.

Although not highly developed intellectually, Anna has been educated as a lady, and treats her schoolmates with aristocratic contempt. Her cousin, Will Brangwen, a lace designer, comes to live near the farm; he appears shy and aggressive, but Lawrence is careful to show him to the reader exclusively through the eyes of Anna. She quickly takes the initiative, and their courtship blossoms in the atmosphere of the farm. The clumsy movement of a horse in the stable, the "explosive bustle" of a hen disturbed in the fowl-loft, and other vivid details lend substance and reality to this picture of first love which is not easily forgotten. At corn harvest the two youngsters wandering in the moonlight find the sheaves lying as the reapers left them, and deciding to put up some shocks, they work together, coming and going, in a rhythm which carries their feet and their bodies in tune, until finally Will overtakes and kisses Anna. The "whole rhythm of him beats into his kisses" and he discovers his desire in a strangely beautiful scene in which the counterpoint of sentence and of paragraph evokes the lovers' unconscious yearnings. Repeated reminders of nature and of the creative pulse obscurely evoke the hidden instincts commanding the physical nature of two young and still unfinished creatures, driven by natural forces to which they submit without ever quite understanding them. The fact that they will never completely become conscious of those forces places them among the incomplete characters described by Lawrence in the "Hardy".[38] The reader may easily be misled by the very beauty of the passages describing their love; in those episodes the novelist preserves complete descriptive neutrality. Yet he later makes it quite clear that they have failed to achieve true being.

The story of their married life, of the cycle of love and hate, attraction and repulsion, played out in ignorance of forces propelling them like puppets, is perhaps too detailed, disproportionate to the novelist's intention. Even the reader engrossed by the sheer interest of the story must often pause to ask himself what Lawrence is really driving at. Autobiographical elements are constantly introduced, many of them purely adventitiously. The honeymoon, for instance, occupies a holiday of "some weeks", most improbably enjoyed by a twenty-year-old industrial lace designer in the late nineteenth century. Will is obsessed with the fear that Anna may leave him as soon as she takes up the thread of social life again by giving her first tea-party![39] Nothing lends plausibility to such a dread, which, however, echoes an all too real fear of Lawrence's at Gargnano. The recital of the young couple's quarrels and reconciliations, on which the novelist seems to dwell with pleasure, is, so to speak, made on two distinct levels: one being the author's personal experience (when Will and Anna are made to behave like Lawrence and Frieda), the other the description of a given couple for the main purposes of the novel. Personal experience frequently invades the narrative, fills in the details, not always in harmony with the broad outlines of the story.

Nevertheless all the key incidents are firmly linked with the main theme, and at times there is also a justified resemblance between the characters and their real-life models. Anna, for instance, is represented as an "aristocrat", whereas Will, a less evolved character, lives unconsciously in the warm, confined atmosphere of the Brangwen family. This contrast is confirmed by the visit which the couple make to Baron Skrebensky, a Polish refugee, and former friend of Lydia and Lensky, who has become an Anglican clergyman. The baron stands out clearly among his mining parishioners as "a fiery aristocrat".[40] As in the "Hardy", Lawrence attributes to this word a mystic, almost racial quality. When the young Brangwens visit the baron before the birth of Ursula, Anna is conscious of the contrast between the rough, plebeian Will and the young English baroness, with her "strange, child-like surety". Skrebensky himself seems to her "so detached, so purely objective", "distinct" and "separate" that "a woman was thoroughly outside him": such are the qualities Lawrence attributes to his "aristocrats"; the very qualities to which the poet aspires in "Manifesto". At home, in contrast, Anna feels "stifled" by the close life of the Brangwens and wonders if "the high sharp air" of the Skrebenskys is not her natural element.[41]

The same opposition directly linked to the ideas expressed in the "Hardy" is taken up once more in the scene of the young Brangwens' visit to Lincoln Cathedral, its symbolism completing the picture of their conflicting immaturities. Will has failed on the plane of independent male activity: he has not been able to finish the work of art he had begun, a wood-carving representing the creation of Eve. With Anna he behaves like a jealous child with its mother; his trips to Nottingham, at first in search of reproductions of works of art, later for less worthy purposes, his efforts to assert his authority over the child Ursula, are all manifestations of this infantilism. After violent quarrels which leave both Anna and himself "shadowed and stained with blood", "pure love" invariably returns to reconcile them. Anna understands that Will is not her "complement" but her "opposite".[42] Each tries to dominate the other, to destroy in the other what makes for separate identity. Will is jealous of Anna's sewing machine, she of his religious feeling, of his "dark, emotional experience of the Infinite, of the Absolute". She makes fun of the Christian symbols he loves, the lamb in the stained-glass window with "its little flag with a red cross".[43]

Lawrence does not seem to have aimed systematically at illustrating contemporary psycho-analytical ideas on the infantile personality, of which he probably did not acquire personal knowledge until after finishing *The Rainbow*. It is not impossible however that some approximate notions may have filtered through to him from Frieda or from Barbara Low. It is far more likely that he was simply drawing on memories of his recent struggles with Frieda, while developing the theme of the opposition between an aristocratic, that is to say more independent character, Anna, and a more plebeian nature, Will. Another background idea, that of the mixture of male and female principles, and its corollary, the notion of "complementarity", already expressed in the "Hardy", is transposed into character in the chapter on the cathedral. In the plebeian Will, the female principle predominates. To Lawrence, this explains his attitude to Anna. He is not her "complement", and since the "male principle" is more developed in Anna than in Will, their union cannot result in true balance.

Aristocrat and plebeian

Lincoln Cathedral becomes the symbol of their divergencies and oppositions. Will's religion is so completely imbued with the "female principle" that to Anna's intense irritation he greets the distant cathedral with a spontaneous "there she is". To Will, the cathedral represents perfect "oneness", the fusion of "before" and "after", "the timeless consummation, where the thrust from the earth met the thrust from heaven and the arch was locked on the keystand of ecstasy". Anna, on the other hand, while conscious of the beauty of the "leaping stone", refuses to let her horizon be bounded by the great vault, conscious of the open sky beyond the roof, and of the space beyond the altar where "stars were wheeling in freedom, with freedom above them always higher". To escape the "ultimate confine", the "perfect womb", of the cathedral she seizes upon the "wicked odd, little faces" carved in stone by the mediaeval artisans, spoiling Will's "passionate intercourse" with the cathedral by her jeers at "the sly malicious" carved figures, which according to Lawrence in the "Hardy", represent a reassertion of the male principle.[44] The aristocrat Anna affirms the modern male principle against her husband's female, Hebraic, monist faith, Lawrence thus using the novel to illustrate the contention made in the essay, itself derived from Weininger and Chamberlain.

Will continues his instinctive superficial existence, without succeeding in becoming "really articulate", in finding "real expression". He continues always in "the old form . . . in spirit, he was uncreated".[45] As a result, Anna is also unable to achieve full individuality and seeks in child-bearing a substitute for salvation. During her first pregnancy she dances, like David naked before his God, a secret ritual dance to consecrate the illusory victory of handing on to the next generation the responsibility of achieving perfect being. This dance has evoked much comment, yet the explanation is quite simple: "Anything that *triumphs*, perishes," as Lawrence was to say in "The Crown".[46] Clearly the pregnant Anna's secret triumph is a consecration of the ultimate failure of her marriage to Will.

The liberation through unbridled sensuality which ends the story of their love differs from the transfiguration undergone by Tom and Lydia. Lawrence shows them united only in a mutual egoism, each seeking his or her own pleasure. Later he makes it clear that these two remain for ever "uncreated", incomplete, despite the success of their union on the plane of procreation and mere sex. As is shown in the scene with the Nottingham "warehouse lass", Will is the type of man who seeks to assert his power over a woman without any regard for her individuality.[47] When he comes home Anna perceives a change and sees him as a sexual adventurer. "Very good," is her reaction; if he was "the sensual male seeking his pleasure, then she was the female ready to take hers". "In one motion they abandoned the moral position", each "seeking gratification pure and simple". This liberation from shame, while comparable to that of Tom, differs in being played out on the plane of "sensuous lust", without "tenderness" or love, just as it also differs from that of Birkin and Ursula in *Women in Love*: with Will and Anna, shame does not disappear, but is accepted as an irreducible fact. It is significant that Ursula's lessons on the different forms of true love will come not from her mother but from her grandmother. Twice married, Lydia has found a peace and reconciliation with life that neither Anna nor her husband will ever know. The rest of the novel is devoted, in the light of these two examples, to the first part of Ursula's apprenticeship.

URSULA

The character of Ursula is the *raison d'être* of *The Rainbow*. With her, the reaerd may legitimately expect to reach the heart of the problem Lawrence set out to treat in this novel: that of "woman becoming individual, self-responsible, taking her own initiative".

Ursula's character evolves on several different planes; the reader is often tempted to analyse the interactions of those planes upon one another, but Lawrence makes this easy neither by his synthetic presentation nor by his theory of allotropic states of the "ego". The character has to be taken for granted rather than understood. Ursula's secondary schooling provides the opportunity for her economic and moral emancipation from her family, and leads to her harsh initiation into the "man's world" as a schoolteacher. Her introduction to love and sex life takes place in three phases, her romantic first love for Skrebensky, her lesbian "crush" on her teacher Winifred Inger, then her liaison with Skrebensky, culminating in his final rejection, after which she thinks she is pregnant, suffers shock and illness, and finally discovers her true self. In the course of her university studies she has repudiated academic science, as well as mechanistic and industrial democracy, in favour of a vitalist romanticism with mystic undertones.

A composite character

The method of composition of *The Rainbow* necessarily made of Ursula a composite character tending more and more to merge with her creator. To begin with, Lawrence "grafts" a physical portrait of Louie Burrows onto a moral portrait of Frieda. The setting of Ursula's family life is that of the Burrows family. Cossethay is the village of Cossal, home of Louie's father, on whom Will Brangwen is modelled, and the house at Beldover, where Will and Anna take their family to live, owes something to one at Quorn, to which the Burrows moved later.[48] The incidents of Ursula's childhood and education are based on those of Louie, while the picture of her career as a teacher is that of Louie's crossed with personal experience. This has not prevented Lawrence from making her mother and grandmother Polish, and giving them "aristocratic" origins which, in his eyes, explain the "curious blind dignity" of the Brangwen girls, the "kind of nobility in their bearing" which, by "some result of breed and upbringing", made them seem "to rush along their own lives without caring that they existed to other people".[49]

But the graft is yet more complex: the closer the identification of the heroine with her creator the more difficult it becomes to distinguish Ursula's soliloquies from those of Lawrence. On the one hand we find scenes transposed from the author's life, but with the sex roles reversed, such as that in which Ursula announces to Skrebensky that she will not marry him.[50] On the other, Ursula's reflections on the Nativity, the Passion and the Resurrection suddenly jump from indirect speech in the past tense to the first person present, and the Brangwen children give way to the Lawrence of Rananim and the earthly paradise.[51] Ursula's social and political ideas scarcely ring true for a girl of her age and generation: the clear traces of Lawrence's own 1915 preoccupations and some echoes of Chamberlain detract from the homogeneity of the character, without making any positive contribution to the novel.[52] Ursula tends to become the mouthpiece of the novelist, who obscures his original theme by launching into destructive diatribes against democratic and industrial society.

This direct grafting of Lawrence onto Ursula is further complicated by the fact that Lawrence seems at times to identify himself not with his heroine, but with Skrebensky. The moonlight love scenes (to which we shall return) are strongly reminiscent of the painful scenes at Robin Hood's Bay and Flamborough, described by Jessie Chambers.[53] Elsewhere Ursula's feeling for Maggie Schofield, very close to that of Lawrence for Jessie, is complicated by her simultaneous attraction to Maggie's young farmer brother, who wants to marry her. Lawrence has drawn so freely on the raw material of his memories that any attempt to disentangle the network of fleeting identification of persons and of experience only risks increasing the obscurity of certain passages expressed in what are, at times, hermetic symbols. After all, what matters is what the author reveals to the reader, the synthesis that is Ursula. Its component elements are of value only in so far as they make it possible to eliminate certain obscurities, or to throw light on certain scenes difficult to understand without their help. Tempting though it is to identify the personal memories used in the synthesis, it should always be remembered that they are, on the whole, subordinate to the creative intention.

From early childhood to the age of twenty-one, Ursula's character is described with a wealth of detail which sometimes obscures the whole, particularly as Lawrence does not hesitate to avail himself of all the facilities offered by his idea of "allotropic states" of the ego. He even sketches a picture of the successive "escapes" of an ego continually shocked by the meanness of her surroundings:

> Then she found that the way to escape was easy. One departed from the whole circumstances. One went away to the Grammar School, and left the little school, the meagre teachers, the Phillipses whom she had tried to love but who had made her fail, and whom she could not forgive.[54]

The life of this eternal adolescent is spent hoping to discover at the next turning point the perfection she has so far failed to find. She feels "superior", her pride, though unconscious, is infinite, and she never shows the least notion of obligation or of a sense of responsibility to others. On the contrary she is completely possessed by the idea that she is predestined to be different, exceptional. As a child she awaits the coming of the Son of God who will choose her for his bride; compared with Maggie Schofield and her farmer brother she thinks of herself as "a traveller on the face of the earth, doomed to go on and on, seeking the goal that she knew she did grow nearer to", ready to break "from that form of life wherein Maggie must remain enclosed".[55] With this asocial romanticism goes a kind of hypertrophy of the ego, all the more complete for a total failure to realize itself in relation to others. Ursula is presented as endowed with a will to "complete independence, complete social independence, complete independence from any personal authority".[56]

The annihilation of Skrebensky

When the son of Baron Skrebensky, a young officer in the Engineers, six years older than Ursula, makes his appearance in her adolescent life, she sees in him one of the Sons of God whose coming she was awaiting: she uses him to explore her own physical female reactions to the male body, without even the illusion of love, the discovery of the nullity of his moral personality being simultaneous with the exploration of his physical being. The chapter entitled "First Love" is devoted to this preliminary skirmishing, which takes the form of passionate kissing, and provides a first indication of the deep difference between the personalities of Ursula and Skrebensky.

This difference is soberly and successfully stated by Ursula after a short dialogue on war and the soldier: "It seems to me as if you weren't anybody— as if there weren't anybody there, where you are. Are you anybody, really? You seem like nothing to me."[57]

A little later Anton's secret is revealed: "Why could he not himself desire a woman so? Why did he never really want a woman, not with the whole of him: never loved, never worshipped, only physically wanted her?"[58]

This passage is one of those where Lawrence is proclaiming, rather than letting the reader discover in action, Skrebensky's basic "nullity"; it provides the key to the curious moonlight scene which follows the wedding of Ursula's uncle, Fred Brangwen. The dancing is led by another uncle, Tom Brangwen, a bachelor and a rake, to whom is attached a slight suggestion of homosexuality, and who in Lawrence's symbolism of corruption and disintegration is represented as some aquatic creature of the marshes. The music comes in waves, and Tom's movements evoke "another element, inaccessible as the creatures that move in the water". Ursula dances with Skrebensky with a "deep, fluid underwater energy", in a "glaucous, intertwining, delicious flux", revealing "a vision of the depths of the underworld, under the great flood". The chapter of "The Crown" entitled "The Flux of Corruption" explains this symbolism. The dance with Skrebensky is not, as has been said, "a representation in physical terms of the ideal relation between a man and a woman: the 'two in one' ".[59] It is an association on a lower plane of being, in corruption and deliquescence, a passing harmony at a sub-human, demonic level. Skrebensky is satisfied by this life of shadows, but Ursula suddenly is "aware of some influence looking in upon her": the watching presence of the rising moon, and she stands "filled with the full moon, offering herself". "She wanted the moon to fill in to her, she wanted more, more communion with the moon, consummation. But Skrebensky put his arm round her and led her away."[60] He wraps her symbolically in a "big, dark cloak" as if to return her to darkness. She wants to "fling away her clothing and flee away, away from this dark confusion and chaos of people to the hill and the moon". But the people stand around her "like stones", Skrebensky himself weighs on her "like a loadstone" and she feels like "bright metal, weighted down by dark, impure magnetism". He is the dross, the people are the dross. If only she could get away to the "clean free moonlight".[61]

The moon here clearly symbolizes consciousness, light, aspiration towards the heights, and Ursula's affinity with the moon is favourably, positively presented. The girl is hard, bright and "intact", as far beyond Skrebensky "as the moonlight was beyond him, never to be grasped". Still he pursues her, trying to "weave himself round her, enclose her in a net of shadow, of darkness, so she would be like a bright creature gleaming in a net of shadows, caught". But Ursula walks back into the moonlight among the "great new stacks of corn glistening and gleaming" under the night's blue sky, and Skrebensky goes with her, still unreal, terrified by the "great moon conflagration of the cornstacks".

The scene which follows has been interpreted in several ways. Comparing it with the later moonlight scene between Ursula and Skrebensky,[62] Professor Daleski deduces a physiological explanation not absolutely essential for an understanding of the whole. Skrebensky is afraid of the full light of the moon because his advances are aimed only at the physical possession of Ursula. She, conscious of the difference between the "chaos" of which he is part and of her own aspirations towards a fuller, purer life, is at the same time sexually excited. She simultaneously tempts and refuses him. She takes the initiative in a long kiss, but the "sudden lust" Anton awakens in her is aimed against his masculinity: she is seized with the desire to "lay hold of him and tear him and make him into nothing", as he presses himself upon her "in extremity". And taking him in a "hard", "fierce", "corrosive" kiss, "seething like some cruel corrosive salt around the last substance of his being", Ursula destroys Skrebensky, whose "soul is dissolved with agony and annihilation".[63]

This scene is too outstandingly written not to correspond in the author's mind to some personal experience. It presents certain analogies with the last love scene between Ursula and Anton, the physiological meaning of which is very much more apparent; but in this case, despite Skrebensky's desire, the actual love play clearly remains at the stage of kisses and close embrace. The essential elements of the scene are the moonlight with its evocative symbolic power; Skrebensky's inadequacy as an individual, afraid as he is of the full light of consciousness; Ursula's auto-eroticism, stimulated by the young man's caresses; and the physical or moral "annihilation" which suddenly deprives Skrebensky of his masculinity, and in which psychoanalysts might be tempted to see the effect of a castration complex.

Coming to herself again, Ursula wonders if she has not been seized with madness, what "horrible thing" can possibly have possessed her? Deliberately, "with all her might", she makes herself loving and protective towards Anton, who, for his part, is conquered, subjected. He has lost the initiative, he has become "reciprocal", "as a distinct male he has no more core", "she had abated that fire, she had broken him".[64]

Since Lawrence is here dealing with an erotic crisis between two adolescents (despite his military experience, Skrebensky is not much bolder or assertive in love than the Lawrence of 1908 to 1910), it seems likely that the personal experience behind this scene is indeed that of the moonlight scenes described by Jessie Chambers on the Lincolnshire coast, when Lawrence, in great physical and moral distress, broke out into violent abuse of the girl who was the innocent cause of his discomfort.[65] But there has clearly been some transposition of the sexes: instead of Will becoming aware of physical desire in the moonlight with Anna, or Lawrence at Mablethorpe with Jessie, it is Ursula who suddenly discovers desire and her femininity, only half understanding what is happening to her. And may not the premature "annihilation" of Skrebensky reflect euphemistically a similar physiological humiliation of Lawrence?

This particular scene remains ambiguous and obscure; that it had a special meaning for Lawrence and recalled personal memories seems probable. But in 1915 he lacked the courage or the skill to say exactly what he meant. Critics therefore tend to interpret such a scene differently, according to which particular aspect of Lawrence's symbolism they wish to emphasize. A simple explanation is, however, possible: Ursula's first, fierce, erotic responses are thwarted by her feeling of the personal inadequacy of the man who arouses them. As a human, Ursula is his superior and she knows it, hence the destructive and egoistic form taken by the erotic excitement which he stimulates against her conscious wish. Lawrence tried to express something similar in The Lost Girl, when Alvina Houghton has her first experience of contact with a man, and behaves rather like Ursula in this scene.

Winifred Inger

After this experience, Ursula's sexual life "flames into a kind of disease within her", settling for a time on Winifred Inger, a twenty-eight-year-old schoolmistress who is the first of a Lawrentian series of intelligent and unsatisfied young women, all more or less lesbian. Winifred serves as a link between several aspects of Ursula's life: she stimulates her philosophical development, she feeds her emotions, she marries her uncle Tom, to whom she is drawn by a corrupt and corrupting scepticism, a disintegration of the psyche, an acceptance of a social system subservient to the machine.

Ursula always keeps her lesbian love for Winifred a closely-guarded secret, "the closed door she had not the strength to open", even to her close friend Maggie Schofield.[66]

Lawrence might quite well have portrayed Winifred, her intellectual influence on Ursula and her marriage to Tom Brangwen, without introducing a Lesbian scene which was ostensibly responsible for the suppression of the novel in 1915. Why then was he so determined to give Ursula this experience, "the secret side-show to her life, never to be opened"? Had his own experience convinced him that any discovery of the self necessarily passes through a phase of ill-differentiated sex activity? There are obvious analogies between this waterside scene and that in which Cyril is rubbed down by George after a swim in *The White Peacock*. Once more the setting is a bathing expedition. A sudden, ice-cold shower of rain pours down on the "flushed, hot limbs" of the women, startling and delicious. It is difficult not to suspect that in introducing this scene at a point when autobiographical memories, including, with the Schofields, the old nostalgia for Haggs Farm, became more pressing, Lawrence was responding to some inner compulsion rather than to any artistic necessity intrinsic to the development of the novel.

Ursula's formal studies receive little attention, and it is from Winifred that she absorbs a philosophy of life and learns to detest a society nevertheless partially imbued with this philosophy. Winifred's education has been both scientific and philosophical. She humanizes Ursula's religion, stripping it of its "dogmas and its falsehoods", showing her pupil that all religion is "but a particular clothing to a human aspiration". She also teaches her that "the human desire is the criterion of all truth and all good", truth being "one of the products of the human mind and feeling". Man has nothing to fear and the enlightened soul "does not worship power" "degenerated to money and Napoleonic stupidity".

Among the "many writings" of which Ursula got the "gist" from talks with Winifred were very probably those of Weininger and Chamberlain, often echoed in this section of the novel, and of Nietzsche: Ursula refuses to accept a mild and gentle God, "neither Lamb nor Dove"; her God is the lion, the eagle, the wild horse.[67]

Winifred is also a feminist, despising men for their impotence. She introduces Ursula to "various men and women, educated, unsatisfied people . . . inwardly raging and mad". Ursula feels swept into something "like a chaos"—thus echoing the very term used of her uncle's wedding dance: a *chaos of people*. Her growing disgust for the society in which she lives is expressed in the very terms of Chamberlain's social and political criticism in *Foundations of the XIXth Century*. Like Lawrence in the "Hardy", she dissociates herself from the feminist movements in which her women friends are involved, on the grounds that she possesses a "strange, passionate knowledge of religion and living far transcending the limits of the automatic system that contained the vote".[68] For her, organized society has become something mechanical, divorced from life.

Rejection of society

Tired of Winifred, and invited to spend a holiday with her uncle Tom (now a Yorkshire colliery manager), Ursula conceives the idea of asking Winifred to go with her and of marrying her off to Tom. This visit brings to a climax her disgust for society, for the "great machine" to which Tom is enslaved, for the "impure abstraction, the mechanisms of matter" explained by Winifred's science. Nevertheless she embarks on the hard teaching apprenticeship described in the long chapter entitled "The Man's World", in which Lawrence has combined memories of his own teaching years with those of Louie Burrows. At college, the process of detachment from society is accelerated, and at the age of twenty-one she is seized with disgust for the university as a "sham workshop", preparing the young for the industrial life of the city. Characteristically, she gives up her study of French in order to concentrate on botany, "fascinated by the strange laws of the vegetable world" which offer her a glimpse of something working entirely apart from the purpose of the human world".[69] At twenty-one, Ursula experiences the same religious and philosophical evolution as Lawrence at twenty-nine. Not only is she aware that outside the circle "lit up by man's completest consciousness" there is a vast area of darkness bristling with "grey shadow shapes" of wild beasts and of angels, but she also discovers that the secret of life lies outside the conscious self. Working at her microscope, she has a sudden revelation of an anti-mechanist and vitalist philosophy, when it comes to her in a flash that the "plant animal" she is examining "intends to be itself":

> But what self? . . . She only knew that it was not limited mechanical energy, nor mere purpose of self-preservation and self-assertion. It was a consummation, a being infinite. Self was a oneness with the infinite. To be oneself was a supreme, gleaming triumph of infinity.[70]

Skrebensky's return

This mystical revelation coincides with Skrebensky's return from the Boer War. He has six months in England before going out to India. Ursula wonders whether he may not be the angel who holds "the keys of the sunshine" to the "gates of freedom and delight". But when they meet again, she feels that they are simply "enemies come together in a truce". The returned Skrebensky is shown as completely foreign in word and in action to Ursula's true self, incapable of admitting his desires, of revealing to himself and to others the depths of his being.[71] Ursula knows that in India he will become "one of the governing class, superimposed upon an old civilization, lord and master of a clumsier civilization than his own". He will make the roads and bridges India needs, but, as she will throw in his face in a subsequent quarrel, only "to make things there as dead and mean as they are here".[72] She knows that this can never be her way.

But still she loves the body of this man whose person she despises. They have in common only a world of darkness, to the call of which she is ready to respond. Lawrence describes at length their springtime and summer liaison, their love play, their doubts, their jealousies and quarrels. Skrebensky wants to marry her, feels himself more and more "a mere attribute" of Ursula, incapable of remaining alone, terrified of that total emptiness of his own being which she seems to have revealed to him. They go to London and Paris. Suddenly Ursula wants to see Rouen and there, under the influence of "the old streets, the cathedral, the age and monumental peace of the old city", Anton feels her escape him. The great cathedral "knew no transience nor heard any denial. It was majestic in its stability, its splendid absoluteness." Ursula's sense of values wins out over her submission to the physical attraction of a man she does not respect.

Panic-striken, he asks her to marry him; they become "engaged" and then spend some time visiting various friends. After several love scenes, involving suggestions of either psychological inadequacy or sexual deficiency on the part of Anton, Ursula announces that she will never marry him, whereupon, like Louie Burrows on a similar occasion, he bursts into tears. Other reminders of Lawrence's own engagement to Louie are difficult to ignore. With his physical charm, and his intellectual and moral nullity, Skrebensky corresponds to Lawrence's idea of Louie. Ursula remains hesitant, and is even inclined to marry him. Visits to friends and family continue and, during a stay on the Lincolnshire coast, the moonlight scenes with Jessie, the brilliance of the rising moon on sea and shore fills Ursula with a kind of manic furor. There "in the great flare of light" she forces her lover to submit to the final physical and moral test from which he emerges vanquished, crushed, obliterated. They part the next day and Anton loses no time in marrying his colonel's daughter.

To H. M. Daleski we owe an admirable analysis of this new moonlight scene. Ursula, for some time unable to bear making love indoors and needing the freedom of the great open spaces, submits Skrebensky to the test of projecting the full light of consciousness, the absolute truth of earth and sea, on a mating hitherto restricted to darkness, never fully faced by their conscious selves. The whole scene centres on Anton's fear of the disclosure of his nullity by total light.

The last two chapters of *The Rainbow* are worked out on two simultaneous and interpenetrating planes. On the factual, practical plane we see the liquidation of the Skrebensky affair as far as Ursula is concerned. On the plane of poetic creation, Lawrence interprets both these facts and Ursula's whole experience to date. Here again Daleski's analysis saves much discussion.

On the practical plane, Ursula, pregnant, writes humbly to Skrebensky asking him to marry her, after which her pregnancy is terminated by an illness brought on by a long, nightmare incident with trampling horses in a downpour of rain. From this crisis she emerges free of all bonds, counting only on herself, like the oak kernel thrusting from the acorn, striving to take new root "to create a new knowledge of Eternity in the flux of Time". No longer will she try to "create" a man "according to her own desire"; she is ready to "recognize a man created by God".[73]

On the poetical plane, the last chapter, as well as the open-air scenes in the preceding one, consist essentially in a symbolic interpretation of Ursula's mental journey, and in so far as this is also Lawrence's journey, his own sexual history. As throughout the novel, memories, fiction and interpretation are intermingled in a recapitulatory effort to sum up and explain the experience of his youth. On the threshold of the great adventure with Birkin, Ursula is very largely Lawrence on the eve of his meeting with Frieda, the poet of the years before *Look! We Have Come Through!* with the addition of certain elements of his experience from 1912 to 1915.

The roads open to Ursula immediately before the completely unreal, wholly symbolic adventure of the horses were as follows: marriage and motherhood with a man she despises (the way of Mrs Morel in *Sons and Lovers*); motherhood without a man, an idea she entertains briefly during her subsequent illness; the creation of an integrated self "consummated" by the creation of "a new knowledge of Eternity in the flux of time"—something of the same nature as the mystic union with Infinite Being of the unicellular creature seen under her microscope. By the artificial intervention of an accident, Lawrence spares his heroine the second solution; the first he excludes by Skrebensky's hasty marriage. His final solution is acceptable, though of doubtful probability. It is clear that what counts for the novelist is not the events but their symbolic meaning.

Lyrical character of The Rainbow

Such is the true originality of *The Rainbow* as a novel: it is less a narrative of events, a chronicle of three generations, than an attempt at an imaginative reinterpretation of the author's whole experience. Invention is subordinated to interpretation. Lawrence may have at one time cherished the illusion that he was trying to give new form to the novel in general as a literary genre. But this was not his real concern when actually he came to write *The Rainbow*. Rather, as he admits in the "Hardy", he felt that each novel must create its own form, its own "law", in the process of composition. Seen from this point of view *The Rainbow* is a highly original novel.

In its last pages, which might seem to have been hastily, artificially connected to the rest of the work, the incident of the horses plays a dual role. Materially, it "explains" the heroine's illness and subsequent regenerative crisis. Symbolically, it resumes, if not actually explains, Ursula's whole experience. The explanations of this scene given by E. L. Nicholes and H. M. Daleski are entirely acceptable,[74] the essential element being, as Daleski stresses, that Ursula escapes from the encircling horses. They symbolize the dark forces of sexual passion; without submitting to them, she succeeds in making them part of her life, as she escapes to the safety of "the high road", between the hedges. She manages to unite the various aspects of her "ego", one which as teacher has accepted the harsh rules of the man's world, another which has yielded to the sudden urges of sex, one which aspires to the light and beauty of nature, and another which seeks darkness. She has achieved a maturity and self-sufficiency which enable her to say:

> I have no father nor mother nor lover. I have no allocated place in the world of things, I do not belong to Beldover nor to Nottingham nor to England nor this world, they none of them exist, I am trammelled and entangled in them, but they are all unreal. I must break out of it, like a nut from its shell which is an unreality.[75]

The opening words express the accession of the integrated, independent ego to maturity. The individual has learned to be alone, to count only on itself. Ursula has achieved that aristocratic "singleness" which her mother Anna so much envied in old Baron Skrebensky, and which her grandfather, Tom Brangwen, had recognized in the distinguished "foreigner" at Matlock.

But the end of this passage introduces a different theme, grafted on to that of woman achieving self-responsibility. Ursula has gained her independence by integrating herself into a man's world. At the same time, ever since her visit to her uncle Tom in the mining town of Wiggiston, we have witnessed her passionate refusal not only of the "great machine" but also of everything in the world around her susceptible of working to improve it from within. Scattered through the second part of the novel is the text of an indictment of industrial, colonizing, democratic England—not a balanced social and political judgment but a passionate denunciation: Ursula (who is almost invariably the author's mouthpiece) never discovers anyone capable of presenting the other side of the question.

The indictment of society

The passionate, irrational aspect of this indictment, superimposed on but not integrated into the psychology of the novel, is evident in every scene in which Ursula expresses her ideas on society and on politics. Her anti-militarism remains in the old democratic and nonconformist English tradition; her denial of the idea of nation and of national interest can still be taken as approaching Keir Hardie's type of socialism. It is not Ursula but Skrebensky who is made to echo the pan-Germanist idea of *Lebensraum*.[76] Yet the fact remains that it never occurs for one instant to Ursula that it might be possible to try to improve the deplorable conditions of the mining town. Her only solution would be to "do without the pits",[77] and Tom and Winifred are despised for not rising in revolt against industrial life, for being aware of its worst aspects without rejecting it outright.

To those of her friends who seek reform, her attitude is entirely negative. She refuses to join in the feminist activities of Winifred, Maggie and Dorothy Russell. Winifred's friends only make her think of "chaos", of the end of the world. The question of votes for women is "never a reality" to her, since it involves submission to the "automatic system"[78] with its whole, vast, inhuman, political machine. Her revolt is not directed towards political action, but remains on a religious, individualist, emotional plane. What Lawrence communicates to the reader is the intensity of his hatred of society, rather than his reasons for it; his whole motivation is passionate and instinctive.

His heroine's disillusionment with university is that of a mind aspiring to greatness and the absolute, suddenly discovering the pettiness and relativity of the learning dispensed at Nottingham: the university appears to her as a mean annexe of the industrial and commercial life of the city, and not as the anticipated temple of knowledge.

Her anti-colonialism is cursory in the extreme: British domination of India revolts her only because it will probably make things there "as dead and mean as they are here"; what she denounces is not so much the domination of an ancient civilization by another as the extension of industrial life.[79] In fact, she has no objection to make to the principle of aristocratic government, preferring "an aristocracy of birth to one of money". "The people" means nothing positive to her: "each one of them is a money interest . . . I hate them . . . I hate equality on a money basis. It is the equality of dirt."[80] Phraseology which may be echoing Houston Chamberlain—and if so, evidence of Lawrence's passionate reaction to the war and hostility to his country's policy—testifies to the irrational, emotional nature of such attitudes, in which Ursula and Lawrence are almost indistinguishable. Both in Ursula's thoughts or conversations, and in Lawrence's comments, we have noted an expression which probably comes straight from Chamberlain: "chaos of people".[81] Another of Ursula's contentions re-echoes the apostle of racialism, the reviler of democracy and denouncer of the power of finance: "Only the greedy and ugly people come to the top in a democracy," she said, "because they're the only people who will push themselves there. Only degenerate races are democratic."[82] And Ursula's discovery, in her microscope, of that vitalist philosophy which reveals to her the secret of individual aspiration to Being, is very close to that vitalism of *Gestalt* which inspires the botanist Chamberlain, and to his aesthetic romanticism. This influence, while it should not be exaggerated, is significant on two counts. First of all, for the affinities it emphasizes between the two writers' mystic vitalism and, second, for the light it throws on Lawrence's violently emotional indictment of English society, proceeding not from a reasoned attitude but from his feelings about the war. Part of the background of thought and feeling in *The Rainbow* relates, in this way, to the circumstances and attitudes of 1914–15.

Ursula's final acceptance of the total isolation of her "ego" thus seems to overshoot the mark, to go beyond the original intention, partially expressed in her struggle to win for herself a career and economic independence. Lawrence, encouraged by the war to follow his own anti-social tendencies of late 1912, has led his heroine beyond self-responsibility, into a refusal of society. There is no discontinuity in this since he first conceived his double novel, but an acceleration due to the war. That he is sensitive to the accusation of being anti-social can, however, be seen in the important passage in which he shows Ursula conscious of the presence of wild beasts stalking the darkness round the bright-lit camp of civilization: he who seeks to "throw a firebrand into the darkness", says Lawrence, will inevitably be "upbraided by the others who cry: Fool, anti-social knave, why should you disturb us with bogeys, . . . how dare you belittle us with the darkness?"[83]

An ambivalent conclusion

As F. R. Leavis has observed,[84] the end of the novel as it appears in the current editions betrays a hesitation: Lawrence hovers on the borderline of the psychological (that is to say, the end of Ursula's search for self-responsibility) and the social (that is to say, the relationship between the self and others). Ursula will no longer seek to create for herself the man of her dreams at the risk of annihilating him, but will try to "recognize a man created by God".[85] It is then she sees the Rainbow linking earth to heaven in a "great architecture of light and colour". To her it promises rebirth not only for herself, but also for all "the sordid people who crept hard-scaled and separate on the face of the world's corruption".[86]

The social optimism of this conclusion seems to contradict the pessimism of the immediately preceding chapters. Nor does it appear to have satisfied Lawrence himself, for on a copy of the novel given by him to his sister Ada, he replaced it in his own hand by the following:

> She knew that the fight was to the good. It was not to annihilation but at last to newness. She knew in the rainbow that the fight was to the good.[87]

This emendation has the advantage of bringing the conclusion to bear exclusively on Ursula's own evolution, without explicitly introducing a doomed society; it refers clearly but discreetly to the theme of the flood, already suggested by the rain in the incident of the horses; it is also a better transition to the mood of *Women in Love* in which the redemption of "the sordid people" is scarcely envisaged. While less well integrated into the psychological theme of the novel, the conclusion as printed is, however, more revealing of the political orientation of Lawrence's messianic urge in the early months of 1915.

THE PLACE OF *THE RAINBOW* IN THE WORK OF LAWRENCE

This novel, written over a period of nearly three years, represents a high point in Lawrence's development. How can we assess its significance in his work as a whole?

In *The Rainbow*, Lawrence has attempted two things: to break away from the old conception of character and to find a new form for the novel, different from the old linear narrative development of most of his predecessors.

His effort to show characters in the form of allotropic states of the same "ego" too often tends, as in certain 1912–13 short stories, to show them in a state of psychological disintegration, cleft by dualism and often behaving almost like somnambulists. They often appear as creatures dissociated by a conflict impossible to resolve for lack of any form of hierarchy between their different states of consciousness.

Tom Brangwen, Will, Ursula, Skrebensky, all to some extent suffer from this psychological inability to unite their selves. Those who know what they want go straight towards their goal—the second Tom Brangwen and Winifred —and are accused of "corruption" and disintegration. In a professedly psychological novel, the dominant psychology is that of Lawrence himself, and the stamp of his own dualism appears in all his characters. The goal of Ursula's odyssey, attainment to an integrated and independent ego, is a little like the quest for an elusive Eldorado. Her long-drawn-out struggle with herself about Skrebensky, that figment of her imagination, comes to an end only as a result of accident and illness. Certain scenes brilliantly demonstrate the "allotropic states" of her being, but the unfolding of her story, from one moonlight drama to another, proves her subject to an illusion under cover of which she seeks to disguise a fundamental dualism between her conscious, waking, social "self" and sexual desires driving her towards a man she cannot respect. Ursula repeats the sexual experience of Mrs Lawrence and her husband, that of Lawrence and Louie Burrows. Even though partially presented as an integration of the ego, her final triumph is in fact no more than an escape towards a new "mystic" state of being. In *Women in Love* we find her once more facing the same problems of adaptation of the self to another; moreover, the idea of an integration of the ego, of the establishment of a hierarchy of psychological states, is contrary to the very idea of allotropic states of equal values. In that sense, Lawrence's experiment ends either in a contradiction of his own psychological theory of character (since *some* states will predominate over others) or in the indefinite continuation of the dualism which besets his characters. *The Rainbow* resolves nothing; in that at least the author is faithful to his programme.

His essential idea on the structure of the novel is indeed that of juxtaposed scenes, side by side in a triptych, without geometry or architecture, "resolving" nothing. But the final image of the rainbow bringing hope and radiance seems to contradict this idea. The Botticelli-like structure is more interesting as a general conception than in actual execution. Lawrence, in fact, did not pursue his search for renewed form, any more than his "allotropic" presentation of characters. And even in this novel, after painting his series of separate scenes à la Botticelli, he ends with a great unifying architecture, that of the rainbow with its message of hope.

A triumph for painter and poet

These intended innovations, not always clear to anyone reading *The Rainbow* without reference to Lawrence's expository works and to his letters, are in any case much less significant than the novel itself, i.e. than the sequence of scenes and incidents which capture the imagination by the beauty, firmness and precision of their execution, and the brilliance of their style. The originality of *The Rainbow* does not lie in its intellectual and psychological structure. The various aspects of the initial idea of woman achieving self-responsibility are not systematically and coherently explored or analysed. The exploration of Ursula's character does not ever really raise the question of the difference, the possible links and contradictions, in a given state of civilization, between a woman's right to an autonomous sexual life, and economic independence.

When he came to write *The Rainbow*, Lawrence seems to have found it impossible to see the problem of modern woman in all its aspects; not only was he obsessed by too many personal memories, too many echoes of his own sexual experience in adolescence and early manhood, but in choosing Frieda as his main model of emancipated woman he was inevitably led to develop her character too exclusively on the emotional and sexual, as opposed to the economic and social, plane. In many ways his heroine falls short of the variety of experience and the humanity of Wells's Ann Veronica. In comparison with Carpenter, or Edith Ellis, he oversimplifies the woman problem, reducing it to the awakening and acceptance of the feminine sexual impulse, stressing the existence in woman of sexual aggression and initiative. Ursula's nostalgic attitude towards Maggie, her refusal to join her friends in active support of the women's movement, are symptomatic of the divorce between Lawrence and the political *avant-garde* of his youth. His heroine, like himself, is too hostile to existing society in England for the development of her personality to be complete, embracing all aspects of feminine life.

But *The Rainbow* is the triumph of Lawrence the painter and the poet: while not making any decisive contribution on the plane of structural aesthetics or experimental psychology, *The Rainbow* undoubtedly contains some of the finest English prose of the century. Particularly in the first third of the novel, going back to his literary roots in Hardy and George Eliot, Lawrence paints pictures which impose themselves so strongly on our memory that on rereading we are astonished to find they are so short: for instance, his portrayal in action of Tom Brangwen's relationship with the old servant Tilly, or the picture of the gradual growth of the bond of affection binding him to his stepchild Anna. Description and action in one, every word, every detail strikes home. Like the unforgettable scenes of Paul Morel's childhood in *Sons and Lovers*, they spring miraculously to life.

The same is true, but to a lesser degree, of some of the scenes he charges with symbolic meaning—Will's and Anna's moonlight race to stack the sheaves of corn, Anna's dance of triumph, Ursula's and Skrebensky's two moonlight confrontations. The intensity of emotion experienced by his characters, as well as that of his own intentions, is conveyed not in the clear terms of verbal evocation, but as an overpowering atmosphere. This is partly due to Lawrence's striving after symbolic meaning, partly to the fact that, either from respect for decency or on account of the inadequacy of his psychological vocabulary, he has to couch in vague or indirect terms the physical and psychic realities he is trying to convey. The style is brilliant, as is the interplay of symbolic suggestion, but the cumulative effect of terms evocative, for example, of light and darkness, while often skilful, is occasionally overworked to the point of causing irritation.

Faced with the task of selecting from *The Rainbow* those pages most worthy of figuring in an anthology, irrespective of any conventional consideration, most people would turn unhesitatingly to passages in the earlier chapters describing life on the Brangwen farm, the childhood of Anna or that of Ursula, or, perhaps, to the visit to Lincoln Cathedral. Although in the later chapters each individual scene, short or long, is well constructed, dialogue and action being skilfully blended, the author intervenes too frequently, too subjectively; and also, each scene being closely linked with the next in a symbolic and lyrical sequence, it becomes difficult to assess separately the value and significance of any one particular episode. An exception, however, may be made for the unforgettable and self-contained classroom scenes described in the chapter "The Man's World".

Limits of The Rainbow

The manuscript of *The Rainbow* bears the mention "End of Volume I",[88] but, as a result of its suppression in 1915, six years in fact elapsed before the appearance of its sequel, *Women in Love*. Critics have always treated it as a separate work, despite the fact that, without *Women in Love*, *The Rainbow* must be considered incomplete, brought to an artificial end. Although Lawrence's aim was synthesis, the portrayal of the new earthly paradise of love presaged by the experience of Tom and Lydia, he in fact takes his heroine only as far as the "bursting" of her consciousness, a rupture followed by no more than the mystical promise of a new world. Art, says Lawrence, resolves nothing; certainly this is true of *The Rainbow*, a work which starts out to illustrate a problem, to achieve a synthesis, but turns into a lyrical confession. Highly revealing of the author's own uncertainties and doubts, it is particularly ill-equipped to resolve those of others. The novel is made up of brilliant descriptions of nature, of simple people and things, placed side by side with affirmations which remain essentially subjective and dogmatic expressions of a negative conception of the social world the characters are meant to illustrate. That this denial of society does not stem from observation of character but, on the contrary, precedes it, becomes more and more evident as the novel develops and as the secondary characters, instead of peopling a more or less traditional background (like Tom's brothers and sisters at Anna's wedding), tend to become protagonists in the drama which obscurely and somewhat gratuitously opposes Ursula to society. The initial effort at artistic objectivity gives way to a destructive attitude, on the part not only of Ursula, but also of the author. The heroine becomes more and more surrounded by puppets—Skrebensky, Ursula's uncle Tom, Winifred, Skrebensky's own family—so that in the end the background is distorted to the point where those who figure in it are hard to recognize as real persons.

Since *Sons and Lovers*, Lawrence has confirmed, rather than affirmed or transformed, his artistic mastery; in that novel a psychological theme was treated with relative objectivity, played out within a framework and by characters the reader could try to evaluate for himself. *The Rainbow*, on the contrary, asserts psychological values outside any objective framework and, except towards the end, apart from any stated hierarchy. The conflict between the individual and society is described without any attempt at explanation or justification. Subjectivity predominates, not without often admirable artistic and poetic effect, but to the exclusion of any serious discussion of a philosophical and social problem. The poetic force, the splendid motion of the prose serve to express emotional disturbance unilluminated by any clear ideology or philosophy. The immense subtlety exercised by various critics in the interpretation of a novel remarkable rather for its poetic vigour than for its content proves that Lawrence's experiment produced one of the outstanding works of the period, but not the innovatory and definitive work to which he aspired. The problems of the female personality treated in connexion with Ursula are restricted, and the psychological evolution of his heroine is not related to the whole of human life. What he does is to lead Ursula to rejection of society, thus preparing her for *Women in Love*, which indeed was what he intended; from that point of view, the success of *The Rainbow* can be judged in relation to the preparation it provides for Ursula's evolution in its sequel. The novelist's real concern remains the couple, but, in the course of studying the development of woman as an individual, his point of view has changed and he no longer believes this development to be desirable: a change confirmed and stressed in *Women in Love*.

13

WOMEN IN LOVE

THE GENESIS OF WOMEN IN LOVE

New themes and old aims

Women in Love does not clearly and decisively proclaim a doctrine or new-world vision. It ends on a note of doubt and dissatisfaction. It raises more problems than it solves. Everything considered, it is more a landmark on the path of Lawrence's progress from *The Rainbow* to the post-war novels and short stories than a climax in his thought and art. The original intention of "The Sisters", which determines the overall pattern of the relations of Birkin and Ursula and the contrast between Ursula's and Gudrun's ways of love, has been overlaid with a variety of other themes, integrated up to a certain point but not enough to form a positive and final synthesis. In spite of its sometimes elaborate structure, this work already reveals its author's tendency to incorporate last-minute elements, and, so to speak, notes from the day's events.

Lawrence's method of work is typical: while still the "priest of love" that he meant to be at the start, his religion has been considerably modified as the novel developed; the bitter critic of English society revealed in the second half of *The Rainbow* reaffirms his position and expands his themes in a portrait of the Midland mining country: the patriot who wanted a "different" England is sometimes visible behind the enemy of the entire human race, who, like Richard Jefferies, would willingly see humanity obliterated from the face of the earth, and for whom death is preferable to certain forms of love. His own failure in the quest for friendship colours darkly the apocalyptic picture of the end of a world replacing the message of joy and hope the novel was originally intended to convey. All the obscurities, hesitations and false trails on which the reader is frequently led spring from this confusion of intention and of theme, and from the vacillations of the principal character Rupert Birkin, a self-portrait marked by the same dualism and instability typical of the wartime Lawrence in his Cornish haven, frailer and more exposed than ever to changes of temper conditioned by ill-health and the realization of his physical weakness.

The problem of the Prologue

The publication in January 1968[1] of an unpublished Prologue to *Women in Love*, after the present chapter was completed in its original French version, raises questions which can be briefly mentioned here. When was the Prologue written, and what were the date of and the reasons for its elimination from the text as published in 1921? The Prologue essentially throws light on two aspects of Birkin's character which the novel as published fails to explain: his relations with Hermione—containing as it does the nearest thing to a full confession of the failure of the author's sexual experiment with Jessie Chambers—and his obsessive homosexual drive, in particular towards "a strange Cornish type of man" and towards Gerald Crich. Taken in its entirety, the Prologue is thus linked both to Lawrence's stocktaking of his youthful loves, and of the reasons for their failure, and to the discovery, which may be dated between 1914 and early 1916, of the significance of homosexual impulses, including his own.

No evidence so far produced is conclusive as to the date of the Prologue, although many of its features suggest, at the least, additions to it which could only have been made in Cornwall, in or after 1916.[1a] It seems that it was part of an early draft (as suggested by the names of certain of its characters, changed in the final version) but revised or rewritten in 1916. Among reasons for its suppression may have been the fear of prosecution because of the openly homosexual nature of Birkin's love for Gerald and of the attraction exercised over him by other men. Another might be the too-candid avowal of Lawrence's sexual failure with Jessie Chambers, in the guise of Birkin's failure with Hermione. This autobiographical element, while making Birkin's behaviour much more intelligible, was certainly too frank for Lawrence's feelings in 1920, and possibly not acceptable to Frieda.

At all events, the suppression of this Prologue shows, as do certain examples of the use of current incidents discussed later in this chapter, that Lawrence probably never gave this novel that last-minute editorial going-over which would have ironed out small inconsistencies and merged the details into the whole. Without it, Birkin and Hermione remain, to a large extent, unexplained; she is more villainous in the novel as published, and less suffering, than the Prologue shows her, and Ursula's reference to Birkin's "foul" sex life with Hermione[2] remains unexplained, whereas the suppressed Prologue makes it reasonably clear.

Primitive civilizations

Women in Love is the first of Lawrence's works to show the impact of primitive civilizations on a twentieth-century mind. By inference, as much as by external evidence, elements can be found of a line of thought possibly not yet fully developed or else still considered too daring for explicit expression, but later to find bolder and more personal expression in *Psycho-analysis and the Unconscious* and *Fantasia of the Unconscious*. Between the beginning of 1915 and the end of 1916, Lawrence seems to have turned a corner, without immediately having seen where it would lead him. After "The Crown", he set to work once more on the "philosophy" to which he attached so much importance, sending a "first half" to Ottoline in February 1916, with the warning that it was suitable reading for "a winter-dark" and not a spring-like day.[3] Notwithstanding Cynthia Asquith's very definite attribution of this title to *Women in Love*, this "philosophy" appears to have been part of a work called "Goats and Compasses". According to Cecil Gray, this was the title of "a treatise dealing largely with homosexuality—a subject . . . in which Lawrence displayed a suspiciously lively interest at that time"—which its author was to destroy in November 1917.[4] Insisting on Lawrence's "dark, sinister, baleful, wholly corrupt and evil" aspect at this time, Gray goes on to enumerate the interests of his friend Heseltine during the weeks he spent with Lawrence and Frieda at Porthcothan and at Zennor.[5] The list includes Peruvian pottery, Javanese puppets, African fetishes, Tibetan painting, William Blake, Jacob Boehme, Thomas Traherne, Eliphas Levi, Hermes Trismegistus and Paracelsus. We also know, thanks to Robert Nichols, that at Oxford Heseltine had read Havelock Ellis, Carpenter (for whom Nichols judged his admiration excessive) and Weininger, to whom he attached great importance. To these names Gray adds those of Whitman, Richard Jefferies and Nietzsche. This list not only includes several of Lawrence's favourite authors, but also gives some idea of the sort of conversations he and Heseltine may have enjoyed in Cornwall, thus throwing light on the intellectual climate in which *Women in Love* was written. Lawrence was already attracted by magic and occultism. In 1917 he was to write to Waldo Frank from Zennor that he found esoteric doctrine "marvellously illuminating, historically". Both in his mind and in his writing a link seems to have existed between esoteric tradition and the Christian symbolism revealed to him by Mrs Jenner.[6] While his main "occultist" period seems to be 1917–18, there are in *Women in Love* indications of earlier contacts with occult literature, and the attraction of Eastern religions can be seen in Lawrence's interest in the Ajanta paintings, known to him by late 1915.

In a novel written in such an atmosphere a certain obscurity is not surprising. It would be idle to expect a character such as Birkin, in particular, to behave and speak according to completely standard norms and in consistent fashion. Like Lawrence, Birkin is disappointed by his fellow-men, disillusioned, imbued with diffuse religious feeling, half seeking for new faiths, simultaneously tempted and repulsed by primitive rites and "savage" art forms, attracted by the mirage of old magical forms of knowledge and repulsed by the mechanistic philosophy of orthodox science. His nihilism, his total rejection of society, extends almost to love itself, which, as we shall see, he wants to renew completely. Only regretfully, half unwillingly, can he admit that the link between a man and a woman can still have any value in a universe seen as doomed to self-destruction. In the vision of Judgment Day painted by Lawrence in *Women in Love* Birkin and Ursula are from the outset marked out by divine grace and can hope to found a new earthly paradise; yet they have themselves but little confidence in this outcome, and their new heaven and new earth go with the final destruction of the vast majority of the human race.

Predominance of satire

Here the pessimism of the last chapter of *The Rainbow* has become, if anything, even gloomier, and turns to a merciless satire of society, or at least as much of it as the author chooses to describe. In February 1915, when still believing in the possibility of an economic revolution, Lawrence wrote to Russell that he would be ashamed to speak of "passionate love" for his fellow-men "before Titan nailed on the rock of the modern capitalist system. Only satire is decent now. The rest is a lie."[7] Fifteen months later the satire of *Women in Love* is so to speak the testament of his youth—written under the joint effects of illness, of the long-drawn-out conflict with Frieda, of the failures of friendship, and of the break between the Messiah and a mankind he no longer hopes to save. A letter to Ottoline written in February 1916 strikes the keynote:

> You cannot *really* do anything now: no one can do anything . . . This world of ours has got to collapse now, in violence and injustice and destruction, nothing will stop it . . . The only thing now to be done is either to go down with the ship . . . or, as much as one can *leave* the ship, and like a castaway live a life apart. As for me, I do not belong to the ship; I will not, if I can help it, sink with it. I will not live any more in this time. I know what it is. I reject it. As far as I possibly can, I will stand outside this time, I will live my life, and, if possible, be happy, though the whole world slides in horror down into the bottomless pit. There is a greater truth than the truth of the present, there is a God beyond these Gods of to-day. Let them fight and fall round their idols, my fellow men; it is their affair. As for me, as far as I can, I will save myself, for I believe that the highest virtue is to be happy, living in the greater truth, not submitting to the falsehood of these personal times.[8]

He is "willing to give people up altogether—they are what they are, why should they be as I want them to be . . . There is my intimate art, and my thoughts, as you say. Very good, so be it. It is enough, more than enough, if they will only leave me alone."[9] As "The Crown" had intimated, art has become his refuge, though a vengeful refuge: a satirical art, marked, whatever he may say, by a certain nostalgia for his earlier reforming zeal, and by the disappointment of failure in dealing with people.

Drawing on current events

The change of atmosphere since the initial conception of "The Sisters" and "The Wedding Ring" is clear from the new titles suggested as the work drew to a close. Lawrence's own idea of "Latter Days", reminiscent of Bulwer Lytton, was followed by Frieda's proposal, "Dies Irae". In November 1917, he considered calling it "Noah's Ark". Lady Cynthia Asquith seems to have discussed with Lawrence a typescript with the title "Goats and Compasses".[10] The title *Women in Love*, the subject of much debate prior to publication in 1921, gives only a partial idea of the content of the novel and is nearer to the original idea of 1913 than to the final version.

Besides partly losing sight of his 1913 plan, Lawrence draws heavily on contemporaneous happenings to illustrate ideas, sometimes even building upon them some key scenes of a novel widely admired for its structural qualities. Three typical examples will suffice to show his method.

Gertler

On 9 October 1916, Lawrence thanks Gertler for having sent him a photograph of his painting "Merry-Go-Round". On 31 October, he sends Pinker what was presumably Chapter XXX, "the conclusion" of *Women in Love*, "all but the last chapter . . . a sort of epilogue".[11] In this chapter is described a frieze by the sculptor Loerke recalling both the subject and the spirit of Gertler's painting. Loerke is a Jew whose father and Austrian childhood recall Gertler's early life, just as the two syllables of his name are not unlike the English painter's. His work and his person seem to Birkin to be "several stages further in social hatred" than Gerald or himself on the way to corruption and dissolution: "He's further on than we are. He hates the ideal more acutely. He hates the ideal utterly, yet it still dominates him. I expect he is a Jew—or part Jewish . . . He is a gnawing little negation, gnawing at the roots of life."[12] Writing to his Jewish friend about "Merry-Go-Round", Lawrence sees in it "a real and ultimate revelation". "I realize how superficial your human relationships must be, and what a violent maelstrom of destruction and horror your inner soul must be . . . You are all absorbed in the violent and lurid process of inner decomposition . . . It would take a Jew to paint this picture." No wonder Lawrence did his utmost to prevent the artist from recognizing himself in the sculptor Loerke.[13] If, as seems probable, Loerke also owes much to Dostoevsky in general and to Svidrigaylov in particular,[14] Lawrence must have created his character by combining at the last moment certain traits of Gertler's personality and work with a model originally inspired by *Crime and Punishment*. He also endowed him with the physical appearance and the "weird glutinous" pronunciation of one of his Gargnano neighbours.[15] But what interests us most is Lawrence's immediate, spontaneous use for literary ends, undeterred by any doubt or scruple, of material which had come into his hands practically while writing the relevant chapter of his novel. The concept of the Jew as negative, as an instrument of moral dissolution, was, of course, an echo from Chamberlain and Weininger.

Katherine Mansfield

The whole of Chapter XXVIII, "Gudrun in the Pompadour", is another last-minute addition drawn from current happenings. Early in September 1916 Lawrence learned of an incident at the Café Royal between Katherine Mansfield and a group loudly making fun of Lawrence's recently published *Amores*. Lawrence had told Pinker his novel was finished on 30 June, so that the chapter based on the Café Royal incident can only have been added as an afterthought, a last-minute inspiration. Gudrun snatches from the hands of the gloating Halliday a letter from Birkin parodying Lawrence's very thought and expression, just as Katherine Mansfield snatched *Amores* from the hands of the Café Royal merrymakers. Koteliansky, who was present when she did so, has confirmed to Cecil Gray that Heseltine was not among them. Lawrence thus merged reality and fiction in the interests of satire, blackening his portrait of Heseltine in the guise of Halliday. It is not impossible that the scene also owes something to Meredith. In *Beauchamp's Career*, an indignant Cecilia hears an inspired letter from Dr Shrapnel to Beauchamp read aloud to an unappreciative audience.

Egyptian ducks

A third detail illustrates Lawrence's successful exploitation of whatever struck his imagination while he was writing. In January 1916, Ottoline sent him a book on Egypt, lent by Juliette Baillot (now Lady Huxley). On 1st February, she received Lawrence's fervent thanks: the book had given him "real pleasure".[16] According to Lady Huxley, the book was Maspéro's *Egypte* in the collection *Ars Una*. But on 7 February, irritated by too many "contentions of learned men", Lawrence reported finding the text "impossible" and asked for a book on early Egypt which would leave more to the imagination! Yet he had carefully studied Maspéro's illustrations, among which two evidently aroused his interest. Figure 92 represents the Meidum Geese. "The details distinguishing the male from the female in each couple", comments Maspéro, "are noted with a precision that astonishes the naturalists; treatment and colour are also admirable, Japanese *and Chinese artists could not have done better.*"[17] [*Italics added.*] Later Maspéro describes the remains of a villa belonging to Amenothes II at Medinet-Habou. On the mosaic floor "fish play in the water and ducks cruise among the lotus".[18] Figure 278 (3 × 5 cm.) represents three ducks swimming among lotus flowers.

Maspéro's ducks have found their way into *Women in Love*. Birkin takes "a Chinese drawing of geese" from Hermione's boudoir and copies it "with much skill and vividness". "The Chinese Ambassador gave it me," Hermione tells him, wondering why he wants to copy it.

"I want to know it," replies Birkin. "One gets more of China, copying this picture than reading all the books . . . I know what centres they live from—what they perceive and feel—the hot, stinging centrality of a goose in the flux of cold water and mud—the curious bitter, stinging heat of a goose's blood, entering their own blood like an inoculation of corruptive fire—fire of the cold-burning mud—the lotus mystery."[19]

While raising the subject to the gracious standards of Garsington by making the drawing a gift from the Chinese ambassador, Lawrence remembers Maspéro's comments and his own criticism of books as opposed to paintings—but he adds yoga and theosophist ideas of the "centres" (*chakras*) and the "lotus mystery"; he also borrows from Heraclitus via Burnet the idea of the corrupting "flux" of cold water and the opposition of damp cold and of flame.[20] These few lines of *Women in Love* show both the artist's power to synthesize disparate elements and the strength of his artistic convictions. Once more he is seeking the spirit of a people or the genius of a painter in the actual muscular movements which have created the work of art, rather than in any abstract conception. They strongly suggest that Lawrence's reading of the theosophists, and perhaps of James M. Pryse, goes back to 1915, or early 1916.[21]

Thus, when engaged in writing a novel Lawrence does not hesitate to make use of anything that comes to hand: the three examples given above show how difficult it is to distinguish in *Women in Love* between an initial structural pattern and last-minute additions. The analytical reader is reminded of a painter who, having settled the broad outline of his picture, adds detail, form and colour under the passing artistic inspiration of the moment. In that light, *Women in Love* emerges not so much as the execution of a master-pattern, the fulfilment of the 1913 plans, the expression of the beliefs or spiritual choices of that moment, but as the mirror of the moods and climate of 1916, i.e. an essentially destructive and satirical work.

During the year in which *Women in Love* was rewritten, Lawrence was reading voraciously. In 1915 he had begun to read Frazer. While the four large volumes of *Totemism and Exogamy* cannot have influenced his thinking profoundly, certain traces of this reading are apparent in *Women in Love*. Not only is Chapter VII entitled "Totem", but Gudrun, seeing Gerald for the first time, repeats to herself, "His totem is the wolf. His mother is an old unbroken wolf."[22]

From *The Golden Bough* Lawrence seems to have taken the idea of the *Dea Syria*, of Cybele, the Great Mother, Weininger providing the complementary idea that eroticism and sexual desire in woman are essentially destructive.[23] Just as he had done in *The White Peacock*, in *Women in Love* Lawrence combines and merges his most recent reading by amalgamating it with ideas absorbed from all his previous reading; and such traces as remain reveal his constant effort to assimilate new images illustrating his own ideas and feelings.

The synthesis, it must however be recognized, is far from complete. From all those component elements, however skilfully combined, there does not emerge a fully independent work of art, a universe fully intelligible and readily accessible to the reader. Like its hero, the novel remains hesitant, its message faltering, its teaching negative, and the way to salvation concealed. This may be due to the inner conflict between the initial 1913 conception and the actual 1916 achievement.

SOME POSITIVE ASPECTS

Regeneration through love

In 1913 Lawrence wanted to be a "priest of love"; a year later, in the "Study of Thomas Hardy", his main preoccupation was with "Being and Not-Being". He still believed in achieving being through love, in regeneration through the union and mutual comprehension of the sexes. By 1916 he was still affirming this regeneration, but not with the same conviction; he was also stressing the forces of disintegration, death and corruption.

Birkin and Ursula, the chosen couple, are, it is true, endowed with some external signs and even premonition of their predestination to be redeemed: nevertheless a doubt subsists. Birkin is never sure of achieving the perfection of being of which he has glimpses and to which he aspires. Yet at no time are the means of accession to it made really clear. An unacknowledged mysticism, an interest in magic, have crept into the novel: the author, like Birkin, operates on two planes, that of regeneration through mysticism, and that of the religion, or black magic, of corruption and death. The affirmation of the mystery of life goes hand in hand with a perverse delight in the idea of death, the key passages being precisely those in which the two planes are linked in a kind of ritual aimed at re-establishing the unity of the ego divided against itself, by the acceptance of death and all that stands for it in life itself. The inner meaning of the work is deliberately esoteric, although the lesson Lawrence is obscurely trying to convey, like that of *Lady Chatterley's Lover*, is basically simple. It is a lesson intended for himself, another effort on his part to free himself from the inhibitions and constraints of his puritan education, to solve his problems of sexual and social adaptation.

As in the original plan for "The Sisters", the main roles are played by two couples: on the one hand Birkin and Ursula, respectively inspector of schools and schoolmistress, on the other Gerald Crich and Gudrun, mine-owner, explorer, soldier, athlete, outwardly the complete Nordic man, the Teutonic hero capable of saving himself if he would, and successful young sculptress. One of these couples will set out in quest of cosmic and angelic equilibrium, the other is doomed to tragedy, to the symbolic death of Gerald. A large part of the book is devoted to their conversations and their loves. The rest is a drastic and at times excessive criticism of the society in which they live. In so far as *Women in Love* is a mystic tale setting in opposition love and self-consciousness, its foundation lies in the contrast between the two couples, and in the quest of Birkin, a modern Parsifal, for the Holy Grail.

Gerald and Gudrun on the one hand, Ursula and Birkin on the other, do not have the same attitudes either towards life and the society in which they live, nor towards their partner in love, nor to love itself. Much of the novel is aimed at marking these contrasting attitudes, as well as the interplay of their reciprocal attractions and repulsions. In the very first chapter the differences between the two girls are shown in a discussion on marriage. Gudrun sees marriage from the practical angle, "the inevitable next step", provided the husband is agreeable and has sufficient means. Ursula, on the contrary, looks to marriage as a step bound to involve and affect her entire person. Gudrun is always shown as on the defensive; Ursula, on the contrary, is self-assured, illumined by an inner light, a constant flame. Lawrence rarely describes her features, but continually characterizes her by this luminescence, this inner glow, which recalls the radiance of the faces of the Ajanta women. At one point Birkin begs Ursula to give him her "golden light".[24]

Gudrun sees in Gerald a means of achieving her selfish ends, while Gerald tries to forget in Gudrun first his dying father, then the emptiness of an existence in the service of a mechanical civilization, of industrial efficiency. He himself envisages relationships with others only as providing instruments subservient to his will: in one of his artistically most successful scenes, Lawrence shows him at a railway crossing forcing his Arab mare to face the "unknown, terrifying" noise of a shunting colliery train. Everything must be bent to his will, everything must serve his needs. Gudrun sees in him the potential instrument of her ambition, of her will to power, until the day when the artist in her finds an equal in Loerke. Every gesture, every word of these two characters stresses the egotism of their relationship, the absence of any submission to a "third", to a mystic presence to whom each renders homage through the other.

Ursula's relationship to Birkin, on the contrary, is marked by the sense of such a higher presence: from the very beginning she feels in Birkin the acknowledgment of a certain spiritual "kinship", a natural, tacit understanding, while he, for his part, is "unconsciously drawn to her". There is "a gleam of understanding between them"; he knows she is "his future", that she is in some way "referred back" to him,[25] although no mention is ever made of any conventional religious belief which might justify these convictions. Birkin is several times reproached for his "Sunday School teacher" moralizing, for his compulsion to try "to save the world".[26] Yet he does not believe in the "old ideals" and, though imbued with religious feeling, accepts no definite revealed religion. Like Lawrence, all he has kept of traditional religion is its basic attitudes and the need to believe. This is shown in the course of his long discussions with Gerald and with Ursula, and the deep understanding which, despite the inadequacies of language, grows up between himself and Ursula: "What was the good of talking, anyway? It must happen beyond the sound of words. It was merely ruinous to try to work her by conviction. This was a paradisal bird that could never be netted, it must fly by itself to the heart."[27] Although no explicit mention of yoga is made anywhere in *Women in Love*, it is clear that Lawrence is trying to place their relationship on several levels of consciousness, at the points of communication between the different vital "centres"; indeed several passages show familiarity with a doctrine partially inspiring Birkin in his search for the earthly paradise.

It is almost always Birkin who develops the main theses, who raises the central issues of the book; but since these are usually introduced in the course of discussion, or in the interplay of character, they are rarely brought out didactically or in abstract fashion. Birkin is depicted as a shifting, chameleon-like "creature of change", externally obedient to social convention, disguising his true nature.[28] Lawrence has chosen not to be didactic—he even lets his hero modify his attitudes out of consideration for Ursula's views—but to reveal what he feels to be the truth little by little, rather than to preach a ready-made doctrine.

Consciousness, sensorial perceptions and sex

Nevertheless the whole novel turns on the quest for a lost paradise, on the relations of the conscious ego with others in love and in friendship; on the relations of the ego with nature and civilization—all of them main themes of

Lawrence's thinking in 1916. Consciousness is accepted from the very first pages as an irreversible fact: it must be widened, completed, not repressed, so as not to degenerate into its egoistic form, self-consciousness. Such is the message Birkin violently brings home to Hermione, who, after listening to a botany lesson, questions the wisdom of rousing children to consciousness by teaching them the facts of vegetable life: "Hadn't they better be animals, simple animals, crude, violent, *anything*, rather than this self-consciousness, this incapacity to be spontaneous?" It is not knowledge, protests Birkin, that makes us "unliving and self-conscious" but the fact of being "imprisoned within a limited, false set of concepts"; to Hermione's intellectual narcissism he opposes true "sensuality", a knowledge of the senses "in the blood", in a "deluge" carrying all before it, a darkness in which man discovers in himself the "demon lover" for whom woman is wailing.[29] While this profession of faith recalls that of Annable in *The White Peacock*, Lawrence refuses to go back, to revert to the animal unconsciousness; what he wants is to rediscover the hidden sources of consciousness, to restore it to its true nature based on the perceptions of the senses. The awakening of consciousness must be accompanied by the faculty of "letting go", of not "watching your naked animal actions in mirrors". The character of Hermione Roddice is a mixture of the liberal and self-proclaimed emancipated lady (Ottoline as she appeared to Lawrence in 1916) and the sentimental intellectual (Jessie Chambers) as seen by a Lawrence freed from her yoke and rationalizing his escape. In *Women in Love* Hermione represents false spirituality, the aberration of love that seeks to dominate a man's mind and emotions. In contrast to Ursula, a woman physically feminine but capable of independence and of giving a man his full autonomy, to Gudrun, an artist exploiting man and nature alike to subject them to her false creative ends, and to Minette, a prostitute using her sex as a means of achieving her petty objects, Hermione appears as the priestess of a false religion, the incarnation of all Lawrence dreads in woman as moulded by civilization.

She needs to touch Birkin to be sure he is really there; she pursues him to the point of going into a class he is in the process of inspecting.[30] She is avid for knowledge which, she says, makes her feel "so uplifted, so unbounded"; to which Birkin sarcastically replies by asking what she wants to feel unbounded for.[31] Birkin, who is in the process of freeing himself from the bonds which have too long tied him to her, reminds her that to her "knowledge means everything":

> Even your animalism, you want it in your head. You don't want to be an animal, you want to observe your animal functions, to get a mental thrill out of them . . . You are the real devil who won't let life exist.[32]

She treats Birkin like a child, as if he belonged to her, making fun of him in front of her guests, wanting to know everything he does, to extract all his secrets.[33] She insists on furnishing his lodgings, pursues him with her attentions even when she knows he wants to be rid of her, even after having tried to kill him by hitting him on the head with a lapis lazuli paperweight in a semi-somnambulistic climax of destruction. Deep down she is devoured by "devastating cynicism", no longer believing either in "her own universals", in an "inner life" which for her has become "a trick, not a reality", nor yet in the spiritual world, which seems to her an "affectation":

> In the last resort she believed in Mammon, the flesh, and the devil—these at least were not sham. She was a priestess without belief, without conviction, suckled in a creed outworn, and condemned to the reiteration of mysteries that were not divine to her.[34]

This ferocious portrait of Hermione precedes her discussion with Ursula on Birkin and his quest for balanced love, and serves, amongst other things, to show Ursula that Hermione will always alternate between domination and slavishness, never reaching balance, never truly female, always ready to betray her womanhood, either treating her partner as an instrument or allowing herself to be so treated.

The text of the cancelled Prologue gives a clue to what had reduced Hermione to this hateful condition. In it Birkin is presented as a writer of "harsh, jarring poetry"

> . . . under which she suffered, and sometimes shallower, gentle lyrics, which she treasured as drops of manna. Like a priestess she kept his records and his oracles, he was like a god who would be nothing if his worship were neglected.[35]

She was jealous of his affection for Gerald, in which he was "belittling his own mind and talent". They had moonlight evenings "of superfine ecstasy of beauty" after which (as for Lawrence at Flamborough Head with Jessie) "there came the morning, and the ash, when his body was grey and consumed, and his soul ill", whereas she "like a priestess, was fulfilled and rich".[36] After thus exploring with her "the pure, translucent regions of death itself, of ecstasy", and although "he did not love any woman. He wanted to love . . . He was consumed by sexual desire, and he wanted to be fulfilled",[37] he had *forced* himself to "have the sexual activity". As for Hermione "she did not want him either. But with all her soul, she *wanted* to want him . . . She prepared herself like a perfect sacrifice to him." But,

> This last act of love which he had demanded of her was the keenest grief of all, it was so insignificant, so null. He had no pleasure of her, only some mortification. And her heart almost broke with grief.[38]

Lawrence's analysis of his failure with Jessie Chambers is both ruthless and candid: it is probably the most truthful description and explanation of what happened to them in 1910.[39]

The Prologue justifies Hermione, and is very revealing about Birkin more explicitly so than any passage in the novel as published: the character of Hermione in the novel remains unexplained, evil in the absolute, whereas in the Prologue she is both Jessie Chambers and Sue Brideshead as explained by Lawrence in his "Hardy", and becomes pathetically intelligible.

On the moral plane, Lawrence's decision to suppress the Prologue resulted in what might be seen as a falsification of the character of Hermione. It may be argued, of course, that the artist need not reproduce his model in all details; but the Hermione of the Prologue strikes one as less of a caricature, more of a suffering, real person, than in the novel as published. On the aesthetic level, Hermione remains an incomplete creation, to a perceptible extent artificial and rigidly allegorical.

After the paperweight scene, Birkin instinctively seeks to "regain his consciousness" in direct, total contact with nature, expression of the creative mystery. He goes off into the open country, takes off his clothes, and sits down naked among the primroses, "seeming to saturate himself with their contact":

> He did not want a woman—not in the least. The leaves and the primroses and the trees, they were really lovely and cool and desirable, they really came into the blood and were added on to him. He was enrichened now immeasurably, and so glad . . . Why should he pretend to have anything to do with human beings at all? Here was his world, he wanted nobody and nothing but the lovely, subtle, responsive vegetation, and himself, his own living self.[40]

This return to the simplest expression of "sensuality", which to Lawrence denotes the use of all the sensations, as opposed to ideas, does not exclude sex. But, as the rest of the novel shows, Birkin tries to put this in its proper place, as an essential but not primordial part of existence: among the other needs of the poet whose satisfactions Lawrence celebrates in "Manifesto". Birkin opposes sensuality to sensuousness, the latter being associated for him with self-consciousness and conceit.[41] In a world devoid of any guiding impulse, in which "the old ideals are dead as nails", only one resource remains to Birkin: "some one *really* pure single activity" such as love. In the Prologue, "his fundamental desire" was to be able to love completely, in one and the same act: both body and soul at once, struck into a complete oneness in contact with a complete woman.[42] That was more explicit, and more directly autobiographical, than his hope in the present scene: to find in "just one woman" the finality of love, that is to say a final self-abandonment. "It seems to me there remains only this perfect union with a woman—sort of ultimate marriage—and there isn't anything else."[43] Although maintaining that God does not exist, when Gerald points out that a woman would not suffice to "make" his life, Birkin accuses him of being "a born unbeliever";[44] which is equivalent to substituting love for God, and takes us back to autobiography. The subsequent account of the Birkin/Ursula relationship is Lawrence's attempt to define this love, what it is, and what it should not be.

Birkin's meditation on love: from protozoa to angel

Love being the only means of escape from the kind of total nihilism which is revealed in his criticism of society, Birkin refuses even to employ the word "love" in his effort to arrive at that understanding with Ursula which will lead to the "ultimate" marriage. His attitude is explained in a lone meditation in his room during a period of convalescence. Not only is this passage more explicit than most others, but Lawrence draws attention to its significance by stressing the particular clarity and sureness of Birkin's ideas whenever he takes to his bed![45]

This meditation throws light on his previous conversations with Ursula, to whom he has declared that he does not believe in love "any more than I believe in hate, or in grief. Love is one of the emotions like all the others— and so it is all right whilst you feel it. But I can't see how it becomes an absolute. It is just part of human relationships, that's all."[46] Thus Birkin offers her not love but "freedom together",[47] a union beyond sentiment and emotion:

> And it is there I would want to meet you—not in the emotional, loving plane—but there beyond, where there is no speech and no terms of agreement. There we are two stark, unknown beings, two utterly strange creatures, I would want to approach you, and you me. And there could be no obligation, because there is no standard for action, there . . . —because one is outside the pale of all that is accepted, and nothing known applies . . . only each taking according to the primal desire.[48]

While Ursula would like to keep the term "love", Birkin refuses, because the word has lost its meaning:

> What I want is a strange conjunction with you—not meeting and mingling . . . but an equilibrium, a pure balance of two single beings:—as the stars balance each other. I did not say, nor imply, a satellite. I meant two single equal stars balanced in conjunction.[49]

In his meditation Birkin rejects "the old way of love" which seems to him "a dreadful bondage, a sort of conscription": he wants neither children nor "the horrible privacy of domestic and connubial satisfaction", while a liaison seems to him only "another kind of coupling, reactionary from the legal marriage".[50] Sex, he admits, is hateful to him:

> On the whole, he hated sex, it was such a limitation. It was sex that turned a man into a broken half of a couple, the woman into the other broken half. And he wanted to be single in himself, the woman single in herself. He wanted sex to revert to the level of the other appetites, to be regarded as a functional process, not as a fulfilment. He believed in sex marriage. But beyond this, he wanted a further conjunction, where man had being and woman had being, two pure beings, each constituting the freedom of the other, balancing each other like two poles of one force, like two angels, or two demons.[51]

Birkin thus aspires to freedom from all compulsive need for emotional union with a woman, from the torment of unsatisfied physical desire. Such desire ought not to worry him any more than thirst in a world abounding in water. What he cannot stand in love is the feeling of being caught up, merged, fused with another. With Ursula he wanted to be "as free as with himself, single and clear and cool, yet balanced, polarized with her".[52] What he fears in women is "the lure for possession, a greed of self-importance in love". He hates in her the *Magna Mater* claiming that "all was hers, because she had borne it". He finds intolerable, even in Ursula,

> . . . the urge to possession at the hands of a woman. Always a man must be considered as the broken off fragment of a woman, and the sex was the still aching scar of the laceration.[53]

But while reverting to a basic "Study of Thomas Hardy" theme, Birkin is adding something new. In 1914 Lawrence followed Weininger in affirming that each individual contains a mixture of male and female principles, sexual union providing the means for an exchange and a purification of the respective partners. Since then he seems to have studied Weininger anew and to have reflected on the conclusions drawn from the first part of his book. What seemed to satisfy him in the "Hardy" now revolts him. And Birkin goes on to proclaim:

> We are not broken fragments of one whole. Rather we are the singling away into purity and clear being, of things that were mixed. Rather the sex is that which remains in us of the mixed, the unresolved. And passion is the further separating of this mixture, that which is manly being taken into the being of the man, that which is womanly passing to the woman, till the two are clear and whole as angels, the admixture of sex in the highest sense surpassed, leaving two single beings constellated together like two stars.[54]

The purification which, according to the "Hardy", took place at the

moment of each perfect physical union is now considered as more or less
final for the elected few.

The theme of twin stars, which recurs constantly in Birkin's discourse,
recalls Carpenter's idea of cellular and spiritual regeneration through love,
thanks to which two beings become twin stars in mutual equilibrium.[55]
Birkin aspires to a permanent and final union of this kind.

His meditation continues with an allusion to "the old age, before sex
was", when each being was "a mixture" of male and female:

> The process of singling into individuality resulted into the great polariza-
> tion of sex. The womanly withdrew to one side, the manly to the other. But
> the separation was imperfect even then.

Now there is to come "the new day", the day of pure beings "fulfilled in
difference": Birkin is the prophet of that new day, of perfect, unmixed
beings, of men like angels or demons, "actual angels" and "good, pure-
tissued demons", the "unseen hosts" in whom he professes to believe.[56]

> The man is pure man, the woman pure woman, they are perfectly polarized.
> But there is no longer any of the horrible merging, mingling, self-abnegation
> of love. There is only the pure duality of polarization, each one free from any
> contamination of the other. In each, the individual is primal, sex is subordinate,
> but perfectly polarized. Each has a single, separate being, with its own laws.
> The man has his pure freedom, the woman hers. Each acknowledges the per-
> fection of the polarized sex-circuit. Each admits the different nature of the
> other.[57]

The evident analogies between this new theory and the ideas expressed by
Carpenter in *The Drama of Love and Death*, particularly in the chapter
entitled "The Beginnings of Love", on the reproduction of protozoa and on
chromosomes, suggest a possible source for Birkin's views on the different
"ages" of sexual differentiation. The idea of purification through individualization is no doubt linked with theosophical ideas, and corresponds to
Lawrence's need to assert his masculinity in opposition to Frieda, the *Dea
Mater*, the devouring mother, or "Queen Bee", as Lawrence was to call
both the Ursula of *Women in Love* and the Frieda of *Sea and Sardinia*.[58] In his
theoretical meditation, Birkin seems to be seeking a love transcending sex,
a union "far beyond the scope of phallic investigation".[59]

Possibly as the result of rereading Weininger, or of deeper reflection on his
earlier reading, the Lawrence of 1916 adopted as his own a number of this
writer's attitudes: his hostility to woman, considered as mother or as
prostitute, as inferior to man, as a human being without logical or moral
values, object rather than subject, matter rather than form, ceaselessly
demanding to be re-created by man; his hostility to love, which "strives to

cover guilt, instead of conquering it", which "elevates woman instead of nullifying her".[60]

If, as seems probable, Lawrence had read Madame Blavatsky's *The Secret Doctrine* before writing *Women in Love*, he may have learned from it that, according to the Zohar, "the first race . . . was imperfect, i.e. was born before the '*balance*' [the sexes] existed, and . . . was therefore destroyed".[61] No doubt in Birkin's mind echoes of this esoteric doctrine are mingled with themes from Weininger and Carpenter, both of whom certainly drank from the same source.

Change of attitude towards woman

Nevertheless, the development of Lawrence's own relationship with Frieda since 1913 is surely the decisive element in this changed attitude towards woman and love, this departure from the initial scheme of "The Sisters" and from the philosophy of the "Hardy". Even in the Prologue Birkin was prepared to find in a complete love a refuge from his inability to love a woman.

Throughout the novel, Birkin's behaviour to Ursula is, in fact, defensive. Despite his attempt to assert his masculine superiority in the scene of Mino's disdainful cuffing of the wild she-cat,[62] when Ursula takes the initiative in one of their love scenes, "to show him she was no narrow prude",[63] Birkin accepts her kisses "with unyielding anguish". He is "afraid of a woman capable of such abandon, such dangerous thoroughness of destructivity",[64] and, when stoning the image of the moon in the lake, it is against Cybele, "the accursed *Syria Dea*", against conscious, aggressive desire in woman that he rails. He refuses to "serve" Ursula's "mere female quality", discourages her from letting herself go "in the Dionysic ecstatic way", which is "like going round in a squirrel cage"; and when his kisses kindle in her "the old destructive fires", he tries to damp them down, wanting only "gentle communion, no other, no passion now".[65] The relationship between this scene and the next—Birkin's reflections on the African fetish which leads him to choose "the way of liberty" and to ask Ursula to marry him—is not clear. Certain links in the author's chain of thought are missing and the problems raised have no apparent connexion with those of the preceding scene. Are Birkin's words and theorizing perhaps masking a reality Lawrence was not ready to face in *Women in Love*, such as the effects of his illness on his sex life, of his fatigue and his inability to respond to Frieda's demands, or the realization, made clear by the Prologue, that he was more attracted physically by men than by women? Such questions inevitably arise from the contrast between Birkin's words and acts, a contrast of which he himself is clearly aware:

> Perhaps he had been wrong to go to her with an idea of what he wanted. Was it really only an idea, or was it the interpretation of a profound yearning?

If the latter, how was it he was always talking about sensual fulfilment? The two did not agree very well.[66]

In this passage Lawrence is in fact underlining the profound difference existing in his novel between a theoretical complete, balanced love, transcending but including sex, still close to his original 1913 concept of "the priest of love", and the practice of Birkin, the hesitant male seeking to impose his conditions on Ursula, and fearful of the consequences of the flames he kindles in her. From the 1913 concept the novel develops into a confession of a half-failure in love, disguised behind a barrage of obscure, mystical theories, and which the unpublished Prologue confirms. For Birkin, as for the pre-1912 Lawrence, woman has become an indispensable, but dreaded, refuge.

Sex as magic ritual

Birkin-Lawrence is thus seeking to free himself from the servitude of sex. When he finds he cannot escape it, he seems to feel a need to confer on it some magic value by inventing an obscure ritual similar to that of "Manifesto" and recalling scenes already studied in *The Rainbow*. But Lawrence built his novel round certain abstract ideas already presented symbolically in "The Crown"; these ideas can help us to grasp at least the main lines of the most obscure of all the scenes between Birkin and Ursula: when, in the parlour of the Saracen's Head at Southwell, they reach total mutual acceptance and final consecration in "a perfect passing away for both of them" which is at the same time "the most intolerable accession into being",[67] a kind of initiation rite for a second birth, suggested, perhaps, by the ethnologists Lawrence read with so much interest.

To understand this scene is not necessarily to admire it: for the vast majority of readers, it must remain obscure, confused, inacceptable. As H. M. Daleski points out in his pertinent and ingenious analysis, Lawrence has failed to communicate his intentions to the reader. The scene requires interpretation, a search for unexpressed ideas. Like other parts of the novel, it reveals a lack of finish, a want of respect for the reader, incompatible with the literary and artistic function of the novel, which should surely be fully, though not necessarily easily, comprehensible. As a work of art, this chapter of *Women in Love* fails to achieve its end: the reader remains perplexed and incredulous, vaguely aware of having been subjected to mystification rather than to mystical experience.

Yet this scene was undoubtedly of great importance to Lawrence: it is part of a series ranging from the "transfiguration" of Tom and Lydia in *The Rainbow*, by way of the liberation of Will, and of the poem "Manifesto" (dated from Zennor and hence contemporary with *Women in Love*), to *The*

Plumed Serpent and *Lady Chatterley's Lover*. It raises the whole problem of the obscure relationship, in the works of Lawrence, between mystic attitudes derived from yoga and the esoterics on the one hand, anal fixations and more or less conscious homosexual tendencies on the other. Between two extremes, religious conceptions on the one hand, quasi-psychotic obsessions on the other, are found also quite commonplace, ordinary ideas. Each element can in fact be traced to Lawrence's preoccupations while writing this book at Zennor. What we are concerned with here is to elucidate as far as possible the language used by him in these extremely obscure passages.

Everything seems to rest on Birkin's concept of "corruption" and of "shame". In order to understand this, it is necessary to go back for a moment to "The Crown". There Lawrence sees two opposing hosts of angels, "the upright, rushing flames, the lofty Cherubim that palpitate about the Presence", and those, "soft and pearly as mist", newts and snakes that "hover on the edge of the last Assumption", the angels of death and corruption.[68] All life is made up of these two currents, the one towards "the upper, ruddy, blazing sun", the other towards obscurity and "universal darkness". Once the flower, which alone is timeless, has leapt "into the upper fiery eternity" in the creative act, the fruit ripens and falls, dark ebbing back to dark and light to light. This process is the "temporal flux of corruption", as the flux together was the temporal flux of creation. "Only the perfect meeting, the kiss, the blow, the two in one", is "timeless and absolute". Those who never know this "consummation into oneness" of light and darkness remain non-beings, like cabbages:

> This is evil, when that which is temporal and relative asserts itself eternal and absolute. This I, which I am, has no being save in timelessness. In my consummation, when that which came from the Beginning and that which came from the End are transfused into oneness, then I come into being, I have existence. Till then I am only a part of nature, I am not . . . But as part of nature, as part of the flux, I have my instrumental identity, my inferior I, my self-consciousness.[69]

The conscious ego is thus part of nature. time-bound, not of the eternal, of the mystic now. The "accession to being" which Ursula and Birkin achieve together is a "consummation into oneness" involving not only "the oneness" of the couple but that of each individual partner. And such oneness is possible only if in each of them, both in relation to themselves and to each other, light is reconciled with darkness, spirit with body, creative forces with those of corruption and disintegration. Each one of them must undergo a true, a second birth, which, according to "The Crown", takes place only when "the soul comes into being in the midst of life, just as the phoenix in her maturity becomes immortal in flame. That is not her perishing: it is her becoming absolute, a blossom of fire".[70] And, as with

Tom and Lydia, "transfiguration" is possible only when each accepts the whole of the other's being, of his or her nature, including its corruption. The "mystic now" of "Manifesto" is accessible only when both recognize and accept as such the time-bound aspects of their being, thus freeing their immortality from their temporality. In simpler terms, the soul accepts the body, but to Lawrence such words are outworn and inadequate to express his mystic experience; he refuses the traditional, the simple, and seeks an over-subtle, esoteric explanation. Not till the mid-twenties will he really dare to express himself in more direct language. What is surprising is Lawrence's insistence, both in "Manifesto" and in *Women in Love*, on the lumbar and anal manifestations of this mutual acceptance. Psychoanalysis can certainly interpret this characteristic localization of the more general concept of "corruption" as applied to the bodily functions. Two passages from an earlier chapter offer some help in discerning the novelist's none too explicit intention.

In the moonlight scene beside the millpond Ursula watches Birkin moving alone and unaware in a wood. A sudden scruple seizes her:

He did not know she was there. Supposing he did something he would not wish to be seen doing, *thinking he was quite private*? But there, what did it matter? What did *the small privacies* matter? How could it matter, what he did? How can there be any secrets, *we are all the same organisms*? How can there be any secrecy, when everything is known to us all?[71] [*Italics added*.]

Ursula here expresses, in everyday terms, what Lawrence later tries to illustrate in mystic form, possibly because he was not yet ready to say straight out exactly what he meant. Immediately after this passage, Birkin, speaking to himself, curses the Syrian goddess Aphrodite, symbolized by the moon reflected in the water: adding at once "Does one begrudge it her? What else is there—?"[72] Thus in the space of a few lines Lawrence associates the thought of excreta and that of the "tribute" man must pay to Aphrodite with the "destructive flames" of woman. Later on in the novel Birkin will associate love-making with "the roots of darkness and shame"—with the fascination of horror. Sex remains an awesome mystery, its degradation redeemed only by religious ritual.

During the water party, Birkin had already spoken to Ursula of the stream of corruption and dissolution within every one of us, in terms very close to those of "The Crown":

"We always consider the silver river of life's rolling on and quickening all the world to a brightness, on and on to heaven, flowing into a bright eternal sea, a heaven of angels thronging. But the other is our real reality."

"But what other? I don't see any other," said Ursula.

"It is your reality, nevertheless," he said; "that dark river of dissolution.

You see it rolls in us just as the other rolls—the black river of corruption. And our flowers are of this—our sea-born Aphrodite, all our white phosphorescent flowers of sensuous perfection, all our reality nowadays . . . Aphrodite . . . is the flowering mystery of the death process . . . When the stream of synthetic creation lapses, we find ourselves part of the inverse process, the flood of destructive creation. Aphrodite is born in the first spasm of universal dissolution—then the snakes and swans and lotus—marsh flowers—and Gudrun and Gerald—born in the process of destructive creation."

"And you and me?" she asked.

"Probably," he replied. "In part certainly. Whether we are that, in toto, I don't yet know."[73]

Birkin constantly uses the words corruption, disintegration, dissolution with reference to the "purely sensual consciousness" symbolized by the African fetish, as well as to Gerald and the mechanical civilization he represents. Ursula, on the other hand, brings him "freedom . . . the paradisal entry into pure, single being, the individual soul taking precedence over love and desire for union". If our interpretation is correct, the problem for Birkin and Ursula is to accept in each other *every sort* of bodily servitude, the "yoke and leash of love", without ever forfeiting each his "own proud individual singleness, even while it loves and yields".[74] And this total acceptance finds expression in caresses on the loins and thighs, symbolizing the unreserved acceptance by each of the complete being of the other—acceptance also of the death and corruption that are part of life itself. These contacts seem to satisfy Birkin's desire to have Ursula "accept him at the quick of death", in all his bodily functions.

Early in the chapter "Excurse" we find him irritated with Ursula, who does not yet know "the depths of passion when one became impersonal and indifferent, unemotional". She "was still at the emotional personal level":

> He had taken her as he had never been taken himself. He had taken her at the roots of her darkness and shame—like a demon, laughing over the fountain of mystic corruption which was one of the sources of her being, laughing, shrugging, accepting finally. As for her, when would she so much go beyond herself as to accept him at the quick of death?[75]

Nothing of what has gone before can explain the phrase "he had *taken* her": the term remains equivocal, and may indeed mean no more than "accepted". But the passage may also be compared with *A Propos of Lady Chatterley's Lover*, where Lawrence insists on Swift's obsession with excreta. For Birkin, it is possible that the "fountain of corruption" simply means woman's sexual desire, which he dreaded and condemned in calling down curses on the *Dea Syria*. But fear of woman's desire is certainly mixed with the repulsion-attraction of excreta.

The mystic acceptance of the other "at the quick of death" is discovered and admitted by Ursula in the Saracen's Head after a scene in which she reproaches Birkin for his liaison with Hermione, his "spiritual brides", the "foulness" of his sex life, accusing him of being "perverse" and "death-eating" (accusations which remain almost meaningless unless the reader can be referred to the suppressed Prologue).[76] Birkin asks himself whether "Ursula's way of emotional intimacy" is not as dangerous as Hermione's "abstract, spiritual intimacy".[77] Whether he does not risk being "absorbed, melted, merged" into Ursula, "the perfect womb", as opposed to Hermione, "the perfect Idea". But in the inn, after their reconciliation, comes their mystic transfiguration. Ursula sees him with "new eyes" which "open in her soul", like a strange creature from another world. He has become one of the Sons of God from "the old magic Book of Genesis". Kneeling on the hearth-rug before him, she puts her face against his thighs, and with her fingertips traces the back of his thighs; following "some mysterious life flow there", she discovers something "more than wonderful, more wonderful than life itself . . . the strange mystery of his life motion, there at the back of the thighs, down the flanks". For Ursula, this is "neither love nor passion" but

. . . a dark flood of electric passion she released from him, drew into herself. She had established a rich new circuit, a new current of passional electric energy, between the two of them, released from the darkest poles of the body and established in perfect circuit. It was a dark fire of electricity that rushed from him to her, and flooded them both with rich peace, satisfaction.[78]

Ursula "seemed to touch the quick of the mystery of darkness that was bodily him". Both "seem to faint" in a "perfect passing away", which is at the same time

. . . the most intolerable accession into being, the marvellous fulness of immediate gratification, overwhelming, outflooding from the source of the deepest life-force, the darkest, deepest, strangest life-source of the human body, at the back and base of the loins.[79]

Quotation is here essential: analysis can only distort by attempting interpretation. Is Lawrence trying to describe a personal experience, as "Manifesto"[80] would suggest, or is he on the contrary endeavouring to translate into action some abstract concept drawn from his readings in ethnology, magic and occultism? Do these curious rites, astonishingly close to those of "Manifesto" and to the spontaneous, less specifically described gestures of Tom and Lydia, correspond to a mystic refinement on some incident in his own sex life? Can these gestures in some way represent a consecration of his distinct, other, individual existence in relation to the beloved but invasive woman, a kind of magic protection against "merging" with the beloved? Any number of hypotheses may be advanced, the most explicit text being that of "Manifesto". In that poem, the woman's contact with the man's "darkest sources" is meant to teach her that the beloved is "other", does not belong to her, is not her "object", but has his own independent being, his own life: Birkin's defensive manœuvres would then appear as a manifestation of Lawrence's new attitude to Frieda as "the devouring mother"—expressed in a previously quoted letter to Katherine Mansfield.[81]

Experience or theory?

This strange scene thus moves on at least two planes: that of the personal experience, strongly suggested by "Manifesto" and by similar scenes in *The Rainbow*: that of a "philosophy" indebted not only to Heraclitus and Burnet, but also to theosophy and yoga. It is difficult to claim any parallel development on the artistic plane, for even Lawrence's most ardent apologists are severely critical or completely silent on this subject. It is, however, only fair to point out the novelist's consistent attempt to depict his characters here as figures in an Indian fresco, hieratic, illumined by an impersonal glow.[82]

Nothing in all Lawrence's known experience or reading can account for this mystic theory of "dark sources", except the yoga theory of the *chakras*, or vital centres, to which he refers specifically in *Psychoanalysis and the Unconscious*,[83] and to which he seems first to have been introduced in his reading (so far undated) of J. M. Pryse's *The Apocalypse Unsealed*. Commenting on the *Upanishads*, Pryse explains that man has two nervous structures, one cerebro-spinal, the other sympathetic or ganglionic. There are seven ganglia, i.e. principal life centres, or chakras, grouped into four areas: (1) the sacral (no doubt Lawrence's "dark source") and (2) the prostatic, both in the "genital area"; next comes the navel region with (3) the epigastric; then the area of the heart with (4) the cardiac chakra; and finally the area of the head, grouping (5) the pharyngeal, (6) the cavernous and (7) the conarium or pineal gland, the "third eye" of the seer (the "new eye" which opened in Ursula's soul!). When Kundalini, the "agent of perfecting work", curled up like a serpent, is roused to activity, it "conquers" the chakras, and two side currents circulate along the spinal cord: in Chapter XXX Lawrence speaks of "the central serpent that is coiled at the core of life" which Loerke has the gift of awakening in Gudrun.[84]

Significant differences do appear between Pryse's interpretation of his "gnostic chart" of the seven chakras and the use made of it by Lawrence. The present comparison merely aims at showing that the scene at the inn in *Women in Love*, with its suggestion of the awakening of occult forces, is vaguely inspired by an esoterism the source of which may well be Pryse, but which may also originate in other occultist literature known to Lawrence, to which there is no specific reference before 1917, but to which Heseltine probably introduced him about a year earlier.

One may well ask how seriously Lawrence is here taking either his new esoteric "knowledge", or indeed his own novel, and the reader. Daleski has rightly drawn attention to the artistic weakness of this whole scene.[85] This aesthetic fall from standards, this incapacity to communicate an experience to the reader in meaningful terms, lead to the conclusion that the novel's "message" on love is at best hermetic, at worst slightly tainted by the ridicule inherent in any pretentious effort to raise the commonplace to the level of the sacred, and that, on this count alone, this chapter fails to be great writing. There are indeed moments when *Women in Love* sinks almost to the level of the novelette: after her mystic experience, Ursula, usually nervous and uncertain when presiding at the tea-table, finds that "the tea-pot poured beautifully from a proud slender spout"![86] Similar examples of Lawrentian symbolism bordering on parody are to be found in his later and notably less inspired novel *Aaron's Rod*.

The lovers return to earth, and that same night, in the heart of Sherwood Forest, they experience the more orthodox and communicable joys of sexual love. Both resign their posts in order to free themselves from the yoke of society, and no more is heard of their love until a day in Austria, after their marriage, when Ursula, confronted by a "bestial", "degraded" Birkin, tells herself that, after all, "they might do as they liked" and that there is no need to exclude "anything that gave one satisfaction":

> Why not be bestial, and go the whole round of experience? She exulted in it. She was bestial. How good it was to be really shameful! There would be no shameful thing she had not experienced. Yet she was unabashed, she was herself. Why not? She was free, when she knew everything, and no dark shameful things were denied her.[87]

Although her sexual dissatisfaction subsists, as well as, so it would seem, the notion of shame, this final message, vehemently put into action in *Lady Chatterley's Lover*, is no doubt the basis of the lesson so laboriously, so slowly spelled out in previous scenes between Birkin and Ursula. Yet the reader remains unconvinced that so much discussion was really necessary to lead to this conclusion, unless the novelist is concealing something about Birkin's psychology—something definitely indicated in the Prologue. It seems that, for Lawrence, accession to a normal sex relationship was conditioned by acceptance of the "other" as a distinct and separate individual acting autonomously and not as an "instrument"; the aim of Birkin's mystico-magical manœuvres is to make sure that he is not treated as an instrument in love but as a being with a separate existence of his own. The clarity and, no doubt, the literary value of the book would have been improved by a more direct treatment of the subject without constant recourse to a somewhat confused symbolism, an esoterism baldly inflicted on the totally uninitiated reader. The only possible conclusion seems to be that Birkin's love is that of an abnormally hesitant man, endlessly manœuvring to delay the physical contacts he cannot do without, struggling against the inhibitions of his puritan upbringing and a "shame" still felt even by the allegedly "enfranchised" Ursula. Although Lawrence either cannot or dare not state this openly, all Birkin's magical and mystical manœuvres are designed to overcome if not eliminate this shame, this fear of woman's normal sexual desires. Even in *Psychoanalysis and the Unconscious* he shrouds his allusions to the lower chakras in verbal mystery, under the pretext of the impossibility of discussing them in public.

As the novel expressing the love Lawrence set out to preach, *Women in Love* fails to achieve its end for the simple reason that the novelist's position had changed with respect to the original aims of 1913 and even of 1915. He neither faces openly nor solves his own conflicts; yet the Prologue shows that they are still present in his very conception of his characters. He no longer believes in love or passion; like Birkin he retreats from conscious love, encompassing both mind and emotion; since he is not ready to accept physical attraction without endowing it with religious character, he feels obliged to attribute religious value to the bodily functions, though without ever explicitly enunciating the new beliefs which make this possible. In so far as it pretends to positive values, this novel of love triumphant does not carry conviction. Birkin's positive philosophy, if indeed he has one, is obscured by his roundabout manœuvres and evasions. How far is Birkin the Lawrence of 1916, and how far is he still a picture of the Lawrence of the pre-Frieda years? Clearly he remains a mixture of the two: the Lawrence of 1916 predominating in so far as Ursula is to some extent a portrait of Frieda, but showing signs of marked regression from the Lawrence of 1913, a year of self-confidence and of love triumphant.

Male comradeship: the wrestling scene

But *Women in Love* is more than a love story: it is also a study of the failure of friendship and a social satire, these last two elements being closely linked.

Birkin conceives of love as the only remaining refuge in a world completely devoid of beliefs and ideals. Having rejected the whole of humanity as doomed to destruction, the loved one is the only acceptable "otherness" remaining, outside male comradeship. Seen from this angle, *Women in Love* appears as a reduction of human relations to their simplest possible expression, with the proviso that Birkin scarcely raises the problem of his own survival in a universe from which human society has been completely eliminated. He himself is able to break away from all professional obligations and begin a wandering life with Ursula, thanks to the unearned income of £400 a year which he enjoys without for a moment questioning its origins: a detail revealing the total unreality of this verbal reduction to essentials. Birkin's experience, like his criticism of society, is invalidated from the very outset by the fact that he accepts from society this £400 while refusing to work, on the grounds that he rejects society and all its goals.

Gerald Crich is the male with whom Birkin makes the experiment of friendship. In the novel as published, no mention is made of the history or nature of this friendship between Birkin and Gerald. The Prologue was much more explicit, and had emphasized the "trembling nearness" of their first encounter, their sudden intimacy which "was between them like a transfiguration", "like a strange, embarrassing fire", as well as revealing Birkin's tortured and secret love of men, of the "beauty of . . . manly limbs".[88]

Gerald, the son of an "industrial magnate" who has rejected Oxford in favour of studies in Germany, is in all respects the tall, blond Aryan, and the novelist lays great stress on his "northern" character and features, his height and air of superiority, his fair hair and blue eyes. From the first he appears as the Wagnerian hero, foredoomed to death, as Ursula is predestined to love and to acceptance of the creative mystery. Gerald is also Cain, having accidentally killed his brother: for Birkin as for Lawrence, there are no accidents.

He is also, symbolically and by education, the Teuton, the Nordic warrior. Birkin's friendship is to be a symbolic effort to redeem Cain, to save humanity from self-destruction. Although this part of the novel is externally based on Lawrence's relationship with Murry at Zennor in 1916, and on the failure of his attempt to persuade Murry to swear eternal friendship in an oath of *Blutbrüderschaft*, the cancelled Prologue suggests that the two men's comradeship recalls older memories of Lawrence's early friendships. In the novel itself the two men are friends, speaking frankly and with mutual respect to each other. Suddenly, in the course of a conversation about death, Birkin finds himself confronted with "a second problem" (the first being that of his relations with Ursula), that of "love and eternal conjunction between two men. Of course this was necessary—it had been a necessity inside himself all his life—to love a man purely and fully. Of course he had been loving Gerald all along, and all along denying it."[89] Whereupon he proposes to Gerald that they swear a *Blutbrüderschaft* like the old German knights, "no wounds, that is obsolete", but an oath "to love each other, you and I, implicitly and perfectly, and finally, without any possibility of going back on it". Gerald is attracted but mistrustful, "resenting the bondage, hating the attraction". Birkin repeats his proposal: "We will swear to stand by each other, be true to each other—ultimately, infallibly—given to each other, organically—without possibility of taking back." But Gerald avoids the issue by asking "in a voice of excuse" to "leave it till I understand it better".[90] In the ensuing silence, Birkin sees Gerald as essentially "limited to one form of existence, one knowledge, one activity, a sort of fatal halfness, which to himself seemed wholeness".[91] Later the two men will come near to what Birkin seeks in a bout of Japanese wrestling, their limbs "interfused" in a "tense white knot of flesh", "mindless at last". The wrestling leaves them exhausted and inert, naked on the carpet. Birkin "comes to consciousness again", raises himself and, putting out a hand to steady himself, touches Gerald's hand, which closes "warm and sudden" over his own. But Gerald's clasp (and Birkin was to remember this significant detail after the final tragedy) was only "sudden and momentaneous".[92]

This wrestling "had some deep meaning" to both of them, "an unfinished meaning". In his best Sunday-school style, Birkin proclaims: "We are mentally, spiritually intimate, therefore we should be more or less physically intimate too—it is more whole." He goes on to admire Gerald's physical beauty: "I think also that you are beautiful, and that is enjoyable too. One should enjoy what is given ... You have a northern kind of beauty, like light refracted from snow, and a beautiful, plastic form. Yes that is there to enjoy as well. We should enjoy everything."[93] He finds Gerald different from himself, as far apart "as man from woman, yet in another direction".[94] But immediately after this comment, perhaps designed to show that Birkin's mind was open to every possible form and manifestation of love, it is Ursula, the woman, who regains "ascendance over his being", Gerald "becoming dim again, lapsing out of him". At the end of the novel, after Gerald's death, Birkin tells Ursula that "to make his life complete" he "wanted eternal union with a man too: another kind of love". "It's false, impossible," says Ursula. "It's an obstinacy, a theory, a perversity." Birkin's evasive rejoinder "I don't think so" suggests that he, for his part, does not necessarily reject "perversity".

Whether these episodes show Lawrence trying to express a fundamental need of his own nature, as is all the more probable in that the first scene with Gerald is inspired by an actual conversation with Murry, or whether his aim was merely to illustrate the theme of complete sexual freedom, in the same way as he was already trying to illustrate a new relationship between man and woman, it must be admitted that the novel once more fails to win over or convince most readers. Both the episodes themselves and their theoretical meaning are obscure; nor is there stylistic value such as to enable them to command attention by sheer artistic merit.

Cecil Gray has stressed Lawrence's contemporary interest in homosexuality. Birkin's attitude to Gerald in these scenes is equivocal, to say the least, and it is possible to interpret it as an attempt to justify homosexual feelings if not practice. But either out of fear of possible consequences after the suppression of *The Rainbow*, or as a result of the fundamental incertitude and ambiguity of his own nature, Lawrence's intentions never emerge from the semi-darkness of vague suggestivity. The Prologue was, of course, much more outspoken, and its suppression may be interpreted in part as a defensive step against interpretations of the Birkin/Gerald relationship which might have been damaging to Lawrence. It is not difficult to see in Birkin's ideas, particularly in his assertion of masculine superiority, the influence of Weininger; but Birkin's position on this point is never made absolutely clear. While it is possible that Lawrence was trying to present Birkin as the "new man" freed from sex advocated by Weininger, no positive proof exists of this intention.

The reader, not having access to the Prologue, was thus reduced to conjecture as to what Lawrence was after. The Prologue does throw some light, not on Lawrence's artistic intentions in the novel as published, but on the state of confusion of the character of Birkin during the 1916 drafting of the novel—a state in which, indeed, he was always to remain. In the Prologue Birkin is shown obsessed by homosexual desires. and some passages are strongly suggestive of the attraction of William Henry Hocking for Lawrence.[95] He is tormented by a "keen desire to have and possess the bodies of some men. He wanted to cast out these desires, wanted not to know them . . . Yet a man can no more slay a living desire in him than he can prevent his body from feeling heat and cold."[96] And in a particularly revealing passage the reader is let into Birkin's inmost privacy:

> . . . this was the one and only secret he kept to himself, this secret of his passionate and sudden affinity for men he saw. He kept this secret even from himself. He knew what he felt, but he always kept the knowledge at bay.[97]

Just like Ursula with the memory of her love for Winifred. One might be tempted to treat this as literary invention, rather than confession, had not Lawrence in "Manifesto" referred to his own "vicious" and shameful desires. Frieda's reply to the present writer, when asked in 1932 whether Lawrence had read Havelock Ellis, assumes special significance in relation to these passages: "No," she said, "I don't think so: he wasn't interested in perversions"—which suggests that to her Havelock Ellis had no significance except as a writer on sexual perversion! Barbara Low, frequently consulted by Lawrence on his health at this time of his life, insisted in conversation with the author in 1934 on the fascination which Murry's good looks exercised on Lawrence. In the light of these facts, much of the Birkin/Gerald relationship appears as a veiled, deliberately obscured confession rather than as literary creation with an autonomous purpose.

Birkin as forerunner of a new race

Evident traces of occultist influence are further proof of Lawrence's failure to merge into a fully coherent and communicable whole the many disparate elements of which this novel is compounded. His satirical aim, the proclamation of the end of a world he hated, constantly gets the better of his desire to announce the coming of a new world, of which Birkin is the prophet and possibly the precursor. There are indications, fully examined in a later chapter, that Lawrence had access to the works of Madame Blavatsky over several years.[98] In *Women in Love* we find suggestions of the coming of a new human race, linked with the idea of dissolution and of angels of destruction, and of the orbital "balance" to which the two sexes must attain before the appearance of the new humanity, which will be like angels.

In Madame Blavatsky, the idea of a new humanity is linked to that of cosmic epochs. In a system ruled by the figure seven, the heavenly bodies all move in groups of seven, each passing through an evolutionary cycle of seven "rounds". After each cycle, every planet enters upon "a certain time of rest", or "obscuration", but in the seventh and last round it begins to die, entering the period of "planetary dissolution" when it must "transfer its life and energy to another planet". During the fourth "round", the Earth hardens, and humanity evolves, man being the first form to appear during this round. During the next three rounds, Earth will once more become spiritualized and "gradually return to its ethereal form", during which time man becomes first Angel, then God. Each earthly round is composed of seven "root-races", beginning with the Ethereal and ending with the Spiritual: the first root-race is that of the "Sons of Heaven" or Lunar ancestors, for the Earth is the daughter of the Moon: these Sons of Heaven are the Sons of God whose coming Ursula awaited.[99]

But on the earth in its fourth round there already exist precursors of future rounds, "fifth rounders" like Plato, or "sixth rounders" such as Buddha:

> Every round . . . brings about a new development and even an entire change in the mental, psychic and physical constitution of man, all these principles evoluting [*sic*] on an ever ascending scale. Thence it follows that persons who, like Confucius and Plato, belonged psychically, mentally and spiritually to the higher planes of evolution, were in our Fourth Round as the average man will be in the Fifth Round, whose mankind is destined to find itself, on this scale of Evolution, immensely higher than in our present humanity.[100]

Still according to *The Secret Doctrine*, fire is "the most perfect and unadulterated reflection, in Heaven as on Earth, of the ONE FLAME. It is Life and Death, the origin and the end of every material thing. It is divine SUBSTANCE."[101] Finally, and this any reader of Lawrence will do well to remember, "to live is to die and to die is to live". Siva, the destroyer, is the creator and saviour of spiritual man, the god who kills "the human passions and physical senses" in order to awaken man's higher spiritual perceptions.

In the light of this doctrine, Birkin can be seen as potentially a fifth or sixth rounder, a precursor of the new age. Not only does he believe "in the proud angels and the demons that are our forerunners" and in the "invisible hosts";[102] not only does he announce that it is time for "mankind to pass away"[103] and that it will be replaced by a new "embodiment" of the "incomprehensible", by something non-human "straight out of fire";[104] he also sees in contemporary corruption "the first spasm of universal dissolution", and predicts the end of the world, "a progressive process" ending in "universal nothing", which means "a new cycle of creation after—but not for us".[105] In his first conversations with Ursula, he either does not yet know, or pretends not to know, that he is one of the predestined beings heralding the next cycle. Whereas Gudrun and Gerald, like "the snakes and swans and lotus", are "born in the process of destructive creation", he and Ursula belong only "in part" to this process: "Whether we are that, in toto, I don't yet know."[106] For next to the "lilies of corruption" there "ought to be some roses, warm and flamy", some of what Heraclitus calls "dry souls".[107] Rosicrucian occultism here seems interspersed with reminiscences of Burnet. Later, in his reflections on the African statuette, Birkin discovers he is *not* completely doomed to dissolution, two aspects of which he then recognizes: one the "long African process of purely sensual understanding, knowledge in the mystery of dissolution", the other that of the white races, "a mystery of ice-destructive knowledge, snow-abstract annihilation".[108] Suddenly he sees another way, "the way to freedom . . . the paradisal entry into pure, single being, the individual soul taking precedence over love and desire for union", submitting "to the yoke and leash of love" without forfeiting "its own proud individual singleness, even while it loves and yields". Just *what* the difference is between "knowledge in the mystery of dissolution" or its Nordic equivalent "snow-abstract annihilation" and Birkin's aim in proposing marriage to Ursula has been the subject of much critical discussion. The scene itself remains obscure and mystifying—and it may be regretted that Lawrence did not put his meaning in English monosyllables, or even in four-letter words. The reader is inclined to suspect that he is being led up the garden path with humourless polysyllables, and the use of occult concepts does not dissipate this disagreeable impression.

In certain scenes, Lawrence's occultist culture helps to explain the character of Birkin. In one such scene, otherwise difficult to understand, after having, so it would seem, abandoned himself entirely to the destructive flames of Ursula's passion, Birkin goes home, triumphant at having achieved "a new spell of life" in "physical passion"; he is both "satisfied and shattered, fulfilled and destroyed";[109] he hears within himself "a small lament in the darkness". Triumphant, he pours scorn upon this "other" lamenting self, which, however, still "hovers" in the background, "somewhere far off and small". If we regard Birkin as the precursor of a humanity partially liberated from the yoke of sex, the opposition of the two "selves", one moving in the physical universe of "destructive" passion, the other seeking a non-human, angelic balance between two beings without any intermixture, explains the antithesis "satisfied/fulfilled" (in the present) and "shattered/destroyed" (on the plane of future being). The scene may then be understood without recourse, above all exclusive recourse, to physiological explanations such as those offered by Eliseo Vivas, or to evocation of the castration rites of the Syrian Goddess.[110] Lawrence's motives are surely complex; and occultist ideas may be a way for him to conceal to himself his own, and his *alter ego*'s, equivocations on sex. But it is important not to underestimate the importance of occultism in the explanation of this scene: the "satisfied" Birkin is a man of our own age; the "destroyed" Birkin is a potential superman, precursor of the race of the future, but he has not yet reached the higher plane of the "balance" between the sexes. His ensuing psychological adventure with Ursula will, however, lead him there, or at least this is what Lawrence seems to be trying to make us understand.

Occultism also helps to provide an explanation for the scene of the stoning of the moon in the millpond. In terms of esoteric cosmic doctrine the moon is the mother of the earth, the *Dea Mater*, the planet which has transmitted its vitality to our own, and which seeks vengeance for this "vampirizing" on the part of her daughter earth. The moon is the image of the "old destructive fires" of love, of the old era when, according to Birkin, individuals were not yet so completely sexually polarized as to be able to attain that "balance", that autonomy, that independence within interdependence without which sex is "a functional process", not a "fulfilment".[111] The reflected white and cold light of the dead planet, image of the mechanical, deliberate, narcissistic consciousness condemned by Lawrence, is immediately though indirectly contrasted with the "golden light" which is in Ursula[112] and which is the glow of true, spontaneous life, of the original divine substance, fire.

Thus over and above problems inherent in the author's personal amatory experience, clearly reflected in Birkin's attitude to love, *Women in Love* offers a systematic if discreet exploration of esoteric doctrine. Just as *The Rainbow* was placed under the sign of Christian symbolism, of themes and illustrations encountered in Mrs Jenner's little manual, *Women in Love* must be numbered among those of Lawrence's works partially inspired by the occult tradition. The source is almost certainly Madame Blavatsky, although direct allusion to works by her and other occult writers occurs only later, in the 1917–18 period: but, as we have already seen in Lawrence's works, it is not rare to find a source emerging explicitly only in later, theoretical. writings, after the completion of a work of art drawing upon that source.

SOME NEGATIVE ASPECTS

We now come to the question of Lawrence's treatment of the architecture of full-length novels. *The Rainbow* had given superb evidence of his endeavour to create form directly related to subject-matter. Its cyclic structure was deeply thought out, indeed almost revolutionary. *Women in Love*, to many critics, seems to take a step backward. To this it is only fair to object that its basic structure, as far as one can make out, had been constructed before *The Rainbow* was even thought of. The structure is closer to that of *Sons and Lovers*, and more conventional—indeed it is relevant to recall that Lawrence had Meredith in mind when constructing his sequence of chapters. Each chapter centres on one main theme, and is usually firmly located in a single town or house, thus achieving a striking atmosphere of concrete reality.

But while the concrete details are coherent, and the overall framework well constructed, the novel nevertheless consists of a curious juxtaposition of scenes or details drawn either from intimate personal experience, or from old and new reading, or again from contemporary episodes, combined with a straining for symbolic meaning in every detail. This constant striving for psychological significance tends to irritate or even to shock the reader, who fails to see why every gesture should be charged with profound meaning. It was one thing to deduce a psychology from the life of Paul Morel, and quite another to attribute deep and universal meaning to conversations with Murry at Zennor. In *Women in Love* and even more so in later novels, we become aware of a tendency to what amounts almost to journalistic exploitation of contemporary incident, not always as portentous as Lawrence tries to make out: a trick most apparent in *Aaron's Rod*. Did Lawrence perhaps lack the stamina for a novel of considerable length? Certain scenes of *Women in Love* are mere accounts of recent incidents, linked to the rest of the novel only by virtue of eliciting comment or interpretation by Birkin, almost always acting as the author's mouthpiece. This aspect is particularly striking in the attempt to convey the positive side, Birkin's quest for love and friendship, which Lawrence never fully explains to the reader, always seeming to keep back something for himself, as if his message were intended for initiates only.

The satirical vision

The satirical, pessimistic view of civilization which represents the negative side of *Women in Love*, if not always convincing, is certainly more incisive. Everything destructive, or representing destruction, is far more surely, more penetratingly conveyed than the corresponding portrayal of the elect. While Lawrence hardly seems to know what he was offering the few, he is quite certain what he condemns, that is to say the whole of contemporary English society, or rather of those sectors of it pictured in his novel.

His satire is directed against bohemian and artistic London, against the intellectual and aristocratic circles known to him mainly through Garsington, and against the industrial and commercial life of the mining country. And it is injected below the surface, into the characters themselves, particularly into those of Gerald, Gudrun and Hermione, the principal figures in the Lawrentian hell, swept along without hope of salvation in a process of death and destruction.

All that is necessary here is to identify the essential nature of this movement towards death, *leitmotif* of the author's social and cultural criticism: Lawrence arrives at his negation not by an empirical, deductive process, leading from an observation of evil to an explanation based on an examination of its origins; on the contrary, he begins with an overall denunciation, followed by selected samples. This makes it possible for him to present only one side of the social and intellectual life of his time, to consider as negligible and vain the efforts of all those who would try to improve from within the system he condemns *en bloc*. While the scope of his criticism has been slightly broadened since *The Rainbow*, the method is essentially the same, based on generalization and violent denial rather than on reason. Since the author's mouthpiece is almost always Birkin, the general tone is set by this character's peremptory declarations. Birkin's dilemma is either to "bust" the present form of life, or to "shrivel inside it, as in a tight skin". Pressed to explain himself, he attacks not only the industrial, mining society which "covers the earth with foulness", but also any human effort to achieve "material things".[113] The fact that the only alternative he can suggest to such utilitarian undertakings is "perfect union with a woman" is significant of the nature and value of his attacks on civilization! His social criticism is purely destructive and negative. It calls upon some favourite Lawrentian themes: the denunciation of patriotism in a nation of shopkeepers, the idea of race, familiar arguments against any form of national defence, attacks on social democracy and egalitarianism. Birkin poses as a "patriot" of the kind who aims at turning his country into something completely different.[114] But he feels the hour for reform and even revolution is past. Mankind must be utterly destroyed:

> If our race is destroyed like Sodom, and there is this beautiful evening with the luminous land and trees, I am satisfied . . . After all, what is mankind but just one expression of the incomprehensible. And if mankind passes away, it will only mean that this particular expression is completed and done. That which is expressed, and that which is to be expressed, cannot be diminished. There it is, in the shining evening. Let mankind pass away—time it did . . . Humanity doesn't embody the utterance of the incomprehensible any more.

Humanity is a dead letter. There will be a new embodiment, in a new way. Let humanity disappear as quick as possible.[115]

Is this "new way" the way of the Sons of God, of the Angels and Demons whose advent Birkin forebodes? While Lawrence is not quite explicit on this point, it is legitimate to think that his old, disappointed, messianic strain is seeking refuge in the idea of a new embodiment of the divine in the form of angels having achieved complete individuality, freed from sex-mixture and "fulfilled in difference". [116] Lawrence's disgust with society and wholesale denial of it leads straight to a prophetic flight of fantasy.

Blind alleys of art: primitivism and the abstract

This negativism is applied to every aspect of society familiar to Lawrence. Birkin partially accepts the moral and intellectual decomposition of bohemian London as described in the chapters "Crème de Menthe" and "Totem" because the artists who compose it "are really very thorough rejecters of the world—perhaps they live only in the gesture of rejection and negation—but negatively something, at any rate".[117] But the novel goes on to mark the difference between this milieu—attracted by African art, by a tradition of pure, soulless technique—and Birkin's religious feeling, his quest for the "way of freedom" in a new embodiment of the inexpressible. This moral irresponsibility and exclusive preoccupation with technique is most strongly shown in the Jewish sculptor Loerke, and in Gudrun, the artist who sculpts "tiny things", animals and "odd, small people", never surrendering herself completely, always remaining on the defensive. These two synthesize what was for Lawrence the supreme abomination, art without inspiration other than the intellect, sex without love or religious feeling.[118] Seen from this angle, *Women in Love* is a translation into characters—Halliday, Loerke, Gudrun—of the ideas on modern art expressed by Lawrence in the "Hardy": the blind alley of the abstract, the impossibility of going beyond Debussy, Mallarmé and Turner. To this idea of the modern impasse, of the end of a world, he adds here that of the blind alley of primitive art, perfect technique without the creative spark,[119] "pure culture in sensation, culture in the physical consciousness, really ultimate *physical* consciousness, mindless, utterly sensual". This is the art and form of civilization Birkin rejects in order to seek with Ursula "the way of freedom", thus returning to the central theme of the "Hardy", the quest for an art based on creative reality, "man-knowledge and woman-knowledge".[120] But the way of freedom is no better defined at the end of the novel than it was at the end of the "philosophy"; as usual, what Lawrence rejects is clearer than what he offers.

The denial of altruism: contempt for man

Lawrence's repudiation of society springs from a systematic attitude, already expressed in the "Hardy": a rejection of all forms of altruism on the pretext that they are only concealed forms of egoism. This means, in fact, refusal to collaborate in any common undertaking:

> Can't you see that to help my neighbour to eat is no more than eating myself. "I eat, thou eatest, he eats, we eat, you eat, they eat"—and what then? Why should every man decline the whole verb. First person singular is enough for me.[121]

This theoretical position dictates the whole of Birkin's behaviour, his resignation from his post of schools inspector (rendered easy by the fact that his eating is assured thanks to anonymous neighbours, i.e. his £400 of unearned annual income), his rejection of the past, of all bonds in the form of

> ... houses and furniture and clothes, they are all terms of an old base world, a detestable society of man ... It is all possessions, possessions, bullying you and turning you into a generalization ... You must leave your surroundings sketchy, unfinished, so that you are never contained, never confined, never dominated from the outside.[122]

This totally inconsequent psychological attitude, blending a rejection of collective action with acceptance of its benefits, underlies the whole social criticism of *Women in Love*, an emotional, affective, irrational criticism, always seen from the point of view of Birkin, the *outsider*. Not one of the characters ever tries to defend, explain or justify society; each, without exception, is more or less consciously a party to the process of corruption and destruction which Birkin observes with savage satisfaction rather than denouncing it: a society devoid of hope, goal or future, held up to constant contempt. In the "Breadalby" chapter Birkin proclaims the inequality of men, echoing the author's conversations with Russell and Ottoline, in a pure caricature of the old Garsington weekends.[123] From the yeoman-farmer and middle-class world of *The Rainbow*, Ursula has risen to mingle with the upper classes and the aristocracy, and the downing of class barriers is occasionally evoked. Most conveniently for the author, Birkin himself is totally classless, and is thus exempt from any sense of loyalty or obligation. Socially he is as much adrift as his enemies Halliday and the Bohemians of the Café Pompadour. In the whole of *Women in Love* there is no vestige of that popular culture, the intellectual life of the working Midlands, that served as guide and inspiration for so much of Lawrence's own youth. All that is forgotten and rejected, just as *The Rainbow* repudiated *en bloc* his college education. The author's infernal, negative vision precludes any continuity with his recent past.

The condemnation of mechanization

The life of the mining country itself, powerfully and accurately evoked in a series of rapid sketches, is also seen through a distorting mirror, no longer observed from inside as in *Sons and Lovers*, but through the eyes of Gudrun and of Ursula who no longer belong there. Gudrun is both attracted and repelled by the life of the mining town: "she hated it, she knew how utterly cut off it was, how hideous and how sickeningly mindless".[124] In this work created by a collier's son, not once does any character show a sign of sympathy or understanding of the common people. Birkin, Gudrun and Ursula all suffer from the ugliness of the industrial landscape, and protest against the defilement of the earth by the pitheads and the slag heaps. Not a word to show the true life of human beings in this setting, their pride, their vitality, their sturdy independence. The social relations of the Crich family with the workers are either paternalistic in the case of the father, distant and haughtily patronizing on the part of the mother; or coldly professional, pitilessly efficient as far as Gerald is concerned. All are stereotypes, devoid of human reality, seen from afar by a man incapable of knowing and appreciating the problems and motivations of a leader of industry. Lawrence's closest personal contact with the Barbers of Eastwood, his models for the Crich family, was through a young aunt of Jessie Chambers, once employed as nursery governess to the Barber children.[125] Thomas Crich, inspired by an obsolete Christian charity and by a futile sense of personal responsibility towards "the poor", is a figure closer to Tolstoy than to the British mining industry. It is indeed curious to find Lawrence, the miner's son, apparently considering working-class men and women merely as "the poor", as beggars for charity, a conception mitigated only by a single passing reference to "the majority" who are "too proud to ask for anything", too independent to come knocking at the door of Thomas Crich.[126] The identification of poverty with mendacity and "creeping democracy" is shockingly clear. The social problem of Thomas Crich's generation is reduced to one of charity and poverty, while the industrial efficiency of Gerald's generation apparently raises no social problems at all as far as Lawrence is concerned. On the whole the miners are satisfied with the mechanization introduced into the mines by their young employer. This acceptance, however, does not meet with Lawrence's approval:

> There was a new world, a new order, strict, terrible, inhuman, but satisfying in its very destructiveness. The men were satisfied to belong to the great and wonderful machine even whilst it destroyed them. It was what they wanted ... Their hearts died within them but their souls were satisfied ... It was the first great step in undoing, the first great phase of chaos, the substitution of the

mechanical principle to the organic, the destruction of the organic purposes, the organic unity, and the subordination of every organic unit to the great mechanical purpose. It was pure organic disintegration and pure mechanical organization. This is the first and finest state of chaos.[127]

This incantatory asseveration contains no analytical criticism, but merely gives vent to Lawrence's hatred of industrial civilization. In Thomas Crich and his son he has embodied ideas, already expressed in *Twilight in Italy*, on the old paternalistic bond between master and servant, king and subject, and the absence of any such mystic organic link in modern industrial society. For him, democracy, equality, any form of humanitarianism other than paternalistic charity to the poor, are merely concessions to "the instinct for chaos", and the egalitarian claims of the workers are as abhorrent to him as Gerald's authoritarian mechanization of the mines: "The desire for chaos had risen, and the idea of mechanical equality was the weapon of disruption which should execute the will of man, the will for chaos."[128]

Women in Love is neither a criticism nor an analysis of early twentieth-century English society, but the translation into a number of highly stylized scenes and portraits of an apocalyptic vision denying any value to industrial change and to the men who accept or execute it. The picture of the mining country proceeds not from observation towards conclusion, but from a preconceived general *Weltanschauung*. The social world of *Women in Love* is a distorted world, a hallucinatory vision rather than a picture of reality. In a novel in which Lawrence has brilliantly succeeded in translating his ideas into action and gesture, albeit symbolic, it is significant that his description of Thomas Crich should be written as a commentary rather than as a portrait in action.[129] However great the errors and misdeeds of industrialization, it would be of little avail to look to *Women in Love* for a rational and truthful initiation to the life of the industrial Midlands on the eve of the First World War.

Equality rejected

The world of *Women in Love* is one of despair, of the denial of all things human. Not a single institution, feeling or activity escapes the desolation, the bitterness of Lawrence's portrayal of society. It is the world of the "Hardy" and "The Crown", but shorn of the impetus which a belief in love gave to those earlier works. In *Women in Love*, this belief has been reduced to its simplest expression, a mere mystic affirmation in the mouth of Birkin: and the author's spokesman, perhaps consciously, stresses the subjectivity of that conception of the world, the absence of any link with objective reality, when he states that "the world is only held together by the mystic conjunction, the ultimate unison between people—a bond. And the immediate bond is between man and woman." This "bond" he opposes to "chaos", to the "nihilism" of liberty in love as in all else; for his criticism of society is based on a nostalgia for the old paternalist or monarchic bond, on the concept of divine right, of an authority which is neither philanthropic and humanitarian like that of Thomas Crich, nor intellectual and mechanistic like that of his son Gerald.

Women in Love constantly harks back to the golden age of sovereign and undisputed authority exercised by a mystic leader dominating female and democratic chaos: its mirage is that of the Wagnerian hero beloved of Weininger, the male alone capable of asserting logical, ethical and aesthetic values.[130] The world to which Lawrence aspires is alternatively a universe in which a single human mind enjoys the beauty of nature, or a world peopled by beings united to the hero by mystic commitments, a romantic hierarchy, a world based on inequality:

> Your democracy is an absolute lie—your brotherhood of man is a pure falsity, if you apply it further than the mathematical abstraction. We all drank milk first, we all eat bread and meat, we all want to ride in motor-cars—therein lies the beginning and end of the brotherhood of man. But no equality.
>
> But I myself, who am myself, what have I to do with equality with any other man or woman? In the spirit, I am as separate as one star is from another, as different in quality and quantity. Establish a state on *that* . . . The minute you begin to compare, one man is seen to be much better than another, all the inequality you can imagine is there by nature. I want every man to have his share in the world's goods, so that I am rid of his importunity, so that I can tell him: "Now you've got what you want—you've got your fair share of the world's gear. Now, you one-mouthed fool, mind yourself and don't obstruct me."[131]

This tirade, exposing Birkin's authoritarian political ideas and fully in line with the anti-democratic, anti-humanitarian attitude of Chamberlain, arouses the inevitable reactions from Hermione and from Sir Joshua Matheson, a caricature of Bertrand Russell as a sociologist preaching the social equality of all men. This passage contains the key to the whole of the social criticism of *Women in Love*, inspired neither by love of nor pity for humanity, but by contempt for the ordinary man on the part of one who believes himself to be predestined. In this respect, *Women in Love* already heralds the power-complex, the anti-democracy of *Aaron's Rod*, *Kangaroo* and *The Plumed Serpent*. The social and political ideas of *Women in Love* are those of a disgruntled megalomaniac: "It sounds like megalomania, Rupert," Gerald tells Birkin at the end of this tirade.[132]

Modern art: Loerke and some ideas of Weininger

An equivocal, even retrograde attitude, as compared with 1913, to love between man and woman; political and social ideas in violent reaction against everything implied by equality and fraternity, such is the emotional climate of this essentially destructive novel. Its ideas on art, though more veiled and more completely merged in dialogue and action, are basically those of the "Hardy", but the final vision of a possible "re-sourcing" of art through the collaboration of the two sexes has by now almost disappeared.

Although in the Prologue he is portrayed as a poet, Birkin, the precursor of the new race, is not shown as a creative artist in the novel. Gudrun and Loerke are the only artists, and they occupy the leading roles in the last scenes of the book. Gudrun is presented as a "spectator" of life, not, like her sister, a "participator". Her art is "strange" rather than deep, no more spontaneous than her character: she restricts herself to carving little objects, animals and birds, seen "through the wrong end of the opera glasses".[133] A gifted but shallow artist, she is both passive and calculating, continually preoccupied with herself and lacking any spark of generosity. At no time, even when at their first meeting she feels herself "singled out" for some kind of union with Gerald Crich, does she lose herself in any deep wave of feeling. Cynical and contemptuous of society, of rich or poor alike, irony is her universal weapon.

The sculptor Loerke, whom she meets when she accompanies Gerald to Austria, appears to her as a fascinating gnome, capable of reaching into her secret nature. For him, his work as an artist is all that counts; he has neither illusions nor spiritual needs. This character, as heavily indebted to Gertler as Gudrun is to Katherine Mansfield,[134] represents for Lawrence the ultimate corruption and decay of modern art. He might have been taken directly from this portrait of the Jew, drawn by Weininger after Chamberlain:

> The true conception of the State is foreign to the Jew, because he, like the woman, is wanting in personality; his failure to grasp the idea of true society is due to his lack of a free intelligible ego. Like women, Jews tend to adhere together, but they do not associate as free independent individuals mutually respecting each other's individuality. . . .

> The Jew is not really anti-moral. But, none the less, he does not represent the highest ethical type. He is rather non-moral, neither very good nor very bad, *with nothing in him of either the angel or the devil* . . . Greatness is absent from the nature of the woman and the Jew, the greatness of morality, or the greatness of evil . . . In the Jew and the woman, good and evil are not distinct from one another. . . .

He is at the opposite pole from aristocrats, with whom *the preservation of the limits between individuals is the leading idea*. The Jew is an inborn communist. . . .

The Jew is of all persons the least perturbed by mechanical, materialistic theories of the world; he is readily beguiled by Darwinism and the ridiculous notion that men are derived from monkeys; and now he is disposed to accept the view that the soul of man is an evolution that has taken place within the human race.[135] [*Italics added.*]

These passages coincide at many points with Birkin's idea of Loerke's materialism, of his hatred of idealism. The sculptor has known poverty and suffered hunger; he is "stages further" than Gerald in "social hatred", living "like a rat, in the river of corruption". Here, too, Birkin's political and social mythology explicitly concurs with Chamberlain's, precisely at the point where he tries to define his aesthetic in contradistinction and opposition to that of Loerke. Like Gudrun's, i.e. that of woman doomed to destruction, Loerke's conception of art is "modern". She sculpts people "in everyday dress"; Loerke has made "a great granite frieze" representing a fair, with peasants and artisans "in an orgy of enjoyment, drunk and absurd in their modern dress, whirling ridiculously in roundabouts, firing down shooting galleries . . . a frenzy of chaotic motion".[136] He wants to bring art into the factory, to build beautiful factories, he sees beauty in "machinery and the acts of labour": "Art should interpret industry, as art once interpreted religion."[137] He practises an almost completely abstract form of art: the horse on which he has placed the statuette of a naked girl "is part of a work of art, a piece of form . . . it was no relation to anything outside that work of art . . . you must not confuse the relative world of action with the absolute world of art".[138] The discussions between Gudrun and Loerke on art, with their common predilection for West African wooden carvings, Aztec and Central American art, show their preoccupation with the "mechanical" action of the mind on natural forms rather than with observation of nature: "Art and Life were to them the Reality and the Unreality." " 'Of course,' said Gudrun, 'life doesn't *really* matter—it is one's art which is central. What one does in one's life has *peu de rapport*, it doesn't signify much.' "[139]

The complicity between these two, who for Lawrence are symbols of the process of reduction, of destruction of the soul and of life, of the absorption of the life force by the destructive intellect, leads Gerald, whom Gudrun has decided to leave for Loerke, to attempted murder and to his death in the eternal snows. Out of his hatred of the abstract intellect, of the presumptuous human mind seeking to impose itself on nature, to change the course of events, Lawrence has created a masterly climax of violence and death amid the gleaming snow. This death had been presaged, foreseen ever since Gerald's first appearance. Given his character, no other choice was open to Gerald. He dies because he denies life and desires death, just as, according to

Birkin, he had desired the death of the younger brother he had "accidentally" killed. And yet the end of the novel never achieves true tragedy, despite the conclusion drawn by Birkin to the effect that the mystery of the universe is not a human mystery. "Man is not the criterion," is his reply to the humanist philosophy Ursula had learnt in her adolescence.[140] God can do without men, as he can do without the ichthyosaurus and the mastodon: "The eternal creative mystery could dispose of man, and replace him with a finer created being."[141] Gerald has died without "the faith to yield to the mystery"; he was a "denier" of the mystery which Birkin recognizes and accepts. The note of nostalgia for friendship on which the novel closes suggests that, despite his acceptance of the end of the human race, Birkin has retained some vestige of the tendency Ursula detected in him, to want to save humanity despite itself.[142]

But while *Women in Love* is still messianic, as Lawrence originally intended in 1913, its messianism is that of despair. Lawrence no longer believes he can save England from itself; he wants its own "special brand of Englishness" to "disappear completely".[143] This pessimistic view of his own country will henceforth remain constant—the divorce between Lawrence and England is now complete—and when he shows Birkin and Ursula on the Ostend Channel steamer, the novelist has already morally left his native land for ever.

Weakness and strength of Women in Love

Women in Love is a direct creation of Lawrence's *Weltanschauung*: the action is drawn from autobiographical memories and contemporary incident. The characters are composite, their external circumstances often based on actual models, their behaviour either invented or modelled on that of the author or his familiars, or on local Eastwood gossip gathered largely from the Chambers household. Hermione Roddice has the physical characteristics, dress and posture of Ottoline Morrell, yet she owes much to Jessie Chambers, who without benefit of the highly revealing Prologue had recognized in Hermione Lawrence's idea of herself. The novel has a life of its own, based on the reality of both persons and places: Shortlands, Breadalby, the Café Pompadour, Halliday's bohemian apartment, Birkin's lodgings at Nottingham and at Willey Water, the hotel in the mountains above Innsbruck. As always, Lawrence excels both in describing places, etched in a few rapid, accurate strokes, and in giving intimate physical reality to such characters as Loerke, "an odd creature, like a troll" with his "quick, full eyes, like a mouse's", his thin legs and "fine-quivering" contemptuous nostrils.[144]

Above all, he excels in conveying the isolation, the sheer animal essence of creatures such as Birkin's tom-cat, the wild she-cat, Winifred's pet rabbit and Gerald's Arab mare, terrorized by its master's bullying. His physical descriptions of persons, animals and things are almost always hauntingly precise. Such admirable realism is spoilt only by a tendency to convey too much, to bully the reader into acceptance of an interpretation of the characters, for instance when the "purely unconscious" Hermione, inspired with a "dynamic hatred of Birkin", tries to kill him with her paperweight. The author's straining to reveal unconscious desire leads to repetition, over-insistence, and ultimately to a brand of expressionism perilously close to caricature. Similarly the portrait of Gerald's mother, "the old unbroken wolf" who wanders about the family estate of Shortlands in a "mutually destructive" relationship with her husband, is forced, obscure, often incomprehensible, because it tries to suggest too much. The novel is marked by a total absence of ordinary, normal people, neither condemned for mediocrity, nor foredoomed to hell or to the limbo of the uncreated. The *dramatis personae* boils down to two potential elect, and a long list of the damned.

Despite these reserves, how many vivid scenes, and how much powerful evocation! Beside certain inflated passages, disproportionately swollen by interpretative pretensions, how many pieces of direct, clear and accurate writing in the style of Lawrence's best post-war short stories! Countless scenes spring immediately to life, each detail, each piece of dialogue carrying conviction: Birkin's visit to Will Brangwen to ask his daughter's hand in marriage, with its comic portrayal of the total lack of comprehension between the two men; or the vivid scene when Gerald, leaving his dying father, furtively creeps into the Brangwens' house, finds his way into Gudrun's bedroom, and is stealthily smuggled out by her at dawn. The narrative skill shown in these episodes, the gift for evoking reality by the use of significant detail, are those of Lawrence the born storyteller, incomparable creator of true and striking images.

The world of *Women in Love* is made up of bits and pieces out of which the novelist has tried but partly failed to make a synthesis, his main ideas not fused into a homogeneous whole, many of his contrasts and oppositions obscure and inconclusive. Lawrence knows what he does not want; he has little idea what he wants instead. Birkin, the demon, the superman, the precursor of a new age, is partially opposed to Gerald, a denier, but also a potential friend, the man whom Birkin could have saved had Gerald so willed it. He is also opposed to Loerke, the artist who would impose his theoretical concepts on nature, the gnome, the absolute denier. Gerald is all will, Loerke all destructive analytical intelligence. Birkin seeks a dual liberation: to free man from the traditional servitudes of sex, as expressed in the ideal of courtly love, of man as servant of the woman,[145] and to free humanity from sexual taboos.[146]

But this dual goal is never clearly or simply presented: the development of the story, of the contrast between the two couples, is too slow, too confused, too trammelled by superfluous detail snatched from everyday life.

As a novel *Women in Love* has the defects of its qualities: if the basic idea fails to emerge, it is because the characters are too firmly based on real life, not sufficiently out of the common run to illustrate unequivocally the novelist's ideas. They seem to live on two never completely connected planes, on the one hand that of abstract symbolism, of interpretation of character and action in the light of ideas, of an attempt at systematization, and on the other that of descriptive realism. The weakest, least convincing passages are those in which the author intervenes clumsily and repetitively, over-insisting in an attempt to interpret and comment, exposing the gap between reality and theory, between the world of observation and that of symbolic ideas and inner themes intended to explain and illumine the outward action of his characters.

Most significant, and the highest proof of the author's talent, are those passages describing things, people and animals, as they are observed by the senses, without the intrusion of psychological interpretation. One of the most successful of many such scenes is that where Birkin and Ursula insist on giving away to a young working-class couple a chair they have just bought. The author's general ideas on man and woman are present, but remain discreetly just below the surface, and the couple are described like two young animals, each physical detail giving rise to a barely suggested interpretation, conveyed by verbal description of actual, observed behaviour, of animal activity just bordering on the human. This is the Lawrence of *Birds, Beasts and Flowers* and of the best post-war short stories, the Lawrence prefigured by the aesthetic of "The Crown". Considered as the second volume of "The Sisters", *Women in Love* fails to correspond to the ambition of 1913; but at the same time it ushers in a new style, that of many of the finest of his later stories.

14

ESCAPES AND HOMECOMINGS

During the war Lawrence wrote few short stories in comparison with his immediate pre-war output. The year 1918, however, is clearly marked by a relatively large crop of stories, primarily written to keep the pot boiling. Together with such 1915 stories as "The Thimble" and "England, My England", they were for the most part taken up again and revised in Taormina in 1921 to form the basis of two collections, *England, My England* (1922) and *The Ladybird* (1923). The play *Touch and Go*, a curious sequel to *Women in Love*, was also written at the end of the war, a time during which Lawrence's imagination seems to have been at a low ebb. While it is difficult to ascertain, in the works revised at Taormina, exactly what was written during the war and what in the happier post-war climate, it is easy to discover, particularly among the Midlands stories—mostly written or conceived at Middleton—some effects of a return to his familiar Midland past which, although short-lived, marks a break between the great 1915–16 novels and those of the post-war years. Like *Touch and Go*, several of the stories are contemporary with the first draft of what was to become *Aaron's Rod*, the novel of ultimate escape also starting in the Erewash Valley but migrating, via literary London of 1917–18, to the British colony in Florence.

Stories of the war and its physical and mental consequences, stories of escape and return, Midland scenes and characters—these minor works are for the most part not only interesting in themselves but for their testimony to Lawrence's unerring talent, his perfect mastery of the short story. Their weakness lies in the author's apparent indecision over the major intent of certain incompletely worked-out plots. But they contain some of the very best Lawrence, describing or showing in action and gesture simple Midland folk, revealed in their physical, almost animal essence, palpably present to the reader; and this is true even before the final touching up at Taormina.

After the pessimistic, infernal vision of *Women in Love*, these stories of wartime England reveal a Lawrence capable of compassion, of human sympathy, and go some way to re-establishing, between the writer and society, the balance broken by Birkin's savage maledictions. It is perhaps significant that this softening, this compassion, coincides approximately with Lawrence's stay in Middleton, that is to say with a period of closer contact with his sisters and their children, the Hopkins and other friends of younger days; a period, too, when Frieda's influence was at so low an ebb that Lawrence seriously entertained the thought of leaving her for ever. In some respects this return to his native Midlands, the abandonment of his doctrinaire and violently anti-English attitude, corresponds to a post-1916 evolution on the part of Lawrence already noted and first expressed in a humble letter which he wrote to Cynthia Asquith on 16 November of that year:

> Believe me, I am infinitely hurt by being thus torn off from the body of mankind, but so it is, and it is right . . . And never again will I say, generally, "the war" only "the war to me". For to every man the war is himself, and I cannot dictate what the war is or should be to any other being, than myself. Therefore I am sorry for all my generalities, which must be falsities to another man, and almost insults.[1]

Scenes of the country in wartime:

Mention may be made here of a sketch dating from before the war: "The Mortal Coil", appearing first in *The Seven Arts* in 1917 and reprinted only in *Phoenix II*, in 1968. It tells the simple story of a young German officer, whose mistress is asphyxiated in his room by fumes from an iron stove. Lawrence proposed it to Pinker in 1916 as "one of my purest creations",[2] by which he may merely have meant one of those least likely to offend the reader. It belongs to the German cycle of "The Prussian Officer" and "The Thorn in the Flesh", and is interesting mainly for the portrait of a sub-lieutenant, a sort of first study for Skrebensky and one who, according to Frieda, was modelled on one of her army cousins. There is no internal evidence to confirm Lawrence's statement that he rewrote this sketch in 1916.

The stories of wartime England fall into two groups: those written before the end of 1916, showing the author's more or less open hostility towards the idea of war against Germany or towards any war, and those of 1917–18, in which he confines himself to describing places and people, to noting changes in contemporary life effected by the war. His earlier striving to express his anti-war attitude symbolically gives way to almost total realism, to a mainly descriptive, factual technique. "England, My England" and "The Thimble" belong to the earlier group; "The Blind Man" falls somewhat outside, or perhaps between the two styles; "Wintry Peacock", "Monkey Nuts", "Tickets Please" and in certain respects "The Fox" and "You Touched Me" make up the second group.

"England, My England"

Two highly different stories appeared successively under the title "England, My England": one in *The English Review* for October 1915; the other gave its title to a collection of short stories published in 1922. Both are set at Greatham, home of the Meynell family, and the differences between them clearly reveal a considerable evolution in Lawrence's art and attitudes between 1915 and 1921. Only the 1915 text will be considered here, except when attention must be drawn to changes introduced in 1921 which have a bearing on 1915 attitudes.

The original text is much shorter than the final version "entirely rewritten" at Taormina in December 1921.³ Roughly sketched-in incidents were later developed and amplified, translated into action or dialogue, in the pure, decanted style of the post-war stories, so different from that of 1915. And, remarkably enough, in the final text, Lawrence's attitude towards the war becomes much more definite, far more characteristic of his own image of himself.

Even the method is different. As if Lawrence in 1915 were experimenting with the "stream of consciousness" technique, the early version begins with a "flashback" in the mind of the hero, a soldier wounded by a bursting shell: "the dream was still stronger than the reality. In the dream he was at home on a hot summer afternoon."⁴ After eleven pages of this dream, Evelyn Daughtry (who became "Egbert" in 1921) regains consciousness and realizes that he is at the front, and wounded. Lawrence subsequently abandoned this flashback technique in favour of a straightforward, and incidentally far better, chronological account.

Evelyn Daughtry is married to Winifred, daughter of a businessman of Quaker stock (in 1921 Lawrence made her father, Geoffrey Marshall, a Catholic, one of a number of changes increasing the resemblance between the Marshalls and the Meynells, Crockham and Greatham). A young man of "decent family", with a modest income of £150 a year, he refuses to increase this income by work, and to "come to grips with life", to face up to his responsibilities as the father of three children. So, like Gertrude Morel, Winifred comes to "reject" him because he "stands for nothing". He works in the garden, happy among the "flamy vegetation and the flowers", resisting his wife's efforts to push him out of the nest, satisfied with a purely physical life. Lawrence describes the latent struggle between husband and wife, their conflict and their passion, in terms strongly reminiscent of his own quarrels with Frieda, and of the love-life of Tom and Lydia Brangwen.⁵ Their eldest daughter cuts her knee on "a sharp old iron" lying about in the garden. In 1921 this accident is clearly blamed on Egbert's negligence; the 1915 text, on the contrary, carries no suggestion of his responsibility. The accident, the infected wound, the crippled child, all serve to aggravate the quarrel between the young couple. Winifred devotes herself exclusively to the child, neglecting her husband. (The story was written at the height of "the trouble about the children" in 1915.) Again like Gertrude Morel, she gives herself up "with ethical rigour to look after the children and to discipline her own flesh".[6]

When war breaks out, Evelyn accepts it with indifference: but it "absorbed the tension of his own life"—possibly another autobiographical admission. His consciousness now has "a field of activity" which makes him aware of "the positive activity of destruction, the seethe of friction" in which he lives as a result of his family tragedy and his conflict with his wife.[7] He enlists in the army, encouraged by his wife and her father, since, as Winifred puts it, there is "nothing to keep you at home".

In uniform Daughtry has become "something" in the eyes of his wife. But he "despises" himself and "detests" his wife for loving him now he is a soldier. He refuses to be taken in by war propaganda, by the sentimental talk of those who think their fighting morally justifiable:

> She tried to tell him he was one of the saviours of mankind. He listened to these things; they were very gratifying to his self-esteem. But he knew it was all cant. He was out to kill and destroy; he did not even want to be an angel of salvation. Some chaps might feel that way. He couldn't that was all. All he could feel was that at best it was a case of kill or be killed. As for the saviour of mankind: well, a German was as much mankind as an Englishman. What are the odds? We're all out to kill, so don't let us call it anything else.[8]

The wounded soldier's internal monologue continues with an account of artillery battle, the action of the men handling the guns being somewhat confused owing to the author's evident lack of first-hand knowledge. Then comes the awakening on the field of battle, the realization that he is lying wounded "on the torn and blood-soaked earth", one leg shot away, "a wet, smashed, red mass".

The story ends in a scene of deliberately exaggerated violence; a group of Germans ride up to survey the battlefield; the wounded man kills three of them before a fourth shoots at him from above, comes at him with a knife and, after stabbing him to death, cuts and mutilates his face "as if he must obliterate it". Does this dénouement represent some sort of concession to the demands of war propaganda, or is it rather another manifestation of the fascination violence held for Lawrence, as illustrated in "The Prussian Officer"? Certainly the horror of the closing scene matches the exaggerated assertion in the 1915 letter when Lawrence declared himself ready "to kill a million, two million Germans".

The portrait of the Meynell family circle in this original version of the story is, on the whole, not too objectionable. The deeper selves of the characters owe as much to Lawrence, Frieda and Lawrence's own family as to Madeline Meynell and her husband Percy Lucas, the models for Evelyn and Winifred. Lawrence has been at some pains to disguise his models, indulging in his usual game of borrowing the outward circumstances of real people but attributing to them feelings drawn either directly from himself or derived out of his own immediate experience. The resemblance to the Meynells is far more marked in the Taormina version, with its vivid descriptions of the countryside, its crisp dialogue, the strong evocatory power of the slightest incident. The 1915 version is scarcely more than a sketch, characteristic in style of the Lawrence of *The Rainbow*, for the most part clear and firm in intent, but without the absolute sharpness and purity of outline which distinguishes the final text. It also lacks the distorted but striking picture of the southern English countryside, the allusions to "the spirit of place" and to psychoanalysis, typical of the 1921 Lawrence. The 1915 vision is still that of post-romantic realism; that of 1921 is more expressionistic, places and characters alike suggesting the presence of occult forces with an intensity not found in the 1915 version. In the first paragraph of the original story, the hero is not even described, and the action is set in a quite ordinary English landscape. The 1921 text makes Egbert almost a double of Gerald Crich, with his keen, blue Viking eyes; over the symbolically snake-infested Hampshire countryside, "the spirit of place lingers on primaeval, as when the Saxons came, so long ago".[9] Between one version and the other can be seen a typical Lawrentian progression, from a simply recounted incident to a triumphal effort aiming at endowing scenes and characters with deep hidden meaning. Egbert's moral isolation plunges him into "the savage old spirit of the place, the desire for old gods, and the mystery of blood sacrifices, all that lost, intense, sensation of the primaeval people of the place, whose passions seethed in the air still, from those long days before the Romans came".[10] If the Evelyn of 1915 is indebted to the Lawrence of Greatham and his quarrels with Frieda, the Egbert of Taormina owes even more to the gardener of Zennor, perhaps to the atmosphere of Sicily, and certainly to the author's prolonged flirtation with the occult and reading of Jung over the intervening years.

By 1921, Lawrence's attitude towards the army and the war had also become much more explicit. In 1915, no overall view relates Evelyn's drama to the war: the attack on British policy and on the army is merely suggested, never quite openly formulated. In 1921, on the contrary, the armed conflict is presented as that of German "military aggression" against the "conquests of peace"—meaning industrialism, Egbert's only choice being between "German militarism and British industrialism". The British Army, imbued with the "mob spirit of a democratic army", is made up of "petty *canaille* of non-commissioned officers—and even commissioned officers".[11]

The difference between these two texts, the absolute mastery over style and description and the relative sobriety of language achieved in the final version, show to what extent Lawrence's art had gained assurance even by 1921, in comparison with the early years of the war. The lessons imbibed from Hardy and the Americans, slowly decanted over the years 1917–19, seemed to bear new fruit in a more favourable climate and relative tranquillity. Nor is the difference merely that between a rough sketch and the finished product: the author of the second version is no longer the confused Lawrence of Greatham in 1915, but a novelist with a mythical but clear vision of the world, professing a psychology based on those occult motivations of behaviour destined to mark the work of his maturity.

"The Thimble"

"The Thimble", suggested by a war wound suffered by Herbert Asquith, is a less successful sketch, which was to be thoroughly, indeed entirely rewritten at Taormina in December 1921, under the title of "The Ladybird". Lady Cynthia Asquith served as model for the heroine, an anonymous "Lady" with a castle in Scotland and an apartment in Mayfair. She is described, with evident sympathy, in the aristocratic atmosphere of her home, with her natural self-assurance, her unyielding sense of responsibility; Lawrence insists particularly on her "slow, unswerving eyes, that sometimes looked blue and open with a childish candour, sometimes greenish and intent with thought, sometimes hard, sea-like, cruel, sometimes grey and pathetic". After being ill with pneumonia in Scotland at the moment her husband was wounded in the face by a bursting shell, she is now sitting on a sofa in her London drawing-room, waiting to see him for the first time since their simultaneous convalescence, wondering with nervous calm what kind of "unknown man", physically disfigured, will be returning to her. In her agitation, she presses her hand down behind the arm of the sofa acquired at an auction sale, and finds "a tarnished gold thimble, set around the base with little diamonds or rubies", engraved with a date and the monogram of an earl. (This anecdote is repeated from a much earlier story in the "Miriam" cycle, "The Shades of Spring".[12]) The maid announces her husband, who surprises her with the thimble on her finger. His jaw shattered by his wound, he speaks in a "mumbling, muffled voice" and their conversation awkwardly revolves around this symbolic object; it slowly reaches important issues such as death and resurrection. Suddenly the husband takes the thimble and throws it out into the murky street, where it is lost to view. This thimble, Lawrence told Lady Cynthia, is the Empire, which he was ready to surrender to Germany if that could end the war. "The fact of resurrection, in this life, is all in all to me now . . . What is the whole Empire, and kingdom, save the thimble in my story?"[13] The mutual embarrassment, the nervousness of the characters, he says, was intended to show that as long as the war lasted no love could be freely expressed.

This story appeared in March 1917 in the American review *The Seven Arts*. A mere preliminary sketch, it has none of the boldness of thought and characterization distinguishing "The Ladybird", nor does it contain any trace of the mystic esotericism of that long short-story. It suggests that Lawrence's creative imagination was at a low ebb at the time. Hepburn, the husband, described in the first pages as "a barrister with nothing to do" and without money of his own, is another Evelyn Daughtry minus the love of gardening and of communion with nature. The dialogue is banal and stiff, Lawrence's attitude towards the war clumsily suggested, for example, by attributing Hepburn's face wound to an *English* shell. The symbolism of the thimble does not emerge clearly from the story, which is at best a sketch for a portrait of Lady Cynthia.

"The Blind Man"

"The Blind Man", like "The Thimble", is based on a war wound. Isabel Pervin is a portrait of Catherine Carswell, and the manor farm on which she lives with her husband, blinded and disfigured in the war, is the parsonage at Lydbrook in the Forest of Dean where Lawrence stayed with the Carswells in 1918.[14] Places and things are faithful copies, described with all Lawrence's talent for evoking atmosphere by a striking choice of precise and significant detail.

Maurice, the blind man, helps their manager with the farm work and the animals; doomed by blindness to a heavy, subconscious, physical existence, he moves about house and farm "carried on a flood in a sort of blood-prescience", possessing the unseen objects "in pure contact", not trying to remember, to visualize: "he did not want to. The new way of consciousness substituted itself in him."[15] The "rich suffusion" of this state "reaches its culmination in the consuming passion for his wife". But he has moments of exasperation, anger and insecurity, of "chaos inside himself" during which he "would compel the whole universe to submit to him".

Isabel has a Scottish cousin, Bertie Reid, a barrister and writer "of the intellectual type, quick, ironical, sentimental and on his knees before the women he adored but did not want to marry". In fact, the exact opposite of Maurice, who "returned the Scotch irony with English resentment" sometimes deepening into "stupid hatred". One day in November, after a long break in their relationship, Bertie has invited himself to stay. From his room Maurice hears him discussing with Isabel the consequences of his blindness. He feels childishly helpless and desolate. At supper, the blind man's gestures and their effect on his wife and friend are minutely described. When Bertie hands Maurice a little crystal bowl of violets to smell, his hand closes "over the thin white fingers of the barrister", whereupon Bertie carefully extricates himself,[16] just as, in *Women in Love*, Gerald Crich breaks away from Birkin's accidental handclasp. The portrait of Bertie is then expanded: he has no mistress, he is "unable ever to enter into close contact of any sort", he cannot "approach women physically". At the core of his being he is "afraid, help-lessly and even brutally afraid".[17]

Later in the evening Maurice goes out on the pretext of having to speak to the farm manager. As he is away some time, Bertie goes out to look for him. He finds him pulping turnips in a dark barn. In the course of a brief conversation about his wounds, Maurice inquires whether he is much disfigured. Suddenly he asks Bertie for permission to touch him, as he "doesn't really know" him. In the darkness, the barrister, who "out of very philanthropy" dare not refuse, allows the blind man to grasp and explore his face, shoulders, arm and hand, later reluctantly agreeing to feel the blind man's eyes and scar in turn. All at once Maurice takes the other man's hand:

> "Oh, my God," he said, "we shall know each other now, shan't we? We shall know each other now."
>
> Bertie could not answer. He gazed mute and terror-struck, overcome by his own weakness. He knew he could not answer. He had an unreasonable fear, lest the other man should suddenly destroy him. Whereas Maurice was actually filled with hot, poignant love, the passion of friendship. Perhaps it was this very passion of friendship which Bertie shrank from most.
>
> "We're alright together now, aren't we?" said Maurice. "It's alright now, as long as we live, so far as we're concerned." "Yes," said Bertie, trying by any means to escape.

Maurice goes in and tells Isabel the news: "We've become friends." "You'll be happier now, dear," she replies, much as Ursula might have replied to Birkin.[18] But Bertie, "like a mollusc whose shell is broken", has only one thought, to flee, to escape the sudden intimacy intruding on his "insane reserve".

Several themes emerge: war wounds and their effects on the marriage relationship and on the self-consciousness of the disfigured man; friendship expressed in physical gesture as offered by Birkin to Gerald, by Lawrence to Murry; the lack of contact of the frigid, isolated lawyer, terrified by the warmth of human touch, to whom Lawrence has seen fit to give the name of Bertie, possibly after Bertrand Russell, and who also brings to mind his 1915 judgments on E. M. Forster;[19] finally, the theme of "blood-prescience", of an immediate "substantial" contact with objects, deeper and more intimate than abstract, visual contact. All the great Lawrentian themes since *The White Peacock* are synthesized in this short story. No clear and self-obvious meaning emerges, but the reader is plunged into a powerful evocation of the author's own emotional universe, the ever-present contrast between life lived in tune with nature and life reduced to a mere mental, abstract, non-physical process. The dialogue and description are welded into a homogeneous whole, and the constant use of detail, never wearying or superfluous, successfully creates a sense of a deeper layer of life beneath the surface. In the more relaxed atmosphere of 1918, Lawrence was already able to speak of the war in the past tense; having abandoned propaganda, he could bring out individual, human tragedy caused by war, without intruding political opinions or polemics. Nor is there any too evident allusion to esoteric doctrine, any attempt at theoretical generalization to confuse the reader or to lead him on false trails. Narrative and dialogue serve exclusively to portray things and people as the artist sees them; the writer's ideas, so often difficult to communicate, remain, in this story, implicit, unobtrusive.

"Wintry Peacock", "Monkey Nuts", are further naturalistic sketches, one of life in the Midlands, the other set in wartime Berkshire. Neither makes any pretension to philosophy or to anything other than painting an exact picture of people and of things: the Derbyshire countryside, the farming talk, the contrast between the standard English of the daughter-in-law and the local dialect of her husband's parents in "Wintry Peacock", and in "Monkey Nuts" the thwarted courting of the recalcitrant soldier by the land-girl, set against the busy loading of hay wagons for the Army. These unambitious slices of contemporary life show Lawrence at his best; even his insinuations concerning the inadequacies of the love-life of the English are conveyed purely by observation, without the slightest hint of preaching, generalization or inordinate effort at interpretation.

"Tickets Please" evokes the war only by its picture of the social atmosphere of the Midlands, at a time when the Bestwood tram drivers were either army rejects or shy and puny youngsters, whereas the conductresses were "fearless hussies" "with a sailor's dash and recklessness", ready to defend themselves against all-comers, but none the less susceptible to masculine charm. Tram-inspector John Thomas Raynor who, no doubt in deference to the public, appeared as John *Joseph* when this story was first published in the *Strand Magazine*,[20] flirts with each in turn until the day when Annie, who has finally succumbed after keeping him at arm's length for many months, engineers a confrontation at the depot between John Thomas (Coddy) and her assembled colleagues. His victims turn on him like harpies, beating and tearing at him until he consents to choose which of them he will marry. He chooses Annie, who turns him down. In the original version, this refusal is final, whereas in the *England, My England* version Lawrence throws a doubt on its genuineness, as though the violence unleashed by Annie had created some sort of link between her and the man she had humiliated. Once again Lawrence has set aside his preconceived ideas, his book-learning and philosophy, even most of his personal problems, to paint the wartime Midlands scene with a realistic humour not far removed from that of Arnold Bennett. The reckless swooping of the trams packed with colliers roaring "hymns downstairs and a sort of antiphony of obscenities upstairs"; John Thomas squiring Annie on the whirling dragons and horses at the Bestwood Statutes Fair; the late halts in the "howling, cold, black, windswept nights", when the tram becomes a haven of refuge: the whole Midlands scene springs to life before our eyes. The raging Bacchantes may be only Nottinghamshire working girls, but the operation of grafting on to the vigorous stem of the mining country a classical theme entirely in line with the writer's 1918 preoccupations is executed with such masterly ease and assurance that the reader, captivated by the narrative, scarcely stops to consider what a strange graft it really is.

These scenes of wartime England thus fall into two groups: the 1915 stories, with their open hostility towards the war; and those in which, the war accepted as fact, Lawrence sets out to observe and describe with sympathy and humour the daily life or feelings of his compatriots. The latter are mainly written in 1918, when Lawrence the artist was beginning once more to prevail over the reformer, preacher and philosopher.

Themes of escape and return:
the assertion of virility

A similar tendency towards realistic objective observation, tinged with a humour not unlike Barrie's, is to be found in several stories centring on a theme long latent in Lawrence's mind which became increasingly predominant after 1917: that of escape in general, and escape to the New World in particular.

His work on American literature probably focused his attention on the question of the psychology of emigration, although to some extent this seems always to have interested Lawrence: the theme of the young misfit leaving hearth and home to join Army or Navy first appears with Arthur Morel in *Sons and Lovers*, and is taken up by Alfred Durant, an early prefiguration of the young Tom Brangwen, in the original version of "Daughters of the Vicar". While Tom Brangwen "escapes" by marrying a Polish woman, Geoffrey, in "Love Among the Haystacks", emigrates to Canada with the woman he cannot marry legally. Running away is recurrent, though not obsessive, in Lawrence's work between 1912 and 1915. In 1917, in the opening chapters of *Aaron's Rod*, we find it amplified in the hero's abandonment of wife and children to pursue his wandering fate and the call of Lilly's friendship.

Three wartime stories show the persistence of the theme. One is "Samson and Delilah", set in a Cornish pub, the Tinner's Rest, in which a mysterious stranger from America visits the landlady, Mrs Nankervis. When this ex-miner returned home to his native Cornwall tries to assert his rights, he is bound hand and foot and thrown out of the pub by its soldier clients with the help of the landlady and her daughter, only to re-enter calmly by the back door and make it up at once with the wife he admires all the more for the

way she has thrown him out. The country pub talk, the fight and reconciliation, each scene is drawn with great simplicity direct from daily life.

But the main theme, expressed entirely in action, without a word of
commentary, is that of the flight of Nankervis, who left his wife and baby
to go to America, and that of his return and reconciliation. This gives
Lawrence occasion to assert masculine authority and the natural right of the
male to dominate the woman he has left to her own devices for so long. The
scene is reminiscent of his own effusions after quarrels between himself and
Frieda, especially this short passage suppressed in the final version:

> He went behind her chair and put his hands over her shoulders on to her full
> soft breasts. She shrank as if struck.
>
> "But I don't think no harm of you for it," came his balanced, soft absent
> voice, as his strong fingers seemed to move her very heart. "You're a darn sight
> too fine a woman for me to bear you any grudge, you are that!"
>
> He put his hand under her soft, full chin and lifted her face. Almost a groan
> of helpless, desirous resentment came from her lips as he kissed her.[21]

Fragments of Lawrence's own life in Cornwall are here merged into a
favourite theme, Nankervis embodying the independent, silent man, the
authoritarian male Lawrence would have liked to be.

The first version of "The Fox", only half as long as the final text rewritten
between 1919 and November 1921, contains a brief portrait of a young
Englishman who, having emigrated to Canada, returns in the autumn of
1918 as a Canadian soldier on leave to find his father's former farm inexpertly
run by two city women, March and Banford. March immediately identifies
Henry with the hen-stealing fox she has lacked the presence of mind to shoot
when, gun in hand, she came face-to-face with it near the farm. The first
twenty-one pages of the final text are almost identical with the earlier version.
Henry asks March to marry him, and she accepts almost at once. But whereas
in the original the marriage takes place without delay, in the final text this
rather flat ending is replaced by a whole new series of incidents. Lawrence
reveals and analyses Banford's jealousy on learning that March has agreed to
marry Henry. March retracts her promise and the story ends with a typical
Lawrentian dénouement: the death of Banford, killed by a tree which Henry
fells after subtly luring his victim to insist on standing exactly where he knew
that it would fall. The equivocal emotional relationship between the women,
the young soldier's will to triumph and its violent climax, Henry's veritable
bewitching of March, fascinated by his resemblance to the fox—these become
the highlights of the final version. The earlier, shorter text is more commonplace, less suggestive of magic or of witchery. The characters of the two
women are not so firmly drawn, the suggestion of Lesbianism less direct.
The character of the young man is also less worked out, and he is not so
vividly depicted as the hunter come from the wide open spaces of the New

World. Reminiscences of the author's reading of Fenimore Cooper, which one would think might have been fresher in his mind when writing the first text, nevertheless find freer expression in the Taormina version, written in 1921, when Lawrence was revising his *Studies in Classic American Literature*.

In this final text, Henry marries March partly out of self-interest, to regain possession of his father's farm, partly actuated by the secret but powerful attraction exercised on a shy young man by a woman eleven years his senior. Out of what was still in the 1918 manuscript a brief, if strongly delineated, sketch, Lawrence later made an admirable short novel not by his usual process of complete rewriting, but by what he himself describes as putting "a long tail to *The Fox*".[22]

In 1918, he was interested not so much in the relationship between the women as in the character and motivations of the man: his timidity with women, his almost unconscious assertion of masculinity, the combination of sordid self-interest and virility. These are also the main characteristics of the hero of another short story written that same year: Hadrian, in "You Touched Me".

The Misses Matilda and Emmie Rockley are turning into old maids as they live with their father by the disused pottery of which he is the owner. After the Armistice, just as their father is dying, their adopted brother Hadrian returns home on long leave. Tired of finding himself "always in a household of women", Rockley had adopted him out of a "Charity Institution" when only six years old. At fifteen Hadrian had set off to lead his own life in Canada, then, like Henry in "The Fox", had enlisted and returned to Europe as a soldier. Just as Henry plots to marry March, Hadrian, with the connivance of their father, decides to marry Matilda, the elder of the two sisters, partly to get a portion of the Rockley heritage, but also on account of a fortuitous incident which has a sudden and decisive effect on his feelings. Thinking her father asleep in his room, whereas in fact the sick man had been moved downstairs and Hadrian installed in his bed, Matilda has caressed Hadrian's face in the darkness:

> The soft, straying tenderness of her hand on his face startled something out of his soul. He was a charity boy, aloof and more or less at bay. The fragile exquisiteness of her caress startled him most, revealed unknown things to him.[23]

All he can say in explanation, in justification of his proposal is: "You touched me." He no doubt has designs on the family fortune, but he knows too that he wants Matilda for herself, not for her money. Subjugated, as March was by Henry, Matilda accepts despite herself.

These short stories of return from exile, of the man who suddenly exerts his virility, are all conceived in the spirit of the relationship of Birkin to Ursula, of the assertion of male superiority. As studies in sex relations they also foreshadow themes in *Aaron's Rod* and *The Plumed Serpent*. Significantly enough, the awakening of these timid males, stirred into self-assertion by a sudden spurt of masculinity, always takes place on their return from an interval of escape into the New World. Similarly all are simple, loutish creatures, devoid of any cultural or intellectual pretensions. Did Lawrence perhaps cherish the secret hope of finding in America that unity of being, that spurt of vitality, perpetual mirage of his "philosophy"? His young men, Hadrian and Henry, are also new embodiments of Annable the gamekeeper; they reveal more clearly than the vacillating Birkin that secret dream of male authority over the female which haunted woman-dominated Lawrence. Significantly again, the first words of the woman over whom these heroes exercise their male superiority are invariably "I could be your mother".

Return to the Midlands

This obsession with escape and return, which also recalls the author's Croydon years and the short stories in which the fledgling Londoner returns to the scenes of his early loves,[24] corresponds exactly to his stay at Middleton and to the use of Midland scenes and events. It also coincides with the deterioration of his relations with Frieda, with his severe late-1918 illness, his reaction against the all-invading *Magna Mater*, the welcome contrast of the careful nursing of his sister Ada. Gone is the literary, apocalyptic vision of the mining country characterizing *Women in Love*, where, as in the "Hardy", men are seen from the outside with the eyes of the anti-democratic, anti-mechanistic, anti-trade-union Lawrence. The prophet of the extinction of man has become once more the native son. The workers and farmers of the Midlands are no longer seen through the tinted glasses of Ursula or Gudrun, carried away in the mystic flood of corruption as in Birkin's dire forebodings.

In "Adolf", a story of the wild baby rabbit reared by the Lawrence children, and in "Rex", that of the fox-terrier puppy entrusted to the keeping of his parents by a pub-keeping uncle, the author is reliving his own childhood. And in a somewhat arid period of literary production these two brief sketches, in which realism replaces the eternal quest for symbolism, rank with the greatest pages of his *Sons and Lovers*.[25] The same gift of evoking local scenes, of conveying the pains and pleasures of simple people, is visible in the brief farm scenes of "Wintry Peacock", in Annie's night at the fair with the tram-inspector in "Tickets Please", and above all in the provincial atmosphere of the nonconformist Midlands evoked in "Fanny and Annie". A story almost devoid of plot, its whole interest lies in the lively character sketches and the vivid scenes of working life in the North Midlands. Fanny returns to her native village to marry Harry Goodall, the full irony of whose name emerges later. For many years she had been a lady's maid in Gloucester. He had waited at home for her to consent to marry him, whereas she had been in love with a "brilliant and ambitious cousin", who had jilted her, and who had died.[26] This theme, reminiscent of "Shadow in the Rose Garden", may indicate that Lawrence was working over an old pre-war sketch.

Fanny arrives home in the lurid light of the blast furnaces: a red glow which, so Lawrence told Katherine Mansfield, prompted the opening scene for this story. She is plunged straight back into the atmosphere of an uncultured industrial working-class neighbourhood, re-establishing contact with her aunt and future mother-in-law. Social differences are marked by the contrast between their local dialect and Fanny's ladylike English, though Fanny's shame at her fiancé's misplaced aitches in an earlier version is later replaced by a passage stressing his physical attraction and Fanny's rebellion against her own desire, which seems to her to drag her down.[27]

Harry is tenor soloist in the choir of the local congregational chapel, and on Sunday afternoon all go to hear him sing the anthem for the Harvest Festival. While he is singing, "a shouting woman's voice" interrupts, accusing him publicly of abandoning her pregnant daughter Annie. The Goodall family gathers to discuss the scandal: Harry admits to having been one of Annie's many lovers; Fanny coolly marks her solidarity with her mother-in-law, thereby confirming her intention to marry Harry, though refusing to return to chapel with him for the evening service.

The whole story hinges on the delicate portrayal of contrasting characters, of Fanny's hesitation between her contempt for the uncouth, uncultured Harry, and her subjugation by his natural charm and sensitivity, "his way of making a woman feel that she was a higher being". The rapid character sketches, the revealing scraps of everyday dialogue in this "slice of life", are nearer to the pre-war disciple of Wells and Bennett than to the Lawrence of 1918. But if, as seems probable, this story was written in 1918, it shows him not only refreshed by contact with his home country but still able to see individuals with objectivity, humour and sympathy, instead of blackening the picture as so often in *Women in Love* and even in *The Rainbow*. A spirit of observation, an appreciation of people, a certain compassion for the narrow limits encompassing their lives, temper his deep pessimism and provide a glimpse of a Lawrence partly reconciled to the burden of humanity.

"The Horse Dealer's Daughter", first written in 1916 as "The Miracle",[28] is another picture of a narrow human milieu illumined by a sense of the miraculous and a compassion rarely found in the author's wartime works. The text may have been revised in 1921, when the original was sent to be typed; there are no clues as to which passages may go back to 1916 and which were rewritten after the war. But this detail may be relevant: when putting the finishing touches to *Women in Love*, Lawrence swore that in future he would "*only* write short stories *to sell*".[29] [*Italics added.*] The gentler, more human tone of certain stories of this period may therefore bear some relation to an effort to come nearer to his public in order to win its sympathy.

Mabel Pervin, the horse dealer's daughter, whose brothers are obliged to sell up and leave the family home, does not know what will become of her. After tending her mother's grave, she deliberately walks into a pond. Fergusson, a young doctor, rescues her, brings her home unconscious, undresses her and warms her before the fire. Coming to, she finds herself naked under a blanket and, when he explains what has happened, springs to the conclusion that he loves her. Quite against his conscious intentions, having accidentally touched her bare shoulder, his heart "yields towards her". The details of awakening and sudden revelation recall both the wrestling scene between Birkin and Gerald (the accidental hand-clasp which makes Birkin aware of his feelings for Gerald) and the transfiguration of Lydia Brangwen as she kneels in front of Tom and puts her arms round his knees and thighs.[30] A brutal disruption of everyday routine, in this case the sudden rescue from death, seems to be required to bring Lawrentian characters face-to-face with one another and their deeper selves, to make them acknowledge hidden feelings at which a meeting of eyes of the doctor and Matilda had hinted in an earlier scene. Lawrence's "physical consciousness", expressed by touch, can only assert itself when "mental consciousness" is momentarily eclipsed.

Here the psychology of "The Horse Dealer's Daughter" continues in the line of The Rainbow and Women in Love. But, as in some of his other contemporary Midland stories, we find a tenderness, a human quality of compassion, which in Women in Love is masked by the bitterness of satire.

Most of these wartime stories bear the mark of revision after 1919. In some of them, notably in England, My England, the interpretation of characters, sometimes amounting to expressionist and symbolist distortion, was added at Taormina in the perspective of self-exile. What remains of the 1918 spirit of partial reconciliation with the Midlands and common humanity is none the worse for not being written in his more consciously typical post-war manner, for remaining, very often, quite close to the springs of his original humanity.

Touch and Go

The play Touch and Go, apart from having a superficial link with Women in Love, also belongs to the "return to the Midlands" cycle, but does not rise to the same level of quality. These three acts were written in 1918 for Douglas Goldring, who was about to found a People's Theatre, revolutionary, pacifist and international in intention.[31] In 1919, Lawrence wrote a preface he intended for the whole series of "Plays for a People's Theatre". He was offended when, instead of Touch and Go, the first play published in the series was Goldring's own revolutionary drama Fight for Freedom.[32] There had been, in fact, total misunderstanding, and Goldring was to discover later that Lawrence detested all that he himself admired, notably "pacifists and idealists".

Read today, the Preface of *Touch and Go* leaves little room for misconception and reveals all the symptoms of a vague political ideology bordering on what became fascism. Written at Hermitage in June 1919, it testifies to the persistence of the mystic anti-democratic racialism which tainted Lawrence's social ideology at its worst moments. Seeking a definition of *people* to whom to present a People's Theatre, he comes out with a statement typical of the dispossessed middle class in a world of economic change: "The proletariat isn't poor. Everybody is poor except Capital and Labour",[33] thus unconsciously defining the predestined followers of fascist movements, jealous both of the rich and of a newly prosperous working class. This, however, was not what he had in mind: what he was after, was "men", heroes according to his conception of "Being and Not-Being": "men who are somebody, not men who are something";[34] by "something" he means employers or miners, capital or labour. Industrial disputes and strikes would result only in "the pulling asunder of the fabric of civilization, and even of life, without any creative issue". And the images he uses to define the strike situation which more or less forms the subject of his play clearly reveal his inmost thought. The British capitalist is an "old bull-dog", holding a bone between his teeth. "That unsatisfied mongrel, Plebs, the proletariat, shivers with rage not so much at sight of the bone, as at the sight of the great wrinkled jowl that holds it." The masses are an "insatiable mongrel", "the shambling servile body in a rage of insurrection against the head"; "the old Shylock of the proletariat" which insists on having its pound of flesh. This self-styled "revolutionary" author of 1919 offers the people the following original solution to social strife:

> If we really could know what we were fighting for, if we could deeply believe in what we were fighting for, then the struggle might have dignity, beauty, satisfaction for us. If it were a profound struggle for *something that was coming to life in us*, a struggle that we were convinced would bring us to a new freedom, a new life, then it would be a creative activity, a creative activity *in which death is a climax in the progression towards new being*. And this is a tragedy.[35] [*Italics added.*]

He would like to make "the great Labour struggle" into an "intrinsic tragedy", offering the masses the "happiness of creative suffering".[36] To workers seeking to improve their condition he proposes the mystic suffering and consolation of "having to pass through death to birth".

The play itself is in the same vein, though the ideas are less clearly, less overtly presented. Gerald Crich is there, renamed Gerald Barlow, whose friend Oliver Turton is a somewhat washed-out Birkin. Gudrun has become

Anabel Wrath. The play is set on the market-place of a Midland mining village, and at the home of the mine-owning Barlows.

Two themes are loosely and dimly intermingled: the return of Gudrun-Anabel and her reconciliation and marriage with Gerald, and the miners' strike. This turns out to be a strike "for nothing", because the pit-workers come out in support of a wage claim of the clerks, which would have been spontaneously granted by the Barlows were it not for the threat of strike. Anabel has left Gerald, with whom she was living in Paris, to share the life of a Norwegian artist, subsequently "killed on the ice". The cause of her separation from Gerald was his friendship for Oliver, with whom he "shared the deepest things"[37]—another, if not quite relevant, instance of Lawrence's preoccupation with the compatibility or incompatibility of friendship and love. Anabel has returned home unknown to Gerald, and is employed as teacher to his sister Winifred. She ultimately marries him, without any explanation either of her return home or of her marriage, as if the play were echoing certain of the author's fantasies or ideas on which he leaves the audience in the dark.

As for the strike and social strife theme, the key role is that of Job Arthur Freer, a modern "Judas", who also makes a brief appearance as a trade-union delegate in the opening pages of *Aaron's Rod*. Obsequious, corrupt, venomous and aggressive by turns, he serves as intermediary between employers and miners, while fanning the flames of discontent. Beaten up by Gerald at the beginning of Act III, he later hands him over to the violence of the miners assembled on the market-place. Gerald is saved from the angry mob by Anabel and Oliver, and the play ends with a series of such platitudes as "We're all human beings, after all" and "Why can't we try really to leave off struggling against one another, and set up a new state of things?" Gerald feebly announces that "the whole system can be altered", provided it is not by "bullying". Some of the talk on social and industrial problems re-echoes, even more vaguely, passages of *Women in Love*, notably on the altruistic and Christian paternalism of Gerald's father, and on the modernization of the mines by the young employer. In so far as Lawrence seems to rally to a social doctrine, it is of the old-fashioned paternalist type rather than socialist or syndicalist. Oliver-Birkin accuses the people of being only "anxious to be rich" and therefore wanting to preserve "the system" much more than do the rich themselves.[38] Gerald thinks the miners are "too stupid" to take control of the industry he runs:

They just simply couldn't control modern industry—they haven't the intelligence. They've no *life* intelligence. The owners may have little enough, but Labour has none. They're just mechanical little things that can make one or two motions, and they're done. They've no more idea of life than a lawn-mower has.[39]

Touch and Go is a play of little if any dramatic or artistic value. But, roughly put together as it seems, it does show Lawrence faced with a real, contemporary social problem—that of strikes for higher wages—completely incapable of sympathizing with, or even presenting objectively, the workers' point of view, and ready to commit himself only to the vaguest of generalities. Viewed as a commentary on *Women in Love*, the play is a monument to the author's intellectual, moral and political confusion, to his social alienation. It differs profoundly from stories such as "Fanny and Annie" or "Tickets Please", which express Lawrence's capacity for sympathetic and humorous portrayal of simple Midland folk. This contrast is typical of the whole of this period and, up to a certain point, of the author's later years. When the artist is left to speak alone, all is humour, compassion, restrained irony: but immediately doctrine or philosophy breaks in, people of flesh and blood give way to puppets, and the "solutions" offered are no more than vague promises of transmuted values. Lawrence's gift is essentially for the observation of people as they are; whenever he takes as his starting-point an idea and not a living model, he is liable to fail piteously, as is shown by *Touch and Go*. Much of his later work confirms this basic incompatibility between a natural, descriptive art and one proceeding from abstraction: an incompatibility which may throw some light on his often-proclaimed hatred of all abstract art.

Aaron's Rod

The first 136 pages of *Aaron's Rod* date from the same period as the last works considered here: the novel was begun in February 1918 during a stay at Hermitage,[40] and Lawrence was probably working on it intermittently during the months spent at Middleton in the neighbourhood of Aaron's native mining country. Certain superficial resemblances with *Touch and Go*, including the person of Job Arthur Freer, suggest some initial hesitation on Lawrence's part as to the exact subject of his new novel.

The opening picture of life in the mining country soon becomes a story of escape, of a flight from invasive love, from social and family responsibilities, into bourgeois and artistic circles such as those in which Lawrence himself moved in 1918. Aaron Sysson, checkweighman in a mine, leaves his wife and children on Christmas night and goes to earn his living as a flautist at Covent Garden Opera House, after making the acquaintance of a group of upper-middle-class guests spending Christmas with the local mineowners, the Bricknells—like the Criches and the Barlows more or less modelled on the Barbers of Lamb's Close. At the opera he meets again Jim Bricknell and his friends, thus gaining entrance into London literary and artistic circles of the late war period. This escape from the mine into London society, through his art, is followed by a series of adventures in Italy, based on Lawrence's 1919 impressions of that country and its English residents, while Aaron's friendship with Lilly (a portrait of Lawrence in his Birkin-like aspects) brings Aaron face-to-face with the problem of male comradeship, above and beyond marriage, or completing it: marriage being an institution which both Lilly and Aaron find in need of "readjustment".

Apart from the theme of escape, the whole of this early section of the novel is an absolutely true and often singularly indiscreet picture of Lawrence's immediate circle in the autumn of 1917, and is particularly enlightening as to Lawrence's use of his sources.

One of these was certainly Cynthia Asquith's *Diaries 1915–18*. That Lawrence had opportunities to read them appears not only from the use he makes in *Aaron's Rod* and "The Ladybird" of certain details, some fairly intimate, but from a note in the diary for 14 June 1915, when Lady Cynthia wrote: "I shan't write anything about my feelings about having him [i.e. her husband] back because the Hun [her name for Frieda] will read my diary."[41]

In the summer of 1917, Lady Cynthia was a guest at a musical house-party at Glynde given by Lady Margot Howard de Walden. Among the guests was the young English composer Cyril Scott, who "at luncheon ... discoursed upon the seven types of humanity—Venusians, Jupitarians, Mercurians, Lunarians, Martians, etc." and "gave us some of his strange creed of yoga, astral planes, and so on".[42] By a strange lapse, Lawrence drew in *Aaron's Rod* a recognizable portrait of Cecil Gray as a young musician, but gave that character the name of Cyril Scott, possibly forgetting that there was an authentic musician of that name!

But even more striking is the adaptation in the chapter "The Lighted Tree" of a real incident occupying much of the time and gossip at this house-party, at which the aristocracy and the rich—Lord Ivor Churchill, Lady Cunard, Lady Diana Manners, foreign diplomats—mingled with "commoners"—musicians, opera singers, painters, stage designers, and literary critics. While some of the party were sleeping out-of-doors, the country sky was lit up by "rocket after rocket", frightening certain of the guests and causing great excitement all round. This entertainment, provided by some army officers in a near-by camp, had been planned as "a most successful and excellent joke" by the hostess and the officers; when this was revealed some of the guests, who had thought a Zeppelin attack was in progress, became very angry. The incident was certainly discussed when the Lawrences accompanied Lady Cynthia and other guests to Covent Garden a few weeks later.

Lawrence's fiction is less daring than reality: the fir tree in the Bricknells' garden is lit up not by army rockets, but by candles and lanterns when one of the guests wants "to make a great illumination" on the estate and the gay party proceeds to "illuminate one of the fir trees by the lawn". At that moment Aaron, who happens to be passing by the estate, looks on and is asked in for a drink, so making the acquaintance of London literary society.[43]

Lawrence thus makes skilful use of the incident at Glynde, not photographically, but to create the atmosphere of life in late 1917. His characters meet at the opera, like Lady Cynthia's friends, and the literary world he conjures up is a mixture of his own circle and that of Lady Cynthia's aristocratic friends. Some of the characters are but thinly disguised: Cecil Gray becomes Cyril Scott; Hilda Doolittle appears as Julia Cunningham; Richard Aldington is portrayed as the mobilized sculptor Robert Cunningham, and Dorothy Yorke as Josephine Ford. Lady Diana Manners, the famous beauty of the day, who in 1919 married Duff Cooper, is barely disguised as Lady Artemis Hooper, and Lawrence and Frieda disport themselves in this exalted company as Lilly and Tanny respectively.[44]

Aaron is not only the native son fleeing the industrial Midlands first for London, then for Italy, but also represents the writer's effort to escape from the yoke and leash of love, to assert his male supremacy:

> The illusion of love was gone for ever. Love was a battle in which each party strove for the mastery of the other's soul. So far, man had yielded the mastery to woman. Now he was fighting for it back again. And too late, for the woman would never yield.
>
> But whether woman yielded or not, he would keep the mastery of his own soul and conscience and actions. He would never yield himself up to her judgment again. He would hold himself for ever beyond her jurisdiction.[45]

And Aaron, like Birkin, wants "life single, not life double", seeking first "clean and pure division", "perfected singleness", which is the only way to "final, living unison".

Thus in treatment and content this novel, quite as journalistic as any of the later or middle periods of H. G. Wells, with its echoes of Lawrence's own conversations, esoteric reading, and other 1918 preoccupations, serves as a bridge between the end of the wartime period and his post-war ideas and themes. Aaron's last quarrel with his wife Lottie is surely an echo of the clash of wills between Lawrence and Frieda, separating—he to Italy, she to Germany—in 1919.

The early pages of this novel are pervaded by the heavy atmosphere of Eastwood and by Lawrence's evident feeling that he has no more to do with it. They mark the end of the cycle of escape and return; and the passage in which Aaron relives his love for Lottie puts paid to Lawrence's ambition to become the priest of love.

In Aaron's subsequent adventure in Italy, as in the London scenes with Lilly, the novel again explores, this time in a 1920 Italian perspective, the themes of common action and male comradeship. These, however, already half-belong to a new period, foreshadowed in the theoretical works of 1918–1919. Once more it is difficult to determine whether the novel, and the experience it translates, proceed from, or follow, this theoretical expression.

While both are inspired by the same preoccupations, the slow gestation of the theoretical ideas suggests that Lawrence sought rather to concretize them *a posteriori* in the novel, when he rewrote it from beginning to end in Italy.

15

THE PITFALLS OF OCCULTISM

Bread and butter, and esoteric philosophy

Between 1916 and 1919 Lawrence as a writer felt the strain of conflicting tendencies. The old messianic spirit was still alive, he still wished to save mankind; yet man had ceased to interest him. The desire to write novels and short stories had died down: "philosophy" alone attracted him.[1] As appears both from the letters and essays of the period, "philosophy" had come to mean to him increasingly the esoteric tradition discussed in letters to Waldo Frank; a secret knowledge he would keep from the "impure herd", and "preserve inviolate" for a future humanity which might deserve access to it. As he himself said later in the Foreword to *Fantasia of the Unconscious*, his art was for "the limited few", for a new race alone worthy of divine secrets:

> I disbelieve *utterly* in the public, in humanity, in the mass. There should be again a body of esoteric doctrines, defended from the herd. The herd will destroy everything. Pure thought, pure understanding, this alone matters— the impure herd is a herd of Gadarene swine, rushing possessed to extinction. But oh, the sheer essence of man, the sheer supreme understanding, cannot we save this to mankind? We must. And it needs a detachment from the masses, it needs a body of pure thought, kept sacred and clean from the herd. It needs *this*, before ever there can be any new earth and new heaven. It needs the sanctity of a mystery, the mystery of the initiation into pure being. And this must needs be purely private, preserved inviolate.[2]

Man must therefore be led to mystic happiness unknowingly and, indeed, despite himself. And in addition to this basic contradiction, Lawrence was also beset by a practical consideration: he must market his writings in order to earn his living. This led him to revive his old idea of limited sale by private subscription. To this end he suggested to Waldo Frank a system of "private publication and private circulation", for initiates only, at a time (July 1917) when America was, in fact, his sole hope of earning money. In the absence of an American Maecenas, he had to fall back on Pinker, and on Harrison's

The English Review which, though paying little, published his essays and stories with remarkable fidelity. With their aid, and a little compromise, he was able to sell some of his esoteric writings:

> Now I am doing a set of essays on "The Mystic Import of American Literature". I hope the title doesn't seem ludicrous, perhaps I shall find a better. These were begun in the hopes of making money: for money is a shy bird. But I am afraid they have already passed beyond all price. It is a pity.[3]

In face of the growing threat of conscription he subsequently attempted to persuade the Minister of Education to find him a civilian job, and to this end sought to prove his competence. G. S. Freeman, director of the *Times Educational Supplement*, having lent a favourable ear to the idea of a set of articles, Lawrence wrote the first four essays of a series entitled "Education of the People". They were rejected without comment in 1919, revised in 1920,[4] and appeared only posthumously in *Phoenix*. Meanwhile, Vere H. Graz Bischoff Collins of Oxford University Press had taken up a suggestion by Lawrence,[5] fresh from a complete reading of Gibbon, to write a history textbook: the result was *Movements in European History*, in which, under a pseudonym, he expressed his "philosophy of history" rather more flamboyantly than was strictly compatible with the demands of a textbook aimed at stimulating the study of European history in English primary schools.

These contradictions and conflicting aims have left their mark on what remains of the theoretical works of 1916 to 1919. Some of these have been lost, others were completely rewritten after the end of the war: witness the *Studies in Classic American Literature*, so very different from the original articles appearing in *The English Review* in 1918. What is left reveals the turmoils and confusions of a mind which was to find peace and charity again only in the relative calm of the post-war years in Italy.

Late wartime theoretical writings

The works surveyed here begin with seven essays entitled "The Reality of Peace", four of which appeared under this title in *The English Review* for May, June, July and August 1917. The other three cannot be traced with certainty, though "Love" (*The English Review*, January 1918) and "Life" (February 1918) may be two of them. "The seven" would seem to have been subsequently developed in a volume entitled "At the Gates", dispatched to Pinker on 30 August 1917, described as "pure metaphysics", but now totally lost.[6]

Immediately after "At the Gates", Lawrence broached his studies in American literature, entitled successively "The Transcendental Element in Classic American Literature" (3 September 1917), "The Mystic Import of American

Literature" (23 September) and finally *Studies in Classic American Literature* (February–March 1918). For some unstated reason, he did not want these essays copied by "the ordinary typist" but entrusted them to somebody "safe", recommended by a friend. In the end several of them, including the original essay on Whitman, were copied in long-hand by Koteliansky.[7] Eight of them appeared in *The English Review* from November 1918 to June 1919—the last, and probably most warranted to shock some of Harrison's subscribers, being "The Two Principles". The essays on Dana and Melville, one of the two on Hawthorne, and the study on Whitman finished in June 1918, did not appear in this series; the reason for the interruption after the eighth essay is not known. Could it be that after "The Two Principles" Harrison feared to exhaust the patience of a public ill-prepared for Lawrence's occultist and Rosicrucian lucubrations? Alternatively, the first version of the Whitman essay may have been thought to involve some risks for the reputation of the author of *The Rainbow*.

"Education of the People", begun in November 1918, was soon completed: Lawrence considered it "most revolutionary".[8] He was working simultaneously on his *Movements in European History*, begun the previous summer and completed in April 1919.

These works may be considered as a whole, together with "Whistling of Birds", an essay written for Murry and published in *The Athenaeum* in April 1919, and "Poetry of the Present", written in 1919 for the American edition of *New Poems*. "The Reality of Peace", "Love" and "Life" are reproduced in *Phoenix* exactly as they first appeared in *The English Review*. The posthumous text of "Education of the People" is undoubtedly longer than the lost original of 1918, while the 1921 edition of *Movements in European History* corresponds to the original manuscript, with slight revisions in accordance with suggestions from Oxford University Press. As for the early studies in American literature, the collection edited by Armin Arnold in 1962 under the title *The Symbolic Meaning* contains the eight original *English Review* versions, an unpublished essay on Hawthorne probably rewritten in Sicily after the war, the unpublished early versions (also written in Sicily?) of essays on *Typee* and *Omoo*, and on *Moby Dick*, and the text of the 1918 Whitman essay, as revised in Sicily in 1920 and published in *The Nation and Athenaeum* on 23 July 1921. This collection thus provides an adequate, if not complete, indication of Lawrence's mental state and interests at the end of the war.

"The Reality of Peace"

In "The Reality of Peace", "Love" and "Life", Lawrence resumes and reworks themes already developed in the "Hardy" and "The Crown". Outwardly at least, he is concerned not with the peace of the warring nations, but with that of the individual; unless he is equivocating, his attitude to the war has been seriously toned down.

He describes the universe as actuated by a motion like "the beating of the everlasting heart", a great "systole-diastole", without aim or explanation; all we know is that "the end is the heaven on earth, like the wild rose in blossom".[9] Some degree of familiarity with Lawrence's mind is required to understand the affirmation "We are like the blood that travels" under the pulse of this everlasting heart. Peace is "the state of fulfilling the deepest desire of the soul"; we know peace if "we fly according to the perfect impulse"; but if we resist this impulse, "we have the gnawing misery of nullification".[10]

In order to flow with this tide of creative direction, it is no use calling upon our will, nor yet our understanding. These must, on the contrary, be submitted "to the exquisitest suggestion from the unknown". Knowledge serves only to map out the past; mechanics and mathematics are useless; courage consists in complete abandonment to "the river of peace which bears us". "Peace is when I accept life."[11]

The social and political ideas emerging from "The Reality of Peace" differ very little from those expressed in the "Hardy". The desire for social change, for a class struggle, "to see the masses rise up and make an end of the wrong old order", like the contradictory desire "to govern them for their own good, strongly", are both represented as death-wishes, for "all strife between things old is pure death". Lawrence seeks salvation rather in "one spark of happiness that is absolved from strife", in "a quick, new desire to have new heaven and earth". Once again he sees social problems through a mystical fog, rejecting both socialism and social conservatism, as in *Women in Love* and *Touch and Go*.

In the third essay, however, Lawrence suddenly ranges himself on the side of the strong. Mankind is but "an obscene whole which is no whole, only a multiplied nullity", weak pullulating insects, a herd of slaves. The "nauseous slaves of decay" have now, alas, "got the upper hand". To subdue them, "we must go forth with whips, like the old chieftain". "It has triumphed, this slave herd, and its tyranny is the tyranny of a pack of jackals. But it can be frightened back to its place. For its cowardice is as great as its arrogance."[12]

Myths of decline and of death

At the very time when, in 1917, Oswald Spengler, also following in the wake of Nietzsche, was writing *The Decline of the West*, Lawrence adopts a similar position, expressing ideas strongly marked by Nietzschean themes as well as by his own occultist reading. Today's humanity is incapable of acceding to true life; the "living dead", the "slug-like sheep", belong to an epoch of decadence and decay: the myth of the end of a human epoch was tormenting Lawrence and Spengler alike:

> When it is autumn in the world, the autumn of a human epoch, then the desire for death becomes single and dominant. I want to kill, I want violent sensationalism, I want to break down, I want to put asunder, I want anarchic revolution—it is all the same, the single desire for death . . . So with very many human lives, especially in what is called the periods of decadence. They have mouths and stomachs, and an *obscene* will of their own. Yes, they have also prolific procreative wombs whence they bring forth increasing insufficiency. But of the germ of intrinsic creation they have none, neither have they the courage of true death . . . These will never understand, neither life nor death . . . The quick can encompass death, but the living dead are encompassed. Let the living dead attend to the dead dead. What has creation to do with them?[13]

This essay ends on an invocation to death which, in 1917, may well have seemed mere rhetoric, but which raises ominous echoes in our ears today. Lawrence launches spontaneously into a stream of thought emanating from Nietzsche and his German disciples: the idea of abandonment to cosmic forces, the belief in the decline of civilizations, the apologia for the wild beast whose nature is to spring upon its willing prey—all this suggests that, drawing upon the same original, mystical, Teutonic creed, Lawrence's "philosophy" was evolving in close sympathy with the Germans of the day. Without wishing to insist unduly on the common elements of his ideas of 1917 and the sources of Nazi theory, one can but be struck by the sinister implications of such passages as this invocation to mass death. Lawrence calls upon "Sweet, beautiful death" to "break in among the herd" and "make gaps in its insulated completion": he implores death to help him "escape from the herd and *gather together against it a few living beings*", to purify them, and cleanse from them the rank stench, the *intolerable oneness with a negative humanity*" [*Italics added.*]:

> Smash, beautiful destructive death, smash the complete will of the hosts of man, the will of the self-absorbed bug. Smash the great obscene unison. Death, assert your strength now, for it is time. They have defied you so long. They have even, in their mad arrogance, begun to deal in death as if it also were subjugated. They thought to use death as they have used life this long time, for their own base end of nullification, swift death was to serve their end of enclosed, arrogant self-assertion. Death was to help them maintain themselves in *statu quo*, the benevolent and self-righteous bugs of humanity.
>
> Let there be no humanity; let there be a few men. Sweet death, save us from humanity. Death, noble unstainable death, smash the glassy rind of humanity, as one would smash the brittle hide of the insulated bug. Smash humanity, and make an end of it. Let there emerge a few pure and single men—men who give

themselves to the unknown of life and death and are fulfilled. Make an end of
our unholy oneness, O death, give us to our single being. Release me from the
debased social body. O death, release me at last; let me be by myself, let me be
myself. Let me know other men who are single and not contained by any
multiple oneness. Let me find a few men who are distinct and at ease in themselves like stars. Let me derive no more from the body of mankind. Let me
derive direct from life or direct from death, according to the impulse that is
in me.[14]

One may also wonder how this meditation would appeal to socialist and
liberal readers of Harrison's review, appearing, as it did, at the very climax
of the third battle of Ypres. Some idea of the Lawrences' total lack of sensitivity to English feelings at the time may, moreover, be gauged by the fact
that Frieda actually envisaged an application for the Nobel Prize for this
remarkable contribution to peace![15]

The fourth section, entitled "The Orbit", to some extent clarifies and
reformulates certain themes, latent in "The Crown" but here more openly
expressed, prior to their further development in the American studies.

The underlying thought is similar to one implicit in *Women in Love*,
greatly clarified in this section of "The Reality of Peace": humanity faces
two possible roads, one leading to death, the other to creativeness and the
earthly paradise. But these two roads are parallel, they never cross: so that
no man can persuade another to follow the road he himself has chosen.
Each has his own road, his predestined "consummation". There was a hint
of this in *Women in Love*, Birkin and Gerald never being *free* to follow the
same road. Liberty, free will permit one only to refuse to follow the road of
one's destiny; hence Lawrence's hatred of "will", the drive towards isolation,
preventing the self from beating in unison with the universal pulse of life
and death. Each individual may either accept life by yielding his "ultimate
will to the unknown impulse", or else remain outside, abiding alone "like
the corn or wheat, outside the river of life". Society is no more than a "vast
colony of wood-lice, fabricating elaborate social communities like the bees
or the wasps or the ants";[16] the choice is not between life and death, but
between accepting one's destiny—be it life or death—and refusing it, which
means nullity, organization, negation, self-preservation. As he goes on to
assert in "Education of the People", Lawrence willingly accepts a restricted
social life for the masses, provided the elect can escape it and follow their own
destiny.

The two principles and polarity

And, as in "The Crown" the two heroic roads—the road to life and the road
to death—are symbolized by two principles, defined later in the essay "The

Two Principles", as fire and water, sun and earth. Having established its own system, Lawrence's symbolism now sets up as a "philosophy" in which echoes of Heraclitus mingle with his new interest in the occult. As in "The Crown", the tiger is a brand of fire, the lion a "golden bonfire", the grass-fed sheep are "sodden mounds of scarcely kindled grey mould", the deer are "the mists of morning", their coolness quenching the flame of the beasts of prey. And man, "rose of perfect being" transcending light and shadow, finds peace not in the impossible reconciliation of the lion and the lamb, but in "the primary law of all the universe", "the law of dual attraction and repulsion", "polarity". The poet is striving to give his thought abstract expression: "There is peace in that perfect consummation when duality and polarity is transcended into absorption";[17] the "lovely, perfect" peace of earth resting on her orbit.

The profusion, one might even say confusion, of images here evoked recalls not only the themes of Birkin's meditation on love, but also the author's own "case history". The poetic use of the first person stresses the "confessional" aspect of this "philosophy". The deep conflict behind it transpires more clearly seen in conjunction with the mutually contradictory tendencies of a Birkin torn between fear of woman and the attraction of Gerald on the one hand, and love for Ursula on the other. Willingly or unwillingly, the Lawrence of 1917 is constantly harking back to the problem of the creation of the ego and sexual differentiation:

> I am born uncreated. I am a mixed handful of life as I issue from the womb. Thenceforth I extricate myself into singleness, the slow-developed singleness of manhood. And then I set out to meet the other, the unknown of woman-hood. I give myself to the love that makes me join and fuse towards a universal oneness; I give myself to the hate that makes me detach myself, extricate myself vividly from the other in sharp passion; I am given up into universality of fellowship and communion, I am distinguished in keen resistance and isolation, both so utterly, so exquisitively, that I am and I am not at once; suddenly I lapse out of the duality into a sheer beauty of fulfilment. I am a rose of lovely peace.[18]

This passage makes sense only in the light of Birkin's meditation: sexually impure, mixed, the individual must achieve singleness, i.e. cease to be both male and female; his love-life will then alternate between attraction and repulsion, and peace lies in admitting the two aspects of his nature, love and hate. Accession to being, to the perfection of the rose, consists in allowing his two component elements to co-exist and balance each other. Lawrence attempts to justify through a general dualism his own idea of a love relation-ship—with its alternation of attraction and reaction, of merging and seeking "separateness" from the loved one.

In the essay "Love", he pursues the idea that love is ebb and flow, reunion and separation, polarity, gravitation. The image of the rose, which exists outside time and space, "perfect in the realm of perfection", is ever present, symbolizing the complete love of man and woman. Of all forms of love this passion alone is complete "because it is dual, because it is of two opposing kinds", "sacred" and "profane". "Love between man and woman is the perfect heartbeat of life, systole, diastole."[19]

In 1917, Lawrence, like Birkin, stresses the destructive aspect of "profane love" which he regards as a refuge from an undifferentiated and confused state of being, rather than as a positive joy. The accent is separation, the desire for isolation of the ego, for independence. The essay ends rather unsatisfactorily with an attack on excessive brotherly love, on fraternity and equality, and with the affirmation that rather than love Christ or Jehovah, who are necessarily jealous Gods, we must accept "the unknown and the unknowable which propounds all creation".

"Life" is in the same vein as the other 1917 essays, aiming "to bring *peace* and *life* in the world".[20] The theme is again the mystic consummation of being, the creation of the individual: man, says Lawrence, is "the quick of creation", "creation itself, that which is perfect". He cannot create himself, but must "submit to the creator" in order to "have being beyond life and beyond death", thus becoming "perfect of both", and comprehending "the singing of birds and the silence of the snake".[21]

What is new here is the idea of death. The two unknowns of the "Hardy" and "The Crown", the beginning and the end, have now become "life" and "death"; the perfect rose uniting them is a human life which obeys the creative impulse; then, "through the bright transition of creation . . . through the transfiguration of perfect being . . . in my completeness of being the two unknowns are consummated in a oneness, a rose of perfect explanation".[22]

This "new creation" comes about "from the unknown, the unknown is added on to me" not by any deliberate effort, "but of my insuperable faith, my waiting". The soul thus reconciled with the unknown no longer fears "the invisible dark hand of death plucking me into the darkness, gathering me blossom by blossom from the stem of my life into the unknown of my afterwards". It feels only "reverence and strange satisfaction".[23] This idea of death accepted as a serene journey into the unknown will reappear towards the end of Lawrence's life. It is significant that in 1917, in the isolation of his Cornish retreat, and after his grave 1916 illness, Lawrence should thus be stressing the idea of death in opposition to love and co-operation between man and woman. Acceptance of life, to him, means acceptance of death— while to reject life and choose death, like Sappho or Empedocles, is not the true choice that leads to peace.

These essays throw some light on the intentions of *Women in Love*, but contribute little in themselves. In spite of some beautiful passages, the symbolism and would-be philosophical abstraction of these essays do not reach a true synthesis; we are always made aware of the author's own eternal problem, the passionate quest for unity of a divided man, deeply conscious of his dualism, endlessly seeking the unifying principle which will enable him to triumph over it.

Occultist investigations, 1916–18

This principle Lawrence apparently believes he has found in his occultist reading; and, while "The Reality of Peace" contains no open reference to such reading, it was certainly in his mind throughout the composition of the essays, as it was throughout the writing of *Women in Love*. Only in the first version of *Studies in Classic American Literature* does this interest in magic fully emerge into the light of day. While his reading of occultist works is not yet fully documented, it can nonetheless be dated with some degree of accuracy as mainly between early 1916 and the end of 1918. Even if, as is possible, it may date back further, perhaps as early as 1912, for Lawrence 1916–18 was undoubtedly a period of renewed interest in esoteric literature. A number of facts, independent of indications in his works of this period and of the veiled hints contained in the Foreword to *Fantasia*, support this view.

As we have already seen, Heseltine was an assiduous reader of the occult writers.[24] He stayed with the Lawrences from January to February 1916 and returned to Cornwall in March of the following year, living for a time near them at Zennor, so that Lawrence was in fact in almost daily contact with him throughout the spring and early summer of 1917.[25] When he stayed in Ireland after July or August 1917, he remained in correspondence with Lawrence. He pursued his occult studies by reading such authors as Eliphas Levi (l'Abbé Constant), the *Book of Abramalin the Wise*, and the works of the pre-Renaissance magician Cornelius Agrippa. At the same time he was trying to find an Irish publisher for "the whole book" from which the "Reality of Peace" essays "were taken". That book was, in his opinion, "the supreme utterance of all modern philosophy, the work of the prophet Ezekiel *redivivus*".[26] He does not make it clear why he thought it impossible to publish the book in England.

Heseltine's correspondence at this time, in particular with Gray, also in close contact with Lawrence, gives some idea of the conversations at Porthcothan and at Zennor and of the letters no doubt exchanged between Lawrence and Heseltine in 1917–18. Besides considering "The Reality of Peace" "a stupendous book", the young composer shows himself convinced that Lawrence had "become the mouthpiece of someone incredibly great". "The real authors", he adds, "are, no doubt, in eternity."[27] Robert Nichols provides some idea of the mental climate in which Heseltine then evolved and the nature of his influence: Heseltine's intellect, he reports, was "of wide range, of sterner mettle, of tougher integrity, of more persistent energy and of more imaginative quality in the metaphysic sense than that of Lawrence. There was something very earthy, very literal about Lawrence's mind. He lacked imagination, as may be seen by the pitiable futility of his views on Shelley."[28]

Now, in August 1918, Heseltine defined art as "the means of communicating spiritual realities to the world of material semblances". For him symbolism in literature "in the special sense ulterior to that wherein all works are symbols, has it roots in the mystical and magical writers from Hermes Trismegistus onwards: it is a little part of a great tradition which has been followed alike by the French Symbolists, by Yeats and by countless others who are not indebted to one another so much as to the central tradition itself".[29] Peter Warlock's ideas on art, and especially on modern art, owe much to Lawrence. On the other hand it seems probable that it is to him Lawrence owes at least part of the interest he was then taking in magic and in occult doctrine, and perhaps even the link here established between esoteric tradition and symbolist art.

How deep did this interest really go? In *Women in Love* we have seen evidence of certain themes inspired by J. M. Pryse, the Dublin theosophist who introduced A. E. and W. B. Yeats to magic and initiation rites. We also found there traces of the secret doctrine as expounded in the two works of Hélène Blavatsky. But all this was still veiled, as though Lawrence did not wish or did not dare openly to reveal the source of certain ideas, the origin of certain images. We shall later find him eager to produce "scientific" evidence in support of statements from occultist sources. Up to 1918, he seems to hover on the brink of esoteric adventure, part of himself—the artist—exploiting certain themes, another part—the believer and initiate—hesitant to reveal his faith, possibly for fear of ridicule. Such, at least, is the impression conveyed by the limited references to occultism contained in his contemporary correspondence.

The off-hand tone of certain letters proves nothing either way. Meredith Starr, an esoteric poet and regular contributor to *The Occult Review*, was living in the neighbourhood of Zennor at the time Lawrence began his studies in American literature. Lawrence met him and his wife and did "not like them very much". Writing to Cynthia Asquith, he refers disdainfully to these "herb-eating occultists, a Meredith Starr and Lady Mary ditto: she a half-caste, daughter of the Earl of Stamford":

They fast, or eat nettles: they descend naked into old mine-shafts, and there meditate for hours and hours, upon their own transcendent infinitude: they descend on us like a swarm of locusts and devour all the food on the shelf or board.[30]

They "make the most dreadful fools of themselves" and Lawrence is at some pains to make it clear to Lady Cynthia that he avoids their company.

Yet other letters written during these same weeks are full of allusions to esoterism, and of terms also used in "The Reality of Peace". While the detailed exposition of ideas remains confused, the deep, emotional vision is clearly discernible. The keynote is destruction: Europe is lost, America is the only hope, the true new world. Not that it is a paradise, but there is a quality in its *sky*, a salt in its *earth* that will, without the agency of man, *destroy* the man of today and "procreate new beings—not men, in our sense of the word".[31] This vision, foreshadowing that of *The Plumed Serpent*, is that of a man who has allowed his imagination, his day-dreaming, if not his conscious thought, to play with the themes of *The Secret Doctrine*, with the traditions regrouped by the theosophists. In April 1918, he told Gertler he had just been reading "*another book* on Occultism", and proclaimed his belief in the "reality" of magic.[32]

Lawrence had certainly read Mme Blavatsky by November 1918. The only letter containing a direct allusion to her books is addressed to Mrs Nancy Henry, then employed by Oxford University Press, who typed the manuscript of *Movements in European History*. Aldous Huxley has placed this undated letter between those of March and May 1919. It bears the indication *Wednesday*, and was written from Chapel Farm Cottage at Hermitage, where Lawrence spent some days in early November 1918.[33] Its date is thus likely to be Wednesday, 13 November, as indeed is proved by the phrase "wonderful that there is peace at last", obviously referring to the Armistice Declaration on 11 November; and by an allusion to the appearance of the first of the American essays "this month" in *The English Review*: the "Spirit of Place" appeared in *The English Review* for November 1918.

Mrs Henry had submitted to Lawrence a short story in which she had tried to create a "subtle atmosphere of unbearable, nauseating or exalting terror"; she had written to him concerning certain "philosophical" problems, about which he preferred to "talk" rather than write letters: "As you feel about your story, so I feel about the reality of the moon, for example. I can hardly talk about it, it goes so deep into one's bowels and makes one a little sick."[34] The reference to occultist ideas is evident: according to the secret doctrine the moon is the mother of the earth, "doomed for long ages to be ever pursuing the Earth, to be attracted by and to attract her progeny":

Constantly *vampirized* by her child, she revenges herself on it by soaking it through and through with the nefarious, invisible and poisoned influence which emanates from the occult side of her nature. For she is a *dead*, yet a *living body*. The particles of her decaying corpse are full of active and destructive life, although the body which they had formed is soulless and lifeless. Therefore its emanations are at the same time beneficent and maleficent . . . And like all ghouls or vampires, the moon is the friend of the sorcerers and the foe of the unwary.[35] [*Italics added.*]

Lawrence was thus given to discussing esoteric secrets with Mrs Henry, whom he saw on his visits to London and who, on one such occasion, provided him with accommodation.[36] The following advice given in November 1918 was clearly written to follow up a previous conversation:

> Try and get hold of Mme Blavatsky's books—they are big and expensive—the friends I used to borrow them from are out of England now. But get from some library or other *Isis Unveiled*, and better still the 2 vol. work whose name I forget. Rider, the publisher of the *Occult Review*—try that—publishes all these books . . . But look in the *Occult Review*. You see, I never owned the books I had—and they are all big, 10/6 and £1.1.0. And they're not *very* much good. But try Rider, he has a good shop.[37]

"I am not a theosophist," he wrote to Waldo Frank, "though esoteric doctrines are marvellously illuminating, historically. I hate the exoteric forms. Magic has also interested me a good deal. But it is all part of the past, and part of a past self in us: and it is no good going back, even to the wonderful things. They are ultimately *vieux jeu*."[38]

The first and fourth sentences echo his December 1914 letter to Campbell on the subject of symbolism: Christian symbols "mean a moment in the history of my soul . . . But it is a moment fixed in context . . . it is necessary to grasp the whole."[39] Similarly, Mme Blavatsky's work was not "*very* much good", and failed to provide a totally acceptable context. Yet, while the symbolism of *The Rainbow* is drawn mainly from the Christian system described by Mrs Jenner, the symbolism of *Women in Love* and of the 1917–18 essays is nearer to that of *The Secret Doctrine*. Heseltine's letter on literary symbolism, quoted above, throws some light on the undoubted link between Lawrence's idea of symbolism, as expressed in 1918, and his esoteric reading.

While it is impossible to date exactly his reading of *Isis Unveiled* and *The Secret Doctrine*, it is certain that the use of symbols inspired by these works, and Lawrence's interest in them, reached its height between early 1916 and the end of 1918. Just as in 1915 Burnet's *Early Greek Philosophy* provided him with an alternative to Christian symbolism, Heraclitus supplying his dualism with new images of opposites, so between 1916 and 1918 his imagination fed on images drawn from esoteric symbolism, destined, in his postwar work, to be fused into an original synthesis with new reading matter provided by Barbara Low and the Eders: works by Jung, and a treatise on the physiology of the nervous system. This synthesis was achieved in *Psychoanalysis and the Unconscious*. But until 1919 Lawrence's work was still under the spell of the magic symbolism of *The Secret Doctrine*. In psychoanalysis he was to seek later a scientific justification for images attracting him, rather than an explanation of his personality and problems. From Blavatsky, as later from Jung, he took what pleased him, images rather than ideas, always secretly and sometimes openly concerned to justify his beliefs by the term "scientific": the sub-title of *The Secret Doctrine*, "The Synthesis of Science, Religion and Philosophy", may indeed have impressed him. What is surprising is not so much the residual scepticism of Lawrence's attitude towards Mme Blavatsky's jumble of beliefs, as the fact that he should have given it as much credit as to Frazer or Tylor. In his assertion that her books are "not *very* much good", the negative is less important than the underlined "very" qualifying the adverb "much".

This ambivalent attitude to esoteric doctrine, very close to that adopted towards Christian symbolism and primitive art, is due to a combination of two factors: on the one hand the fascination exercised on the poet by image and by symbol, and on the other the conviction that the human spirit should free itself of beliefs that have had their day and can no longer satisfy the intellect. But at the moment of writing the original studies on American literature, the fascination of occultism was predominant, and blended with notions of psychoanalysis, derived less from any intensive reading than from conversations with the Eders and with Barbara Low.

THE SYMBOLIC MEANING:
THE 1918 AMERICAN STUDIES

Of the thirteen essays published in 1962 under the title *The Symbolic Meaning*, twelve concern us here: the eight from *The English Review* of November 1918 to June 1919; the second essay on Hawthorne, and the two on Melville, all three probably revised in Sicily; and finally the "Whitman" written in 1918, revised in Sicily in 1920 and published in the *New Statesman* in July 1921.

These essays have certain points in common with the "Hardy": undertaken as literary criticism, they rapidly assume the form of a confession, becoming at once philosophy, cosmology, psychology, analysis of sex, theory of art and symbol, and criticism of mechanistic and materialist society. And, like the "Hardy", they have the added interest of being a free and frank confession, a commentary by a creative writer on ideas and beliefs throwing light on his own creative processes, while also explaining the authors under study.

Wartime spiritualism and Lawrence's 1917 mood

Why did Lawrence in 1917 and 1918, when writing these essays on American literature, thus openly reveal his interest in occultism and in magic? Since late 1914, his esoteric ideas had been largely concealed in certain phrases of the "Hardy", in a few poems, and in the character of Birkin. There is nothing in his letters, nor in the biographical evidence from his familiars, to enlighten us on this change. Reticence may be linked to his preoccupation with sexual problems—to which he was seeking an esoteric explanation. The new openness, on the other hand, may be explained by two facts. First of all, a reading of anthropologists such as Frazer, Tylor and Frobenius, and of psychologists (whom, according to what Barbara Low told the present writer, he never studied deeply but may have read about 1916, though introduced to Jung only in the autumn of 1918) may have given him the feeling, expressed in a letter already quoted, of the "historical" value of esoteric doctrine. This may have helped free him of the shame he may well have felt at being attracted by such beliefs.[40]

Secondly, account must be taken of the spiritualist revival in England in 1917 and 1918 as a result of the heavy death toll taken by the war. Many of the bereaved strove to enter into contact with the spirits of the fallen. The spiritualist works of Sir Oliver Lodge, the wireless scientist, who himself tried to communicate with his dead son Raymond, aroused wide interest at this time.[41] Lawrence's personal sympathy had been gained by a letter from Lodge on the occasion of the suppression of *The Rainbow* and a certain, if negative, interest in his work is proved by a letter to Edward Marsh in May 1919 in which he expresses his distaste for "the Oliver Lodge spiritualism—hotel bills and collar studs".[42] Apropos of *Fantasia of the Unconscious*, the American Leo Stein noted the coincidence of Lawrence's ideas with Lodge's, when he commented in a 1921 letter: "the hour of war spiritualism is running to its end . . ."[43] Lawrence often claimed a "scientific basis" for some of his own concepts in much the same spirit as that evinced by Lodge. He may well have found encouragement in a dual current sympathetic to his own tendencies—the anthropological-psychological stream, and the spiritualist stream—which may have seemed to him not so very far removed from psychoanalysis, particularly if, as seems probable, it was Dr Eder who had lent him his books on occultism.

The indirect influence of Sir Oliver Lodge is palpable in his efforts to assert the "scientific value" of certain of his most daring ideas: the concept of "polarity" not only appears and reappears constantly in his vocabulary, but is freely associated with other scientific and non-scientific terms to become "the great mystic-magnetic polarity".[44] Montezuma's foreknowledge of the coming of the Europeans is attributed to "fine vibrations in the ether"; he considers the "mystery of prophecy" to be "no more absurd than the sending of a wireless message".[45] The writer who, particularly in *Fantasia of the Unconscious*, was to denounce science as passive, dead and abstract,[46] here asserts no less than five times the "scientific exactitude" of St John's description in the Apocalypse of the "conquest of the lower or sensual dynamic centres by the upper or spiritual dynamic consciousness":[47] a "scientific value" attested in this instance by J. M. Pryse, from whom Lawrence here borrows generously while he fails to mention him. His tone suggests he was in need of frequent reassurance against his own critical judgment. In a fit of pseudo-scientific enthusiasm, he seems under a compulsion to borrow from contemporary science a number of concepts used completely out of context: ether, magnetism, radio-activity. "Our plasmic psyche", he asserts, treating spiritualist "psychometry" on the same level as psychoanalysis,[48] "is radio-active", "connecting with all things".

Earth, salt and sky: the spirit of place

Beneath this pseudo-scientific façade a whole "system" is elaborated: we are no longer faced with symbols throwing light on the past of man's mental life, but rather with a would-be explanation of the universe, of human psychology, and, of course, of the mysteries of sex. Love between man and woman will vary in value according to whether it corresponds to the "youth" or "crumbling" of a human or a cosmic era. Indeed the dominant theme, the overall concern, remains the great Lawrentian problem: the explanation of the individual's relationship with "otherness".

The "spirit of place", a theme much on Lawrence's mind since the summer of 1917, is one of the leading ideas of the American essays. America attracts him because "there is a new sky above it". Once more cloaking his metaphors in scientific language reminiscent of alchemy, he hopes that "the strange salt which must be in the American soil and the different ether which is in the sky will feed a new mind in us".[49] The first American essay, entitled "The Spirit of Place", propounds a dual theory: on the one hand, "All art partakes of the Spirit of Place in which it is produced"; on the other, modern man being divided, the "mystic", "transcendental", unconscious message of a work of art differs from its intentional, exoteric message: "the deliberate ideas of the man veil, conceal, obscure that which the artist has to reveal", the artist is "a somnambulist", sincere in his own "intention", unconscious of his "duplicity", "contravened and contradicted by the wakeful man and moralist who sits at the desk"[50]—an idea which may have been reinforced by conversation with the Eders and Barbara Low, but also encouraged by his interest in the occult. The "Spirit of Place" offers a preliminary synthesis between these early psychoanalytical contacts, contemporary spiritualism and Lawrence's hermetic reading. And, as will appear later from his two books on the unconscious, the influence of the mystics was to prove far deeper, much closer to his personal inclinations, than that of the psychoanalysts.

He finds in American literature an "alien" quality, "not inherent in the English race" but belonging "to the American continent itself": it shows a "difference and otherness"; beyond a "oneness" which is "historic only", there exists "a reality of untranslatable otherness".[51] The esoteric message of early American literature unconsciously reveals the existence of a "new race". In all its vagueness this idea of race varies little from that expressed by Lawrence in the "Hardy". "Race", he affirms, "is ultimately as much a question of place as of heredity . . . The place attracts its own human element and the race drifts inevitably to its own psychic and geographical pole."[52] Similarly for Houston Chamberlain race was *Gestalt* at its purest, as determined by "the blood" and "the ideal". As we shall see, to Lawrence blood is the cosmic element *par excellence*, the link between man and the cosmos, and hence between man and his geographical and mystic environment, between man and his deepest ideal. This conception also owes something to *The Secret Doctrine*, since to Lawrence "race" evokes the advent of a new era, thanks to a "slow and terrible process of transubstantiation" of Europeans on American soil: "their subtlest plasm" being "changed under the radiation of new skies, new influence of light, their first and rarest life-stuff transmuted".[53]

Atlantis and the great migrations

Lawrence quotes the occultists in support of his mystic theory of place and historic mutations. He explicitly links their concepts to those of the psychologists concerning "the understanding of symbols", and refers to their doctrine according to which mankind once possessed "a universal mystic language", known to the priesthood of the whole world, "perhaps before the Flood".[54] That language expresses in ideograms or symbols a common idea of cosmic creation: hence the universality of mystic, abstract symbols such as the circle, the *crux ansata* and the circled cross of the Rosicrucians.

The true universal language (and here the artist in Lawrence clearly gains the upper hand over his obsession with the occult) is "art-speech", which is also "a language of pure symbols", standing not for "a thought or an idea, a mental *concept*":

> . . . a pure experience, emotional and passional, spiritual and perceptual all at once. The intellectual idea remains implicit, latent and nascent. Art communicates a state of being . . . art speech is a use of symbols which are pulsations on the blood and seizures upon the nerves, and at the same time pure percepts of the mind and pure terms of spiritual aspiration.[55]

He does, however, allow himself to be seduced by the idea of an esoteric doctrine common to mankind, returning to it once more apropos of Melville.[56] The myth of Atlantis fascinates him,[57] although at first he treats it purely as myth, without any implication of reality. His attitude towards the problem of ancient esoteric doctrine, known to the initiated, as revealed in connexion with this myth, shows signs of his usual ambivalence: at one point he gives a modern explanation of Atlantis, at another states the myth as fact, in a manner implying belief: "the savages, we may say all savages, are remnants of the once civilized world-people, who had their splendour and their being for countless centuries in the way of sensual knowledge, that conservative way which Egypt shows us at its conclusion, mysterious and long-enduring".[58] The savages are "old", it is "we from the North, starting new centres of life in ourselves, who have become young": an assertion which recalls Birkin's dilemma before the African fetish[59]—except that in *Women in Love* the man from the North is Gerald, and Birkin, harbinger of future man, insists more on the "return to sensual centres" than on their harmonization with the new centres, those of the brain. Either Lawrence's thought is clearer in didactic, explanatory form than imaginatively expressed in his novel, or he has characteristically shifted his ground since writing *Women in Love*.

He explains migrations as the effect of deep, inexplicable, and certainly unconscious drives. Mankind is directed by mystic "circuits": in Roman times the Rome-Milan-Gaul axis followed the Rome-Carthage circuit; then there was the "divergent" axis Rome-Byzantium. In the Middle Ages the Rome-Trèves axis, the great "German-Italian circuit of vital magnetism", constituted "the main polarity of Europe". And when Italy was exhausted by the Renaissance, Europe and America became "the great poles of negative and positive vitalism". "On the wings of this new attraction" the European navigators discovered America: "they had no choice, because the influence which was upon them was prior to all knowledge and option".[60]

The Celts and Iberians, "dissociated from the circle of Italian-German culture", in "mystic opposition" to the civilizing principle of the rest of Europe, always "existed in the spell of the vital magnetism of the unknown continent", and were unconsciously drawn by this attraction at the very moment when Montezuma, guided by a kind of "race clairvoyance", a projection of "race-memory" into the future, was filled with mystic apprehension: for the Aztecs "knew the future" not in symbols, but in "plain, direct, prescience".

As for the Pilgrim Fathers, they "did not sail to America in search of religious freedom"; this was no more than a "specious reason", "a sufficient pretext". They were no more Christian than the "dark and violent Spaniards of the Inquisition". In answering the call of the American continent, what they were really seeking was not liberty "but a gloomy and tyrannical sense of power"; they

> . . . wanted to have power over all immediate life, to destroy and mutilate
> life at its very quick, lusting in their dark power to annihilate all living
> impulses, both their own and those of their neighbour. America, dark, violent
> aboriginal would lend them force to satisfy their lust of anti-life.[61]

And in this they succeeded, controlling the life-impulse and mechanizing existence to become "good businessmen", like the Jews, who had also conquered and destroyed within themselves instinctive, impulsive being. This again seems to echo Chamberlain's mystic, vitalistic, anti-Semitism, as well as offering a foretaste of the philosophy of history soon to be expressed in *Movements in European History*.

Duality of the cosmos

For the first time, Lawrence here unveils the whole of his hermetic thought and reveals his fervid search for a total explanation of creation. His recent reading seem to have encouraged him to bring into the open all that was suggested in the "Hardy" and in certain passages of *The Rainbow*, *Women in Love* and "The Crown", with the result that he reveals the links existing between his mystic theory of nature and artistic creation on the one hand, and on the other the cosmogony taken direct from *The Secret Doctrine* and Rosicrucian theory. Not only was he emboldened to express ideas haunting him for some time past, but the writings of Mme Blavatsky provided him with a mystico-esoteric synthesis, which seems, at least for the time being, to have given him satisfaction.

In order to explain his ideas on the role of the sea in Dana and in Melville, he devotes a whole essay, "The Two Principles", to the basic duality of the cosmos and expounds his gnostic idea of the creation of the world. He expresses it with the usual ambiguity of vocabulary of such mystic statements —one and the same word being used either with its usual meaning, or with some totally different import. For instance, the beginning is not a beginning, "the Waters" means water, but also Earth; the "unnamable cosmic Fire" is a "dark flame", and so on. The few basic ideas which do emerge may be summed up as follows:

The creative reality or "living cosmos" first divides into "an inexplicable first duality", into "two great valves of the primordial universe" between which moves "The Spirit of God".[62] "The mystic Earth is the cosmic Waters, and the mystic Heaven the dark cosmic Fire." The Spirit of God moving between the Waters and the Fire "brings forth the first created apparition, Light". "Surely," adds Lawrence, disarmingly, "this is true, scientifically, of the birth of light."[63]

This first division is "perpendicular" (*sic*); a second division intervenes, "when the line of the firmament is drawn", and this is horizontal, giving the elements of the Rosy Cross ⊕, which represents the Universe on the "Second Day of Creation". Central within this "fourfold division" is "the creative reality itself", like the body of a four-winged bird, two wings being "opposite Waters", and two "opposite Fire".

On a more material level, the sun is the effect of a centripetal movement of waters and dark fire: space, that of a corresponding centrifugal movement. Here metaphor becomes indistinguishable from belief, when Lawrence asserts that "invisible waters steal . . . right up to feed the sun" and that "new waters are shed away from the sun, into space"; that an "invisible dark fire" rolls its waves to the sun and "new fire floods out into space", and that all this is "scientific", "physically, actually perfect".[64] Here he seems to admit a difference between the "actual" and the symbolic, and, in order either to convince himself or to win the assent of his reader, he endeavours to prove that there is no difference!

But he denounces the "palpable" error of a scientific cosmogony which sees life itself as no more than "a product of reactions in the material universe". God did not withdraw from the universe after creation, but remains immanent within it, filling it in the form of a homogeneous "rare *living* plasm", a "living self-conscious ether", a "creative singleness", the substance of which "divides and subdivides into multiplicity", as an egg subdivides.

This leads him to a cabbalistic notion, traces of which we have already noted in the "Hardy",[65] and which he may well have absorbed from Blake or Swedenborg: "At each new impulse from the creative body, All comes together with All: that is, the one half of the cosmos comes together with the other half, with a dual result." At this point, his argument becomes particularly hard to follow, but it seems that this "coming together" gives birth simultaneously, on two different levels, vital and material, to a new living individual, and to "a new chemical element", a gem. "Every new thing is born from the consummation of the two halves of the universe, the two great halves being the cosmic waters and the cosmic fire of the First Day." A mystic link thus exists between the "two germs of the male and female", which "epitomize the two cosmic principles", and the material elements, water and fire: "Life plasm mysteriously corresponds with inanimate matter." But life plasm, the essence of being, is primordial. The inanimate world is dead matter, "released from the dead body of the world's creatures", the "static residue of the living conscious plasm. Thus the material universe is born of the death of the living universe."[66]

This throws light on the symbolism of "The Crown", *Women in Love* and "The Reality of Peace": merging Blavatsky and Heraclitus, Lawrence sees the universe as a constant dual flux of fire and water. Life is "midway between fire and water" and the two elements must "exquisitely balance, commingle and consummate in the living creature". If either fire or water predominates, it is a sign that "life has withdrawn itself". "Liquid" water is not pure, but already mingled with fire; ice, snow crystals, and "that infinitely suspended invisible element which travels between us and the sun", constitute "the true cosmic element". Air is the product of the living plasm, Earth is its "incalculable and indefinite residuum".

Polarity, sex, and cosmic dualism

Lawrence then asserts the "mystic dualism of pure otherness", which, he says, extends through everything, "even through the *soul* or *self* or *being* of any living being", and from this principle of "duality and otherness" he deduces "the scientific dualism of polarity".[67] The "fourfold activity" of the two cosmic elements, mystic attraction, centrifugal movement in infinite space, is the basis of all creation, and on this "root of four" is established all "law and understanding". On these "supreme truths" the Pythagoreans based their philosophy "of symbolic numbers". They also provide the explanation of the mystic symbols: the Rosicrucian cross within the circle; the Egyptian symbol of life; Aphrodite's circle resting on a cross. How foolish, remarks Lawrence, to give these great signs "a merely phallic indication"!

Yet the sex division is "one of the first mysteries of creation"; while it is not quite true to say that "the one sex is identical with fire, the other with water", there is "some indefinable connexion" between sex and the cosmic elements. The duality of sex parallels the dualism of the cosmic elements. Aphrodite is born of the waters, and Apollo is the sun-god; yet certain races, men and women alike, derive from the sun and have the fiery principle predominant in their constitution (we are reminded of Ursula's "golden light"), whilst others (e.g. Gerald) "blonde, blue-eyed, northern are evidently water-born, born along with the ice-crystals and blue, cold deeps, and yellow, ice-refracted sunshine".[68] Lawrence has adopted mystic forms of reasoning, to which the principles of analytic thought—identity and causality—are never rigorously applied.

The duality of sex, "the mystery of creative *otherness*", is "manifest", and, "given the sexual polarity", sex illustrates the fourfold motion of cosmic creation: "The coming-together of the sexes may be the soft delicate union of pure creation, or it may be the tremendous conjunction of opposition, a vivid struggle, as fire struggles with water in the sun."[69] This coming-together results always in a "birth": in the first case the birth of "a softly rising and budding soul", "harmonious and at one with itself"; in the second, that of a "disintegrative soul, wherein the two principles wrestle in their eternal opposition". This not only provides a mystic and cosmic explanation of Lawrence's own conflicts, but at the same time gives the clearest and most accessible exposition we have of the distinction felt by the novelist between the love of Birkin and Ursula and that of Gudrun and Gerald. It holds the key to the basic contrast on which rests the plot of *Women in Love*, and reveals the esoteric meaning of this novel in so far as it relates to the idea of the decline of the West:

The first kind of birth takes place in the youth of an era, in the mystery of accord: the second kind preponderates in the times of disintegration, the crumbling of an era. But at all times beings are born from the two ways and life is made up of the duality.[70]

In 1934, Barbara Low intimated to the author that while she could not in strictly medical terms say that she had psychoanalysed Lawrence, she had studied him closely over many months. Aldous Huxley in a 1920 letter to his father refers to Lawrence having been "analysed for complexes, dark and tufty ones, tangled in his mind";[70a] this, which reflects London gossip, must relate to events prior to late 1919. Of all the doctors who had anything to do with Lawrence, Barbara Low certainly is the one who knew him best in his darkest hours. Although, from frequent conversations with her and the Eders, Lawrence must surely by this time have increased his knowledge of psychoanalysis, it seems that in 1918 he was seeking elsewhere than in scientific psychology the explanation of his own tendency towards a "disintegration" of personality: a mystic cosmogony seemed to him to hold the answer he was seeking. Lawrence's latent but constantly recurring aversion to all forms of analytical science is demonstrated by this fervid quest for a transcendental explanation, capable of relieving him of the burden of his personal problems by raising them to the cosmic level. His need was to justify rather than explain his own nature, to make it appear consistent with a universal norm, to attribute his own conflicts to the working of a general principle. A psychoanalytical explanation, it must be stressed, does not seem ever to have occurred to him.

Levels of consciousness and their bodily location

On to the affirmation of the fourfold movement of the two principles he proceeds to build a complete psychology, organized around a twofold duality, within which the indications gathered from his psychoanalyst friends are transformed and integrated into his own dualist conception.

Duality and polarity, says Lawrence, assert themselves within the individual psyche by means of the "fourfold creative activity". His own adolescent conflict between the spiritual and animal being is explained by an attempted localization of the different levels of consciousness indebted more to Pryse and to yoga than to modern neuro-psychology. The sole interest of this attempt lies in its revelation of Lawrence's struggle to overcome and justify his own dualism. Meanwhile his analysis of the individual psyche also throws some light on the symbolic vocabulary of his works from *Women in Love* onwards:

> Man is divided, according to old-fashioned phraseology, into the upper and lower man: that is, the spiritual and sensual being. And this division is physical

and actual. The upper body, breast and throat and face, this is the spiritual body; the lower is the sensual. By spiritual being we mean that state of being where the self excels into the universe, and knows all things by passing into all things. It is all blissful consciousness which glows upon the flowers and trees and sky, so that I am sky and flowers, I, who am myself. It is that movement towards a state of infinitude wherein I experience my living oneness with all things.

By sensual being, on the other hand, we mean that state in which the self is the magnificent centre wherein all life pivots, and lapses, as all space passes into the core of the sun. It is a magnificent central positivity, wherein the being sleeps upon the strength of its own reality, as a wheel sleeps in speed on its positive hub. It is a state portrayed in the great dark statues of the seated lords of Egypt. The self is incontestable and unsurpassable.

. . . But in the lower part of the body there is darkness and pivotal pride. There in the abdomen the contiguous universe is drunk into the blood, assimilated, as a wheel's great speed is assimilated into the hub. There the great whirlpool of the dark blood revolves and assimilates all unto itself. Here is the world of living dark waters, where the fire is quenched in watery creation. Here, in the navel, flowers the water-born lotus, the soul of the water begotten by one germ of fire. And the lotus is the symbol of our perfected sensual first-being, which rises in blossom from the unfathomable waters.[71]

The seat of "blood-consciousness" is in the lower body, source of "our strongest self-knowledge", of "the passional self-consciousness". In the nerves, on the other hand, "we pass out and become the universe": but beyond this first duality, breast (the great sympathetic) and bowels (blood, blood-consciousness), there is a deeper and higher duality, face and loins:

All the time, there is some great incomprehensible balance between the upper and lower centres, as when the kiss of the mouth accompanies the passionate embrace of the loins . . . The face and breast belong to the heavens, the luminous infinite. But in the loins we have our unbreakable root, the root of the lotus. There we have our passionate self-possession, our unshakable and indomitable being. There deep calls unto deep.[72]

When there is balance "in first being" between breast and belly, loins and face, "then, and only then, when this fourfold consciousness is established in the body, do we come to full consciousness of the mind". "Full consciousness" thus requires the complete action of a "fourfold consciousness", and it is itself the "conclusive apex" of the "sacred pentagon", the synthesizing and creative agent "perfecting its finite thought and idea as the chemical elements are perfected into finality from the flux". Psychology of a kind mixes here with alchemy, and once more it leads straight to Lawrence's basic aesthetic concept, that of the individual achieving timeless, final perfection, the perfection of the rose, the poppy and the gem. But in this case the idea is based on a mystic interpretation of the body and the dualism of our psychic and physical natures. Lawrence does not deny the spirit, indeed he accords it the place of honour, but he associates it intimately with the equipoise, the harmonization of all the elements of the twofold duality of the living being.

The self and otherness

Besides the mystery of artistic creation, the transmutation of the ephemeral into the eternal, another mystery remains to be explained: that of "otherness": the behaviour of the *self* in relation to *another*. Lawrence seeks an explanation in the "dual polarity" of the body. While hardly intellectually satisfying, this theory at least has the merit of illuminating his symbolism, from "The Crown" to *Women in Love* and beyond. The last few paragraphs of "The Two Principles" throw considerable light on the vocabulary and images of these works, particularly on Birkin's reaction against "oneing" love, and on the language used to describe the character of Gerald Crich; they also enlighten us on the mystic significance of the poem "Manifesto", and the corresponding scenes in *The Rainbow* and *Women in Love*.

"The great sympathetic activity of the human system" is polarized with the "voluntary system": "The front part of the body is open and receptive, the great valve of the universe. But the back is sealed, closed. And it is from the ganglia of the spinal system that the *will* acts in direct compulsion, outwards":

> The great plexuses of the breast and face act in the motion of oneing, from these the soul goes forth in the spiritual oneing. Corresponding to this, the thoracic ganglion and the cervical ganglia are the great centres of spiritual compulsion or control or dominion, the great *second* or negative activity of the spiritual self. From these ganglia go forth the motions and commands which *force* the external universe into that state which accords with the spiritual will-to-unification, the will for equality. Equality, and religious agreement, and social virtue are enforced as well as found. And it is from the ganglia of the upper body that this compulsion to equality and virtue is enforced.
>
> In the same way, from the lumbar ganglion and from the sacral ganglion acts the great sensual will to dominion. From these centres the soul goes forth haughty and indomitable, seeking for mastery. These are the great centres of activity in soldiers, fighters: as also in the tiger and the cat the power-centre is at the base of the spine, in the sacral ganglion. All the tremendous sense of power and mastery is located in these centres of volition, there where the back is walled and strong, set blank against life.
>
> So the division of the psychic body is fourfold. If we are divided horizontally at the diaphragm, we are divided also perpendicularly. The upright division gives us our polarity, our for and against, our mystery of right and left.

Any man who is perfect and fulfilled lives in fourfold activity. He knows the sweet spiritual communion, and he is at the same time a sword to enforce the spiritual level; he knows the tender unspeakable sensual communion, but he is a tiger against anyone who would abate his pride and his liberty.[73]

Thus in the chapter "Excurse" it is by acting on the sacral ganglion that Ursula unleashes in Birkin the dominating activity which will make of him a "Pharaoh", a complete being no longer limiting himself to seeking a "merging" with woman but asserting his "otherness", his separate existence. The vague caresses of Lydia and Tom Brangwen, apparently also liberating the individuality of both partners, are succeeded by more definite gestures, the mystic significance of which now becomes clear, even if they also correspond to a psychological idiosyncrasy of Lawrence's. Similarly in "Manifesto", the poet, "touched" by his wife where he is most "other", is freed from the painful feeling of being an object belonging to this woman, of being "confused" with her; both are then enabled to become "freer than angels", to live in the fullness of the moment, in the "mystic NOW". This liberation is achieved by the acceptance by each partner of the total otherness of the other, shorn of all desire for domination or submission:

> We shall love, we shall hate,
> but it will be like music, sheer utterance,
> issuing straight out of the unknown,
> the lightning and the rainbow appearing in us unbidden, unchecked,
> like ambassadors.[74]

The psychology of the chakras thus corroborates his desire to rediscover spontaneity of being, to love without shame, without the humiliation of feeling subjected to the woman. Spontaneity in love is achieved through the perfect equipoise of yoga.

The symbolic import of art

For Lawrence a mystic universe exists at the very core of the physical universe. Matter and spirit are fused into one. Manifestations of perfection, —gems, flowers, beasts, and certain humans—are the result of perfect balance, perfect harmonization of the two principles, of a dualism constantly recurring in an infinite number of dichotomies, which are seen as complementary whereas to small minds they may seem contradictory. How far is this a poetical game, and where does belief begin? At the time of writing "The Two Principles", Lawrence was certainly carried away into belief, even to a greater extent than in *Fantasia of the Unconscious*, in which, despite the suggestion of a game implicit in the title, he adopts towards "official science" a pose of detachment, asserting that his intuitions are worth far more than any analytical effort. Yet these are still ambivalent attitudes; the thirsting after certainty, the lure of poetry and of the flashing image, the need for some ultimate explanation and justification of his own contradictory impulses are still subject to the watchfulness of a critical mind and practical intelligence. The desperate will to believe is there, the longing for an assured faith, for a total explanation of his universe.

In "The Two Principles" he succumbs to the lure of occultism, and of a fanciful brand of neuro-psychology. And yet his starting-point was that of a literary critic conscious not only of the value of symbols, but also of their limits. As always his thought revolves around the two poles of sex and artistic creation, but in the 1918 studies the latter is mercifully predominant.

"Art speech, art utterance", he asserts, is and will always be "the greatest universal language of mankind, greater than any esoteric symbolism".[75] He also affirms the pre-eminence of spontaneous art, based on "pure experience", over a system of "authorized" symbols founded on "a thought or an idea, some *mental* concept".[76]

Reduced, diminished by analysis to its "didactic capacity", a work of art appears as "a subtle and complex idea expressed in symbols". And "for certain purposes, it is necessary to degrade a work of art into a thing of meanings and reasoned exposition. This process of reduction is part of the science of criticism." By applying it to American writers, Lawrence distinguishes in their works on the one hand their didactic import, "the development of the orthodox European idea on American soil", and on the other their "profound symbolic import", which proceeds from the writer's "unconscious or subconscious soul as he works in a state of creation which is something like somnambulism or dreaming".[77]

Here we have come full circle back to his critical starting-point: having first postulated an active unconscious, conditioned by the spirit of place, he has identified matter and spirit as the unity beyond universal dualism; the gems of art, which stem from the subconscious, are identified with the gems of the earth, produced by a mystic transmutation of men and souls under the effects of the spirit of place. Nature is the source of all art, as of all creation, of all life: the aesthetic of "The Crown" is thus confirmed, and directed towards that which is purest and most original in Lawrence, whether in poetry or in prose:

> Every great locality expresses itself perfectly, in its own flowers, its own birds and beasts, lastly its own men, with their perfected works. Mountains convey themselves in unutterable expressed perfection in the blue gentian flower and in the edelweiss flower, so soft, yet shaped like snow-crystals. The very strata of the earth come to a point of perfect, unutterable concentration in the inherent sapphires and emeralds. It is so with all worlds and all places of the world. We may take it as a law.[78]

Blood-consciousness and instinct:
the myths of art

The spirit of place is transmitted to human beings directly through the blood, without passing through the nervous system:

> What we call "instinct" in creatures such as bees, or ants, or whales, or foxes, or larks, is the sure and perfect working of the primary mind in these creatures. All the tissue of the body is all the time aware. The blood is awake: the whole blood-system of the body is a great field of primal consciousness . . . When a bee leaves its hive and circles round to sense the locality, it is . . . establishing a primary *rapport* between its own, very tissue and the tissue of adjacent objects.[79]

In the nervous system this "primal consciousness" is localized, specialized. Each nerve centre has "its own peculiar consciousness, its own peculiar mind, its own primary percepts and concepts, its own spontaneous desires and ideas". The "primary *rapport*" between the "tissue" of the bee and "the tissue of adjacent objects", is a "physical thought", a "sensual concept".[80]

This subliminal, physical, sensual thought is expressed in myth:

> The primary or sensual mind of man expresses itself most profoundly in myth . . . Myth is the utterance of the primary self-knowledge of the dynamic psyche of man . . . [which] . . . utters, in terms more or less monstrous, its own fundamental knowledge of its own genesis. Owing to the great co-ordination of everything in the universe, the genesis of the psyche of the human species is at the same time the genesis of the sun, the moon, and the thunderbolt: indeed, the genesis of everything . . .

Because everything in the universe is "co-ordinated" "the genesis of the psyche of the human species is at the same time the genesis of the sun, the moon, and the thunderbolt . . . And the clue or active quick of the creative mystery lies in the human psyche."[81]

This is tantamount to asserting that nothing exists except in the human mind. But so great is Lawrence's mistrust of abstract knowledge that this idealism is reached only by way of affirming that the actual matter of the body is spiritual in nature, by asserting a monism of spirit and matter. It is "in the human soul, the human psyche, the human anima" that the quick of the creative mystery lies; hence "the only form of worship is to be: each man to be his own self, that which has issue from the mystery and takes form as an inscrutable self. In the soul, the self, the very man unto himself, the god-mystery is active and evident first and foremost."[82]

Man's conscious understanding of the world is a dual progression. The "sensual mind" that has its seat in the lower centres creates first myth, then art, while the "reasoning" mind, starting from the great cosmogonies of the ancient world, tries via the natural sciences "to gain an inkling of the connexion between scientific reality and creative, personal reality". Gradually there comes about "a pure unison between religion and science", a "harmony between the two halves of the psyche". Myth, which is repugnant to reason, and scientific cosmogony, rejected by the "passional psyche", must be reconciled, so that man "can really begin to be free, really to live his whole self, his whole life, in fulness". The role of art is to liberate the individual in a synthesis: "When the unison between art and philosophy is complete, then knowledge will be in full, not always in part as it is now."[83] Art is the supreme synthesis, the creative act of the individual.

Confessions of an artist approaching a synthesis

Lawrence's discussion of the various American writers teems with such ideas, more or less haphazardly expressed. The system expounded is neither complete nor coherent, and it would be easy to point to important discrepancies between passages referring to various forms of consciousness. Lawrence's position in regard to esoteric myths varies according to whether he lets himself be carried away by his artistic imagination to expound ancient cosmogonies and the yoga doctrine of the vital centres, or whether he reacts as a man of the twentieth century not totally disrespectful of the scientific turn of mind. He is still impressed by science—witness his rhetorical appeals for scientific confirmation of his wildest assertions—but it does not satisfy his mind. In measured terms, he affirms the supremacy of art, as a synthesis of all forms of knowledge. The reader who makes comparisons can but be struck by the poise and serenity of the passages on myth, science and art in the first essay on Hawthorne, in sharp contrast with the truculent attitude later adopted in *Fantasia of the Unconscious* and in the first essay on Melville,[84] revised in Sicily in 1920 and characterized by an increasing irritation with science. An important feature of Lawrence's philosophical and critical work of 1918 is this quest for a synthesis of myth and science, surely a step in the direction of a certain equipoise, and probably encouraged by reading, or talks with Dr Eder, on the subject of psychoanalysis.

More strongly than the American studies published in volume form in 1924, after they had been rewritten twice and in some cases three times (in Sicily in 1920 and in America in 1923), the *English Review* essays mark a definite advance in Lawrence's development, a step towards a synthesis between his deepest aspirations and his new reading. Just as at the age of twenty-four he assimilated the technique and themes of George Moore, and between 1910 and 1915 absorbed Nietzsche, the Russian novelists and

Chamberlain, so between 1916 and 1918 he digests Pryse and Blavatsky, taking from them whatever corresponds to his preconceived ideas, to his needs. That he also had some contact with the psychoanalysts is proved by the use of terms like "sublimation", certain ideas on myth and legend, at least one clear allusion to the Oedipus complex, and even one to Jung, possibly added on the proofs since the article appeared in April 1919, and he does not seem to have read Jung until late 1918.[85] Just as in 1914, when seeking artistic renewal and adjusting his conception of character and his style before rewriting *The Rainbow*, he chose Hardy as a subject of study, so in 1917 he turns to the Americans, the men of the New World, whom he then sees as harbingers or founders of a new humanity. In Fenimore Cooper, Hawthorne, Melville and Whitman, then his heroes, he is still seeking the psychological foundations of Rananim, whereas Franklin and Crèvecœur are seen as "asserting the triumph of materialism", of political and economic abstraction, "the triumph of the will of man and of the laws of the mechanical universe, over the creative mystery itself".[86] They are seen as agents of "reduction" of a democratic America which he already finds repellent, and which by 1923 will be an object of hatred.

His interest is naturally attracted by the origins and development of American puritanism, at a time when he himself is endeavouring to formulate a personal religion in opposition to the Calvinism in which he had been brought up and in which he sees the origin of his maladjustment to life. In attacking Franklin's egalitarianism and economic democracy, his real target is the Calvinist heritage of the Pilgrim Fathers. Hence his denunciation of their unconscious "gloomy and tyrannical sense of power", their desire to "annihilate all living impulses", their "dangerous negative religious passion of repression".[87] Just as America had originally given Spain "the impulse to religious cruelty", which explains the Inquisition, so it *called to* the Pilgrim Fathers, offering them what their puritanism craved, a spirit of place which "would lend them force to satisfy their lust of anti-life".[88] No doubt with Chamberlain's lessons in mind, Lawrence here makes a distinction between Bernard of Clairvaux, St Francis of Assisi and Martin Luther, all liberators of the human soul, and puritan Calvinism, the anti-life religion which perpetuates the Jewish "assertion of control over the natural functions" demonstrated in the rite of circumcision, in the frenzied self-mutilations of St Simeon or St Anthony.[89] He reproves as one and the same error the Calvinism of the New England colonists and the mechanization of production "which is the clue to Western democracy", substituting for the "rich, passional contact" between men "the vast mechanical concord of innumerable machine parts".[90] Egalitarian democracy is anti-life: "as long as we believe in Equality, so long shall we grind mechanically till, like most Jews, we have no living soul, no living self but only a supermachine faculty which will coin money".[91] Faced with a democratic, mechanized America, in which the "natural impulsive" has withered and been replaced by "the deliberate, self-determined being, the perfect businessman", the American who, "like the Jew", suffers from a "torturing frictional unease, an incapacity to rest", Lawrence falls to prophesying: just as the England of Lloyd George is not the true nation of his dreams, so the America of Woodrow Wilson is not the true, the primitive America:

> This is not the reality of America. It is only the reality of our own negation that the vast aboriginal continent reflects back at us. There will come an America which we cannot foretell, a new creation on the face of the earth, a world beyond us. The early Christianity produced monstrous growths, monstrous reflections of the world then dying, distorted and made huge by the new spirit. These monstrosities, like enormous horrifying phantoms that men do not care to remember, disappeared, leaving the new era to roll slowly on to the European summer. So the mechanical monstrosity of the West will presently disappear.[92]

Lawrence is here venting his disappointment and rancour at America's entry into the war: this passage is his goodbye to Rananim. Already he turns to Australia as a last desperate hope. The conflict between puritanism, the triumph of will over instinctive being, and the emanations of the American earth and sky, such is the subject of the new lyric confession poured out in this first version of the studies in American literature. Much more measured and balanced than his 1923 judgments, these analyses of the great New England writers contain many scraps of confession, many revealing phrases. While discussion of Lawrence's considered attitudes to those writers belongs to a later period, certain traits noted in 1918 are of interest here because they are in fact his own recognized in them.

Crèvecœur is seen as a precursor of *Birds, Beasts and Flowers*. To Lawrence he is essentially a master in the art of painting nature: "He can only see insects, birds and snakes in their own pristine being."[93] Fenimore Cooper is mystically linked with the aboriginal American warriors in the same way as the pure Englishman Birkin felt himself linked with the Germanic Gerald. "All futurity for him lay latent, not in the white woman but in the dark, magnificent presence of American warriors, with whom he would be at one in the ultimate atonement between races."[94] This sentence may perhaps even explain Lawrence's intent in making Gerald, with his German university education, the representative of the blond Nordic race.

Also apropos of Cooper, Lawrence predicts the "slow, implacable revenge" of nature, of the Spirit of Place, on a civilization which sterilizes the creative world.[95] Poe symbolizes for him the decline of the Western soul, the inevitable death of "the great psyche which we have evolved through two thousand years of effort" and which must die "by a long, slow process of disintegration". Poe's *Fall of the House of Usher* is used to illustrate his theory of the blood that has its "sympathies and responses to the material world, quite apart from seeing".[96] In Hawthorne we catch a glimpse of Ursula and her devastation of Skrebensky, of Gudrun and her death-like effect on Gerald: "The woman isolate or in advance of man is always mystically destructive."[97] In Melville he discovers the affirmation that "the sea is the material home of the deep sacral-sexual consciousness".[98]

Whitman, woman and male comradeship

In this first or second version, his admiration goes instinctively to Whitman, the guide and master of his youth, well known to him through Willie Hopkin and possibly through the works of Carpenter:[99] in the 1924 text, on the contrary, Lawrence will hold Whitman up to ridicule, as though ashamed of the earlier self who had admired and imitated him.

The 1918 manuscript is lost but the 1921 text remains relatively close to Lawrence's chief preoccupations at the time he probably wrote the first version, that is to say before reading Jung, but already in violent reaction against "merging" with a woman, against the *Magna Mater* recognized in Frieda. The aesthetic of poetry expressed in this second version is also close to that of the "Hardy", of "The Crown" and of the 1919 preface to the American edition of *New Poems*.[100] The value of this essay as a confession, a revelation of Lawrence's deepest personal anxieties, is such that, together with this preface, it constitutes perhaps the clearest commentary on those poems—"New Heaven and Earth" and, up to a point, "Manifesto"—which express the quintessence of Lawrence's emotional life and esoteric thought from 1916 to 1919.

While Whitman is "the greatest of the Americans" and "one of the greatest poets of the world", some "element of falsity", says Lawrence, still troubles us in him. The Christians have tried "to *annihilate* the sensual being in man", by affirming that he is, in reality, pure spirit. The sensual being once conquered, man tends to "provoke mental reactions in the physical self" . . . "from the mind, and nothing spontaneous". This is what "the aesthetes and symbolists, from Baudelaire and Maeterlinck and Oscar Wilde, and nearly all later Russian, French and English novelists" have done: hence "a vicious living and spurious art"; idealism puts an end to spontaneity.

This, continues Lawrence, is also true of Whitman; but while sometimes affected, over-self-conscious, Whitman goes further, "in actual living expression", "in life-knowledge", than any other: "it is he who surmounts the grand climacteric of our civilization".[101] Here both language and thought are reminiscent of Pryse, as are allusions to St John the Evangelist and the Greek esoteric writers:

Whitman enters on the last phase of spiritual triumph. He really arrives at that stage of infinity which the seers sought. By subjecting the *deepest centres* of the lower self, he attains the maximum consciousness in the higher self: a degree of extensive consciousness greater, perhaps, than any man in the modern world.[102]

Lawrence's commentary on Whitman here derives straight from Pryse's description of the "conquest" of the chakras by the "seer" who can then "know the eternal realities":[103] the very terms of St John's initiation as described by the Irish theosophist. This interpretation of Whitman may also owe something to Edward Carpenter's *The Art of Creation*, Chapter IV, "The Stages of Consciousness". Carpenter here quotes another of Whitman's disciples, Dr R. M. Bucke, the American alienist whose book attempts, as did Lawrence after Carpenter, to find a physiological location for "cosmic consciousness".[104] Lawrence may well have known of this work through the Hopkins; Bucke's list of heroes achieving cosmic consciousness, including Whitman and Carpenter, both personal friends of Bucke, includes many of Lawrence's own heroes.

For Lawrence, as for Carpenter, Whitman's greatness lies in his attainment to "a state of infinite comprehension" of life:

> The quick is the living being, the quick of quicks is the individual soul. And it is here, at the quick, that Whitman proceeds to find the experience of infinitude, his vast extension, or concentrated intensification into Allness. He carries the conquest to its end . . . The great oneness, the experience of infinity, the triumph of the living spirit, which at last includes everything, is here accomplished.[105]

Whitman's paean "of praise and deliverance and accession" is "man's maximum state of consciousness, his highest state of spiritual being. Supreme spiritual consciousness and the divine drunkenness of supreme consciousness." Thus Whitman becomes "in his own person, the whole world, the whole universe, the whole eternity of time".

Here, however, Lawrence parts company with Whitman: "Even at his maximum a man is not more than himself. When he is infinite, he is still himself. He still has a nose to wipe."[106] A man is himself, and only himself, that is the first and essential truth. And the second is that Whitman's "En-Masse, his Democracy", is only "an enormous half-truth". To democracy Lawrence opposes authority, Pharaoh, the conqueror. The other half is "Jehovah, and Egypt and Sennacherib: the other form of Allness, terrible and grand, even as in the Psalms".[107] Whitman's way to Allness is through "endless sympathy, merging"; but, says Lawrence, every systole has its diastole, all life alternates between two poles, "the shuttle comes and goes". "The direction is twofold. Whitman's *one direction* becomes a hideous tyranny once he has attained his goal of Allness. His One Identity is a prison of horror, once realized."[108] The same horror which comes over the poet of "New Heaven and Earth" when, after identifying himself with all things to the point of desiring death:

> Creator, I looked at my creation;
> created, I looked at myself, the creator;
> it was a maniacal horror in the end.[109]

A prison of horror in which the "motion of merging" becomes "disintegration", and expansion into unification breaks down "into slime, imbecility, epilepsy and vice, like Dostoevsky".

But in attaining to his "infinite state" Whitman shows himself a precursor, a pioneer opening up "a new field of living": he drives on to the very centre of life and sublimates even this into consciousness"; he lives in "the ecstasy of *giving himself*"; he treats woman as "a great function—no more", "a submissive function . . . no longer an individual being with a living soul . . . Function of sex, function of birth."

This is a remarkably long way from the original conception of "The Sisters", "woman becoming an individual". The man of the future, the Lawrentian hero (*Aaron's Rod* was begun at about this time) will dispense with woman:

> Acting from the last and profoundest centres, man acts womanless. It is no longer a question of race continuance. It is a question of sheer, ultimate being, the perfection of life, nearest to death. Acting from these centres, man is an extreme being, the unthinkable warrior, creator, mover and maker.
>
> And the polarity is between man and man. Whitman alone of all moderns has known this positively. Others have known it negatively, *pour épater les bourgeois*. But Whitman knew it positively, in its tremendous knowledge, knew the extremity, the perfectness and the fatality.
>
> . . . And he tells the mystery of manly love, the love of comrades. Continually he tells us the same truth: the new world will be built upon the love of comrades, the new great dynamic of life will be manly love. Out of this inspiration the creation of the future.[110]

This passage, possibly rewritten in 1920, may owe something to the first stirrings of Italian fascism; however this may be, it certainly evokes many deep Lawrentian echoes, from the bathing scene in *The White Peacock*, the wrestling between Birkin and Gerald, to the scenes with Murry at Higher Tregerthen, and the evenings passed in company with William Henry Hocking. Weininger's gospel of Lohengrin-like liberation from the female yoke seems also to have left its traces, merged no doubt with Wagnerian mysticism. The passage is essentially a synthesis of various influences which, in the Lawrence of *Aaron's Rod* and other post-war novels, fuse with certain undercurrents of the writer's ambiguous self.

Lawrence remains faithful to his admiration of Whitman right up to the end of this essay. The poet of "Calamus" has touched "the confines of death", for "creative life must come near to death to link up the mystic circuit. The pure warriors must stand on the brink of death." How much this means to Lawrence in 1918 appears from a contemporary letter in which he sees "in Calamus and Comrades one of the clues to a real solution—the next adjustment".[111]

The Lawrence of the Nietzschean invocation to death in "The Reality of Peace" is here speaking with emotion of the poet of the Civil War. His passing homage to marriage gains full significance only if we recall his own feelings for his wife in 1918: marriage "the external orbit", so he says, comes *after* asexual friendship, family, clan and nation but *before* "love between comrades, the manly love which alone can create a new era of life". Does this mean that love between men is not asexual? Marriage should not supersede "friendship, family and nationality" but "fulfil" them. "A wife or husband who sets about to annul the old, pre-marriage affections and connexions ruins the foundations of marriage." Is this meant personally?

Similarly friendship between men should not destroy marriage:

> The ultimate comradeship is the final progression from marriage; it is the last seedless flower of pure beauty, beyond purpose. But if it destroys marriage it makes itself purely deathly. In its beauty, the ultimate comradeship flowers on the brink of death. But it flowers from the root of all life upon the blossoming tree of life.[112]

Whitman thus appears as the harbinger of the "great life-circuit which borders on death in all its round", of the great and sacred "relationship of comrades" on which depends "the future of mankind", of the truth "beyond marriage". The new era now dawning will be the era of "the new perfect circuit of our being", the epoch of the establishment of the "love of comrades, as marriage is really established now", of the "starry maturity" of man. More than any other of the American writers studied in the 1918 essays, Whitman provides Lawrence with the occasion for reflection on themes which have been perplexing and troubling him in various ways since 1912, inspiring a train of thought slow and uncertain in finding full expression.

Whitman was the master and inspirer of Carpenter. In his *Days with Walt Whitman*[113] Carpenter stresses the exclusively male nature of the poet's loves, his feigned liaisons with women and his pretence at having fathered children. In this essay Whitman emerges clearly as advocate of "the seedless flower", the cult of the tree of life on the very brink of death. Can it be because the essay contained in fact a confession of his own true desires that

Lawrence hesitated to publish it? In a letter to his American publisher condemning the activities of "smut hunters"[114] he expressed the thought that Huebsch might find it "politic" not to publish the essay on Whitman, in which case it should be cut altogether since Lawrence did not want it altered. This letter suggests that the 1921 version may not have been greatly altered as compared with the 1918 text.

"Poetry of the present"

In 1918, Whitman still represents to Lawrence the model, the ideal of an aesthetic based on the beauty of the mystic moment, the spontaneous accord between the self and the universe. In the last pages of this essay we find the clearest, purest, simplest message of this early version of the studies in American literature:

> Whitman, at his best, is purely himself. His verse springs sheer from the spontaneous sources of his being. Hence its lovely, lovely form and rhythm: at the best. It is sheer, perfect human spontaneity, spontaneous as a nightingale throbbing, but still controlled, the highest loveliness of human spontaneity, undecorated, unclothed. The whole being is there sensually throbbing, spiritually quivering, mentally, ideally speaking. It is not, like Swinburne, an exaggeration of the one part of being. It is perfect and whole. The whole soul speaks at once, and it is too pure for mechanical assistance of rhyme and measure. The perfect utterance of a concentrated spontaneous soul. The unforgettable loveliness of Whitman's lines![115]

Lawrence was then seeking in American literature what he had already found within himself: the expression of "pure present":

> . . . the most superb mystery we have hardly recognized: the immediate, instant self. The quick of all time is the instant. The quick of all the universe, of all creation, is the incarnate, carnal self.[116]

Despite the lure of the esoteric and occultist beliefs, which led to the digressions of the essays as published in *The English Review*, he returns in the end to the modern and essentially personal aesthetic of "Poetry of the Present" and of the Whitman essay; in the last resort the creative instinct, the sense of beauty snatched from the eternity of the universal flow count more for him than the wild rhetoric of magic "explanations". But for every gem created, how much dross, and how much barren waste!

"EDUCATION OF THE PEOPLE"

Between 1918 and 1919 Lawrence thus appears to be torn in two opposite directions: one the true, pure way of an aesthetic of the present, of enjoyment of the immediate; the other, impure, way towards leadership of a despised mankind, the lure of power. After a temporary eclipse in 1916, the ending of the war seems to have renewed the attraction of the second path. "Education of the People", and, to some extent, *Movements in European History*, show a survival of the ideas of 1915 and the persistence of the authoritarian, pessimistic, socially conservative ideas of an author who had originally thought he had leanings towards evolutionary socialism.

The text of "Education of the People" published in the posthumous collection *Phoenix* bears evident marks of its revision and expansion in Taormina in June 1920, when Lawrence had just finished writing *Psychoanalysis and the Unconscious*.[117] In September 1918 he reported having written "three little essays" under this title; by December they had become four.[118] After *The Times Educational Supplement* had refused them Lawrence entertained the idea of turning them into a book which Barbara Low was to have submitted to Stanley Unwin.[119] The first four essays differ considerably from the bulk of the other eight, and all allusions suggesting either Italy or the post-war period are to be found exclusively from the fifth essay onwards. Knowing Lawrence's methods of work, it is of course possible he may have been expanding texts first drafted in 1918-19. However that may be, up to and including the fourth essay, he is writing for H. A. L. Fisher, President of the Board of Education, whereas as from the fifth, and above all the sixth, he is writing for himself, taking up and reformulating his own ideas on psychology, on mother and child, on the coming of a new era, on the supreme role the future reserves for male friendship and martial exercise. The themes developed in the later essays are the same as those of the "Whitman" and of certain passages of *Aaron's Rod*. They provide further evidence of the persistence of certain of his obsessions between 1918 and 1921.

Confirmation of certain subsisting tendencies rather than new developments thus characterizes both "Education of the People" and *Movements in European History*, written at the same time, ostensibly in response to the same financial needs, but covertly pursuing the same ideological ends. Both works reveal the essentially anti-social nature of his message at the end of the dark years marking the close of his young manhood.

Lawrence's late 1918 social criticism, like that of Ursula in *The Rainbow*, is dominated by the idea of the poor, "the human implements of industrialism", and it is striking to note to what extent this rebel, this would-be liberator, accepts and takes for granted a social stratification almost as rigid as that later satirically portrayed in Aldous Huxley's *Brave New World*. To

Lawrence the educator, "the people" are synonymous with "the poor", for ever destined to irremediable degradation. Granted, they are also the humble possessors of a spark of "the divine nature", whose feet the Pope washes "in symbolic recognition"; but the programme of education that Lawrence the realist draws up for them is essentially utilitarian and conservative, and is inspired by contempt, social pessimism and despair.

Instruction a social danger

Elementary education, Lawrence asserts, aims at producing (1) the perfect citizen and (2) the perfect individual. But neither citizenship nor self-expression is clearly defined for the teachers; Lawrence concentrates his attack on the inanities of self-expression as practised in schools, and advocates "pitching them overboard" in favour of a purely utilitarian elementary technical education:

> Every teacher knows that it is worse than useless trying to educate at least fifty per cent of his scholars. Worse than useless: it is dangerous, perilously dangerous . . . For the uninstructible outnumber the instructible by a very large majority.[120]

Young helots of seven to twelve will thus be taught reading, writing and "a modicum" of arithmetic, as well as "martial exercises and the rudiments of domestic labour", prior to being "apprenticed to some trade" at fourteen, and to earning their own living at sixteen.

In secondary schools, two years' study will suffice to distinguish "those who are apparently 'complete' as far as mental education can make them", who will then be drafted into "some apprenticeship for some sort of semi-profession, such as school-teaching and all forms of clerking".

The remaining scholars, "of the third or highest class", will at the age of sixteen be drafted into colleges, until the age of twenty, after which they will be given two years of "final training" as "doctors, lawyers, priests, artists and so on".[121]

Such an educational set-up would no doubt result in a social stratification somewhat on the lines of that recommended in a memorandum produced by a Committee of the Federation of British Industries, and attacked as reactionary in a *Daily News* article by R. H. Tawney in February 1918, under the title "Keep the Workers' Children in their Place".[122]

All education would be State education, on a strictly egalitarian basis, teachers being selected "for their power to control and instruct children, not for their power to pass examinations". Headmasters would always be men of the highest education, and, once established, "will be like a magistrate in a community", responsible for judging the scholars and deciding "the next move" for the child, who would be consulted, although the headmaster and, ultimately, the inspector, would always have "the final word".

The existing system of education was "extravagantly expensive, and simply dangerous to our social existence" because it produced "a lot of half-informed youth" who "despise the whole business of understanding and wisdom and who realize that in a world like ours nothing but money matters".[123] What if the system proposed put too much power into the hands of the masters and inspectors? "Better there than in the hands of factory owners and trade unions." Someone must choose for the children, who cannot choose for themselves. Dictatorship by "wise" men: such was the apparent aim of a reformer prepared to "shut up all the elementary schools at once" and keep them shut: elementary education had been "fatal" because it had not paid sufficient attention to differences in intelligence between children: "We've got to shape our course by some just idea. We shaped it by a *faulty idea of equality and the perfectibility of man*. Now for the true idea: either that or the precipice edge."[124] [*Italics added.*]

For "in no sense whatever are men actually equal": Lawrence's doctrine of the "pristine incomparable nature of every individual soul"[125] goes hand-in-hand with a contempt for those he judges his "inferiors". Since every man should have "every opportunity to come to his own intrinsic fulness of being",[126] and since "his own nature is his destiny, not his purse", equality and fraternity are no more than empty words, destinies being neither equal nor convergent. Each being is "single, starrily single, . . . not to be blurred or confused" with any other. "We want quality of life, not quantity", "distinct individuals" which are "incompatible with swarms and masses. A small, choice population, not a horde of hopeless units."[127] All of which amounts in fact to allowing "fulness of being" only to a small, elect minority.

The new era will therefore need "life-priests", leaders, inspectors "deeply initiated into the mysteries of life, adepts in the dark mystery of living, fearing nothing but life itself, and subject to nothing but their own reverence for the incalculable life-gesture".[128] Thus, as inspector of schools, a Birkin will be a dictator of human destinies, an archangel designating the elect. "Education of the People" confirms the profound significance attached by Lawrence to the character of Birkin, at once harbinger and magus of a new society.

Education in a caste-ridden society

The educational system he recommends will "inevitably produce distinct classes of society".[129] Shaped like a pyramid of castes the base is "the great class of workers", from among whom will be recruited "the masters of industry, and, probably, the leading soldiers". Next comes "the clerkly caste", elementary teachers, minor professionals, local government officials. Thirdly we have "the class of the higher professions, legal, medical, scholastic". And finally "the small class of the supreme judges: not merely legal judges but judges of the destiny of the nation".

In a social system "primarily religious and only secondarily practical", educators, as the supreme judges of human destinies, will take as criteria for assigning a man to a particular caste not his professional aptitudes, but his "profound natural life-understanding", his "profound life-quality . . . his soul-strength and his soul-wisdom, which cause him to be a natural master of life . . . The highest quality will be living understanding, not intellectual understanding."[130] For egalitarian democracy, for an oligarchy of wealth, Lawrence substitutes a vitalist theocracy, a system "established on the living religious faculty in men". A benevolent dictatorship, a despotism illuminated rather than enlightened, founded on an anti-evolutionist conception of the individual, on a mystic acceptance of inequality, leading to a kind of shamanism, a charismatic conception of the social structure:

> The great volcanoes stand isolate. And at the same time the life-issues concentrate in certain individuals. Why it is so, we don't know. But why should we know? We are, after all, *only* individuals, we are not the eternal life-mystery itself.
>
> And therefore there will always be the vast, living masses of mankind, incoherent and almost expressionless by themselves, carried to perfect expression in the great individuals of their race and time. As the leaves of a tree accumulate towards blossom, so will the great bulk of mankind at all time accumulate towards its leaders. We don't want to turn every leaf of an apple tree into a flower. And so why should we want to turn every individual human being into a unit of complete expression? Why should it be our goal to turn every coal-miner into a Shelley or a Parnell? We can't do either. Coal-miners are consummated in a Parnell, and Parnells are consummated in a Shelley. That is how life takes its way: rising as a volcano rises to an apex, not in a countless multiplicity of small issues.
>
> Time to recognize again this great truth of human life, and to put it once more into practice. Democracy is gone beyond itself. The true democracy is that in which a people gradually cumulate, from the vast base of the populace upwards through the zones of life and understanding to the summit where the great man, or the most perfect utterer, is alone.[131]

"*The most perfect utterer*", the supreme interpreter of a non-revealed religion, of "passionate consciousness"—this is what Lawrence would oppose to the egalitarian reduction of humanity to the lowest common denominator, that of the pay packet: in place of this "mechanistic", automatized unit, he wants to construct an "organic" social system, depending on "the profound spontaneous soul of man",[132] and to establish such a system, even at the price of revolution, he will begin by introducing "compulsory instruction of all teachers in the new idea";[133] by reducing schooling to the strict minimum—the three Rs, domestic work and martial exercises—and by slashing the education budget!

Anti-evolutionism and contempt for man

It is not difficult to understand Freeman's lack of enthusiasm for these articles designed to appear in his *Times Educational Supplement* at a time when H. A. L. Fisher was preparing to make education more democratic than after the 1902 reform—to which, incidentally, Lawrence owed his schooling and his career. Of the great democratic impulse of wartime England Lawrence fails to see anything but the meaner side, the demagogic aspects and the claims for higher wages. He sees no potentialities of individual development outside his mystic vitalism, and relegates to second place, or even excludes completely from the range of education, man's intellectual development or the extension of knowledge, which he considers harmful and would subordinate to the religious development of the individual. Having rejected the dogma of his own childhood religion, Lawrence quickly reverts to authoritarian and hierarchic doctrines, in the name of a religion of life, and seeks in botany, in static forms of life, the stability of species and of individuals invariably invoked by those denying the perfectibility of man. For Lawrence, interpreting in his own way the Lamarckian idea of exfoliation dear to Whitman and to Carpenter, is denying evolution:

> There is no evolving, only unfolding. The lily is in the bit of dust which is its beginning, lily and nothing but lily: and the lily in blossom is a *nec plus ultra*: there is no evolving beyond . . . So also, a pure Chinaman: there is no evolving beyond, only a slipping back, or rather rotting back, through all the coloured phases of retrogression and corruption, back to nought. This is the real truth. Man was man in eternity, has been man since the beginnings of time, and is man in the resultant eternity, no evolution only unfolding of what *is* man. And the same with the Chinaman: no evolution beyond the Chinaman, none, none, none . . . There are animal *principles* in man, which totemism recognizes, but these have nothing evolutionary.[134]

This theory shows the link between his occultism, his educational theories, and Birkin's attitude towards mankind: despair and contempt, a refusal to believe in the possibility of salvation save for a few predestined beings. It will be for the high priests and the judges to discover the elect, who in turn can be given responsibility for the destiny of the race: in fact he sees no hope except for the predestined. Whatever he may say to the contrary, the development of the individual is for Lawrence a question not of intelli-

gence and of education, but of revelation. When he expresses the wish that
"a man's destiny shall be shaped into the natural form of that man's being,
not as now, where children are rammed down into ready-made destinies,
like so much canned fish", his conception is static: the real aim is the detection
of those destined for priesthood. "Big classes will not matter. The *personal*
element, personal supervision is of no moment."[135] In other words, he is
ready to dispense a mass-produced elementary education to a blind and
docile rank and file, and to dissociate arts and crafts from any form of
intellectual activity. This form of mass education on the cheap is conditioning
rather than education, and is based on a pessimism which, without going so
far as to assert that the people has no soul, is none the less convinced that "it
will never know, by itself, what to do with its own soul":

> The populace partakes of the flower of life: only leaves of grass. And shall
> we hew down the Tree of Life for the sake of the leaves of grass?[136]

He sees no hope for the masses: they will follow the path of blind technique without soul or intelligence, seen by Birkin in the African statuette.

Towards Fantasia of the Unconscious

In the eight following sections, Lawrence returns to themes he would
certainly not have wished to expound in the columns of *The Times Educational
Supplement*. Many of these he will treat yet again in *Psychoanalysis and the
Unconscious* and *Fantasia of the Unconscious*, with additions which show
traces of his study of the psychoanalysts. But most of the themes were
already in his mind by 1918.

First of all, the old esoteric motif of "the end of an era": the human soul is
approaching the end of one of its "great phases"; it is therefore necessary to
"discover a new mode of human relationship . . . a new morality".[137]
The old Christian creed according to which man is "*essentially* and *finally* an
ideal being" must be abandoned.[138]

There follows a brief exposition of the fanciful neuro-psychology of
"Two Principles": the solar plexus, the cardiac plexus, and the two corresponding ganglia, lumbar and thoracic, all borrowed by Lawrence from
yoga via J. M. Pryse; and finally the theory of a primary, solar, cardiac
consciousness and a secondary, mental consciousness.

After this Lawrence launches into an attack on mothers and maternal love,
culminating in the war-cry "*Down with mothers! A bas les mères!*" and its
Lawrentian corollary "No more soul". The style of this passage is, however,
characteristic of 1920 and not of wartime Lawrence. Nothing suggests that
in 1918–19 Lawrence had cut himself free from filial piety. He goes on to

expand his theory of the physical "sightless, mindless" bond of polarity between mother and child. In Section VII he expounds at length the idea of a healthy "primal consciousness" based on the bodily centres and not the head, for which Christianity has substituted a "mental consciousness", which "automatizes" the affective centres. In the next section he once more takes up the theme of Birkin's rejection of "merging" with the "other" in love, actually re-employing certain images evoked in the "Hardy" or *Women in Love*.

Basing himself on his psychology of "volitional" and "affective" centres he develops a sado-masochist theory of "spontaneous" corporal punishment designed to "shock the feeble volitional centres" of the lower body "into life again". Unlike "mental punishment", physical blows stimulate a "living healthy" reaction of anger: "Spank the little tail, till at last the powerful dynamic centres of the spinal system vibrate into life out of their atrophied torture."[139] And after recommending that every child be taught independence by learning "to do all it can for itself", not to depend on parents or servants, Lawrence pursues his idea of martial games: not Swedish drill but "living naked battle, flesh to flesh contest" with "profound mystic delight in unified motion": "teach fencing, teach wrestling, teach ju-jitsu, every form of hand-to-hand contest, and praise the wounds . . . Rouse the old male spirit again. The male is always a fighter."[140] After which he proceeds to bid the English "put your guns in the fire and drown your explosives", and to extol the martial spirit of German student games!

Male comradeship and martial games

What will be the spirit of the new era? In the first place man and woman must assert their "difference", find "equipoise in difference". Let men realize that

> . . . they must go beyond their women, projected into a region of greater abstraction, more inhuman activity.
>
> There, in these womanless regions of fight, and pure thought and abstracted instrumentality, let men have a new attitude to one another. Let them have a new reverence for their heroes, a new regard for their comrades: deep, deep as life and death . . . And the extreme bond of deathless friendship supports them over the edge of the known and into the unknown . . . Marriage and deathless friendship, both should be inviolable and sacred: two great creative passions, separate, apart, but complementary: the one pivotal, the other adventurous: the one, marriage, the centre of human life; and the other the leap ahead.[141]

Lawrence's treatise on popular education, like his essay on Whitman, ends with the mirage of Birkin's nostalgia for a friendship transcending the slavery to which woman tends to reduce man. And where does his promised "leap ahead" lead humanity? Straight to the religious rites of the *Plumed Serpent*. Except for certain stylistic details, it is impossible to distinguish in the later sections of these essays on education the ideas of 1917–18 from those of 1920 and later.

MOVEMENTS IN EUROPEAN HISTORY—GIBBON OR HOUSTON CHAMBERLAIN?

Movements in European History springs from the same roots and reveals the persistence throughout the duration of the war of anti-humanist themes and theses which, for want of a better description, can only be called "reactionary". The mystic theory of history propounded by Lawrence, putting man entirely in the grip of unconscious and uncontrollable movements, could lead only to a defence of dictatorship. In it are clear echoes of Carlyle's heroes and hero-worship, of Chamberlain's mystic theory of race and of great leaders, of his hatred of the French Revolution and of all forms of egalitarian democracy.

Certainly Gibbon provided the starting-point, the original inspiration; certainly too, as Harry T. Moore has pointed out,[142] Lawrence drew widely on the English historian for details, adapting him with considerable skill. That the resemblance goes no deeper is, however, clear from the following letter to Cecil Gray in July 1918:

> I feel in a historical mood, being very near the end of Gibbon. The chief feeling is, that men were always alike, and always will be, and one must view the species with contempt first and foremost, and find a few individuals, if possible—which seems, at this juncture, not possible—and ultimately, if the impossible were possible, to *rule* the species. It is proper ruling they need, and always have needed. But it is impossible, because they can only be ruled as they are willing to be ruled: and that is swinishly or hypocritically.[143]

Apology for dictatorship

This work, designed for "adolescents" in their last year of elementary school, begins with a preface addressed to the teacher and setting the general tone: history is an ebb and flow of "impersonal" movements which have no deducible origin . . . no reasonable cause".[144] Such "welling up of unknown powers" was the "naked cause" of the Crusades, of the Renaissance, unpredictable events defying all logic just as earthquakes do and, "like them", . . . "unaccountably related to man's psychic being and dependent on it". History cannot explain, but "can note with wonder and reverence the tides which have surged out from the innermost heart of man", and watch "the great gestures" of life.[145] From Ancient Rome, by way of Byzantium and the dawn of Christianity, nineteen chapters lead the pupil to the end and climax—the unification of Germany. On the way the author exalts the Teutonic warriors indomitably resisting the Roman legions and finally besieging Rome itself: "The two opposite races of Europe have now met. The dark-eyed, swarthy, wine-loving men from the sun lands met with the fierce, blue-eyed men . . ." born of the northern sea, the "beautiful blue of ice". Lawrence then sings the praises of the Germans, their love of freedom and of "separateness", their fierce war councils, their scorn for agriculture, their respect for woman and for marriage,[146] their religion, foreshadowing that of *The Plumed Serpent*: "The tree worship, the worship of the Tree of Life seems always to have entailed human sacrifice. Life is the fruit of that Tree. But the Tree is dark and terrible, it demands life back again."[147]

When he arrives at Charlemagne and the Franks, Lawrence's prejudices become quite blatant: the Gauls once reduced to slavery, the reader is suddenly presented with the vision of Chamberlain's chaos of peoples:

> We are bound to feel that these Gallo-Romans, ancestors of the modern French, were during this period spiritless, made for slavery . . . Charlemagne struggled to improve the condition of the great servile mass of these serfs or villeins. But they were too apathetic, and the Franks were too contemptuous of them altogether to trouble about them. The Gallo-Romans dragged on their degraded existence, caring nothing for freedom, filled with strange and some-times horrible superstitions, loving to make pilgrimages to shrines, neglecting all work, desiring to inflict strange penances on themselves, and performing mysterious rites before trees and groves and springs, using charms and practising magic, and willing to commit strange crimes.[148]

Such is the power of words that, when performed by ancestors of the French, these rites become debased, whereas, with the Germans, human sacrifice before the Tree of Life possessed profound religious significance. When practised by the Gallo-Romans, even magic loses its attraction.

The French Revolution gets no more sympathetic or objective treatment: the Third Estate is reproached with "claiming to act for the whole nation, the populace acting for king and nobles and asking for no consent".[149] Napoleon is presented as the Saviour putting an end to "mob rule": the only effect of the Revolution, according to Lawrence, being that in France "the God-made kings and nobles were destroyed" for ever, and replaced by "man-made" leaders: "Money ruled instead of birth, that was all."

The rise of Prussia is treated sympathetically, whereas the Italian liberation movement meets with serious reserves: "You can't save mankind by politics. Liberty isn't salvation." "No wonder liberty so often turns to ashes in the mouth, after being so fair a fruit to contemplate. Man needs more than liberty."[150]

The last chapter reveals the author's basic idea: the unification of Germany has at last shown Europe the way to its true future. But this future will only be achieved around the pivot of a great leader:

> But Germany and Russia step from one extreme to the other, from absolute monarchy such as Britain never knew, straight to the other extreme of government, government by the masses of the proletariat, strange, [and] as it seems, without true purpose: the masses of the working people governing themselves they know not why, except that they wish to destroy all authority, and to enjoy all an equal prosperity.[151]

Lawrence here invokes a "law of life" which requires that "as soon as the appetite for martial adventure and triumph in conflict is satisfied, the appetite for peace and prosperity manifests itself and vice versa":

> Therefore a great united Europe of productive working-people, all materially equal, will never be able to continue and remain firm unless it unites also round one great chosen figure, some hero who can lead a great war, as well as administer a wide peace. It all depends on the will of the people. But the will of the people must concentrate in one figure, who is also supreme over the will of the people. He must be chosen, but at the same time responsible to God alone. Here is a problem of which a stormy future will have to evolve the solution.[152]

Thus Tree of Life, mysticism, esoterism and anti-evolutionism lead to the same result as did in 1915 the quest for Rananim: men are to be delivered into the hands of a superman, himself directly obedient to the word of God. Lawrence's theocracy, translated into terms accessible to elementary-school children, culminates in political shamanism, in movements such as those which were to pave the way for Fascism and Nazism. Psychologically, the Lawrence of 1919 is ready for the between-wars period and for his *Plumed Serpent*, the synthesis of his spiritual, mystic and political aspirations.

16

LAWRENCE IN 1919

"It was in 1915 the old world ended":[1] *Women in Love*, in 1916, was Lawrence's celebration of the death of *his* old world. External circumstances prolonged the agony of his youth until 1919, through years of waiting and postponement. Arid and frustrated so far as literary production was concerned, these were also years of wide new reading, of slow maturation of ideas and assimilation of a new mental universe which was to assert itself in the writings of the post-war years.

The aridity shows most, as we hope appears from the last chapter, in the uneven quality and bitter inspiration of his didactic and theoretical essays. The whole of his prolific didactic output of 1917–19 counts for next to nothing in Lawrence's literary reputation. Most of it consists of preliminary sketches, subsequently to be entirely recast or greatly modified. Indeed, in certain cases, one is entitled to question whether Lawrence would have wished them to be published, since some of these essays seem to have escaped his memory in the post-war years when he was sending publishers almost anything he could lay hands on. They do, however, throw light on the intentions underlying his novels and short stories, as well as revealing his personal uncertainties and contradictions. They also raise fundamental questions which the critic has to face when attempting an assessment of the social and moral pretensions of Lawrence's works and of the value of his prophesyings.

How far does his art point towards solutions to the problems he aspired to solve, not only for himself, but for all men? To what extent does he deal with real problems, correctly stated, applicable to mankind? Do Lawrence's pre-1919 novels and poems help the reader to know or understand himself more fully, to adapt his behaviour and emotions to his natural and social environment? Did the redemptory mission suddenly revealed in 1913 succeed? Was Lawrence able to transmit the radiant message of love proclaimed at the beginning of his liaison with Frieda? And, if he was not, what are the causes of the confusion, corruption or distortion of his intended message?

The preceding chapters have tried to provide, often in Lawrence's own words, the answers to these questions. Like the legendary shrinking skin, the vision which, in relatively happy months, led to the original idea of *Women in Love* and *The Rainbow* was later to wither and shrivel. Paul Morel's deep-seated conflict had not only survived but had grown deeper; Lawrence's ego, eager for contact and communion, had withdrawn into itself, cutting him off for ever from the springs of social life.

To sum up and conclude the present work, it remains to seek out this ego in the most revealing of Lawrence's works, his novels, poems and short stories, and with their aid to attempt to define the scope and limitations of his art in 1919.

As we have seen, throughout this youthful formative period, content, form and aesthetic theory all remain closely linked to the fundamental conflict of his personality. On the one hand the futility of his theoretical efforts at explanation and justification demonstrates his inability to understand this conflict objectively. On the other, the source of all these efforts, as of his lyricism, lies in this same suffering, in this struggle, in his will to live and to triumph, to prove himself and accede to integrated being and communion with others. The synthesis so passionately sought by him in ideas, symbols, and images drawn from outworn doctrines, attractive to him mainly because they seemed more "natural" than the abstract constructions of science and the pure intellect, surely lay nearer at hand in his own great gift for perceiving and expressing the vital essence of things and beings, in his aesthetic of the present.

But deep and fundamental contradictions remain between the aesthetic theory of pure enjoyment of the present and his messianic ambition, between the poetic message itself and all that continues to veil and to obscure it— between the basic simplicity of the poet's song or the novelist's narrative and the pretensions to a "metaphysic" or a psychology aiming both at preaching reform and at dehumanizing the individual through severing him for ever from every social link.

Persistence and generalization of an internal conflict

By the time he came to write the second half of *The Rainbow*, clouds were already beginning to obscure the relatively clear, pure vision of 1913; in the "Hardy", as in the rest of his didactic output, new signs appeared of an internal conflict, a conflict which, in the last poems of *Look! We Have Come Through!* and in *The Symbolic Meaning*, takes the form of a struggle with woman and with the very idea of love. While on the face of it this conflict is no longer that of Paul Morel, in reality this same struggle persists through the discussion of Hardy's characters and up to the quest for a new heaven and new earth on American soil and in the creative unconscious of the New England writers. Lawrence's inner life, his love-life, his experience as an artist, the feeling that something essential lies outside his reach, lead him continually to seek a solution to the problems of relationship between self and other, in love, in friendship and in literary expression.

Why does he insist so much on the futility of "looking before and after", on the necessity of living in the present in order to re-create one's unity of being? Is it not precisely because, aspiring ardently to a unity he can conceive but rarely achieve, except for brief instants, he can neither sustain nor savour it with unadulterated joy? Like Birkin, who both loves and despises England, who alternately vows mankind to total extinction and tries to save it, he never gives up all hope of being a man of destiny, the prophet of a new era. He never ceases to believe that the conflict cleaving him in two is a symptom of a generalized modern malady to which he has found the cure. Thus the man who suffers, who feels himself the victim of a deep-seated disorder of the self, who seeks both to justify and to understand himself, goes hand-in-hand with the creative artist who, by creating, tries not only to cure himself, but also to enter into the eternal joy of the present and live at last in harmony with the universe, offering to others the secret of his cure.

The problem of the self and of otherness is thus linked to a theory of aesthetics, to the Lawrentian concept of lyric creation. The predominance of satire in *Women in Love* and in the short stories of the war years, the didactic nature of so much of his writing after 1915, while undoubtedly revealing a certain aridity, also testify to a passionate effort at integration with the universe, to a return to the springs of the lyricism which remains Lawrence's outstanding characteristic and greatest claim to lasting fame. His social criticism was bound to become rapidly outdated in an England undergoing rapid transformation; already it seems to us nearer to the Victorian past than to present realities. His descriptive lyricism, on the contrary, is as alive today as yesterday, and ranks him among the great poets of the English language. During the war years, his lyricism broke slowly and painfully through, despite the persistence of his long-drawn inner conflict, and his ceaseless attempt to establish with the many forms of "otherness" that ever-elusive "relatedness" symbolized for him by the song of the lark or the poetry of Whitman.

During this period, obsession with the relation between self and others too often intervenes to mask Lawrence's intelligence and descriptive lyricism, an obsession dispelled only in the relative calm of his last works, as death approached and the poet gradually renounced all ambition and aspiration other than that of enjoyment of the present. Thus his 1914–19 works continue the process of self-justification begun not so much in *Sons and Lovers* itself as in the postscript to that novel, not too aptly dubbed a Foreword.

The autobiographical *Sons and Lovers*, having failed to lay the ghosts of the past, did no more than reveal to Lawrence the depth and extent of his wounds. According to Barbara Low, who knew him well in the war years, Lawrence at this time loathed Paul Morel and all he represented of his own past self; so that *Sons and Lovers* never had the cathartic effect of a true analysis, of a self-revelation capable of reconciling him to a self already dead and buried. The discussion of Sue and Arabella in the "Hardy", certain scenes of Ursula's youth in *The Rainbow* and, in *Women in Love*, the character of Hermione in so far as it resembles Lawrence's idea of Jessie Chambers, are evidence of the persistence of the old wounds to his self-respect, of a lasting inability to face up to his share of responsibility in the failure of his first love.

From 1914 onwards these old sores were reopened by the ceaseless fight with Frieda, by the deep and lasting conflict on the emotional and also, very probably, on the physical plane. Existing analyses of this conflict, notably those made by Daleski and Vivas[2] in the light of the confessions contained in Lawrence's own novels, make it unnecessary for us to go into detail. Suffice it to say that, in *The Rainbow* as in *Women in Love*, the accent is not on the triumph of love Lawrence wished to celebrate in 1912, but rather, as in *Sons and Lovers*, on the failure of physical relations in love.

The very basis of Lawrentian love, if Birkin and Ursula are intended as a norm, is failure. At the end of the novel, even after allegedly having known total liberation from shame of both her body and her desires, Ursula remains unsatisfied. The novelist presents this failure as being her own fault:

> She could give herself up to his activity. But she could not be herself, she *dared* not come forth quite nakedly to his nakedness, abandoning all adjustment, lapsing in pure faith with him . . . They were never *quite* together, at the same moment, one was always a little left out.[3]

Even if it did not correspond to Birkin's typical dread of Aphrodite unleashed and the *Dea Syria*, the reason for this deep discordance between the perfect couple is partly elucidated by a confession made by Lawrence to Compton Mackenzie in 1920.[4] Lawrence expressed worry over "his inability to attain consummation simultaneously with his wife". Marriage, he said, was "still imperfect, in spite of all they had both gone through". Despite Mackenzie's reassurances, Lawrence "became more and more depressed about what *he* insisted was the only evidence of a perfect union", and confessed that he had known perfect love "with a young coal-miner" (*sic*) when he was about sixteen.

Lawrence's theoretical works, the flight towards esoteric tradition, the obsessive need to formulate his own "philosophy", are thus revealed as a prolongation of the effort begun in the Foreword to *Sons and Lovers* to explain and justify the deep-seated dualism of a self tortured by a sense of something missing. The rejection of Freud, to be more clearly expressed in *Psychoanalysis and the Unconscious*, and in *Fantasia*, goes hand-in-hand with the temptation to adopt the images and concepts of a Blavatsky, and to substitute for analysis a system of analogies and images less wounding to his self-esteem. His didactic works thus correspond to an effort at self-integration by the creation of a cosmogonic model consecrating in religious form a universal dualism both reflecting and justifying a divided self. In the long run, after 1919, this integration was to come about thanks to his spontaneous art and intelligence rather than to this form of analogical reasoning: but in 1919 Lawrence was not yet ripe for the ultimate simplification and purification of themes then assailing his mind and imagination.

In the first place he was not free to write as he would have liked: pursued by lack of money, he was forced to undertake jobs unlikely to show him at his best and often in fact seeming to bring out the worst of his qualities. Next, and partly as a result of the painful warning conveyed by the suppression of *The Rainbow*—but also partly owing to the fact that by the time he came to write *Women in Love* his own faith was no longer absolute—the joyful message on love he had wanted "The Sisters" to convey had become confused and indeed altogether lost in certain scenes of that novel which leave the reader uneasy and perplexed. Only after years of success, financial independence and, even more important, almost complete liberation from his own inhibitions, was Lawrence to be bold enough to try to say openly in *Lady Chatterley's Lover* what he considered his essential message, and, by speaking of physical love in physical terms, to rid himself for ever of the Christian symbolism which permeates *The Rainbow* and of the esoteric dross clogging the thought of *Women in Love*. In 1919 Lawrence still depended too much on the force of symbols inherited from his early years, was still too Wagnerian, his style over-encumbered with the repetitious litanies and incantations that mark the weakest passages of *Women in Love*, such as his presentation of Hermione. Only with *Fantasia of the Unconscious* in 1922 was he to achieve both artistic detachment with regard to the esoteric themes on which he freely draws, and the purified, untrammelled style of his maturity already presaged in the best of his late wartime short stories. Only then was he to learn to be himself, without seeking self-justification in any kind of "metaphysic".

Creative vision and esoteric pattern

The Lawrence of 1919, like the Lawrence of *Women in Love* and of the last poems of *Look! We Have Come Through!*, was still relying on a philosophico-religious system to explain the relationship between himself and the universe. From 1914 onwards, the spontaneity of the beginning of this cycle of poems gave way to a relatively obscure expression of the problems of relationship between self and other, drawing upon ideas foreign to the poem itself. This poetry is living illustration of the Lawrentian contradiction concerning the spontaneity of creation, independent of a "philosophy" allegedly developed *a posteriori* on the basis of experience: a standpoint certainly more in line with the more detached, more self-assured Lawrence of 1922. True, he wrote primarily because he was tortured by certain problems, because his temperament, his sincerity drove him to try to understand his own motives and emotions. Nor was he wrong in 1922 to insist on the primordial role of experience in his motivations as a writer, to assert that from his reading he remembered only "hints" and then proceeded "by intuition";[5] i.e. by exploitation of the images, myths and allegories encountered in his reading, especially any which profoundly affected his own emotions, such as the myth of the moon as mother and vampire of the earth. We have seen to what extent, in "The Spirit of Place" and "The Two Principles", myth and idea are intermingled, and to what extent mythology threatens to take the place of thought, emotion to triumph over reason, even when the writer is seeking to justify his myths by trying to prove them "scientific".

Could novels like *The Rainbow* and *Women in Love*, which attempt to construct out of experience a systematic structure aimed at explaining human destiny, ever have been conceived either independently of or prior to the interpretative systems to which they correspond? We have tried to show here that their genesis was at least concomitant with that of analogical models or "systems" suggested by the author's reading; the characters created out of the novelist's personal experience were both explained by the mythical "model" and served to reinforce it by their very existence, thus being both created by the system and contributing to its illustration. We witness the creation of an imaginary universe from certain elements of external reality, but a universe in which the characters act according to motivations very different from those of daily life.

Today, in the light of the last fifty years of novel-writing, it may be felt that Lawrence probably did not aim at "realism"; as contemporary reviews show, his readers may have been in fact misled by the intense realism of his physical descriptions. The author of *Women in Love* lived and moved in a mythical universe of his own creation, that of the illustrated bestiary of "The Crown" and of "The Reality of Peace", a world transcending the physical environment so faithfully drawn. His characters with legendary names—Gudrun, Loerke, Gerald—are essentially symbolic creatures, inhabiting this universe on an equal footing with the symbolic beasts: the wolf, totem of Gerald, the rat symbolizing Loerke, Winifred's obscene pet rabbit, Gerald's arab mare, the potent, magic moon whose image Birkin would destroy.

Thus "out of experience"—but also out of the myths and structures of an analogical form of thought "remembered" from Pryse, Blavatsky, or Burnet's Heraclitus—the novelist creates a universe in which he plays the part of demiurge, a vision of the Last Judgment with himself as god and archangel. But in this vision images borrowed from his reading are substituted for ideas; images turned, so to speak, into visual abstractions, and as such not subject to the critical exigencies of precise comparison with the world of ordinary perception. But, thanks to the realism of description of places and people, the legendary, mythical creatures of the novelist's imagination participate in the physical universe. Typical of this procedure are the portraits of Heseltine, transformed into Halliday, of Ottoline, who becomes Hermione with traits of Miriam, or again the picture of the mining town. Lawrence's abstract, mythical world has its existence somewhere on the confines of sensory images and of the emotions they evoke, and not in the realm of ideas, of intellectual concepts. This explains why he insists on calling his abstractions "experience", denying that they are abstractions, convinced that they are superior in value to intellectual concepts because they seem to him rooted in the immediate, not intellectually processed, data of his consciousness. As early as 1914 he was claiming objectivity for free symbols emanating direct from the subconscious, as opposed to the "voluntary" and artificial character he attributed to mechanistic and abstract thought, to the scientific working of the mind. He opted for an explanation of the world satisfactory to his emotions, as opposed to any explanation based on scientific reasoning. Hence in 1922 he found it imperative to insist that his ideas came "out of experience", and not from books.

Rejecting *en bloc* the Renaissance, the Calvinism in which he was steeped, and modern scientific methods of thought, he felt the attraction of occultism at a time when ethnological descriptions by Frazer, Tylor and Frobenius, and the studies of the psychoanalysts, were throwing fresh light on primitive forms of thought—on the mental structures of primitive peoples or of neurotics. Dissatisfied with his own epoch, hostile to a mechanistic society into which he had been unable to integrate, passionately anxious to justify his instinctive rebellion, but, as a true inheritor of puritanism, still requiring religious sanction for revolt—primitive thought offered him a way of escape from the prison of the Hebrew, biblical and Calvinist heritage, of Greek analytical thought, of the narrow spirituality of his adolescence, of all that he had been and that he blamed for being, as he thought, the cause of the malady from which he suffered.

At all costs this spiritual ego has to be destroyed, or at least suppressed, replaced by a self able to give free expression to the vital instinct; a self free from dualism, solidly anchored in the realities of both the body and the blood. To "intellectual" spirituality, he opposes a "soul" situated in the body, since he cannot do without the soul, yet rejects everything which proceeds from the "mind", or at least everything he considers to be both mental *and* disembodied. Hence the opposition he constantly seeks to surmount between the emotions of the higher centres, and the deep impulses of the lower "pivotal" centres; hence his need to find the perfect expression of the creative urge in flowers, beasts, birds and snakes. Hence also his search in such living forms for a type of abstraction different from that of the mind, an "intuitive" sympathy with the cosmos, with sensual life, independent of words and abstract thought. Yet when all is said and done, was he not also offering an abstraction—one proceeding from certain types of sensations, which he pretended was different from the abstraction of the intellect? In his own way, he was thus led to recreate a primitive mode of thought, with structures of its own, because he rejected "civilized" and "abstract" forms of thought. His analysis stops short and fails to see that "savage thinking" follows the same laws as scientific, civilized thinking. Even more than that of *The Rainbow*, with its rejection of geometry in favour of dynamic, cyclic and rhythmic form, the symbolist structure of *Women in Love* is in itself a structure of primitive thought; but a structure none the less, although it seeks to escape traditional forms of thought. The symbolism of expression should not make us overlook the framework, which is not immediately perceptible to the reader, since Lawrence has chosen, so it seems, not to communicate his experience in immediately accessible terms. It is nevertheless a structure based on a mystic theory of race and blood, of place and nature, of love and friendship, and above all on a mystic theory of predestination. For the old Calvinistic predestination leading to eternal salvation he substitutes Birkin's continual annunciation, if not definition, of a new era; and Christian quietism is replaced by a humble and expectant waiting for the divine breath to inspire the predestined few. Puritan themes and attitudes have thus found their way into the esoteric religion absorbed by Lawrence in irregular doses since 1914 or even 1912, and reinforced by some ethnology and a limited dose of psychoanalysis viewed and understood from a religious standpoint rather than for its intrinsic interest. From all these he extracts only such elements as feed the flame of his own intuitive faith. The particular significance attached by Lawrence to Hawthorne and his Roger Chillingworth lies in the mixture of sorcery, alchemy and puritanism in which he seems to have recognized his own 1918 self.

Self and non-self: "bursting the world-consciousness"

The central, crucial theme of Lawrence's writing from 1914 to 1919 is that of self in relation to otherness, a theme closely linked to that of the accession of the self to being. Onto it are grafted those of the relations of man with woman as mother or as lover, with man and with society; while "accession to being" is an aspect of the relationship of the self to the divine. Lawrence has expressed his experience of these problems in two poems which illuminate both his artistic motivations and his limitations: "New Heaven and Earth" and "Manifesto".

As poet, novelist or philosopher, Lawrence invariably takes as his starting-point both the facts of his own experience, and an interpretation of those facts, constantly harking back to the experience. So that when he describes the actions and emotions of his characters, he is always referring more or less explicitly to scenes of his own life, engraved for ever in his memory, or to successive interpretations of these scenes. Similarly, when he advances a theoretical explanation, for instance of the different values of the love relationship in "The Two Principles", it is always in relation to his mother's or his own intimate experience. Hence an intensity and a profound sincerity, but also a limitation of the field of experience, and a feeling on the part of the reader that life must offer other emotions, other knowledge, other riches: a feeling growing in intensity whenever the author moves away from basic relationships—parent and child, man and woman—to deal with more complex social relationships. At this point, the perspective of the most ambitious of all his novels, *Women in Love*, or of the early chapters of *Aaron's Rod*, becomes distinctly restrictive and distorting. Not only is the problem of the self central, but the ever-present, all-pervasive self, like a demiurge, usurps the place of the universe it is seeking to explain: avowing, asserting that it *is* the universe.

No doubt the literary world of 1919 was not ripe for such an affirmation, for such total subjectivity: indeed, was Lawrence himself altogether prepared for what he was attempting? He had no fully formed theoretical conception of what he was about; he did not see to what extent his universe was limited by his own self; if he did, would he have gone on seeking, beyond the conscious self, an "objective" otherness in which he hoped to discover his new heaven and new earth? An otherness in relation to which he could exist objectively, that is to say, for him, unconsciously, free from the burden of "mental" consciousness? Significantly enough it is in woman that he seeks this otherness, just as the newborn infant seeks it in the mother. "New Heaven and Earth" is the poem of the discovery of otherness and of the solitude of the soul in a "New World" in which it achieves distinct existence, separated from the matrix in which are embedded souls which have not known how to detach themselves from the mass:

And so I cross into another world
shyly and in homage linger for an invitation
from this unknown that I would trespass on.

I am very glad, and all alone in the world,
all alone, and very glad, in a new world,
where I am disembarked at last.

I could cry with joy, because I am in the new world, just ventured in.
I could cry with joy, and quite freely, there is nobody to know.

And whosoever the unknown people of this unknown world may be
they will never understand my weeping for joy to be adventuring among
    them
because it will still be a gesture of the old world I am making
which they will not understand, because it is quite, quite foreign to them.[6]

    This new world is one in which the non-self exists independently of the self, in which the individual achieves distinct, differentiated being, escaping from the obsession identifying him with all things: the poet was "weary of the world" because "everything was tainted with [his own] self":

Skies, trees, flowers, birds, water,
people, houses, streets, vehicles, machines,
nations, armies, war, peace-talking,
work, recreation, governing, anarchy,
it was all tainted with myself, I knew it all to start with
because it was all myself.
When I gathered flowers, I knew it was myself plucking my own
    flowering.
When I went in a train, I knew it was myself travelling by my own
    invention.
When I heard the cannon of the war, I listened with my own ears to
    my own destruction.
When I saw the torn dead, I knew it was my own torn dead body.
It was all me, I had done it all in my own flesh.[7]

    The poet is "Creator and creation", "God and the creation", a creature beholding itself as creator; he is seized with "maniacal horror":

I was a lover, I kissed the woman I loved,
and God of horror, I was kissing also myself.
I was a father and a begetter of children,
and oh, oh horror, I was begetting and conceiving in my own body.[8]

    Then came death: "I buried my beloved; it was good, I buried myself and was gone",[9] the "beloved" being the poet's mother. Next came war, an orgy of murder in which the poet is both murderer and victim "Till it is almost enough, till I am reduced perhaps", "dead and trodden to nought in the sour black earth of the tomb", "trodden quite to nought", "absolutely to nothing". And then the resurrection:

                . . . then I am here
. . . risen, not born again, but risen, body the same as before,
new beyond knowledge of newness, alive beyond life,
. . . living where life was never yet dreamed of, nor hinted at,
here, in the other world, still terrestrial
myself, the same as before, yet unaccountably new.[10]

Having thus in death rejected from his consciousness the whole universe that filled it, having "burst the world consciousness in the individual",[11] the poet sets out on a voyage of discovery of the non-self, of "the unknown, the real unknown, the unknown unknown". He puts out his hand and feels that which "verily was not I". This unknown is the flank of his wife, perceived without the aid of mental consciousness: "a thousand nights" he has touched her before, and "all that previous while, she was I, she was I":

> Yet rising from the tomb, from the black oblivion
> stretching out my hand, my hand flung like a drowned man's hand on
>   a rock,
> I touched her flank and knew I was carried by the current in death
> over to the new world, and was climbing out on the shore,
> risen, not to the old world, the old, changeless I, the old life,
> wakened not to the old knowledge
> but to a new earth, a new I, a new knowledge, a new world of time.[12]

"Mad with delight" at this new universe, the poet explores the mystery of the "other", that "land that beats with a pulse", these "valleys that draw close in love", the "strange sheer slopes and white levels". The woman, recognized as "other" than himself, opens to him "sightless and strong oblivion in utter life":

> The unknown, strong current of life supreme
> drowns me and sweeps me away and holds me down
> to the sources of mystery, in the depths,
> extinguishes there my risen resurrected life,
> and kindles it further at the core of utter mystery.[13]

This poem, written at Greatham in 1915, expresses more clearly than any other of Lawrence's writings what he meant by his new heaven and new earth. Implicit in it, as in Ursula's meditation on the Resurrection at the end of Chapter X of *The Rainbow*, is what was to become the theme of "The Man who Died": "The Resurrection is to life, not to death."[14]

The Lawrentian myth of death and resurrection stands for the death of mental, abstract consciousness, falsely affirming the supremacy of the spirit, and for the resurrection of instinctive and spontaneous man, living in the fullness of his being, both corporal and spiritual.

All-devouring "self-consciousness" is what the poet seeks to destroy in order to find peaceful communion with the other, with the non-self, without the intolerable and permanent assertion of the self and its identity with the other, of which even Whitman is finally accused in *Studies in Classic American Literature*.

But the effort to subjugate mental consciousness, the need to stress the death of the conscious self in the higher centres, is too intense. By stressing so heavily the suppression of self-consciousness the poet tends to suggest that only the corporeal survives. The fact that Lawrence's doctrine is not regressive, does not aim at the suppression of the spiritual, was not always clearly perceptible, and hence liable to misinterpretation not only in 1915, but long afterwards.

This ceaseless quest for acceptance of non-self without identifying it with, absorbing it into the ego (one might almost say the quest for an *objective* attitude of the self towards the non-self) expresses itself in a struggle for independence from the beloved: Will Brangwen is typical in this respect, his successive "rebirths" never culminating in the creation of a genuine, autonomous personality. His moral, emotional dependence on Anna, similar to Paul Morel's dependence on his mother, to Skrebensky's on Ursula, and Gerald's on Gudrun, illustrates what Birkin is trying to avoid when he recoils in horror from the idea of "merging" in love, of identification with the beloved.

Out of his intuitive knowledge of his own personality, of the continual and vital need, like that of the infant for its mother, which he experiences for the beloved, Lawrence depicts these infantile personalities, incapable of enduring solitude, distraught at the idea of their own emotional void when not subjected to and supported by the loved one. With a distrust of psychoanalysis typical of those refusing analysis because it would delve too deeply into their weaknesses, he seeks a mystic, cosmogonic explanation to the destructive love which, so he maintains, is experienced by souls in the process of cosmic disintegration: but, as in the poem just analysed, he is more successful at describing the encroaching spirit which accuses the other of encroachment, than the cured, adult spirit, capable of enduring solitude. His new heaven and new earth is not really a paradise where love flourishes. It is rather a promise of autonomy and balance for the individual, thanks to which he will cease to intrude or be dependent on his lover. In *The Rainbow*, Lawrence gave signs of perceiving that this was a question of upbringing and of social training; but he did not pursue this promising idea, his "philosophical" turn of mind leading him to prefer cosmogonic explanations.

"Manifesto": a claim for autonomy

The logical sequel to "New Heaven and Earth" is "Manifesto", written at Zennor either at the same time as *Women in Love* or very soon after. It is at once a song of accession to fullness of being, and of mystic assertion of the poet's autonomy in regard to the beloved. We know how certain ritual gestures, more magic than erotic, are held to liberate Lawrentian lovers, by convincing them of their inalienable, fundamental otherness, of their distinct and separate existences. Such are the gestures performed by Birkin and

Ursula in that extra-erotic communion of the bodies which unleashes in Birkin the mystic energy of the serpent Kundalini, source of the life of the human body.[15] After such gestures the lovers become "detached",

> . . . moving in freedom more than the angels,
> conditioned only by our own pure single being,
> having no laws but the laws of our own being.[16]

The strangeness of this ritual should not be allowed to obscure the meaning of the whole poem, a manifesto of belief in the complete, balanced human being. All that is strange is the by-ways by which the puritan seeks to attain such balance; that is to say, his own acceptance of all functions of physical and moral being.

For clearly all the functions are involved, including the highest. In "Manifesto", the poet expresses his thanks to "the good generations of mankind" for never having known hunger, thirst, or cold. He also evokes other reasons for rendering thanks to man:

> Then the dumb, aching, bitter, helpless need,
> the pining to be initiated,
> to have access to the knowledge that the great dead
> have opened up for us, to know, to satisfy
> the great and dominant hunger of the mind;
> man's sweetest harvest of the centuries, sweet, printed books,
> bright, glancing, exquisite corn of many a stubborn
> glebe in the upturned darkness;
> I thank mankind with passionate heart
> that I just escaped the hunger for these,
> that they were given when I needed them,
> because I am the son of man.
> I have eaten, and drunk, and warmed and clothed my body,
> I have been taught the language of understanding,
> I have chosen among the bright and marvellous books,
> like any prince, such stores of the world's supply
> were open to me, in the wisdom and goodness of man.
> So far, so good,
> wise, good provision that makes the heart swell with love.[17]

Then comes sexual hunger, the shame, terror and madness of unsatisfied desire, which one woman alone has satisfied.[18] Having thanked her, the poet proceeds to put the ultimate question, the question of "Study of Thomas Hardy" and "The Crown", that of Birkin, and of "The Reality of Peace":

> To be, or not to be, is still the question.
> This ache for being is the ultimate hunger.[19]

For his fulfilment to be complete it still remains for him "to be known even as I know", to be recognized by his wife as "other", to become "two and distinct" instead of merging. This ultimate need corresponds to Birkin's phobia for love as "merging", an indiscriminate mingling of two beings. But the quest for the separateness of mystically linked stars, in angelic freedom and perfection, here remains obscure. None of the possible explanations is entirely satisfying: the psychological peculiarities of the man himself, anal fixation, the theory of the stimulating action of the lower chakras, nothing fully explains the motivation of the poet in Section VII of "Manifesto". The explanation advanced above[20]—a final crumbling of the wall of shame erected round the individual by a puritan upbringing—offers the most plausible interpretation both of this passage and of similar scenes in *The Rainbow* and *Women in Love* and, at a later stage, in *Lady Chatterley's Lover*. Indeed, one may well ask whether the poet's experience is such as to be helpful to the reader.

For the man whom Lawrence is trying to kill in himself in order to live, to have "no laws but the laws of our own being", is the very man he attacks in *The Symbolic Meaning*; the puritan, heir to Calvin and to a Judaism continually "lusting spiritually for utter repression" of the "sensual psyche", of the "blood consciousness", of "the primal impulsive being in every man".[21] Chillingworth, Hester, Dimmesdale,[22] are the "triangle of destruction" and the Lawrentian explanation of *The Scarlet Letter* is both passionate and penetrating because it expresses his own deep-seated malady, his own struggle against the dikes constructed by his education around his inner being, his passionate ego. Despite the obscurity of the mystic ritual which liberates the poet, "Manifesto" remains the key work of this period, an imperfect, obscure, but complete confession of the psychological infirmity of the poet and his effort to triumph over it. But in 1917 esoteric obscurity seems to have been his sole recourse; and ten years were to pass before he dared, in *Lady Chatterley's Lover*, to speak out clearly, and in so doing confess how inhibited he had been before.

While trying to escape from puritanism, from the bodily shame of which he also speaks in the poem "She said as well to me", he is struggling, like Birkin, to overcome his fear of woman, manifested by a withdrawal as of a startled animal, observed by Hilda Doolittle. In this poem his wife asks him why he is ashamed of his body and, admiring it, endeavours to inspire him with self-confidence. But she cannot free him from his shame. Like Paul Morel when accidentally touched by Miriam, he draws back, exclaiming:

Don't touch me and appreciate me.
It is an infamy.
You would think twice before you touched a weasel on a fence
as it lifts its straight white throat.
Your hand would not be so flig and easy.

The woman would not touch "the adder we saw asleep with her head on her shoulder . . . though she looked rarely beautiful", nor "the young bull in the field":

> Is there nothing in me to make you hesitate?
> I tell you there is all these.
> And why should you overlook them in me?[23]

This withdrawal goes hand-in-hand with the demand to be recognized as "the terrible *other*", the "terrible other flesh", and shows his determination to defend himself against invasive, protective, maternal love, against the active, demanding "non-self". Hence the importance of the concepts of polarity, of twin orbits, of astral interdependence between self and other, later to give way to the idea of the necessity for the subordination of the woman, an idea assuming cosmic significance in "The Two Principles", for does not Aphrodite rise from the waters, is not the Sun God Apollo?

After *Women in Love* the accent will be on masculine superiority, shortly to be proclaimed in *Aaron's Rod* and other works of 1918–25, in a return to the themes of male comradeship and leadership, of male activities outside the framework of man's relationship with woman—"He for God only, She for God in him".

The danger threatening the self in its relationship with the "other" is that of merging, of emotional subjection: as is testified by the evolution of the original theme of "The Sisters" from its conception in 1913 to its realization as *Women in Love*. In its relationship with another man, the self is also threatened, for Lawrence can conceive the other man only in one of two roles: disciple or Judas. Like love, male comradeship can only be theoretically conceived as the conjunction of two orbits; in practice, as will be stressed in *Aaron's Rod*, *Kangaroo* and *The Plumed Serpent*, one of the partners is always nearer to God than the other. But in 1919, the Judas theme, already suggested in *Touch and Go* and the early chapters of *Aaron's Rod*, has not yet assumed the important place it will later occupy in Lawrence's work. Gerald's refusal of Birkin's offer of eternal friendship is tainted not with treachery, but rather with a hint of impotence. The dream of domination, of action for the salvation of mankind, the messianism of 1913, with all its ambiguities and reserves, is still alive; the ritual, almost magic nature of the wrestling scene between the two friends in *Women in Love* stresses the curious mixture of religion, mysticism and the lure of the forbidden fruit entering into Birkin's motivation. Similarly the suppressed Prologue to *Women in Love*, the essays on Whitman, the stress on hand-to-hand wrestling in "Education of the People", all suggest that Lawrence either did not dare, or did not wish, to reveal his real feelings on male comradeship. To say the least, he admits the existence of a problem in male relationships, even without physical contacts; but both in the wrestling scene and in "The Blind Man", as in his proposals of *Blutbrüderschaft* to Russell and to Murry, he shows himself unable to conceive such relationships without an emotional bond ritualized in some form of physical contact. It may be objected that this proves no more than Lawrence's abhorrence of the abstract in social relations. The facts as he himself presents them speak, however, for themselves. Without the sanction of caresses or blows (the fight with Baxter Dawes, the eulogy of corporal punishment in "Education of the People"), relations between men are for Lawrence tainted with the vice of civilization: abstraction and mechanism. It is perhaps worth noting that this conforms closely to his attitude to women: he reverts spontaneously to the state of the infant dependent on his mother, even if he rebels from time to time in order to assert his supremacy; with men, his role is that of prophet, harbinger or Messiah, and any deviation by the other from the path allotted by Lawrence is felt to be treachery. Hence his morbid need for certitude, for some form of magic ritual binding him to his disciple.

Social criticism and alienation

This fundamental inability to form human links on a footing of equality, combined with the Calvinist tradition of predestination, conditions the whole of Lawrence's social criticism which, as we have already seen, is based not on analysis but on sudden, brutal, passionate affirmation, on sudden disgust such as sweeps over Ursula during her second year at university. The sordid conditions of the working classes do occasionally provoke his revolt, but this is far less frequent than expressions of his contempt for men because they are not concerned to save themselves, to accede to fullness of being. In this respect, the "Study of Thomas Hardy" is his most revealing work. Lawrence denies the social problem, rejects all collective action to improve the fate of men, because the true problem is to him ethical, religious, personal. Rananim, the refuge of the elect, is his sole reply to the problem of the relations between self and society. And in "Education of the People" he advocates a reactionary doctrine, a caste-ridden society, a cut-price education.

The social perspective of *Women in Love* is equally narrow and restrictive. The Midlands, the industrial town, are invariably presented through a distorting lens, such as the confused and ill-digested Christian charity of Thomas Crich, or the economic, mechanistic vision of his son, Gerald. Society is seen not as a collectivity of "selves" seeking expression, but as the reflection of a given "self", the mine-owner or his son, on the collectivity. Men are seen as sheep or wolves, according to whether they accept or revolt, but no effort is made to present them individually, in all their human dignity and suffering. Lawrence's preoccupation with the salvation of the elect, excludes intuitive presentation of the reality of the life of the mining town.

The novelist inhabits a higher sphere, where his chief characters commune with the divine. Society is one vast non-self, as foreign to the self as the woman or the friend who declines to be bound to Lawrence by a mystic link: governed by "abstract" principles, it inevitably "reduces" its members to non-being.

The quest of the Lawrence of Rananim, as of the Birkin who resigns from his post of schools inspector "to be free, in a free place, with a few other people",[24] is a quest for true being, for identity with pure being; in other words, for the divine. The true, the only relationship wholly satisfying to Lawrence is that of the self with the divine, which, since he does not believe in any personal God, can in the last analysis only mean the relationship of the self with its own vital impulses. His 1913 messianism is neither dissipated nor rejected. At most, it has slightly changed its form as a result of the great débâcle of 1915, of the collapse of his dreams of revolution, of the rebirth of England. "To be or not to be": ever since 1912 this question has been haunting Lawrence, and his reply is always the same: a denial of all organized non-self, i.e. all forms of non-being, with its corollary, a glorification of a self receptive to the impulses of the vital urge. The impersonal deity of Lawrence's childhood religion speaks through the mouth of the poet: "Not I, not I, but the wind that blows through me."[25]

"The Reality of Peace" urges the abandonment of the self to the "ultimate will", to the "unknown impulse" of the "river of life". *Movements in European History*, like *The Symbolic Meaning*, is dominated by a fatalistic, heroic conception of history, showing weak and despised humanity a prey to irresistible, convulsive, cosmic movements that only men of destiny can dominate and direct. This Puritan of Cromwell's own sect is in direct communication with the guiding spirit of those cosmic changes, and the deity expresses its intentions through him.

Escape into lyricism: poetry of the present

But the need for explanation and for certitude dominates the urge to action. Lawrence has neither the physical strength nor the self-assurance necessary to lead mankind. And while he may not perhaps recognize his weakness, at least he knows his true powers. Therefore it is in art that he seeks refuge, in a world of his own making. His personal theory of aesthetics, already amply stated in "The Crown", subsequently confirmed but never modified, proceeds partly from his own internal conflict, the bitterness of his sense of failure, and partly from his conception of the relationship between self and non-self. His reading on occultism, ethnology and psychology was not to bear fruit until later. While swift to seize upon a suggestion, never hesitating to exploit a fresh idea, he always moved slowly towards the complete and original artistic creation which is the mark of true assimilation. During these apparently arid years he, in fact, acquired many of those ideas and images he was to make his own after 1920, when he felt his American public ripe to follow him. In 1919, Lawrence is still in transition. In *Women in Love* he had already found the social world he was to satirize, but had not yet discovered the primitive country in which to establish in imagination his personal religion. He had perfected both technique and style, and formulated his aesthetic of the present, of the mystic now, in which his religion and his talent converge. This aesthetic theory is an admirable expression of both his potentialities and his limits. Its positive essence is expressed in "Poetry of the Present".

It is an aesthetic of the mystic, creative moment, of the ephemeral communion of the self with the cosmos and the "quick" of creation, outside all theorizing, all constraint of form and structure. By 1919 Lawrence had already fully formulated a theory of art characteristic of his post-war period: owing much to the Symbolists and the Impressionists, it leads to the total disintegration of conventional structures. The self seeks spontaneous expression outside all traditional form. Reverting to images he had used in "The Crown", Lawrence defines a "poetry of the beginning" and a "poetry of the end", the one turned towards the past, the other towards the future: the symbol of one the nightingale, of the other, the lark. These two poetries are "in the realm of all that is perfect", "of the nature of all that is complete and consummate", and this "finality" and "perfection" are expressed in the symmetry and rhythm of "exquisite form".

But there is another kind of poetry:

> ... the poetry of that which is at hand: the immediate present. In the immediate present there is no perfection, no consummation, nothing finished. The strands are all flying, quivering, intermingling into the web, the waters are shaking the moon. There is no round, consummate moon on the face of running water, nor on the face of the unfinished tide. There are no gems of the living plasm. The living plasm vibrates unspeakably, it inhales the future, it exhales the past, it is the quick of both, and yet it is neither. There is no plasmic finality, nothing crystal, permanent. If we try to fix the living tissue, as the biologists fix it with formalin, we have only a hardened bit of the past, the bygone life under our observation.[26]

Lawrence here returns to his favourite images, expressing his idea of "ever-present", non-crystallized life: the perfect rose, a living flame, the water-lily, incarnation of the ever-swirling flood, the smiling face of disintegration. The poetry of "transcendent loveliness", he goes on to explain, must include everything: "Let me feel the mud and the heavens in my lotus." It will have not "the qualities of the unfading, timeless gems" but the "whiteness that is the seethe of mud", of mutation "swifter than iridescence", haste, not rest, inconclusiveness, not fixity, "without dénouement or close".

There must be the rapid momentaneous association of things which meet and pass on the forever incalculable journey of creation: everything left in its own rapid, fluid relationship with the rest of things.[27]

This pointillist conception of poetry of the present, the undisputed master of which, for Lawrence, is Walt Whitman, converges with the idea of character expounded to Garnett apropos of "The Sisters", owing something to the Futurists, something to Meredith, and much to Edward Carpenter. It is an aesthetic of movement, of the eternal mutation of the creative flux, without finality or "resolution", like that of the characters in *The Rainbow* and *Women in Love* and the short stories of this period. Theoretically, it is an aesthetic of "direct utterance", daring to tell all, to speak of love as a total reality, in all its aspects. Such is the principle, even if in practice its boldness becomes tempered, to the point of seeming timid, hesitant and at times obscure.

It is also an aesthetic of poetry, of free verse, of spontaneity and immediacy, of the short story rather than of the novel. It is not difficult to conceive of poetry as "a spasm, naked contact with all influences at once. It does not want to get anywhere. It just takes place."[28] But it is quite a different matter to apply this doctrine to a novel like *Women in Love*, constantly proclaiming rebirth but resolving nothing except in death. In "Poetry of the Present", Lawrence is, in fact, defining the art of his remaining years: the poetry of beasts and flowers, the late short stories; at the same time he presages the loose, sometimes incoherent structure of his coming novels.

Messianism and an aesthetic of the present:
a contradiction

By 1919 Lawrence had grasped more clearly than in "The Crown" in 1915 the special nature of his inspiration, if not the limits of his temperament and of his talent. Was he perhaps conscious of a contradiction inherent in this aesthetic between the messianism of 1913 and the idea of an art of the fleeting, the ephemeral, the almost incommunicable? It is a contradiction of which Birkin seems obscurely aware, when he abandons mankind to its fate; but one which Lawrence does not pursue in *Women in Love*, or in the escapist short stories nor yet in *Aaron's Rod*. Escape into mystic enjoyment of the present, flight from a despised society, from a hurtful "non-self" towards the illusory but more docile "non-self" of artistic creation, does not yet appear to Lawrence incompatible with messianic ambitions. Only after circling the globe, after the artistic experience of *The Plumed Serpent*, at the approach of a calmly accepted death will he be ready to admit enjoyment of the present in all its completeness and simplicity. But long before this, beginning with *The Rainbow* and *Women in Love*, his messianism tended to find satisfaction in the creation of a universe of which the Messiah was both demiurge and hero. Not until some years after the war was Lawrence to define his critical attitude towards the novel. And to this end he was to expand an idea already present in the "Hardy", that is to say the link there established between the actual construction of a novel and a "philosophy". "Poetry of the Present" defines a poetical aesthetic, Lawrence's supreme aesthetic, that of his most directly, most purely characteristic work, and in particular of *Birds, Beasts and Flowers*, the poems best expressing his feeling for the essence and individuality of living forms. How far is this compatible with his conception of the novel?

Lawrence himself was perfectly well aware of a difficulty if not an incompatibility. The poet, he says, is not "divided against himself":

> It is the novelists and dramatists who have the hardest task in reconciling their metaphysic, their theory of being and knowing, with their living sense of being.

Because each novel is a "microcosm", because the universe can only be explained "in the light of a theory, therefore every novel must have the background or the structural skeleton of some theory of being, some metaphysic". And with a deep sense of the perils which await him, the novelist continues:

> And the danger is, that a man shall make himself a metaphysic to excuse or cover his own faults or failure. Indeed, a sense of fault or failure is the usual cause of a man's making himself a metaphysic, to justify himself.[29]

In Tolstoy he sees a "flagrant example" of the error that consists, in his eyes, of moulding the world according to a metaphysic instead of "applying the metaphysic to the world". While never expressly relating this stricture to his own novels, in "The Spirit of Place" he provides some valuable indications on this point. The "deliberate" ideas of the artist, "veil, conceal, obscure" the "revelation" it is his mission to reveal: he is unconscious of the "quality of duplicity" which runs through "so much of the art of the modern world". Although "sincere in his intentions" the artist "writes as a somnambulist, in the spell of pure truth as in a dream", but "is contravened and contradicted by the wakeful man and moralist who sits at the desk".[30]

This contradiction between the intellect and the subconscious self, between conscience and the deep-seated aspirations of the artist, finds expression in the use of symbols, of what Lawrence calls "*art-symbol or art-term*" in contradistinction to "conventional" symbols representing "mental concepts":

> The art-symbol or art-term stands for a pure experience, emotional and passional, spiritual and perceptual, all at once ... Art communicates a state of being ... [the] work of art is a subtle and complex *idea* expressed in symbols.[31]

In the nineteenth-century American writers he sees a "profound symbolic import" which proceeds from a writer's "unconscious or subconscious soul, as he works in a state of creation which is something like somnambulism or dreaming".[32] Clearly it is in his own name and that of his own art that he here proclaims the modern doctrine, for he immediately adds, exactly in the spirit of "The Reality of Peace", that "we must wake and sharpen in ourselves the subtle faculty for perceiving the greater inhuman forces that control us".[33]

His symbolism thus leads to a theory of an art of the unconscious, as well as of the present. In 1914 Lawrence had written that "symbolism avoids the I and puts aside the egotist".[34] He was then referring to the interpretation of Christian symbols of the type which in 1918 he was to call "authorized" or conventional. Did his passage from an official, traditional to a free, individual symbolism make it possible to restore "the I and the egotist" to their true place?

Did Lawrence consider his novels, essentially symbolic constructions, as a spontaneous upsurge of free symbols, or as an organized whole? The structure of *Women in Love* provides the answer to this question. The Christian symbols which on the whole dominate *The Rainbow* up to the time of Ursula's adolescence are replaced by a new symbolic system, borrowed partly from Frazer and Heraclitus, partly from theosophist doctrine; but the corresponding liberation of his symbolism leads to a quasi-somnambulist writing in which the conscious and deliberate plan of the novelists does, in fact, go hand in hand with a certain number of unconscious patterns.

Structure as a message from the unconscious

Several structures are thus superimposed on one another, a phenomenon illustrated even more clearly in *Women in Love* than in *The Rainbow*. Each scene has its individual symbolism, witness little Winifred's tame rabbit, representing to Gerald and to Gudrun the sexual instincts they neither master nor acknowledge, their secret sadism and complicity. Each character too has his or her own symbol—as, for example, in the case of Gerald and his mother, whose totem is the untamed wolf. Similarly, the ultra-phallic ritual performed by Birkin and Ursula corresponds to a symbolic pattern revealing personal obsessions also expressed in certain parallel scenes of *The Rainbow* and in "Manifesto".

To what extent is the choice of symbol, flower, animal, object, premeditated and deliberate? Where does prearranged plan end and subconscious self-revelation begin?

All Lawrence's youthful works, especially his novels, reveal a deep infrastructure resulting from the obligation to construct a plot and to abandon the protection afforded in poetry and the short story by his aesthetic of the present. A novel is not a moment, but a succession of moments, and unless the novelist pushes the use of the interior monologue to its logical conclusion, as Lawrence never does, he must either accumulate, associate and combine events, or else follow a more or less chronological pattern as in *Sons and Lovers*. Thus Lawrence's novels are among those of his works most revealing of the world of his dreams, his failures and desires, and are rich in precious indications of his unconscious drives and his conflicts and glimpses of self-revelation. While the poems, and to a certain extent the short stories, are translations into words, images and symbols of actual moments of joy and pain, the novels, by Lawrence's own admission, are closely associated with his theoretical works, are part of the same effort to explain and justify himself, to construct a universe in which his innermost self can find expression. Unlike the majority of the poems, they are not "pure passionate *experience*", if *experience* is to be taken to mean a feeling produced by *events*; they are quite as much the expression of the unconscious in action: the "acting out" of the psychoanalysts.

In his four great novels from *The White Peacock* to *Women in Love*, Lawrence treats themes undoubtedly issuing from his unconscious, his neurosis, his perplexity in face of the internal contradictions of his being. In 1919, when about to resume in *The Lost Girl* and *Aaron's Rod* the themes of flight and escape evident in his last series of short stories, he renounces the idea of any pact with social "otherness", and the compromise he reaches with the "otherness" of Frieda is a *modus vivendi* revealing his physical and emotional dependence, his incapacity to free himself from the infantile bond with the *Magna Mater*, to prove himself the triumphant male of his dreams.

Art thus becomes a double refuge: a spontaneous, immediate refuge in poetry and the natural beauty of flowers, beasts and the singing of birds; an artificial refuge, a dream world, in the secret structure of his novels. His poetry gives expression in words and rhythm to the docile, reassuring "otherness" represented by the beauties of nature, token and promise of rebirth and *ewige wiederkehr*. The novels, by the use of satire, of affirmation rather than description, reveal his faith in a rebirth reconciling self and other: paradisal love, true friendship, a society of men freed from material care and psychological barriers to fullness of being. For Lawrence, a sick and tortured man, conscious that he is a prisoner of his own past, of his upbringing, of his poverty, perhaps of his inadequate masculinity, "to be or not to be" is and will remain the fundamental question. Caught also between his alienation from society and his desire to contribute to its reform, after the suppression of *The Rainbow* he is obliged to recognize that he is powerless to change it. He therefore sets out to destroy it by satire, at the same time trying to lay the foundations of a new faith drawn from beyond the hated

Western heritage in which Judaism, Christian spirituality and Greek intellectualism are combined. He returns to the mystic springs extolled by
Houston Chamberlain as containing the future of the whole white race.
This revulsion from the Western heritage was to culminate years later in
The Plumed Serpent, the final artistic expression of a political and religious
trend of thought he first expressed in the "Study of Thomas Hardy", and
again in *The Symbolic Meaning*. But in 1919 Lawrence was still and above
all at grips with the problem of the individual's relations with immediate
otherness, i.e. man or woman.

From 1911 to 1916, his novels constantly bear on this problem, in a way
revealing permanent psychological features of his personality. *The White
Peacock*, written under the triple influence of his mother, of Alice Dax and of
Jessie Chambers, is the novel of a young man's perplexity before woman,
who, in fact, inspires him with both fear and contempt: the attitude of Cyril,
as well as of Annable. Men, on the other hand, i.e. George and Annable,
attract and fascinate Cyril, torn between friendship and love almost to the
point of homosexuality. *The White Peacock* reveals an ambivalence of the
psychic attitudes in its adolescent author, haunted by the phantasm of an
absent father.

Sons and Lovers, thanks successively to Jessie Chambers and to Frieda,
marks the novelist's realization of his own psychological problem: but side
by side with a faithful portrait of Paul Morel, he paints a false and self-
justifying picture of the girl, Miriam, aided and abetted in the final stages
of revision by Frieda's jealousy and her very primary psychology. The
attempt at self-analysis is a failure, not as a novel, but as a cure: it does not
enable Lawrence to make a new start. The obsessive male Lawrentian
character, sometimes an image of the father with whom no filial bond has
been established, sometimes the husband or lover of the adulterous woman,
bursts into this novel in the form of Baxter Dawes, Paul's rival, as was his
father; the novel ends weakly on a scene intended to assert Paul's vitality,
but on a vague promise and not on the achievement of balanced relationships.
Paul is left alone and vulnerable.

The Trespasser is haunted not only by the ghost of the rival, but also by
that of the lover's impotence in face of the unsatisfied female psyche. *The
Rainbow* gives the reader at first the impression that entirely new ground
is being broken, that the gates are opening into a paradise reached by Tom
and Lydia after their first unsuccessful strivings. But this is shortly followed
by the fall of Will and Anna, portraits of a man and woman incapable of
accession to true being, to regeneration through fullness of love. The contrast
between these two couples marks a climax in Lawrence's positive optimistic
concept of love. But with Ursula's story, conceived at first as an advance
towards complete individuality, we return once more to the fundamental
concept of *The White Peacock*, the mingled fear of and contempt for woman:

this is perceived when Lawrence secretly identifies with Skrebensky as lover, if not as soldier. The spectre of homosexuality prowls once more, unexplained, around Ursula and her Uncle Tom.

Although intended to lead to earthly paradise, *Women in Love* brings one couple to catastrophe, leaving the other a prey to a nostalgia for "something more" in addition to love accepted by Birkin only with certain ritualistic restrictions, and with fears similar to those of Cyril in *The White Peacock*. The erotic nature of woman must be restrained, subordinated to man. The message of Weininger the woman-hater would seem to have prevailed over that of Carpenter, who defended homosexuals but whose all-embracing psychology of love in all its forms had made him the friend and counsellor of many a sufferer. Weininger's views no doubt answered a deep-seated predisposition of Lawrence, a fundamental failure to adapt to the male social role; and indeed there is evidence that at the same time of his life his interest in Carpenter's writings on homosexuality had increased. Most readers will agree with Ursula when, unsatisfied in her love, she accuses Birkin of "perversity" as he mourns for the friendship he had hoped to maintain with Gerald. The novel as finally published does not explicitly admit the passionate, physical attraction which underlay this friendship. The recent publication of the Prologue shows that Ursula was right.[35]

The short stories of 1914–19 are mainly scenes of escape and of flight, flight into death as in "England, my England", of resignation to a life of mediocrity as in "Fanny and Annie", of a blind quest for contact with "the other" as in "The Blind Man". The opening chapters of *Aaron's Rod* and *The Lost Girl*—the latter just preceding, the former closing this same period—are tales of flight from the mediocrity of a North Midlands reminiscent of Arnold Bennett, of inadaptation and revolt; in both novels sex—positively with Alvina Houghton, negatively for Aaron—plays a primary role in their rebellion. Seeking a subconscious link between these stories, we find a constant failure to adapt to communal life, revealing itself in the impossibility of a normal love relationship, and a nostalgia for "touch" most strikingly manifested in "The Blind Man". In this story, as in "England, My England", the war is merely accessory, revealing as it does a profound incompatibility, a nostalgia for a mystic relationship between beings not satisfied by ordinary social links. *Kangaroo*, and above all *The Plumed Serpent*, will subsequently pursue this quest for a social relationship at once binding, absolute and sacred. They will also pursue on the political and religious plane a quest for a definitive relationship between self and other.

Psychoanalysts have their own explanation for this anxiety, this ceaseless quest for an absolute link with mother, woman, man: namely that Lawrence never "accepted the father", as some critics think Paul Morel does at the end of *Sons and Lovers*, when he turns to face the city and the world of men.[36]

Without wishing here to enter into a purely psychological discussion, we would merely observe that while *Sons and Lovers* may lead *in extremis* to some kind of catharsis, Lawrence, who portrayed himself in the guise of Paul, nevertheless continued to create characters incapable of choosing the world of men, or of forming simple, balanced relationships. The psychology of Birkin and Ursula is one of escape; they are united in a quest for a mythical paradise. The psychology of the hero of "England, My England" is that of a flight into death. The characters of the late war short stories all flee towards the New World with a woman "who could have been their mother". Aaron's flight from his wife leads him to friendship with Lilly, the charismatic leader; "Manifesto", too, is a poem of flight, describing as it does a relationship with the beloved outside all normal emotions or contacts, a flight into the obscurity, the near-mystification, of a magic ritual derived from theosophy and yoga.

The self incapable of normal human relationships, simply offered and accepted, thus takes refuge in mystification. Some see perversity in the scenes just alluded to, and in the subject of *The Plumed Serpent*. What they reveal above all, however, is the tragedy of an asocial personality, deformed from infancy, but fortunately endowed with a talent so exceptional as to redeem by spontaneous artistic creation all that was incurably distorted in its human relationships.

Destructive ardour

Love, friendship, social life being impossible, the novelist and theorist hovers between two poles: satire of what is, vision of what should be. But the painter and realist prevails over the utopist: satire predominates, and reaction triumphs over action. The Lawrence of 1915, like the Lawrence of 1919, was a true reactionary, a pessimist despising human activities because they are mean and relative, preferring the mythic majesty of some vague future absolute. "Otherness", being a form of non-being, must submit to the self. Here the Lawrence of 1916 and later differs from the Lawrence of 1914–15, who still believed sincerely in the possibility of finding jointly with a woman, in perfect equipoise, the expression of the "law" of being. That is the doctrine of the "Hardy", of the first half of *The Rainbow*. Disillusionment, the return to isolation, to the will to subjugate the other, begin with Ursula's adolescence, and the theory of twin stars, balanced love, in *Women in Love* is no more than a mirage to which Lawrence was henceforward to refer more and more rarely. He was in fact to become progressively more and more absorbed by the problems of the identification of the self with the cosmos; to be reached not through love, but only by blind submission to the divine breath, of which love is only one manifestation among countless others, all of which exclude and extinguish the conscious, deliberate ego. During a later phase, Lawrence's sense of critical reality will lead him to denounce as falsehood this identification, this last refuge of spiritualist abstraction, of the desire for "merging" in the all-self. His relentless attack upon Whitman's remaining traces of spirituality in 1923, his passionate affirmation of the flesh as opposed to spirit, that flesh which, in Lawrentian psychology, is the seat of the soul, is, with added bitterness and vehemence, but an aspect of his dissatisfaction with the abstract, disembodied spirituality of his youth.

A clouded message

By 1919 Lawrence had not fully and satisfactorily worked out the message of his last years: complete integrity of soul and body, and joyful recognition of one's partner's integrity. The dross of ambition, of dreams of domination over others, still obscured the message, and vaguely religious aspirations veiled any manifestation of human sympathy. The Puritan in revolt was still hampering the plain man longing for a free and integrated life.

Thus Lawrence's message to his compatriots concerning sex—which is substantially the same as those of Sir Richard Burton, translator of the *Kama Sutra* and *The Arabian Nights*, of Havelock Ellis and of Carpenter— remains confused, hesitant, constricted by the remnants of Victorian prudery, a certain greenhorn reticence, enveloped in a cloud of esoteric trash. The most daring love scenes, from *Sons and Lovers* to the end of *Women in Love* by way of the three generations of Brangwens in *The Rainbow*, do not throw much light on what Lawrence was trying to convey in his descriptions of the motivations and manifestations of sex. The clearest affirmations are those appearing in *Women in Love*: "We should enjoy everything", says Birkin after declaring his admiration for Gerald's physical beauty. "How could anything that gave one satisfaction be excluded?" asks Ursula after the revelation of Birkin's "bestiality".[37] The message of *Lady Chatterley's Lover*, which, coming after Burton and Ellis, is essentially the liberation of the individual from puritan inhibitions, is contained in *Women in Love*, but masked and obscured by one-sided social criticism and by the ideology and ritual magic of a hesitant and tormented Birkin. The Lawrence of 1916 and 1919 was still far from having accomplished his mutation, his personal liberation. While his aesthetic is resolutely modern, the formulation of his love ethic retains a note of provincial, if not Victorian timidity.

Lyricism

Close analysis of Lawrence's uneven literary output of the war years reveals all that is still confused and passionately arbitrary in his thinking; a large part of this output is the result of an effort to see clearly in an internal universe perturbed by problems of self-adaptation, an effort based not on a clear and lucid analysis of the problems themselves, but on images or patterns springing from the emotion-charged wisdom of the ages rather than from ideas organized rationally and logically. The rejection of science, of scientific philosophy, of humdrum academic knowledge, in favour of passional explanations, religious cosmogonies, and psycho-ethnological myths, was no accident, but was inherent in the writer's character, in his craving for certitude, his search for faith and hope of salvation. Lawrence's intelligence, his poetic gift, were functioning in a pre-scientific mental universe, guided by affective logic serving as basis for a highly personal system of images and symbols, rationally incommunicable, and weakened or deadened by any attempt at explanation. Lawrence was well aware of the art form best adapted to his temperament: "poetry of the present", the lyrical expression of intense states of communion, of unison with nature, of any "quick" incarnation of the divine, of hate and rebellion against all that seemed to him to deny life.

His 1914–19 poetic output, very slight apart from the cycle of *Look! We Have Come Through!*, contributes no new theme of importance apart from "New Heaven and Earth" and "Manifesto". Indeed the war had but little direct effect on his poety: his occasional verses, the few passing references to "Tommies in a Train", to the fate of soldiers at the front or to London in the blackout, naturally lack the impact of the war poems of a Wilfred Owen or Siegfried Sassoon. The genuine suffering inflicted on Lawrence by the war is expressed elsewhere, and in "New Heaven and Earth" assumes personal, totally subjective expression. Not until his return to Italy and his life in New Mexico, was he to find inspiration in a poetry combining love of living forms, satire, and animal symbolism.

But even during these relatively arid years, his prose works abound in pure lyric passages: the rhythmic scenes of *The Rainbow*, the vivid descriptions of animals in *Women in Love*, in "Rex" and "Adolf", the evocation of nature and the fabulous denizens of the Lawrentian bestiary in "The Crown" or in "The Reality of Peace". Children, beasts, birds and flowers, all living creatures, spontaneous in their unconscious natures, their psychic individuality and their perfect harmony with the creative mystery, such are the very substance of his purest, most individual art.

But while the detail springs from pure lyricism, the global message remains confused, obscure: the writer fails to break his bonds. The new heaven and earth which he proclaims are not yet firmly and unreservedly placed within the grasp of those who live on this earth and under these skies. Several more years will elapse before he is able to translate into works of imagination, less bitterly, less satirically and less obscurely, his love of a constantly renewed and ever-glorious life, his faith in human tenderness shorn of all reticence and freed of all metaphysic. The Lawrence of 1919 is still a prophet denouncing the wickedness of man and proclaiming the coming of a better era. But how much more convincing is he when, as in "Whistling of Birds", his short essay celebrating the end of the war, he simply expresses his confidence in the return of springtime, not in some far-distant paradise but in the here and now:

> We may not choose the world. We have hardly any choice of ourselves. We follow with our eyes the bloody and horrid line of march of extreme winter, as it passes away. But we cannot hold back the spring. We cannot make the birds silent, prevent the bubbling of the wood-pigeons. We cannot stay the fine world of silver-fecund creation from gathering itself and taking place upon us. Whether we will or no, the daphne tree will soon be giving off perfume, the lambs dancing on two feet, the celandines will twinkle all over the ground, there will be a new heaven and a new earth . . . Who can thwart the impulse that comes upon us? It comes from the unknown upon us, and it behoves us to pass delicately and exquisitely upon the subtle new wind from heaven, conveyed like birds in unreasoning migration from death to life.[38]

This is the gentle voice of the poet, only to be heard when the shrill cry of the prophet is stilled, when, ceasing to rend himself asunder, he consents to live and make the most of life. This voice, with that of other great English poets of life and nature, will be heard by future generations little concerned with his relentless battle against his inbred puritanism, against that personal dualism which, despite all efforts to persuade himself that his malady was that of his whole epoch, remained an individual burden.

Personal significance of the early works

If Lawrence's poetry, novels and short stories did not force themselves upon our attention by the vigour of his passionate sincerity, if his works did not spring clearly from life and from experience, if they were always fully intelligible without the help of an interpretation based on his biography and theoretical works, the present study would have little object. Its justification lies in their obscurities, distortions, hesitations. This amounts to saying that except for certain short stories, and including *Sons and Lovers*, the most autonomous, the most independently alive of all his novels, Lawrence's youthful work is profoundly marked not so much by his epoch as by the particularities of a personality which, it is true, *was* sensitive to certain contemporary trends. But his works are so marked by his personal circumstances that the critical battle which has raged around him has, in fact, rarely risen above biographical considerations; witness, among many others, even such a study as *D. H. Lawrence, novelist*, by F. R. Leavis.

In the first place Lawrence stands out in contemporary English literature by his working-class origin: in the first twenty years of this century in England, only a man of the people could so completely escape scholastic, university and social conditioning, at the same time remaining so deeply marked by puritan nonconformism. Any man reared in the traditional scholastic pattern, outside the family setting, would not to the same degree have been branded puritan, and would have experienced less intensely the desire for liberation so confusedly but constantly noticeable in Lawrence.

Most important for his psychic development is the predominant influence of the family environment and its conflicts, resulting in the association of opposing tendencies of his parents, with certain contrasting ideas, ways of life, philosophies. Father and mother images become symbols of antithetic views, the one puritanic and socially aspiring, the other naturistic, tending towards easy acceptance of life, devoid of the will to change or to improvement. A traditional English education would have removed the boy from such conflicts, rapidly encouraging an independence of character which Lawrence, no doubt also partly by virtue of his temperament and hypersensitivity, was never to approach. The effort to free himself was to be all the harder for the bonds of affection linking him to mother, sisters and the Chambers household, and for the fact that his adolescent intellectual maturation was to coincide and become indissolubly associated with the slow growth of love, thus creating not so much the seed of his deep personal conflict as the very ground out of which it was to develop.

From this conflict he sought to escape by means of flight, by change of woman, of country, of climate and of social milieu. In 1919 he still hoped to alter his personality by changing countries, even though he no longer wished to change his woman, or even to believe in complex marriage. Flight, not revolt, is the keynote of his work: flight into the anonymously divine creative instinct, into the song of eternal rebirth; flight from social responsibility; from painstaking construction of a world of stable relationships: flight into art, symbolized by Lawrence's favourite images of the phoenix rising from its ashes, and of the singing, solitary, soaring lark. This poet of Life, of the creative impulse, remains essentially the poet of individual, solitary life. Thus by 1918 this self-styled priest of love, this reputed prophet of sexual freedom, could portray only tortured, indecisive love, powerlessly obsessed by the problems of human relations between lovers, filled with a nostalgia for the inhuman, i.e. a reduction, if not the absolute negation, of love. Birkin, with his compulsive dread of "merging", is surely the ultimate witness to this reductive notion of love.

For sheer lyrical force, for power of physical evocation of things and beings, and, beyond the physical, of what he himself calls soul, Lawrence has no equal among his contemporaries. His bitter, passionate, satirical talent is at the service of an undiscriminating criticism of society, entirely negative and devoid of all attempt to understand or sympathize with any form or category of social life. The satire is not that of a child of the people directed against the upper classes and the aristocracy, but an attack upon society as a whole by a man rejecting *en bloc*, in an access of self-mutilation, a society to which he feels himself a total stranger. *Women in Love* is no place to seek a balanced picture of twentieth-century English society: all we find is a series of firmly drawn caricatures. A symbolic portrait, it may be objected, an imaginative re-creation, a form of expressionism. Perhaps, but what use is such a portrait if it does not correspond to the realities of a recognizable world, if it shows only one side of the society it pretends to depict?

A marked tendency of Lawrentian criticism is to try to justify and defend rather than evaluate this writer. In 1930, no evaluation was possible: the problems and conflicts were still too close for judgment. Lawrence's reputation has grown with the years, as his critical and artistic preoccupations have become better understood. No one will contest the greatness of the novelist of *Sons and Lovers*, of the poet of the early years. Agreement is less unanimous concerning *The Rainbow* and *Women in Love*—more ambitious works, the perspective and aim of which were modified in the course of composition, not so much on account of the war as of a certain slackening of the original love inspiration. Yet they remain two great novels, showing an effort towards new form, a search for symbolic expression of states of consciousness or of the unconscious which contemporary psychology scarcely knew how to describe, let alone express: works ahead of their time, exploiting to the utmost limits the Wagnerian and Symbolist heritage; works which, in spite of frequent faults, irritating repetitions and exaggerated insistence upon symbol, remain monuments of an English style admirable at its best. But the fact that the intentions of these novels cannot be fully understood without a biographical gloss, and without reference to their author's theoretical works and to ideas acquired from his reading, does detract from their value as works of art. The reader remains torn between admiration, and the sense of frustration and incomplete achievement, perhaps because of Lawrence's very originality and promise. To point this out in conclusion in no way detracts from his significance.

NOTES

For D. H. Lawrence's works, all now published by William Heinemann Ltd, references are to the earlier Secker thin-paper edition, unless otherwise indicated. The following abbreviations are used in the Notes below:

Am.	*Amores*, Poems by D. H. Lawrence, Duckworth, 1916.
Apoc.	*Apocalypse*, Martin Secker, 1932.
A.R.	*Aaron's Rod.*
Ass. Art.	*Assorted Articles*, Martin Secker, 1930.
Bib. Com.	Noyes, John Humphrey, *Bible Communism*, Brooklyn: Oneida Community, 1853.
Brewster	Brewster, Earl and Achsah, *D. H. Lawrence, Reminiscences and Correspondence*, Martin Secker, 1939.
B.T.W.	Murry, John Middleton, *Between Two Worlds*, Jonathan Cape, 1935.
C.L.	*Collected Letters*, Heinemann, 1962.
Col. P.	*Collected Poems*, Martin Secker, 1928.
C.P.	*Complete Poems*, Heinemann, 1964.
C.S.St.	*Complete Short Stories*, Heinemann, 1955.
Delavenay, *D.H.L.*	Delavenay, Emile, *D. H. Lawrence: L'Homme et la Genèse de Son Œuvre: Les Années de Formation: 1885–1919*, Paris: Klincksieck, 1969.
Diaries	Asquith, Lady Cynthia, *Diaries, 1915–1918*, Hutchinson, 1968.
E.L.	Lawrence, Ada, and Gelder, Stuart, *Young Lorenzo, the Early Life of D. H. Lawrence*, Florence: Orioli, 1932.
E.T.	*D. H. Lawrence, a Personal Record*, by E.T. (i.e. Jessie Chambers), Jonathan Cape, 1935.
E.T. (I)	"The Literary Formation of D. H. Lawrence", by E.T., *European Quarterly*, May 1934.
Fantasia	*Fantasia of the Unconscious*, Martin Secker, New Adelphi Library, 1930.
Foundations	Chamberlain, Houston S., *The Foundations of the XIXth Century*, a translation from the German by John Lees with an Introduction by Lord Redesdale, John Lane, 1911.

H.A.S.	Noyes, John Humphrey, *History of American Socialisms*, 1870 (reprint, New York: Hillary House, 1961).
H.O.	Home Office documents.
Int. H.	Moore, Harry T., *The Intelligent Heart*, Penguin, 1960.
L.	*The Letters of D. H. Lawrence*, edited by Aldous Huxley, Heinemann, 1932.
L.A.H.	*Love Among the Haystacks, and other Pieces*, Nonesuch, 1930.
L. in T.	Luhan, Mabel Dodge, *Lorenzo in Taos*, New York: Knopf, 1932.
Lk.	*Look! We Have Come Through!*, Chatto and Windus, 1917.
L.P.	*Love Poems and Others*, Duckworth, 1913.
M. & C.	Lawrence, Frieda, *Memoirs and Correspondence*, Heinemann, 1965.
M.E.H.	*Movements in European History*, Humphrey Milford, 1921.
M.L.	*A Modern Lover*, Martin Secker, 1934.
M.S. (I) M.S. (II)	Two unpublished manuscript memoirs prepared for the author by Jessie Chambers, extracts from which can be found in Delavenay, *D.H.L.* 1969 (see above).
Nehls	Nehls, Edward, *D. H. Lawrence, A Composite Biography*, University of Wisconsin, 3 vols, 1957, 1958, 1959. (All references to Vol. I unless otherwise stated.)
N.G.	Corke, Helen, *Neutral Ground*, Arthur Barker, 1933.
Not I . . .	Lawrence, Frieda, *Not I, but the Wind*, Heinemann, 1935.
N.P.	*New Poems*, Martin Secker, 1918.
P.G.B.	Aldington, Richard, *Portrait of a Genius, But . . .*, Heinemann, 1950.
Ph.	*Phoenix*, Heinemann, 1936.
Ph. II	*Phoenix II*, Heinemann, 1968.
P.O.	*The Prussian Officer and Other Stories*.
Ps. U.	*Psychoanalysis and the Unconscious*, Martin Secker, New Adelphi Library, 1931.
R.B.G.	Asquith, Lady Cynthia, *Remember and be Glad*, Barrie, 1952.
R.D.P.	*Reflections on the Death of a Porcupine*, Philadelphia: The Centaur Bookshop, 1925.
RW.	*The Rainbow*.
S. and L.	*Sons and Lovers*.
S.C.A.L.	*Studies in Classic American Literature*, Martin Secker, 1924.
S.M.	*The Symbolic Meaning*, Arundel: Centaur Press, 1962.
S.P.	Carswell, Catherine, *The Savage Pilgrimage*, Chatto & Windus, 1932.
T.H.	"Study of Thomas Hardy", in *Phoenix*.
T.I.	*Twilight in Italy*, Traveller's Library, Jonathan Cape, 1926.
T.L.S.	*The Times Literary Supplement*.

Tres.	*The Trespasser.*
Wh. P.	*The White Peacock.*
W.L.	*Women in Love.*
Zytaruk	Zytaruk, George, *The Quest for Rananim*, McGill–Queen's University Press, 1970.

CHAPTER I

1. "Nottingham and the Mining Countryside", *Ph.* 133; cf. *Int. H.* 27–8
2. *E.L.* 3
3. *S. and L.* 17; *E.L.* 12
4. *E.L.* 11
5. ibid. 23
6. *S. and L.* 114
7. ibid passim; "Autobiographical Sketch", *Ass. Art.* 146–7
8. *S. and L.* 66 ff.; *E.L.* 26
9. *S. and L.* 21 ff.; 38 ff.; 59–60, 63–4, etc.
10. *E.L.* 26–7
11. ibid 9
12. *S. and L.* 7, 10
13. ibid 8–9; cf. *E.L.* 10; *Col. P.* 80, "Whether or not"
14. *S. and L.* 9–11; *E.L.* 10–11
15. *S. and L.* 33 ff.; *E.L.* 22
16. *S. and L.* 52
17. Cf. *E.L.* 20–1
18. *S. and L.* 50 ff.
19. ibid 59 ff.
20. ibid 89; cf. also *Col. P.* 17, "The Collier's Wife"
21. *S. and L.* 1–2, "The Bottoms"
22. *E.L.* 17–18
23. *S. and L.* 60–1; cf. *Col. P.* 13, "Discord in Childhood"
24. *S. and L.* Ch. I and II passim; cf. also *Wh. P.* 43
25. Brewster, 310
26. *S. and L.* 37
27. ibid 37
28. ibid 36
29. ibid 58
30. ibid 38
31. Letter from Mrs Clarke to the author, 17 December 1934
32. *S. and L.* 77; *E.L.* 33 ff. and additional information given to the author by Mrs Clarke
33. *S. and L.* 70–2
34. ibid 72–3
35. *P.O.* 267–80
36. *The Lost Girl*, Ch. I; *T.I.* 192

37. *E.L.* 57; *Apoc.* 2; *Ass. Art.* 162
38. *E.L.* 57
39. "Hymns in a Man's Life", *Ass. Art.* 160–1
40. *Apoc.* 15
41. "Pomegranate", *C.P.* 278
42. *Apoc.* 5
43. "Hymns in a Man's Life", *Ass. Art.* 163; cf. *C.P.* 143, "Piano"
44. "Hymns in a Man's Life", *Ass. Art.* 159
45. ibid 156
46. ibid 160
47. Information given by Mrs Clarke, 26 August 1932
48. *E.L.* 60
49. Information given by H. Goddard Esq., master at Nottingham High School
50. *Ass. Art.* 118–25
51. *S. and L.* 89
52. *RW.* Ch. X passim; cf. 248 ff.
53. *E.L.* 58
54. Information given by H. Goddard Esq.
55. cf. *S. and L.* 89
56. cf. ibid 89 ff.

CHAPTER 2

1. The chronology of Lawrence's youth as given by his sister Ada in *The Early Life of D. H. Lawrence*, and in the Biographical Notice figuring in the first collected edition of his *Letters* is far from reliable. His own "Autobiographical Sketch" (*Ass. Art.* 148) is a better guide. In the present and following chapters documentary evidence, supplied by Nottingham University College and the Davidson School, Croydon, has been used to complete these sources. The author has also drawn upon the following published and unpublished material from Jessie Chambers Wood:
   (1) *D.H.L., a Personal Record* by E.T.;
   (2) "The Literary Formation of D.H.L." by E.T. in *European Quarterly*, May 1934;
   (3) Two unpublished manuscripts loaned to the author from which substantial extracts are published in Delavenay, *D.H.L.*, 1969, Appendix IV (M.S. [I] and M.S. [II]);
   (4) Letters from Jessie Chambers Wood to the author, also in Delavenay, *D.H.L.*, 1969, Appendix IV;
   (5) Replies from Jessie Chambers Wood to eight questions by the author, unpublished except the reply to Question 8 in Delavenay, *D.H.L.*, 1969, Appendix IV.
2. *S. and L.* 91; *E.L.* 70–1
3. *S. and L.* 97
4. *E.L.* 71
5. *S. and L.* 90–3
6. ibid 96
7. ibid 140–1
8. ibid 141
9. ibid 150

10. *RW*. 348–9
11. *Ass. Art.* 148
12. *RW*. Ch. XIII
13. *S. and L.* 159
14. *The Teacher*, Vol. II, No 58, 280–4
15. M.S. (I) 21; cf. also E.T. 74
16. *The Teacher*, loc. cit.
17. M.S. (I) 22
18. cf. Plate 3, showing D.H.L. at twenty-one
19. Letter from Enid Hilton to the author, 18 January 1969
20. E.T. 16, 20, 21–2
21. M.S. (I) 5
22. *S. and L.* 125
23. ibid 147–9
24. ibid 143, 148
25. ibid 148 ff.
26. *E.L.* 65
27. *S. and L.* 150
28. ibid; cf. also *Wh. P.* II, Ch. 8, "A poem of friendship"
29. *S. and L.* 158, 232; cf. also *C.L.* 24
30. *S. and L.* 226–7
31. *C.L.* 1100
32. *S. and L.* 150–2
33. See below, Ch. 4, 84
34. Letter No 2 from Jessie Chambers in Delavenay, *D.H.L.* 1969, 668
35. ibid 668–9
36. *S. and L.* 125
37. ibid 143; *Wh. P.* 413
38. *S. and L.* 153
39. ibid 153, 189; *Wh. P.* 21
40. *S. and L.* 154–5
41. ibid 127–8, 150–2
42. ibid 127
43. ibid 148
44. ibid 144
45. ibid
46. ibid 143
47. ibid 144
48. ibid 149
49. ibid 124
50. E.T. 91
51. M.S. (I) 14; *S. and L.* 159–60, etc.; also E.T. 33
52. *S. and L.* 158; M.S. (I) 17–18; E.T. 55
53. M.S. (I) 18
54. M.S. (I) 19–20
55. cf. *A Collier's Friday Night*, 4
56. E.T. 92

57. *S. and L.* 160, etc.
58. E.T. (I) 37; cf. also E.T. 96
59. E.T. 96
60. Nehls, 44, George H. Neville
61. M.S. (I) 16–17
62. *S. and L.* 168
63. ibid 170
64. E.T. 95
65. ibid 99
66. E.T. (I) 40; cf. also *Ass. Art.* 155
67. M.S. (I) 24; cf. E.T. 38–9
68. E.T. 57
69. E.T. 101–2
70. E.T. 56–7
71. E.T. 59
72. M.S. (I) 24–5; cf. E.T. 61
73. *S. and L.* 173
74. E.T. 62–3
75. Letter No 7 from Jessie Chambers, Delavenay, *D.H.L.* 1969, Appendix IV
76. *S. and L.* 162–3
77. ibid 173
78. M.S. (I) 30–3; cf. E.T. 65–7
79. M.S. (I) 30–3
80. M.S. (I) 35
81. See below, Ch. 3, 45 ff.
82. See below, Ch. 4, 82–3
83. See above, Ch. 1, 7; also *S. and L.* 32, 36, 79, 102, etc.
84. *S. and L.* 257
85. *S. and L.* 100 ff., 116, 121, 129, 134
86. ibid 185
87. ibid 88, 121 ff., 164, etc.
88. ibid 89, 176, 181 ff., etc.
89. ibid 162, 212–13
90. ibid 162, 175, etc.
91. ibid 257
92. Mrs Ada Clarke in conversation with the author, August 1932
93. cf. L. 28–9
94. E.T. 125–6
95. *S. and L.* 169, 175, 180, 204
96. ibid 143 ff., 154
97. Letter No 6 from Jessie Chambers, Delavenay, *D.H.L.* 1969, Appendix IV, 673

CHAPTER 3

1. "Autobiographical Sketch", *Ass. Art.* 148
2. E.T. 75–6

3. Board of Education, *Regulations for the Training of Teachers and for the Examination of Students in Training Colleges*, 1906
4. Letter No 17 from Jessie Chambers, Delavenay, *D.H.L.* 1969, Appendix IV; cf. *E.L.* 249–68 and *RW.* 407 for Ursula Brangwen's study of the "theory of education"
5. cf. *T.I.* Part II, Ch. V
6. E.T. 82 and E.T. (I) 43
7. E.T. 80; cf. *E.L.* 52–3
8. *Wh. P.* 23, 39, 80, 82, 169, 378, 419, 446, 460
9. *E.L.* 269 onwards; see below p. 49
10. E.T. 107
11. M.S. (I) 70
12. *E.L.* 48
13. *RW.* 411; cf. also 408
14. E.T. 107; E.T. (I) 41; *Lawrence in Love, Letters to Louie Burrows*, Ed. James T. Boulton, University of Nottingham, 1968, 84
15. E.T. (I) 40–1; E.T. 106
16. E.T. 135
17. ibid 134; see below 48 ff
18. *Wh. P.* 33, 46, 47; cf. *P.O.* 172
19. cf. *Not I, but the Wind* passim and *C.L.* 110, 137, 142, 188, 205, 336, 524, 528, etc.
20. *C.L.* 1100 (to J. D. Chambers) see above p. 23
21. E.T. 78; cf. *Lawrence in Love* 2, 3
22. *RW.* 406
23. ibid 407
24. ibid 410; cf. also *Pansies* 80: "Nottingham's New University"
25. Reply by Jessie Chambers to Question No 4, Delavenay, *D.H.L.* 1969, Appendix IV; cf. also *A Collier's Friday Night* 37–8
26. Document communicated by the late Professor J. D. Chambers of Nottingham University College
27. E.T. 88
28. *Wh. P.* 90, Ch. II passim, 173–4
29. *RW.* Ch. XIV
30. "A Modern Lover", in the volume so entitled, 22
31. ibid 19
32. E.T. 108, 110, etc.; E.T. (I) 42–3
33. *S. and L.* 172
34. *S. and L.* 173–4
35. M.S. (I) 46
36. *S. and L.* 178–9
37. M.S. (I) 40–1
38. *S. and L.* 227
39. *Ass. Art.* 159
40. *S. and L.* 193, 227
41. E.T. 86; *E.L.* 47
42. Essays of Schopenhauer (translated by Mrs R. Dirks), Walter Scott Publishing Co Ltd, 1903
43. See below, 95
44. *M.L.* 19

45. E.T. 112–13
46. By Thomas Hood
47. *S. and L.* 209–10. Note the three misquotations, which may well be deliberate
48. E.T. 107, 134
49. Havelock Ellis, *A Study of British Genius*, 173
50. *E.L.* 66
51. In Liverpool Museum; cf. *E.L.*, Reproduction No 6
52. *Wh. P.* 42–5
53. *E.L.* 84
54. *Wh. P.* 243; cf. E.T. 110
55. *Wh. P.* 245
56. E.T. 112–13
57. M.S. (I) 63
58. E.T. 112–13
59. *S. and L.* 193
60. ibid 208
61. E.T. 135
62. E.T. 130
63. *S. and L.* 228
64. cf. *S. and L.* 189–90, 195, 208, 218 ff. etc.
65. E.T. 130–1
66. *Wh. P.* 106
67. M.S. (I) 51; cf. *S. and L.* 280, 209–10, etc.
68. See below 72 ff.
69. M.S. (I) 53; cf. E.T. 142–3
70. H. T. Moore, *Int. H.* 131
71. Nehls, 135
72. *C.L.* 5, 6, 7, 9, 12, 14, 19, etc.
73. *C.L.* 19
74. *C.L.* 14
75. Letter to the author from Enid Hilton, 18 January 1969
76. *C.L.* 7
77. Letter No 5 from Jessie Chambers in Delavenay, *D.H.L.* 1969

CHAPTER 4

1. *C.P.* Note, 2, 8
2. *Wh. P.* III, 361–2, 380: cf. also "Last Hours", *Col. P.* 35
3. M.S. (I) 66–7
4. E.T. 151; cf. also *Wh. P.* 395–6
5. *C.P.* 64, 73; E.T. 157
6. *Wh. P.* 401–2; cf. also *C.P.* 50, 52, 53, 57, 58, 70, etc.
7. *C.L.* 38
8. Information given to the author by A. W. McLeod, a fellow-teacher of Lawrence at Davidson Road School

9. *C.P.* 74, 92, 94, etc.; cf. also *RW.* 361–4
10. *E.L.* 95–7
11. *C.L.* 31
12. "Last Lesson in the Afternoon", *C.P.* 74
13. "A Snowy Day in School", *C.P.* 76
14. "The Punisher", *C.P.* 94
15. "The Best of School" (1st version), *Love Poems,* 37
16. "Discipline" (1st version) *Am.* 34; final version, *C.P.* 92
17. Reply by Jessie Chambers to Question 5, Delavenay, *D.H.L.* 1969, Appendix IV
18. From a letter from Helen Corke to the author, 9 October 1968
19. *E.T.* 120
20. *Lawrence in Love,* 145
21. *E.T.* 122
22. *Wh. P.* 450
23. *Lawrence in Love,* 42
24. *C.L.* 84, 88, 94
25. Information from A.W. McLeod; *E.L.* 233–4
26. Information from P. F. Smith
27. *E.T.* 155
28. *Lawrence in Love,* 38, 42, 43
29. M.S. (I) 15
30. *E.T.* 156–60
31. *E.T.* 163, *C.L.* 58, 163
32. *C.L.* 12
33. ibid 44–5
34. ibid 45
35. *E.T.* 160, 163 and M.S. (I) 79–81, 83
36. *Lawrence in Love,* 37
37. *C.L.* 59
38. *E.T.* 164–8; M.S. (I) 85–7
39. *Am.* 11
40. *C.P.* 106
41. *C.P.* 70
42. *Am.* 52; *C.P.* 179
43. *E.T.* 130
44. *Wh. P.* 340–1
45. *E.T.* 153
46. M.S. (I) 72–3; cf. *E.T.* 153
47. *S. and L.* 276
48. *RW.* 13–14
49. M.S. (II) 1–2; cf. *E.T.* 180
50. *M.L.* 11–44
51. ibid 19
52. ibid 22
53. ibid 25
54. ibid 41
55. ibid 43; cf. *S. and L.* 281–5

56. M.S. (II) 11
57. *M.L.* 15; cf. also "Forecast", *C.P.* 91 ("Epilogue "*Am.* 31)
58. *M.L.* 23
59. *S. and L.* 285
60. *RW.* 13
61. *C.L.* 55
62. *C.L.* 59
63. *C.L.* 60
64. *Lawrence in Love*
65. M.S. (II) 3
66. ibid 4
66a. M.S. (II)
67. "Scent of Irises", *C.P.* 90
68. "Scent of Irises", first version, *Am.* 39
69. "Lilies in the Fire", *C.P.* 87
70. *S. and L.* 292
70a. Letters 18 and 20 from Jessie Chambers, Delavenay, *D.H.L.* 1969, Appendix IV
70b. *Ph. II* 94
70c. ibid 97
70d. ibid 99
70e. M.S. (II)
70f. *Ph. II* 99–100
70g. ibid 101
71. *N.G.* 259
72. M.S. (II) 5–6
73. *N.G.* 261 ff.
74. Helen Corke, *Lawrence and Apocalypse*, Heinemann, 1933, 44, 128; cf. *N.G.* 260, 265, etc.
75. *Lawrence and Apocalypse*, 77; cf. also 'The Yew Tree on the Downs", *C.P.* 114
76. *C.L.* 61; *L.* 2–4; M.S. (II) 6; E.T. 181
77. *N.G.* 262, 274 ff.
78. *S. and L.* Ch. XIV, "The Release"
79. *C.P.* 99, 100
80. "The Bad Side of Books", *Ph.* 232
81. *C.L.* 66
82. *S. and L.* 387
83. "The Appeal", *C.P.* 86
84. *L.P.* 30
85. "Lotus and Frost", *C.P.* 113
86. M.S. (II) 8–9; "Excursion", *Am.* 101; "Excursion Train", *C.P.* 116
87. *C.P.* 116
88. "Reproach", *Am.* 95; "Release", *C.P.* 117
89. *C.P.* 117
90. *Am.* 106; "These Clever Women", *C.P.* 118; cf. also *Lady Chatterley's Lover*, Secker, 223
91. *S. and L.* 378
92. "Reminder", *C.P.* 103; *S. and L.* 393

93. *C.L.* 70
94. M.S. (II) 9; cf. E.T. 184
95. "The Witch à la Mode", *M.L.* 103–28
96. *Lawrence in Love*, 67 (20 October 1910)
97. ibid 89 (1 April 1911)
98. ibid 98
99. *C.P.* 27, and 116–30 "Kisses in the Train"; "Turned Down"; "Snap-Dragon"; "Come Spring, Come Sorrow"; "The Hands of the Betrothed"; "A Love Song"; "Twofold"; "Tarantella"; "Under the Oak"
100. *C.P.* 127
101. *C.P.* 129
102. *L.* 17 (30 November 1911)
103. *C.L.* 77; *E.L.* 88, 89–90
104. *C.P.* 131
105. *E.L.* 91
106. *C.L.* 79–81
107. *C.L.* 66–90, particularly 85 and 88
108. *Lawrence in Love*, 124–8
109. M.S. (II) 11
110. ibid; cf. also E.T. 186 ff.
111. *C.L.* 82, 84
112. *C.L.* 73
113. E. D. McDonald, *A Bibliography of the Writings of D. H. Lawrence*, Philadelphia: The Centaur Book Shop, 1925, 126–7
114. *C.L.* 82
115. *E.L.* 83; *C.L.* 62, 88, 89
116. *M.L.* 11 ff.
117. ibid 17–18
118. ibid 30; cf. also 19–20
119. "The Soiled Rose", *Forum* XLIV, March 1913, 324–30; cf. *C.L.* 91
120. cf. *P.O.* 158 and 172
121. M.S. (I) 70
122. M.S. (I) 72
123. E.T. 168, 176
124. cf. *S. and L.* 256–7
125. E.T. 163–4
126. *S. and L.* 97–8
127. *Wh. P.* 375
128. *Not I . . .* 34
129. E.T. 79
130. *S. and L.* 258, 423; cf. also "Call Unto Death", *C.P.* 134
131. cf. *S. and L.* 97
132. *E.L.* 90–1
133. *E.L.* 81, 82, 89
134. *L.* 7
135. *E.L.* 89
136. *E.L.* 79, 80, 82–4, 88

137. *C.P.* 47, 62
138. "End of Another Home Holiday", *C.P.* 64
139. "The End . . ." *C.P.* 100
140. "The Bride", ibid 101
141. "The Virgin Mother", ibid 101
142. "Note", ibid 28
143. "Sorrow", ibid 106
144. "Brooding Grief", ibid 110; cf. *S. and L.* 413
145. "Grey Evening", *C.P.* 135
146. "Piano", ibid 148; cf. also "Twenty Years Ago", ibid 152
147. "Silence", ibid 109; cf. also "Listening", ibid 110
148. "Troth with the Dead", ibid 114
149. "The Shadow of Death", ibid 132
150. "Call unto Death", ibid 134
151. "In Trouble and Shame", ibid 134
152. "The Inheritance", ibid 108; cf. also "Silence", ibid 109
153. "At a Loose End", ibid 115
154. *S. and L.* 415
155. ibid
156. "Dolour of Autumn", *C.P.* 107
157. "Drunk", ibid 105
158. ibid 106
159. "Late at Night", ibid 140
160. *S. and L.* 414
161. ibid 422–3
162. *C.L.* 89–90
163. *C.L.* 87 (17 December 1911)
164. *Lawrence in Love*, 165
165. "The Dreaming Woman, Helen Corke, in conversation with Malcolm Muggeridge", *The Listener*, 23 July 1969
166. *C.L.* 98, 100, 101; *C.P.* 196, 198–200
167. *C.L.* 100
168. *RW.* 440–1
169. *C.L.* 93, 96 (19 and 29 January 1912)
170. ibid 66 (18 September 1911)
171. *P.O.* 62–137; *C.L.* 81 (2 October 1911); cf. also *C.L.* 78 (12 June 1911)
172. Letter No 5 from Jessie Chambers, Delavenay, *D.H.L.* 1969, Appendix IV; cf. also E.T. 194, 197
173. E.T. 186 and M.S. (II) 10
174. Letter No 5 from Jessie Chambers, Delavenay, *D.H.L.* 1969, Appendix IV; cf. E.T. 190–3
175. "The Soiled Rose" and "A Modern Lover"
176. *C.P.* 122; *Am.* 116; Letter No 5 from Jessie Chambers, Delavenay, *D.H.L.* 1969, Appendix IV; cf. E.T. 195–7
177. *S. and L.* 415–21; in particular 420
178. M.S. (II) 11–16; cf. also E.T. 195 ff.
179. *Not I . . .* 4

180. M.S. (II) 15–16
181. *C.L.* 107–8, 110–11
182. M.S. (II) 15–16; E.T. 216
183. M.S. (II) 19–22
184. *Lawrence in Love*, 171
185. M.S. (II) 19–20
186. Letter No 5 from Jessie Chambers, Delavenay, *D.H.L.* 1969, Appendix IV
187. Frieda Lawrence, *M. & C.* 246. For the meaning of the reference to "morphia", see below p. 146. See also *L.* p. 49 where the dash stands for (Mrs) Dax

CHAPTER 5

1. cf. *C.L.* 78; 102
2. M.S. (I) 37; *C.L.* 61
3. M.S. (II) 5; *C.L.* 66, 91, 96; see above 69, 82
4. See above 75, 82 ff.; *C.L.* 66, 101, 102, 106, 124, 135, 141, 147, 153, 154
5. E.T. 113
6. *P.O.* 138–52; cf. E.T. 113
7. E.T. 113–14; see below 193 ff.
8. *P.O.* 208–22
9. Jessie Chambers in conversation with the author
10. G. H. Neville, *London Mercury*, March 1931
11. cf. *E.L.* 44–55
12. *Wh. P.* 153, 157, 191, 485
13. ibid 13
14. ibid 11–12; cf. "Piano", *C.P.* 148
15. cf. E.T. 103
16. cf. *Wh. P.* 266–9; cf. also *Wh. P.* Part II, Ch. V
17. cf. E.T. 181
18. *Wh. P.* Part I, Ch. IV
19. ibid 199, 388–9
20. ibid 460
21. ibid 475 ff.
22. ibid 419, etc.
23. ibid 423
24. *E.L.* 79; cf. also *The Athenaeum*, 25 February 1911
25. *P.O.* 141, 146, 150–2; cf. also "Cherry Robbers", *C.P.* 36
26. *Wh. P.* 29
27. ibid 47–8; cf. "Love on the Farm", *C.P.* 42
28. Mrs Clarke in conversation with the author
29. Delavenay, *D.H.L.* 1969, Appendix IV, Letter No 5, 672; cf. E.T. 117–18
30. *Wh. P.* 202
31. ibid 224
32. ibid 228–32
33. ibid 231; cf. also *Women in Love*, 27
34. Delavenay, *D.H.L.* 1969, Appendix IV, Letter No 5, 672

35. *Wh. P.* 229–30
36. Delavenay, *D.H.L.* 1969, Appendix IV, Letter No 5, 672
37. *Esther Waters,* 198 ff.
38. *Wh. P.* 227
39. *Esther Waters,* 373
40. *Wh. P.* 200, 206, 227
41. ibid 198
42. ibid 401–2
43. See above, Ch. 3, 47
44. *Wh. P.* 3, 240–2, 270, 89–90, 380–1, 49, 396, 401, etc.
45. ibid 321, 322, 343
46. ibid 238
47. ibid 334–5
48. ibid 487
49. ibid 486–7; 422
50. ibid 174–5, 198, 155, 167, 173–4, 271–2, etc.; cf. E.T. 119
51. See above 69
52. *Neutral Ground,* 226–8
53. *Tres.* 64–6; *N.G.* 229; *Tres.* 120; *N.G.* 233–4
54. *N.G.* 229
55. *Tres.* 64
56. cf. in particular *Tres.* 40–5
57. cf. *Tres.* Sections I and XXI, 176–94
58. *Tres.* 51
59. ibid 26–7, 51, etc.
60. ibid 51; 56; 53
61. ibid 35, 53, etc.
62. ibid 158
63. ibid 162
64. ibid 52, 54
65. cf. *C.L.* 58
66. *Tres.* Sections II and XV; *N.G.* Part II, Ch. XI, etc.
67. See above 5, 7, etc.
68. *C.L.* 61
69. *N.G.* 284; cf. also 263, 264–5
70. *Tres.* 107, 161 ff.; 212, 224, 229, etc.
71. ibid 160
72. *Tres.* 189–90; 214; 204–5
73. ibid 118–19, 120; 158; 159
74. ibid 138
75. ibid 127–8
76. ibid Sections XXVII, XXVIII
77. See above 58
78. *Tres.* Sections III and IV
79. See above Ch. 4, 58
80. *Tres.* 57–8
81. ibid 59–64

82. *C.L.* 88, 96; cf. also *C.L.* 88, 91, *L.* 19

83. cf. *C.L.* 88, 78

84. *L.* 19

85. *C.L.* 83, 101

86. *C.S.St.* Vol. 1 and the first story in Vol. 2

87. "New Eve and Old Adam" is certainly later; see below 151, 190.

88. See above 61; *E.T.* 166

89. *C.P.* 58; cf. *A Collier's*, etc., 40

90. *A Collier's*, etc., 44

91. *C.L.* 218, 223

92. *C.L.* 223, 224

93. *M.L.* 103–28; see above, Ch. 4, 72

94. *M.L.* 116

95. See above 63

96. The *New Statesman*, 16 August 1914; also in *Ph. II*

97. *P.O.* 176–88, *C.L.* 20

98. *The English Review*, February 1912, 188

99. See above 76

100. "The Soiled Rose", *Forum* XLIX, March 1913, 324–40

101. *P.O.* 163

102. See above 84. Lawrence rewrote the story in 1914.

103. *M.L.* 15; cf. also *L.* 49

104. *M.L.* 20, 26

105. cf. *A Collier's*, etc., Introduction, p. vi, Act I passim; Act III, 70–6

106. *The English Review*, June 1911; *P.O.* 281–310

107. cf. *C.L.* 953

108. *The English Review*, June 1911

109. *The English Review*, June 1911; cf. "The Bride", *C.P.* 101

110. cf. "A Man who Died", *C.P.* 55

111. *P.O.* 307–10

112. *The Plays of D.H.L.*, Secker, 1933

113. ibid 75

114. *C.L.* 76

115. *The Plays of D.H.L.* 64, 65, 67, etc. and *Riders to the Sea*, in *The Tinker's Wedding and other plays*, G. Allen & Unwin, 73 ff.

116. See below 110

117. "Two Marriages", supplement to *Time and Tide*, 24 March 1934, 393

118. ibid 393–9; *P.O.* 62–137

119. See below 187

120. *Time and Tide*, 393–9

121. ibid 395

122. ibid 394

123. *P.O.* 257–66

124. *M.L.* 75–83; *Westminster Gazette*, 6 September 1913, "Strike Pay I, Her Turn"

125. *M.L.* 87–100, "Strike Pay II, Ephraim's Half Sovereign"

126. cf. *C.L.* 106

127. "The Miner at Home", in *The Nation*, 6 March 1912; cf. *Ph.* 775

128. *M.L.* 47–71; cf. Delavenay, *D.H.L.* 1969, Appendix I, B
129. *M.L.* 71
130. *Wh. P.* 95–6, 224; *A Collier's*, etc., 73 ff.; *The Widowing of Mrs Holroyd*, 34 ff.
131. *S. and L.* 59–60
132. Delavenay, *D.H.L.* 1969, Appendix IV, Letter No 5
133. See below 149. Cf. *C.L.* 116
134. See below 113
135. cf. *M.L.* 47
136. *L.* 19
137. *L.A.H.* 17
138. ibid 27
139. "Toil of Men", 113–15
140. See below 188 ff.
141. *L.A.H.* 5
142. ibid 37
143. ibid 47
144. ibid 38
145. cf. "Restlessness", above 62; "A Fragment of Stained Glass", *Wh. P.* Part II, Ch. 4, "Kiss when she is Ripe for Tears"; *The Trespasser*, 238 ff; see also above 91
146. *Am.* 33
147. "The Old Adam", *M.L.* 48–53
148. *L.* 95–102
149. *L.* 76–7
150. See below 166 ff.
151. cf. *L.* 5
152. cf. *C.L.* 74
153. *E.T.* 190–3
154. *S. and L.* 3–7
155. cf. *E.L.* 10–11
156. *S. and L.* 49, 67, 65–6, 201; see above 24; *S. and L.* 186
157. cf. *Not I . . .* 52
158. cf. above 83
159. cf. *Not I . . .* 52
160. See above 104 ff.
161. *S. and L.* 208, 222, etc.
162. ibid Ch. XI
163. ibid 295–9
164. ibid 421; *E.T.* 196
165. *Not I . . .* 3, 4, 52
166. *C.L.* 166–71
167. *S. and L.* 352
168. ibid 354–6
169. ibid 362
170. See above 66, 85; *E.T.* 202; *S.P.* 7
171. See above 69
172. *C.L.* 101; *S. and L.* 352; 404 ff.; *S. and L.* 362
173. *S. and L.* 91–2

174. ibid 100–1
175. *C.L.* 90
176. *S. and L.* 118 ff.; 131 ff.
177. *C.L.* 161
178. *S. and L.* 6
179. ibid 66–7, 141, etc.
180. ibid 143 ff.
181. ibid 354 ff.
182. ibid 58–9
183. ibid 213, 216, 223, 227, 251, etc.
184. ibid 212 ff.
185. ibid 409, 317, 363
186. ibid 366 ff.
187. ibid 389, 404 ff.
188. ibid 390
189. ibid 394 ff.

CHAPTER 6

1. *Coriolanus*, V, III, 158–9; cf. E.T. 61–2
2. Longfellow, *Hiawatha*; M.S. (I), 18
3. E.T. 63
4. E.T. 98
5. *C.P.* 52–3 "Dreams Old and Nascent: Old"
6. E.T. 161
7. *Fleurs du Mal*, Lemerre, 103
8. cf. *S. and L.* 38
9. *Tres.* 106–7
10. *L.* 2
11. *Tres.* 108
12. *L.* 7
13. E.T. 109
14. See above 66
15. *C.L.* 62
16. E.T. 137, 141, 189, 152, 200
17. *Wh. P.* 198
18. *Tres.* 107–8
19. *Studies in the Psychology of Sex*, Vol. III, Ch. 2, "Love and Pain", 109; cf. also ibid 172
20. *S. and L.* 353, 362
21. *M.L.* 13
22. Delavenay, *D.H.L.* 1969, Appendix IV, 666; cf. E.T. 213–14
23. M.S. (II) 8; *S. and L.* 248
24. *S. and L.* 296, 422; Delavenay, *D.H.L.* 1969, Appendix IV, 665
25. M.S. (II) 11, 10; cf. E.T. 185
26. *C.L.* 97
27. E.T. 197

28. ibid 182
29. *E.L.* 90
30. J. M. Barrie, *Sentimental Tommy*, Cassell, Ch. XVI, 187
31. E. Delavenay, *D.H.L.* 1969, Appendix IV, 666; cf. *S. and L.* 193
32. *M.S.* (I) 56
33. *M.L.* 32; cf. "The Shades of Spring", *P.O.* 168
34. *M.S.* (I) 63–4
35. ibid 58
36. ibid 64; *S. and L.* 97, 154
37. *Tres.* 107
38. ibid 107; *Wh. P.* 320
39. *M.L.* 34–5
40. *S. and L.* 258
41. *E.L.* 86 (Letter of 9 April 1911)
42. *S. and L.* 353, para. 3
43. *Wh. P.* 131
44. *M.S.* (II) 10
45. *M.L.* 12

CHAPTER 7

1. *E.T.* 199, 200, 213
2. *Not I . . .* 4
3. *C.L.* 107–8
4. *Not I . . .* 4, 5
5. ibid 5
6. ibid 5–6
7. ibid 9–10, *C.L.* 109–10; cf. *Daily Mail*, 20 October 1913, p. 4, col. 4
8. *C.L.* 109
9. *Not I . . .* 10
10. *E.T.* 214
11. cf. "New Eve and Old Adam", in *M.L.* 132, 138, etc.
12. *C.L.* 107
13. *Not I . . .* 34–6
14. *Int. H.* 155 ff.
15. *L. in T.* 103–4; cf. also *C.L.* 122, 123, 124 and 125, and *S.P.* 8; *Not I . . .* 3, *M. & C.* 89; on Otto Gross, cf. R. Hoops, *Der Einfluss der Psychoanalyse auf die Englische Literatur,* 73
16. *Not I . . .* 5
17. *Not I . . .* 4–5; *S.P.* 9
18. cf. also *L. in T.* 104; *S.P.* 8–9
19. cf. *RW.* 15, 25, 27, etc.; also "Love Among the Haystacks", 5–6
20. cf. J. M. Murry, *Between Two Worlds*, 292; *C.L.* 107, 115, 124–5, 245, etc.; *S.P.* 4
21. *Not I . . .* 6, 7, 8; *C.L.* 114, 133, 137
22. *Not I . . .* 11–12, 13
23. *Not I . . .* 14

24. Uncollected letter quoted in *News of the World*, 19 October 1913 and *Daily Mail*, 20 October 1913; cf. also *Not I . . .* 13
25. *Not I . . .* 13
26. *C.L.* 114–15, 125; *Not I . . .* 14–17
27. *Not I . . .* 20; 18; cf. "Bei Hennef", *C.P.* 203
28. *Not I . . .* 24
29. ibid 28; 21
30. ibid 21, 23; *Letters*, 39–40, 42, 44, 85
31. *Not I . . .* 24
32. ibid 21
33. ibid 23, 24
34. ibid 21–3
35. ibid 25
36. cf. *C.L.* 125; *Not I . . .* 19, 27
37. *Not I . . .* 27
38. ibid 24–6
39. ibid 22, 24
40. *E.L.* 109
41. *C.L.* 127–8, 129–30, 138, 140, 141–2, 146–8; *Not I . . .* 31, 55
42. *C.L.* 175–6, 181–4
43. *L.* 116–17; *C.L.* 209–10, 212, 217; *Not I . . .* 61
44. *Not I . . .* 61–2; *C.L.* 150, 211; *L.* 130; *C.L.* 181, 184, 214; *B.T.W.* 261
45. *T.I.* 165–224; *C.L.* 224
46. *C.L.* 219–21, 227
47. *C.L.* 282, 286, 287; *The Daily Telegraph*, 18 October 1913, 5; *The Times*, 28 April 1914, 3, col. 3; cf. also *Daily Mail*, 20 October 1913 and *News of the World*, 19 October 1913.
48. *C.L.* 130
49. ibid
50. *C.L.* 129; cf. also "First Morning", *C.P.* 204
51. *C.L.* 132; "Gloire de Dijon", *C.P.* 217; cf. also "Once" in *Love Among the Haystacks*, 85–6, 89
52. *C.L.* 132
53. *C.P.* 209. The spelling "Frohnleichnam" is Lawrence's
54. *C.L.* 132
55. "First Morning", *C.P.* 204
56. cf. *Not I . . .* 17
57. "And oh, that the man I am", *C.P.* 205
58. "In the Dark", *C.P.* 210–12; cf. *Not I . . .* 33–4
59. *Not I . . .* 56, 57; *C.L.* 133, 135, 137, 141; *L.* 70
60. "She looks back", *C.P.* 205–8; cf. *Not I . . .* 38
61. *C.L.* 134, 137; *M. & C.* 184; cf. "Quite Forsaken"; "Forsaken and Forlorn", *C.P.* 220
62. "Mutilation", *C.P.* 212–13
63. "Humiliation", *C.P.* 214–15
64. "A Bad Beginning", *C.P.* 230; "Why does she weep", ibid 231; "Lady Wife", ibid 234; *C.L.* 132, 134, 172, 173, etc.
65. *C.L.* 209, 235, etc.
66. *C.L.* 145, 152

67. *Not I* ... 34, 36–7, 41; *C.L.* 215
68. *C.L.* 153; cf. also *C.L.* 80, 111, 232, 155; cf. *Lawrence and Brett* passim; "New Eve and Old Adam", *M.L.* 140, etc.
69. *C.L.* 176, 195, 198
70. cf. "Once", *L.A.H.* 88, 94; "Shadow in the Rose Garden", *P.O.* 205; "New Eve and Old Adam", *M.L.* 137; cf. also "Lady Wife", *C.P.* 234–5
71. "New Eve and Old Adam", *M.L.* 145
72. Moore and Roberts, *D.H.L. and his World*, 35
73. Murry, *Son of Woman*, 61–91, 106–22
74. "New Eve and Old Adam", *M.L.* 131–66
75. ibid 165–6
76. ibid 131, 135
77. ibid 141
78. ibid 139–40
79. ibid 139; 134–5
80. ibid 133, 136–7, 154
81. ibid 155–6
82. ibid 136
83. "Once", *L.A.H.* 85, 96
84. "New Eve and Old Adam", *M.L.* 163
85. ibid 169
86. ibid 144–5
87. ibid 158–60
88. "Daughters of the Vicar", *P.O.* 105–37; cf. *L.* 136
89. *RW.* 19, 21, 22; *Ph. II*, 98–100
90. "Daughters of the Vicar", *P.O.* 105
91. ibid 106
92. "New Eve and Old Adam", *M.L.* 147
93. *C.L.* 133
94. *C.L.* 169–70
95. "Lady Wife", *C.P.* 234–5
96. "Song of a man who is not loved", *C.P.* 222
97. "Song of a man who is loved", first version, *Not I* ... 42
98. "New Eve and Old Adam", *M.L.* 162
99. "Second Best", *P.O.* 183; cf. also *Tres.* 63
100. "Daughters of the Vicar", *P.O.* 129
101. cf. *Tres.* 160
102. cf. above Ch. 4, 60 ff., 67–8
103. S. Vere Pearson, M.O., M.R.C.P., "The Psychology of the Consumptive" in *The Journal of State Medicine*, 1932, Vol. XL, 477–85 (A Study of R. L. Stevenson, Lawrence, Mrs Browning, Chekhov, Keats and Thomas Mann's *Der Zauberberg*.)
104. cf. *RW.* 13–19, 22 ff.; cf. also "Love Among the Haystacks", above, 114
105. cf. "Frohnleichnam", *C.P.* 209
106. "First Morning", *C.P.* 204
107. "She Looks Back", *C.P.* 207
108. cf. "Sinners", "On the Balcony", "Frohnleichnam", *C.P.* 223, 208, 209
109. "River Roses", *C.P.* 217

110. "The Primrose Path", *England, My England*, 181–98; cf. also *C.L.* 257
111. "The Primrose Path", *England, My England*, 196
112. ibid. 196–8; cf. a somewhat similar scene in "New Eve and Old Adam", *M.L.* 160–5
113. "The Primrose Path", *England, My England*, 198
114. ibid 144
115. "A Bad Beginning", *C.P.* 230
116. "Winter Dawn", *C.P.* 230
117. *Not I . . .* 33; cf. "I am like a rose", "Rose of All the World", *C.P.* 218; "Song of a man who is loved", first version, *Not I . . .* 42
118. *Not I . . .* 38; *C.L.* 135; cf. "On the Balcony", *C.P.* 298; "Frohnleichnam", *C.P.* 209–210; "Sinners", *C.P.* 223; "Rose of All the World", *C.P.* 218
119. *Not I . . .* 34; *C.L.* 133
120. "Both sides of the Medal", *C.P.* 235
121. "Argument", *C.P.* 191
122. *Wh. P.* 285, 415, 422; *S. and L.* 143
123. *Wh. P.* 124
124. cf. "Forecast", "Amores", "Epilogue", *C.P.* 91; 31
125. Line 1 of "Song of a man who has come through", *C.P.* 250
126. See above 105
127. *C.L.* 139–40, 141
128. *C.L.* 146, 151, 154
129. *C.L.* 234, 254, 262; *L.* 181
130. *C.L.* 150, 151, 164–5, 230, 233, etc.
131. *C.L.* 231, 232
132. *C.L.* 160; *L.* 81, 110. As my later examination of the M.S. suggests, Garnett's cuts went rather further.
133. *C.L.* 141, 145, 147, 150
134. ibid 133
135. ibid 137
136. ibid 152, 155, 161, 181: cf. *The Complete Plays of D.H.L.*
137. *C.L.* 176, 178, 183, 200, etc.
138. See below 174 ff.
139. *C.L.* 211, 229
140. *C.L.* 199; *L.* 137
141. *C.L.* 230
142. ibid 214–15
143. ibid 148 etc.; 265, 270
144. *E.L.* 105–14. (Many of those letters are misdated in *E. L.*)
145. *C.L.* 156, 158–60, 164, 171, 179, etc.; 180, 188–9; *L.* 113
146. *C.L.* 219, 235–7
147. *C.L.* 170
148. *C.L.* 116–256 passim; *L.* 81, 171, 174, etc.
149. *C.L.* 165, 171, 176; *L.* 174–5; *C.L.* 266; *M. & C.* 190
150. *C.L.* 249, 253, 260; *L.* 174; *Not I . . .* 65
151. Nehls, 215–22
152. *C.L.* 220
153. ibid 240, 248

154. ibid 176
155. L. 130
156. C.L. 265
157. C.L. 169
158. ibid 173, 203, etc.
159. ibid 141-2, 158
160. ibid 210
161. ibid 137
162. ibid 234
163. C.L. 237, 246; L. 130
164. C.L. 200, 201
165. C.L. 203, 180; cf. L. 124
166. C.L. 230, 241, 269
167. ibid 139
168. ibid 180
169. ibid 179
170. ibid 183
171. L. 96
172. ibid 96
173. ibid 98
174. ibid 96
175. C.L. 156
176. L. 97
177. ibid 97
178. ibid 96
179. ibid 98
180. ibid 98
181. cf. *Not I . . .* 57
182. ibid 56
183. L. 99
184. ibid 99-100; cf. also E. Carpenter, *Love's Coming of Age*
185. L. 100
186. ibid 100-1
187. ibid 101-2
188. cf. Delavenay, *D.H.L. and Edward Carpenter*, Heinemann, London, 1970
189. "I saw in Louisiana a live oak growing", *Leaves of Grass*
190. "I sing the body electric", *Leaves of Grass*; L. 100
191. L. 102
192. Herbert Spencer, *First Principles*, 110, may be a source here
193. "Rose of All the World", *C.P.* 218-19
194. Murry, *Son of Woman*, 65
195. cf. Havelock Ellis, *Studies in the Psychology of Sex*, Vol. V, 148; Edward Carpenter, *Love's Coming of Age*, 27-8
196. *S. and L.* 288
197. cf. *S. and L.* 178-9, 256
198. cf. *Twilight in Italy*, 10, 11, 22
199. *S. and L.* 288; cf. "In the Dark", *C.P.* 210

200. cf. "A Young Wife", *C.P.* 215; "First Morning", *C.P.* 204
201. "Don Juan", *C.P.* 196
202. *C.L.* 176
203. ibid 170, 172
204. ibid 193, 200
205. ibid 200, 197, 208
206. ibid 200
207. ibid 203
208. ibid 199
209. ibid 200
210. cf. E. Delavenay, *D.H.L. and Edward Carpenter*, Heinemann, 1971
211. *C.L.* 251
212. ibid 251-2
213. ibid 259
214. ibid 281-3
215. ibid 280
216. ibid 281-2
217. cf. *The Daily Telegraph*, 15 November 1915, 12, col. 2; *C.L.* 296, 346-7
218. *C.L.* 272
219. cf. *C.L.* 269, 272, etc.
220. *C.L.* 275 to J. M. Murry
221. ibid
222. *C.L.* 286

CHAPTER 8

1. "French Sons of Germany", "Hail in the Rhineland", *Ph.* 71-81
2. *C.L.* 137, 141
3. cf. *Women in Love*, 113 ff.
4. *Ph.* 71
5. *Women in Love*, 221, 248-50, 261, 489
6. *C.L.* 115; cf. also *Not I* . . . 19, 25
7. *Westminster Gazette*, 22 March 1913; *Ph.* 82-6
8. *T.I.* 7-23: "The Crucifix across the Mountains"; cf. also "Meeting among the Mountains", *The English Review*, February 1914, 306; *Not I* . . . 48-9
9. *Ph.* 84
10. ibid 84
11. *L.A.H.* 57-70, 71-82
12. ibid 69
13. ibid 80-1
14. ibid Introduction xii
15. *The English Review*, Vol. XV, 202-3
16. ibid 206
17. ibid 209
18. ibid 209
19. ibid 215

20. ibid 202–3, 228–9; "The Lemon Gardens" passim
21. *The English Review*, Vol. XV, 215
22. ibid 212
23. ibid 229
24. ibid 224
25. *C.L.* 178
26. *C.L.* 218, 254
27. *P.O.* 267–80; *The Smart Set*, February 1914, 81–5
28. cf. *L.* 201
29. *P.O.* 267–80
30. ibid 62–137; see above 109, 152
31. *P.O.* 104
32. ibid 104
33. *L.A.H.* 16
34. *Not I . . .* 4
35. *L.A.H.* Introduction ix
36. ibid 83–96
37. "New Eve and Old Adam", *M.L. C.S.St.* I, 71–94
38. *The Smart Set*, March 1914, 71–7; *P.O.* 189–207
39. cf. *P.O.* 191; cf. also Delavenay, *D.H.L.* 1969, Appendix IV, 694
40. cf. *C.L.* 144
41. *The Smart Set*, October 1914, 97–108; *P.O.* 223–56; cf. *E.T.* 113–14
42. *The Smart Set*, 102
43. *C.L.* 156
44. *Le Brave Soldat Chveik*, N.R.F., 242
45. *Int. H.* 156
46. *C.L.* 156
47. ibid 209
48. *P.O.* 1–33; *The English Review*, August 1914, 22–43; cf. *L.* 202, 213
49. *P.O.* 34–61
50. *The English Review*, June 1914, 298–315; cf. *L.* 201–2; *C.L.* 287
51. *P.O.* 54–8
52. ibid 245–6
53. *S. and L.* 285
54. ibid 287–8, 291
55. ibid 318
56. ibid 354
57. ibid 354–5
58. ibid 288 and above 173
59. E. Delavenay, *D.H.L. and Edward Carpenter*
60. *S. and L.* 182–3, 342–3; *P.O.* 70
61. "The Thorn in the Flesh", *P.O.* 49–50

CHAPTER 9

1. D. Garnett, *The Golden Echo*, 264
2. *B.T.W.* 290
3. *C.L.* 284
4. ibid 284
5. *S.P.* 19, 31, etc.; cf. *C.L.* 336
6. *C.L.* 209
7. ibid 293
8. ibid 336
9. ibid 345–6
10. *C.L.* 246; *L.* 236
11. *C.L.* 379; *L.* 276
12. *P.G.B.* 174; cf. *C.L.* 380, 386, 388, 390
13. *C.L.* 395, 397, 433, 461–2, 457, 489; *L.* 320, 319; cf. Nehls, 405
14. *C.L.* 496, 497
15. ibid 515–16; *L.* 413
16. *C.L.* 527; *R.B.G.* 101
17. *C.L.* 538
18. ibid 541–2; cf. Nehls, 492
19. *C.L.* 548; Asquith, *Diaries*, 418
20. *C.L.* 551
21. ibid 557
22. ibid 559; Gertler, *Selected Letters*, edited by Noël Carrington, Rupert Hart-Davis, 1965, 161
23. *Int. H.* 347; *C.L.* 587; cf. also *Int. H.* 347–8
24. Leonard Woolf, *Beginning again, an Autobiography of the years 1911–18*, Hogarth Press, 1964, 231; *Downhill all the way, an Autobiography of the years 1919–39*, Hogarth Press, 1967, 63
25. D. Garnett, *The Flowers of the Forest*; G. C. Mackenzie, *The Four Winds of Love, The South Wind*, 272–3; cf. Nehls, 570, n. 41; *C.L.* 297; Gertler, *Selected Letters*, 77. F. A. Lea, *The Life of John M. Murry*, Methuen, 1959, 42; *C.L.* 306, 307
26. *C.L.* 314; George Zytaruk, *The Quest for Rananim, D. H. Lawrence's Letters to Koteliansky, 1914 to 1930*, McGill-Queen's University Press, 1970, 25; *C.L.* 325, 330, 333, 335, 344–345, 315, 357; cf. Nehls, 269–70; Asquith, *Diaries*, 58
27. *Not I . . .* 77; *L.* 329
28. Nehls, 447; cf. also *S.P.* 95
29. *C.L.* 536; cf. *C.L.* 540, 548, etc.
30. Nehls, 454–7; *C.L.* 536
31. *C.L.* 552–3
32. *B.T.W.* 304; *S.P.* 15; R. Aldington, *Life for Life's Sake*, Cassell, London, 1968, 139–42; *C.L.* 293, 306, 316, 321, 330, 331–2; Zytaruk, 39
33. *C.L.* 309, 333
34. ibid 339
35. *C.L.* 377, 399; Cecil Gray, *Peter Warlock*, 89, 106; *S.P.* 34
36. *C.L.* 411

37. Nehls, 355
38. ibid 356
39. C.L. 416
40. ibid 422 (7 February 1916)
41. M. & C. 198; C.L. 428, 430, 449
42. B.T.W. 417; cf. ibid 403–5, etc.; S.P. 59–78; C.L. 483
43. C.L. 486
44. ibid 458
45. Dr Muriel Radford in Nehls, 414; L. 408; C.L. 530, 541, 567, 581; Garnett, The Flowers of the Forest, 190; J. M. Murry, Reminiscences, 96; M. & C. 215
46. C.L. 581
47. Int. H. 470
48. K. Mansfield, Journal, 146; cf. also Nehls, 475
49. R.B.G. 136; Asquith, Diaries, 18–19; P.G.B. III; H. T. Moore, A D. H. Lawrence Miscellany, 130–2
50. B.T.W. 305
51. Leonard Woolf, Beginning again, 251–2
52. B.T.W. 306; cf. Asquith, Diaries, 58; cf. R.G.B. 139–40; S.P. 67
53. M. & C. 341
54. S.P. 71; cf. M. & C. 184; B.T.W. 411; Mackenzie, The Four Winds of Love, The South Wind, 279
55. C.L. 295
56. M. & C. 195–7; Gertler, Selected Letters, 162; M. & C. 196
57. Gertler, Selected Letters, 77–9
58. F. A. Lea, The Life of J. M. Murry, 42; B.T.W. 322; cf. "H.D." (Hilda Doolittle), Bid me to Live, 111, 121, 137, 163
59. L. in T. 51
60. "H.D." Bid me to Live, 75–90; C.L. 529, 531, etc.; Int. H. 255; Cecil Gray, Musical Chairs, 131–40, in Nehls, 433.
61. Aldington, Life for Life's Sake, 233
62. Kangaroo, 239
63. L. 379
64. See below 298–303
65. cf. Nehls, 234–7 and notes
66. C.L. 289
67. Nehls, 242
68. C.L. 290, 296
69. ibid 290
70. L. 208
71. cf. B.T.W. 339; C.L. 350, Not I . . . 76, 81, etc.; Doolittle, Bid me to Live, 86–9
72. C.L. 292 (13 October 1914); C.L. 314, 337, 505, etc.
73. ibid 309–10
74. ibid 340
75. ibid 337
76. Garnett, The Flowers of the Forest, 7–9; cf. Nehls, 240–1; Mackenzie, The Four Winds of Love, The South Wind, 277–80; Milton Rosmer in Nehls, 264; cf. Not I . . . 74
77. C.L. 316

78. *Int. H.* 248; F. M. Ford, *Portraits from Life*; Nehls, 288, n. 107; Violet Hunt, *I have this to say*, 259–60; *M. & C.* 389

79. *S.P.* 90; Gray, *Musical Chairs*, 127, in Nehls, 429, etc.; B.B.C. Broadcast, 1953, in Nehls, 426; *R.B.G.* 142; Asquith, *Diaries*, 369

80. cf. *Int. H.* 294

81. *C.L.* 312, 317, etc.; 320

82. ibid 323, 338, 336

83. ibid 348–9

84. ibid 328

85. *RW.* 292; cf. *M. & C.* 208

86. *Int. H.* 259

87. *RW.* 309

88. ibid 418–19

89. *L.* 219

90. *C.L.* 356

91. ibid 346

92. J. M. Murry, *Reminiscences*, 130

93. *Daily News and Leader*, 5 October 1915, "Literature"

94. *The Sphere*, 23 October 1915, 104, "A Literary Letter"; *Star*, 22 October 1915, 4, "Books and Bookmen"

95. *C.L.* 385

96. ibid 376, 385

97. ibid 376, 377–8

98. ibid 378; Asquith, *Diaries*

99. *C.L.* 378

100. Letter from Frieda to Lady Cynthia Asquith, December 1916; *M. & C.* 208

101. Aldington, *Life for Life's Sake*

102. Letter from Methuen to Thring, *T.L.S.* 27 February 1969, 216

103. *T.L.S.* 216 (27 February 1969)

104. ibid

105. Letter from Mr Derek Muskett, 22 February 1967

106. H.O. 45/13944, p. 2, minute 210/PB/589, from Commissioner of Metropolitan Police to Sir John Anderson

107. Conversation with Mr J. Alan White, April 1967, after he made inquiries into Methuen's financial records

108. *The Daily Telegraph*, Monday, 15 November 1915

109. *C.L.* 398

110. Aldington, *Life for Life's Sake*, 209

111. Parliamentary Debates, House of Commons, 5th Series, LXXV, 18 November 1915

112. See above 233

113. Introduction to *Apocalypse*, vii

114. Letter to Harry T. Moore, 1952, in *Int. H.* 258

115. *T.L.S.* 27 February 1969, 216

116. Parliamentary Debates, House of Commons, 5th Series, LXXVI, 1 December 1915

117. *C.L.* 392

118. Asquith, *Diaries*, 6 October 1915, 85

119. *C.L.* 372, 373, 378; Asquith, *Diaries*, 95; *C.L.* 373

120. L. 284; C.L. 395; 397
121. M. & C. 209
122. C.L. 490, 491, 493; Letter to Dollie Radford in Nehls, 408–9
123. C.L. 499
124. ibid 496, 8 January 1917
125. ibid 501, 12 February 1917
126. P.G.B. 162; cf. L. 222–3, see below 559 n. 145
127. C.L. 459
128. Kangaroo, 240, 255
129. ibid 259
130. Gray, Musical Chairs, 129
131. S.P. 91
132. C.L. 516
133. Gray, Musical Chairs, 131; C.L. 513, etc.; M. & C. 211
134. T.L.S. 20 December 1917, reproduced with author's signature T.L.S. 21 September 1967
135. Kangaroo, 251–3, which seems to be Aldington's only source, P.G.B. 193
136. B.T.W. 402
137. cf. Nehls, 365, 367, 384–5, 409–10, 425–8
138. Kangaroo, 274
139. C.L. 527
140. ibid 528–9
141. Asquith, Diaries, 257
142. Aldington, P.G.B. 200–1; Gray, Musical Chairs, 128–31
143. Letter to C. Carswell quoted by H. T. Moore, Int. H. 302; C.L. 563
144. L. 453
145. Kangaroo, 282–7
146. H. A. L. Fisher, then Minister of Education
147. C.L. 563

CHAPTER 10

1. C.L. 116
2. R.B.G. 133–4, in Nehls, 207–9, 411–17; I. R. Rosmer and M. Rosmer, in Nehls, 264; S.P. 15; Ottoline Morrell, The Nation and Athenaeum, XLVI, 22 March 1930, 859
3. Quoted by Muriel Radford, in Nehls, 292–3
4. The London Magazine, II, 4 April 1955
5. K. Mansfield, Letters of K.M. 79; ibid 215
6. B. Russell, Portraits from Memory, IX, 104
7. Murry, Reminiscences, 49–50
8. Ottoline, The early memoirs of Lady Ottoline Morrell, Faber & Faber, 1963; C.L. 305; ibid 313; Garnett, The Flowers of the Forest, 33–7, in Nehls, 266–8; cf. C.L. 308
9. The Golden Echo, The Flowers of the Forest, The Familiar Faces
10. Garnett, The Flowers of the Forest, 54, in Nehls, 299–302
11. J. M. Keynes, Two Memoirs, 80, in Nehls, 287
12. Quentin Bell, Bloomsbury, Weidenfeld and Nicolson, 1968, 70–6

13. *S.P.* 55 and *C.L.* 469
14. Gray, *Musical Chairs*, 131, in Nehls, 431
15. *Not I . . .* 66
16. ibid 79; *S.P.* 22; Letter to Koteliansky No 26, Zytaruk, 21, cf. *C.L.* 305; *B.T.W.* 33
17. *C.L.* 314
18. See below 286, 310
19. Edward Carpenter, *Civilization, Its Cause and Cure*, 1899
20. *C.L.* 307
21. cf. also "Study of Thomas Hardy", and below 286, 326
22. *C.L.* 311–12
23. Lady Glenavy, *Today we will only gossip*, 1964, 99
24. See below 304
25. *C.L.* 302–3
26. ibid 291
27. *Ph.* 405–6
28. *C.L.* 319–20
29. ibid 318–19
30. ibid 319
31. Nehls, 569
32. "Nathaniel Hawthorne, (I)", in *S.M.* 134–58
33. C. Mackenzie, *My Life and Times: Octave Five: 1915–1923*, 167
34. *H.A.S.* 62–6
35. 1 Cor. 6.12
36. *H.A.S.* 630
37. ibid 360–1
38. ibid 632
39. ibid 636
40. ibid 637
41. *Bib. Com.* 40
42. ibid 48
43. See below 351; *C.L.* 393–4
44. See above 260–1
45. *Bib. Com.* 48; cf. the form of *coitus reservatus* practised by Cipriano in *The Plumed Serpent*
46. ibid 51
47. *C.L.* 349, 354
48. ibid 316
49. ibid 330
50. ibid 324
51. ibid 351
52. ibid 352
53. Lea, *The Life of J. M. Murry*, 42
54. *A.R.* 96–107
55. Murry, *Reminiscences*, 50, 56; *C.L.* 300–4; 269
56. *C.L.* 321
57. *B.T.W.* 332
58. ibid 332–3
59. Murry, *Son of Woman*, 100–5

60. *B.T.W.* 351
61. *R.D.P.*, "Note to The Crown"; cf. Murry, *Reminiscences*, 68, 72; also *C.L.* 363, 367, 369; *L.* 257, 259
62. *B.T.W.* xxviii; *Reminiscences*, 74–81, etc.
63. cf. Edward Carpenter, *Love's Coming of Age*, "The Sex Passion", 18 ff., 115–16, etc.
64. *B.T.W.* 409; *Reminiscences*, 79
65. *B.T.W.* 413
66. ibid 416
67. Russell, *Portraits from Memory*, 104
68. ibid 12
69. ibid 104
70. "Study of Thomas Hardy", *Ph.* 406
71. *C.L.* 313, 314, 327, 328, etc.
72. ibid 323; Russell, *Portraits from Memory*, 104
73. *Ph.* 426–7
74. *C.L.* 305, see above 256, 259, etc.
75. ibid 317, 320
76. ibid 327
77. Keynes, *Two Memoirs*, 78, in Nehls, 346; see above 253 ff.
78. *Not I . . .* 76
79. *C.L.* 329, 330
80. ibid 343
81. ibid 346, 347
82. ibid 352
83. Burnet, *Early Greek Philosophy*, 140–1
84. *C.L.* 354
85. ibid 354; see below, 314, for Jane Harrison
86. ibid 355–6
87. ibid 362
88. *M. & C.* 390, cf. *C.L.* 326; *Not I . . .* 76
89. *C.L.* 365
90. ibid 366
91. Russell, loc. cit. 107
92. cf. *C.L.* 316–20, *M. & C.* 196
92a. *C.L.* 355–6, 352, etc. Russell, loc. cit. 105
93. *R.B.G.* 142; Gray, *Peter Warlock*, 89–90 (in Nehls, 329, 331, 346, 354); *C.L.* 381; Gray, 90; *C.L.* 402, *L.* xxix
94. Gray, 108; ibid 109; 112
95. *C.L.* 416 and 455; Gray, 119; cf. *C.L.* 414, 427, etc.
96. cf. *C.L.* 529, 531, 539, 545, 549
97. *Kangaroo*, 265
98. B.B.C. Talk, November 1953, in Nehls, 365
99. *P.G.B.* 196; *Not I . . .* 81
100. *S.P.* 89; *L.* 408; *C.L.* 482
101. cf. *C.L.* 539, 550; *P.G.B.* 199, 202; "H.D.", *Bid me to Live*, 143–69; *C.L.* 447
102. *C.L.* 530, 531; ibid 543; ibid 525, 571, 27 December 1918
103. Gertler, *Selected Letters*, 43

104. cf. *C.L.* 291; also above 260
105. *C.L.* 477
106. Gertler, *Selected Letters*, 127, 133
107. Gray, *Peter Warlock*, 117, etc.
108. Gertler, *Selected Letters*, portrait facing p. 144, L. Woolf, *Beginning again*, 247–53
109. Gertler, ibid 161–2
110. *M. & C.* 195 ff.
111. D. Goldring, *Life Interests*, in Nehls, 492
112. "H.D.", *Bid me to Live*, 75–90
113. *C.L.* 468
114. "H.D.", *Bid me to Live*, 84
115. *Kangaroo*, 279
116. *S.P.* 37–8
117. cf. *C.L.* 331; 567
118. *Kangaroo*, 278
119. *C.L.* 311, 321, 325
120. ibid 326
121. ibid 381
122. ibid 488
123. ibid 502, 548; cf. *C.L.* 542, 540, 543; *C.L.* 559
124. Gray, *Musical Chairs*, 133, in Nehls, 433
125. *C.L.* 531–2
125a. *Ph.* 510
126. B. Campbell, Lady Glenavy, *Today we will only gossip*, 92
127. Nehls, 275
128. *C.L.* 309; cf. above 229
129. ibid 341
130. ibid 349, 361, 370, 127, 372
131. ibid 375
132. cf. *L.* 349; *C.L.* 483, 501; *L.* 378, etc.
133. *C.L.* 501, 536, 554–5, 382
134. Carpenter, *Love's Coming of Age*, 121
135. *C.L.* 307, see above 258
136. *C.L.* 311–12; 323; 382
137. ibid 467
138. ibid 565

CHAPTER 11

1. *M. & C.* 277, 445
2. *Fantasia*, 10
3. ibid 11
4. *Ph.* 512–14
5. *M. & C.* 446, etc.
6. See above 174 ff.
7. *C.L.* 519

8. ibid 485

9. ibid 183

10. ibid 193

11. cf. *C.L.* 287, 290, 292; *Ph.* XX–XXI; *Book Collector's Quarterly*, January–March 1932; S. Foster Damon, *Amy Lowell, a Chronicle*, New York, 1935, 279

12. *C.L.* 290

13. Damon, loc. cit. 279

14. *C.L.* 324, 327, 329

15. *The Times*, quoted in advertisement in Chamberlain's *Immanuel Kant*, John Lane, 1914

16. *Fabian News*, June 1911, 53

17. cf. *The Ravings of a Renegade*, War Essays of H. S. Chamberlain, translated from the German by Ch. H. Clarke, Jarrold, 1916, a typical production of British counter-propaganda

18. Ernest Seillière, *D. H. Lawrence et les Récentes Idéologies Allemandes*, Paris, 1936

19. Armin Arnold, "The German Letters of D. H. Lawrence" in *Comparative Literature Studies*, Vol. III, No 3, 1966

20. cf. Lawrence's essay on "Fallen Leaves", by V. V. Rozanov, *Ph.* 392

21. *C.L.* 250

22. *Ph.* 448

23. *Foundations*, II, 301–2

24. See below 311

25. *Foundations*, I, 269

26. ibid 297–8

27. ibid I, 542, II, 228

28. ibid II, 563, I, LIV

29. ibid II, 31, 41–2, "Mythology of Inner Experience"

30. ibid II, 363

31. *Ph.* 515–16; *C.L.* 280

32. *Foundations*, II, 241

33. *Ph.* 479

34. *Foundations*, II, 411, 436

35. ibid 422

36. ibid 242–3

37. *L.* 101

38. *Ph.* 415, 399

39. ibid 402

40. ibid 413–14

41. *L.* 237; Jakob Boehme, *Aurora, oder die Morgenröte im Aufgang*, 1612

42. *RW.* 106; *C.L.* 304; see above 256, 260

43. *C.L.* 302, 304

44. *Ph.* 442

44a. Private information

45. *Poetry and Prose of William Blake*, Ed. Geoffrey Keynes, London, The Nonesuch Library, 1927, 618

46. *Ph.* 404; cf. Blake, loc. cit. 753, and St Paul, 1 Cor. 6, 12

47. ibid 405, 460; "The Crown", 52–61, 65, 66, 75–6, 80, etc.; *T.I.* passim, etc.

48. St Matthew 25–9; *Ph.* 404

49. Now in the National Museum, Warsaw
50. *Ph.* 432
51. ibid 432
52. ibid 282–3
53. ibid 433
54. ibid 434
55. ibid 439
56. ibid 441
57. ibid 442
58. ibid 443–4
59. ibid 444
60. Otto Weininger, *Geschlecht und Character* (1903), translated as *Sex and Character*, London, Heinemann, 1906
61. Gray, *Peter Warlock*, Ch. II "At Oxford" by Robert Nichols, 67; *Ph.* 391–2; cf. also Janko Lavrin in *European Quarterly*, August 1934, "Sex and Eros (on Rozanov, Weininger and D.H.L.)"
62. Conversation with the author, 1934
63. *Ph.* 479
64. ibid 445
65. ibid 445–6
66. ibid 446
67. ibid 446; *C.L.* 179
68. *Ph.* 447
69. ibid 469, 448, 449
70. ibid 450
71. ibid 448
72. cf. J. Réal, "The religious conception of race: Houston Stewart Chamberlain and Germanic Christianity", in *The Third Reich*, 1955, 267, quoting *Grundlagen des XIX Jahrhunderts*, 51, 52, 53, 477, 638, etc.
73. *Foundations*, II, 41, 42
74. *Ph.* 449
75. Réal, loc. cit. 268, 263
76. *Ph.* 451–3
77. ibid 452
78. ibid 453
79. *C.L.* 300–4 quoted in part below, 315
80. *Ph.* 453
81. cf. Réal, loc. cit. 256; *Ph.* 453–4, 465
82. *Ph.* 457–60, 641, 463–4
83. ibid 515
84. ibid 515–16
85. See above 302
86. Jane Harrison, LL.D., D. Litt., *Ancient Art and Ritual*, Oxford, Home University Library of Modern Knowledge, 1913. cf. *C.L.* 249, 250
87. Harrison, loc. cit. 216
88. *Ph.* 449–50, 460, 447
89. ibid 455

90. Harrison, loc. cit. 211, 212, 214; cf. *Ph.* 398, 400, 403
91. ibid 465
92. cf. *C.L.* 302
93. *C.L.* 302; cf. "Mythology of Inner Experience", *Foundations*, II, 31–41
94. *Ph.* 465–6
95. Carpenter, *Love's Coming of Age*, 151, 160
96. See above 307; cf. also *Ph.* 492 for another passage (at the end of the first paragraph) which suggests familiarity with gnostic or cabbalistic ideas on universal love
97. cf. Saurat, *Blake and Modern Thought*, Constable, 1929, 98–106
98. *C.L.* 170, 172–3
99. *Ph.* 459, 481
100. ibid 468
101. ibid 464–5
102. ibid 465
103. ibid 468–9
104. ibid 470
105. Carpenter, *Love's Coming of Age*, 165; see above 288, 290
106. *Ph.* 474
107. ibid 475
108. ibid 477
109. ibid 477–8
110. ibid 406
111. ibid 426–9
112. Mallock, *C.L.* 495; Gissing, *C.L.* 87; Shelley and Godwin, *L.* 237, *C.L.* 404, 495; and *Ph.* 426, 427, 429, probably inspired by Brailsford's *Shelley, Godwin and their Circle*
113. *Ph.* 407
114. ibid 410
115. Jane Harrison, loc. cit. 199; *Ph.* 415
116. *Ph.* 415
117. ibid 419
118. ibid 434–40
119. ibid 479
120. ibid 481
121. ibid 460; cf. also Carpenter, *The Intermediate Sex*, 170, 189
122. *Ph.* 483, 488
123. ibid 489
124. ibid 490
125. ibid 494
126. Garnett, *The Golden Echo*, 254–5
127. *Ph.* 496–7; cf. *C.L.* 326 and above 286
128. *Ph.* 500
129. ibid 507; cf. above 67–9
130. ibid 509–10
131. *R.D.P.* 84
132. *C.L.* 352
133. *R.D.P.* 10; *The Signature*, I, 9
134. *R.D.P.* 17

135. ibid 24
136. ibid 37
137. ibid 38
138. ibid 47–8
139. ibid 51–4
140. See above 261
141. *R.D.P.* 13
142. ibid 46
143. ibid 46–7
144. ibid 69–70
145. ibid 72–4; cf. *L.* 222, misdated by Aldous Huxley, in view of its reference to the formation of the coalition government, May 1915
146. ibid 78
147. cf. letter from Frieda to Cynthia Asquith, *M & C* 208, in which she asserts it "does not matter" if "hundreds of dull young men die early"
148. *The Signature*, III, 4–8; *R.D.P.* 39–46
149. *R.D.P.* 25–6
150. ibid 74
151. ibid 91
152. *C.L.* 327
153. *R.D.P.* 93
154. ibid 94
155. ibid 99
156. *C.L.* 351, 353
157. Burnet, *Early Greek Philosophy*, 145
158. *R.D.P.* 35–6
159. *C.L.* 364
160. ibid 361
161. ibid 386, 369; cf. also *L.* 358
162. *C.L.* 374; cf. also *C.L.* 369–71
163. *C.L.* 375–6
164. *T.I.* 52
165. ibid 7
166. ibid 171, 212
167. ibid 10–11
168. cf. *Foundations*, I, Ch. VI, "The Entrance of the Germanic People into History", II, Ch. VIII B, 6, "The Mystics"; 7, "Art", etc.
169. *T.I.* 11–12
170. *Ph.* 85; *T.I.* 20–1
171. *T.I.* 27
172. *Foundations*, II, 188
173. *T.I.* 47, 50; cf. also "The Theatre"
174. *Foundations*, I, LXIV, LXVII
175. *T.I.* 53
176. ibid 54–5
177. ibid 55–6
178. ibid 12, 14, 15

179. ibid 72
180. ibid 73
181. *C.L.* 255–6, 360–3, 351; cf. *Foundations*, II, 377
182. *T.I.* 93–4; cf. Nietzsche, *Le Gai Savoir*, N.R.F., 1950, 358, "La Jacquerie de l'esprit"
183. *T.I.* 96
184. ibid 100
185. Letter to Harry T. Moore, *Int. H.* 483; *The Observer*, 11 February 1934, Rolf Gardiner's reply to a Berlin dispatch entitled "D.H.L. in a Black Shirt"
186. cf. *C.L.* 325–7

CHAPTER 12

1. *C.L.* 272, 273; *M. & C.* 190
2. *C.L.* 273
3. ibid 172–3
4. O. Weininger, *Sex and Character*, Ch. II, "Male and Female Plasmas"
5. *C.L.* 280
6. ibid 281; *Drama of Love and Death*, 120
7. *C.L.* 282
8. ibid 282
9. ibid 282
10. ibid 179–80
11. ibid 291
12. ibid 334; cf. *Ph.* 478–9
13. *C.L.* 393
14. ibid 393; *Ph.* 468
15. *Sex and Character*, 217–18
16. *C.L.* 422
17. *RW.* 437–40
18. *C.L.* 519
19. ibid 519
20. *RW.* 106, 261; Jenner, loc. cit. 5, 74
21. *Ph.* 410
22. ibid 515–16
23. ibid 460–1
24. *C.L.* 302
25. *RW.* 30–4
26. ibid 38, 86, 87, etc.
27. ibid 114, 135, 223
28. ibid 3
29. ibid 48, 53–4
30. *RW.* 85–8; *W.L.* 392 ff.; *Lady Chatterley's Lover*, 297 ff.; *C.P.* 262–8
31. *RW.* 75
32. ibid 85–6
33. *C.P.* 264
34. Carpenter, *Love's Coming of Age*, 224–5

35. Carpenter, *The Drama of Love and Death*, 239
36. *RW.* 127–8
37. ibid 242–3
38. *Ph.* 429 ff.
39. *RW.* 141
40. ibid 90
41. ibid 186–7
42. ibid 158–9
43. ibid 148–50, 160–2, etc.
44. ibid 188–93; cf. *Ph.* 454
45. *RW.* 194
46. *R.D.P.* 17
47. *RW.* 216–18
48. cf. *C.L.* 263; Nehls, 556 n. 97; *Int. H.* 79–80, Moore, *The Life and Works of D. H. Lawrence*, New York, Twayne, 1951, 362
49. *RW.* 248
50. cf. *C.L.* 100; *RW.* 400–1
51. *RW.* 263–5
52. ibid 435
53. *E.T.* 127–8, see above 46 ff.
54. *RW.* 248
55. ibid 394
56. ibid 315
57. ibid 293
58. ibid 298
59. H. M. Daleski, *The Forked Flame*, 110
60. *RW.* 300
61. ibid 300
62. *RW.* 451–3; Daleski, loc. cit. 291–2
63. *RW.* 303
64. ibid 303–4
65. See above 46 and *E.T.* 127–8
66. *RW.* 384
67. cf. Weininger, *Sex and Character*, 160–2; also *Foundations*, I, 550
68. *RW.* 323, 383, 408
69. ibid 411
70. ibid 416–17
71. ibid 418
72. ibid 419, 435
73. ibid 464
74. Daleski, loc. cit. 122–4
75. *RW.* 464
76. ibid 291–2
77. ibid 328
78. ibid 383
79. ibid 435
80. ibid 435

81. See above 375
82. *RW.* 434
83. ibid 479
84. F. R. Leavis, *D.H.L., Novelist*, 142
85. *RW.* 466
86. ibid 467
87. Transcribed by the author from a copy of *The Rainbow* belonging to Mrs Ada Clarke
88. Lawrence Clark Powell, *The Manuscripts of D.H.L.* 5

CHAPTER 13

1. *Ph. II*, 92–108. Examination of the holograph manuscripts at Austin, Texas, confirms that the Prologue was written in Cornwall in 1916
2. *W.L.* 323
3. *L.* 328
4. Gray, *Peter Warlock*, 114; Asquith, *Diaries*, 415
5. Gray, loc. cit. 122
6. *C.L.* 519; cf. ibid 302
7. ibid 317
8. *L.* 317
9. *C.L.* 409–10
10. ibid 477, 480, 532; Asquith, *Diaries*, 417
11. *C.L.* 477, 480
12. *W.L.* 451
13. *C.L.* 477–8, 490
14. G. A. Panichas, *Adventure in Consciousness*, 151–9
15. *C.L.* 152
16. ibid 420, 425
17. Maspéro, *Egypte*, 55 and Fig. 92
18. Maspéro, op. cit. 165 and Fig. 278
19. *W.L.* 91
20. ibid 180; for the chakras see below 408
21. On this see W. Y. Tindall, *D. H. Lawrence and Susan his Cow*, 1939; J. M. Pryse, *The Apocalypse Unsealed*, 1910, and Brewster, 141
22. *W.L.* 15
23. ibid 258; *The Golden Bough*, 348–9
24. *W.L.* 8, 9; cf. *C.L.* 404; *W.L.* 261–2
25. *W.L.* 21, 94, 134, 208
26. ibid 133
27. ibid 262
28. ibid 95; cf. also ibid 25, 26
29. ibid 41–4
30. ibid 22, 38
31. ibid 87–8
32. ibid 42–4

33. ibid 88–9
34. ibid 308
35. *Ph. II*, 94
36. ibid 97
37. ibid 99
38. ibid 100
39. see above 67 ff.
40. ibid 111; see above 62 and the poem "Restlessness", *C.P.* 179
41. *W.L.* 46
42. *Ph. II*, 103
43. *W.L.* 58–9
44. ibid 59
45. ibid 210
46. ibid 133
47. ibid 136
48. ibid 151–2
49. ibid 153–7
50. ibid 208
51. ibid 208
52. ibid 209
53. ibid 209–10
54. ibid 210
55. Carpenter, *Love's Coming of Age*, 121
56. *W.L.* 210, 132
57. ibid 210
58. ibid 209; *Sea and Sardinia*, "The Q.B." standing for the "the Queen Bee", passim
59. *W.L.* 266
60. Weininger, *Sex and Character*, XII, "Woman and her significance", 300
61. H. Blavatsky, *The Secret Doctrine*, 1888, II, 2
62. *W.L.* 156
63. ibid 195
64. ibid 159
65. ibid 265
66. ibid 265
67. ibid 331
68. *R.D.P.* 35–7, etc.
69. ibid 37–8
70. ibid 38
71. *W.L.* 258
72. ibid 258
73. ibid 178–80
74. ibid 217
75. ibid 320–1
76. ibid 323–4
77. ibid 326
78. ibid 329–30
79. ibid 331–2

80. See above 362–3
81. See above 291
82. cf. *W.L.* 329
83. *Ps. U.* 112 ff; 127–8
84. Pryse, *The Apocalypse Unsealed*, 14–26; *W.L.* 476; see Plate 28
85. Daleski, loc. cit. 176–80
86. *W.L.* 331–2
87. ibid 435–6
88. *Ph. II*, 92, 93, 104
89. *W.L.* 216
90. ibid 216
91. ibid 217
92. ibid 285
93. ibid 286
94. ibid 287
95. *Ph. II*, 95–6
96. ibid 105–6
97. ibid 107
98. See below 458 and letter to Amy Lowell, quoted Nehls, 478
99. H. Blavatsky, *The Secret Doctrine*, I, 155 ff.
100. ibid 162
101. ibid 162
102. *W.L.* 132–3
103. ibid 60
104. ibid 132
105. ibid 180
106. ibid 179
107. ibid 180
108. ibid 266–7
109. ibid 195
110. H. Daleski, *The Forked Flame*, 169–71; E. Vivas, "The Substance of *Women in Love*",
    The Sewanee Review, 66, Autumn 1958, 620
111. See below 460; *W.L.* 208
112. *W.L.* 261
113. ibid 55–7
114. ibid 29, 30, 31, 418, etc.
115. ibid 60
116. ibid 210
117. ibid 61
118. ibid 484–5
119. ibid 266, 81
120. *C.L.* 280
121. *W.L.* 57
122. ibid 376
123. ibid 106–7
124. ibid 119
125. Letter No 13 from J. Chambers quoted in Delavenay, *D.H.L.* 1969, Appendix IV, 684

126. *W.L.* 226
127. ibid 242
128. ibid 237
129. cf. *W.L.* 224–9
130. Weininger, loc. cit. Ch. VI, VII, VIII, IX, XII and XIII: *Judaism*, passim.
131. *W.L.* 106–7
132. ibid 106–7
133. ibid 97, 172, 96, 40, etc.
134. See above 390
135. Weininger, loc. cit. 307–8, 311, 314–15, cf. also *C.L.* 518
136. *W.L.* 97, 446–7
137. ibid 448
138. ibid 454
139. ibid 474
140. *RW.* 322
141. *W.L.* 504–5
142. ibid 133
143. ibid 418
144. ibid 429, 445, etc.
145. ibid 263
146. ibid 286, 435

CHAPTER 14

1. *L.* 379
2. *C.L.* 480
3. ibid 680, 689
4. *The English Review*, October 1915, 238
5. ibid 241; cf. *RW.* 85, and above 360 ff.
6. ibid 243
7. ibid 243
8. ibid 245
9. *C.S.St.* II, 303
10. ibid 323
11. ibid 327
12. ibid 203
13. *C.L.* 372–3
14. *S.P.* 105–6
15. *C.S.St.* II, 355
16. ibid 358
17. ibid 359
18. ibid 363–5
19. *C.L.* 315–18
20. *Strand Magazine*, April 1919, Vol. 57, 287–93; *C.S.St.* 334–6
21. *The English Review*, March 1917, 224
22. *C.L.* 678

23. *C.S.St.* II, 402
24. See above 64, 104
25. *Ph.* 7–13, 14–21
26. *C.S.St.* 459
27. *Hutchinson's Magazine*, V, November 1921, 461–9; *C.S.St.* 465–6
28. *L.* 378, 380
29. *C.L.* 469
30. *C.S.St.* II, 452–3; *R.W.* 85–6
31. Goldring, *Life Interests*, quoted in Nehls, 493
32. *S.P.* 127–30
33. *Plays of D.H.L.* 83
34. ibid 85
35. ibid 88–90
36. ibid 90
37. ibid 309
38. ibid 124
39. ibid 145
40. *C.L.* 543
41. Asquith, *Diaries*, 43
42. ibid 338, 340
43. ibid 341 ff.; *A.R.* 34
44. *A.R.* 135–6
45. ibid 136

CHAPTER 15

1. *C.L.* 514
2. ibid 520, 27 July 1917
3. ibid 526
4. *Int. H.* 312
5. *C.L.* 550, 553, 561
6. *L.* 414
7. *C.L.* 560–1; Zytaruk, *The Quest for Rananim*, 191–4
8. Letter to Catherine Carswell, quoted by H. T. Moore, *Int. H.* 312
9. *Ph.* 669
10. ibid 669
11. ibid 670–4
12. ibid 675 and 686
13. ibid 682–4
14. ibid 686–7; cf. also *C.L.* 519
15. *M. & C.* 211
16. *Ph.* 688
17. ibid 693
18. ibid 694
19. ibid 153
20. *C.L.* 506

21. *Ph.* 695
22. ibid 697
23. ibid 698
24. See above 388
25. Gray, *Peter Warlock*, 169
26. ibid 168
27. ibid 181
28. R. Nichols, in Gray, *Peter Warlock*, 86-7
29. R. Nichols in Gray, op. cit. 186, letter from Heseltine, 30 May 1918
30. *C.L.* 523
31. ibid 525
32. ibid 551
33. Letter to Amy Lowell, 5 November 1918, in Nehls, 478
34. *L.* 454-5
35. H. Blavatsky, *The Secret Doctrine*, 1888, Vol. I, 155-6
36. cf. *L.* 455, 476
37. ibid 476
38. *C.L.* 519
39. ibid 302
40. Barbara Low, conversation with the author, 25 December 1934. For Jung, cf. *C.L.* 565; for Freud, *C.L.* 291
41. Lodge, *The War and After*, 1915; *Raymond, or life and Death*, 1916; *Christopher, A Study in Human Personality*, 1918
42. *C.L.* 587
43. *L. in T.* 11
44. *S.M.* 20, 23
45. ibid 23, 24
46. *Fantasia*, 135-6, 141, etc.; cf. *S.M.* 163 concerning the alchemists
47. *S.M.* 75; cf. ibid 176, 177, 178, etc.
48. ibid 176, 18
49. *C.L.* 501, 518
50. *S.M.* 16-18
51. ibid 16-17
52. ibid 20
53. ibid 29-30
54. ibid 18
55. ibid 19
56. ibid 221
57. ibid 22-3; cf. also *Fantasia*, 8
58. ibid 223
59. See above 406
60. *S.M.* 20-1
61. ibid 22-5
62. ibid 176
63. ibid 177
64. ibid 178
65. See above 316

66. *S.M.* 179–80
67. ibid 183
68. ibid 185
69. ibid 185
70. ibid 185
70a. *Letters of Aldous Huxley*, 187
71. *S.M.* 186–7
72. ibid 188
73. ibid 188–9
74. *C.P.* 268
75. *S.M.* 18–19
76. ibid 19
77. ibid 19
78. ibid 30
79. ibid 135
80. ibid 135
81. ibid 136–7
82. ibid 137
83. ibid 138
84. ibid 223
85. ibid 135, 136–7, 125
86. ibid 58
87. ibid 25
88. ibid 25; cf. also above 466
89. ibid 24–7
90. ibid 27
91. ibid 85
92. ibid 28–9
93. ibid 61
94. ibid 96
95. ibid 99
96. ibid 116, 126
97. ibid 143
98. ibid 235
99. *C.L.* 556
100. *Ph.* 218; *C.P.* 181
101. *S.M.* 255–6
102. ibid 256
103. Pryse, *The Apocalypse Unsealed*, 22–3, 60–1, etc.
104. R. M. Bucke, *Cosmic Consciousness*, Philadelphia, 1901
105. *S.M.* 257
106. ibid 257–8
107. ibid 258
108. ibid 259
109. *C.P.* 257
110. *S.M.* 260–1
111. ibid 262; cf. Nehls, 501, letter to Godwin Baynes

112. *S.M.* 263
113. E. Carpenter, *Days with Walt Whitman, with some notes on his life and work*, George Allen, 1906
114. *C.L.* 595
115. *S.M.* 264
116. "Poetry of the Present", *C.P.* 185
117. *C.L.* 399, 625, Tedlock, *The Frieda Lawrence Collection of D. H. Lawrence Manuscripts*, Albuquerque 1948, p. 90
118. *C.L.* 566; *S.P.* 106–7
119. *C.L.* 577
120. ibid 596
121. *Ph.* 598
122. Tawney, *The Radical Tradition*, Penguin, 1966
123. *Ph.* 599
124. ibid 600
125. ibid 602
126. ibid 603
127. ibid 606
128. ibid 607
129. ibid 607
130. ibid 607
131. ibid 609
132. ibid 611–12
133. ibid 611–12
134. *C.L.* 518, 21 July 1917
135. *Ph.* 613
136. ibid 610
137. ibid 615
138. ibid 615–16
139. ibid 639–40
140. ibid 657–8
141. ibid 664–5
142. H. T. Moore, *Life and Works of D.H.L.* 172–3
143. *C.L.* 561, 3 July 1918
144. *M.E.H.* vii
145. ibid viii
146. ibid 49–50
147. ibid 53
148. ibid 111–12
149. ibid 239–40
150. ibid 272, 291
151. ibid 305–6
152. ibid 306

CHAPTER 16

1. *Kangaroo*, 342
2. Daleski, *The Forked Flame*; E. Vivas, "The Substance of *Women in Love*" in *The Sewanee Review*, 66, 620
3. *W.L.* 459–60
4. Mackenzie, *My Life and Times, Octave Five: 1915–1923*, Chatto & Windus, 1966, 167–8
5. *Fantasia*, 8
6. *C.P.* 256
7. ibid 256–7
8. ibid 257
9. ibid 257
10. ibid 258
11. cf. *C.L.* 519
12. *C.P.* 260
13. ibid 260
14. *RW.* 264
15. See above 408 and *W.L.* 330–511
16. *C.P.* 267
17. ibid 263–4
18. ibid 263–4
19. ibid 265
20. See above 363
21. *S.M.* 27
22. N. Hawthorne, *The Scarlet Letter*; cf. *S.M.* 134 ff.
23. *C.P.* 255–6
24. *W.L.* 333
25. *C.P.* 250
26. ibid 182
27. ibid 183
28. ibid 185
29. ibid 479
30. *S.M.* 18
31. ibid 19
32. ibid 19
33. ibid 19
34. *C.L.* 302
35. See above 387, 413; *Int. H.* 282; *Ph. II*, 92–108
36. cf. Daniel A. Weiss, "The Mother in the Mind", in *Oedipus in Nottingham: D. H. Lawrence*, University of Washington Press, 1962; in Tedlock, *D.H.L. and Sons and Lovers*, 1965
37. *W.L.* 286, 435
38. *Ph.* 4–6

BIBLIOGRAPHICAL NOTE

Apart from Section I, this lists works and articles cited in the present study. Where reference was made to a later edition of a book, the date of the first edition is given in brackets. (Works in the Martin Secker thin-paper edition are now published by William Heinemann Ltd.)

I. BIBLIOGRAPHICAL WORKS ON D. H. LAWRENCE

Aldington Richard, *D. H. Lawrence, A Complete List of His Works with a Critical Appreciation*, Heinemann, 1935.

Beebe, Maurice and Tommasi, Anthony, "Checklist of D. H. Lawrence Criticism" in *Modern Fiction Studies*, Vol. 5, No 1, spring, 1959.

McDonald, Edward D., *A Bibliography of the Writings of D. H. Lawrence*, Philadelphia: The Centaur Bookshop, 1925.

McDonald, Edward D., *The Writings of D. H. Lawrence, A Bibliographical Supplement*, Philadelphia: The Centaur Bookshop, 1931.

Powell, Lawrence Clark, *The Manuscripts of D. H. Lawrence*, Los Angeles: The Public Library, 1937.

Roberts, F. Warren, *A Bibliography of D. H. Lawrence*, Rupert Hart-Davis, 1963.

Sagar, Keith, *The Art of D. H. Lawrence*, Cambridge University Press, 1966.

Tedlock, E. W., Jr, *The Frieda Lawrence Collection of D. H. Lawrence Manuscripts*, Albuquerque: University of New Mexico, 1948.

White, William, *D. H. Lawrence, A Checklist*, Detroit: Wayne University Press, 1950.

II. WORKS BY D. H. LAWRENCE

Poetry

The Complete Poems of D. H. Lawrence, Collected and edited with an Introduction and Notes by Vivian de Sola Pinto and Warren Roberts, Heinemann, 1964, 2 vols, pp. vii–1062.

Whenever variants not collected in the above are concerned, reference is made to versions of the poems in the following earlier collections:

Collected Poems, Martin Secker, 1928, 2 vols.
Love Poems and Others, Duckworth, 1913.
Amores, Duckworth, 1916.

Novels
(All references are to the Martin Secker thin-paper edition)

The White Peacock (1911), 1930
The Trespasser (1912), 1927.
Sons and Lovers (1913), 1930.
The Rainbow (1915), 1930.
The Lost Girl (1920), April 1930.
Women in Love (1921), April 1930.
Aaron's Rod (1922), August 1929.
Kangaroo (1923), March 1930.

Short Stories
(All references are to the Martin Secker thin-paper edition unless otherwise indicated. When early versions under the same title but offering significant variants are cited from periodicals, the full reference is given in the first footnote)

The Prussian Officer and Other Stories (1914), 1929.
England, My England (1924), April 1930.
Love Among the Haystacks and Other Pieces, The Nonesuch Press, 1930.
A Modern Lover, Martin Secker, 1934.
The Complete Short Stories, Heinemann, 1965–66, 3 vols.
"Two Marriages", Supplement to *Time and Tide*, 24 March 1934. (Early version of "Daughters of the Vicar".)
"The Soiled Rose", *Forum*, March 1913. (Early version of "The Shades of Spring".)

Plays

The Plays of D. H. Lawrence, Martin Secker, 1933.
A Collier's Friday Night, Martin Secker, 1934.

Travel

Twilight in Italy (1916), Jonathan Cape, The Travellers' Library, 1930.

Essays, Criticism, etc.

Movements in European History, by Lawrence H. Davison, Oxford University Press, 1921

Psychoanalysis and the Unconscious (1923), Martin Secker, 1931.

Fantasia of the Unconscious (1923), Martin Secker, 1930.

Studies in Classic American Literature (1923), Martin Secker, 1924.

Apocalypse (1931), Martin Secker, 1932.

Phoenix, The Posthumous Papers of D. H. Lawrence, Edited by Edward D. McDonald, Heinemann, 1936.

Phoenix II, Uncollected, Unpublished and Other Prose Works by D. H. Lawrence, Edited by Warren Roberts and Harry T. Moore, Heinemann, 1968.

The Symbolic Meaning, The Uncollected Versions of Studies in Classic American Literature, Edited by Armin Arnold, Arundel: Centaur Press, 1962.

Letters

The Letters of D. H. Lawrence, Edited and with an Introduction by Aldous Huxley, Heinemann, 1932.

The Collected Letters of D. H. Lawrence, Edited with an Introduction by Harry T. Moore, Heinemann, 1962, 2 vols.

Lawrence in Love, Letters from D. H. Lawrence to Louie Burrows, Edited with an Introduction and Notes by J. T. Boulton, Nottingham: University of Nottingham Press, 1968.

The Quest for Rananim, D. H. Lawrence's Letters to Koteliansky, 1914–1930, Edited by George J. Zytaruk. Montreal: McGill Queen's University Press, 1970.

News of the World, 19 October 1913; *Daily Mail*, 20 October 1913: Fragments of an uncollected letter from D. H. Lawrence to Ernest Weekley.

The Teacher, Saturday, 25 March 1905, Vol. 2. No 58, pp. 280–4: D. H. Lawrence's first known letter.

III. BIOGRAPHICAL SOURCES

(In the lists which follow, the letter (L) designates works containing letters from D. H. Lawrence.)

I. Works on D. H. Lawrence

Aldington, Richard, *Portrait of a Genius, But . . .*, Heinemann, 1950.

Brett, Dorothy, *Lawrence and Brett, A Friendship*, Martin Secker, 1933.

Brewster, Earl and Achsah, *D. H. Lawrence, Reminiscences and Correspondence*, Martin Secker, 1939. (L)

Carswell, Catherine, *The Savage Pilgrimage, a Narrative of D. H. Lawrence*, Chatto and Windus, 1932. (L)

Chambers, Jessie ("E.T."), *D. H. Lawrence, A Personal Record*, Jonathan Cape, 1935. (L)

Chambers, Jessie ("E.T."), Memoirs and letters to the author, in Delavenay, *D. H. Lawrence: L'Homme et la Genèse de Son Œuvre, etc.*, Paris: Klincksieck, 1969, Appendix IV.

Chambers, Jessie ("E.T"), "The Literary Formation of D. H. Lawrence", "D. H. Lawrence's Student Days", "D. H. Lawrence's Literary Debut", *European Quarterly*, May, August, November 1934.

Corke, Helen, *D. H. Lawrence, The Croydon Years*, Austin: University of Texas Press, 1965.

Corke, Helen, *Lawrence and Apocalypse*, Heinemann, 1933.

Corke, Helen, *D. H. Lawrence's Princess, A Memory of Jessie Chambers*, Thames Ditton: The Merle Press, 1951.

Lawrence, Ada (Clarke) and Gelder, Stuart, *Young Lorenzo, Early Life of D. H. Lawrence*, Florence: G. Orioli, 1932; Martin Secker, 1932. (L)

Lawrence, Frieda (von Richthofen, Weekley, Ravagli), *Not I, But the Wind . . .*, Heinemann, 1935. (L)

Lawrence, Frieda (von Richthofen, Weekley, Ravagli), *The Memoirs and Correspondence*, Edited by E. W. Tedlock Jr, Heinemann, 1961.

Litvinov, Ivy (Ivy Low), "A Visit to D. H. Lawrence", in *Harper's Bazaar*, No 2818, October 1946.

Luhan, Mabel Dodge, *Lorenzo in Taos*, New York: Alfred A. Knopf, 1932.

Moore, Harry T., *The Life and Works of D. H. Lawrence*, New York: Twayne, 1951.

Moore, Harry T., *The Intelligent Heart*, Penguin Books, 1960. (L)

Moore, Harry T., *Poste Restante, A Lawrence Travel Calendar*, Berkeley and Los Angeles: University of California, 1956.

Moore, Harry T. and Roberts, Warren, *D. H. Lawrence and His World*, Thames and Hudson, 1966.

Murry, John Middleton, *Son of Woman*, Jonathan Cape, 1931.

Murry, John Middleton, *Reminiscences of D. H. Lawrence*, Jonathan Cape, 1933. (L)

Nehls, Edward, *D. H. Lawrence, A Composite Biography*, Madison: The University of Wisconsin Press, 1957, 1958, 1959, 3 vols. (L)

Neville, George H., "The Early Days of D. H. Lawrence" in *The London Mercury*, XXIII, No 137, March 1931.

Tindall, William York, *D. H. Lawrence and Susan his Cow*, New York: Columbia University Press, 1939.

2. *Memoirs, Biographies, etc., Containing Information on Lawrence and his Times*

Aldington, Richard, *Life for Life's Sake. A Book of Reminiscences*, Cassell, 1968.

Asquith, Lady Cynthia, *Haply I May Remember*, James Barrie, 1950.

Asquith, Lady Cynthia, *Remember and be Glad*, James Barrie, 1952.

Asquith, Lady Cynthia, *Diaries 1915–1918*, Hutchinson, 1968.

Asquith, Herbert, *Moments of Memory; Recollections and Impressions*, New York: Scribner, 1938.

Corke, Helen, *Neutral Ground, A Chronicle*, Arthur Barker, 1933.

Damon, S. Foster, *Amy Lowell, A Chronicle*, New York: Houghton Mifflin, 1960. (L)

Doolittle, Hilda (H.D.), *Bid me to Live, a Madrigal*, New York: Grove Press, 1960.

Douglas, Norman, *Looking Back*, Chatto and Windus, 1933.

Farjeon, Eleanor, "Springtime with D. H. Lawrence" in *The London Magazine*, II, 4 April 1955.

Ford, Ford Madox, *Return to Yesterday*, Gollancz, 1931.

Ford, Ford Madox, *Mightier than the Sword. Memories and Criticisms*, Allen and Unwin, 1938.

Garnett, David, *The Flowers of the Forest*, Chatto and Windus, 1953.

Garnett, David, *The Golden Echo*, Chatto and Windus, 1955.

Garnett, David, *The Familiar Faces*, Chatto and Windus, 1962.

Gertler, Mark, *Selected Letters*, edited by Noël Carrington, Rupert Hart-Davis, 1965.

Glenavy, Beatrice (Campbell), Lady, *Today we will only gossip*, Constable, 1966.

Goldring, Douglas, *The Nineteen Twenties: A General Survey and some Personal Memories*, Nicholson and Watson, 1943.

Goldring, Douglas, *Life Interests*, Macdonald, 1948.

Gray, Cecil, *Musical Chairs, or Between Two Stools*, Horne and Van Thal, 1948.

Gray, Cecil, et al., *Peter Warlock: A Memoir of Philip Heseltine*, Jonathan Cape, 1934.

Hunt, Violet, *The Flurried Years*, Hurst and Blackett, 1926.

Keynes, John Maynard, *Two Memoirs*, Rupert Hart-Davis, 1949. (L)

Lea, F. A., *The Life of John M. Murry*, Methuen, 1959.

Mackenzie, Compton, *The South Wind of Love*, Rich and Cowan, 1937.

Mackenzie, Compton, *My Life and Times, Octave Five: 1915–1923*, Chatto and Windus, 1966. (L)

Mansfield, Katherine, *Journal*, Constable, 1954.

Mansfield, Katherine, *Letters*, Constable, 1928.

Mansfield, Katherine, *Letters to John Middleton Murry*, Constable, 1951.

Marsh, Edward, *A Number of People. A Book of Reminiscences*, Heinemann and Hamish Hamilton, 1939. (L)

Morrell, Ottoline, *Ottoline, The Early Memoirs of Lady Ottoline Morrell*, edited by Robert Gathorne Hardy, Faber and Faber, 1963.

M(orrell) O(ttoline) "D. H. Lawrence, 1885–1930", in *The Nation and Athenaeum*, XLVI, 25, 22 March 1930.

Murry, John Middleton, *Between Two Worlds*, Jonathan Cape, 1935.

Russell, Bertrand, *Portraits from Memory*, Allen and Unwin, 1956.

Russell, Bertrand, *The Autobiography of Bertrand Russell, 1872–1914*, Allen and Unwin, 1967. *1914–1944*, Allen and Unwin, 1968.

Woolf, Leonard, *Beginning Again, An Autobiography of the Years 1911–1918*, Hogarth Press, 1964.

Woolf, Leonard, *Downhill all the Way, An Autobiography of the Years 1919–1939*, Hogarth Press, 1967.

IV. CRITICAL STUDIES

Daleski, H. M., *The Forked Flame, A Study of D. H. Lawrence*, Faber and Faber, 1965.

Delavenay, Emile, "Sur un exemplaire de Schopenhauer annoté par D. H. Lawrence", *Revue Anglo-Américaine*, XIII, February 1936, 234–8.

Delavenay, Emile, *D. H. Lawrence and Edward Carpenter, A Study in Edwardian Transition*, Heinemann, 1971.

Hoops, Reinald, *Der Einfluss der Psychoanalyse auf die Englische Literatur*, Heidelberg: Carl Winters, 1934.

Leavis, F. R., *D. H. Lawrence, Novelist*, Chatto and Windus, 1955.

Panichas, George A., *Adventure in Consciousness, the Meaning of D. H. Lawrence's Religious Quest*, The Hague: Mouton, 1964.

Seillière, Ernest, *David Herbert Lawrence et les Récentes Idéologies Allemandes*, Paris: Boivin, 1936.

Vivas, Eliseo, "The Substance of Women in Love", in *The Sewanee Review*, Vol. 66, No 4.

Weiss, Daniel A., *Oedipus in Nottingham*, Seattle, 1962.

V. OTHER WORKS CITED

Baillot, A., *Influence de la Philosophie de Schopenhauer en France*, Paris, 1927.

Balfour, Arthur J., "Creative Evolution and Philosophic Doubt", in *The Hibbert Journal*, X, October 1911–July 1912, No 37.

Barrie, Sir James M., *Sentimental Tommy* ⎱ The Uniform Edition of the Works
Barrie, Sir James M., *Tommy and Grizel* ⎰ of J. M. Barrie, Cassell.

Belt, Thomas, *Naturalist in Nicaragua* (1874), Dent, Everyman edition.

Bergson, Henri, "Life and Consciousness" (The Huxley Lecture, University of Birmingham, 29 May 1911) in *The Hibbert Journal*, X, October 1911–July 1912, No. 37.

Blake, William, *Poetry and Prose*, edited by Geoffrey Keynes, complete in one volume. Nonesuch, 1927.

Blavatsky, Hélène P., *The Secret Doctrine: The Synthesis of Science, Religion and Philosophy*, Theosophical Publishing Co, 1888.

Blavatsky, Hélène P., *Isis Unveiled*, New York: J. W. Bouton, 1877.

Brailsford, H. M., *Shelley, Godwin and their Circle*, Oxford: Home University Library, 1913.

Bucke, R. M., *Cosmic Consciousness, A Study of the Evolution of the Human Mind*, Philadelphia, 1901.

Burnet, John, *Early Greek Philosophy*, Black, 1892.

Carpenter, Edward, *Civilization, its Cause and Cure, and Other Essays* (1889), eighth edition, Swan, Sonnenschein, 1903.

Carpenter, Edward, *Love's Coming of Age* (1896), sixth edition, Swan, Sonnenschein, 1909.

Carpenter, Edward, *The Art of Creation, Essays on the Self and its Powers*, George Allen, 1904.

Carpenter, Edward, *Days with Walt Whitman, with some Notes on his Life and Work*, George Allen, 1906.

Carpenter, Edward, *The Intermediate Sex: A Study of Some Transitional Types of Men and Women*, Swan, Sonnenschein, 1908.

Carpenter, Edward, *The Drama of Love and Death, A Study of Human Evolution and Transfiguration*, George Allen, 1912.

Carpenter, Edward, *Intermediate Types among Primitive Folk: a Study of Social Evolution*, George Allen, 1914.

Carpenter, Edward, *The Healing of Nations and the Hidden Sources of their Strife*, George Allen and Unwin, 1915.

Chamberlain, Houston Stewart, *The Foundations of the XIXth Century*, a translation from the German by John Lees with an Introduction by Lord Redesdale, John Lane, 1911, 2 vols.

Chamberlain, Houston Stewart, *The Ravings of a Renegade*, being the War Essays of H. S. Chamberlain. Translated from the German by Charles H. Clarke, Jarrold, 1916.

Chamberlain, Houston Stewart, *England*, 1915.

Chamberlain, Houston Stewart, *Germany*, 1915.

Ellis, Henry Havelock, *Studies in the Psychology of Sex*, Vols 1–6, Philadelphia: F. A. Davis, 1905.

Ellis, Henry Havelock, *A Study of British Genius*, Hurst and Blackett, 1904.

Frazer, Sir James G., *The Golden Bough*, Macmillan, 1890—1915.

Frazer, Sir James G., *Totemism and Exogamy*, Macmillan, 1910.

Frobenius, Leo, *The Voice of Africa*, Hutchinson, 1913, 2 vols.

Harrison, Jane, *Ancient Art and Ritual*, Oxford: Home University Library, 1913.

Jenner, Mrs Henry (Katherine Lee), *Christian Symbolism*, Little Books on Art, Methuen, 1910.

Jung, Carl Gustav, *Collected Papers on Analytical Psychology*. Authorized translation edited by Constance E. Long, Baillière and Co, 1916.

Jung, Carl Gustav, *Psychology of the Unconscious. A study of the transformations and symbolism of the Libido. A contribution to the history of the evolution of thought.*

Authorized translation, with introduction, by Beatrice M. Hinkle; New York: Moffat, Yard and Co, 1916; London: Kegan Paul, 1916.

Lavrin, Janko, "Sex and Eros (on Rozanov, Weininger, and D. H. Lawrence)", in *The European Quarterly*, Vol. 1, No 2, August 1934, pp. 88–96.

Maspéro, G., *Egypte*, Paris: Hachette, Collection Ars Una, 1912.

Meredith, George, *Beauchamp's Career*, Chapman and Hall, 1876.

Moore, George, *Esther Waters*, Walter Scott, 1894.

Moore, George, *Evelyn Innes*, T. Fisher Unwin, 1898.

Moore, George, *Sister Teresa*, T. Fisher Unwin, 1909.

Noyes, John Humphrey, *History of American Socialisms* (1870) (reprint of 1870 edition), New York: Hillary House, 1961.

Noyes, John Humphrey, *Male Continence*, New York: Oneida, 1872.

Noyes, John Humphrey, *Dixon and His Copyists*, New York: Oneida, 1871.

Occult Review (*The*)

　XX–1. July 1914, pp. 30–2. Review by Havelock Ellis of Carpenter, *Intermediate Types among Primitive Folk*.

　XXII–1. July 1915: discussion of Carpenter's *Love's Coming of Age*, new edition (Methuen).

　XXIV–3. September 1916. Review of *My Days and Dreams*, by Edward Carpenter.

　XXIV–5. November 1916. Review of Carpenter, *Never Again!*

　XXII–1. July 1915. Review of *Reincarnation in the New Testament* by J. M. Pryse, by H. S. Redgrove.

Oneida Community, *Bible Communism*, Brooklyn, 1853.

Pryse, James Morgan, *The Apocalypse Unsealed*, John M. Watkins, 1910.

Querido, Israel, *Toil of Men*, translated by F. S. Arnold, Methuen, 1909.

Reade, Winwood, *The Martyrdom of Man* (1872), John Lane, 1912.

Réal, Jean, "The Religious Conception of Race: Houston Stewart Chamberlain and Germanic Christianity", in *The Third Reich*, Weidenfeld and Nicolson, 1955.

Saurat, Denis, *Blake and Modern Thought*, Constable, 1929.

Schopenhauer, Arthur, *Essays, translated by Mrs Rudolf Dircks*, Walter Scott, 1903.

Thompson, Francis, *Shelley*, Burns and Oates, 1909.

Tylor, Sir Edward Burnett, *Primitive Culture: Researches into the Development of Mythology, Philosophy, Religion, Language, Art and Custom*, John Murray, 1871.

Unwin, Sir Stanley, *The Truth about Publishing*, George Allen and Unwin, 1926.

Weininger, Otto, *Sex and Character*, Authorized translation from the sixth German edition, Heinemann, 1906.

Zytaruk, George, *The Quest for Rananim, D. H. Lawrence's Letters to Koteliansky, 1914 to 1930*, McGill Queen's University Press, 1970.

INDEX OF PROPER NAMES AND TITLES CITED IN THE TEXT

Names preceded by an asterisk are those of characters in works by D. H. Lawrence
Titles of works by D. H. Lawrence are identified by a dagger
Abbreviations of D. H. Lawrence titles as in the list of abbreviations on pp. 525–6.